In the first collection of its kind, Paul Drew and John Heritage bring together the latest advances in the application of conversation analysis to the study of language and interaction in institutional settings. Leading American and European scholars contribute to *Talk at Work* original empirical research into the interactions between professionals and "clients" in a wide variety of settings, including doctor–patient consultations, legal hearings, news interviews, visits by health visitors, psychiatric interviews, and calls to the emergency services. Taken together, their reports are an illuminating exploration of how key aspects of an organization's work are managed through talk and of the distinctively asymmetric character of institutional discourse. The use of a method at the forefront of research, on recordings of naturally occurring interactions in the settings under scrutiny, uncovers the relationships between social contexts and social actions and offers invaluable insight into the traditional concerns of the sociology and ethnography of organizations, sociolinguistics, and pragmatics.

D0096028

Studies in Interactional Sociolinguistics 8

General Editor: John J. Gumperz

Talk at work

Studies in Interactional Sociolinguistics

Talk at work

Interaction in institutional settings

Edited by PAUL DREW

University of York

and JOHN HERITAGE

University of California, Los Angeles

CAMBRIDGE
UNIVERSITY PRESS

Published by the Press Syndicate of the University of Cambridge
The Pitt Building, Trumpington Street, Cambridge CB2 1RP
40 West 20th Street, New York, NY 10011–4211, USA
10 Stamford Road, Oakleigh, Victoria 3166, Australia

First published 1992

Printed in Great Britain at the University Press, Cambridge

A catalogue record for this book is available from the British Library

Library of Congress cataloguing in publication data

Talk at work : interaction in institutional settings / edited by Paul
   Drew and John Heritage.
         p.   cm. – (Studies in interactional sociolinguistics)
      Includes bibliographical references and indexes.
      ISBN 0-521-37489-8 (hardback) – ISBN 0-521-37633-5 (paperback)
      1. Oral communication.   2. Interpersonal relations.   3. Social
   interaction.   4. Sociolinguistics.   I. Drew, Paul.   II. Heritage,
   John.   III. Series.
   P95.T28   1992
   302.3' 46 – dc20   91–44627 CIP

ISBN 0 521 37489 8 hardback
ISBN 0 521 37633 5 paperback

FP

72181

Contents

Contributors

Dr. J. Maxwell Atkinson, Henley Management College, UK, and Visiting Professor, School of Social Sciences, University of Bath.

Professor Jörg R. Bergmann, Institut für Soziologie, Giessen, Germany.

Dr. Graham Button, Department of Social and Political Sciences, Polytechnic of the South West, Plymouth, UK; and EuroPARC, Cambridge.

Professor Steven E. Clayman, Department of Sociology, University of California, Los Angeles, USA.

Dr. Paul Drew, Department of Sociology, University of York, UK.

Dr. David Greatbatch, Department of Sociology, University of Nottingham, UK.

Professor John J. Gumperz, Department of Anthropology, University of California, Berkeley, USA.

Dr. Christian Heath, Department of Sociology, University of Surrey, Guildford, UK; and EuroPARC, Cambridge.

Professor John Heritage, Department of Sociology, University of California, Los Angeles, USA.

Dr. Gail Jefferson, Juckemawei 29, 9015 KA Rinsumageest, The Netherlands.

Dr. John R. E. Lee, Department of Sociology, University of Manchester, UK.

Professor Stephen C. Levinson, Research Group for Cognitive Anthropology, Max-Planck Institute for Psycholinguistics, Nijmegen, The Netherlands.

Professor Douglas W. Maynard, Department of Sociology, University of Wisconsin-Madison, USA.

Professor Emanuel A. Schegloff, Department of Sociology,
University of California, Los Angeles, USA.
Dr. Sue Sefi, Radcliffe Infirmary, Oxford, UK.
Professor Don H. Zimmerman, Department of Sociology,
University of California, Santa Barbara, USA.

Acknowledgments

We gratefully acknowledge the continuing support for this project by successive editors at Cambridge University Press, namely Sue Allen-Mills, Penny Carter, Marion Smith, and most recently Judith Ayling. Ian Taylor, of Computype, York, has given invaluable technical assistance in preparing the data extracts included in this book. And we are especially grateful to the series editor, John Gumperz, for his very considerable encouragement and advice. The professionalism of all these has contributed greatly to what has emerged.

We are grateful to the American Sociological Association for permission to reprint the chapter by Button (ch. 7), which is a slightly revised version of a paper first published in the *Social Psychology Quarterly*, 50 (1987), pp. 160–71; to Mouton Publishers, for permission to reprint the chapter by Levinson (ch. 2) from *Linguistics*, 17 (1979), pp. 365–99; and to the North Holland Publishing Company, for permission to reprint the chapter by Jefferson and Lee (ch. 15), which first appeared in the *Journal of Pragmatics*, 5 (1981), pp. 399–422.

PART 1

Theoretical orientations

1

Analyzing talk at work: an introduction

PAUL DREW and JOHN HERITAGE

1 Overview

This book is a collection of studies of social interaction and language use in a variety of institutional contexts. The interactions that are analyzed here are basically task-related and they involve at least one participant who represents a formal organization of some kind. The tasks of these interactions – ranging from the examination of a witness in court to a health check in a new mother's home – are primarily accomplished through the exchange of talk between professionals and lay persons. So the title of this volume, *Talk at Work*, refers to this: that talk-in-interaction is the principal means through which lay persons pursue various practical goals and the central medium through which the daily working activities of many professionals and organizational representatives are conducted. We will use the term "institutional interaction" to refer to talk of this kind.[1]

Institutional interactions may take place face to face or over the telephone. They may occur within a designated physical setting, for example a hospital, courtroom, or educational establishment, but they are by no means restricted to such settings. Just as people in a workplace may talk together about matters unconnected with their work, so too places not usually considered "institutional," for example a private home, may become the settings for work-related interactions. Thus the institutionality of an interaction is not determined by its setting. Rather, interaction is institutional insofar as

We would like to thank Max Atkinson, Steven Clayman, Charles Goodwin, David Greatbatch, Per Linell, Doug Maynard, and Manny Schegloff for their comments on an earlier draft of this Introduction.

participants' institutional or professional identities are somehow
made relevant to the work activities in which they are engaged. The
studies in this volume seek to describe the institutional nature of the
tasks and relevances that inform conduct in a variety of work
settings. They examine how these relevances are established and
how specific tasks are discharged through such conduct. And they
depict the consequences which both may have for the character of
the interaction and its outcomes.

. This collection is unusual in at least two respects. First, the
contributions are not studies of the same institutional domain.
Whereas it has been usual in the literature to focus on one particular type of institutional setting (e.g. doctor–patient interaction
[Fisher and Todd 1983; Heath 1986; Silverman 1987] or courtroom language [Atkinson and Drew 1979; Maynard 1984; Levi
and Walker 1990]), this volume contains studies of a wide variety
of different institutional contexts. We believe that this diversity
encourages a comparative perspective from which it is possible to
develop a range of analytical and thematic connections. And this
may encourage a greater degree of theoretical coherence and cumu-
lativeness in research than has previously obtained in this field.

The other respect in which this collection is distinctive also
relates to the hope of developing a coherent, cumulative research
perspective. All the studies here arise from a single research tradition, that of conversation analysis (henceforth CA).[2] It may
perhaps seem surprising that a perspective which, as its very name
suggests, is associated with the analysis of ordinary conversation
between peers in everyday contexts should be applied to interactions which are evidently not "ordinary conversation" in quite this
sense. Yet the data and research enterprises of CA have never been
exclusively focused on ordinary conversation. On the contrary, CA
research has been developed in relation to a wide range of data
corpora.[3] Indeed it is for this reason that the term "talk-in-interaction" (Schegloff 1987a) has come to be generally used, in preference to "conversation," to refer to the object of CA research. There
is nothing about the perspective and techniques associated with the
sequential analysis of ordinary conversation which is inimical to the
analysis of institutional talk. Part of our purpose in this chapter is
to outline how it is that CA has generated the kind of studies
exemplified in this collection, and how the distinctiveness of CA's

approach may yield special insights into how persons conduct their
affairs in institutional contexts. Our hope is that this collection may
help to consolidate a specifically conversation-analytical approach
to the analysis of institutional interaction.

The contributions to this volume focus on conduct that is in
various ways shaped or constrained by the participants' orientations to social institutions either as their representatives or, in
various senses, as their "clients." These orientations have traditionally been researched in a variety of ways: through questionnaires
and unstructured interviews, through ethnographic observation
and participants' commentary to researchers in workplace contexts, and through self-reports and diary studies. By these procedures, sociologists have attempted to get inside the "black box"
of social institutions to gain access to their interior processes and
practices.

In contrast to such methods, the studies collected here attempt to
gain access to institutional processes and the outlooks that inform
them by analyzing audio and video records of specific occupational
interactions. The objective is to describe how particular institutions
are enacted and lived through as accountable patterns of meaning,
inference, and action. The direct focus on recorded conduct has the
advantage that it cuts across basic problems associated with the gap
between beliefs and action and between what people say and what
they do (Deutscher 1973; Stimson and Webb 1975; Abell and
Gilbert 1983; Gilbert and Mulkay 1984). At the same time, this
form of research may be regarded as a complement to more traditional observational and participant ethnographic methods of
dealing with the same problems.[4] Insofar as recorded data from
institutional settings can be subjected to repeated inspection which
can enhance analytic treatments ranging from the interpretative to
basic forms of quantification, an opportunity exists to bring new
insights to traditional sociological analyses of institutional settings
with additional data and with new and powerful investigative techniques.

In what follows, we sketch the position of CA as an approach to
institutional talk within a more general set of approaches to action
and interaction, outline the methodological and analytical framework represented in this approach, and describe the major growing
points of research in the field. Readers who wish to proceed directly

to an outline of the contents of this volume should turn to section 8
of this "Introduction" (p. 53).

2 Convergences in the development of research on institutional interaction

The analytic outlooks expressed in this volume emerge in part from
distinctive, but converging, lines of investigation in sociology, anthropology, and linguistics. There are two central tendencies in this
convergence: (a) the development of sociolinguistic approaches to
language that address the contextual sensitivity of language use;
and (b) the emergence of analytic frameworks that recognize the
nature of language as action and which handle the dynamic features
of social action and interaction.

2.1 Context in talk: sociolinguistic perspectives

Sociolinguistic research into discourse and social interaction
emerged in a context of competition with linguistic traditions that
treat the constituent units and levels of organization of speech as if
they were isolated both from one another and the interactional
contexts in which they might occur. Banished from the ideal order
of *langue* to the disorderly domain of *parole* where, Chomskian
orthodoxy had it, little that was systematic was to be found: the
sociolinguistic study of interaction initially seemed to have little to
recommend it.[5]

Early indications from sociolinguistics that the world of *parole*
might be more orderly than expected emerged in empirical studies
of linguistic phenomena below the level of a sentence, for example
the phoneme (Labov 1966) or address terms (Ervin-Tripp 1969). In
his study of English in New York, for example, Labov (1966) found
it necessary to take account of the dialogic contexts in which his
data occurred. In noting the change from the unpronounced (r)s in
fourth floor when a salesperson was first asked directions, to the
voiced (r) in response to a request to repeat the direction, Labov
connected a systematic phonetic variation to a change from a
"casual" to a "careful" speech context. This was an important
early step in the recognition that "purely" linguistic phenomena –
here, the phonetics of speech – are not autonomous from their
dialogic context in interaction.[6]

Thus, when linguists, in part, perhaps, stimulated by the results of CA within sociology, began in the 1970s to take seriously the collection and analysis of data which were not contrived but naturally occurring, and which were not limited to single sentences but included sequences of discourse, they were not just responding to the recognition that levels of linguistic structure and organization are interrelated. They also acknowledged that fundamental linguistic phenomena are significantly influenced by the interactive or textual context in which they are produced (Brown and Yule 1983; Stubbs 1983). With the developing acknowledgment of naturally occurring talk as appropriate data for linguistic analysis (Labov 1972), it became apparent that conceptions of sociolinguistic context had also to be modified. Apart from categorizing speech situations as either formal (status-marked) or informal, sociolinguistics had initially treated context in terms of the social attributes speakers bring to talk – for example, age, class, ethnicity, gender, geographical region, kinship, and other relationships. The impact of these attributes was treated as somewhat monolithic, drawn, as Goffman memorably remarked, "directly and simply from chi squaredom" (1964: 134). However, studies of data from natural social settings soon showed that the relevance of these attributes depended upon the particular setting in which the talk occurred – that is, whether the talk was conversational, took place in school, in courts, in business negotiations, and so on – and also upon the particular speech activities or tasks speakers were engaged in within those settings. In some cases, it was found, the nature of the social setting heightened the relevance of speakers' social attributes (e.g. Cazden 1970); in others, however, the activities in which persons were engaged influenced the talk in ways that overwhelmed the relevance of their social attributes (Goffman 1964).

A second major impetus to connect linguistic structure with social context derives from anthropological linguistics which, from Malinowski (1923) onwards, has stressed the sociocultural context of utterance as central to meaning and action (Duranti 1988; Goodwin and Duranti 1992). This perspective gained prominence with the emergence of the ethnography of speaking (Hymes 1964) within anthropology. Hymes's development of the concept of communicative competence (Hymes 1972b; see also Hymes 1972a, 1974) expressed the growing confidence and sophistication with

which the contextualization of speech and language was being
treated within anthropology and his 'SPEAKING' (1972a) model
systematized the major growing points in the analysis of that contextualization. At the same time, a key collection of papers, *Directions in Sociolinguistics* (Gumperz and Hymes 1972), contained a
range of studies that gave empirical substance to these connections.

In this context, a particular debt is owed to the work of Gumperz and his collaborators, who stimulated a reassessment of the
dynamic nature of social contexts and the importance of linguistic
details in evoking them. Gumperz (1982) demonstrated that any
aspect of linguistic behavior – lexical, prosodic, phonological, and
syntactic choices together with the use of particular codes, dialects,
or styles[7] – may function as a *contextualization cue*, indicating
those aspects of the context which are relevant in interpreting what
a speaker means (1982: 162). By signaling interpretively significant
aspects of the social context, they enable interactants to make inferences about one another's communicative intentions and goals.
Using data from a wide variety of social contexts, Gumperz (1982)
indicated the complex ways in which, in interethnic interactions,
inferences from linguistic behavior are miscued through ambiguities and mismatches in these cues. The notion of "contextualization
cues" thus offered an important analytic opening to grasp the relationship between language use and speakers' orientations to context and inference making. It embodied a more complex and dynamic view of context than hitherto, and suggested that a wide
range of linguistic detail might be implicated in the contextualization process.

There is a significant convergence between the linguistic concept
of "contextualisation cues" as outlined by Gumperz, and the sociological concept of "frame" developed by Goffman (1974; see also
Bateson 1972). Goffman's notion of "frame" focuses on the definition which participants give to their current social activity – to
what is going on, what the situation is, and the roles which the
interactants adopt within it. In this analysis, behavior, including
speech, is interpreted in the context of participants' current understandings of what frame they are in. His related notion of "footing"
(Goffman 1981) addresses the reflexive and fluctuating character of
frames, together with the moment-by-moment reassessments and
realignments which participants may make in moving from one

frame to another.[8] These are sociological concepts that focus on the social organisation of individuals' experience of the situation or "context" which informs their own conduct and their interpretations of the conduct of others. They are, however, linguistically relevant in so far as participants negotiate frames and communicate changes in footing through "cues and markers" in speech (Goffman 1981c: 157). Tannen and Wallat (1987), for example, have usefully analyzed how a pediatrician selects and shifts between different linguistic registers according to whether she is speaking to a child or to the mother, and according to her particular activity (i.e. whether she is examining the child, explaining to the mother, recording her diagnosis, etc.). They further show that certain detailed aspects of the pediatrician's speech can be understood as the products of her managing the demands of two competing frames, the frame of consultation and that of examination (1987: 212).[9]

Goffman's frame theory has contributed to an increasingly sophisticated and dynamic approach to the analysis of social context. Instead of treating context as unitary and invariant, he has suggested a conceptual framework which captures the changing activity frames with their associated systems of relevance that can emerge within a given setting. In studies such as that by Tannen and Wallat, Goffman's sociological insights are combined with linguistic analysis to show the ways in which the details of language use are related to specific activities within an institutional setting.

Gumperz's notion of "contextualizing" and Goffman's conception of "frame" both relate specific linguistic options to the social activity for which language is being engaged. In combination, they have done much to advance and develop a more complex and dynamic analysis of the "context" of interaction. Their analyses of the relation of linguistic choice to context are resonant with Garfinkel's (1967) discussion of the indexical and reflexive characteristics of talk and behavior, with the precepts of "context analysis" (Kendon 1990), and with the conversation-analytic notion of "recipient design" (Schegloff 1972).

Overarching these particular gains, these studies and the wider "ethnography of speaking" framework with which they articulate have consolidated a key sense both of the contribution of cultural contextualization to the understanding of language and, more generally, of the relationship between language and the sociocultural order. The record is less clear-cut, however, in the analysis of action. Hymes (1972a) invoked the conception of speech acts to handle this, observing that "the level of speech acts mediates immediately between the usual levels of grammar and the rest of a speech event or situation" (1972a; 57). But while many studies in the ethnography of speaking show how actions are shaped by the cultural contextualization of utterances, there has not been an equivalent emphasis on the organization of social action *per se*. Rather, the nature of social action and its sequential organization have been explored more extensively from other perspectives, to which we now turn.

2.2 Talk in context: speech acts and discourse analysis

Perhaps the most vivid point of convergence between language and social organization arises at the level of *speech acts*. In *How to Do Things with Words*, Austin (1962) developed the view that in the production of an utterance a speaker performs an action, and aspects of his analysis were developed in a more systematic and technical way by Searle (1969).[10] Searle's speech-act theory, with its focus on the rules and conditions through which a sentence is understood as a particular kind of action, involves a more restricted focus than the "activity" or "speech-event" domain addressed by the work of Gumperz and his colleagues. However, because activities or speech events are built out of particular component actions, speech acts are arguably central to the analysis of all forms of interaction. And, since analysis of the organization of social action has always been a central focus of sociological research, the emergence of speech-act theory was a promising development for sociology. It held out the prospect of a real and empirically grounded interface between linguistics and sociology that could, in turn, contribute to the emerging body of work on discourse and social interaction.

Labov and Fanshel's (1977) study of a psychotherapeutic interview represented a major effort to apply speech-act analysis to institutional discourse. The study was motivated by two distinct objectives. The first was to demonstrate that, in the way they perform their actions, therapist and patient give expression to their proper roles in therapy. This goal involved detailed interpretative analysis; for example, Labov and Fanshel demonstrated the ways in which the patient, in making an evaluation, uses language which specifically displays her adherence to the therapeutic objective that patients should "be in touch with their emotions and be aware of what they are feeling" and gain insight into these feelings, including feelings of guilt (1977: 138 and 185; also Wootton 1977).

Labov and Fanshel's second, and more fundamental, objective is a theoretical one. It arises from their observation that coherence in discourse is not primarily a product of either the surface structure or the content of utterances. Rather, it is achieved in the connections between the actions which particular linguistic expressions perform (Labov and Fanshel 1977: 69–70). As Labov and Fanshel saw it, the production of discourse involves two distinct processes: (a) the speaker's analysis of a surface form as a given speech action; and (b) an analysis of its connections to other actions. Their objective, therefore, was to account for discourse coherence (a) in terms of rules which "translate" what is actually spoken into the speech act thereby performed and (b) in terms of rules that provide for linkages between actions. Both sets of rules are necessary to show how surface form, often through very indirect means, achieves a given speech action.[11]

The conjunction of these two objectives in a context of interaction which is, by common consent, often veiled and highly indirect led to a number of interlocking difficulties in Labov and Fanshel's analysis. First, in addressing the pervasively indirect character of much of the dialog, they were obliged to get from the surface form of utterances to their character as actions by means of contextually triggered "translation rules" (Gordon and Lakoff 1975). Yet, as Levinson (1980, 1981a, 1981b, 1983) notes, an indefinitely large number of such rules are apparently required to achieve this goal, which is consequently unattainable.[12] Moreover, the utterances in Labov and Fanshel's corpus can function as actions which can be understood differently at a number of different levels. The researchers made considerable efforts to formulate rules which account for different understandings of an utterance. But, as Taylor and Cameron (1987: 49ff.) observe, it was often difficult for Labov and Fanshel to determine how a particular utterance was actually understood by the participants and how the recipient's understanding of the utterance squared with the speaker's intention in producing it. As a result, it was difficult to validate the empirical applicability of any particular analytical rule. Here Labov and Fanshel often had recourse to the speaker's intentions in producing some utterance, and commonly supported their reading of them by reference to talk occurring much later in the session. But this procedure is vitiated by the fact that the later "validating" utterances emerged in their own interactional contexts. Often, it appears, Labov and Fanshel were reduced to "reading history backwards" in an attempt to secure an interpretative foundation for their analyses. And this methodology is no less questionable in the study of interaction than it is in the study of historical events.

The problems of Labov and Fanshel's analysis reflect deeper and more enduring difficulties inherited from the Searlian speech-act paradigm. These difficulties made speech-act theory an unlikely complement to the new context-sensitive forms of sociolinguistics and discourse analysis. In an unfortunate parallel with Chomskian linguistics, speech-act pragmatics was developed from considerations of idealized sentences – originally construed as occurring in a "null context" (Searle 1969)[13] – and resulted in attempts to model the pragmatic presuppositions or extra syntactic knowledge and conventions which must function if a sentence is to be not only well formed but also "meaningful."

In thus viewing meaning as fundamentally emergent from the sentence or utterance, this approach is drastically decontextualized. There can, by now, be no serious doubt that sentences and utterances are designed and shaped to occur in particular sequential and social contexts and that their sense as actions derives, at least in part, from such contexts (Schegloff 1984). In particular, utterances are interpreted in terms of whether, or to what extent, they conform to or depart from the expectations that are attached to the "slots" in which they occur. These expectations are of two types. First, there are expectations which are "perlocutionarily" established by a previous turn at talk (Sacks 1964–72; Schegloff 1972, 1984; Grice 1975). Thus a question establishes the relevance of an answer, a greeting expects a reply and so on. The obvious importance of these expectations may be glossed by noting that they can make silences – which are *prima facie* meaningless because no spoken action is undertaken – into highly significant events. The second type of expectation derives from the more general context of the interaction, the social identities of the participants, and the assumptions about the scope of conduct that conventionally attach to such events as a casual conversation, a news interview, or a medical consultation. It is these expectations which can make an *oh*, for example, something to be avoided in a news interview (Heritage 1985) or a medical consultation (ten Have 1991), and correspondingly noticeable in such contexts when it occurs.

No analysis that begins from the isolated sentence and undertakes to "translate" it from a hypothetical "null context" meaning into a social action has any real chance of grasping even these elementary phenomena. Indeed, the lesson that should properly be taken from Labov and Fanshel's study is that, rather than starting from sentence meanings, analysis should begin from the study of sequences of actions and the ways in which context forms a resource in their interpretation. Any other approach is liable to misconstrue what is at stake in the analysis of situated social interaction.

A speech-act-based approach that was more directly focused on the sequential organization of action was developed by the Birmingham discourse analysis group, which examined classroom and medical interaction (Sinclair and Coulthard 1975; Coulthard 1977; Coulthard and Montgomery 1981; Stubbs 1983). Like Labov and Fanshel, the Birmingham group focus on discourse coherence, viewing it in essentially "grammatical" terms (Sinclair and Coulthard 1975). Just as well-formed sentences can be treated as the products of the rules of syntax, so coherent and meaningful discourse can be generated by a syntax of action specified, in Sinclair and Coulthard's model, in terms of hierarchically organized sets of acts, moves, exchanges, and transactions. In their analysis of classroom interaction (Sinclair and Coulthard 1975), interactional coherence is most extensively treated at the level of the exchange structures, the most cited of which is the initiation–response–feedback (I–R–F) exchange.[14] The Birmingham studies represented a move towards a more dialogic analysis of language in institutional settings. Interaction is specified through descriptions of sequential patterns – the sequences of moves making up exchanges that are characteristic of particular settings such as the classroom – and the predictions or expectations that these patterns engender. Three-part structures similar to those discussed by Sinclair and Coulthard have also been identified by others working on classroom discourse (notably Mehan 1979: Ch. 2; also Drew 1981).

Despite the analytical advance represented by the Birmingham approach, it is vulnerable to a number of basic criticisms. Conceptually, the Birmingham authors' attempt to develop a formal analysis of the utterance–action relationship through "translation rules" appears to be vulnerable to the same criticisms that Levinson (1981a, 1981b, 1983) levels against the Labov and Fanshel approach. Moreover, in the wake of Grice's (1975) discussion of conversational implicature, the notion that sequences of discourse can be abstractly specified in terms of well- or ill-formedness is no longer defensible (Levinson 1981b, 1983; Taylor and Cameron 1987: 76–9). Goffman (1981b: 68–72), for example, playfully illustrates the difficulties of specifying rules for a determinate well-formed discourse with two pages of possible responses to the utterance *Do you have the time?* And, in a different way, Garfinkel's (1967: 76–103) analysis of his "student-counselling experiment" illustrates the adroitness with which some contextual element can be invoked to give sense to an apparently bizarre interactional contribution.

With respect to empirical analysis, the focus of the Birmingham group on institutional discourse was less advantageous than may at first appear. There is an important sense in which the I–R–F analysis depends for its cogency on the constraints of the classroom and medical contexts it models. It is doubtful that such a model would have been attempted for more free-flowing conversational interaction, where participants have a greater range of opportunities to act and options among alternative courses of action. Moreover, the socially constrained context of classroom interaction may have encouraged hopes for a relatively simple formalism which could be, in turn, extended to other social contexts without too much difficulty.

These formalistic hopes were, in retrospect, distracting. In their preoccupation with the rules for discursive action within a context, the Birmingham group tended to ignore the task of analyzing how mutual understandings are achieved by the participants – thereby mirroring a central weakness of Parsonian normative sociology (Garfinkel 1967; Heritage 1984a). This engendered a related failure to specify in their model how participants show their orientations to the particular institutional context in which they are interacting. For example, because the investigators did not look at question-answer-feedback sequences in a variety of settings (see Levinson, this volume ch. 2; Heritage 1984a: 280–90), their analysis failed to disclose the ways in which successive elements of the I–R–F sequence *constitute* its "instructional" character.[15] There was thus a deep incompatibility between the Birmingham investigators' underlying assumption of an association between a fixed social context and a formal syntax of action, on the one hand, and the active context-cueing approach embodied in Gumperz and Goffman's analyses, in the more general tradition of "context analysis" (Kendon 1979, 1982, 1990) and indeed in the then emerging perspective of conversation analysis on the other.

These various difficulties came to a head in two related analytic failures. First, although the I–R–F model was originally developed specifically to render formal descriptions of sequences of "exam" questions in classroom interaction, its fundamental analytic categories were fatally general and imprecise. This generality permitted the extension of the model to other institutional domains, such as doctor–patient interaction, but without serious attention being given to how these various settings are differentiated. As a result, notwithstanding their very real social differences, the two settings could not be differentiated in formal terms.

Second, the I–R–F model tended to obscure the social relations of the environments it described. The classroom context that Sinclair and Coulthard (1975) deal with, for example, is one that most educators would describe as "traditional" (McHoul 1978; Taylor and Cameron 1987). In their pursuit of a formal model to describe interaction in this context, the Birmingham group specified, as features of "coherence" in discourse, behaviors that might preferably be viewed in terms of a regime of conduct underpinned by a particular pedagogical theory and enforced, if need be, by threat. There was, in short, a tendency to conflate linguistic rules and social relations. And, in an analysis that was apt to slip between descriptive and prescriptive views of rules (Taylor and Cameron 1987: 74–80), to treat conduct that is clearly informed by considerations of task and teaching philosophy as something that could be treated in exclusively linguistic terms.

In sum, the last two decades have witnessed a broad range of conceptual innovation in the study of dialog. The impact of the ethnography of speaking and of speech-act models of dialog on the analysis of social interaction may be summarized as follows. The ethnographic studies, with their background in cultural anthropology, have created a richly textured sense of the role of sociocultural context in ordinary understandings of utterances and events. They have contributed to a broader and more detailed sense of how context structures and shifts the meaning of utterances and is itself structured and shifted by them. However, with their primary emphasis on the cultural background of language use, the ethnographers of communication generally have not developed analyses that combine a focus on the organization of specific sequences in social interaction with a treatment of the understandings and practical reasoning that inform these sequences and are engendered by them.

The speech-act theorists, on the other hand, recognize the importance of sequence in interaction and have worked to establish formal models of the linkages between one spoken action and the next. Yet the effort to develop analyses of these linkages using linguistic frameworks and metaphors that denied the relevance of contextual considerations has resulted in flawed conceptual tools and empirical analyses. In particular, analytical formalism was bought at the cost of empirical purchase on the detailed fabric of the social world of interaction.

Contemporary with both of these analytic frameworks, C A emerged with an approach to sequence in social interaction that avoided the sterile formalism that has constricted speech-act approaches to dialog. At the same time, in its analysis of specific organizations of social actions, C A has from the outset found ways of admitting the enriched sense of context in utterance that ethnographic approaches have insistently advocated. In what follows, we sketch the nature of the C A approach to interaction as a prelude to focusing on its application to institutional talk.

3 Conversation analysis: a brief overview

Conversation analysis combines a concern with the contextual sensitivity of language use with a focus on talk as a vehicle for social action. With its grounding in the study of ordinary talk between persons in a wide variety of social relations and contexts, C A has been in a particularly strong position to develop analytic tools for the study of talk-in-context. Indeed, as Schegloff (ch. 3) notes, CA represents a consistent effort to develop an empirical analysis of the nature of context. Here, we briefly summarize four major features of the CA perspective which have a particular relevance for the analysis of talk in institutional settings.

3.1 The activity focus of conversation analysis

The decisive feature that distinguishes the CA treatment of interaction and language use from others that are current in the field is what may be termed its *activity focus*. In contrast to perspectives that begin, at one pole of the analytic enterprise, with a treatment of culture or social identity or, at the other pole, with linguistic variables such as phonological variation, word selection, syntax, etc., CA begins from a consideration of the *interactional accomplishment of particular social activities*. These activities are embodied in specific social actions and sequences of social actions. Thus the initial and overriding CA focus is on the particular actions that occur in some context, their underlying social organization, and the alternative means by which these actions and the activities they compose can be realized.[16]

3.2 Sequential analysis: an interactional approach to the units of discourse

The activity focus described above emerged directly from the core interests of CA in "structures of social action" (Atkinson and Heritage 1984). These interests embodied an ethnomethodologically inspired concern to investigate the procedures and resources by which actors can engage in mutually intelligible social interaction whose organization is assured through an architecture of intersubjectivity and moral accountability (Heritage 1984a). These investigations could only be pursued through intensive analysis of particular interactional events because the data of CA – ordinary conversational actions in everyday contexts – proved quite resistant to treatment in terms of normal sociolinguistic variables and indeed to premature quantification more generally (Schegloff in press).

The emerging CA perspective developed through detailed qualitative analysis of naturally occurring data. Its analyses rapidly led to the conclusion that the sense of an utterance *as an action* is an interactive product of what was projected by a previous turn or turns at talk and what the speaker actually does. This analytic integration of what linguists would terms the "illocutionary" dimension of a current utterance with the "perlocutionary" dimension of its prior has been a hallmark of CA data analysis from its inception. It represents a wholesale departure from the analytic outlook of speech-act analysis as presently practised and it further required a focus on units that were larger than the individual sentence or utterance. These units were conceived as *sequences of activity* and their component unit turns as turns-within-sequences.

3.3 The conception of context

The interactional framework of CA also embodies a particular analytic attitude towards the notion of context in interaction. Within this framework, as Heritage (1984a) summarized it, utterances – and the social actions they embody – are treated as doubly contextual. First, utterances and actions are *context shaped*. Their contributions to an ongoing sequence of actions cannot be adequately understood except by reference to the context in which they participate. The term "context" is here used to refer both to the immediately local configuration of preceding activity in which an utterance occurs, and also to the "larger" environment of activity within which that configuration is recognized to occur. This contextual aspect of utterances is significant both because speakers routinely draw upon it as a resource in designing their utterances and also because, correspondingly, hearers must also draw upon the local contexts of utterances in order to make adequate sense of what is said. Second, utterances and actions are *context renewing*. Since every current utterance will itself form the immediate context for some next action in a sequence, it will inevitably contribute to the contextual framework in terms of which the next action will be understood. In this sense, the interactional context is continually being developed with each successive action. Moreover each current action will, by the same token, function to renew (i.e. maintain, adjust, or alter) any broader or more generally prevailing sense of context which is the object of the participants' orientations and actions.

Entailed in this view of context is the abandonment of what may be termed the "bucket" theory of context in which some preestablished social framework is viewed as "containing" the participants' actions.[17] Instead, the CA perspective embodies a dynamic approach in which "context" is treated as both the project and product of the participants' own actions and therefore as inherently locally produced and transformable at any moment. Thus the methodological constraints raised by Schegloff (ch. 3) concerning the relevance of particular social identities and the procedural consequentiality of context are generic to CA approaches to the analysis of social interaction. The study of institutional interaction cannot by any means be exempted from this constraint (Heritage 1984a: 280–90).[18] It is this abandonment of the "bucket" theory of context that marks an important point of contrast between CA and the perspective of the Birmingham school of discourse analysis.

3.4 Comparative analysis

CA research has, in part, been inspired by the realization that ordinary conversation is the predominant medium of interaction in the social world. It is also the primary form of interaction to which, with whatever simplifications, the child is initially exposed and through which socialization proceeds. Thus the basic forms of mundane talk constitute a kind of benchmark against which other more formal or "institutional" types of interaction are recognized and experienced. Explicit within this perspective is the view that other "institutional" forms of interaction will show systematic variations and restrictions on activities and their design relative to ordinary conversation (Sacks, Schegloff, and Jefferson 1974: 629; Atkinson and Drew 1979; Atkinson 1982; Heritage 1984a). The study of ordinary conversation, preferably casual conversation between peers, may thus offer a principled approach to determining what is distinctive about interactions involving, for example, the specialisms of the school or the hospital or the asymmetries of status, gender, ethnicity, etc. A clear implication is that comparative analysis that treats institutional interaction in contrast to normal and/or normative procedures of interaction in ordinary conversation will present at least one important avenue of theoretical and empirical advance. This comparative focus is manifest in a number of the contributions to this volume.

4 Analyzing institutional talk; methodological aspects

In analyzing specific features of interaction in social institutions, most of the contributors to this volume begin from the perspective expressed by Schegloff (ch. 3) concerning the interrelationship of interaction and social organization, of talk and social structure. As Schegloff observes, most students of interactional data readily acquire an intuitive sense of the particular social identities or attributes (e.g. gender, ethnicity, status, occupational role, power, etc.) which the parties treat as significant in the course of their interaction. And, as Atkinson (1982) points out, this sense can be overwhelming in institutional talk.[19] The question that Schegloff raises, however, is how are these institutions to be translated into empirically warranted findings? In this context, he observes, following Sacks's (1972a) discussion, that persons can be correctly described in numerous different ways. This raises what he terms the issue of "relevance": given that mere "factual correctness" cannot motivate the analytic use of one particular description over another, the analyst is faced with the task of finding some other warrant for some specific description of the parties. Like Schegloff, the contributors to this volume do not look for solutions which Schegloff terms "positivistic." Rather they are concerned to show that analytically relevant characterizations of social interactants are grounded in empirical observations that show that the *participants themselves* are demonstrably oriented to the identities or attributes in question.

In the context of institutional talk, this means that empirical analysis must first accomplish the normal CA tasks of analyzing the conduct of the participants including their orientations to specific local identities and the underlying organization of their activities. Additionally, however, analysis will normally be concerned to show that the participants' conduct and its organization embody orientations which are specifically institutional or which are, at the least, responsive to constraints which are institutional in character or origin. This additional task is by no means a straightforward one. Although it is easy enough, on an intuitive basis, to identify a variety of ways in which activities seem to be "done differently" in institutional settings, it is much more difficult to specify these differences precisely and to demonstrate their underlying insti-

tutional moorings. These difficulties are further compounded by the
fact that, as noted above, CA works with an elaborate and complex
approach to the analysis of social context. Given the abandonment
of the "bucket" concept of context in favor of a more dynamic
"context renewing" one, CA researchers cannot take "context" for
granted nor may they treat it as determined in advance and independent of the participants own activities. Instead, "context" and
identity have to be treated as inherently locally produced, incrementally developed and, by extension, as transformable at any
moment. Given these constraints, analysts who wish to depict the
distinctly "institutional" character of some stretch of talk cannot be
satisfied with showing that institutional talk exhibits aggregates
and/or distributions of actions that are distinctive from ordinary
conversation. They must, rather, demonstrate that the participants
constructed their conduct over its course – turn by responsive turn
– so as progressively to constitute and hence jointly and collaboratively to realize the occasion of their talk, together with their own
social roles in it, as having some distinctively institutional character. Although there is, it appears, no single "royal road" to such
demonstrations because the character of institutional interaction
varies widely across different institutional tasks and settings, a
major resource in such demonstrations is comparative analysis, to
which we now turn.

5 Institutional talk and ordinary conversation: activities, goals, constraints, and inferences

In the following discussion, we will address some aspects of interaction which are often cited when analysts seek to distinguish "institutional talk" from "ordinary conversation." We stress that we do
not accept that there is necessarily a hard and fast distinction to be
made between the two in all instances of interactional events, nor
even at all points in a single interactional event. Nor do we intend
to offer a definition of "institutional talk,' nor to make any attempt
at synoptic description. Rather, our aim here is to point to some
features that may contribute to family resemblances among cases of
institutional talk that are predominantly addressed in the chapters
that follow.

In his contribution to this volume, Levinson (ch. 2) develops an analysis of some basic features of what he terms "activity types" in social interaction. Although his conception of activity types is broader in scope than our present concern with institutional interaction, it forms a valuable point of departure. Arising from Levinson's discussion, although construing the issues he raises within the terms of the *participants' orientations* to institutional context, we propose that:

1 Institutional interaction involves an orientation by at least one of the participants to some core goal, task or identity (or set of them) conventionally associated with the institution in question. In short, institutional talk is normally informed by *goal orientations* of a relatively restricted conventional form.
2 Institutional interaction may often involve *special and particular constraints* on what one or both of the participants will treat as allowable contributions to the business at hand.
3 Institutional talk may be associated with *inferential frameworks* and procedures that are particular to specific institutional contexts.

In what follows we will briefly elaborate on each of these points.

5.1 Institutional talk is goal-oriented in institutionally relevant ways

It is abundantly clear in the studies presented in this volume that the participants organize their conduct by reference to general features of the tasks or functions of particular social institutions as they understand them within either a vernacular or technical competence. Whether in a medical consultation, or an emergency call to the police, in a job interview or a cross-examination in court, both lay and professional participants generally show an orientation to institutional tasks or functions in the design of their conduct, most obviously by the kinds of goals they pursue.[20]

In this context however, it is useful to note the range of variation in the kinds of goal orientation that are evident in the interactions described in this volume. (a) Zimmerman's analysis (ch. 13) of emergency calls to the police, for example, deals with interactions whose manifest purposes – the request and dispatch of emergency assistance – are for the most part clearly and definitely oriented to by the participants from the outset to the completion of the call. In contrast, Heritage and Sefi (ch. 12) discuss nurse visits to new mothers whose tasks are various and generally ill-defined. In the emergency calls, the participants appear to operate with a pre-defined "top-down" conception of the interaction. In the com-munity-nurse visits, by contrast, the participants seem to negotiate their way in "bottom-up" fashion towards a sense of what the interaction will be about. Moreover, (b) the contributions to this volume show that, even where the participants share a stable under-standing of the general tasks or goals of their interaction, the specifics of their implementation may fluctuate in the local con-tingencies of interaction and that this is so regardless of whether the goals are presumptively cooperative (as in a visit to a doctor) or conflictual (as in a courtroom cross-examination). Additionally (c) we may note virtually inevitable differences in the goals pursued by lay and institutional participants. The latters' conduct, in particu-lar, is shaped by organizational and professional constraints and accountabilities which may be only vaguely known or entirely opaque to lay participants.

5.2 Institutional talk: constraints on contributions

A central theme of Levinson's discussion concerns the ways in which conduct in institutional settings may be shaped by reference to constraints that are goal-oriented or functional in character. In papers dealing with several kinds of institutional contexts, most notably courtroom conduct (Atkinson and Drew 1979; Drew, this volume, ch. 14) and news-interview interaction (Heritage 1985; Clayman 1988; Greatbatch 1988; Heritage and Greatbatch 1991), it has been shown that the participants shape their conduct by reference to powerful and legally enforceable constraints which impart a distinctly "formal" character to the interaction (Atkinson 1982). By contrast, in other institutional settings, for example nurse–mother or doctor–patient interaction, the participants are often oriented to more local and negotiable understandings about the ways in which the tasks or other institutional aspects of their activities may limit allowable contributions to the business at hand. In such contexts, the understandings (and the constraints on con-duct that are associated with them) are often quite variable from interaction to interaction and from phase to phase (or task to task) in any given interaction (Heath 1986; Heritage and Sefi, this volume, ch. 12).

A number of chapters in this volume detail the ways in which institutional contexts are manifested in, and in turn shape, the particular actions of both professional and lay interactants. These chapters go some way towards meeting Schegloff's (ch. 3) injunction that researchers document the "procedural consequentiality" of the participants' orientation to an institutional context by showing how this orientation has consequences for the "shape, form, trajectory, content or character of the interaction that the parties conduct" (111). As is noted in what follows, such consequentiality may be "positive" in the sense that certain actions, which might be inhibited in a conversational context, may be promoted in institutional contexts. Or, alternatively, it may be "negative" in the reverse sense that certain conversational actions may be strongly avoided in particular institutional contexts.

5.3 The special character of inference in institutional contexts

In a context where particular institutional goals may be the object of the participants' orientations and where the participants' conduct departs in various ways from ordinary conversational conduct, Levinson argues, there will also tend to be special – "institutional" – aspects of the reasoning, inferences, and implicatures that are developed in institutional interaction. For example, a number of kinds of institutional interaction (including legal, medical, and news-interview environments – see the contributions by Atkinson, Button, and Clayman to this volume) embody a constraint on the "professional" to withhold expressions of surprise, sympathy, agreement, or affiliation in response to lay participants' describings, claims, etc. Such withholdings would be interpreted as disaffiliative in a conversational context, but often are not clearly so interpreted in these professional encounters. Similarly, comparatively "innocuous" conversational remarks may be interpreted as threatening in an institutional context (Heritage and Sefi, ch. 12). In each case, considerations of social identity and task reconfigure the interpretive "valence" that may be attached to particular actions in institutional contexts by comparison to how they are normally understood in ordinary conversation. Still more tangled and complex interpretative issues arise in interactions, such as those described by Gumperz (ch. 10), where the participants to an institutional interaction (a job interview) do not share common cultural or linguistic resources.

In sum, these three dimensions of interaction – (a) orientations to institutional tasks and functions; (b) restrictions on the kinds of contributions to the talk that are, or can be, made; and (c) distinctive features of interactional inferences – are the primary features of talk that are focused upon here as evidencing distinctively institutional orientations in talk at work. Their analysis will very often involve an element of (explicit or tacit) comparison with the conduct and organization of ordinary conversation.[21] In what follows, we begin by distinguishing two main avenues of comparative research in this area.

6 Approaches to the analysis of institutional interaction

6.1 Formal settings

Among published studies that have focused on institutional talk, several of the more significant and influential have dealt with data in which the institutional character of the interaction is embodied first and foremost in its *form* – most notably in turn-taking systems which depart substantially from the way in which turn taking is managed in conversation and which are perceivedly "formal" in character. Following Sacks, Schegloff, and Jefferson's (1974) initiative, interactions in courtrooms (Atkinson and Drew 1979), classrooms (McHoul 1978), and news interviews (Greatbatch 1988) have been shown to exhibit systematically distinctive forms of turn taking which powerfully structure many aspects of conduct in these settings.

The studies which have reported these findings have been influential for two reasons. First, turn-taking organizations – whether for conversation or institutional contexts such as courtroom interaction – are a fundamental and generic aspect of the organization of interaction. They are organizations whose features are implemented recurrently over the course of interactional events. This characteristic gives them a special methodological interest for

students of institutional talk. For if it can be shown that the participants in a vernacularly characterized institutional setting such as a
courtroom pervasively organize their turn taking in a way that is
distinctive from ordinary conversation, it can be proposed that they
are organizing their conduct so as to display and realize its "institutional" character over its course and that they are doing so *recurrently and pervasively*. The "problem of relevance"raised by Schegloff (ch. 3) is thus resolved – at least at the grossest level – at a single
stroke.

The second source of interest in institutional turn-taking systems
also derives from their generic and pervasive character. To the
extent that the participants' talk is conducted within the constraints
of a specialized turn-taking system, other systematic differences
from ordinary conversation tend to emerge. These differences commonly involve specific *reductions* of the range of options and
opportunities for action that are characteristic in conversation and
they often involve *specializations* and *respecifications* of the interactional functions of the activities that remain. The ensemble of
these variations from conversational practice may contribute to a
unique "fingerprint" for each institutional form of interaction – the
"fingerprint" being comprised of a set of interactional practices
differentiating each form both from other institutional forms and
from the baseline of mundane conversational interaction itself.
Both severally and collectively, the members of each ensemble of
practices may contribute to what Garfinkel (Garfinkel, Lynch, and
Livingston 1981) has termed the "identifying details" of institutional activities.

These institutionalized reductions and specializations of the
available set of conversational options are, it should be stressed,
conventional in character. They are culturally variable; they are
sometimes subject to legal constraints; they are always vulnerable
to processes of social change; they are discursively justifiable and
are often justified by reference to considerations of task, efficiency,
fairness, and so on in ways that the practices making up the conversational "bedrock" manifestly are not. Associated with these various institutional conventions are differing participation frameworks (Goffman 1981c) with their associated rights and
obligations, different footings (ibid.) and different patternings of
opportunities to initiate and sanction interactional activities. The

special character of these conventions is also associated with subjective sentiments. Those elements of "formal" institutional interaction which are experienced as unusual, irksome, or discomforting are experienced as such against a tacitly assumed background which is supplied by the workings of ordinary conversation (Atkinson 1982).

In several of these "formal" forms of institutional interaction – most notably "formal" classroom interaction, courtroom interaction, and news interviews – turn taking is strongly constrained within quite sharply defined procedures. Departures from these procedures systematically attract overt sanctions. The pattern of turn taking in these settings is uniform and exhibits overwhelming compliance with these procedures. In the case of courtroom and news interview interaction, for example, it can sometimes be difficult to locate the "deviant cases" with which to exhibit the normativity of the procedures under investigation.[22] It is notable that these settings all involve the production of "talk for an overhearing audience." In two of the settings (courtrooms and classrooms), the audience is copresent and the turn-taking system is designed, at least in part, to control or curtail the nature of audience participation in any ongoing exchange (McHoul 1978; Atkinson 1979, 1982; Mehan 1979). In all three settings, the presence of an audience whose members may assess the moral character of the focal participants may help to limit the extent to which the latter depart from formal turn-taking procedures. In contrast, there are other types of institutional interaction where neither turn-taking organization nor other aspects of the talk exhibit the qualities of formality and uniformity so far described and it is to these that we briefly turn.

6.2 Non-formal settings

In a variety of less formal forms of institutional interaction – commonly occurring in medical, psychiatric, social-service, business, and related environments – patterns of interaction exhibit considerably less uniformity. Although they may show distributional asymmetries in the patterning of activities between role incumbents (e.g. as between doctors and patients in the asking, and answering, of questions in private consultations [Byrne and Long 1976; West

1984; Frankel 1990]), these asymmetries are apparently not the
products of turn-taking procedures that are normatively sanction-
able. These interactions, for the most part, take place in private
rather than public contexts. There is room within them for considerable negotiation and/or stylistic variation as to how they will
come to be managed (Byrne and Long 1976; Heritage and Sefi, this
volume, ch. 12). In many cases, although the talk in these settings is
clearly institutional in that official task-based or role-based activities occur at least some of the time, turn-taking procedures may
approximate conversational or at least "quasi-conversational"
modes.[23] When considered in turn-taking terms at least, the boundaries between these forms of institutional talk and ordinary conversation can appear permeable and uncertain.[24]

These characteristics have the following methodological consequence. It is unlikely that a single recursive procedure (such as is
found in special turn-taking procedures) can be found that would
pinpoint the participants' turn-by-turn instantiation of institutional
role-based identities at a single stroke. Accordingly, the participants' orientation to the institutional task- or role-based character
of their talk will be located in a complex of non-recursive interactional practices that may vary in their form and frequency. Systematic aspects of the organization of sequences (and of turn design
within sequences) having to do with such matters as the opening
and closing of encounters, with the ways in which information is
requested, delivered, and received, with the design of referring expressions, etc. are now beginning to emerge as facets of the ways in
which the "institutionality" of such encounters are managed (Maynard 1984, 1991; Heritage 1985; Whalen and Zimmerman 1987;
Clayman 1989; Watson 1990; Boden forthcoming; and in this
volume, Atkinson, ch. 6; Bergman, ch. 4; Heath, ch. 8; Maynard,
ch. 11). Other studies deal with activities that are more particularly
tied to specific institutional contexts – the physical examination in a
medical consultation (Heath 1986: 99–137; 1988) is a case in
point.

In what follows, and in a spirit of exploration rather than *ex
cathedra* pronouncement, we outline five major dimensions of
interactional conduct that seem to us to constitute foci of research
into institutional talk at the present. These are: (a) lexical choice;
(b) turn design; (c) sequence organization; (d) overall structural

organization; and (e) social epistemology and social relations. In considering these themes, we will discuss a range of research drawn from C A and the cognate traditions of research outlined earlier.

7 The organization of talk in institutions: dimensions of research

7.1 Lexical choice

Lexical choice is a significant way through which speakers evoke and orient to the institutional context of their talk. Numerous studies have documented the incidence of "lay" and "technical" vocabularies in such areas as law and medicine, and it is clear that the use of such vocabularies can embody definite claims to specialized knowledge and institutional identities (Korsch and Negrete 1972; Meehan 1981; Waitzkin 1985).[25] The following extract is from the Heritage and Sefi health-visitor corpus and occurs during the first visit to the home of a two-week-old infant by a type of community nurse known in Britain as a health visitor. Here, a mother's description of the birth of her first child contains enough technical terminology to claim considerable medical expertise:

```
(1)  [HV:3A1:2]
  1   M:        And I was able to push her ou:t on my ow::n,=
  2   HV:       =Goo:d.
  3   M:        And um (0.6) I didn't have an episiotomy so:,
  4             (0.3)
  5   HV:       O::h s ┌u:per.
  6   M:              └I had a (0.3) tiny little tea:r it wasn't a
  7             perineal one (0.2) it was a (sort of      )=
  8   HV:       =Mm
  9   M:        And um (1.5) but otherwise everything was fi:ne (.) and
 10             the epidural made it lovely at the e:nd because I was
 11             able to pu:sh still ˙hhh but I had no pai:n and it was
 12             (.) super, it was lo:vely,
```

The relevance of lexical choice to institutional contexts is, however, far more wide-ranging than the use of technical jargon. Choices among descriptive terms are almost universally context-sensitive. For example, the choice between *cop* and *police* is, as Jefferson (1974) and Sacks (1979) have both noted, a consequential one for a variety of contexts including court proceedings (Jefferson 1974), though neither term is, of course, a technical one.

segment8
30 Paul Drew and John Heritage

In noticing issues to do with lexical choice, many studies document how speakers select descriptive terms which are fitted to their roles within an institutional setting. A clear illustration, noted by Sacks (1992 [fall 1967]: lecture 11), is that when speaking as a member of an organization, persons may refer to themselves as *we*, rather than *I*. Examples of this phenomenon are ubiquitous. Those that follow are cases of two-party interaction where organizational representatives refer to themselves as *we*. The first is from a study of household interviews for the US General Social Survey and National Health Interview Survey (Suchman and Jordan 1990).

```
(2) [Suchman and Jordan 1990:238](I = interviewer, Mrs = householder)
1   Mrs:        Uh huh. I guess the problem I'm having with the
2               question is, when you say cut down his activities
3               does that mean that, that he really, you know,
4               wasn't:: doing things actively or that he wasn't
5               doing what he would normally do::
6   I:     →    Well we, uh, we take the thing that the person would
7               normally do. . .
```

And in the next datum – a call to the emergency services for paramedic assistance (J. Whalen, Zimmerman, and Whalen 1988: 344) – both parties use *we* as a medium of self-reference.

```
(3) [Whalen et al 1988: 344](D = desk, C = caller)
1   D:          Hello? What's thuh problem?
2   C:     →    We have an unconscious, uh:, diabetic
3   D:          Are they insiduv a building?
4   C:          Yes they are:
5   D:          What building is it
6   C:          It's thuh adult bookstore
7   D:     →    We'll get somebody there right away
```

In instances such as these, speakers use the self-referring *we* to invoke an institutional over a personal identity, thereby indicating that they are speaking as representatives, or on behalf, of an organization.[26] The last instance, from an emergency-services call, is interesting in this respect. The emergency services are called up by members of the public, who may themselves not have any institutional identity relevant to their calling. However, here the caller self-refers with "we" (line 2): it turns out that for this caller *his* institutional identity – a shop assistant – *is* relevant to the matter of how he comes to be calling. The person for whom assistance is sought is not connected to the caller other than that he has lost consciousness in the shop at which the caller works ("It's thuh adult book store"). Notice as well that the emergency-services desk operator also uses the institutional *we*.

These observations, in turn, open up a rich vein of analysis which can focus on the use of *we* and *I* by incumbents of institutional roles (see Maynard 1984; Silverman 1987; West 1990); for example, in the following a doctor is recommending a test to the parents of a child with a heart condition:

(4) [Silverman 1987:58]
```
1   Dr:          Hm (2.0) the the reason for doing the test
2         →      is, I mean I'm 99 per cent certain that all
3                she's got is a ductus
4   F:           Hm hm
5   M:           I see
6   Dr:   →      However the time to find out that we're
7                wrong is not when she's on the operating
8                table
```

Here the switch from *I* to *we* is significant not merely as a shift from a more to a less "democratic" referring expression (Silverman 1987: ch. 3), but also as a means for the doctor to avoid saying *the time to find out when I'm wrong is not ...*, which would overtly raise the possibility of his being personally responsible for a clinical error.[27]

Temporal references are a further illustration of the ways in which lexical choices can formulate context (Schegloff 1972). There can be differences between what is an appropriate descriptive term in conversation, on the one hand, and some institutional context on the other; for example, Mishler cites this extract as an instance of conflict between doctor and patient about how appropriately to describe "how long."

(5) [Mishler 1984:165]
```
1   Dr:          How long have you been drinking that
2                heavily?
3   Pt:          Since I've been married
4   Dr:          How long is that?
5   Pt:          (giggle) Four years
```

The two versions of "how long" which the patient gives arise from different pragmatic formulations of time, the first being biographical or "personal" time, the latter being "calendar" time (Sacks 1992 [spring 1972]: lecture 5). In ordinary conversation, recollecting when or how long ago something happened may involve placing that in relation to the events of one's own biography or experience (Button 1990). But in more "formal" contexts, time is often more appropriately formulated in terms of a universalistic or "objective" measure. The patient in the extract above first responds in terms of her biographical time ("Since I've been married"), which, of course, may simultaneously offer an account for *why* she started drinking heavily. The doctor's redoing of the question treats her "conversational" version as not appropriate to the norms of the clinical setting and, by her revised answer, she acquiesces in this treatment. The conflict between "conversational" and "institutional" formulations of time here is also the carrier for the participants' very different agendas for this encounter. While the patient apparently seeks to raise complainable aspects of her life circumstances, the doctor declines their elaboration.[28] Studies of courtroom interaction are similarly replete with examples of conflicts between biographic and calendar formulations of time and with the tangles that witnesses get into when required to translate between the two.

In the present volume, Bergmann's (ch. 4) analysis of questioning in psychiatric intake interviews includes a sustained discussion of a particular reference form ("litotes") as a means of accomplishing a particular institutional task tactfully or "discreetly." Drew (ch. 14) also discusses the use of lexical formulations through which descriptions are designed to be heard as "competing" with one another as a witness' strategy in contesting evidence in the restricted context of cross-examination in the courts. In several of the other contributions, discussions of lexical choice are embedded within analyses of the closely related issue of turn design.

7.2 Turn design

The analysis of turn design addresses two distinct phenomena: (a) the selection of an activity that a turn is designed to perform; and (b) the details of the verbal construction through which the turn's activity is accomplished.

7.2.1 Selecting an action

A crucial feature of turn design concerns the selection of the activity to be accomplished in a turn at talk. The following extract is from the Heritage and Sefi health-visitor corpus. In it, a father and mother respond to a remark from the health visitor by performing quite different actions:

```
(6) [HV:4A1:1]
 1   HV:          He's enjoying that ⌈ isn't he.
 2   F:      →                      ⌊°Yes, he certainly is=°
 2   M:      →      =He's not hungry 'cuz (h)he's ju(h)st (h)had
 4           →      'iz bo:ttle ˙hhh
 5                  (0.5)
 6   HV:            You're feeding him on (.) Cow and Gate
 7                  Premium.
```

When the visitor remarks "He's enjoying that," she is presumably noticing the baby sucking or chewing on something. This is certainly the gloss which the mother gives to *enjoy* when she responds "He's not hungry ..." In replying that way, she treats the health visitor's remark as implying that the baby is "enjoying" whatever he is sucking or chewing because he might be hungry – an implication which she rebuts with the account that the baby has just been fed. The mother's response is a *defense* against something which she treats as implied in the health visitor's remark. The father, by contrast, simply *agrees* with the health visitor. Thus, in designing their responses differently (quite apart from the particular design of their turns), the mother and father elect to perform alternative activities. Both activities, of course, have a "logic" as relevant next actions: the father treats the health visitor's remark as an innocent "conversational" one; the mother, who is oriented to the health visitor's advisory tasks in the visit, employs a different inferential schema (Levinson, ch. 2) and finds a more pointed implication regarding the proper care of her baby. Her response is one that is oriented both to the institutional role of the health visitor as an observer and an evaluator of baby care and to her own responsibility and accountability for that care. It may be added that the parents' different responses also reflect an underlying conventional gender-based family division of labor, together with sensitivities to other institutional orders that cannot be further elaborated here.

7.2.2. *Selecting the verbal shape of an action*

In designing a turn, a selection is made between alternative ways of saying something or performing the same action. In extract (6) we saw that a mother and father performed very different actions in response to a health visitor's observation. In another instance later in the same visit, they perform broadly the same action, agreeing with the health visitor, but design their agreements quite differently.

```
(7) [HV:4A1:2] (HV is a health visitor; M the mother and F the father)
 1   HV:        It's amazing, there's no stopping him now,
 2              you'll be amazed at all the di ⌐ fferent things=
 3   F:                                        ⌊(hnh hn)
 4   HV:        =he'll start doing.
 5              (1.0)
 6   M:         Yeh. They ⌐ learn so quickly don't they.
 7   F:                   ⌊ We have noticed hav'n't w–
 8   HV:        That's right.
 9   F:         We have noticed (0.8) making a grab for your
10              bottles.
11              (1.0)
12   F:         Hm ⌐::.
13   HV:           ⌊Does he: (.) How often does he go between
14              his feeds?
```

Here the health visitor has been asking the parents whether the baby has begun to look around and "fix" on them and they confirm that he has. At lines 6 and 7 in this extract, the mother and father each produce an utterance designed to agree with the health visitor's suggestion that they will be "amazed" at the child's progress and they do so nearly simultaneously. However, the mother's agreement refers to the development of children in general ("They learn so quickly don't they"), while the father refers to their experience of their own child's progress ("We have noticed hav'n't w-"). The fact that the parents perform the same action somewhat independently of one another is evidence for the intersubjective relevance of that action in that slot.[29] The differences in the design of the two agreements point to the fact that these actions can be fashioned in alternative ways.[30]

The alternatives that may be involved in turn design are rarely as exposed as they are in extract (7), where different speakers employ

different designs to achieve the same broad end. More usually, the
choices involved in turn design can be teased out by looking at the
details of a turn's components and determining their interactional
purpose or import. In the following datum, AC is an attendance-
office clerk at an American high school. Part of her job is to call the
homes of children who have missed classes at school and who are
therefore suspected of being truants. The following is the first part
of one such call.

(8) [Medeiros 5] (AC is the attendance clerk; M his mother, F is father)
```
 1    AC:        Hello this is Miss B from W
 2               High School calling
 3    M:         Uh hu:h
 4    AC:        Was Charlie home from school ill today?
 5               (0.3)
 6    M:         ˙hhhh
 7               (0.8)
 8    M:         ((off phone)) Charlie wasn't home ill today
 9               was he?
10               (0.4)
11    F:         ((off phone)) Not at all.
12    M:         No:.
13               (.)
14    AC:        N ┌o?
15    M:          └No he wasn't
16    AC:        ˙hhh (.) Well he wz reported absent from his
17               thir:d an' his fifth period classes tihday.
18    M:         Ah ha:h,
19    AC:        ˙hhh A:n' we need him t' come in t'the office
20               in the morning t' clear this up
```

When, after checking with the father, the mother confirms that
their son has not been home ill that day (lines 12 and 15), the
attendance clerk informs her of the boy's absences from certain
classes (lines 16–17). Here it is noticeable that the clerk does not
say *he was absent from his* ... Instead, she says "he wz reported
absent from ..." and thereby evokes an "official" or bureaucratic
dimension to the transfer of information she describes. Moreover,
by including "reported" the clerk cites an (unspecified) source for
the information she is relaying and this imparts a certain equivocality to that information (Pomerantz 1984b). Had she said simply *he
was absent from* ..., the clerk would be heard to announce an
established, known fact. Since "reports" need to be confirmed

before becoming "facts," the equivocality to be found in "reported" suggests that the information has yet to be checked and confirmed. Hence the selection and inclusion of "reported" in line 16 introduces an equivocality, the interactional import of which is to announce a suspicion of absence. The determination of the full facts of his absence awaits further investigation (Pomerantz 1990/1).

The way in which the clerk refers to this investigation (in lines 19–20) is also consistent with the cautiousness which "reported" lent to her announcement of the absence. In saying "we need him" to come into the office, the clerk describes the organization's bureaucratic procedure for dealing with such cases. Alternative possible forms such as *he needs to, he should,* or *you should send him* might have more plainly implied the child's responsibility in remedying a shortcoming in his conduct. Similarly "t'clear this up" avoids presupposing the child's guilt. It is a neutral way of referring to the inquiry relative to such alternative forms as *to explain why,* which would treat his absence or truancy as established fact. Thus the clerk consistently uses expressions which convey the equivocality or still-to-be-determined status of the nature and extent of the child's absence, together with the child's culpability in the matter.

In sum, our second dimension of turn design arises from the fact that, because there is always a range of alternative ways of saying something, a speaker's selection of a particular formulation will, unavoidably, tend to be heard as "motivated" and perhaps chosen.[31] The syntactic, lexical, and other (e.g. prosodic) selections by a speaker are aspects of a turn's *design*. When, for instance, the clerk includes "reported" in announcing the child's absence from school, she designs that announcement to be cautious about the facts of the case. Thus turn design can articulate with the performance of organizational tasks (see below).

Turn design, then, embodies both an action selection and a selection of how the action is to be realized in words. Issues of turn design are often highly sensitive to issues of institutional incumbency. Chapters in this volume that have a particularly explicit or systematic focus on these topics include those by Clayman (ch. 5), Greatbatch (ch. 9), and Drew (ch. 14), but the topic has a centrality that renders it a major subtext in almost all the chapters in this collection.

7.3 Sequence organization

All analyses of institutional interaction – from ethnographic to
sociolinguistic – connect talk to its institutional context by citing
extracts of interaction in order to exhibit features of action and
social relations that are characteristic of particular settings. In these
analyses, whether CA-oriented or not, it is apparent that the
phenomena through which the institutionality of the talk is sub-
stantiated are most often *sequential* phenomena. For example, in an
investigation of a cleft-palate clinic, Silverman (1987) discusses a
doctor's attempt to determine whether a young patient wants to
undergo further surgery. He focuses on the misunderstandings that
can arise in this process by reference to the following:

```
(9) [Silverman (1987:165)] (C = consultant, D = 12 year old male patient)
 1   C:        Now then. This has got rather an ugly scar line
 2             hasn't it? It's rather (1.0) rather a lot of stitch
 3             marks.
 4             (1.0)
 5   C:        Isn't terribly handsome, is it? What do you think
 6             about your looks, Barry?
 7             (3.0)
 8   D:        I don't know.
 9   C:        You ((laughs)) Doesn't worry you a lot. You don't
10             lie awake at night worrying about it or anything?
11   D:        No
12   C:        No, no. It could be improved er because I think
13             that scar line isn't brilliant (1.0) but it's,
14             you're the customer, if you're happy with things the
15             way they are then that's
16   D:        Well I hope to have it done
17   C:        Oh you would oh. All right well (0.5) we'll see
18             about that (shortly). Now what about this nose of
19             yours...
```

Silverman's analysis focuses on the misunderstanding by the consultant (C) of the child's (D) "noncommittal" answer "I don't
know" (line 8), which C mistakenly interprets as meaning that D is
"happy with things the way they are" (14–15). In order to correct
this, D "has to resort to an interruption ... in order to convey his
real wishes" (line 16). After this point, "the discursive format of the
interview is re-asserted by the doctor's exercise of his interviewer's
rights to control the agenda by means of closing the topic and

beginning another" (Silverman 1987: 168) – the new topic being
D's nose (lines 18–19). Three "institutional" properties of talk are
thus taken to be evident in the data: (a) the misunderstandings
which can arise from the consultant trying to find out the patient's
preference indirectly (lines 5–6) rather than directly asking him if
he wanted a further operation; (b) the difficulties created for the
patient by the discursive format of the consultation which limits his
rights and opportunities to speak; and (c) the doctor's control over
the agenda of talk. Each of these is identified through an ordinary
conversational phenomenon, namely a *misunderstanding* (which
becomes apparent through a *repair* of that misunderstanding in the
next turn), an *overlap/interruption*, and a *topic change*.

This summary does not do justice to Silverman's analysis of this
extract to show how "[Clinical] discourse ... can create uncertainty
about the space available for the patient's speech" (1987: 168). But
it does illustrate the way in which analysis commonly draws upon
basic conversational phenomena in identifying patterns of talk that
are institutional in character.[32] Our point in raising this issue (and
of the list in note 32) is to underscore our earlier suggestion that the
study of institutional interaction very often involves an explicit or
implicit comparative dimension. Basic conversational organizations
(in this case centering on repair, interruption, topic shift, and the
rest) are used by the participants in institutional settings to manage
particular role-specific activities. Here nonspecialized or conversational organizations are being fitted or adapted to specialized
interactional tasks in institutional contexts. Significant light can be
shed on institutional data by showing, for example, *how* nonspecialized conversational procedures are being thus adapted; how they
might be altered in some respects as compared with their use in
conversation; whether or how they are being used to novel effect
in a specialized setting; and how such conversational forms are
otherwise being systematically and recurrently mobilized to perform some specialized role-related or "strategic" task in that setting.

This comparative perspective is not always sufficiently acknowledged in the CA literature. Nor perhaps does it play a sufficiently
explicit role in non-CA discussions of research methodology.[33]
However, it is fundamental for two reasons: first, whether overtly
or tacitly, comparative judgments shape analytic interpretations of

how nonspecialized interactional procedures function in specialized institutional settings; second, the more specialized elements of institutional conduct which are often referred to in the literature in this area can themselves only be fully understood in a comparative context.

CA, with its body of findings about the sequential organization of ordinary conversation, has the potential to develop explicitly comparative studies of institutional talk. As noted earlier, many of these studies have so far focused on formal, public forms of interaction. They have dealt with the features of specialized institutional turn-taking systems, with the ways in which these systems are at least partially constitutive of, and fitted to the external constraints of, the activities they shape as "legal" or "broadcast talk" or "educational," and with the impact which these systems inevitably have on the design of actions and sequences of action (McHoul 1978; Atkinson and Drew 1979; Mehan 1979; Heritage 1985; Clayman 1988, 1989, 1991; Greatbatch 1988; Garcia 1991; Heritage and Greatbatch 1991). All of these studies focus on turn-taking systems which, in their different ways, are organized through the preallocation (Sacks, Schegloff, and Jefferson 1974; Atkinson and Drew 1979) of questions and answers — most often to the institutional and lay participants respectively.

Although question–answer sequences in many other institutional settings are not so formally organized, they are often a dominant form within which interaction proceeds. In a study of medical consultations, for example, Frankel (1990: 239) notes that fewer than 1 percent of the patients' utterances were initiatory in character — a figure which is highly comparable with statistics for more formal environments such as court proceedings (Adelsward *et al.* 1987; Linell, Gustavsson, and Juvonen 1988). Thus the normative outlooks and the local organization of doctor–patient interaction — a somewhat "nonformal" type of interaction — may generate skewed distributions of activities with quite the same efficacy as rules of formal turn taking in a legal setting.

These specialized but nonformal interactions often involve discernable transitions from a more "conversational" mode into a series of questions and answers. This is nicely illustrated in Erickson and Shultz's (1982: 77ff.) study of counseling interviews. Although there is no formal stipulation that these events be or-

ganized through question–answer sequences, the authors show
clear junctures at which the shift from introductory conversation to
the questioning part of the interview, as well as transitions from
one kind of questioning to another, are concertedly managed by the
participants. Similar transitions are reported for doctor–patient
interaction by Heath (1981), for survey interviews by Suchman and
Jordan (1990), and for health-visitor–mother interaction by Sorjonen and Heritage (1991).[34] Closely related to turn-taking restrictions also are the special opening (Turner 1972; Whalen and Zimmerman 1987; Levinson, this volume ch. 2) and closing (Clark and
French 1981; Greatbatch 1988; Clayman 1989) procedures that
are commonly associated with institutional talk.

Turn taking and the restriction of participants within a
question–answer framework are only the starting point for a consideration of the sequential organizations that are particular to
various forms of institutional talk. A useful point of entry into this
domain can be found in the variations in the third turns of three-
part sequences that emerge in many institutional environments.

During the instructional phase of classroom lessons, for
instance, teaching is managed through question–answer sequences
in which the third turn is often partly occupied with some kind of
evaluation. A prototypical case is the following:

(10) [Sinclair and Coulthard 1975:21]
```
1   T:        Can you tell me why do you eat all that food
2             Yes
3   S:        To keep you strong
4   T:        To keep you strong. Yes. To keep you strong.
5             Why do you want to be strong...
```

Here the evaluation consists of a repeat of the answer to confirm its
correctness, together with an accepting "Yes." The teacher then
initiates a new question–answer sequence with "Why do you want
to be strong?" Classroom instruction can thus consist of a recursive
chain or progression of such three-part sequences. This distinctive
sequential pattern is characteristic of talk in classrooms because it is
associated with the core activity in that setting, namely instruction.
We here underscore an important point: the three-part sequence is
characteristic of the setting (classroom) *only* because it is generated
out of the management of the activity (instruction) which is the
institutionalized and recurrent activity in the setting. Thus, where

the same activity is performed in other and possibly noninstitutionalized settings, as when parents instruct their children in the home, there also may be found similar three-part sequence structures (see Drew 1981). The sequence structure is the instrument through which the activity is accomplished on any given occasion (Heritage 1984a: 280–90).

Underlying this argument is a comparative point. Although it is not uncommon for an answer to be acknowledged by the questioner in conversation, it would be somewhat unusual, bizarre even, if the questioner were subsequently to evaluate the correctness of the recipient's answer, in the way that teachers ordinarily do in the classroom. Teachers, with certain institutionalized claims to superior knowledge (Mehan 1985), generally ask questions to which they already know the answers to test or extend students' knowledge.[35] Their evaluations of students' answers repeatedly reaffirm both the claim to superior knowledge and their role as testers of students. In conversation, by contrast, where questioners normally seek information which the recipient has to give, no such claim is in point.

The distinctiveness of conversational questions emerges clearly in such responses to question–answer sequences as *oh*. *Oh* is a common way in which speakers may indicate that they have been informed about something by what another has said. Heritage (1984b) terms *oh* a "change-of-state token," a resource through which speakers indicate that they have undergone a change in their locally current state of knowledge of awareness (see also Schiffrin 1987). *Oh* is often used to indicate receipt of information or of "news" of some kind, and contrasts with acknowledgments such as *that's right* that specifically avoid such indications (see Heritage and Sefi, ch. 12). Heritage also reports (1985: 96–101) that *oh* is very largely absent from talk in such institutionalized settings as radio or television news interviews, or classroom or courtroom interaction. This absence arises from the dual role of *oh* in conversation, where it indicates both that what the other has just said is news to the speaker and, in virtue of this, accepts the truth or adequacy of that news.[36] However, in news interviews and court rooms, for example, the questioners – that is, interviewers and lawyers respectively – are briefed beforehand and are expected to have a broad grasp of what the interviewees' or witnesses' answers are likely to be. For these questioners, answers are not and should not properly be "news." Furthermore, the primary recipients of the answers are the radio or television audience, or the jury: it is *they* who are to be informed, not the questioner. In such contexts, *oh* receipts are withheld and questioners therefore define themselves as the elicitors of talk, but not its recipients (Heritage 1985).

In sum, something of the distinctiveness of talk in classrooms as compared with conversation, and compared also to news interviews and courtroom examination, is visible in the different patterns of question–answer sequences in each setting. And this further underscores the value of comparative sequence analysis as a means of investigating the identifying characteristics of the activities associated with different institutional settings.

A number of the contributions to this volume discuss departures from routine conversational sequences in institutional settings. For example, Atkinson (ch. 6) shows that in Small Claims Courts, arbitrators respond to what plaintiffs say in such a way as to avoid affiliating or disaffiliating with them, thereby sustaining a neutral stance towards the evidence while it is being given. Similarly, Button observes (ch. 7) that job interviewers, by withholding response to interviewee's answers, avoid giving any indication as to their assessment of them. Maynard (ch. 11) details a questioning procedure which is particularly fitted to the telling of bad news in medical settings. Heath's chapter on the medical encounter (ch. 8) shows that patients are unresponsive to diagnostic information to an extent that would be remarkable in a conversational context. Greatbatch's chapter (ch. 9), perhaps the most explicitly comparative of all of the contributions to this volume, shows the ways in which departures from a specialized turn-taking system for news interviews which move the talk towards a conversational mode represent a method of escalating disagreement which is nonetheless generally "safe" in the context of the news-interview framework as a whole. Finally, Heritage and Sefi (ch. 12) outline the quite unusual ways in which advice is initiated by health visitors in comparison with its initiation in ordinary conversation (Jefferson and Lee, ch. 15), and argue that the advice is acknowledged and resisted in ways that are consistent with the social relations of the encounter.

7.4 Overall structural organization

A further level at which the institutionality of an interaction may manifest itself is in its overall structural organization. Many kinds of institutional encounters are characteristically organized into a standard "shape" or order of phases. Conversations, by contrast, are not. With the exception of the opening and closing stages of conversations, which are often shaped through a standard series of sequences, it does not appear that conversations ordinarily progress through some overarching set of stages. The locally contingent management of "next moves" in conversation, and the options speakers have even within particular sequences or activities, ensure that there is no "standard pattern" for the overall organization of conversations. The activities conducted in many kinds of institutional interactions, by contrast, are often implemented through a task-related standard shape. In some instances that order may be prescribed, for instance, by a written schedule or formal agenda of points which an inquirer may be required to answer when requesting a service (Frankel 1989). But equally, the order may be the product of locally managed routines (Zimmerman, ch. 13).

The impact of task orientation on the overall structural organization of an encounter is perhaps clearest in the 9–1–1 calls for police or emergency assistance discussed by Zimmerman (ch. 13). Here every aspect of the call – from the specialized opening (Whalen and Zimmerman 1987) onwards – is geared to the earliest possible completion of the task. Zimmerman points out that, regardless of the extent to which callers are questioned about their emergencies and the contingencies that the questioning raises, such calls are based on a single adjacency pair – a request for help from the caller and response from the emergency center (see also Schegloff 1990). The task focus of these calls is intense and precise: for example, the provision of a response is treated by the caller as the closing of the call.

Related arguments can be made for other task-oriented interactions, such as medical consultations and other institutional encounters that are characterized by functionally oriented phases. Some notable examples of the characteristic overall organizations which can be discerned in specific institutional interactions are provided by Erickson and Shultz (1982) for student–counsellor interviews, Byrne and Long (1976) and Davis (1988) for doctor–patient consultations, Mehan (1979) for classroom lessons, J. Whalen, Zimmerman, and Whalen (1988) for calls to an emergency-services agency, and Maynard (1984) for courtroom plea-bargaining.

One of the most comprehensive accounts of the overall organization of a form of institutional interaction is Byrne and Long's ordered sequence of six phases in family practice doctor–patient consultations (1976: ch. 3). In contrast to the kind of "invariant sequence" which Erickson and Shultz (1982: 22, 60) found in student–counsellor interviews, the Byrne and Long model is an idealized one. The six-stage sequence rarely appears in full and in its canonical order because certain stages are optional and the overall structure may be disordered by a range of contingencies. So, while the overall pattern – with its functional and dysfunctional elements – is discernible for all consultations, the optionality of particular stages accommodates the diversity of circumstances in which patients visit doctors.

Here, then, is some indication of the kinds of functionally related standard sequences which are beginning to be found to characterize certain institutional interactions, and which give them the kinds of overall structure which conversations generally do not have.[37] As Zimmerman stresses, the production of such overall organizations, the relevance of a given phase, and the move from one phase to a next are locally managed by participants in a given interaction. Nevertheless, the recurrence of such organizations across ranges of instances, persons, etc. indicates the extent to which participants may be jointly oriented towards an overall structural organization in their encounters.[38]

The existence of these standard patterns in institutional encounters is likely to owe much to the direction and initiative of the institutional professional. The professional may participate in many such interactions in a day, the client perhaps only one in a lifetime. In this context, professionals tend to develop, for better or worse, standard practices for managing the tasks of their routine encounters (Byrne and Long 1987; Emerson 1981). The progression of the interaction through a standard series of sequences certainly requires the collaboration of noninstitutional participants, who may, of course, also resist that progression. Nevertheless, the overall organization of such sequences into the kinds of standard patterns described above tend to be shaped primarily by the professional. Here an individual client may be confronted with an organization's routine for processing cases in a context where the routine itself emerges in and through the professional's ability to direct the talk (see below). Professional control here manifests itself as a pattern of sequences through which clients may find themselves being led.

7.5 Social epistemology and social relations

With this last category we mean to raise themes and issues that are often generally distributed across broad ranges of conduct in institutional settings and manifest themselves in and through the features of institutional interaction addressed above. These themes are not necessarily attached to any specific sequence of action; rather, they may emerge in any or all sequences. We begin with an illustration that evokes several contributions to this volume.

7.5.1 Professional "cautiousness" in interaction

Earlier in this chapter we discussed datum (8) below, and it emerged from that discussion that the school-attendance officer designed her turns in ways that were cautious.

(8) [Medeiros 5] (AC is the attendance clerk; M his mother, F is father)

```
 1   AC:        Hello this is Miss B from W
 2              High School calling
 3   M:         Uh hu:h
 4   AC:        Was Charlie home fron. school ill today?
 5              (0.3)
 6   M:         'hhhh
 7              (0.8)
 8   M:         ((off phone)) Charlie wasn't home ill today
 9              was he?
10              (0.4)
11   F:         ((off phone)) Not at all.
12   M:         No:.
13              (.)
14   AC:        N ┌o?
15   M:             └No he wasn't
16   AC:        'hhh (.) Well he wz reported absent from his
```

```
17                    thir:d an' his fifth period classes tihday.
18     M:            Ah ha:h,
19     AC:           ˙hhh A:n' we need him t' come in t'the office
20                    in the morning t' clear this up
```

This cautiousness emerges in a number of ways. First, the child's absence from school is introduced in a most indirect way (Pomerantz 1988). Rather than asserting that the child has not been at school, the attendance clerk asks "Was Charlie home from school ill today?" (line 4), thus avoiding stating outright that the child is absent. Further, the clerk's inquiry offers the most normal (Sacks 1984b; Pomerantz 1988) and legitimate account for the child's absence. The clerk's utterance is thus triply cautious. (a) The inquiry avoids stating outright that the child is not at school. The mother is permitted, even invited, to *infer* that her child has not been at school but the clerk's inquiry remains compatible with the possibility that the child is at school but has not been recorded as such. (b) If the child is ill, it permits the mother to establish that through an affirmative utterance that "confirms" the clerk's inquiry rather than through a sequentially "defensive" excuse or account. (c) Even if the child is, in fact, a truant, the inquiry specifically avoids drawing any conclusions about the child's absence from school and, in particular avoids any accusation of truancy.

This cautiousness is sustained at line 16, after the mother has confirmed that child was not at home. Here, as we have noted, instead of asserting that the child had been absent from school that day, the clerk announced to the mother that "he wz reported absent," the element of equivocation in her statement conveying the possibility, rather than a direct accusation, of truancy and leaving its determination, and its full extent, to subsequent investigation. Finally, in lines 19–20, where the clerk moves to propose how the absence should be dealt with, she preserves (with the words "t'clear this up") the possibility that there may yet be a legitimate explanation for the child's absence. This cautiousness, then, is something that inhabits the attendance clerk's orientation to her institutional tasks in all the details of this call. Lexical choice, turn design, and sequence organization are all here harnessed to the same end.

It is not only in these calls that professional cautiousness appears to be a feature of institutional talk. Many of the chapters of this collection suggest that the professional participants in institutional interactions design their talk so as to maintain a cautiousness, or even a position of neutrality with respect to their co-participants. In his study of news interviews, Clayman (ch. 5) identifies elements of question design which enable news interviewers to incorporate controversial or hostile opinions within the framework of their questions while avoiding any endorsement of those opinions. This design permits interviewers to ask challenging questions while nonetheless maintaining a "neutralistic" position (Heritage and Greatbatch 1991), remaining personally disengaged from the substance of the opinion being put to the interviewee. Atkinson, as noted above, shows (ch. 6) that, in the context of Small Claims Courts, arbitrators respond to claimants' statements in a distinctively neutral fashion. The chapters by Bergmann and Maynard provide further exemplification of professional cautiousness, respectively in the way psychiatrists design their quesions in psychiatric intake interviews and by clinicians when interviewing parents of children who have tested positively for developmental disabilities. Zimmerman reports (ch. 13) a related kind of cautiousness in certain types of calls to the emergency services. Where callers wish to alert the police to events in which they are not directly involved, they may work to display the innocent and unmotivated way in which they have discovered the untoward event – this being but a facet of what Zimmerman terms the "practical epistemology" of these communications (see also M. Whalen and Zimmerman 1990).

7.5.2. Interactional asymmetries in institutional settings

A central theme in research on institutional interaction is that in contrast to the symmetrical relationships between speakers in ordinary conversation, institutional interactions are characteristically asymmetrical. Underlying this research is a widespread acceptance that ordinary conversation is premised on a standard of "equal participation" between speakers and that this standard is departed from in talk in institutional settings. And, while there are significant differences in the literature concerning how to relate the interactional asymmetries of institutional talk to social-structural relations (Maynard 1991), the documentation of the asymmetries themselves continues to develop apace.

Linell and Luckmann (1991) have cautioned, however, that this dichotomy between the symmetries of conversation and the asymmetries of institutional discourse oversimplifies the nature of asymmetry and overlooks the ways in which conversational participation may be asymmetric. As they observe: "if there were no asymmetries at all between people, i.e. if communicatively relevant inequalities of knowledge were non-existing, there would be little or no need for most kinds of communication!" (Linell and Luckmann 1991: 4). Viewed from a perspective that asks which persons participate in talk and to what effect, it is apparent that ordinary conversation can embody asymmetries that have several dimensions. Conversational asymmetry exists, however temporarily, between the speaker and the hearer of a turn at talk; between the initiator and respondent in a sequence of interaction; between those who, more broadly, are active in shaping topics and those who are not; and between those whose interventions are decisive for the outcomes of conversations and those who are not (Linell 1990; Linell and Luckmann 1991). From this standpoint, the contrast between the putative symmetry of ordinary conversation and the asymmetry of institutional discourse is indeed oversimplified: all social interaction must inevitably be asymmetric on a moment-to-moment basis and many interactions are likely to embody substantial asymmetry when moment-to-moment participation is aggregated over the course of an encounter or, indeed, many encounters.

Yet the claim that there is a fundamental distinction between the symmetry of ordinary conversation and the asymmetries of institutional interaction emerges as a significant one when we consider ordinary conversation as a normative institution; for it is clear that the rules of conversation operate in ways that are, in principle at least, independent of the extradiscursive identities of the participants. Notwithstanding the several studies that have, for example, reported an association between power and status and asymmetries in conversational turn-taking violations (Zimmerman and West 1975; West and Zimmerman 1983; West 1984; Kollock, Blumstein, and Schwartz 1985), it is clear that the turn-taking rules themselves operate in terms of locally constructed discourse statuses rather than, for example, position in a social hierarchy.[39] Indeed, if this were not the case, the reported asymmetries in the distribution of violations might not seem so flagrantly unjust.

In many forms of institutional discourse, by contrast, there is a direct relationship between status and role, on the one hand, and discursive rights and obligations, on the other. As we have detailed, institutional interactions may by characterized by role-structured, institutionalized, and omnirelevant asymmetries between participants in terms of such matters as differential distribution of knowledge, rights to knowledge, access to conversational resources, and to participation in the interaction. In ordinary conversation between friends or acquaintances, by contrast, this is not normally the case. In a range of ways, patterns of institutional discourse indicate important asymmetries between professional and lay perspectives, and between professional and lay person's capacities to direct the interaction in desired and organizationally relevant ways. Here we briefly discuss asymmetries arising from restrictions on the participation rights of organizational and lay parties, asymmetries of knowledge and rights to knowledge, and asymmetries arising from differential access to organizational routines and procedures.

An important dimension of asymmetry between the participants in institutional interaction arises from the predominantly question–answer pattern of interaction that characterizes many of them. In such contexts, there may be little perceived opportunity for the lay person to take the initiative (Linell, Gustavsson, and Juvonen 1988; Frankel 1990) and professionals may gain a measure of control over the introduction of topics and hence of the "agenda" for the occasion. A common finding in this literature is that institutional incumbents (doctors, teachers, interviewers, family social workers, etc.) may strategically direct the talk through such means as their capacity to change topics and their selective formulations, in their "next questions," of the salient points in the prior answers (Heritage 1985: 101–4; Tannen and Wallat 1987: 303–6). In both ways, professionals may prevent particular issues becoming topics in their own right. This is a common theme in the literature on medical consultations, where examples are frequently cited to demonstrate that doctors cut short patients' apparent attempts to talk about aspects of their experience which doctors regard as irrelevant to a strictly medical assessment of their problems (Byrne and Long 1976; Mishler 1984; Tannen and Wallat 1987). Doctor's use of questioning and other resources to control the initiative are also a means by which doctors maintain control over what topics are deemed medically relevant, over what is talked about, and at what length (Byrne and Long 1976; West 1984; Davis 1988). Moreover, insofar as patients may be unaware of the purposes lying behind particular questions, they may not grasp the line of inquiry which the doctor is pursuing in questions about what might seem to be unconnected topics. Doctors' control over the initiation and shaping of topics, together with patients' lack of access to the "hidden agenda" of doctors' questioning, represent significant avenues of research into the asymmetry of participation in medical interaction (Shuy 1983; Fisher 1983; Silverman 1987: 184–5). Parallel asymmetries associated with "hidden agendas" have been reported for other institutional contexts, notably educational ones (Stubbs 1976).

A further dimension of professional–client asymmetry concerns the participants' differential states of knowledge. In conversation, the participants generally assume that, while they may not always be equally knowledgeable and informed about every topic, such asymmetries will be short-lived and will shift among the speakers from topic to topic; but in many professional–client interactions that assumption cannot be made. Once again, this kind of asymmetry is best documented for medical consultations. The literature shows that even where patients have considerable medical knowledge, they may orient to such knowledge as belonging to an authoritative professional (Strong 1979) by, for example, the tentative or uncertain use of medical terminology (Silverman 1987; Drew 1991; Maynard 1991). The literature frequently accounts for differences between doctors' and patients' perceptions and assessments of ailments in terms of the different bodies of knowledge that the parties bring to the encounter. Much of the misunderstanding and conflict which discourse researchers have identified in doctor–patient interaction may be attributable to differences between medical definitions of problems and patients' lay versions of their experience of these problems (Cicourel 1983; Mishler 1984; Silverman 1987; Tannen and Wallat 1987; Davis 1988; Frankel and West 1991).

A third asymmetrical property of interactions between institutional professionals and the lay public is worth mentioning, although it is given rather little attention in the literature. This arises from the difference, and often tension, between the organizational perspective that treats the individual as a "routine case," and the client, for whom his or her case is unique and personal. All agencies have procedures for the routine management of multiple cases, for "processing"cases by assigning them to routine categories, and so on. However, the clients – whose inquiries, troubles, illnesses, claims, and the like constitute an organization's routine cases – are not generally themselves aware of, or concerned with, the pattern into which their individual cases fit. The client's perspective often arises out of the particular circumstances which bring him or her into contact with the organization, perhaps for the first or only time, or at least not frequently enough to have developed a self-conception as a routine case.

A striking instance is Sudnow's ethnographic study of the routine management by hospital personnel of patients' deaths. Sudnow describes how the status of routine case is assigned to dying patients, what the interactional consequences are of being so assigned, and what communicational differences (and other differences in medical intervention) emerge when a dying patient is treated as a non-routine case (Sudnow 1967). Similarly, Sacks (1992 [April/May 1971]) shows that in calls to suicide-prevention agencies, the agency member's organizational need for "face sheet data" may influence the kind and order of questions and topics that may be raised in calls to the center. Whalen (1991) has similarly argued that, in 9–1–1 emergency calls, such contingencies as the current position of the cursor on a menu-driven computer screen can influence the pattern of the call.

These themes associated with asymmetry are evident in several contributions to this volume. Maynard's discussion of a particular procedure used by doctors prior to giving parents negative diagnoses about mental disability – a procedure that involves first asking the parents for their view of the child's disability – points to the ways in which an unquestionable disparity in medical authority can be exploited to prepare a parent for the worst. As Maynard shows, the procedure is initiated in the hope that the negative medical diagnosis can be done as an agreement with the parents' views. But the doctors risk inviting a view that may contradict their own, secure in the knowledge that it is the medical diagnosis that will prevail. In a different vein, Heritage and Sefi point to the unilateral ways in which health visitors may initiate advice giving to new mothers and the ways in which the latter display resistance to the advice that is given. This resistance overwhelmingly takes a passive form rather than outright rejection, and is, Heritage and Sefi suggest, calibrated to and reflects the disparities in knowledge and power between the parties. Finally, Heath, as noted earlier, documents the striking finding that, at the point in the consultation when doctors announce their diagnoses, patients typically withhold responding, neither commenting upon nor questioning the diagnosis. Patients thereby orient to and preserve the asymmetry between their own lay opinion and the authoritative medical knowledge embodied in diagnosis. All three studies suggest the complex interplay between knowledge, interaction patterns, social relations, and power which constitute an important intersection between studies of language and of social relations.

The topics taken up in this section are, of course, just illustrations of what is probably a quite general kind of asymmetry in professional–client interactions. Space prevents further consideration of what in more particular circumstances may be special sources of asymmetry – notably those associated with the linguistic and interactional norms, and interpretative procedures, of different speech communities, especially racial or ethnic communities (Gumperz, this volume ch. 10). The misunderstandings or misperceptions which such asymmetries may generate in interethnic interaction are an increasing focus of research (Erikson and Shultz 1982; Gumperz 1982).

We have been able here to give only a truncated account of the character and consequences of interaction processes identified in the literature on institutional interaction. It is clear that an important theme in this area is that the overall balance which may usually obtain, at least in the aggregate, between co-participants in ordinary conversation, in terms of shared interpretive procedures, knowledge, access to action opportunities, etc. is simply not a feature of institutional interactions. Indeed, every substantive contribution to this volume documents some form of institutionalized asymmetry in conduct.

In keeping with Schegloff's remarks, however (ch. 3; see also Drew 1991; ten Have 1991; Maynard 1991), we would stress that it is not enough to rely on exogenous explanations – for example, professional authority over clients – as an automatic explanation for such asymmetries, nor to attribute in an *ad hoc* fashion a particular event in the talk to participants' asymmetrical relations. Research needs to show both the specific ways in which the participants' talk is oriented to role-related asymmetries and the consequences of such orientations for talk-in-interaction and its outcomes. Alternatively, it should demonstrate, by thorough comparative analysis, that particular features of talk in institutional contexts embody systematic asymmetries that are not ordinarily found in mundane conversation. Given the ease with which asymmetries in conduct can be interpreted in terms of exogenous variables, their analysis should properly begin by addressing those features of the interaction to which the participants' conduct is demonstrably oriented. Only when these considerations are exhausted should analysis turn to factors that are exogenous to the interaction. Analytic approaches that start with endogenous features of interaction have the additional advantage of treating institutional asymmetries in an analytic context that must necessarily embrace the broadest range of aspects of the talk. Maynard observes (1991: 486) that "the asymmetry of discourse in medical settings may have an institutional mooring, but it also has an interactional bedrock, and the latter needs sociological appreciation as much as the former." There will be gains in our understanding of asymmetries in institutional discourse when their particulars are grasped as embedded in the larger tasks and frameworks of the interaction order.

8 The organization of the present volume

CA research has made a very substantial contribution to each of the themes reviewed in the previous section. Indeed, for some of those themes, its contribution has arguably been preeminent. This collection brings together a range of original studies of interaction in institutional settings and reflects our view that CA offers an especially powerful and coherent perspective from which to investigate the activities making up the life of social institutions. We believe that these studies offer new information about the ways in which a range of institutional activities are transacted in contemporary society, and that they embody new analytic outlooks on how such transactions may be described and investigated reliably and reproducibly.

In keeping with our concern to display the application of a common methodology to a range of diverse institutional settings, we have organized the chapters analytically rather than in terms of institutional domain. In all the interactions analyzed in this volume, the talk between the participants is predominantly characterized by question–answer sequences in which the professionals largely ask the questions and the lay "clients" respond with answers. Accordingly, we have organized the empirical chapters into sections based on whether they focus primarily on the activities of the (professional) questioner, on the activities of the one answering questions, or on the interplay between questioner and recipient. We should emphasize that chapters have been included in particular sections only according to their *primary* focus. In no instance is a chapter's sole concern or focus captured by the title of the section in which it appears. But, although there may be an element of approximation in this organization, we are confident that it is informative about the substance of the constituent chapters.

We complete the present section of the collection, "Theoretical orientations," with a theoretical study by Levinson and a methodological one by Schegloff. Levinson's chapter (ch. 2) was the first of a series (see also Levinson 1980, 1981a, 1981b) dealing with the nature of speech as social action and with speech-act theory in particular. Here he addresses the essentialism of Searlian speech-act analyses of questions in the light of the very varied kinds of interactional work that questions can actually accomplish. This variety, which is evidenced in the contributions to this volume, raises the question of what analytical and inferential resources participants might use and rely upon to understand and produce question–answer sequences of various types. Levinson's analytic sketch of the issues, here developed through the notion of "activity types," is a most valuable starting point for anyone beginning to consider work in this area, and is justly regarded as a classic contribution.

Schegloff's chapter (ch. 3) deals with some of the major methodological constraints which need to be observed by researchers who want to venture empirically into the analytic terrain sketched by Levinson. In particular, he asserts the importance of demonstrating the local revelance for participants of their institutional contexts and identities. Schegloff matches this strongly "emic" approach with an equal insistence on empirical pay-off from analytical decisions to characterize participants in "institutional" terms. Research should be able to show the impact of institutional contexts and identities in "procedurally consequential" terms – that is, in terms of institutionally distinctive conduct produced by the participants – and Schegloff sketches what such an analysis might look like with data from a news interview.

Turning to the empirical studies, part 2 focuses on the activities of the professional *questioner* and includes chapters by Bergmann, Clayman, Atkinson, and Button. Bergmann's chapter (ch. 4) analyzes questioning during psychiatric intake interviews. He shows that the design of questions through which psychiatrists explore the states of mind of interviewees displays a caution or indirectness which amounts to what he calls "discretion." This discretion emerges in relation to both lexical choice and turn design, which Bergmann demonstrates to have a striking symmetry. In a neo-Simmelian conclusion, Bergmann points to some of the ambiguities that inhabit this form of "discretion" in psychiatric conduct.

The theme of "caution" is also addressed in Clayman's study of news interviews (ch. 5). Clayman notes that interviewers may confront interviewees with controversial positions which are often directly contrary or hostile to those of interviewees. The interviewers' problem in engaging in this adversarial questioning is essentially that of avoiding the assertion of positions on their own behalf, thereby sustaining a formally neutral or "neutralistic" (Heritage and Greatbatch 1991) position. Clayman details a range of features of question design that permit interviewers to achieve this aim.

While Bergmann and Clayman both discuss aspects of the design of questions, the contributions by Atkinson and Button focus particularly on the ways questioners deal with responses to their prior questions (i.e. the third turns in sequences initiated by the questioners). However, both authors continue the theme of professional caution by describing practices through which questioners avoid taking up positions with respect to those answers. Both chapters involve an element of contrast with ordinary conversation. In conversation, where affiliative responses to answers-to-questions are commonplace, the kind of "neutral" conduct documented by Atkinson and Button would be regarded as odd or downright hostile (see Heritage 1985).

In his study of Small Claims Courts (ch. 6), Atkinson shows that arbitrators acknowledge witnesses' statements using forms of receipt that avoid giving any indication about their assessment of what they have heard. In Button's chapter (ch. 7) the absence of affiliative responses to interviewees' answers is also documented, together with the avoidance even of clarification by the interviewers when it appears that the interviewee might have misunderstood the question. It is significant that the conduct documented in these two chapters is often justified by reference to fairness, impartiality, and objectivity. Yet the similarities in the conduct described (and its justification) should not be allowed to obscure the rather different roles which it plays in the two environments with their different tasks and inferential frameworks.

The chapters in part 3 focus principally on the tasks, constraints, and rationales of those *answering* questions. Heath's chapter (ch. 8) documents the remarkable fact that, in British general-practice medical consultations, patients systematically withhold responses to doctors' announcements of their diagnoses. Even when doctors offer their diagnoses in such a way as to invite patients to reply, for example in question format, patients appear reluctant, except under very specific circumstances, to do anything that would extend talk about the nature of the doctor's diagnosis. In conse-quence, patients tend to be less informed about their condition and less involved in treatment decisions than might otherwise be the case.

Greatbatch (ch. 9) examines the means through which news interviewees in panel interviews – interviews involving two or more persons who hold opposing positions about some issues – can escalate their disagreements with one another through aspects of the design and placement of their turns. Greatbatch has been in the forefront of those who have analyzed institutional talk in terms of very specific constraints on conduct that are distinctive from those applying to ordinary conversation. In this context, it is particularly interesting that he reverses perspective to focus on what, despite the rules and constraints, the participants can in fact get away with. But he also shows that, even where the participants break free of the question–answer framework of the news interview, this framework nonetheless tacitly underlies their freedom of maneuver.

Finally, in the context of interviews associated with a job-train-ing program, Gumperz (ch. 10) shows that applicants from ethnic minorities are disadvantaged in comparison with native English speakers by their apparently cryptic answers to questions. Gumperz traces the character of such answers, and of the misunderstandings which may arise between South Asian applicants and native English interviewers, to the culturally based differences in communication patterns between them. These differences appear in a wide range of contextualization cues, particularly those associated with prosody, which are important for the ways in which each makes inferences about what the other is asking or saying.

Part 4 of this volume consists of chapters which focus on the interplay between the activities of questioners and answerers. This is quite explicit in Maynard's analysis (ch. 11) of the "perspective display series" with which clinicians often preface their reports of diagnosed developmental disorders to parents of young children. Maynard identifies the perspective display series as one in which clinicians – instead of directly or straightforwardly revealing their diagnoses – first ask the parents for their observations about their child's difficulties and progress, and subsequently try to present the clinic's diagnosis so as to confirm and elaborate the parents' view. Thus clinicians elicit parents' views so as to, as Maynard puts it, "co-implicate" parents in an already completed diagnostic decision and thereby avoid the kinds of resistance that such diagnoses might otherwise engender.

There is some overlap of concern between Maynard's chapter and the one which follows it by Heritage and Sefi (ch. 12). The latter describe some of the ways in which community nurses manage the delivery of advice to first-time mothers about various aspects of baby care. Their chapter identifies a "stepwise" pattern in advice-giving sequences. Here, in the context of a "trouble-shooting" series of questions, the nurses use the mothers' replies, and particularly any indication that problems might have arisen, as a warrant for the delivery of advice. Heritage and Sefi identify a range of dilemmas for both nurses and mothers, in which the identities of each are somewhat at stake, which inform the type and frequency of forms of advice delivery and the forms of response to it.

The chapter by Zimmerman (ch. 13) reports an investigation of calls to emergency dispatch centers for medical or other emergency assistance. He shows that the overall shape of the calls, the ways in which such calls develop and are concluded, is the product of how the participants – both the call taker in the emergency center and the caller – manage the call-processing requirements and policies of the particular dispatch organization, and the variable circumstances and contingencies which are specific to each call. In such calls, callers may have very widely differing needs and callers and call takers have varyingly different relevances. Yet, notwithstanding this variety, emergency calls have an underlying range of organizational similarities which are locally achieved and managed. Zimmerman documents the achievement of alignment and collaboration through the phases of emergency calls through which these abstract but locally achieved patterns are realized.

The study by Drew of cross-examination of a witness in a criminal trial (ch. 14) focuses on the way in which the development of a line of questioning initiated by the questioner, here a lawyer, is contingent upon the answers given by the witness. But in this case, the interaction between them is far from collaborative. Indeed, one of the principal contingencies with which the lawyer has to deal is a series of attempts by the witness to forestall his hostile line of questioning. Drew identifies a sequentially managed device designed by the lawyer to undermine these attempts by the witness, and in turn to discredit her evidence.

The final chapter in this volume, by Jefferson and Lee, is rather different from previous chapters insofar as it deals primarily with ordinary conversation. In their analysis of troubles tellings in conversation, the authors show that troubles tellers are frequently offered advice by their recipients – advice which is systematically resisted or disputed by the troubles teller. They also note a divergence between troubles tellings and some service encounters. In the latter, the troubles teller is often seeking advice, and continues detailing their troubles only until the advice giver (i.e. some agency personnel) starts to deliver their advice. They suggest that there can be particular difficulties when official or quasi-official organizational representatives try to "humanize" the delivery of advice. This observation indirectly highlights the dilemmas discussed in the Heritage and Sefi chapter. In contexts such as social work and community nursing, where the professional may seek to establish a "befriending" relationship, the different styles of soliciting and delivering advice that are appropriate to "personal" and "pro-

fessional" interactions respectively may become fatally compounded leaving, the participants interactionally discomforted and
unable to resolve their difficulties.

Here, then, are a range of attempts to map the details of institutional conduct and its underlying orientations. We believe that
they offer considerable insight into the ways that interaction is
conducted within organizations. They represent an important avenue of contemporary development in the growing field of CA, and
one which holds a range of possibilities for social-scientific development in the future. That future is an open one. Although the
methods employed in the present studies are not always readily
compatible with those of ethnography or survey research,[40] the
contributions to this volume sketch the kinds of possibilities that
can emerge when CA techniques of analysis are applied to institutional interaction. It is in a spirit of openness to these future
possibilities that the present volume is undertaken.

Notes

1. In keeping with the contents of this volume and with general usage as it
   has emerged within the conversation-analytic literature, we here restrict the term *institutional interaction* to interactions that are work- or
   task-oriented and "non-conversational" in ways that will be clarified
   over the course of this Introduction. Our use of the term does not
   extend to persons who engage in mundane conversation about everyday topics while they happen to be working, for example, on an
   assembly line or in a food processing outlet. Notwithstanding the standard sociological usage within which the family is also a social institution, we will also avoid using the term to describe activities that
   would be glossed as family dinners, picnics, and the like. The term
   would, however, encompass activities that involve communication in
   complex, technologically mediated environments such as airports,
   experimental laboratories, subway systems, etc. This kind of communication is now the object of interesting and significant new
   research (Brun-Cottan 1990; Jordan 1990; Goodwin 1991; Goodwin
   and Goodwin forthcoming; Suchman forthcoming).
2. For summaries of the CA perspective, see Heritage (1984a: 233–92),
   Levinson (1983: 284–370), Zimmerman (1988).
3. It is worth recalling that the origins of CA go back, a little over twenty-
   five years ago, to Sacks's investigations into calls made to a suicide-
   prevention center. These calls were collected by the Los Angeles SPC as

part of a program of research designed to increase the effectiveness of the service (Litman 1972). These calls, together with recordings of group psychotherapy sessions, continued to be the principal source of data for Sacks's lectures for many years. It was from these materials that he developed CA's focus on the sequential organization of talk-in-interaction (Sacks 1989, 1992; Schegloff 1989). Data from institutional contexts have been similarly important to other pioneering work in CA – for instance, Jefferson's use of group-therapy data, and Schegloff's work on calls to a police department.

There is, moreover, a more general connection with ethnomethodological investigations of a range of work environments: for example, the study of jurors' deliberations in arriving at verdicts in criminal trials (Garfinkel 1967: 104–15) motivated further such studies as those by Zimmerman of bureaucratic procedures in a social-welfare office (Zimmerman 1969), by Pollner of traffic-court hearings (Pollner 1974, 1975, 1979), by Sudnow (1965) of plea-bargaining, and by Wieder (1974) of a "half-way" house for convicts. For a fuller account of these mutually informed developments in ethnomethodology and CA, see Heritage (1984a: esp. chs. 7–9).

4. We stress here the complementarity of the techniques involved; for while the analysis of recorded data presents opportunities for qualitative and quantitative rigor that may elude direct observational techniques, there are many aspects of organizations which cannot be directly or easily caught on tape but can only be grasped through ethnographic fieldwork.

5. See Sacks (1984a) and Garfinkel (1988) for some discussion of parallel sociological treatments of the everyday world of social action as inherently disorderly.

6. This perspective is now developing in a reevaluation of aspects of phonetic analysis (Kelly and Local 1989).

7. On aspects of style, see also Labov and Fanshel (1977: 35–7).

8. Fur a further discussion and elaboration of the implications of Goffman's notion of footing for linguistic analysis, particularly of deixis, see Levinson (1988) and especially Hanks (1990).

9. On a related sense of frame, as marking and establishing phases within classroom lessons, see also Sinclair and Coulthard (1975:22) and in therapeutic interviews, Labov and Fanshel (1977: 37).

10. For a comprehensive and critical overview, see Levinson (1983: 226–83) and the debates in Searle (1991).

11. For an assessment of these objectives, see Levinson (1983: 286–9, 294, and 352–3).

12. For a parallel discussion in relation to sociological analyses of the relationship between rules, contexts, and action, see Heritage (1984a: 103–34).

13. Though Searle (1979) later repudiated this view.

14. In common with Labov and Fanshel, Sinclair and Coulthard are also interested in identifying the rules which translate surface linguistic form (e.g. a teacher's declarative *I can hear someone laughing* into a speech action (a command to stop laughing; 1975: 32–3). But from a discourse-analysis perspective, discourse is orderly through the more general moves which such acts constitute, and the regularly occurring patterns of moves that make up exchange structures.

15. The ambivalences of the model between an emic and etic stance and between a descriptive and prescriptive orientation have been widely noted in the literature (Levinson 1983; Taylor and Cameron 1987).

16. Thus the very first lecture by Harvey Sacks (1992 [1964]: lecture 1) deals with two alternative procedures by which a counselor at a crisis-intervention center can attempt to solicit the name of the caller.

17. This abandonment is strongly canvassed in Garfinkel's (1967) analytic writings. See also Heritage (1984a, 1987) for some explication of Garfinkel's arguments.

18. Several recent papers deal with dramatic breakdowns in the normal or routine ways that "institutional" interaction generally proceeds. In relation to the news interview, Schegloff (1988/9) and Clayman and Whalen (1988/9) discuss aspects of the breakdown of an encounter between CBS anchor Dan Rather and (then) Republican Vice-President George Bush from a "news interview" to a "confrontation." Similarly, J. Whalen, Zimmerman, and Whalen (1988) discuss a disastrous telephone call to an emergency hotline in Dallas, Texas, in which, as a result of an interactional breakdown, an ambulance was not sent to a dying patient. These studies illustrate the generic methodological point that a "context" of interaction – whether conversational or institutional – is something that is coconstructed by the participants to an encounter and that "routine" exchanges – whether conversational (Schegloff 1986) or institutional (Whalen and Zimmerman 1987) – must always be treated as the contingent outcomes of a collaborative achievement between the participants.

19. In a parallel discussion, Wilson (1991) addresses this same theme in his warning of the dangers of a too hastily assembled conclusion that particular "obviously relevant" institutional identities are informing courses of action.

20. The task agendas of many forms of institutional discourse became a theme in the CA literature almost as soon as institutional talk became an object of systematic analysis. (Atkinson and Drew 1979; Maynard 1984; Heritage 1985). Maynard's (1984: 11–12) observations on plea bargaining were particularly trenchant in this regard:

    it is impossible to ignore that plea bargaining occurs in a particular institutional environment. Relatively unexplored in conversational analysis is how such an environment provides instrumental tasks to which members must attend by way of their talk and action . . . the setting of plea bargaining is more than an incidental part of the discourse. It is a feature of the criminal-justice process that *results* – in the form of decisions about criminal defendants and their cases – must always be produced. This feature has consequences for the patterns of talk that emerge in plea bargaining ... organized aspects of the discourse are often occupied with meeting the participants' institutional mandate to process cases.

21. Analytically, these comparisons should ideally be explicit. However, the question of whether they model elements or processes of comparison which are in any sense "real" to the participants is a very complex topic. There are moments when, in their conduct (Heritage and Greatbatch 1991) or reports of it (Atkinson 1982), participants in institutional interaction directly appeal to the special character of the interactional framework in which they are participating and/or to some specific aspect of it which is "nonconversational" or different from conversation. In grasping the meaning of some utterance or action however, participants may simply see the action at a glance as "an-action-in-a-different-organization or system-of-relevances" (see Wieder 1974). Such a grasp could involve a "gestalt seeing" that involves no conscious or intentional (in a phenomenological sense) entertaining of comparisons.

22. Although it is sometimes difficult, illuminating "deviant cases" can almost always be found: for example, while it can be difficult to find departures from news-interview turn-taking rules in data with only one interviewee, the presence of two or more interviewees expands the range (and the motivation) of possibilities for departure as Greatbatch (ch. 9) shows.

23. Perakyla and Silverman (1991a, 1991b) document a range of comparatively exotic turn-taking procedures associated with such counseling methods as the *Milan School Family Systems Theory* (Perakyla 1991). Their data also indicate some of the difficulties of sustaining this turn-taking framework without relapsing into more "normal" conversational modes.

24. A fine ethnographic study of encounters between social workers and clients (Baldock and Prior 1981) evokes a wide-ranging permeability between a "conversation" and a task-oriented encounter as a general feature of social-worker–client interaction and notes a consequence of this permeability – a corresponding uncertainty, among many clients at least, about the purpose of the encounter.

25. Interestingly, Strong (1979) notes that medical professionals may comport themselves as lay people when attending pediatric clinics in a parental capacity. In such cases, the presentation of a lay self is, in part, managed by the avoidance of jargon.

26. This observation is dramatically illustrated in the following account, from *The Independent* in which a British resident of Beirut recounts how she was told – we now know, incorrectly – that her husband had been killed by hostage takers.

He said to me: "You're Mrs. Mann, aren't you?" And when I said "yes," he said, "I'm very sorry but I've got some very bad news for you." I asked him what it was, and he said: "We have to tell you your husband is dead." My knees were like jelly. I just sank down into a chair ... It was only later that I realised the man had referred to "we" as if he was some kind of intermediary.

(*The Independent*, 9 September 1989)

27. This datum illustrates that incumbency of an institutional role may not preclude the use of a self-referring *I*, which may be used to invoke a stance or identity that is somewhat less "institutionally" weighted. In institutional contexts, the choice between a self-referring *I* or *we* is not "determined" by the setting; rather, both formulations are available to the institutional incumbent, who can achieve a variety of actions and communicational outcomes by selecting between them.

28. See Turner (1976) for analysis of a closely parallel case to the datum discussed here. The issue of medical vs. social/emotional agendas in medical consultations is usefully discussed in Byrne and Long (1976).

29. On intersubjectivity in CA see, *inter alia*, Schegloff and Sacks (1973), Heritage (1984a: 254–60), and Schegloff (1992).

30. As in datum (6) discussed above, the M and F's turn designs embody different stances towards the health visitor and her assertions. The HV offers the remark on lines 1–2 of the datum having already asked the parents a string of questions about the baby's behavior. It is noticeable that neither parents take up the HV's claim that they will be "amazed" at all the different things their child will start doing. The mother responds with a remark offering the same view as a previously held general expectation about all children – thereby avoiding the "expert–novice" stance that the HV's remark might be seen as expressing. The father, by contrast, agrees with the HV's remark by asserting that they have already and independently noticed their child's rapid development. Significantly, while the father (putatively the junior partner in the family's child-care arrangements) appears eager to show their competence in noticing the details of their child's behavior, the mother's response avoids any indication that she will hold herself accountable to the HV for such skills.

31. For a sociological background to these observations see Garfinkel and Sacks (1970), Heritage (1984a: 144–57), Schegloff (1989).

32. Topic initiation and (rapid) topic shifts feature analytically also in Cicourel (1987: 222), Fisher (1983: 213–19), Shuy (1983), Erickson and Shultz (1982: 72–85), and frequently elsewhere, as do overlaps and "interruptions" (Fisher 1983: 210–12; Davis 1988: 268; Mishler 1984: 108–9; Gumperz 1982: 175–7), and other phenomena such as correction of a co-participant (Fisher 1983: 207; Tannen and Wallat 1986: 302–3), greetings sequences (Gumperz 1982: 175–7; Silverman 1987: 165–8), insertion sequences in response to (indirect) requests (Labov and Fanshel 1977: 155–67; Erickson and Shultz 1982: 24–5), and dysfluencies such as hesitancy, self-repair, and pauses (Mishler

1984: 72–5; Labov and Fanshel 1977: 313–14; Gumperz 1982: 177).
33. But see Gumperz (1982: 176) for an important exception to this.
34. On this transition from conversational mode into the "business," as it were, conducted trough professional questioning, Suchman and Jordan (1990) observe a related phenomenon in the General Social Survey and National Health Survey interviews they studied. Respondents were often misled by the interviewers' opening "chatty" remarks into believing that they could treat the occasion as an extended conversation, for example, tell the interviewer stories. The interviewer had then to reorient the respondent just to answer the question.

[The respondent] initially takes the interview to have a kind of talk show format, wherein she is to provide her opinions in the form of a commentary on topics raised by the interviewer. The extensive and elaborate opening remarks by the interviewer contribute to this expectation and appear to be heard as an invitation to produce a response in kind. But what this respondent hears in the first question as an invitation to talk, to give her opinion, she discovers to be a fixed choice between items, where the possible terms of her answer are already decided and are non-negotiable. The interview comes to be transformed from an interactive "talking with" someone, to the solitary production of acceptable answers to questions: answers whose adequacy for the interview purposes respondents come to be able to evaluate, but in which they may have little personal investment.

(Suchman and Jordan 1990: 236)

35. A further variation of this "exam question" sequence involves the *withholding* of evaluative response to answers. This is characteristic of yet another somewhat related activity – educational testing (Marlaire and Maynard 1990).
36. In this respect it is significant that both doctors and therapists generally refrain from responding to patients' reports with *oh* (Labov and Fanshel 1977: 137; ten Have 1991).
37. Though see Jefferson (1980b, 1988) for a delineation of particular kinds of sequences within conversations, notably "troubles tellings," that may have some such "standard components on a standard order of occurrence."
38. The tendency of lay participants to orient towards some task-related overall structure of interaction is underscored by the common complaint by social-work clients (Baldock and Prior 1981) that their interviews with social workers were such amorphous conversations that they had little idea of their agendas, of what was expected of them during the encounter, or, indeed, what it might take for the encounter to be complete.
39. This issue is extendedly discussed in Sack's lectures on turn-taking (1992 [fall 1967]) in which he compares the locally constructed basis for conversational turn taking with the hierarchically based rules described by Albert (1962) for turn taking among the Burundi. See also Sacks, Schegloff, and Jefferson (1974).

40. Though see Strong 1979), Maynard (1984), Moerman (1988), Ochs (1988), Conley and O'Barr (1990), and, most significantly, M. H. Goodwin (1990) for very serious efforts to combine the analysis of discourse with the use of ethnographic techniques and findings.

2

Activity types and language

STEPHEN C. LEVINSON

1 Introduction

Wittgenstein in a number of places (1958b; 1958a: I, 23) suggests
that understanding a language, and by implication having a grasp
of the meaning of utterances, involves knowing the nature of the
activity in which the utterances play a role. This, of course, is part
of the well-known doctrine of "language games," which by the
later writings had "come to mean the study of any form of use of
language against a background context of a form of life" (Kenny
1973: 166).

Now part of what Wittgenstein was getting at has since been
captured in the concept of speech acts, although there is, of course,
considerable disagreement about how to handle speech acts theoretically. Some (Searle 1969, for example) would try to reduce the rest
of language to speech acts. Others would try to reduce speech acts
to the frameworks of analysis that handle the propositional core of
language (e.g. Lewis 1972; Sadock 1974; Lakoff, 1975). Yet others
would accept a fundamental distinction between speech acts and
propositional context, and apply Wittgenstein's "language games"
mode of analysis only to the former (for an elegant version of such
an account see Stenius 1967). In any case, the majority of linguists,
and philosophers too, would reject the later Wittgenstein's reduction of meaning to usage in favor of the earlier Wittgenstein's

An earlier version of this chapter appeared in Pragmatics Microfiche vol. 3, Fiche
3–3 pages D.1–G5, May 1978. My thanks are due to Jay Atlas, Terence Moore, and
Gerald Gazdar for reading and commenting on an almost illegible first draft; some
of the suggestions have been incorporated without further acknowledgment, so not
all errors are necessarily my own!

semantical theory, complemented, if needs be, by a pragmatic theory of speech acts.

But there is more implied in Wittgenstein's language-games analogy than can be captured in a theory of speech acts: the list of language games given by Wittgenstein in *Philosophical Investigations* includes describing objects, giving measurements, constructing an object from a measurement, telling jokes, acting plays, praying, guessing riddles, greeting, and so on (see also Kenny 1973: 165).

The intuitions that underlay Wittgenstein's emphasis on the embedding of language within human activities have not been accounted for in any modern theory of how language is used and understood. The purpose of this chapter is to document from empirical materials that Wittgenstein's intuitions have a basis in fact, and moreover that his failure to make the distinction between speech acts and speech activities was not just an oversight – the two are interconnected in such fundamental ways that only a thorough-going pragmatic theory will be adequate to describe both phenomena.

To see the force of Wittgenstein's preoccupations with the matrix activity within which language usage takes place, consider a simple case that should jog the intuitions. In a game of cricket there is a general rule of silence during play, but there are a number of distinct cries that punctuate the proceedings, for example *howzat*, *LBW*, *over* (there are also appreciations of play, and instructions from the captain to the team, of the sort *John, the slips*). Now it would be simply and straightforwardly impossible to describe the meaning or the function of these cries without referring to aspects of the game and their role within the game – so, for example, *howzat* functions as a claim directed to the umpire by one of the fielding side that one of the batsmen is "out," while *over* functions as both a statement that six turns at bowling have now transpired since the last such cry and as an instruction to reverse the direction of bowling, and so on.

The immediate reaction to such cases will no doubt be that they are exceptional, in no way typical of language usage or indeed of language, and parasitic on more ordinary uses of language. And certainly the reduction of meaning to moves within a language game is not going to provide us with any account of the key intuition that sentences have meanings partially independent (not totally, of course) of the circumstances in which they are used. But holding a more conservative and traditional theory of meaning (of the sort that pairs meanings with well-formed formulae, *in vacuo*) is not going to rescue us from the dilemma that many, indeed probably most, situations in which language is used have an aspect precisely similar to the cricket case. The common feature, of course, is the extent to which the understanding of what is said depends on understanding the "language game" in which it is embedded, over and beyond whatever meaning the words or sentences may have *in vacuo*.

As an intermediate case consider the following utterances recorded during a basketball game:

(1) 1 Alright Peter.
     2 Here!
     3 Farewell people.
     4 C'mon Peter.
     5 Beautiful tip!
     6 Right over here.

Now understanding these utterances seems to require two things in particular: we need to know the meaning of the words; and we need to know the kind of utterances that typically occur in such a game. It would be helpful, of course, to have a visual picture of the state of play at each utterance, but lacking this we can still reconstruct the probable function given the two kinds of knowledge above. So utterances 1, 2, 4, and 6 could function as claims that the speaker is in a good position to have the ball passed to him, and thus as requests to do so; while utterance 5 is an appreciation of another player's move, and 3 something more like a war cry, a shout of defiance by the player with the ball.[1] In assigning functions to the utterances (signals to pass, exhortations, applause, and so on) we depend both on the meaning of the words which serve to differentiate the utterances, and on the possible roles that utterances can play within such a game. In this case we can see that the main reason that we have to rely on information about the game is massive ellipsis, but, as we shall see, this is only one source of such contextual dependence.

But before proceeding, let us turn to clarify a concept that will be basic to what is to follow.

2 Activity types

I want to introduce as a term of art the notion of an "activity type." There are various terms that are employed by sociologists and anthropologists engaged in the study of language usage which are roughly equivalent, especially "speech event" and "episode" (see e.g. Gumperz 1972; Hymes 1972a). My notion is to be preferred for present purposes because it refers to any culturally recognized activity, whether or not that activity is coextensive with a period of speech or indeed whether any talk takes place in it at all (see Sacks, Schegloff, and Jefferson 1974 for some useful distinctions here). In particular, I take the notion of an activity type to refer to a fuzzy category whose focal members are goal-defined, socially constituted, bounded, events with *constraints* on participants, setting, and so on, but above all on the kinds of allowable contributions. Paradigm examples would be teaching, a job interview, a jural interrogation, a football game, a task in a workshop, a dinner party, and so on.

The category is fuzzy because (as with bad examples of the color red – see Berlin and Kay 1969) it is not clear whether it includes a chat (probably) or the single telling of a joke (probably not). It appeals to the intuition that social events come along a gradient formed by two polar types, the totally prepackaged activity, on the one hand (e.g. a Roman Mass) and the largely unscripted event on the other (e.g. a chance meeting on the street). There is some (incomplete) correspondence between this gradient and another, that between the poles of a highly formal activity on the one hand and a very informal one on the other. However formality is properly described (and see here E. O. Keenan 1977; Irvine 1978), it certainly seems to involve greater levels of preplanning both in action and in speech together with greater social distance between participants. The evidence for this is that style changes accordingly: for example, the more elaborate higher diglossic varieties of a language with diglossia (Ferguson 1964) or address forms conventionally implicating social distance (see Levinson 1977) will tend to occur in formal situations. Thus my colleagues may address me as *Steve* in the common room, *Dr. Levinson* in a faculty meeting. So style or mode of address can be one index of a change of activity.

A further dimension on which activities vary clearly crosscuts the other two: this is the degree to which speech is an integral part of each activity. On the one hand, we have activities constituted entirely by talk (a telephone conversation, a lecture, for example); on the other, activities where talk is nonoccurring, or if it does occur is incidental (a game of football, for instance). Somewhere in between (though this dimension of variation is not simply a linear scale like the other two) we have the placing of bets, or a Bingo session, or a visit to the grocers. And there are sometimes rather special relations between what is said and what is done, as in a sports commentary, a slide show, a cookery demonstration, a conjuror's show, and the like. Then there are the peculiarities of rituals, where words and acts are related and integrated in most complex ways (the best descriptions of exotic cases are still those of Malinowski in *Coral Gardens and their Magic*; 1966, vol. II).[2]

There is one discipline that has set itself the task of describing the different uses to which speech is put in different activities in different societies, namely the ethnography of speaking, as conceived originally by Hymes (1962) and exemplified by the collection of essays in Bauman and Sherzer (1974) (see also Blount and Sanches 1975). Hymes suggested eight key variables that would function as a classificatory grid for crosscultural comparison: each activity should be described, he suggests, as particular constraints on setting, participants, ends (or goals), acts (including specified sequences), key (or tone), instrumentalities (the varieties of language employed, in particular), norms (concerning, for example, attenuation or interruption), and genre (poetic, mythic, prosaic, etc.).

The results of such investigations are important for anyone interested in giving Wittgenstein's intuitions about "language games" some flesh. But there is a drawback to Hymes's taxonomic approach, for not all of the variables he adduces are of equal significance or importance. I would choose to divide the pie a little differently, making a first distinction between the *structure* of the event in question, and the *style* in which it is conducted. Only the former is germane to the issues raised in this chapter, and I deal with the latter elsewhere.

Elements of the structure of an activity include its subdivision into a number of subparts, or episodes as we may call them (e.g. a seminar usually involves first a presentation, followed by a discussion, while a court case is divided into a statement of the case, cross-examinations, the passing of sentence, etc.), and within each any prestructured sequences that may be required by convention, the norms governing the allocation of turns at speaking, and so on. There may, further, be constraints on the personnel and the roles they may take, on the time and the place at which the activity can properly take place. There are also more abstract structural constraints, having to do with topical cohesion and the functional adequacy of contributions to the activity.

In general, wherever possible I would like to view these structural elements as rationally and functionally adapted to the point or *goal* of the activity in question, that is the function or functions that members of the society see the activity as having. By taking this perspective it seems that in most cases apparently *ad hoc* and elaborate arrangements and constraints of very various sorts can be seen to follow from a few basic principles, in particular rational organization around a dominant goal. This analytic approach is distinct from the taxonomic and descriptive one employed in the ethnography of speaking. The dangers of the latter can be most clearly seen in the extreme atomism and particularism in applications to problems of second-language teaching, where it is considered necessary to teach the pupil studying the foreign language in its culture each and every structural detail of some activity, even though these details are often direct and simple means of achieving the relevant goals (see e.g. Munby 1978).

But for present purposes our interest in the structure of activities can be confined to one particular important question: *in what ways do the structural properties of an activity constrain (especially the functions of) the verbal contributions that can be made towards it?* This will be one dominant theme of the succeeding discussion, and it will be useful to have a paradigm case in mind. A simple example is provided by Labov's (1972b) description of the activity of "sounding" among the Black community of New York. Essentially, this consists in the competitive exchange of ritual insults governed by structural constraints of two types. The first of these is that "sounds" or turns at ritually insulting should be constructed in a specific fashion, which Labov (1972b: 153) represents as follows:

T(B) is so X that P

where T is the target of the sound, normally a relative (typically the mother) of B, the addressee, X is a pejorative attribute like *fat*, *poor*, *dirty*, etc., and P is some proposition that must, when applied to T, be false (otherwise the ritual insult would become a genuine insult). The second type of structural constraint governs appropriate sequencing: if A sounds on B, B should reply with a sound based on A's sound but which "tops" it (i.e. is considered more ingenious), and, if possible, A should then try to top that, or alternatively try another kind of sound. After each stage the audience makes a vocal assessment of the sound (ibid.: 146). So an exchange might begin as follows:

(2)   A: your mother so old she got spider webs under her arms.
      C: awwww!
      B: your mother so old she fart dust
      C: Ho lawd!

The point here is that there are strict constraints on what counts as a sound: the target should not be the addressee directly nor should the proposition describing the target be true, for example. Moreover, sounds should relate to prior sounds in specific ways if they are to be positively evaluated. If these constraints are not met, the activity breaks down.

3 Activity types and inference

One important fact about activity types, then, is that there are constraints on what will count as allowable contributions to them.[3] Now there is another important and related fact, in many ways the mirror image of the constraints on contributions: namely, the fact that to each and every clearly demarcated activity there is a corresponding set of *inferential schemata*. These schemata are tied to (derived from, if one likes) the structural properties of the activity in question.

Let us start with some straightforward examples. As Turner (1972) has pointed out, the possible ways of starting an activity are contingent on aspects of its structural organization. So an utterance like:

(3)   It's five past twelve.

can serve to start proceedings just in case the activity is scheduled to begin by then and all necessary personnel are present. Notice that if the activity was a university lecture then (3) could only function as the initial utterance of the activity if it was uttered by the lecturer (or his introducer if he was a visitor), who we can designate the "pivotal person" in this activity; in addition there would have to be at least some partial complement of listeners. Now contrast:

(4)   We seem to all be here.

which could only serve to initiate a different kind of activity: namely, one in which a full complement of persons is required (e.g. a committee meeting). Now, as Turner points out, if activities were bounded by silence there would be no problem: the first turn at talking would initiate the proceedings. But such is not the case; normally, there is talk of another kind right up to the moment the activity begins. The problem then is to account for the fact that utterances like (3) and (4) have the *force* of announcing the beginning of an activity, and whatever the details of the account it will clearly have to refer to the mutual knowledge among participants of the particular conditions that must be met in order for the specific activity to begin. Exactly the same sort of remarks, of course, can be made about ways of terminating a given activity. The following three utterances could function as ways of ending a seminar, a lecture, and a committee meeting respectively:

(5)   It's one o'clock.

(6)   Next week I'll be looking at another approach to the same problem.

(7)   Jim's got to go.

These examples are both like and unlike the initial and terminal whistles in a soccer game; they are alike because they have the same sort of force, and they are unlike in that they do so via referring to the necessary prerequisites of the activity in question, thereby making a knowledge of those prerequisites essential for the understanding of their function.

Now let us consider an example of a slightly different kind, that can be found in the following exchange recorded in a grocer's shop (where S is the shop-assistant and C the customer):

(8)   S: (to last customer): Bub-bye.
      C: Some apples please. Just help myself is that alright?
      S: Yes they're all fine.
      C: Yes they look good.
      S: // // There, that's eighteen, orright?
      C: uhuh. You've just got the one kind of lettuce?
      S: Yes. Cos.
      C: That's a nice one.
      S: Yes. They are getting proper now aren't they. Thirty six please.
           // // thank you very much.
      C: Thanks. Goodbye.

The utterance of interest here is C's "That's a nice one," which was
accompanied by a gesture of pointing. The interesting thing is that
this utterance *counted as* selecting a lettuce, requesting that it be
wrapped, and undertaking to pay for it. As one can see there were
no further negotiations about the lettuce. How did the utterance
function in the way that it did? The answer is that it had the force
that it had by virtue of the expectations governing the activity of
shopping in small stores, here specifically the expectation that the
customer will only pick out and select goods that he intends to buy.
The corollary is that the shop-assistant can take any identification
of a piece of merchandise as a selection with intent to purchase,
unless there are contrary indications.

  With these examples in mind let us turn to the theoretical implications of these observations. There are at least four main
approaches to the study of inference in discourse which are worth
reviewing as a background to this study. The first of these is Grice's
(1975) attempt to isolate some basic background assumptions of
cooperation that underlie talk across differing situations. These
general assumptions are so strong that apparent violations give rise
to inferences that would preserve them. Another approach, in part
inspired by Grice's, has been current in linguistics, where to handle
inferences to indirect illocutionary force specific rules for formulating indirect expressions of particular kinds have been proposed (see
e.g. Gordon and Lakoff 1975; Heringer 1972; Fraser 1975). In
fact, as suggested by Searle (1975) and Brown and Levinson (1978),
these specific principles can generally be reduced to Grice's more
general principles. A third distinct approach is current in artificial
intelligence, where the emphasis is on using massive amounts of
detailed factual knowledge about the world as extra premises to

derive inferences made in discourse (see e.g. Charniak 1972). A problem that then has to be solved is how to bring the relevant facts in at the right moment, a solution to which seemed to be Minsky's idea of a "frame" or block of knowledge that could be called up (see articles in Schank and Nash-Webber 1975). And finally, the fourth and very different approach comes from analyses of conversation by ethnomethodologists, and especially by Sacks, Schegloff, and their associates (see e.g. Sacks, Schegloff, and Jefferson 1974; Turner, 1974; Schegloff 1984). The emphasis here is on structural information about conversational organization, and the way in which such information predisposes participants to see utterances as fulfilling certain functions by virtue of their structural location. There are inferences, then, from the structure of a conversation to the role that any one utterance plays within it.

I suspect that, with the possible exception of the second, each of these approaches catches some aspects of the nature of inference in discourse. On methodological grounds, though, there are reasons to prefer the approaches favored by Grice and Sacks and Schegloff to that favored by workers in artificial intelligence. For the former focus on structural properties of talk as the source of inferences, while the latter concentrate on the substantive content of background beliefs. And there is reason to presume that such structural properties are fewer and simpler than participants' general belief and knowledge of the world, and thus both more conducive to study and more likely to be the sort to thing that participants have to learn initially in order to converse. (Of course, there is no reason why these structural kinds of knowledge cannot be subsumed within the artificial intelligence, and in particular the frames, approach, provided that the special role they play in inferences can be captured; but so far this has not been done.)

Let us return now to the kinds of inferences that are tied to the structural organization of particular activities. The knowledge that is required to make the appropriate inferences is clearly not provided by Grice's maxims alone, for these are (implicitly) supposed to hold across different kinds of activity. Nor is it provided by the general structural expectations that have on the whole been the focus of work by Sacks, Schegloff, and their colleagues. The knowledge in question, rather, seems to be a distinct and further kind of structural expectation that lies behind inference in discourse. The knowledge is much more specific than the kind that Grice had in mind, but much more general than the immense array of facts that workers in artificial intelligence generally assume to be involved in inference.

Now there may, in fact, be some relation between Grice's maxims of conversation and particular expectations associated with particular activities. Grice's maxims of quality, quantity, relevance, and manner are supposed to outline preconditions for the rational cooperative exchange of talk. But one thing we can observe is that not all activity types are deeply cooperative. Consider an interrogation: it is unlikely that either party assumes the other is fulfilling the maxims of quality, manner, and especially quantity (requiring that one say as much as is required by the other). Inferences that in fully cooperative circumstances would go through (namely conversations implicatures) may no longer do so. Consider the following extract from Haldeman's testimony before the Senate committee that conducted the Watergate hearing (*New York Times* 1973: 577).

(9)   Q: You saw all of the papers that were being reviewed, did you not?
      A: Not all the working papers of the committee. I saw the
           recommendations that went to the President.
      Q: Did you read the recommendations that went to the President?
      A: I am not sure I did or not. If I did it was not in any detail.

Now I take it that in more cooperative and perhaps more normal circumstances the following exchange is bizarre (or has specific implicatures different from those in (9)):

(10) A: Did you see last week's Newsweek?
      B: Part of it.
      A: Did you read that part of it?
      B: I'm not sure whether I did or not.

What is strange about (10), of course, is that if X says he *saw* some reading matter then he generally implicates that he *read* it, the rationale for a stronger reading being that the questioner is much more likely to be interested in whether the respondent knows something about the content rather than the visual form of the reading matter, and, this being mutually assumed, it would be uncooperative to understand the question in the other way, so that an answer to the question can be taken to be an answer as to whether or not the respondent *read* the material in question. Hence A's second question is redundant, and thus conversationally bizarre by Grice's maxim of quantity; while B's response to the second question treats it as nonbizarre, thus doubly confusing the reader trying to understand this as an ordinary conversation.

Now the point is that strange as (10) is, it is precisely parallel to (9). So that in understanding (9) we have to cancel the implicature from X *saw* some reading matter to X *read* it. And we understand the implicature to be cancelled because, given our understanding of legal inquiries, we know it is often not in the interests of a defendant to cooperate beyond the minimum required to escape contempt of court.[4] In particular, we know that he may try to avoid committing himself to any definite statement of fact; knowing which, the interrogator cannot be content with implicatures that can later be denied – hence he has to ask the second question, that seeks assent for the inference from *saw* to *read*. That the inference is not assented to by Haldeman is further indication of the extent to which these proceedings are more like zero-sum games than games of pure coordination (see Luce and Raiffa 1957; Lewis 1969, respectively).

The example indicates that there could be some quite interesting relations between Grice's maxims and different kinds of activities, of a sort where some of the maxims are selectively relaxed to varying degrees in activities of specific types. To take another simple, but rather extreme example, consider the kind of talk that takes place in group-therapy sessions. Here is an extract from Perls (1969: 189):

(11) M: I said within myself "You know, you don't matter so what are you talking to me for?" And the other one was I felt.
    F: What was the sentence "You don't matter?"
    M: I felt I didn't talk directly to you.
    F: You said some words like, "You don't matter".
    M: Yes. This is what I said to myself.
    F: I know. Can you say it again, "You don't matter?"
    M: Yes. You don't matter.
    F: Say this again.
    M: You don't matter at all.
    F: Say it again.
    M: You don't matter at all.
    F: Say it to a few more people.
    M: You don't, you don't really matter...

There are a number of features that make this very different from
ordinary conversation. The repetition of "You don't matter" is a
violation of the nonredundancy required by Grice's maxim of
quantity. More complex is some violation of ordinary notions of
relevance; for example, the third utterance is in no way directly tied
to the preceding query. And there seem, in fact, to be for such
activities some rules of precedence that allow statements about
feelings, especially feelings about what has been said, to supersede
direct responses. In other cases the notion of relevance may be
preserved intact while complex additional premises (the therapeutic
theory) that are unstated link what are apparently unconnected
utterances.

   Now, although these may be extreme examples, paler things of
the same sort seem to go on in ordinary everyday activities. For
example, in a casual encounter harmless simplifications may be
untruths that, strictly speaking, violate the maxim of quality (see
e.g. Sacks 1975). And at the dinner table a question may be responded to with an unrelated *Would you like some more soup?*
These "violations" are principled in the sense that the degree of
cooperation, the ranking or precedence of topics, and so on are
intrinsically related to the nature of the activity in question. Must
we then reject Grice's attractive and influential theory on the
grounds that it does not apply to the empirical facts about the way
in which talk is organized? I think that would be hasty: it has
already given us a preliminary way of talking about some of the
ways in which talk is different in different activities. There are two
ways in which the conflict between Grice's general principles of
conversation and the particular expectations of specific activities
can be reconciled. The first is to seek for a more sophisticated
statement of Grice's principles that will allow differing degrees of
application of each maxim and the corresponding adjustment of
implicatures. The second is to accept Grice's maxims as specifications of some basic *unmarked* communication context, deviations
from which, however common, are seen as special or *marked*. And
there are various observations that suggest that the notion of basic
unmarked communication context may be essential to pragmatics:
for example it seems required by the facts of deixis (where the
unmarked deictic center seems to be the speaker, and his or her
temporal–spatial location at coding time; see Fillmore 1975), and

by the way in which turn taking is organized in conversation (where the system seems organized around or biased towards two-party conversation without preallocation of turns – see Sacks, Schegloff, and Jefferson, 1974), and by a number of other pragmatic factors. In any case, more empirical work on activity types will be required to settle the issue.

Let us turn to a final issue concerning special inferences due to activity types, which was raised at the beginning of the section, when we claimed that particular modes of inference were the "mirror image," as it were, of the structural constraints on each activity. What exactly is the relation between the structure of an activity and the inferences special to it? Presumably, exactly the same kind of relation that holds between Grice's maxims and the inferences they generate. In that case the maxims set up specific expectations such that, if they are apparently violated, an inference that would preserve them is derived, and if contributions are adequate, they are strongly interpreted as cooperative (the latter is the kind of inference involved in the transition from *five* to *only five* in the exchange: A: *How many children does John have?* B: *Five*; see Horn 1972).

In a similar fashion the structural properties of specific activities set up strong expectations. Because there are strict constraints on contributions to any particular activity, there are corresponding strong expectations about the functions that any utterances at a certain point in the proceedings can be fulfilling. For example, in a basketball game it is understood that utterances will relate only to the game, and moreover will be restricted to a limited set of functions including, for example, applause/abuse, exhortations, directions positioning players, and signals to pass the ball. Given these constraints an utterance like *Here! Peter* or *Right over here* can (with appropriate prosodics) be understood best as a signal to pass the ball in the direction of the caller. The inference from the elliptical expression to the instruction or request relies on the constraints on the functions that utterances should have within that activity. Exactly the same kind of remarks hold for example (8) above, where the utterance "That's a nice one" counted as selecting a lettuce for purchase by virtue of the strong expectations about the sorts of things that utterances in such a shop are doing.[5]

4 Some activities where questions have a focal role

There are some activities where questions play a central role, for example an interview, a press conference, a legal case, greeting sequences, classroom teaching, seeking advice from a bureau, and so on. It is worth looking at some of these activities in detail to see precisely what role questions play in each.

The focus on questions has been chosen with some design. It is possible, (but mistaken, I believe), to view many other kinds of illocutionary force with their associated paradigmatic linguistic forms as having no interactional component. Austin (1962) would have disagreed, of course: he stressed the role of "uptake" – the recognition by the other party of the force in question – in the felicity of illocutionary acts. For him a threat, an order, a statement, a bet made to the winds are simply defective even if other felicity conditions are met; if I bet you sixpence that I can outrun you, but you fail to hear, I cannot be said truthfully to have betted you sixpence. In any case with questions (and imperatives too, of course), the case is clearer: the force of a question *is* (on the whole) an attempt to elicit a particular kind of answer. And a question–answer pair *is* an interactional sequence; such an important one, in fact, that it plays a special role in the ontogeny of verbal interaction (Keenan, Schieffelin, and Platt 1978) and in the organization of adult discourse (Sacks 1992: *passim*; Pope 1975; Merritt 1976). So in the case of questions anyway the concept of illocutionary force takes us beyond the bounds of a sentential utterance into a consideration of the role that such utterances can play in a discourse.

It is worth pointing out that even the formal, that is logical, treatment of questions leads in the same direction. A simple way to treat questions logically is to think of them as open sentences, closed by an appropriate answer; so a question–answer pair can denote a truth value just like an indicative sentence (see e.g. Hull 1975). Alternatively, one can think of them as the declarative disjunction of their possible answers (see e.g. Harrah 1961; Belnap 1963).[6] But if questions can only be characterized in relation to their answers, and question–answer pairs are normally distributed across parties to a conversation, then we are back to the essentially interactional nature of questions. Even if we allow that questions can be answered by their poser, we are still irrevocably beyond the sentence and involved in the characterization of sentence properties by reference to their discourse properties.

Our purpose now is to show that the discourse properties involved in the definition of a question are subject to the nature of the activities in which questions are used: in short, that the role, and thus the nature, of a question is in part dependent on the matrix "language game."

By way of introduction let us consider the different roles that questions play in an exotic society – among the Gonja of West Africa, as reported by E. Goody (1978). This is not simply a catalog of all the indirect usages to which questions are put; although the interrogative form and its uses are the focus of the report, all the uses described have some family resemblance to the illocutionary force that we paradigmatically associate with questions, more so, I understand, than English questions like *can you please pass the salt?* There are strong social constraints in Gonja in the use to which questions can be put in various circumstances; some of these constraints derive from the activity type in which the questions are being used, others are related more closely to the social relations between the interlocutors. Taking those uses of questions that are clearly constrained by the nature of the activity, we may note the following special uses. In greetings, questions are asked about activities and the health of relatives, but the "information that can pass is minimal, for the statement or question is standardized, as is the reply", for "in Gonja a single answer can suffice for all these salutations: *awo* 'it is cool.' This is the equivalent of 'all right,' 'fine,' 'ok' " (Goody 1972: 47). Further examples of such special treatment of questions in greetings can be found in other societies of course – see, for example, Irvine (1974) on greetings among the Wolof, and Sacks (1975) on greetings between (American) English speakers.

Another special usage in Gonja is the use of rhetorical questions in court cases. An elder may say in such circumstances things like "Is it one parent only who creates a child?"; this is interpreted as an attempt to establish the relevance of norms associated with co-parenthood to the judicial case in process. If other elders presiding do not think the norms referred to have relevance to this particular case, they do not answer; on the other hand, if they concur with the questioner they provide an affirmative answer of the sort "No, it is not only one parent who creates the child," thereby conceding the judicial point in question (Goody 1978: 30). There are also special uses of questions in divination, although we are not told much about them; from my own fieldwork in South India I am familiar with a system of questioning restricted to *yes/no* questions that could be answered by configurations in the divinatory objects, and perhaps in Gonja divination works in the same sort of way.

Other uses of questions in Gonja are more closely related to types of social relationship than to activities. Perhaps intermediate is the use of questions to express what anthropologists call a "joking relationship" as typically holds between potential affines. In Gonja, a man may say to a visiting marriageable girl things like the following:

Man: Have you prepared your trousseau yet?
Girl: How can I? You haven't given me anything towards it.

where the man's question refers to the possibility that the girl could be his next wife, and her reply jokingly "chides him for not having courted her" (Goody 1978: 28).

Now each of these uses are understood as questions in some sense, indeed in a primary sense because the response to each is or can be an answer in logical terms. But if, like Searle (1969), we hoped to capture a common feature, the illocutionary force of questioning, in terms of a set of shared felicity conditions, we should be rudely disappointed. We shall return to this point below.

I now wish to look in detail at two special uses of questions in English and I shall try and show that the particular uses are closely tied to – indeed, derived from – the overall goals of the activities in which they occur.

The following extract comes from the cross-examination of a rape victim by the defendant's lawyer in an English court of law (this and other extracts are reprinted in Toner 1977: 156ff).

(12) 1 Your aim that evening then was to go to the discotheque?
      2 Yes.
      3 Presumably you had dressed up for that, had you?
      4 Yes.
      5 And you were wearing make-up?
      6 Yes.
      7 Eye-shadow?
      8 Yes.

9   Lipstick?
10 No I was not wearing lipstick.
11 You weren't wearing lipstick?
12 No.
13 Just eye-shadow, eye make-up?
14 Yes.
15 And powder presumably?
16 Foundation cream, yes.
17 You had had bronchitis had you not?
18 Yes.
19 You have mentioned in the course of your evidence about
    wearing a coat?
20 Yes.
21 It was not really a coat at all, was it?
22 Well, it is sort of a coat-dress and I bought it with trousers, as a
    trouser suit.
23 That is it down there isn't it, the red one?
24 Yes.
25 If we call that a dress, if we call that a dress you had no coat on
    at all had you?
26 No.
27 And this is January. It was quite a cold night?
28 Yes it was cold actually.

Now this is a dialogue constructed of questions and answers. Our
initial question is: what exactly is the nature of these questions? An
immediate puzzlement is that many, in fact most, of these questions
request details that are already known to the questioner. This is
clearer, perhaps, in the second extract:

(13) 1   ...you have had sexual intercourse on a previous occasion
          haven't you?
      2   Yes.
      3   On many previous occasions?
      4   Not many.
      5   Several?
      6   Yes.
      7   With several men?
      8   No.
      9   Just one.
      10 Two.
      11 Two. And you are seventeen and a half?
      12 Yes.

Here the girl's age is asked, even though the basic facts of the case,
including this one, would be known to all parties. The point of the

question is not to learn something from the answer, although it is in part to obtain the answer, to get the witness to state the answer. What can be the point of getting the witness to state what is already known to all present? It could be to obtain a confession, but in this case a statement of one's age is hardly a confession. We could spin the conundrum out, but the point, of course, is that the function of the question does not lie within utterance 11 (or the answer in 12), but in its *juxtaposition* with what has gone before. By careful juxtaposition 11 does the job of suggesting that a girl of seventeen who has already slept with two men is not a woman of good repute.

Turning back to extract (12), we see that juxtaposition there too provides our understanding of what some of these questions are doing. Take utterance 17 for example: here a question about the girl's health follows those about her make-up on the night of the crime, and is succeeded by questions about whether on that occasion she had a coat and how cold the weather was. Again the fact questioned in utterance 17 was known to both questioner and respondent, as indicated by its form – a tagged assertion; the point of asking the question was to obtain an acknowledgment of the fact *at this particular locus* in the cross-examination.

In what kinds of discourse is it appropriate, and perhaps necessary, to state things that may already be known in a certain order or sequence? One answer is: in the presentation of an argument, of course. And now we are in a position to state succinctly what our intuitions have already told us about extracts (12) and (13): *the functions of the questions here are to extract from the witness answers that build up to form a "natural" argument for the jury.* The argument that is thus extracted from the girl's answers in (12) goes something like this: the victim was dressed to go dancing, she was heavily made up – something of a painted lady, in fact – and, despite the fact that she had been ill, she was wearing no coat on the cold winter's night. The implicit conclusion is that the girl was seeking sexual adventures.

But to obtain this argument, or anything like it, we have had to make some basic assumptions about the intentions of the questioner – namely, that he wishes to convey an argument, and moreover an argument that will show the facts of the case in a certain light. We can make these assumptions with surety because the nature of the activity – the cross-examining of the victim by the defendant's lawyer – assigns a particular role, a class of intentions, in fact, to the questioner. To see the connections between these different levels of discourse organization, first note that if the questions were randomly picked out of a hat, then we could not understand the sequence of questions as an argument designed by the questioner. Second, note that if the sequence of questions is understood as designed to convey an argument, the conclusion of the argument could be different in different activities. If (13), for example, was constructed from the questions posed by a concerned auntie to her modern niece, the implicit conclusion might be something like "well I do disapprove of modern mores". Or even if the roles in the courtroom were reversed, and the respondent in (12) was the defendant accused of luring lorry-drivers into deserted lay-bys where accomplices could hijack the goods, the implicit conclusion would again be different – what else could the siren be doing on a January night underdressed?

I hope, then, to have established that our understanding of these extracts as designed to elicit an argument of a certain kind with specific conclusions rests on our knowledge of the kind of activity the talk occurs within. We know that in a rape case it is the job of the defendant and his lawyer to show that the girl asked for it, and the goal of the victim and her counsel to resist this and establish that the defendant committed the crime intentionally and against the girl's resistance. Each of these conflicting goals specifies a class of strategies, and it is the location of these that gives us our understanding of what is going on.[7] For example, it will be in the defendant's best interests to obtain the most damaging admissions from the victim; his counsel will therefore ask the strongest version of the relevent question first, and failing to obtain assent, will come down one notch and so on. A structure of this sort can be seen in (13), where the cross-examiner first asks whether the girl has had sexual intercourse on many occasions, to which there is dissent, falls back on several, which is again resisted, and so on. We understand too, of course, why the girl resists: her understanding like ours rests on a reconstruction of the intended line of argument, and, given the goals that the activity assigns to her, she must try to thwart that line of argument. In the case in question she was sometimes relatively successful at this, as indicated by the following extract (Toner 1977: 158):

(14) 1   ...you guessed by then this was a man who wanted to make
          advances to you, didn't you?
      2   Well, I didn't think of it straight away.
      3   I know you didn't think of it straight away. I am now asking
          you about the time when you missed the turning and started
          talking, according to you, about going to Taunton?
      4   Well, I thought about it, but I just sort of kept it at the back of
          my mind. You know, I didn't really want to think about it.
      5   You thought about it, and your evening having fallen flat you
          were not adverse to it, were you?
      6   I don't understand what you mean.
      7   Well, you didn't mind?
      8   Of course I minded.
      9   I want to make this quite clear. You did not say, 'Stop the car'
          because you didn't want the car stopped?
     10   I did.

This example should make clear the way in which our understanding of what is going on requires reference to the underlying strategies or plans employed by both parties, which in turn are derived
from the nature of the activity and the goals that it assigns the
various participants. There is a way in which the question–answer
format is invariant and insensitive to all of this; together with an
assignment of questioner/answerer roles it constructs a turn-taking
organization that gives control of topical organization entirely to
the questioner, thus making the format a possible vehicle for the
expression of an argument. But there is another way in which the
role and the function of each question is relative to the goals and
strategies of the participants: the questioner hopes to elicit a response that will count as part of an implicit argument, the answerer
will try to avoid such a response. The questions may be rhetorical,
in the sense that both know the answer (cf. utterances 23 in (12), 11
in (13)); they may appear to seek information when in fact the
information is already known (as perhaps in 25 in (12)), or they
may appear merely to seek confirmation when in fact they seek
information, and so on. In each case the particular role that we see
them playing is established by reference to the strategies we assume
the questioner to be utilizing by virtue of the role he is playing in a
particular kind of activity.

   Let us turn now to another activity type where questions play an
important role: teaching children in the classroom. Interestingly,
questions are not integral to the teaching process in all cultures;

Gonja society again provides some useful crosscultural perspectives here (see Goody 1978: 40–1). Nevertheless, it is clear that questions are an invaluable resource in the classroom: firstly, because they require answers they enjoin participation; secondly, because they provide feedback they can be used to test for knowledge acquired in particular; and thirdly, because they allow the pupil to express the location of any puzzlement he or she may feel. But in what follows we shall be particularly concerned with questions uttered by the teacher, and with the larger discourse structures that are involved with these questions.

We may start with a piece of constructed data (T denotes teacher, C1 first child, and so on):

(15) T: What are the names of some trees?
      C1: There are oaks.
      C2: Apples!
      T: Apple-trees, yes.
      C3: Yews.
      T: Well done Johnny!
      C4: Oak trees!
      T: No Sally, Willy's already said that.

The example illustrates that to participate properly in this activity you have to know more than just how to answer questions. For C4's utterance was a valid and truthful answer to T's question, but the response by T indicates that it was not a valid move in this particular language game. Note too that T's rejoinder does not entirely make explicit the language game: the game could still consist of uttering any tree name Willy has not already said. T is merely alluding to the rules of the game, not stating them.

Now let us turn to a piece of real data that will illustrate the same sort of thing in greater detail and veracity. The data and some of the insights come from a study of classroom interaction by Gumperz and Herasimchuk (1975: 109ff.).

(16) T: Jane, how do you spell *Ann?*
      J: A, N, N.
      T: A, N, N. What kind of an A?
      J: Capital.
      T: Why is it capital?
      J: Cause it's a name.
      T: Of a?

J: Girl.

T: OK, Ivy, do you see a name on that page you know?

I: Ann.

T: That's the one that Jane just named. How do you spell *Ann?*

I: A, N, N.

T: How do we say A?

I: (no response).

T: Jane, do you want to help her?

C: I know.

J: The letter capital A.

T: Capital A, N, N. Why do we say 'capital', Ivy?

I: (no response).

T: Why should we put a capital A on *Ann,* Esmé?

E: Because it's someone's name.

T: It's the *name* of someone, Ivy. So we make it special.

E: A girl, the name of a girl.

T: Would you see any other name, Ivy, that you know?

C: I see a name, a *Ben.*

T: (to Ivy):   ...any other name? Let Ivy find one.
     D'you see a name you know there?

I: (pause) *Ken?*

T: All right, *Ken.* That's right. How do you spell *Ken?* Don't
     forget what you'd say to that first letter. How do you spell *Ken?*

A: Where is *Ken?* K,C, K, E, er..

T: Alex, Ivy is spelling it. Capital K–

I: Capital K.

C: (to other child) You messin up the raser already!

T: E.

I: N.

T: Right. *Ken.* Do you see any word that you know there, Bill,
     anyone's name?

B: *Pat.*

T: Where do you see *Pat?* do you see an *ae* sound in there?

B: No.

T: What sound do you see?

B: Pat.

T: Do you see an *ae* sound?

B: No.

T: What sound do you see?

B: *Pet.*

I: *Peter?*

T: Is there an *er* on the end?

I: Is it *Peter?*

T: Ivy's helping you. She's given you a clue. But is there an *er* on the
     end of that?

C: (inaudible).

> T: What's the word?
> C: (inaudible).
> T: What?
> C: *Pete.*
> T: That's right. How do you spell it?

In this extract I think it is clear that the teacher's questions are *requests to follow a procedure.* The procedure in question, which is recursively applied, has three parts: first one should identify names in the text; then one should spell them; and thirdly one should attend to the capitalization of the first letter. The teacher, in getting the children to go through the procedure, also requires that the children's contributions must *prove* (a) that they can identify names, (b) that they can spell them, and (c) that they know about capital letters.

It is because it is necessary in this language game to prove that one can identify a name or spell it that one cannot repeat an identification or spelling, since one might do that by imitation. And this explains the particular role that we understand T's utterances like the following to be playing: "That's the one that J just named"; "A, I is spelling it." Notice that, as in the prior constructed example, the rules of the language game are presumed even in these corrections, and not taught. In order to understand these two utterances of the teacher as having the force of dismissing the prior contribution one would need already to know what the rules of the language game are. We are left with what is here, and elsewhere I think throughout the range of activities in a culture, a genuine puzzle: how are the rules of a language game ever learnt?

Even within our culture teaching styles and methods vary a great deal, partly, of course, in relation to subject-matter, educational ideology within the school, and approaches favored by particular teachers. Let us take another example of a rather different type, where questions play a different role. The following extract from a science lesson comes from a large corpus gathered by the Birmingham (UK) discourse project.[8]

(17) T: Now tell me: why do you eat all that food? Can you tell me why do you eat all that food?
        Yes
     C: To keep strong.
     T: To keep you strong. Yes. To keep you strong. Why do you want to be strong?

C: Sir, — muscles.
T: To make muscles. Yes. Well what would you want to do with your muscles?
C: Sir, use them.
T: You'd want to —
C: Use them.
T: You'd want to use them. Well how do you use your muscles?
C: By working.
T: By working. Yes. And when you're working, what are you using apart from your muscles? What does that food give you? What does the food give you?
C: Strength.
T: Not only strength; we have another word for it. Yes.
C: Energy.
T: Good girl. Yes. Energy. You can have a team point. That's a very good word. We use — we're using —energy. We're using — energy When a car goes into the garage, what do you put in it?
C: Petrol.
T: You put petrol in. Why do you put petrol in?
C: To keep it going.
T: To keep it going; so that it will go on the road. The car uses the petrol but the petrol changes to something, in the same way that your food changes to something. What does the petrol change to?
C: Smoke.
C: Water.
C: Fire.
T: You told me before.
C: Smoke.
C: (inaudible.)
T: Again.
C: (Energy).
T: Energy. Tell everybody.
C: Energy.
T: Energy. Yes. When you put petrol in the car, you're putting another kind of energy in the car from the petrol. So we get energy from petrol and we get energy from food. Two kinds of energy.

Despite the fact that this extract shares with (16) the fact that it is structured primarily by the teacher's use of questions, it is clearly a very different "language game" in the sense that there are different strategies and procedures in employment. Specifically, the discourse in (17) appears to be a variant of the Socratic method: the teacher attempts to make explicit a selected part of the implicit knowledge that he assumes pupils to have, by means of a dialog of questions and answers. The selected knowledge that the teacher hopes to make explicit is an analogy or parallelism, best expressed by the proportion:

(18)   food : humans :: petrol : cars

where the underlying symmetry is that the first part of each pair is the energy source for the second part. There is a parallel here to the way in which in the courtroom questions were used to extract answers that would amount to a specific argument. One difference, of course, is that whereas in the courtroom a cross-examination is more like a zero-sum game, where one party's losses are the other party's gains, here it is at least the hope of the teacher that the game is perceived as more like one of pure coordination, where both parties stand to lose or gain together. That is, the teacher hopes that by directing questions and selecting answers he will get the pupils to see in what direction he wants them to answer. And there is a presumption of cooperation. The game then consists in trying to get the pupils to see the proportion in (18) and to state the underlying rationale for it.

It is important to note to what extent the procedure here is cooperative and dependent on the pupils foreseeing the *kind* of answer that the teacher has in mind. The answer to the teacher's first question, for example ("Can you tell me why do you eat all that food?"), could equally well have been *Hunger* or *Mother cooks it* or a host of other responses in the wrong direction. Nevertheless, these might be truthful answers. Similarly, to the question "When a car goes into the garage, what do you put in it?" there would be many correct but useless answers – useless in that they would not advance the game – like *Air, Water, Oil*, and so on. The game could not proceed efficiently, if at all, simply by a selection of randomly produced answers. To play the game the pupils must know the kind of thing the teacher is trying to do, they must foresee the general line of reasoning, and they must cooperatively help to build it.

The discussion so far has in fact oversimplified the nature of the game in (17), and thus the amount of knowledge that the children require in order to play it effectively. Consider how the children are meant to come to a realization of the proportion in (18), and what will count as a display of that realization. They are meant to use the same linguistic category to express the relation between humans and food and between cars and petrol. We see from T's rejection of C's answer "Strength" to the question "What does food give you?" that the relation must be expressed by the word *energy* to count as a winning move in the game. The game has then a metalinguistic element. An interesting thing about this element is that it seems to commit the teacher to holding a special view of the relation between language and the world, something approximating to that held by Wittgenstein in the *Tractatus Logico-Philosophicus*. For only on such a view would the activity of placing two events, objects, or relations under the same linguistic description amount to saying something about the relationship between those two events, objects, or relations in the real world. This Tractarian assumption then, seems to underlie the insistence on the use of the word *energy*.[9]

We are now in a position to state the knowledge that the child needs in order to play in this particular language game. He must know that not just any truthful answer to the teacher's questions will count as a valid move; he must attempt to foresee the line of argument so that his answer will contribute towards it. Moreover, he needs to see that not just any expression of his contribution will do, and specifically here that parallelisms should be expressed under an identical verbal relation. To do this, he must be able to recognize sameness of linguistic description, and his understanding of the relevance of this will certainly be aided by a grasp of the teacher's Tractarian views (without this grasp the activity will appear to be a purely linguistic game rather than a science lesson).

I have talked loosely of "language games" at two levels: on the one hand, one has the activity type which in part determines the role that language will play; and on the other hand, one has particular strategies or procedures within the activity – like teaching spelling in a particular way, or drawing out the pupils' implicit knowledge about energy sources of various sorts. Does the existence of these lower-order structures indicate that the notion of activity alone is not predictive of (or explanatory with regard to) the rules of language use in an interesting way? I think not, because there are intrinsic connections between the two layers of organization. For example, there are certain goals that seem to be taken as central to teaching. One of these is to impart knowledge, but more importantly to organize knowledge, especially by drawing out important parallels – let us call this the gnomic function; another is to impart abilities, or knowledge of procedures, like spelling, counting, and so on. Now, given some other aspects of the activity, especially that one functionary (the teacher) has control both in task setting and turn taking while the rest must try to do whatever task the teacher assigns, various detailed features of the teaching strategies or procedures can be seen to follow – in the sense that they seem to be rationally adapted to achieving the overall goals. For example, the procedure used in (16) where each child was called upon to demonstrate the ability to identify and spell proper names was a rational way of testing whether that ability had been acquired, and perhaps of enhancing that ability by practice. So it is ultimately against the background of the goals of the activity as a whole and the derivative structures and pedagogical strategies that detailed features of the organization make sense. So an utterance of the form "A, B is spelling it" can function as a command for A to shut up, because it is understood that the teacher T schedules the events, that T has asked B to spell it in order to ascertain whether B has learnt the relevant procedure, and that T is therefore not now interested in A's ability.[10]

It seems, then, that the various levels of organization within an activity cohere, and can be seen to derive as rational means from overall ends and organizational conditions. It may be that the means chosen only *seem* rational to the participants at the time, or are assumed to be on the basis of received wisdom, or more often are rational but turn out to be ineffective because other conditions have not been taken into account. In any case the coherence of the different levels seems to reside in a general tendency towards rational organization.

In the light of the very different usages of questions in these examples, let us return to examine the definition and characterization of a question. Our basic problem is this: can we factor out from all these different usages a common core which we can continue to think of as part of the semantics of questions? Or is there no such core, but rather only a set of language games in which they play roles related by "family resemblance"?

One influential way of thinking about the properties that indivi-

duate different illocutionary forces is to factor out the set of necessary and sufficient conditions for the nondefective performance of
the relative speech act. This is the characterization of speech acts by
means of the specification of their "felicity conditions" as advocated by Austin (1962) and Searle (1969, 1976). After stating that
"there are two kinds of questions (a) real questions, (b) exam
questions" (1969: 66), Searle produces the following felicity conditions for "real questions" (the corresponding ones for exam
questions are presumably as I have indicated in brackets):

(19) Propositional content condition: any proposition or proposi-
      tional function.
      Preparatory conditions: (a) S does not know "the answer"
                              (exam Q: S knows the answer but does
                              not know whether H knows it).
                              (b) It is not obvious to both S and H
                              that H will provide the information at
                              that time without being asked.
      Sincerity condition: S wants this information (exam Q: S
                              wants to know if H knows the infor-
                              mation).
      Essential condition: Counts as an attempt to elicit this infor-
                              mation from H.

It is clear that in line with Searle's method one could go on elaborating the conditions; for instance, for real questions there seem to
be other preparatory conditions to the effect that S has reason to
think that H might know the answer, that S expects H to provide a
response, and so on. The notion of 'answer' can be independently
characterized as an assent or dissent to the proposition of a *yes/no*
question, or the completion of the open proposition in the case of
Wh-questions.

The problem for us is that many of the questions that we have
examined do not fit into this schema as either "real" or "exam"
questions. For example, the utterance 11 in the courtroom example
(13) ("And you are seventeen and a half?"),[11] does not fit the first
preparatory condition, the sincerity condition, or the essential condition: both parties know the answer and know that they know the
answer, the speaker does not want the information nor does he
want to know whether the hearer knows it, nor is he attempting to
elicit the information although he is attempting to elicit a response
(namely the answer). We could say that this is a rhetorical question,

in that these properties are typical of such questions, and that rhetorical questions are "really" statements (see Sadock 1974, for one such line). However, the fact that a response that is an answer is expected and given distinguishes this question from rhetorical questions where responses are inappropriate or optional.

Take another of our questions, the first utterance in example (17) ("why do you eat all that food?"). Again both parties know a wide range of truthful answers to this question and know that they do – so it does not fall within Searle's category of exam questions. The questioner does not want the information, nor does he want the children to show that they know it, he merely wants a response drawn from the pupils' tacit knowledge that will advance and make explicit his argument about a specific analogy.

Most of the other questions in our examples will also fail to fit Searle's schema in one way or another. Consider the questions in greetings (*How are you?*), where the answers are more or less prescribed so that all the felicity conditions concerning knowledge, information, and desire for it must be wrong. Consider too the special uses in Gonja between joking relatives, or in law courts, as described at the beginning of this section. It is really hard to see a common core to all these kinds of questions, except that they elicit responses of specific kinds. But that will hardly distinguish questions from bets, offers, and so on. Moreover, some questions do not seem intended to elicit responses, unless we consider silence a response – consider the use of sentences like *How could you do that to me?* in a quarrel. Nor will the usual strategy for the rescue of the concept of speech act from the diversity of discourse – namely, to identify a paradigmatic type and then consider other usages "indirect speech acts" (see Gordon and Lakoff 1975; Searle 1975) – work very well here: the questions in the courtroom, for example, are not easily understood as other kinds of speech acts masquerading in question from. Nor is the distinction between direct and indirect speech acts so clear in practice: consider the first utterance in (16) for example ("J, how do you spell Ann?"): is this an imperative ("Go through the procedure of spelling Ann!") in question form? But how else would you answer the question except by demonstrating how to spell Ann?[12] Sometimes it is easier to demonstrate an "answer" than to describe it.

Other linguistic approaches to the analysis of questions tend to accept the existence of well-defined felicity conditions; the problem is, then, where in a linguistic description these should be accommodated. If one accepts the performative analysis (Ross 1970; Sadock 1974; Lakoff 1975), then they can be seen as presuppositions of the higher verb of saying. Even those who have avoided that analysis have tended to see their job as dismantling the hybrid theory of speech acts and parceling out the felicity conditions to either the semantic or pragmatic component, where they are thought more properly to belong (see e.g. Katz 1977). But if felicity conditions are variable in relation to discourse context, then none of them are the sort of thing one wants in an orderly semantics in any case.

Is there anything left that one could claim to be the semantics of questions? Note that if one rejects the performative analysis, and there are now a great number of arguments why one should (see e.g. Gazdar 1976 and references therein), then there is reason to think that illocutionary force has nothing to do with semantics, and should rather be handled entirely in pragmatics. Not all linguists seem to see this. Katz (1977), for example, while rejecting the performative analysis, argues that because one has to provide the semantics for *ask* in such statements as *John asked Mary what the time was*, one should assimilate the same semantics to the *question form* in direct questions. But the argument seems confused: one might as well argue that because one has to provide the semantics for *kick* in sentences like *John kicked Bill*, one should provide the same semantics for the action of kicking. Reports of acts have semantic characterizations, acts do not.

If there is a role for semantics to play in the characterization of questions it is probably in the characterization of the logical relation between questions and answers. But since there are also pragmatic constraints on adequate answers (of the sort outlined by Grice 1975, as well as the sort specific to activities), and since there are many appropriate responses to questions that are not answers, the precise role that this relation will play in the definition of a question is certainly not clear to me.

If, on the other hand, the illocutionary force associated with questions is an entirely pragmatic affair (as for example in Stennius's 1972 account), then there is no reason to resist the fact that the nature of questions can vary in relation to the particular language games in which they play a role. In that case Wittgenstein's failure to make a distinction between speech acts and the activities they are used in would have a more principled basis than is currently thought.

5 Conclusions

We have argued that types of activity, social episodes if one prefers, play a central role in language usage. They do this in two ways especially: on the one hand, they constrain what will count as an allowable contribution to each activity; and on the other hand, they help to determine how what one says will be "taken" – that is, what kinds of inferences will be made from what is said. Both of these issues are of some theoretical and practical interest. For example, knowing the constraints on allowable contributions will be an important part of what Hymes (1962) has called *communicative competence*, the knowledge required to use language appropriately in cultural situations. The inferential side to these constraints adds an important further element to our understanding of, and appreciation of the importance of, inference in discourse. In addition to the very general principles outlined by Grice (1975), and the very specific organizations of background knowledge emphasized by workers in artificial intelligence, there are *activity-specific rules of inference*. Again having a grasp of the latter will play an important role in the reception side of communicative competence, the ability to understand what one hears. And because these activity-specific rules of inference are more culturally specific than other sorts, they are likely to play a large role in crosscultural or interethnic miscommunications, an area of growing interest (see e.g. Gumperz 1978). Computer models of language understanding are also likely to prove disappointing if such bases for inference are not taken into account.

The apprehension will no doubt be that a full understanding of the ways language usage is inextricably entangled with social activities will require the description of a heterogeneous mass of arbitrarily varied, culturally determined language games. Certainly, compared to simple overarching principles of a Gricean sort, this is something of a Pandora's box. Nevertheless, as we proceeded through the examples we were able to show that many features of these language games are not unprincipled. Rather there seems to be a healthy tendency towards the rational construction of language games as organizations functionally adapted to achieving certain goals – the main purposes of the activity in question. A very good idea of the kind of language usage likely to be found within a given activity can thus be predicted simply by knowing what the main function of the activity is seen to be by participants. If that is the case, then all the details of constraints on language usage within each activity need not be taught to the foreign-language learner, or incorporated into a language-understanding program; it will suffice to specify the general goals and any special unpredictable constraints.

And finally we have tried to show that Wittgenstein's abstention from a distinction between speech acts and speech events, both of which fell under the rubric of "language games," was more principled than speech-act theorists would have us believe. To quote him:

But how many kinds of sentence are there? Say assertion, question, and command? – There are *countless* kinds: countless different kinds of use of what we call "symbols," "words," "sentences." And this multiplicity is not something fixed, given once for all; but new types of language, new language-games, as we may say, come into existence, and others become obsolete and get forgotten ... Here the term "language-*game*" is meant to bring into prominence the fact that the speaking of language is part of an activity, or of a form of life.   (1958a: I.23)

We explored this doctrine through an analysis of questions and their usages in various activities. And we may take as an epitaph to that investigation another quote:

If you do not keep the multiplicity of language-games in view you will perhaps be inclined to ask questions like: "What is a question?" – Is it the statement that I do not know such-and-such, or the statement that I wish the other person would tell me ...? Or is it the description of my mental state of uncertainty?   (1958a: I.24)

Notes

1. Those more familiar with basketball tell me that I have assigned the wrong functions to some of these utterances, on a mistaken analogy to soccer. They tell me that (1)1 is obviously a commendation, (1)4 a critical encouragement. But my mistake only illustrates the point – how specialized the uses of language can be to the particular activities within which they are employed.

2. I have in mind distinctions like Searle's "Word to World" versus "World to Word" fit: a sports commentary mirrors a nonspeech event, but magical rites are often held to create the world they describe. Another distinction can be made between cases where concurrent actions describe or illustrate the words, and cases where the words describe the actions. Consider, for instance, how the same set of photographic slides of, say, Venice could be used to illustrate a lecture on architecture or to describe a holiday trip: in the one case the slides merely illustrate the talk, in the other talk merely amplifies the slides.

3. Recollect that I have confined my remarks to the structural rather than the stylistic properties of speech events; here the constraints on contributions that I have in mind are especially those on the functions that utterances will be understood – if possible – to have.

4. It may be argued, incorrectly I think, that the implicature from *saw x* to *read x* (where *x* is reading matter) is *particularized* in Grice's sense, that it only holds in certain special circumstances. Its cancellation might then not be dependent on certain levels of cooperation, but due simply to the absence of those special circumstances. However, precisely analogous arguments to those I am making here can be made from other examples that have indubitably *generalized* conversational implicatures. For example, *three* generally implicates "no more than three," and so the following exchange is expectable only in noncooperative situations like legal settings:

A: How many men were with you?
B: Three.
A: No more than three?
B: Well, perhaps as many as five.

5. A final issue that arises in connection with inference can be a very real interactional problem, that faces conversationalists: how does one ascertain *which* activity one is in at any one point in an ongoing interaction? Sometimes the gross facts of physical setting, time, copresent personnel, etc. are insufficient to determine the activity. Then one may work backwards, so to speak, from the nature of verbal contributions to a determination of what kind of activity the other participants, at least, think they are in. The need for this kind of inference frequently arises where one kind of activity comes embedded within another, for example joking sequences within work talk, or business transactions conducted at a cocktail party. A good locus for the study of such activity-identifying processes is where misunderstandings arise due to different cultural or subcultural origins of participants: John Gumperz and associates have done some important work in this areas (see e.g. Gumperz 1978; Gumperz and Tannen 1979). My lack of attention to this problem of "frame invocation" is a gross oversimplification if it is taken to imply that the determination of the activity one is in is unproblematic, but that is not my intention. In this chapter my main aim is to establish that the activities within which utterances occur play

a central role in the assignment of function or import to those utterances. If this can be established, the question of how activities are
recognized becomes, of course, all the more important.

6. More recently we have the formal treatment of questions as the sets of
   possible, or true, answers by Hamblin (1973) and Karttunen (1977).
   Another long-standing tradition, of course, is to think of questions as
   imperatives to tell specific answers; there is a rather sophisticated treatment along these lines by Hintikka (1974) incorporating an epistemic
   element – a *yes/no* question gets paraphrased essentially as "bring it
   about that I know that p or not-p." The interactional element here is
   also clear: an answer will only be adequate relative to the asker's
   epistemic state. The problem with this line of attack is that it assigns a
   very specific pragmatic function to questions, while empirically they
   seem to have a very wide range of functions, as will be fully documented below.

7. I am reminded by Carlotta Smith that it would be useful here to
   distinguish and relate *constraints* on activities from the *strategies* that
   may flourish within them. We may take constraints to be normatively
   imposed, and maintained at least in part by the fact that failure to
   conform may yield quite unintended misinterpretations. Strategies, on
   the other hand, may be seen as optimal or self-maximizing patterns of
   behavior available to participants in particular roles, *under* the specific
   constraints of the relevant activity.

8. The example is cited here by kind permission of Malcolm Coulthard.
   These and other materials appear in Brazil, Coulthard, and Johns
   (1980).

9. It is a Tractarian game, Jay Atlas points out to me, insofar as the
   syntax of language is *made* to mirror the structure of the world. The
   emphasis on the metalinguistic element in this game derives directly
   from Jay Atlas's comments on a version of this paper given to a
   seminar in Cambridge.

10. Much of this discussion ties into the controversy over the nature of
    indirect speech acts; for some discussion and many references see
    Brown and Levinson (1978: 137ff.). The classic articles are reprinted
    in Cole and Morgan (1975).

11. I have not always distinguished between what are syntactically
    questions and what are only prosodically marked as questions,
    although there are clearly some pragmatic differences here. But in most
    cases we could substitute syntactic questions for those marked by
    other means in our examples without changing those aspects of the
    text that we are interested in here. In any case the argument here could
    be conducted equally well with syntactic questions, drawn from a
    wider range of data.

12. Let us ignore the other readings of the manner adverbial implicit in
    how, as revealed in such joke answers (this one produced by Jay Atlas)
    as "Correctly every time."

3

On talk and its institutional occasions

EMANUEL A. SCHEGLOFF

1 Introduction

Whether starting from a programmatic address to the structure of face-to-face interaction or from a programmatic concern with the constitutive practices of the mundane world, whether in pursuit of language, culture, or action, a range of inquiries of several social-science disciplines (most relevantly anthropology, sociology, and linguistics) have over the past twenty-five to thirty years brought special attention to bear on talk in interaction. It is not unfair to say that one of the most focused precipitates of this broad interest has been that family of studies grouped under the rubric "conversation analysis." It is, in any case, with such studies of "talk" that I will be concerned in reflecting on "talk and social structure."

The reflections discussed in most of this chapter were prepared to serve as the opening presentation of a conference on "Talk and Social Structure" held at the University of California, Santa Barbara, March 1986, and most of the paper (and an additional section omitted here) have been published as "Reflections on talk and social structure" in D. Boden and D. Zimmerman (1991). In some places that paper, and the present minor revision of it, address once again matters taken up in an earlier paper (Schegloff 1987a), but different facets of those matters or in a more detailed fashion. My thanks to Jennifer Mandelbaum for contributions of tact and clarity in the preparation of the paper in its earlier published form. I am also indebted to Deirdre Boden, Paul Drew, Douglas Maynard, and especially Jack Whalen, whose reactions to an earlier draft of that paper, or to the reactions of others to it, helped in my efforts to arrive at a text which might be understood as I meant it.

In place of one section of the aforementioned paper, I have included a segment of another paper (Schegloff 1988/9) which may serve to give some empirical and analytic focus to what may otherwise appear merely theoretic and policy programs. The passage from the previous papers to this one has been facilitated, even motivated, by the tender ministrations of Paul Drew and John Heritage, for which I am in their debt.

Although itself understandable as a sustained exploration of
what is entailed in giving an analytic account of "a context" (as in
the phrase "in the context of ordinary conversation"), various
aspects of inquiry in this tradition of work have prompted an
interest in neighboring disciplines in relating features of talk-in-
interaction to "contexts" of a more traditional sort – linguistic
contexts, cultural contexts, and institutional and social structural
contexts. At the same time, investigators working along conversation-analytic lines began to deal with talk with properties which
were seemingly related to its production by participants oriented to
a special "institutional" context; and, wishing to address those
distinctive properties rather than ones held in common with other
forms of talk (as Sacks had done in some of his earliest work based
on group-therapy sessions), these investigators faced the analytic
problems posed by such an undertaking.

The interest in the theme "talk and social structure" comes,
then, from several directions – the most prominent being technical
concerns in the analysis of certain forms of talk, on the one hand,
and an impulse to effect a rapprochement with the concerns of
classical sociology, and to do so by relating work on talk-in-interaction to those social formations which are referred to as "social
structures," or generically as "social structure," on the other hand.
My reflections will have this latter impulse as their point of departure, but will quickly seek to engage it by formulating and confront-
ing the analytic problems which it poses.

Of course, a term like "social structure" is used in many different ways. In recent years, to cite but a few cases, Peter Blau (1977)
has used the term to refer to the distribution of a population on
various parameters asserted to be pertinent to interaction, claiming
a derivation from Simmel and his notion of intersecting social circles. Many others have in mind a structure of statuses and/or roles,
ordinarily thereby building in an inescapable normative component
of just the sort Blau wishes to avoid. Yet others intend by this term
a structured distribution of scarce resources and desirables, such as
property, wealth, productive capacity, status, knowledge, privilege,
power, the capacity to enforce and preserve privilege, etc. Still
others have in mind stably patterned sets of social relations,
whether formalized in organizations or more loosely stabilized in
networks.

The sense of "social structure" intended in the thematic concern with "talk and social structure" does not range across all these usages. But almost certainly it includes a concern with power and status and its distribution among social formations such as classes, ethnic groups, age-grade groups, gender, and professional relations. It is this sense which has animated, for example, the work by West (1979) and Zimmerman and West (1975) on gender and interruption and West's work (1984) on doctor–patient interaction. It includes as well a concern with the structured social relations which comprise organizations and occupational practice and the institutional sectors with which they are regularly identified (e.g. in Atkinson and Drew's treatment of the courts [1979], in the work of Zimmerman and his associates on the police [e.g. Zimmerman 1984; Whalen and Zimmerman 1987], Maynard's work [1984] on the legal system, that of Heritage [1985] on mass-media news, or Boden's (forthcoming) on organizations). Mehan's studies of decision making in the context of educational bureaucracies (Mehan, Hertweck, and Meihls 1986; Mehan 1991) touch on both usages (as, of course, do some of the other studies which I have invoked to exemplify one or the other).

The work which engages with these classical sociological themes and incorporates reference to and treatment of them in studying talk-in-interaction has revived for me some concerns which were deep preoccupations some twenty-five years ago, when work on the analysis of talk-in-interaction, of the sort now referred to as "conversation-analytic," was getting underway. In these reflections, I want among other things to review, restate, and update some of those considerations, and ask how contemporary efforts to engage these topics stand with respect to some of these older concerns. Do the old concerns still have the force they once had, or have they faded in perceived significance? Are there now solutions to the problems as once formulated? Or can the results of current work at the interface of conversation and social structure be usefully enriched or constrained by engaging these issues?

Whatever answers we arrive at to these questions, there is one point I want to make before taking them up. Whatever substantive gains there are to be had from focusing on the relationship between talk and social structure in the traditional sense, this focus is not needed in order to supply conversation analysis with its sociological credentials. The work which is focused on the organization of talk-in-interaction in its own right – work on the organization of turn taking, or on the organization of sequences, work addressed to the actions being done in turns and the formats through which they are done, work on the organization of repair, and work directed to the many discrete practices of talking and acting through talk which do not converge into domains of organization – this work is itself dealing with social organization and social structures, albeit of a different sort than in the received uses of those terms, and is no less sociological in impulse and relevance (Schegloff 1987b).

For some, the fact that conversation analysis (henceforth, CA) concerns itself with the details of talking has meant that it is a form of linguistics. Perhaps so, but certainly not exclusively so. If it is not a distinctive discipline of its own (which it may well turn out to be), CA is at a point where linguistics and sociology (and several other disciplines, anthropology and psychology among them) meet. For the target of its inquiries stands where talk amounts to action, where action projects consequences in a structure and texture of interaction which the talk is itself progressively embodying and realizing, and where the particulars of the talk inform what actions are being done and what sort of social scene is being constituted. Now, from the start, one central preoccupation of sociology and social theory has been with the character of social action and what drives it (reason, passion, interest, utility) – this is familiar enough. Another concern has been with the character of interaction in which action is embedded, for it is observations about some aspects of the character of interaction that motivated such hoary old distinctions as those between *Gemeinschaft* and *Gesellschaft*, between status and contracts, and the like. "Action in interaction" is, then, a longstanding theme of social analysis.

CA's enterprise, concerned as it is with (among other things) the detailed analysis of how talk-in-interaction is conducted as an activity in its own right and as the instrument for the full range of social action and practice, is then addressed to one of the classic themes of sociology, although, to be sure, in a distinctive way. Of the several ways in which CA shows its deep preoccupation with root themes of social science and sociology in particular, these standing conversation-analytic preoccupations resonate more with the title of the recent Atkinson and Heritage collection (1984); they are concerned with "structures of social action" – structures of single actions and of series and sequences of them. Atkinson and Heritage's title is, of course, a thoroughly unveiled allusion to the title of Talcott Parsons' first major work, *The Structure of Social Action* (1937), the work which launched the enterprise of Parsonian action theory. The difference between Parsons's title and the Atkinson and Heritage allusion, *The Structure of Social Action* vs. *Structures of Social Action*, may suggest some of the distinctiveness.

Parsons's tack was conceptual and global. For him there was "*the* structure . . .," and it was arrived at by theoretic stipulation of the necessary components of an analytic unit – the "unit act," components such as "ends," "means," "conditions." This was a thoroughly conceptual enterprise on a thoroughly analytic object. The Atkinson and Heritage title, "Structures of . . .," suggests not only multiplicity of structures, but the empirical nature of the enterprise. The units are concrete activities, and the search for their "components" involves examination and description of empirical instances.

But with all the differences in conception, mode of working, etc., there is a common enterprise here, and it has long been a central one for sociology and the social sciences more generally. It is one of getting at the character of social action and social interaction. In addressing this theme and the varied problems and analytic tasks to which it gives rise, CA is itself engaged in *echt* sociology; its sociological credentials are grounded by this undertaking, even without the introduction of such other traditional sociological concerns such as "social structure." Of course, CA may go on to address itself to the relationship between talk-in-interaction (and the action and conduct which it realizes) and social structure as traditionally conceived, but this is an extension of its sociological office, not its basis.

The reasons for thinking about the relationships of talk and social structure are ready to hand. Both our casual and our studied examination of interaction and talk-in-interaction provide a lively sense of the occasions on which who the parties are, relative to one another, seems to matter, and matter to *them*. And these include senses of "who they are" that connect directly to what is ordinarily meant by "social structure" – their relative status, the power they differentially can command, the group affiliations they display or can readily have attributed to them such as their racial or ethnic memberships, their gender and age-grade status, their occupational status and its general standing and immediate interactional significance, and the other categories of membership in the society which can matter to the participants and which fall under the traditional sociological rubric "social structure."

The issue I mean to address is not "Is there such a thing as gender/class/power/status/organization/etc.?" or "Does it effect anything in the world?" Rather, the question is: whatever observations we initially make about how such features of social organization as these work and bear on interaction, how do we translate them into defensible, empirically based analyses that help us to get access to previously unnoticed particular details of talk-in-interaction, and appreciate their significance? For the lively sense we may all share of the relevance of social structure along the lines I have mentioned needs to be converted into the hard currency of defensible analysis – analysis which departs from, and can always be referred to and grounded in, the details of actual occurrences of conduct in interaction.

Again, I do not mean to be addressing myself to two apparently neighboring stances, although there may well be implications for them. I am not centrally concerned with those investigators whose primary analytic commitment is to social structure in the received senses of that term, and who mean to incorporate examination of talk into their inquiries because of the role attributable to it in the "production" of social structure. And I do not take up the position (apparently embraced in Goffman 1983) in which the *prima facie* relevance of social structure to the organization of interaction is in principle to be disputed (although I do suggest that some received notions may not be sustainable when required to come to terms with the details of actual occurrences.) Rather, I mean to formulate and explore the challenges faced by those attracted to the interaction/social-structure nexus. A solution must be found to the analytic problems which obstruct the conversion of intuition, casual (however well-informed) observation, or theoretically motivated observation into demonstrable analysis. For without solutions to these problems, we are left with "a *sense* of how the world works," but without its detailed explication.

So what *were* those problems? Or, rather: what *are* those

problems? My discussion will be organized around two main themes:[1] the problem of relevance and the issue of "procedural consequentiality." After a discursive explication of these themes, I will exemplify their upshot in a brief "case study" of an episode of talk-in-interaction.

2 Relevance

First, *relevance*. Here I draw directly from among the earliest contributions to conversation analysis, the first systematically developed work of Harvey Sacks, now over twenty years old (1972a, 1972b, but the arguments were developing as early as 1964–5). Let me remind you of some issues he raised with respect to how "members" characterize, identify, describe, refer to, indeed "conceive of" persons in talking to others.

The original focus of the work by Sacks which I mean to recall was the way in which persons engaged in talk in interaction did their talk, specifically with respect to reference to persons. Sacks noted that members refer to persons by various category terms – as man/woman, protestant/catholic/jew, doctor/patient, white/black/chicano, first baseman/second baseman/shortstop, and the like. He remarked that these category terms come in collections. In presenting them above, they are inscribed in groups: [man/woman], [protestant/catholic/jew], and so on, and that is the correct way to present them. It is not [man/woman/protestant], [catholic/jew]. This is what is being noted in the observation that the category terms are organized in *collections*.

Some of these collections Sacks called "Pn adequate"; they were adequate to characterize or categorize any member of any population, however specified, whether or not it had been specified (e.g. counted, characterized, or bounded) in some fashion (1972a: 32–3). Other collections were not "Pn-adequate." [Male/female] *is* Pn-adequate; [first baseman/second baseman/shortstop...] is *not* Pn-adequate, because the latter is only usable on populations already specified or characterized as "baseball teams," whereas the former is not subject to such restrictions.

One of Sacks' main points was that there are demonstrably many Pn-adequate category collections. The collection of category terms for gender/sex and age are the most obvious ones, and these two alone serve to allow the posing of the problem of relevance. The point is that since everyone who is an instance of some category in one of those collections is necessarily (for that is the import of Pn-adequacy) also an instance of some category in the other, or *an* other, the fact that someone *is* male, or *is* middle aged, or *is* white, or *is* Jewish, is, by itself, no warrant for so referring to them, for the warrant of "correctness" would provide for use of any of the other reference forms as well. Some principle of relevance must underlie use of a reference form, and has to be adduced in order to provide for one rather than another of those ways of characterizing or categorizing some member. That is the problem of relevance: not just the descriptive adequacy of the terms used to characterize the objects being referred to, but the relevance that one has to provide if one means to account for the use of some term, the relevance of that term relative to the alternative terms that are demonstrably available.

Now, this problem was developed by Sacks initially in describing how members talk about members. It showed the inadequacy of an account of a conversationalist's reference to another as a "cousin" by reference to the other "actually being a cousin." But, once raised, the point is directly relevant to the enterprise of *professional* analysts as well. Once we recognize that whoever can be characterized as "male" or as "protestant," or as "president" or whatever, can be characterized or categorized in other ways as well, our scholarly/professional/scientific account cannot "naively" rely on such characterizations, that is, cannot rely on them with no justification or warrant of their relevance.

Roughly speaking, there are two types of solution to this problem in the methodology of professional analysis. One type of solution can be characterized as the "positivist" stance, in one of the many senses in which that term is currently used. In this view, the way to warrant one, as compared to another, characterization of the participants (for example, in interaction) is the "success" of that way of characterizing them in producing a professionally acceptable account of the data being addressed. "Success" is measured by some "technology" – by statistical significance, a preponderance of historical evidence, and so forth. Sometimes there is an additional requirement that the characterization which produces "successful" analysis be theoretically interpretable; that is, that the selection of descriptive terms for the participants converges with the terms of a professional/scientific theory relevant to the object of description. In this type of solution, which I am calling "positivistic," it does not matter whether or not the terms that are used to characterize the participants in some domain of action, and which have yielded "significant" results, are otherwise demonstrably oriented to or not by the participants being described. That is what makes this solution of the problem "positivist."

The alternative type of solution insists on something else, and that is that professional characterizations of the participants be grounded in aspects of what is going on that are demonstrably relevant *to* the participants, and at that moment – at the moment that whatever we are trying to provide an account of occurs. Not, then, just that we see them to be characterizable as "president/ assistant," as "chicano/black," as "professor/student," etc. But that for them, at that moment, those are terms relevant for producing and interpreting conduct in the interaction.

This issue should be of concern when we try to bring the kind of traditional sociological analysis that is implied by the term "social structure" to bear on talk-in-interaction. Much of what is meant by "social structure" in the traditional sense directly implicates such characterizations or categorizations of the participants as Sacks was examining. If the sense of social structure we are dealing with is the one that turns on the differential distribution of valued resources in society, whether status or power or money or any of the other "goods" whose distribution can be used to characterize social structure, then that implies a characterization or categorization of the participants on that occasion as one relevantly to be selected from that set of terms. But then the problem presents itself of the relevance of those terms to the participants for what they are doing. Without a show of that warrant, we are back to a "positivistic" stance, even though the animating concerns may be drawn from quite antipositivistic theoretical sources or commitments.

Now let us be clear about what *is* and what is *not* being said here. The point is not that persons are somehow *not* male or female, upper or lower class, with or without power, professors and/or students. They may be, on some occasion, demonstrably members of one or another of those categories. Nor is the issue that those aspects of the society do not matter, or did not matter on that occasion. We may share a lively sense that indeed they do matter, and that they mattered on that occasion, and mattered for just that aspect of some interaction on which we are focusing. There is still the problem of *showing from the details of the talk or other conduct in the materials* that we are analyzing that those aspects of the scene are what the *parties* are oriented to. *For that is to show how the parties are embodying for one another the relevancies of the interaction and are thereby producing the social structure.*

The point here is not only methodological but substantive. It is not just to add a methodological apparatus supporting analyses already in hand. It is, rather, to add to, and potentially to transform, the analysis of the talk and other conduct itself by enriching our account of it with additional detail; and to show that, and how, "social structure" in the traditional sense enters into the production and interpretation of determinate facets of conduct, and is thereby confirmed, reproduced, modulated, neutralized, or incrementally transformed in that actual conduct to which it must finally be referred.

This is not, to my mind, an issue of preferring or rejecting some line of analysis, some research program or agenda. It is a problem of analysis to be worked at: how to examine the data so as to be able to show that the parties were, with and for one another, demonstrably oriented to those aspects of who they are, and those aspects of their context, which are respectively implicated in the "social structures" which we may wish to relate to the talk. If we treat this as a problem of analytic craft, we can use it as leverage to enhance the possibility of learning something about how talk-in-interaction is done, for it requires us to return again to the details of the talk to make the demonstration.

So, one issue posed by the theme "talk and social structure" is relevance.

3 Procedural consequentiality

The issue just discussed with respect to the characterization of the participants in some talk-in-interaction also is relevant to a characterization of "the context" in which they talk and interact. "Context" can be as much a part of what traditionally has been meant by "social structure" as attributes of the participants are. So, for example, remarking that some talk is being conducted "in the context of a bureaucracy," "in a classroom" "on a city street," etc. is part of what is sometimes intended by incorporating the relevance of social structure.

Such characterizations invoke particular aspects of the setting and not others. They involve selections among alternatives, and among subalternatives. For example, one type of formulation of context characterizes it by "place," and this is an alternative to various other sorts of context characterization. But within that context type, various forms of place formulation are available, all of which can be correct (Schegloff 1972). So, although the details of the argument have not been fully and formally worked out for the characterization of context or setting in the way that Sacks worked them out for the characterization of participants, it appears likely that the issue of relevance can be posed in much the same way for context as it has been for person reference.

What I want to do here is add something to this relevance problem for contexts. It concerns what I am calling the "procedural consequentiality" of contexts.

Even if we can show by analysis of the details of the interaction that some characterization of the context or the setting in which the talk is going on (such as "in the hospital") is relevant for the parties, that they are oriented to the setting so characterized, there remains another problem, and that is to show how the context or the setting (the local social structure), *in that aspect*, is procedurally consequential to the talk. How does the fact that the talk is being conducted in some setting (e.g. "the hospital") issue in any consequence for the shape, form, trajectory, content, or character of the interaction that the parties conduct? And *what is the mechanism by which the context-so-understood has determinate consequences for the talk?*

This is a real problem, it seems to me, because without a specification of such a linkage we can end up with characterizations of context or setting which, however demonstrably relevant to the parties, do little in helping us to analyze, to explain, to understand, to give an account of how the interaction proceeded in the way in which it did, how it came to have the trajectory, the direction, the shape that it ended up having.[2] When a formulation of the context is proposed, it tends *ipso facto* to be taken as somehow relevant and consequential for what occurs in the context. Yet it is nonetheless the analyst's responsibility either to deliver analytic specifics of that consequentiality or to abjure that characterization of the context. Otherwise, the analysis exploits a tacit feature of its own discursive format, but evades the corresponding analytic onus. A sense of understanding and grasp is conveyed to, and elicited from, the reader, but is not earned by the elucidation of new observations about the talk.[3]

So, this is an open question, somewhat less formally stated than the other: how shall we find formulations of context or setting that will allow us (a) to connect to the theme that many want to connect to – social structure in the traditional sense, but (b) that will do so in a way that takes into account not only the demonstrable orientation of the participants, but, further, (c) that will allow us to make a direct "procedural" connection between the context-so-formulated and what actually happens in the talk, instead of having a characterization that "hovers around" the interaction, so to speak, but is not shown actually to inform the production and grasp of the details of its conduct.

As with the issues of "relevance," I am here putting forward not principled objections to the invocation of social structure as context, but jobs to be taken on by those concerned with the intersection of talk and familiar senses of social structure. They challenge us to be alert to possible ways of showing such connections. I will just mention a few possible directions here.

Some formulations of setting do the sort of job I have in mind because they capture features of the setting that fall under the general rubric of "speech exchange systems" (Sacks, Schegloff, and Jefferson 1974: 729ff.). They satisfy this concern because they characterize a setting or context both in ways that connect to our general notions of social structure and in ways which directly refer to aspects of the practices by which the participants organize their talk. Some such settings carry with them as well a set of relevant identifications for the participants.

Consider, for example, the case of the courtroom in session (see Atkinson and Drew 1979; my remarks here rest on a much looser, vernacular, and unstudied sense of the setting). To focus just on the turn-taking organization, it *is* the "courtroom-ness" of courtrooms in session which seems in fact to organize the way in which the talk is distributed among the persons present, among the *categories* of persons present, in the physical setting. So, for example, onlookers (members of the "audience") are not potential next speakers, as the official proceedings go on. And among the others who *are* potential next speakers at various points – the judge, the attorneys, the witness, and the like – there are socially organized procedures for determining when they can talk, what they can do in their talk, and the like. It could be argued, then, that to characterize some setting of talk-in-interaction as in "a court-in-session," characterizes it with a formulation of context which can not only be claimed to connect to the general concern for "social structure" (for it certainly relates to institutional context), but can be shown to be procedurally consequential as well. Insofar as members of the audience sitting behind the bar never get up and talk but rather whisper to one another in asides, whereas the ones in front of the bar talk in defined and regular ways, by the very form of their conduct they show themselves to be oriented to the particular identities that are legally provided by that setting and show themselves to be oriented to "the court-in-session" as a context.[4]

We have to be careful here to see what sorts of characterizations of context will satisfy these requirements. It is clear to me that vernacular accounts or formulations of context, even if informed by social-scientific considerations, will not necessarily do it, if they do not specify how the talk is organized. For example, one not uncommon kind of proposed context description of talk-in-interaction is "an experiment" or "in a laboratory setting." Those terms sound like an adequate formulation of a kind of setting, and for some concerns perhaps they are. But these characterizations do not satisfy the concerns we have been discussing; under the rubrics "laboratory" or "experiment" very different sorts of organization of talk-in-interaction can be conducted.

Consider, for example, a study of repair published by the Dutch psycholinguist Willem Levelt (1983). Levelt had conducted an experiment on the so-called "linearization problem" (organizing a mass of simultaneously presented information into a temporally organized, hence linearized, format in talk). He had a number of subjects look at a screen on which were projected different shapes – circles, triangles, and the like – which were connected by lines of various sorts. Their job was to describe these figures so that someone else (not present) would be able to retrieve the figure from the description. The descriptions were all tape-recorded. Levelt noticed that in the course of producing the descriptions, people regularly "mispoke"; they started to say one thing, cut themselves off, and went back and "fixed" it. Levelt recognized these as self-repairs (Schegloff, Jefferson, and Sacks 1977), and he wrote up a separate paper on various aspects of the placement and organization of self-repair and the evidence it gives about processes of self-monitoring by speakers.

But it seems to me that the findings of this work, at least with respect to the organization of repair, have an equivocal status at the present time. Why? Not simply because the talk was produced in a laboratory or experimental context. That the data come from laboratory-produced protocols does not tell us what consequences for the character of the talk are entailed. For example, it does not tell us what the speech-exchange system was in which this talk was produced. As it happens, this *was* consequential, and has a bearing on the topic of the research report.

The speech-exchange system in which this talk was produced was one whose turn-taking organization denied anyone else the right to talk besides the experimental subject. That is to say, within the boundaries of "the experiment," there was no possibility of a sequence in which current speaker's turn (e.g. subject's) is followed by a next turn in which some recipient (e.g. experimenter or laboratory assistant) could have initiated repair. That is, this speech-exchange system's turn-taking organization transforms the familiar organization by which opportunities to initiate repair are ordered (Schegloff, Jefferson, and Sacks 1977). In fact, one of the classical rationales for the insistence on the methodology of experiments, *formal* experiments, is precisely to exclude the talk or other "extraneous" conduct of the experimenter. The whole point was to hold everything (except the variables of interest) constant. And one part of holding everything constant is to keep the experimenter or the experimenter's agent from talking in potentially varying ways to the different subjects, thereby introducing extraneous, and unmeasured, effects into the experimental results. So the whole point of this sort of experimental format *requires* the denial of the possibility of a next turn in which recipient/experimenter could talk.

We have, then, a very different turn-taking organization that

seems to be subsumed by the formulation of context that we call
"laboratory" or "experiment," with various sorts of consequences
for the organization of repair. Aside from general organizational
considerations that relate next-turn repair to same-turn repair
(Schegloff 1979b), more specific analytic issues are implicated, only
one of which can be mentioned in passing here. It is that the
sequential possibility of a next turn by another participant, and
orientation to such a possibility, adds a wholly different *sort* of
position for initiating repair from the ones incorporated into
Levelt's account. He describes the positions in which repair is
initiated *within* a turn in terms of their relationship to that which is
being repaired (as do Schegloff, Jefferson and Sacks [1977] with
respect to the initiation of repair *across* turns). However, he does
not (and with his materials he *can*not) formulate the placement of
the initiation of repair relative to the structure of the turn in which
it occurs. For example, the initiation of repair cannot be formulated
relative to possible completion of the ongoing turn by current
speaker and possible start of a next turn by another (the relevance
of which is analytically instantiated in Schegloff 1987b: 111), a
matter we would expect to be strategic if there is a "preference for
self-correction."[5]

Until someone does a parallel analysis on talk from ordinary
interaction, and sees whether the findings about same-turn repair
come out the same way or not, we will not know the status of
Levelt's findings about how same-turn repair is organized (where
repair is initiated relative to the trouble-source, how far back
people go when they are going to reframe the trouble-source, and
the like), or how substantial a contribution to our understanding of
repair it can be.

In this case, I think the notion of "the laboratory as context"
raises some serious concerns about particular research that was
conducted under its auspices. But this is by virtue of the particular
speech-exchange system which composed it on that occasion,
which provides the link of procedural consequentiality to the particular features of the talk being focused on in the research.

Compare with this the data addressed in such work as that
reported in Zimmerman and West (1975) and Maynard and Zimmerman (1984). These data are also referred to as occurring in a
"laboratory" context. But the speech-exchange system involved

here is a wholly different one: that speech-exchange system provided for the parties (in this case, two "subjects") to talk to each other. The organization of the talk did not render any speaker free of the contingency of someone talking next (with the opportunity, in principle, of initiating repair). Were one to use those tapes to study self-repair, I do not think the results would be subject to the concerns raised above about Levelt's results, even though both of those settings can be characterized by a single context descriptor: "laboratory." The vernacular terms do not do the work. In one case "laboratory" is, and in the other case it is not, procedurally consequential *for the particular phenomena being studied.*[6]

In the search, then, for characterizations of context which will link talk to social structure, we cannot necessarily rely on the social-structural terms we have inherited from the past. Some of them will be procedurally consequential, and some of them will not, just as some will be demonstrably relevant to the participants and some will not. We have to find those terms for formulating context which are both demonstrably relevant to the participants and are procedurally consequential for the aspects of the conduct being treated, *on any given occasion.*

But it is not necessarily our *loss* that we cannot just appropriate terms from the traditional lexicon of "social structure" to understand talk; for we come thereby to use our data as a test of the relevance and viability of our sociological inheritance. We should be prepared to find that some of what we have received from the past, however, cherished theoretically, culturally, politically, or ideologically, will not pass this test, and must therefore not be incorporated into our analysis. Rather, we should exercise our capacity to address the details of conduct, and exploit our data as challenges to our theoretical and analytic acumen, to enhance and expand our understanding of what "social structure" could consist of, as a robust and expanding tool of analysis rather than as an inheritance from the disciplinary past.

4 An exemplification: the Bush–Rather television encounter

The concerns for relevance to the participants and procedural consequentiality so far introduced as general considerations have a bearing on studies of talk at work as well. As with other settings, not everything *in* the setting is *of* the setting. Not all talk at work is work talk. Further, sometimes the parties are not at all oriented to the relevance of the work setting and the related identifications of themselves. Sometimes, although they *are* oriented to its relevance, the setting does not directly contribute to the production of the talk; it is not procedurally consequential. But *some* talk in work settings is fully taken up with working, and that has substantial consequences for the talk. Indeed, it is through the ways in which the talk (and other conduct) is produced that the work setting is realized (by and for *its participants*, in the first instance) as a concerted interactional accomplishment.

A satisfying account of such a realized work setting should, of course, provide evidence of the work setting's relevance to the participants in the interaction being examined, and a description of the practices in which its procedural consequentiality is displayed. Thus, for example, the relevance of a courtroom context may be established, and a distinctive turn-taking system for "formal courtroom proceedings" characterized, for example, as involving a preallocation of turns to classes of participation (Atkinson and Drew 1979: ch. 2). The account of the procedurally consequential, however, must finally explicate the realization-in-their-course of those practices by which the setting is animated as a work context.

In what follows I offer a brief exemplar of how a course of talking in interaction for a while amounts to *doing* a news interview, and, as the talk practices change, the occasion slips from being an interview to being what was generally received as a "confrontation." The occasion which supplies the material for this account is an encounter between then Vice President George Bush, one of several contenders for the Republican nomination for president of the United States in the 1988 election, and CBS news anchor Dan Rather.[7]

Although it may initially seem puzzling, the need for explicating the characterization of this episode as "an interview" will quickly become apparent, and, I hope, exemplary for other such characterizations. The point of departure is that their social-structural location does not by itself endow occasions of interaction with a genre identity. The Bush–Rather affair offers eloquent *prima facie* testimony to the observation that labeling and announcing an occasion of talk-in-interaction as an interview (*post hoc* by commen-

tators or even *on the occasion* as part of the occasion itself) does
not *ipso facto* make it one, nor does it guarantee that what begins
as one will remain one.

All of which is to note that both the aspect of this event as an
interview and its aspect as a confrontation (if that is what it
became) require explication as *achievements*, as *outcomes* of practices of conduct in interaction (Schegloff 1987a: 218–28). And that
is to ask, how did the parties to this event conduct themselves so as
to make of the occasion, to constitute it, first as an interview, and
then as a confrontation – how did they "do interview"; how did
they "do confrontation?"

The achievement of such analyses can sometimes be made more
difficult by their very situatedness in a recognizable social-structural context. For that context may "normalize," "naturalize," and
make very nearly invisible those particular practices of talk and
conduct in interaction by which the distinctive stamp of that type of
work-realizing talk is achieved. Paradoxically, then, it is the very
goal of relating talk to its social-structural and work-organizational
context which may most recommend the bracketing of those
aspects of context, lest they help mask how the participants procedurally realize that context through their activities.

If there is a single, most fundamental component of what is
considered an "interview," both in vernacular or common-sense
conceptions of that term and in more technical accounts,[8] it is that
one party asks questions and the other party gives answers. An
orientation to this feature by the participants, it might be argued, is
at least partially constitutive of an occasion of talk as "an interview."

Note the tack being taken here. It is not that, in interviews, it is
an empirically established regularity that one party asks questions
and the other answers. But that an occasion is progressively and
methodically constituted and "realized" as an interview by, among
other things, an orientation by its participants to having one of
them be doing questions and the other answers. It is by virtue of
their orientation to, and practice of, so conducting themselves that
what I formulated at the start of this paragraph as an empirical
regularity comes to be the case. But putting it this way allows us to
see *how it comes to be the case.*

Let me illustrate this point from the Bush–Rather episode, by examining the first exchange between the two participants.[9] In doing so, I intend to be explicating how at the outset they constitute this occasion as an interview, and deliver "the context," and the "definition of the situation," which has been announced (Schegloff 1987a: 220–6).

Among the questions that parties to talk-in-interaction in general may undertake to do – and *not* just in interviews – some appear to their speakers to require some "background," some "leading up to." In ordinary conversation, this can present a problem because of the way the organization of turn taking for ordinary conversation appears to work. Participants who undertake to produce a turn can ordinarily *count on* getting to produce only a single, recognizably complete unit (like a clause or sentence).[10] If they undertake to "lead up" to a question, they may find any possible ending of a unit in their "leading-up" talk treated as the end of their turn, with others starting up turns of their own at that point. And, even worse, talk which is innocuous enough as "background" may have a very different interpretation if taken to be what the speaker meant to say in its own right.

Consider, for example, the following exchange (taken from Schegloff 1980: 117–20) between two janitors, one of whom – Vic – has swept up a mess of broken glass at the building of the other, James. Now Vic wants his garbage pail (which he had left at James's building) back, as well as a little credit for the good turn he has done James.

(1) [US:45-46]

```
1    V:    1→   The pail is in yuh hallway, ⌈(uh,)
2    J:                                     ⌊I know it
3               hu(hh)h!
4    V:    1→   The-the- I didn' have a broom wit' me, if I
5               adduh hadda ⌈broom I'd uh swept ⌈up.
6    J:    2→               ⌊e(hh)h!            ⌊That's
7          2→   alright.
8    V:         so ⌈(dat's, right on).
9    J:    2→      ⌊That's a'ri'- Somebody-
10         2→   ⌈got it up, I don't know who.
11   V:    3→   ⌊(Look). But do me a favr- Do, me, one
12         3→   fa:vuh, I ⌈cleaned it up!
13   J:               ⌊Yeh hh
14   J:         Yeh right. I- ih-deh ca:n, (I- brought de) can
```

```
15              (I'll) set it dehr own the sidewalk. ⌐Izzat
16              ehkay=                              |
17    V:                                           ⌊No.
18    J:        =⌐No.
19    V:        =⌊Didjeh ⌐sweep up duh rest a' duh me⌐ss.
20    J:               ⌊(        )              ⌊NO I
21              didn' sweep up nothin!
22    V:        Well o⌐kay well that's why I left the=
23    J:              ⌊Leave ih deh.
24    V:        =can⌐innuh hallway
25    J:           ⌊I'll do it (early) ⌐innuh maw:ning.
26    V:                            ⌊-so if you hadda
27              br⌐oo:m then you c'd=
28    J:          ⌊Yeh right.
29    V:        =sweep up duh dust ⌐(        )-
30    J:                          ⌊Very, uh- very good I
31              ⌐appreesh- ˙hhh
32    V:        ⌊-the glass,
33    J:        I apprecia⌐te that Victuh,
34    V:                 ⌊Tomorruh I-
35    V:    4→  No. ⌐Tomorruh I want my pail back.
36    J:           ⌊E(hh)h yeh.
37    V:        Dass a⌐ll.
38    J:              ⌊Ye(hh)h!
39    J:        I don'know I may keep dat pail.
```

For Vic, as we come to see in the sequel at arrow 4, the talk at the start of this sequence (at the arrows numbered 1) is leading up to a request for the return of his pail. But James hears it as said in its own right, and, far from giving Vic credit for a favor done, he understands Vic to have apologized, accepts the apology, and credits some anonymous person for cleaning up the glass (at the arrows numbered 2).

So "leading up" to something, or doing talk as prefatory to something else, can pose problems of sequential organization for the participants in ordinary conversation. And, indeed, by virtue of the structurally recurrent character of this possibility, there are specific practices of talking in interaction which are addressed to it. One of these I have had occasion (1980: 116) to dub a "pre-pre," a preliminary to a preliminary; it is an utterance which marks what directly follows it as said not in its own right, but as preliminary to something which will follow. One way of doing a "pre-pre," for example, is to formulate in advance the type of utterance or action being led up to, and that is done by an "action projection" such as *Can I ask you a question?* In Vic's dealing with James, he follows the "misunderstood" talk with such an action projection (at arrow 3: "do me one favor"), after which his preliminaries get heard as preliminaries, and his request gets registered as a request (ibid.: 117–20 for a fuller analysis). All this, recall, is in ordinary conversation.

Now when we shift our attention from ordinary conversation to a different "speech-exchange system" like "interviews," or more specifically "news interviews," a different turn-taking system may produce different problems and different opportunities of sequential organization. If one constitutive property of interviews is that one of the parties – ordinarily a particular predesignated one – asks questions, then the turn-taking system may obviate the "problem of preliminaries" without the services of a "dedicated solution" like "preliminaries to preliminaries." On this view, the designated questioner's turn is not "over" in a sequentially relevant sense, and it is not its recipient's turn to talk, until a question has been asked. And it *is* over, and it *is* the other's turn to talk, when a question *has* been asked. In that case, one of the ways in which the parties could – in concert – accomplish the occasion *as an interview* would be by organizing the talk to display that some such orientation was being jointly sustained. They would be doing it with one another, showing it *to* one another, showing it to the audience, and to us as technical onlookers as well.

With this theme in mind, examine (2), the transcript of the first exchange of the Bush–Rather episode following the end of a prepared videotaped feature, and parse the surface of its turn-taking and sequence-organizational structure.

(2) [Bush/Rather, 00:00]

```
1    Rather:      ...Today, Donald Gregg still works inside the
2                 White House as Vice President Bush's trusted
3                 advisor. ((End of feature; start of live
4                 broadcast.))
5                 (1.0)
6    Rather:      ˙hh Mister Vice President, tha:nk you for
7                 being with us toni:ght, ˙hh Donald Gregg
8                 sti:ll serves as y'r tru:sted advi#sor,=he
9                 w'z dee:ply involved in running arms t'the
```

```
10              Contras an' he didn' inform you.=
                 { (0.5) }
11   Rather:    {=.hhhh}⁺Now when President Rea:gan's, (0.2)
12              trusted advisor: Admiral Poindexter: (0.6)
13              failed to inform hi:m, (0.8) the President-
14              (0.2) fired'im.hh
15              (0.5)
16   Rather:    Why is Mister Gregg still: (.) inside the
17              White Hou@se'n still a trusted advisor.=
18   Bush:      =Becuz I have confidence in im, (0.3) en becuz
19              this matter,Dan, ...
```

\#   Bush brings hands together and mouth opens.
⁺   Bush separates hands.
@   Bush's lips part (with in-breath?).

Rather begins with an appreciation/greeting (lines 6–7); no question, no next turn taken by Bush. Rather next produces, as a first preliminary to a projected question, what amounts to a bridging repetition of the last sentence of the video-tape lead-in, including its key terms, "Donald Gregg" and "trusted advisor." At the possible completion of the unit, Rather employs a practice used in ordinary conversation to interdict a possible start-up by another and to extend the current speaker's turn (see Schegloff 1982) – he rushes into the start of a next unit (line 8), here marked by the "=" between "advisor" and "he w'z dee:ply involved." But although there is some evidence that Bush has monitored this spot in the talk as structurally a place where a next speaker might otherwise start (the evidence being a slight postural adjustment and an opening of the mouth – marked in the transcript by "#"), he does not actually move to start talking here.

In fact, Rather produces additional talk coming to a quite decisive-sounding possible completion, at "inform you" (line 10). Here he stops to take a big in-breath, one lasting about half a second – quite a long time, conversationally speaking. To be sure, the long audible and visible in-breath projects an "intention" on Rather's part to continue, but such gaps are not infrequently exploited by aspiring next speakers. Not here, however, although Bush again gives some indication of registering the opening, the possibility, by another adjustment of the position of his hands (marked in the transcript by "+").[11]

Next, at lines 11–14, Rather produces the second preliminary, the second component of the problem with which he means to confront Bush. There are several pauses here – of 0.2, 0.6, 0.8, and 0.2 seconds respectively, but these are internal to units of turn construction, and are not in the first instance places for an interlocutor to enter the talk.

But the silence at line 15 is quite another matter. Here, another unit of talk has been brought to recognizable possible completion, *and*, furthermore, the second element of Rather's problem/challenge has been articulated. Here is an eminently ripe place for Bush to enter in. But the question itself, however strongly adumbrated, has not yet been posed. And here we have the apex of Bush and Rather together doing a display of the occasion as interview. It is virtually choreographed: Rather leaves a yawning gap with the challenge glove off his hand but not yet thrown to the floor, and relies on Bush to withhold entering the lists. And Bush, raring to go, withholds until such a unit of talk is done as properly occasions his response. And, indeed, at the first possible completion of Rather's actual question at line 16–17 – at the word "House" – Bush's lips part in an apparent preturn in-breath, and directly on the next possible completion of the question, with not a moment of gap, Bush begins his turn, designed from its very outset to reveal itself as "an answer" – a "because" to fit to Rather's "why."

Here, in this first turn of the occasion, we see Bush and Rather orienting to the constitutive properties of "interview," and organizing their conduct to produce them. It is by virtue of such orientations and conduct that they collaborate here to produce an exchange, a potential statistical "case," if you will, in which one asks a question and the other answers. For Bush clearly *"could have"* talked earlier, at the several junctures which I have mentioned. And then it would *not* have been one of the cases which lead to the conclusion that in interviews one party asks questions and the other gives answers.

But as long as they proceed as they have at the first exchange, participants will produce interviews in which overwhelmingly one party produces questions and the other answers, because the latter party will not talk where talk might otherwise be done if a question has not been asked, and the former party will provide that type of turn which will allow the occasion properly to proceed from turn to turn and phase to phase. And thereby the participants constitute –

do – the context which might otherwise be thought of, indeed is often described as, "supplying" the setting for their talk (Schegloff 1987a; see also Clayman 1988: 479–80; Greatbatch 1988: 409–13).

But we need not conjecture about Bush hypothetically talking at the earlier junctures in the "development" of a question. The Bush–Rather affair supplies us with actual occurrences. Shortly after the initial exchange which has just been briefly examined, Bush does precisely that; he talks at those earlier junctures. Which is at least part of how we come to understand this occasion as "an interview which turned into a confrontation."[12] It is not possible here to track step by step the devolution, or reversion, of this occasion of talk-in-interaction from "interview" back to a version of ordinary conversation,[13] but it may be useful to explicate one of the forms which this transition takes. Rather's first question engenders a long response from Bush, which itself engenders a number of touched-off sequences, including ones in which Bush complains about the video-taped feature which had preceded the "interview" and challenges Rather in various other respects. This, clearly enough, is a departure from the interview format, and is the occasion for several flurries of overlapping talk. At the end of one such spate of contentious talk, about three minutes into the interview, Bush appears to key the resumption of "interview" talk explicitly by returning the floor to Rather by inviting/demanding a question. The consequence affords a telling display of the ways in which "interview" requires realization in practice and in conduct, and not merely institutional settings and declared intentions.

(3) [Bush/Rather, 03:00] (See Appendix A for a fuller text)

```
 1   Bush:      … ˙hh An' I've answered every question put
 2              before me.=now if you have a question, (0.2)
 3                         ⌈ ˙hh what is it. ⌉
 4   Rather:    ⌊ I do have one. ⌋
 5   Bush:      Ple⌈ase.
 6   Rather:    ⌊ I- ⌋ I have one.
 7   Bush:      Please ⌈ f i r e  a w a y . ⌉ (          )
 8   Rather:    ⌊ You have said that ⌋ y- if you had
 9              know:n: you sed th't'f hed known: this was an
10              a:rms for hosta⌈ges swap, ˙hh that you would
11   Bush:      ⌊ Yes
```

```
12   Rather:      have opposed it.=
13   Rather:      ='hhh You've a:lso ┌said that- that you┐=
14   Bush:                            └Exactly. (M a n y-)┘
15   Rather:      =┌did not┐ kno::w that you:┐
16   Bush:        =└May I-┘ May I May I  ┘answer that.
17   Rather:      Tha┌t wasn't a ques┐tion. It was=
18   Bush:           └(Th- right      ┘
19   Rather:      ┌=a statement.┐
20   Bush:        └Yes it was ┘a statement,=
21                =┌an' I'll a:nswer it.= T h e President=┐
22   Rather:       └Let me ask the question if I may first.┘
23   Bush:        =created this progra:m, 'hh has testifie- er:
24                stated publicly, 'hh he di:d no:t think it
25                was arms fer hostages.
26   Bush:        'hh ┌It  w a s  o n l y  l a:┐ter that-
27   Rather:          └That's the President. ┘ Mr. Vice ┌President┐
28   Bush:                                               └and that's┘
29                me.
30                (.)
31   Rather:      ┌'hh Well-
32   Bush:        └Cuz I went along with it becuz-=
33                =<y'know why Dan, { 'hhh/(0.2)}
34                becuz ┌I  w o r r i e d  w h e n ┐ I saw=
35   Rather:            └That wasn' the question ┘Mister
36                ┌Vice President┐
37   Bush:        └=M i s t e r::┘'hhh Mister Buckley, 'hh
38                uh'r heard about Mister Buckley being
39                <tortured ta death.>Later admitted as
40                the CIA chief. 'hh So if I erred, I erred on
41                the side of tryin' ta get those hostages
42                outta there.=
43   Bush:        =┌'hh And the who:le story has been to:ld┐=
44   Rather:       └Mister Vice President, you set thee:-    ┘
45   Bush:        =┌to  t h e  C o n g r e s s.┐
46   Rather:       └you set the rules for this::┘ this
47                talk here. >I didn' mean to step on
48                yer line there,< 'hhh but you insisted that...
```

In response to Bush's invitation/demand for a question, Rather begins as he had done at the outset, by laying the groundwork for the question with some preliminaries (lines 8–12). His procedure appears to be the same as before: he will introduce two, claimably incompatible, events or assertions and challenge Bush to reconcile them (Pomerantz 1988/9). The talk at 8–12 is the first of these, much like that at lines 7–10 in (2) above. But unlike the earlier

instance, Bush does not allow the production of the second preliminary. Indeed, before the first preliminary has been completed, there
are indications of trouble for "the interview."

First, well before the first preliminary has come to possible completion, even before the grammatical juncture of its initial con-
ditional clause, Bush interpolates a receipt token of sorts. Most like
a "continuer" or "backchannel" response, its ordinary use in conversation is to pass, on behalf of its speaker, a place at which that
party might otherwise talk. Its use in the Bush–Rather episode at
line 11 is in any case somewhat special, because even in ordinary
conversation, this would not be (in strictly turn-taking terms) a
place for Bush to talk;[14] passing an opportunity to talk would,
then, not ordinarily be an issue at such a point.

But such an interpolation, and the one at the start of line 14, is
particularly anomalous in the context of a news interview. In news
interviews, neither party (albeit each for a different reason) ordinarily registers what the other has said with recipient tokens, either to
register receipt of information, or to pass an opportunity to talk
(see Heritage 1985). One does not find continuers in news interviews,[15] because interviewers do not treat themselves as the true
recipients of interviewee's talk (ibid.), and interviewees only respond to questions, whereas continuers specifically pass the opportunity to do a full turn, such as "answering." As early as midway
through the first of Rather's preliminaries, then, there is evidence in
Bush's continuer that commitment to the practices of "doing interview" has broken down.

Furthermore, as soon as Rather has projected, and begun producing, a continuation of his preliminaries, Bush interrupts at line
14/16, proposing to "answer." When Rather explicitly invokes the
constitutive property of interviews to block Bush's talk: "That
wasn't a question. It was a statement," and "Let me ask the
question if I may first," it appears that he may not. Bush seems to
concur that it was a statement, but insists on "answering" in any
case (thereby adhering at least rhetorically to the constraint that
interviewees should only do "answering"). And here we have
empirically what we had earlier conjectured hypothetically: Bush
(and interviewees generally) *can* talk at earlier junctures preceding
production by the interviewer of a question. When they do so, the
interview *qua* interview breaks down.[16]

The career of this episode suggests a methodological canon. Establishing relevance and establishing procedural consequentiality cannot be "threshold issues", that is, once you have "enough" to show it you are finished. Rather, they are questions for continuing analysis. And not necessarily in the "loaded" form, "how are they now doing 'interview'?"; but in "open" form – "what does the form of the talk show about recipient design considerations and about orientation to context (institutional, social structural, sequential, or whatever)?"

If the focus of inquiry is the organization of conduct, the details of action, the practices of talk, then every opportunity should be pressed to enhance our understanding of any available detail about those topics. Invoking social structure or the setting of the talk at the outset can systematically distract from, even blind us to, details of those domains of events in the world.

If the goal of inquiry is the elucidation of work institutions, one might think that quite a different stance would be warranted, and one would want to give freer play to the effective scope of social-structural considerations, and do so free of the constraints I have been advancing. Though this stance has much to recommend it, it could as well be argued that one does not best serve such an undertaking by attributing to social-structural constraints or features properties which are better understood as the outcomes of the procedures of ordinary interaction. In any case, the understanding of social structure will be enhanced if we explicate how its embodiment in particular contexts, and on particular occasions, permeates the "membrane" (Goffman 1961a) surrounding episodes of interaction to register its stamp within them.

5 Concluding remarks

These, then, are some of the issues mobilized for me when the talk turns to "talk at work." We may share lively intuitions, in general or with respect to specific details, that it matters that some participants in data we are examining are physicians or news interviewers; that they are working at tasks which are constrained by the law, or by economic or organizational contingencies, or by their material setting. However insistent our sense of the reality and decisive bearing of such features of the work institution or setting, there remains the relevance of anchoring our "grasp" in a methodic explication of the objects of our inquiry, cast, so to speak, from the inside. To reprise these themes:

> 1 How can we show that what is so loomingly relevant for us (as competent members of society or as professional social scientists) was relevant for the parties to the interaction we are examining, and thereby arguably implicated in their production of the details of that interaction?
>
> 2 How can we show that what seems inescapably relevant, both to us and to the participants, about the "context" of the interaction is demonstrably consequential for some specifiable aspect of that interaction?

In brief, the issue is how to convert insistent intuition, however correct, into empirically detailed methodic analysis.

This is a heavy burden to impose. Meeting it may well lead to exciting new results. But if it is not to be met in one or more respects, arguments will have to be put forward that the concerns I have discussed are no longer in point, are superseded by other considerations, or must yield to the new sorts of findings that are possible if one holds them in abeyance. Simple invocation of the burden of the sociological past will not suffice.

With respect to social structure, then, as with respect to other notions from social science's past such as intention, the stance we might well consider is treating them as programmatically relevant for the parties, and hence for us. In principle, some one or more aspects of who the parties are and where/when they are talking may be indispensably relevant for producing and grasping the talk, but these are not decisively knowable *a priori*. It is not for us to *know* what about context is crucial, but to *discover* it, and to discover *new sorts* of such things. Not, then, to privilege sociology's concerns under the rubric "social structure," but to discover them in the members' worlds, if they are there.

Otherwise, we risk volunteering for a path which has led close inquiry into social life astray in the past, but which we now have an opportunity to avoid. In the past, one has needed a special warrant or license to examine closely the details of ordinary life and conduct. Whether it was the defectiveness of the people involved as with the mentally ill or retarded or physically handicapped, their moral taint as with criminals, delinquents or other versions of "evil," or the possibilities of enhanced efficacy as in the improvement of production processes or bureaucratic administration, or enhanced justice or fairness, there was always a "good reason" for looking closely at the details of conduct.

With the license came a shaped focus, either on a target population, a target set of behaviors, or a target aspect of conduct which one examined. What was found was then generally attributed to the license under which one found it. Thus, early investigations into the language of schizophrenics (e.g. Kasanin 1944) came upon the phenomenon of a spate of talk being touched off by the sound of some word in a prior utterance (so-called "clang association"), a phenomenon which students of conversation will recognize as not uncommon in ordinary talk. But having found it through the close examination of schizophrenic talk (talk which could be so closely examined by virtue of its speakers' diagnoses), it was taken as specially characteristic of such talk. So also with children's talk, etc.

If the study of conversation and talk-in-interaction is once again required to be "licensed," whether by practical concerns or by the institutionalized interests of traditional disciplines, then we may well find ourselves attributing – now to "social structure" – what are the indigenous features of talk-in-interaction. Should we not give the latter a chance to be recognized in their own right, especially since they constitute their own sociology in any case?

Appendix A

[Bush/Rather, 03:00]

```
 1   Bush:      ...'hh An' I've answered every question put
 2              before me.=now if you have a question, (0.2)
 3                       ⌈'hh what is it. ⌉
 4   Rather:    ⌊I do have one.⌋
 5   Bush:      Ple⌈ase. ⌉
 6   Rather:       ⌊I- ⌋   I have one.
 7   Bush:      Please⌈f i r e   a w a y.⌉ (        )
 8   Rather:         ⌊You have said that⌋ y- if you had
 9              know:n: you sed th't'f hed known: this was an
10              a:rms for hosta⌈ges swap, 'hh that you would
11   Bush:                     ⌊Yes
12   Rather:    have opposed it.=
13   Rather:    ='hhh You've a:lso ⌈said that- that you ⌉=
14   Bush:                         ⌊Exactly. (M a n y-)⌋=
```

```
15  Rather:      ┌did not┐ kno̲w:: that you:┐
16  Bush:       =└May I-┘May I May I ┘ an̲swer that.
17  Rather:     Tha┌t wasn't a ques┐tion. It was=
18  Bush:          └(Th- right      ┘
19  Rather:     ┌=a statement.┐
20  Bush:       └Yes it was  ┘a statement,=
21              =┌an' I'll a:nswer it.= T h e  President=
22  Rather:      └Let me ask the question if I may first. ┘
23  Bush:       =crea̲ted this progra:m, ˙hh has testifie- er:
24              s̲tated publicly, ˙hh he di:d no:t think it
25              was arms fer hostages.
26  Bush:       ˙hh ┌ It   was  only  la:┐ter that-
27  Rather:         └That's the President.┘ Mr. Vice ┌President
28  Bush:                                            └and that's
29              me.
30              (.)
31  Rather:     ┌˙hh Well-
32  Bush:       └Cuz I went along with it becuz-=
33              =<y'know why  Dan, ˙hhhhh
34              becuz┌I  w o r r i e d  w h e n┐ I saw=
35  Rather:         └That wasn' the question ┘ Mister
36              ┌Vice President┐
37  Bush:       └=M i s t e r : : ┘˙hhh Mister Buckley, ˙hh
38              uh'r hea̲rd about Mister Buckley being
39              <to̲rtured ta death.>Later admitted as
40              the CIA chief. .hh So if I erred, I erred on
41              the side of tryin' ta get those hostages
42              o̲utta there.=
43  Bush:       =┌˙hh And the who:le story has been to:ld┐
44  Rather:      └ Mister Vice President,  you set thee:- ┘=
45  Bush:       =┌t o  t h e  C o n g r e s s.┐
46  Rather:      └you set the rules for this::┘ this
47              talk here. >I didn' mean to step on
48              yer line there,< ˙hhh but you
49              insisted that this be li̲:ve, en
50              ┌you know (th't)>we have a limited amount of┐
51  Bush:       └E x a c t l y.  T h a t' s  w h a t  I :-┘=
52  Rather:     =time.< =
53  Bush:       =┌>That's why I wan┌na get my share< i̲n: he:re,
54  Rather:      └=˙h h h h       └Now
55  Bush:       ┌on something  ┐ o̲ther than whatch u̲ wanna talk=
56  Rather:     └The President-┘
57  Bush:       ┌=about.
58  Rather:     └The President- (.) h's- has spoken for
59              hi̲m:self.=I'm asking you: to speak ┌for you̲r:=
60  Bush:                                          └Please
```

```
61   Rather:    =self, which you have not been willing
62              t'do in the pa:st,= ⌈if I m- =
63   Bush:                         ⌊(      )
64   Rather:    =if I may- u- suggest th't- that- this is what
65              leads people to sa:y, .hh quote, "Either
66              George Bush wz irrelevant, (0.3) or he
67              w'z ineffective= >he said himself he
68              wz outta the loop< = >now lemme give
69              ⌈an example, you said to ask you a question<⌉
70   Bush:      ⌊(              ) o u t t a  t h e  l o o p ⌋
71              May I explain "outta the loo:p." No:=
72              =operational ro:le. Go ahead.
73   Rather:    Now. You've said that if you'd known it wz 'n
74              arms fer hostages swap you would've opposed
75              it.=You said the first you knew it was an arms
76              fer hostages swap wz in <December of Nineteen
77              Eighty Six> ⌈(correct?)⌉
78   Bush:                 ⌊ w h e n ⌋the who:le thing
79              became brie:fed ta me by Senator
80              Duerrenburger,
81   Rather:    Exact⌈ly
82   Bush:           ⌊and the pro:ximity of arms to hostages
83              ˙hh much closer. ⌈than we had thought, on these=
84   Rather:                     ⌊But Mr. Vice President, you
85              went ta Israel in  ⌐<July of Nineteen Eighty=
86   Bush:      =hearings that w-⌡
87   Rather:    ⌐=Six?>⌉
88   Bush:      ⌊ Yes ⌋
89   Rather:    ˙hhhh And- a member of your own sta:ff Mister
90              Craig Fuller.- ((swallow/(0.5))) has verified.
91              And so did the o:nly other man the:re. Mister
92              Ni:r. Mister Amiron Nir, ˙hh who's the
93              Israeli's ˙hh to:p anti-terrorist man,
94   Bush:      ⌐Ye: ⌐s.
95   Rather:    ⌊˙hh ⌊Those two men >were in a meeting with
96              you an' Mister Nir not once,< but three:
97              times. three times, underscored with
98              you that this was a straightout arms
99              ⌐fer hostages swap.⌉ = ˙h h h
100  Bush:      ⌊W h a t   t h e y::⌋(.) were doing.⌡=
101  Rather:    =Now ⌐how do you- How⌝ do you reconc-⌝I have =
102  Bush:           ⌊Read the memo⌋ Read the memo.⌡What =
103  Rather:    ⌐(sir)
104  Bush:      ⌊they::⌋ were doing.
105  Rather:    How: can you reconci:le that you were
106             there<Mister Nir a- underscored three::
```

```
107              separate occa:sions, 'hh that it was a- arms
108              fer hostages swap an' to:ld you we were
109              dealing with the most ra:dical elements in
110              Iran:. You were dealing straightaway with the
111              Ayatollah ⌐Khomeini
112   Bush:               ⌊I was told what they: were doing,
113              and not what we were doing en that's the big
114              difference...
```

Notes

1. For a penetrating treatment of many of the issues taken up here, cf. Heritage (1984a: 280–90).
2. A similar argument is made for explicating how cultural/linguistic context has the consequences attributed to in (Schegloff 1987c). Aspects of prosody may well have consequences for misunderstanding in crosscultural interaction (e.g. Gumperz 1982), but understanding how they issue in the particular misunderstandings which ensue will require explicating what in the structure of talk-in-interaction converts that prosody into that *type* of misunderstanding.
3. Reasons both of relevance and procedural consequentiality motivated a decision not to characterize the "Opening up closings" paper (Schegloff and Sacks 1973) as contextually specific to American culture, as had been requested by an anthropologically oriented referee (see footnote 4, p. 291, and also Sacks, Schegloff, and Jefferson 1974, footnote 10, p. 700, on the same issue). That request invoked on behalf of anthropology a cultural sense of "context," parallel to the invocation by sociologists of social-structural senses of "context."
4. A penetrating account along these lines of the constituting of a speech-exchange system through practices of talking, in this case of "the job interview," may be found in Button this volume ch. 7.
5. I leave aside here the exclusion of interactional considerations (Jefferson 1974) which can bear on where and how repair is initiated, an exclusion which allows the depiction of the initiation of repair in strictly grammatical terms.
6. One could harbor a concern that the setting of the Zimmerman–Maynard data *is* procedurally consequential for the organization of topic talk which is their focus, since the participants in their experiment were asked to talk while knowing they were to be interrupted for the start of an experiment in a "few minutes" (Maynard and Zimmerman 1984), a prospect which may well constrain the sort of topic talk participants undertake. There are naturalistic settings which are in many respects similar (e.g. medical waiting rooms, though there is no injunction to talk there) in which the seriousness of this concern might be assessed.

7. The account by Clayman and Whalen (1988/9) tracks the transform-
ation of the Bush–Rather episode rather further than does the present
one. The two accounts are in accord where they address the same parts
of the data. Greatbatch (1988) and Heritage and Greatbatch (1991)
offer a systematic account of the news interview as a speech-exchange
system, and of a distinctive turn-taking organization as a systematic
solution to some of the problems of analysis posed in the text of the
present chapter.
8. For example, on the employment interview see Button (1987b); on the
medical interview, see Frankel (1990); and, most relevant here, on
news interviews see Heritage (1985), Clayman (1988), Greatbatch
(1988), Heritage and Greatbatch (1991).
9. The whole of the Bush–Rather episode (not including the prepared
video feature shown before the beginning of the "interview") lasts
approximately nine minutes. I transcribed no further than the first
seven minutes, and only about two-and-a-half of those first seven
minutes. As with all transcripts, the one with which I am working is
virtually endlessly revisable. However, in the respects which matter for
the discussions in this chapter, I believe it is reliable. The full transcripts on which I am relying may be found as appendix I in Schegloff
(1988/9).
10. Of course, in point of fact they may end up producing more, but
prospectively they are systematically assured of but a single "turn-
constructional unit" (Sacks, Schegloff, and Jefferson 1974).
11. It is not just that he marks these places by adjustments of hand positioning; to this point he has not moved except at such "structural
joints" in the talk.
12. Another might be the actual reversal of the questioning "role," as in
the following exchange about six minutes or so into the talk:

Bush: … 'cause I wanna talk about why I wanna be
Presidenh. ˙hh why those forty one per cent
a' the people are suppo:rting me,=
[= ˙hh en I don' think it's fair to judge a who] le=
Rather: [And Mister Vice President, these questions()]
Bush: =caree:r, ˙hh it's not fair to judge my: whole
caree:r by a rehash on Iran.<˙hh How wouldju like
it. (0.2) if I judge your career by those seven
minutes when you walked off the set in New York.
(1.0)
Rather: Well[Mis–
Bush: [Wouldju like tha:t?

13. Clayman and Whalen (1988/9) address themselves to this development.
14. But see Lerner (1987) for the juncture between "if" clauses and their
consequents as an "opportunity space" for collaborative completion

by a recipient of current speaker's talk. Furthermore, production of such continuers or "backchannels" and leaving room for them can have uses relevant to accomplishing particular activities and alignments in the talk, uses which may get them placed at just such turn-taking junctures.

15. See Greatbatch (1988: 411–13). For this observation, and many others in this paragraph, I am indebted to John Heritage. For discussion of the "hostile" use of continuers in the segment, see Heritage and Greatbatch (1991).

16. This can be seen in the rather more extended excerpt provided in the Appendix. The talk initiated through Bush's intervention continues to line 43/5, and engenders further talk to line 72. At line 73, Rather tries again, repeating the first preliminary from 8–12 at 73–5, followed by some more preliminary talk, with the question which Bush invited at lines 2–3 finally being delivered at lines 105–11.

PART 2

The activities of questioners

4

Veiled morality: notes on discretion in psychiatry

JÖRG R. BERGMANN

1 Introduction

The phenomenon that I consider here came to my attention in the course of working on tape recordings of psychiatric intake interviews in various mental hospitals in (West) Germany. In these interviews the psychiatrists' official work assignment was to decide whether a person should be – voluntarily or involuntarily – hospitalized as a mental patient on the basis of that person's observable behavior during the interview. The psychiatric examination did not usually include any physical check-up or formal testing of the candidate patient; instead, it consisted of talk – talk which seemed to be organized into the well-known series of preallocated "questions" and "answers"; simply enough, the psychiatrist asks and the patient answers.

As I studied these recorded and transcribed interviews it became clear that "questions" and "answers" is too narrow a formulation, since regularly the psychiatrists did not interrogate the patients directly, but rather chose other forms of inquiry. That is to say, very often the psychiatrist produced talk in response to which, without having been literally "asked" for it, the candidate patient proffered information. This form of exploration could roughly be described as the psychiatrist seeking information not by *asking*, but by *telling* the candidate patients something about themselves. An example of

Earlier versions of this chapter were presented at the International and Multidisciplinary Conference on Interaction and Language Use, Plymouth, Britain, July 1984, and at the Conference on Everyday Culture and Professional Culture, Linköping, Sweden, May 1988. I can hardly express my gratitude to Gail Jefferson for advice and detailed comments, to Emanuel Schegloff for his insightful suggestions, and to Paul Drew, Christian Heath, and John Heritage for recommendations and encouragement, all of which is just a recent acknowledgment of a long history of indebtedness.

this method of interrogation can be found in data segment (1), which comes from an intake interview in which a psychiatrist and a married couple are talking about the problem of whether or not the wife, who is the candidate patient, should be committed to the mental hospital. The data segment is the very beginning of that intake interview:[1]

(1) [INTAKE:A-13:II:1/Free translation](Dr.F. just finished a phone call with the medical doctor who referred Ms.B. to the mental hospital, and turns now to Ms.B.)

```
 1   Dr.F:      (I just) got the information, (0.8)
 2              (that you're) not doing so well.
 3   Ms.B:      Yea::h well that is ⌈the  opinion
 4   Dr.F:                          ⌊Is that correct?
 5   Ms.B:      of Doctor Hollmann.
 6   Dr.F:      I ⌈see
 7   Ms.B:        ⌊but it isn't mine.
 8   Dr.F:      It isn't your ⌈s.
 9   Ms.B:                    ⌊No: :
10   Mr.B:      (                    )
11   Ms.B:                    ⌊I'm doing very well.
```

Two interrelated events occur in this segment which are of immediate interest. I shall only deal with one of them, but I shall approach it by mentioning the other, as analyzed by Gail Jefferson (1981a).

Working on this selfsame piece of talk, Jefferson noticed a phenomenon which struck her as very odd; in line 4 the interviewing psychiatrist seems to be soliciting a response ("Is that correct?"), when, in fact, the recipient has already started to produce one (line 3: "Yea::h well that is // the opinion ..."). Jefferson took that to mean that a response is asked for despite the fact that a response is already on its way. She called this phenomenon "post-response pursuit of response", and in her paper she thoroughly analyzed this object and a range of related phenomena.

To get at the object with which I am concerned, let me look at Jefferson's object in a different way. Suppose that line 4, "Is that correct?" is simply a continuation of the doctor's turn, showing that his prior talk was a preparatory turn part leading up to a question. It might then be asked why in the first place Ms. B. starts her response at the point she does. Could that simply be a precipitate reaction? Could it be just a quirk of this particular speaker? Just an idiosyncratic personal habit, of no sociological interest at all?

Or is it possible to identify in the doctor's utterance some sequential implications which allow or even oblige the recipient not to wait for a direct question to be added, but to respond to it right there and then? Ms. B.'s response in line 3 would not, then, be precipitate; it would be not "verrückt,"[2] but precisely timed and positioned, so that the doctor's "continuation" would indeed be subject to the sort of consideration Jefferson has given it. In that case the event observed should be produced in other situations and by other interlocutors, and it should occur with a certain kind of regularity.

The search for other instances in which a recipient produces a response without having been directly asked for it turned out not to be very difficult. In fact, an instance occurs in the very next exchange between the doctor and Ms. B. Half a minute later, Dr. F., who had turned to the husband and engaged in talk with him (perhaps in response to the husband's utterance at line 10) turns back to Ms. B. and the following exchange occurs:

(2) [INTAKE:A-13:II:2/20 sec. later/Free translation](Having told Mr.B. that he first wants to talk to his wife, Dr.F. now turns again to Ms.B.)

```
31   Dr.F:        ((to Mr.B.)) We've got time ┌to talk about
32   Mr.B:                                    └(          )
33   Dr.F:        that afterwards.
34   Dr.F:  →     ((to Ms.B. again)) ˙hh okay u::h I mean I can
35          →     see (from) your face that the:- (1.0) mood (.)
36          →     apparently is not ba:┌d.
37   Ms.B:                             └˙hhh yea:h now let me
38                tell you this.
39                ( . )
40   Ms.B:        If you:-
41                (1.0)
42                know-
43                (1.0)
44                God-
45                (0.8)
46                is my fa:ther;
47                ( . )
48   Dr.F:        Hm ┌m,
49   Ms.B:           └I am his child;....
```

In this segment the doctor's utterance

```
34   Dr.F:                                        I can
35               see (from) your face that the:- (1.0) mood (.)
36               apparently is not ba:d.
```

does not directly ask the candidate patient for any information (i.e. it is not an interrogative form); neither is it continued by a follow-up question. But just like the doctor's initiating move in segment (1) it nevertheless leads to an immediate response from the recipient, the immediacy of which is manifest in the onset of Ms. B.'s inbreath (line 37). From the vantage point of segment (2), the possibility arises that both of the psychiatrist's initiating utterances were designed to elicit talk from the candidate patient about her condition. The first would have been an unsuccessful attempt in that its implicit assertion ("[you're] not doing so well") was disconfirmed by its recipient, who furthermore moved to a counterassertion ("I'm doing very well"). The second might, then, constitute a renewed attempt to elicit such talk. In segment (2) the psychiatrist has adjusted himself to the candidate patient's position. Whereas he suggested in his first attempt that Ms. B. is "not doing so well," he now suggests that her "mood apparently is not bad." This opportunistically reshaped second attempt not only gains confirmation by the recipient, but an elaborate account for her good mood.

2 Exploring by "fishing"

Comparing each of these two initiating turns by the psychiatrist:

> "(I just) got the information, (0.8)
> (that you're) not doing so well."

> "I can see (from) your face
> that the:– (1.0) mood (.) apparently is
> not ba:d."

it can be seen that they both have a number of features in common; for the moment I want to mention two of them:

> Both turns include a report to the recipient about the recipient, more specifically a report to the recipient about her personal state of affairs: that is, her state of health and her mood, respectively. With regard to these personal states of affairs the recipient can be taken to have first-hand knowledge.

> In both turns the speaker indicates that he has only indirect knowledge, an outsider's knowledge of the referred-to facts.

This is done by including in the utterances a description of the
sources of his knowledge. In segment (1) reference is made to
a nonpresent third party from whom the speaker says he
"(just) got the information". In segment (2) the speaker
makes mention of an observable part of the recipient's
appearance ("can see [from] your face"), which provides the
grounds for his inference about her internal state ("mood").

Having observed and described these two features which are
held in common to the two initiating utterances, it turns out that I
am dealing here with an utterance format which not only occurs in
psychiatric interviews and other interrogative contexts, but which
is familiar in everyday interaction, too. That, and how, such a
telling of an experience may serve as an elicitor of information has
already been considered by Anita Pomerantz (1980). In her paper,
" 'Limited access' as a 'fishing' device," Pomerantz draws attention
to instances such as the following.

```
(3) [NB:II:2. 1:quoted from Pomerantz, 1980]
1   B:              Hello::,
2   A:              HI:::.
3   B:              Oh:hi::'ow are you Agne::s,
4   A:        →     Fi:ne. Yer line's been busy.
5   B:              Yeuh my fu(hh)- 'hh my father's wife called
6                   me. 'hh So when she calls me::, 'hh I always
7                   talk fer a long time. Cuz she c'n afford it'n
8                   I can't. hhhh heh 'ehhhhhh
```

Simply by saying "Yer line's been busy" the speaker may successfully attempt to have the recipient disclose the identity of the party
to whom she was talking and the reason for talking such a long
time. This maneuver of getting an interactant to volunteer information has been called "fishing" by Anita Pomerantz, and she
suggests that these information-eliciting tellings operate with
regard to certain knowledge constraints. A speaker, referring with
an assertion to an event about which he himself has only indirect
knowledge, indicates that he has only "limited access"; but at the
same time he invokes the fact that the recipient, given he is a
"subject–actor" in that event, has direct knowledge and "authoritative access" to it. In describing the occasioning of my knowledge
of an event, I am referring to an "objective event", of which my

report can only give an outsider's version or – to use Pomerantz' expression – a "my side telling." "Telling 'my side' when the recipient is an object in the told experience is a speaker's device for casting the recipient into the position of speaking as a subject–actor in the referred-to event" (Pomerantz 1980: 193).

It can now be seen that each of the transcribed segments of a psychiatric intake interview includes an instance of "fishing." In each segment the doctor refers with an assertion to a personal state of affairs (state of health, mood) to which he as an outside observer has only limited access. In describing the source of his restricted knowledge (outside information, the candidate patient's appearance), the doctor invites or provides for the candidate patient to present – so to speak, "voluntarily" – an authoritative version, and an account of her personal state of affairs.

A search through the corpus of about a hundred transcribed intake interviews provided a large collection of instances in which psychiatrists do not formulate direct questions, but instead try to get whatever it is they might want to know from the candidate patients by information-eliciting tellings. In these instances a range of techniques can be found which a speaker may use for marking his restricted access to the events or circumstances he is focusing on.

One device a speaker may apply is to point out the specifically *derivative character of his knowledge*. This can be accomplished by referring to a third party or a case file as the origin of one's knowledge, instances of which may be found in segments (1) and (4:3):

```
(1)
1    Dr.F:        [(I just) got the information,]
2                 (0.8) (that you're)

(4:3) [INTAKE:A-13:II:7/Free translation]
11   Dr.F.:       [Doctor Hollmann told me] something like
12                you were running across the street
```

Another way of showing the specifically derivative character of one's knowledge is to describe this knowledge as a product of one's observation or impression. This may be done by mentioning the process of perception itself:

```
(2)
34   Dr.F:                    .....u::h I mean [I can
35                 see (from) your face ] that the:- (1.0) mood
```

or by formulating the referred-to facts as an outward appearance (as is the case in utterances like: "You look a little bit nervous" or "You sound kind of depressed").

A second device which a speaker may use to mark restricted knowledge consists in pointing out the *uncertain character of this knowledge.* Again this can be accomplished in several possible ways. In segment (2)

(2)
34   Dr.F: ..... I mean I can
35   see (from) your <u>face</u> that the:- (1.0) mood (.)
36   apparently is not ba:d.

we find an instance where, through the insertion of the qualifier "apparently," an assertion of fact ("the mood is not bad") is turned into a statement of what *seems* to be the case (in contrast to a possible statement of what *is* the case). And in segment (4:2)

(4:2) [INTAKE:A-13:II:7/Free translation]
 7   Dr.F: .... and somehow
 8   also a behaviour seems to have occurred
 9   where you really- (0.4) uh acted a little bit
10   (.) peculiar.
11   Ms.B: ˙hhh ⌐u:hm-
12   Dr.F: ⌊Doctor Hollmann told me something like
13   you were running across the street not so
14   completely dressed or something like that,

the speaker not only qualifies his assertion with "somehow" (line 7), but he also uses the phrase "a behaviour seems to have occurred" (line 8); furthermore, he completes his utterance with the expression "or something like that." In all these instances the speaker is taking pains to indicate that his assertions rest on fragmentary and uncertain knowledge and could therefore be regarded only as possibly correct descriptions. Presenting his knowledge as fragmentary and uncertain may be seen as a speaker's method for inviting or inducing the recipient to deliver an authentic version, should he know better.

3 The usefulness of indirectness in the context of psychiatric exploration

Having partially described what may be called the technology of information-eliciting tellings, the question remains why this device is so frequently used in the context of psychiatric exploration. At first sight the frequent occurrence of "my side tellings" in intake interviews may appear strange since interviews and examinations are usually seen and described as speech-exchange systems whose main feature is that, whatever is done there, has to be done in the sequential environment of questions and answers. So why should a psychiatrist attempt to examine a candidate patient in an indirect, "fishing" manner, given that all his turns will be treated as questions anyway?

For the present my argument is that there are several structural reasons for the observably rich occurrence of information-eliciting tellings in psychiatric intake interviews. I shall describe two of them:

1 In carrying out an exploratory interview the psychiatrist faces a task and is provided with a resource which together may be seen to facilitate, if not predetermine, the employment of "my side tellings." To describe the resource first: there are many sources from which the psychiatrist usually derives knowledge about the candidate patient well before the intake interview. These include phone calls with the referring doctor, with a social worker, or with the police; conversations with a member of the candidate patient's family, as well as the letter of admission or the already existing patient's file, all of which provide the psychiatrist with a variety of information which may be retrieved when he starts the interview with the candidate patient. In the course of an intake interview the psychiatrist's prior knowledge about the candidate patient is relevant insofar as it is representative of all the voices and actions which accompanied the patient's psychiatric trajectory, or were instrumental to it. These pieces of prior information are then supplemented by the psychiatrist's observations of the candidate patient's behavior during the actual interview.

While knowledge arrived at in this fashion will provide outside versions of the case at hand, it is the psychiatrist's work task to get access to the candidate patient's view during the course of the exploratory interview. Instead of starting from zero in asking the candidate patient for his first-hand version of an event, which the psychiatrist could then compare with already known versions of other parties, he can opportunistically use his prior information as

an economical and efficient means for the elicitation of authoritative descriptions. Taken together, the psychiatrist's task of getting
access to the candidate patient's view, and his resource of having
available prior external knowledge about him appear to be an
extremely apt constellation for the employment of an utterance
format the operating principle of which is to achieve exactly that
type of task by using exactly this type of resource.

2 A second structural reason for the affinity between information-
eliciting tellings and the context of exploratory talk can be found in
segment (5):

(5) [INTAKE:B-15:5/Free translation](Dr.D. is reading through the candidate
patient's file, and letter of admission)

```
1    Dr.D:    →   Uh you've already been with us.
2                 I ⌈ s that right.
3    Ms.P:          ⌊ On:ce:.
4                 ( . )
5    Dr.D:        Fou:r ti:mes!
6    Ms.P:        °Or four ti ⌈ :mes.°
7    Dr.D:                      ⌊ Four times.
```

In response to the telling "Uh you've already been with us" the
recipient does not simply produce a confirmation or disconfirmation, which may be seen and treated as an accountable withholding.
Instead, she "voluntarily" announces the precise number of her
past admissions ("On:ce:"). In the ensuing talk she is confronted by
a quite different version of the number of times she has been
admitted, in the doctor's exclamation "Fou:r tii:mes!" By confirming this statement (line 6) the candidate patient implicitly confesses
that she was caught lying, further evidence for which may be found
in the transition from her determined "On:ce:" to a subdued "Or
four ti:mes."

   This telling of a lie – whatever its particular motive may have
been – has as a general structural condition its placement after a
"my side telling." Casting the recipient into the position of
someone who is invited to present, then and there, an authoritative
correct version may lead the recipient to "confess"; and the general
readiness for confessions after information-eliciting tellings is
indeed surprising. But the same feature may also lead the recipient
into the temptation of telling – under the cloak of assigned auth-

ority – an expectably successful lie. However, an information-eliciting telling does not reveal what knowledge the speaker has beyond that which is shown in the utterance itself. This is, of course, a general constraint on the production of a lying response, since the danger of lie detection becomes an imponderable matter.

In the intake interview from which segment (5) originated, the candidate patient may have found evidence that Dr. D. does not have any knowledge of the case at hand beyond that which is displayed in her telling. Dr. D.'s utterance starts with the turn-initial token "Uh," which is used to index that just at that moment its producer at last and to his surprise found something out that he was searching for.[3] Thus the token "Uh" displays realization, that the knowledge which is reflected in Dr. D.'s assertion is locally emergent, not based on prior information, and therefore uncertain knowledge which is in need of confirmation. In this situation it may appear to be a safe move for the candidate patient Ms. P. to "volunteer" the precise but wrong number of her past admissions, thereby making her present contact with a psychiatric institution a second slip instead of the fifth in a series of commitments. But she was trapped.

I want to claim that, given their operational structure, information-eliciting tellings can successfully be used as a lie-detecting device and are therefore highly suitable for exploratory interviews, examinations, and interrogations (e.g. police interrogations). The recipient is addressed as someone who has authoritative access, and with this local identity he may be tempted to tell a profitable lie. But the speaker who presents himself as someone who has limited access may have derived further knowledge from a variety of other sources, knowledge which enables him to doubt or contest the recipient's supposedly authoritative version, or even to reject it as having been a lie.

4 Methodological interlude

The description of two structural conditions for the affinity of "my side tellings" to psychiatric intake interviews can only be a first step in the analysis. Were these analytic considerations to stop at this point they would necessarily share some of the shortcomings which tend to occur when conversation analysis is used to study institutional interaction. In my view the study would be subject to two serious methodological objections:

> Simply identifying utterances as instances of "my side tellings" is a way of proceeding which is governed by a peculiar type of logic which is characteristic of legal action and which may be called the "logic of subsumption" (Ulrich Oevermann).[4] This expression denotes a way of proceeding in which events in the social world *a priori* are sorted and arranged under aspects of general, preconstructed concepts. No attention is paid to the question of how the structure of a concrete social object is reproduced in and through the course of action.
>
> A second shortcoming is commonly associated with this logic of subsumption: namely, the tendency towards what might be termed the "Balesianization" of conversation analysis. I mean to describe with this horribly Germanic term the process whereby the concepts which have been introduced and developed in conversation analysis lose their processual, "local production" (Garfinkel) character and are inclined to be treated like Robert Bales's system of categories; that is, they come to be treated canonically and are used with the aim of determining the distribution of prespecified conversational objects in various social settings.

In my view, if the analysis of interaction in task-oriented, formal organizations is to be worthwhile and rewarding, then these shortcomings should as far as possible be avoided. But that is not an easy task; there are no recipes which guarantee success. One way to avoid these shortcomings may be to let oneself not be satisfied prematurely with so-called "findings," findings which often leave the more interesting issues unexplicated. For example, in talking about the "affinity" of information-eliciting tellings to exploratory interviews I might be perceived as treating both objects as independent entities, whose covariation is at issue. But the question remains, of course, what is the substantial meaning of that "affinity"? Another example: starting with the identification of a clearcut conversational object, the "my side telling," may have the consequence that the focus on the psychiatric intake interview, as the interactional context, is minimized to the extent of becoming only a marginal condition for the application of conversational norms. Proceeding in that way may provide some answers to the question of what makes those psychiatric intake interviews instances of psychiatric *talk*, but it certainly could not tell us what makes those intake interviews *psychiatric* talk.

These considerations encourage me to take a second run on my data. The leading question for this second attempt will be: is it possible to identify and describe features of the interaction which are locally produced in the sense that they are the result of the interactants' analysis of and orientation to the context, which simultaneously is reproduced in and through their actions?[5]

5 Descriptive practices (I): "litotes" formulations

To answer this question, I return to the instances of information-eliciting tellings in the first two segments, but now with the aim of discovering whether these two exploratory utterances

> "(I just) got the information, (0.8)
> (that you're) not doing so well."

> "I mean I can see (from) your <u>face</u>
> that the:– (1.0) <u>moo</u>d (.) apparently is
> not ba:d."

have some other significant features in common, which make it possible to analyze these as instances of specifically *psychiatric* interaction. A previously unmentioned but salient feature of these two utterances is that in both cases what is reported to the recipient is described by using a certain rhetorical form which in classical rhetorics is called litotes. Litotes describes the object to which it refers not directly, but through the negation of the opposite. So in segment (1) Dr. F. uses the expression "not so well" instead of the possible *verbum proprium*, *bad*; and in segment (2) he tells the candidate patient that her mood apparently is "not bad," where he could have said instead *good* or *excellent*.

Litotes is quite frequently used by psychiatrists within the intake interviews, at least frequently enough to pose the question as to what this rhetorical figure is doing there. For example:

(4:1)
1   Dr.F: Okay. d'hh there are obviously- (1.0) your

```
2                husband is [not ( . ) of the same opinion] as
3                you: and u:h
```

```
(4:3)
12    Dr.F:      you were running across the street [not so
13               completely dressed] or something like that,
```

The account given in various rhetorical textbooks reveals a picture of the rhetorical figure litotes which is – to put it aptly – "not very clear." The following considerations may contribute to a generic conception of this rhetorical device (which is especially popular in academic discourse).

The initial accomplishment of the element of negation in the litotes figure is twofold: on the one hand, the negation ensures that an indefinite nonspecific indirect or inexplicit description occurs at the functional slot where a more direct or inexplicit description might otherwise be due; on the other hand, it provides for the possibility that the ongoing interaction can be continued without the production of such a description, which otherwise is a prerequisite for such a continuation. That means: with litotes one can go on talking without specifying what one is talking about.

Secondly, by its very relinquishment, a speaker's avoidance of a more direct or explicit description creates the possibility that the co-interactant will be the first to introduce such a description and, by doing so, show openness and honesty. Take, for example, segment (4):

```
(4) [INTAKE:A-13:II:7/Free translation]
11    Dr.F:      Doctor Hollmann told me something like
12               you were running across the street [not so
13               completely dressed] or something like that,
14    Ms.B:      (h)yes: that's:- I am a child of God;=
15               =I am his child;
16               ( . )
17    Ms.B:      Does a- does-=
18               =Do you have children Doctor Fisch ┌er?
19    Dr.F:                                         └Yes:
20    Ms.B:      Yes what age,
21    Dr.F:      uh around s-seven eight ┌ and eleven
22    Ms.B:                              └ yes and when they
23               were small these children,
24    Dr.F:      Yes ┌:,
25    Ms.B:          └didn't they sometimes run around [naked]
```

26		because they don't yet- because they
27	Dr.F:	t(hh)u(h)
28	Ms.B:	don't (.) know that they must not do that.

In this segment Dr. F. uses in his information-eliciting telling (line 11–13) the litotes phrase "not so completely dressed." In her response to this "fishing," Ms. B., the candidate patient, then uses the term "naked" (line 25) to describe the very same event to which Dr. F. was referring. And if one follows the ensuing talk

(6) [INTAKE:A-13:II:9/15 sec. later/Free translation]
```
1    Dr.F:  →   So you ran- (0.5) like a child naked in
2                the (0.5) ⌈u:h stree-
3    Ms.B:              ⌊In the street?=I was in the
4                hallway
```

it transpires that a few seconds later the psychiatrist also uses this *verbum proprium*. So it seems to be the case that by using the form of litotes, a speaker not only abstains from describing an object in direct terms, but does so in the service of his recipient, insofar as the recipient is invited and given the opportunity to go first in properly denominating the referred-to object. Once the object is named by the recipient, the speaker can take over.[6]

Thirdly, this means that a speaker who is referring to an object in the indefinite form of litotes thereby displays a certain kind of caution and defensiveness. The litotes presents the description in which it is used as a cautious description. It avoids the proper naming of an object and leaves that instead to the recipient.

Furthermore, the avoidance of a proper reference form may imply that there are good reasons for such an avoidance: that is, the not-naming of an object may be an accountable matter. In using a litotes, a speaker may indicate that there is something "special," something "peculiar" in the referred-to object which motivated the indirect manner of its denomination. What that "special feature" is is left unclear in the description and has to be decided by the recipient.

It is evident from the features described so far that litotes is a rhetorical device which is typically used for the purpose of alluding or hinting. Referring to an object with the negation of the opposite is a way of dealing with presumably delicate, touchy, or embarrassing matters, where the delicacy of the matter is constituted by the very fact of talking about it allusively.

Alluding to a delicate issue can only be successful if the recipient correspondingly has the knowledge necessary to decode this indirect method of reference. That is to say, litotes works on the basis of shared knowledge; or, more precisely, litotes displays that its producer has knowledge of something delicate, about which he presupposes that his recipient also has knowledge. Therefore litotes claims intimacy and may generally be regarded as an "Intersubjectivity Invoking Device."

Taking all my remarks together, I want to claim that the rhetorical figure litotes is one of those methods which are used to talk about an object in a discreet way. It clearly locates an object for the recipient, but it avoids naming it directly. I will come back to the issue of discretion shortly.

In closing my remarks on the issue at hand I want to reintroduce the fact that all of the instances of litotes I am dealing with here occur in the doctor's information-eliciting tellings. This is relevant insofar as now a very stunning resemblance may be detected: the rhetorical figure litotes reproduces exactly the structure of the turn type it is used in. In the same way that an information-eliciting telling may solicit a response while avoiding the production of an overt question, so the litotes formulation may refer to some matter while avoiding a direct or explicit description of it. So the speaker, that is the psychiatrist, not only avoids directly asking about something, but he also avoids naming that "something" explicitly.

6 Descriptive practices (II): mitigators and euphemistic descriptors

Litotes is not the only descriptive practice which regularly occurs in psychiatrists' exploratory utterances. There are at least two other practices which are of interest here, but it is not possible to treat them at this point in as detailed a way as litotes. Some observations and remarks must suffice.

In addition to litotes, psychiatrists' descriptions of an event in which the candidate patient is a subject-actor are very often interspersed with elements which may be grouped together as mitigators. Mitigators are descriptive elements which generally weaken a claim or diminish the directness or roughness of an assertion. Examples may be found in the following segments:

(4:2)
```
 6   Dr.F:        the surroundings neither, and somehow
 7                also a behaviour seems to have occurred where
 8                you really- (0.5) uh acted [a little bit]
 9                (.) peculiar.
```

(4:3)
```
11   Dr.F:        Doctor Hollmann told me something like
12                you were running across the street [not so
13                completely] dressed or something like that,
```

(7) [INTAKE:D-19:2/Free translation]
```
 1   Dr.F:        °You're [kind of] irritated [a little bit?°]
 2   Ms.W:        Pardon?
 3   Dr.F:        You're [kind of] irritated [a little ⌐bit,]
 4   Ms.W:                                           ⌊Yes
 5                because I'm living there in a house with
 6                lunatics....
```

Here the psychiatrist does not say to the candidate patients that apparently they acted in a peculiar fashion, nor that they ran around undressed and were irritated; instead, he describes them as having acted "a little bit" peculiarly, as having been "not so completely dressed" and "kind of irritated a little bit." In the same manner as litotes, these mitigators operate in a defensive way, thereby trying to head off a possibly upcoming disagreement by the psychiatrist's co-interactant.

The third descriptive practice which can be found in psychiatric information-eliciting tellings comes to the surface quite clearly in segment (8):

(8) [INTAKE:A-6:10/Free translation](Dr.B. is reading the letter of referral)
```
 1   Dr.B:   →    Obviously you withdrew very much.
 2                ( . )
 3                recently.
 4                ( . )
 5                in your flat.
 6                (0.7)
 7   Ms.K:        Hu! That's private business. There is nothing
 8                to talk about!.=
 9                =Withdrew.=I can do what I want.
10                (0.8)
11   Dr.B:   →    Well here ⌐it says you had yourself -
12   Ms.K:                  ⌊S a y i n g   s u c h   th ings.=
```

```
13   Dr.B:   →   =Here it says you had yourself barricaded
14               and (.) you we ┌ re-
15   Ms.K:                      └ Pardon?
16               (.)
17   Dr.B:      you had simply disappeared in your flat
18              and had no longer shown up, and uh
19              (1.5)
20   Dr.B:      ┌ and were-
21   Ms.K:      └ I can do what I want,
22              that's really ridiculous what (        )
```

The interesting thing that happens here is that Dr. B. delivers,
one after the other, two quite different descriptions of the event he
focuses on. One feature of these two descriptions is that they are
accompanied by two different knowledge claims. The first description is introduced with the qualifier "Obviously" (line 1), claiming
thereby that the description given is based on common knowledge
without the need for specific evidence. In contrast, the second
description is prefaced by the remark "Here it says" (line 11/13),
which makes reference to the candidate patient's case record and
which claims an officially confirmed validity for this latter version.
With this shift Dr. B. can be seen to upgrade the authoritativeness
of his knowledge.

In connection with the change of knowledge claims, the event
itself is reformulated in the psychiatrist's second version. Whereas
in the first version (line 1: "you withdrew very much") the
referred-to event is described as a strange-but-nevertheless-
possibly-normal-and-understandable event, the second formulation
(line 13: "you had yourself barricaded") recasts the same event as a
documented-bizarre-and-crazy behavior. This shift exhibits that in
his first version, the speaker withheld a description which is (or
would have been) much more offensive and embarrassing for the
recipient than the one which was actually used. Thus, the first
telling can retrospectively be seen as one which is built on what I
want to call a "euphemistic descriptor." In all cases in which the
actually used descriptor is not reformulated in the subsequent
course of talk by an evidently less sympathetic descriptor, it is, of
course, difficult to show that it was euphemistic in character.
Nevertheless, I would claim that many descriptors which can be
found in the psychiatric information-eliciting tellings can be taken to
be at least somewhat euphemistic. Take, for example, segment (5),

(5)
```
1    Dr.D:       Uh you've already been with us.
2                I ⌜s that right.
3    Ms.P:        ⌊On:ce:.
```

where the phrase "with us" could easily be replaced by some more
direct (and possibly derogatory) descriptors such as "in the hospital", "in the mental hospital".

Let me summarize now the last part of my chapter: I have identified
and laid out a group of observable descriptive practices which
regularly occur in psychiatric information-eliciting tellings: namely,
the rhetorical figure "litotes," a range of "mitigating" elements,
and the use of "euphemistic descriptors." All three practices are
used in the description of events and circumstances in which the
candidate patient is a subject-actor and which presumably were
instrumental to the commitment of the candidate patient to the
psychiatric institution. The common effect of these practices is that
the object to which they refer is described with discretion. So my
use of the term "discretion" is intended to convey two points simultaneously: on the one hand, it implies that within psychiatric interviews the *act of exploration* is regularly done indirectly in the
format of information-eliciting tellings. And, on the other hand, it
implies that the *object of exploration* is regularly described in these
tellings in an indirect, cautious, and euphemistic manner.

Given this pervasive character of discretion, we need to enquire
further into what it is doing and how it is related to the psychiatric
locality of its occurrence. In answering these questions I am not
interested in trying to find out what motivated the speaker to use
these discreet forms of exploration. My way of proceeding is
instead to take these elements of discretion reflexively as providing
for an implicit account of their use. By describing something with
caution and discretion, this "something" is turned into a matter
which is in need of being formulated cautiously and discreetly.
Viewed sociologically, there is not first an embarrassing, delicate,
morally dubious event or improper behavior about which people
then speak with caution and discretion; instead, the delicate and
notorious character of an event is constituted by the very act of
talking about it cautiously and discreetly.[7]

7 Psychiatric discretion: between medical and moral version

I want to claim – and this leads to the title of my chapter – that the pervasive element of discretion in psychiatric interviews must be viewed and analyzed as a phenomenon, in which the peculiar and paradoxical meaning structure of present-day psychiatry is reproduced.

Evidence for this claim is derived from the observation that a discreetly exploring utterance in psychiatric interviews is usually treated by the recipient, that is, the candidate patient, as one of two very different types of activity. The first option is that such an utterance is seen as a considerate, affiliative invitation to the recipient openly to formulate private problems, to disclose personal feelings, and to talk about their troubles. The recipients are not directly asked or obliged to answer; they are, instead, solicited in a mild way to give authentic descriptions, to put feelings into words and to relieve their hearts. They are given the opportunity to talk about issues which they themselves would not have dared to topicalize in the first place; and this way of prompting implicitly assures them that whatever they are going to disclose will find understanding and affirmation. They are offered the right to talk about their problems in their own words and to unfold parts of their interior life, which is usually hidden. In this sense, the psychiatric "my side tellings" imply a component of empathy, of *Mitgefühl*, of affiliation; and it is therefore not surprising that this utterance format is frequently used in various types of psychotherapy (especially nondirective psychotherapy), and among those groups whose members like to "psychologize" everything. Let me call this first option the *medical* version of the discreetly exploring utterance.

Now the same utterance type may, on the other hand, be treated by the recipient in a very different manner. By telling a candidate patient something about himself and thereby gently urging him to give away more or less voluntarily information and opinions about an issue he is involved in, the psychiatrist is intruding on his co-interactant's private, personal sphere. He draws attention to something which in the first place is not his but his recipient's business. The psychiatrist thereby deprives his recipient of his right to decide for himself what part of his personal life he wants to disclose and share with a stranger. The psychiatrist transgresses borders of responsibility; his "fishing" attempt may therefore be seen as an insidious strategy to make the recipient disclose experiences, feelings, or information which the candidate patient might have preferred to keep to himself.

In addition to this character of intrusion, the psychiatrist's discreetly exploring utterances have a further and more strongly offensive meaning: in reporting an event a speaker makes of that event a reportable event. To mention something makes this a mentionable something, that is, a something worth mentioning. So a discreetly exploring utterance displays that the event it topicalizes must somehow be worth talking about; but by its very construction it conspicuously avoids giving the speaker's reason for turning just this event into a topic of talk. In this situation the pervasive character of discretion becomes an important interpretive resource for the candidate patient. The very fact of discretion may lead the candidate patient to suspect that the exploratory utterance topicalizes behavior which needs to be formulated with discretion, that is some improper, deviant, or morally questionable behavior. At the same time this supposed impropriety can be seen as the psychiatrist's unformulated reason for drawing attention to just this behavior in the first place. So the very discretion with which the improper character of a referred-to behavior was disguised and covered may be used by the candidate patient to detect and to uncover the fact that the psychiatrist is dealing with the topic he has just introduced in moral terms. Let me call this second option the *moral* version of the discreetly exploring utterance.

Because of its indirectness and because of its suggestive telling-format, a discreetly exploring utterance can be regarded as a prototypical carrier of insinuation – insinuating in the official medical version some trouble, and in the unofficial moral version some improper behavior. The seemingly innocent, helpful, and affiliative utterances with which a psychiatrist attempts to induce a candidate patient to disclose his feelings and opinions have structurally an inbuilt hidden or veiled morality.

Candidate patients may, of course, respond solely to the medical version of psychiatrists' discreetly exploring utterances. But if recipients voluntarily give the information such an utterance is asking for, they not only accept what is being insinuated in that utterance, but also that it is conveyed to them via insinuation. By responding in a "neutral" and friendly way to the psychiatrist's "fishing" attempts, a candidate patient avoids rejecting but instead implicitly accepts the veiled morality and the incipient suggestion of wrong-doing in that utterance. Given this situation, many candidate patients do not join the insinuation game but choose instead to turn against the psychiatrist, protesting – quite often in an unarticulated way – against the kind of business they are drawn into, as in lines 11–14 of the following example.

(9) [INTAKE:D-20:5/Free translation]

```
 1   Dr.F:   →   ˙h thh. You feel angry about being committed
 2               by Doctor ⌈Kluge. (      )
 3   Ms.K:              ⌊˙hhh No:: I don't feel angry about
 4               h- being committed by Doctor Kluge ˙hh but
 5               that you somehow-
 6               (1.0)
 7   Dr.F:   What?
 8               (0.6)
 9   Ms.K:   hhh
10               (3.0)
11   Ms.K:   Mhh(a)hh(a)h please.
12               ((Ms.K. sweeps the doctor's papers with a
13               wave of the hand off the table))
13   Ms.K:   I:-  ( . ) can't stand you Doctor Fischer.
```

Discreetly exploring utterances are extremely vulnerable to being heard by the recipient in moral terms and may therefore trigger uncontrollable, interactionally disastrous social situations. That is, an utterance which not only looks quite innocuous but also seems sympathetically to assist the recipient may lead to a kind of explosive reaction. Since such reactions in the psychiatric intake interview will unavoidably lead the psychiatrist to the judgment that the candidate patient is showing strange if not aggressive behavior, and in any case is in need of treatment, the psychiatric discretion which triggered that reaction may be called fatal.

Of course, I do not mean to blame the psychiatrists for playing dirty tricks on the candidate patients. The psychiatric discretion is an object in which the contradictory meaning structure of present-day psychiatry is crystallized into a unique phenomenon. The discreetly exploring utterances reproduce in their duality of medical and moral versions the character of psychiatry as an institution with two conflicting frames: on the one hand, as a subdiscipline of medicine, psychiatry has to deal in a neutral, disengaged way with what psychiatrists themselves have come to call "mental illness"; on the other hand, psychiatry has to deal with people whose improper behavior in our culture was treated, is treated, and – as I would claim – will be treated in moral terms. Psychiatry is an institution caught and twisted between medicine and morality; and detailed analysis reveals that this contradictory structure materializes itself at the level of turn-by-turn interaction in the various manifestations of psychiatric discretion.

Appendix: original German transcripts

(1) [INTAKE:A-13:II:1](Der Aufnahmearzt Dr.F. hat soeben ein Telefongespräch mit dem einweisenden Arzt beendet und wendet sich nun an Frau B.)

```
 1   Dr.F:     (Ich hab) g'rad Nachricht, (0.8) (daß es
 2             Ihnen) nich' ganz gu:t geht.
 3   Frau B:   Ja:: also das ist ┌dann die Ansicht┐
 4   Dr.F:                        └Is' das zutreffen┘d?
 5   Frau B:   dess Herrn Doktor Hollmann.
 6   Dr.F:     A ┌ja
 7   Frau B:      └also meine ist es nicht.
 8   Dr.F:     Ihre isses nich ┌t.
 9   Frau B:                    └Nei ┌:n
10   Herr B:                         └(            )
11   Frau B:                              └mi:r geht es se:hr
12             gut.
```

(2) [INTAKE:A-13:II:2/20 sec. später](Nachdem er Herrn B. kurz erklärte, daß er zunächst mit dessen Ehefrau sprechen möchte, wendet sich Dr.F. wieder an Frau B.)

```
31   Dr.F:     ((zu Herrn B.)) Wir könn' uns ┌nachher drüber
32   Herr B:                                 └(        )
33   Dr.F:     noch unterhalten.
34   Dr.F:     ((wieder zu Frau B. gewandt)) ˙hh ja ä::h ich
35             mein' ich seh Ihrm Gesicht aus daß die:- (1.0)
36             Stimmung (.) anscheinend nicht schlecht ┌is::.
37   Frau B:                                           └˙hhh
38             jaa jetzt will ich Ihnen mal was sa:ng.
39             (.)
40   Frau B:   Wenn Sie:-
41             (1.0)
```

```
42                 wissen-
43                 (1.0)
44                 Gott(h)
45                 (0.7)
46                 ist mein Va:ter;
47                 (.)
48    Dr.F:        Hm ⎡m,
49    Frau B:          ⎣ich bin sein Kind;....
```

(4) [INTAKE:A-13:II:7]

```
1     Dr.F:        Ja. d˙hh nun: gibt's ja offenba:r- (1.0) is
2                  Ihr Mann nicht (.) ganz der gleichen Meinung-g
3                  wie Sie: ⎡u  n  d          ä : : h ⎤
4     Frau B:               ⎣Nei:n also=mein=Mann ⎦=ist=bestimmt=
5                  nicht=der=gleichen= ⎡Meinung.    ⎤
6   ˴ Dr.F:                            ⎣die Umge ⎦bung-g auch
7                  nicht grade, und es schein' ja irgendwie auch
8                  Verhaltensweisen vorgekomm' zu sein wo: Se
9                  doch:- (0.4) ah sich 'n bissl (.) auffällich
10                 verhalten haben.
11    Frau B:      ˙hhh ⎡ä:hm-
12    Dr.F:             ⎣der Doktor Hollmann sagte mir was Sie
13                 seien da über die Stra:ße gelaufen nich so
14                 ganz angezogen oder so,
15    Frau B:      (h)ja: das:- ich bin ein Kind Gottes;=
16                 =ich bin sein Kind;
17                 (.)
18    Frau B:      Läuft e- läuft-=
19                 =Haben Sie Kinder Herr Dokter Fisch ⎡er?
20    Dr.F:                                            ⎣Ja:
21    Frau B:      Ja wie alt,
22    Dr.F:        ah so: s-sieben acht ⎡und elf
23    Frau B:                           ⎣ja und wo sie klein
24                 waren diese Kinder,
25    Dr.F:        Ja ⎡:,
26    Frau B:         ⎣sind die nicht auch mal nackt irgendwoher
27                 gelaufen ⎡weil se ja noch- weil se ja nicht
28    Dr.F:                 ⎣t(hh)a(h)
29    Frau B:      (.) wissen daß sie das nicht dürfen.
30                 Ja und genauso: muß man das sehen in meinem
31                 Verhältnis zu Gott
```

(5) [INTAKE:B-15:5](Dr.D. liest im Einweisungsschreiben und in der Krankenakte)

```
1     Dr.D:        Ah Sie waren scho:n mal bei uns.
```

```
2                    S ⌜timmt das.
3      Frau P:         ⌞Ei:nmo:l.
4                    ( . )
5      Dr.D:        V:ie:rma:l!
6      Frau P:      °Oder vierma ⌜:l.°
7      Dr.D:                      ⌞Viermal.
```

(6) [INTAKE:A-13:II:9]
```
1      Dr.F:        S' sind also- (0.6) wie ein Kind nackt auf der
2                    Stra:ße (0.5) ⌜a:h (rum)-
3      Frau B:                     ⌞auf der Straße?=Ich war im
4                    Hausflur war das.
```

(7) [INTAKE:D-19:2]
```
1      Dr.F:        °S' sind so:'n bißchen gereizt?°
2      Frau W:      Was?
3      Dr.F:        S' sind so:'n bißchen ge ⌜reizt,
4      Frau W:                                ⌞Ja weil ich da eben
5                    in e'm Haus bei Verrückten läbe...
```

(8) [INTAKE:A-6:10](Dr.B. liest im Einweisungsschreiben)
```
1      Dr.B:        Sie haben sich offensichtlich sehr
2                    zurückgezogen.
3                    ( . )
4                    in der letzten Zeit.
5                    ( . )
6                    in Ihrer Wohnung.
7                    (0.7)
8      Frau K:      Ha! das ist doch Prifa:tsache da gibt's nix
9                    darüber zu re:den.=
10                   =Zurückgezogen.=Ich kann machen was ich will.
11                   (0.8)
12     Dr.B:        Also hier ⌜steht Sie hätten sich ⌝-
13     Frau K:                ⌞S o : was zu sa ⌟:gen.=
14     Dr.B:        =Hier steht Sie hätten sich verbarrikadiert
15                   und (.) Sie hä ⌜tten-
16     Frau K:                      ⌞Bitte?
17                   ( . )
18     Dr.B:        Sie seien einfach in Ihrer Wohnung
19                   verschwunden und hätten sich nicht mehr .
20                   gezeigt, und äh
21                   (1.5)
22     Dr.B:        ⌜und hätten-
23     Frau K:      ⌞Ich kann doch machen was ich will,
24                   das ist doch l-lächerlich was da    (     )
```

(9) [INTAKE:D-20:5]
```
 1   Dr.F:        ˙h thh. Sie ärgern sich drüber daß Dokter
 2                Kluge Sie einge ⌐wiesen hat. (    )
 3   Frau K:                      ⌊ ˙hhh Nei:n ich ärgere mich
 4                nicht daß i- daß mich Doktor Kluge
 5                eingeliefert hat.hh sondern daß Sie irgendwie-
 6                (1.0)
 7   Dr.F:        Wa:s?
 8                (0.6)
 9   Frau K:      hhh
10                (3.0)
11   Frau K:      Mhh(a)hh(a)h bitte.
12                ((Frau K. fegt mit einer Handbewegung die vor
                  ihr liegenden Dokumente des Arztes vom Tisch))
13   Frau K:      Ich:- (.) mag Sie nicht leide' Herr Doktor
14                Fischer.
```

Notes

1. All extracts in the main text are free translations of the original German transcripts that appear in the Appendix at the end of this chapter. The fragments numbered 4:1–4:3 are taken from extract 4 in the Appendix, and are numbered according to their order of occurrence in that extract.
2. The meaning of the German expression *verrückt* is twofold; literally it means "dislocated," but its usual metaphorical sense is "crazy."
3. Instead of the German particle *oh* the German token "uh" spoken with a cut-off at the end may thus – at least in some situations – be more equivalent to the English particle *oh* which has been shown by Heritage (1984b) to propose a change of state in the knowledge of the speaker.
4. The logic of subsumption which is prevalent in social research and its affirmative function, for example in traditional mass-media research, are a major target of Oevermann's (1983: 267ff.) critique out of which he developed his conception of an "objective hermeneutics."
5. An early formulation of what I have in mind here can be found in Schegloff (1972: 115):

   It is being proposed that the much invoked "dependence on context" must be investigated by showing that, and how, participants analyze context and use the product of their analysis in producing their interaction. To say that interaction is context-sensitive is to say that interactants are context-sensitive, and for what and how that is so is an empirical matter that can be researched in detail.

6. This may be seen as an instance of the [X–Y–Y] series of consecutive references, which Gail Jefferson (1987) described as "embedded correction." There seems to be a special relation between this by-the-way form of correction and the litotes format, insofar as by virtue of its being a

"defensive" or even overdefensive description the use of litotes may be regarded by the recipient as an invitation to substitute a more "offensive" or direct one.

7. An early formulation of this view within the tradition of sociology can be found in the work of Georg Simmel, for example in his essay on the poor:

> From a sociological perspective it is not the case that poverty is first given and thereupon benefit is effected. This is nothing else than fate in its personal form. Instead, he who gets benefit or should get it according to his sociological constellation, even if by chance it fails to come, he is called the poor.
>
> (Simmel 1908: 371; my translation, JRB)

5

Footing in the achievement of neutrality: the case of news-interview discourse

STEVEN E. CLAYMAN

1 Introduction

In the course of talking interactants encounter a variety of assess-
able matters, matters about which they may express a viewpoint,
interpretation, or perspective. But rather than straightforwardly
commit themselves to a particular perspective, interactants may
choose to be more cautious or circumspect; for example, by systematically delaying their assertions in various ways (Maynard 1989a,
1991a, this volume; Pomerantz 1984a), or producing them as com
paratively modest statements of experience rather than strong
declarations of fact (Pomerantz 1984b), speakers can exercise varying degrees of interactional caution when expressing their views. In
the process, they can achieve a variety of practical ends, such as
minimizing interpersonal disagreement while maximizing agreement (Pomerantz 1984a; Maynard this volume) and mitigating
critical, accusatory, and other sensitive actions (Pomerantz 1984b).

There is one setting in which expressive caution is practiced with
extraordinary consistency: the television news interview. Like other
journalists, news interviewers are supposed to be objective in their
work. This means, among other things, that they should not allow
their personal opinions to enter into the interviewing process; to the
best of their ability, they are supposed to remain neutral as they
interact with public figures (Lewis 1984: 122–4). While neutrality
is a concern for reporters generally, it is a particularly pressing issue
for those who interview for television. Their work practices are
commonly broadcast "live" without the benefit of editorial review,
and are thus open to the immediate scrutiny of fellow journalists,

I am grateful to Paul Drew and John Heritage for commenting in detail on an earlier
version of this chapter. This research was supported in part by grant MH 14641
from the National Institute of Mental Health.

government officials, social scientists, and a mass audience with diverse interests and ideological sympathies. Many viewers have a practical interest in monitoring news programming for the presence of bias. Accordingly, news interviewers continually face the problem of sustaining the accountability of their conduct under widespread critical scrutiny.

This chapter is concerned with one interactional practice and its role in addressing this problem within the television news interview. The practice in question involves altering what Goffman (1981b) has referred to as a speaker's interactional "footing." The end it achieves is the maintenance of a formally neutral or "neutralistic" posture for news interviewers (see also Clayman 1988: 482–7).[1] This analysis represents an extension of a growing body of research on the organization of news-interview discourse, research that has been concerned with a wide range of conventional interviewing practices, including those that figure in the process by which interviewers maintain a neutralistic stance in interaction with their guests (Heritage 1985; Clayman 1988; Greatbatch 1988; Heritage and Greatbatch 1991).

Since the footing concept derives from Goffman's work, I will first briefly outline the concept's origins and discuss its relevance to the phenomenon of neutralism. Footing will then be examined empirically in news-interview discourse, beginning with interviewers' management of footing to achieve a neutralistic posture. I will also consider the role of the interviewees in this process, paying particular attention to how they can collaborate to preserve interviewers' neutralism. Finally, I will explore how the credibility of the interviewers' assertions can become an issue for both parties, with interviewers commonly working to enhance the credibility of their claims while interviewees seek to cast doubt on them.

2 The concept of footing

A preliminary discussion of footing can be found in Goffman's *Frame Analysis* (1974: 496–559), and the spirit of the concept – if not its literal application – appears much earlier in his writings (e.g. in the notion of "role distance"; see Goffman 1961b). Yet it received its most focused treatment in his 1979 paper by that name, later reprinted in *Forms of Talk* (1981: 124–57; see also Levinson

1988). Goffman introduced the footing concept in order to explore the nature of involvement and participation in social interaction. For Goffman participation in interaction is not a simple either/or affair in which one party speaks while another listens. There are varying forms and degrees of participation, and the roles of speaking and hearing can be broken down analytically into more specific interactional "footings." Speakers, for example, may take up various footings in relation to their own remarks. By employing specific "production formats" (1981: 145) they may convey distinctions between the (a) animator, (b) author, and (c) principal of what is said. The "animator" is the person who presently utters a sequence of words. The one who originated the beliefs and sentiments, and perhaps also composed the words through which they are expressed, is the "author." Finally, the "principal" is the person whose viewpoint or position is currently being expressed in and through the utterance.

It is not uncommon for a single speaker to embody all three of these identities simultaneously.

(1) [West 16:3:27]
     A1:   So I figured it'd be a good cla:ss to take.

As the speaker of this utterance, BD is self-evidently its animator. He also appears to have composed these words (author) to express a personal viewpoint (principal). BD thus exhibits all three of these identities through his turn.

In contrast, interactants may act primarily as animators when they speak, deflecting the other identities away from themselves and (commonly) onto some other party. The following extract contains several illustrations of this practice (arrowed), beginning with a comparatively mild footing shift that is subsequently upgraded.

(2) [Frankel:TC:I:1:25-26]
```
1   G:   →    ... we don't wanna see one another, (.) ˙hh
2              on a weekend where we just have (.) y'know
3              two da:ys if┌even tha┐:t.
4   S:               └Right, ┘
5              (.)
6   S:         tch I ┌don't blame you.┐
7   G:          └tuh relate tuh o┘ne another. ˙hh Y'know
8        →     we'd like- (.) a little bit longer than tha:t.
9              (0.2)
```

```
10   S:          Right,=
11   G:          =I mean I don't (.) really care that much.
12        →      But he does.
```

G first speaks on behalf of herself and her boyfriend by using the pro-term "we" (lines 1–3, 8). She thus indicates that she is not solely responsible for the viewpoint she is reporting; she is expressing the sentiments of the couple as a unit, with both parties sharing the identities of author and principal. Notice that this footing also becomes an issue for S, who in the course of expressing sympathy and affiliation (at line 6) must indicate with whom she is affiliating. Thus, S uses the pro-term "you," which can refer to G and her boyfriend as a collection (although it can also refer exclusively to G). At any rate, G eventually distances herself further from this perspective (lines 11–12) by observing that it reflects her boyfriend's feelings more than her own. The segment ends (line 12) with a more decisive footing shift in which G is animating the sentiments of her partner.

Speakers can also shift footings in a less direct manner, without overtly stating that another party authored or endorses what is being said. For example, by using transparently imitative phrasing (e.g. aphorisms, renowned quotations, or other statements known in common), or by adopting a mocking style of speech, interactants can show that their words are not entirely their own (Goffman 1981: 150; see also Sacks 1992 [1966]). Both of these resources are employed in the following (see lines 8–16).

```
(3) [HG II:26]
 1   N:          …I still think he might write you,
 2               (0.3)
 3   N:          It just takes 'm awhi:le,
 4               (.)
 5   H:          ˙h-hh-hhe writes one word a day, hhih ⌈hn
 6   N:                                              ⌊yeahhh
 7               (.)
 8   N:          Dear? hh nex' day. Hanna,=
 9   H:          =h h ˙hhh
10               (.)
11   N:          Ho:w?
12               (.)
13   H:          ˙hhhi:⌈nh⌉heh-heh,
14   N:                ⌊A:⌋re?
15               (.)
16   N:          You.
```

Speaker N mocks the opening of a hypothetical letter from Hanna's friend (lines 8, 11, 14, 16), and she does so in part by using stereotypical letter-writing words. She also alters the rhythm of her talk to satirize the idea of a letter being written at the rate of "one word a day." Thus, after saying "nex' day" between the first and second words (line 8), she inserts a little space between each of the succeeding words (lines 9–10, 12–13, 15) to evoke the image of a painfully slow process of composition. The imitative character of this action is also projected at the outset by her comment that he "writes one word a day" (line 5), but these mocking lexical and rhythmic features within the talk further contribute to its intelligibility as a shift of footing.

Goffman called attention to the existence of diverse speaker footings, and he commented on their presence in formal lecturing and radio announcing (1981: 173–86, 280–314). However, he did not examine how they operate in more interactive circumstances. This is significant, because by conceptualizing footing analytically, and examining it empirically in lectures and other monologous forms of talk, interest in footing came to focus quite naturally on the actions of individual speakers. Witness, for example, Goffman's suggestion that speakers achieve specific footings by designing their utterances in accordance with particular "production formats." Similarly, while some studies of news-interview talk have called attention to the fact that interviewers shift footings (e.g. Greatbatch 1986b: 106–7; Harris 1986: 67–8; Jucker 1986: 134–6), these analyses remain speaker-centered in focusing on production formats. What has not yet been examined is how footing operates in interaction: the ways that recipients may orient to a speaker's footing during its production (see Goodwin 1984) and in their subsequent responses to it (see Zimmerman 1990) by either ratifying it, contesting it, or ignoring it, thus shaping the trajectory of the interaction. What is needed, then, is an analysis of the interactional organization by which footing is achieved, sustained, and altered over the course of an encounter.

The television news interview is a fertile setting in which to examine this phenomenon, partly because interviewers shift footings with some regularity, and also because this practice seems to be bound up with matters of neutrality and professionalism that journalists routinely face. As we shall see, it is in part because interviewers have the ability to shift footings that they can maintain a

neutralistic posture even during the production of strongly evaluative or opinionated statements. Hence, these data can yield insight
into the organization of a generic interactional device, while showing how this device may be wielded to accomplish a specific institutional task indigenous to the context of broadcast journalism.[2]

3 How interviewers shift footings

News interviewers usually ask questions of their guests. This practice is characteristic of the interview as a speech-exchange system,
for that system specifies that interviewers (henceforth IRs) and
interviewees (henceforth IEs) should restrict themselves to producing turns that are at least minimally recognizable as questions and
answers, respectively (Greatbatch 1988; see also Clayman 1988).
This form of turn-type preallocation does not mean that IRs cannot
produce statement-formatted utterances, such as assertions, assessments, and the like; but when they do, they usually embed them
within questioning turns and only occasionally allow them to stand
freely. In either case, IRs commonly shift footings during their
production, thereby placing some degree of distance between themselves and their more overtly opinionated remarks. For example, in
the following the IR produces a nonquestioning assertion (lines
9–12) regarding the manageability of nuclear waste; but before
doing so he attributes the statement, and the point of view it
expresses, to a third party (lines 6–9).

```
(4) [Nightline 6/6/85: 19-20]
 1    JS:      ...And if you look et- simply thuh record in
 2             thuh low level waste field over thuh last
 3             fifteen tuh twenty years... thuh record is
 4             not very good (0.3) an' it doesn't give one
 5             a cause for optimism.=
 6    IR:      =You heard what Doctor Yalow said earlier in
 7             this broadcast she'll have an opportunity to
 8             express her own opinions again but she seems
 9             to feel that it is an EMinently soluble problem,
10             and that ultimately that radioactive material
11             can be reduced, to manageable quantities,
12             'n put in thuh bottom of a salt mine.
13    JS:      Thuh p- thuh point that she was making earlier
14             about (.) reprocessing of: thuh fuel rods goes
15             right to thuh heart (.) of thuh way a lotta
16             people look at this particular issue...
```

In this case the cited party is another IE ("Doctor Yalow"), whose previously expressed views are now being animated by the IR in a new context. The IR does not merely attribute a set of words to Yalow; by saying that "she'll have an opportunity to express her own opinions again," he makes a special point of indicating that the viewpoint being expressed through these words "belongs" primarily to this third party and thus is not necessarily his own.

3.1 Footing in pursuit of neutralism

IRs shift footings at specific junctures as a way of adopting a locally neutralistic posture. Part of the evidence for this stems from the fact that IRs frequently take such measures when making assertions. But stronger evidence can be marshalled to demonstrate that neutralism is specifically at issue, and that footing is an oriented-to resource for achieving this posture. This will require examining the footing shift in somewhat finer detail. In this regard, several observations are in order.

1. *Footing shifts tend to be restricted to relatively controversial opinion statements.* This pattern is observable in the following, where an initial "factual" statement is asserted directly (beginning at arrow 1), while the more contentious assertions that follow (arrows 2–3) are produced on a different footing.

(5) [Meet the Press 12/8/85:18] (The IE here is Robert Dole, then Senate majority leader for the Republican party.)

```
 1  IR:    1 →   Senator, (0.5) uh: President Reagan's elected
 2               thirteen months ago: an enormous landslide.
 3               (0.8)
 4          2 →   It is s::aid that his programs are in trouble,
 5               though he seems to be terribly popular with
 6               the American people. (0.6)
 7          3 →   It is said by some people at thuh White House
 8               we could get those programs through if only we
 9               ha:d perhaps more: ˙hh effective leadership
10               on on thuh hill an' I ⌈suppose⌉ indirectly=
11  RD:                              ⌊hhhheh ⌋
12  IR:           =that might (0.5) relate t'you as well:. (0.6)
13               Uh what d'you think thuh problem is really.
14               is=it (0.2) thuh leadership as it might be
15               claimed up on thuh hill, er is it thuh
16               programs themselves.
```

The initial statement (arrow 1, lines 1–2) that Reagan was elected "thirteen months ago" in "an enormous landslide" has the character of a relatively concrete declaration of historical fact; its content is a matter of public record. By way of contrast, the subsequent claim that Reagan's programs are "in trouble" (arrow 2, lines 4–6) and the suggestion that the IE is to blame for this (arrow 3, lines 7–10, 12) are both evaluative in character, and are thus arguable by comparison. As might be expected, the IR distances himself from these more contentious assertions by prefacing them with an attributive verb in the passive voice ("It is said ..."). He thus indicates that they derive from another source which remains unnamed in the first case (arrow 2), but which is loosely identified as "some people at thuh White House" in the latter (arrow 3).

It would be incorrect to view the controversial character of these items as something that is purely intrinsic to their "nature," for their contentiousness becomes visible in part through the special manner in which they are treated. Consider that the IR shifts footing at particular points within his talk, and like any action this is accountable in terms of its sequential placement. Hence, observers can notice that he is selecting particular items from the turn for special handling by taking extra care to distance himself from them. These items might well be contentious or objectionable in themselves, but the move to an animator stance works reflexively to mark them as such. The footing shift thus achieves more than neutralism for its speaker; it simultaneously endows the attributed item with qualities that would otherwise threaten that posture.

2 *Footing shifts are renewed during specific controversial words.* In the following, for example, the IR begins (at arrow 1) by attributing an upcoming assertion in its entirety to a third party ("the Ambassador"). This footing is later renewed within the assertion itself (arrow 2) just prior to a specific descriptor ("a collaborator") which is reattributed to that party.

(6) [Nightline 7/22/85: 17] (Discussing violence among Blacks in South Africa)
```
1   IR:     1 → Reverend Boesak lemme a- pick up a point uh
2               the Ambassador made.
3               What- what assurances can you give u:s ˙hh
4               that (.) talks between moderates in that
5               country will take pla:ce when it see:ms thet
```

```
 6                    any black leader who is willing to talk to
 7                    thuh government is branded
 8          2 →       as the Ambassador said a collaborator
 9                    and is then punished.=
10    AB:             =Eh theh- thuh- thuh Ambassador has it wrong.
11                    It's not thuh people who want to talk with
12                    thuh government that are branded collaborators
```

As a way of characterizing Black leaders who negotiate with the
South African government, "collaborator" has strong morally
judgmental overtones. The IR is thus going to extra lengths to
disavow any personal attachment to strategic items within the
assertion even though he had already altered his footing at the
assertion's beginning.

3 *IRs execute self-repair to shift footings.* It is not uncommon for
IRs to abort their utterances in midstream and revise them so that
they are attributed to a third party (arrowed in the following
extract).

(7) [MacNeil/Lehrer 6/10/85a:CT:4] (Discussing the U.S. decision to continue
to honor the SALT II arms control treaty with a Reagan administration official.)

```
 1    IR:             How d'you sum up thuh me:ssage. that this
 2                    decision is sending to thuh Soviets?
 3    KA:             'hhh Well as I started- to say:: it is ay- one
 4                    of: warning an' opportunity. Thuh warning
 5                    is (.) you'd better comply: to arms control::
 6                    agreements if arms control is going to have
 7                    any chance of succeeding in thuh future.
 8                    Unilateral compliance by thuh United States
 9                    just not in thuh works...
10                    ((Four lines omitted))
11    IR:      →      But isn't this- uh::: critics uh on thuh
12                    conservative- side of thuh political argument
13                    have argued thet this is:. abiding by thuh
14                    treaty is:. unilateral (.) observance. (.)
15                    uh:: or compliance. (.) by thuh United States.
```

IR begins to respond to KA's assertion by producing an interrogative preface ("But isn't this . . ."), which is commonly used by news
interviewers prior to assertions of various sorts (Clayman 1988:
476). The turn-initial *but* indicates, more specifically, that a disagreement is about to be produced. In this instance, however,
employing the standard format for correcting errors (Jefferson

1974), IR aborts the turn and restarts on a different footing, such
that the subsequent viewpoint is attributed to "critics uh on thuh
conservative- side of thuh political argument." This revised version
is no longer formatted as a question, the interrogative preface having been omitted; it is now a free-standing assertion, one that
disputes the IE's previous point, but now does so on someone else's
behalf.

A more complex instance of self-repair to shift footings is the
following (arrowed).

(8) [Nightline 7/22/85: 7] (Allen Boesak, a black South African spokesperson,
is explaining blacks' involvement in recent violence in that country.)

```
 1    AB:          … what you find in thuh black townships it
 2                 seems to me is thuh kind of reaction of thuh
 3                 people to thuh violence of thuh police and
 4                 this is thuh situation in which we find
 5                 our selves.
 6    IR:              [·hhhh ] Well you- you may argue that
 7                 it- that it is a result of apartheid thuh
 8                 violence, it certainly was not s- uhhh
 9                 apartheid is uh- is uh- system (.) imposed
10                 by thuh goverment but
11         1 →     thuh violence itself was not started by thuh
12                 goverment,
13         2 →     thuh violence now st- (.) thuh violence thuh
14                 government now says has to be stopped ·hh
15                 before ANything else can happen an thuh state
16                 of emergency is necessary (0.3) tuh do that.
17                 (.)
18    AB:          ·hhh Well I donno what they me:an you see...
```

After reformulating the gist of AB's prior turn ("Well you- you may
argue that it- that it is a result of apartheid thuh violence"), the IR
proceeds to challenge this point of view. He packages the challenge
in the form of a common rhetorical device: the contrast (Atkinson
1984; Heritage and Greatbatch 1986; Clayman 1988: 478). The
first part of the contrast is initiated at arrow 1 in negative form,
while the second positively formatted part begins at arrow 2 with
"thuh violence now st-." Given the parallel lexical and intonational
constructions, this appears to have been designed to complete the
contrast, and is presumably leading towards blaming the current
violence on Blacks rather than the government. That is, he seems to
have been about to say that "the violence now started *because of*

the actions of blacks," or words to that effect. This counterassessment could be heard as a personal attack here, given that the IE is himself a Black South African and is present to speak under the auspices of that categorical identity. It is not completed, however, for IR aborts the utterance in midstream (notice the glottal stop at "st-"), and revises it so that the point is weakened (in the new version, Blacks are not overtly blamed for the violence), and is ascribed to "thuh government."

As Jefferson (1974) has observed, self-repair is not merely directed to problems of correctness and grammatical coherence. It is also aimed at repairing "interactional errors"; that is, mistakes in the attempt to speak appropriately to particular recipients in particular circumstances. The issue here is clearly not the correctness or coherence of the utterance, but its properly neutralistic footing.

4 IRs avoid affiliating with or disaffiliating from the statements they report. By means of the footing shift, IRs are able to indicate that the viewpoints they report originated elsewhere; in Goffman's terms, "authorship" is overtly deflected. But in addition to this basic action, IRs also systematically refrain from either endorsing or rejecting these views, so that the attributed party is nominated as the sole "principal" across the turn. A cursory examination of extracts (4)–(8) above will demonstrate that IRs simply do not comment on the views that they animate. This contrasts with what occurs in other contexts, where speakers may affiliate with or against opinions that ostensibly originated elsewhere. For example, in the following extract, taken from an ordinary conversation about windows, a speaker first asserts that a type of sliding window is "just as effective" (line 1), after which she animates the similar views of a third party who owns such windows (line 2). Hence, the animated assertion is introduced as evidence to support a position that the speaker has already taken (see also Pomerantz 1984b).

(9) [Rah:C:2:JSA(18):3]
1   J: It's (.) just as effective isn't it.
2   At least these people said it was,

And in the following (taken from a psychiatric intake interview) the speaker *first* animates the words of her husband (lines 1–2) and *then* exhibits equivocal agreement/disagreement (line 3).

```
(10) [PI:1]
 1    C:          An he says that my place is home with thuh
 2                children.=
 3                =I agree:. But I w- I need a rest.
```

News interviewers, in contrast, systematically refrain from aligning with or against the opinions they report. They do not reveal their own views before invoking the views of others, and they do not follow such views with their own comments. Accordingly, by declining to affiliate with/against statements involving others as principals, IRs do not project themselves as principals in their own right.

Of course, viewers may assume that the IR actually agrees (or disagrees) with what is reported. Such assumptions may be founded on impressions that the IR has "given off" (Goffman 1959: 2ff.) through facial expressions or tone of voice, background knowledge of his or her opinions, or even on the basis that "everyone agrees with that." But by virtue of the footing device, the IRs own position is (a) not stated, (b) not officially "on record" in the discussion, and, as a consequence, (c) the animated viewpoint is not something for which the IR or the employing news organization can be held responsible.

3.2 Contexts and uses of footing shifts

IRs make opinionated statements in a variety of contexts to accomplish a range of distinguishable activities. The footing device enables them to perform these tasks while maintaining a neutralistic posture. I shall briefly examine the most common activities for which the footing shift is used.

1 *Initiating a topic.* On many occasions, IRs make provocative statements to open the discussion, or to initiate a new topical line of talk. The following interview is opened by this procedure. In the taped "sound bite" that preceded this opening segment, Bishop Desmond Tutu expressed his view that the state of emergency recently imposed by the South African government would inhibit the achievement of peace. After introducing an IE (line 1–3) (who plainly represents the "other side," the position of the White South African government), the IR uses a particularly contentious assertion by Tutu (lines 5–6) to lead up to an opening question (line 7) concerning the state of emergency.

(11) [Macneil/Lehrer 7/22/85:1]

```
  1    IR:              ˙hhhhh We hear fir:st from thuh top South
  2                     African official in thuh United States. the
  3                     ambassador designate, Herbert Beukes. ˙hhhh
  4                     Mister Ambassador, (.)
  5    →               Bishop Tutu jus' said you cannot get peace
  6                     at the end of a gun.
  7                     Why is the state of emergency so necessary.
```

Bold assertions of this kind are convenient resources with which to
establish the relevance of an opening question and, by virtue of the
footing shift, IRs can utter them without being responsible for the
positions that they embody.

2 *Presenting the other side.* IRs also produce opinion statements to
counter an IE's previously stated position. These actions occur
within an IE/IR/IE turn sequence. In the following, HB's claim that
the intent of the state of emergency is to curb violence (lines 13–21)
is subsequently countered by the IR (lines 23–8), who invokes the
perspective of "thuh critics" (arrowed) to suggest that the real
purpose is to "suppress political dissent."

(12) [MacNeil/Lehrer 7/22/85a: 5]

```
  1    IR:              tch ˙hhh Why was it necessary to impose uh::
  2                     restrictions on thuh press both inside South
  3                     Africa an' outside South ⎡Africa.⎤
  4    HB:                                       ⎣˙hhhh ⎦Uh- (0.4)
  5                     it is: uh:- (0.3) not- anything unique...
  6                     ((6 lines omitted))
  7                     ... we have similarly considered those
  8                     ⎡necessary. ⎤
  9    IR:              ⎣˙hhhhhhhh ⎦ Under thuh theory that uh::
 10                     information causes people to act more
 11                     violent? or- or ⎡what is thuh the ⎤ory there.=
 12    HB:                              ⎣˙hhhhhhhhhh (um)⎦
 13    HB:              =W- w- we have eh seen on: uhm- f- film footage
 14                     ˙hh where people would be exploiting those
 15                     circumstances. Pa- participants in violence.
 16                     ˙hh that at times it is not clear whether some
 17                     of those ˙hh uh innocent people might become
 18                     victims ˙hh uh because of circumstances
 19                     created by eh- publicity. ˙hh and we would
 20                     just want to avoid any possible ˙hh uh
 21                     situation that might lead to more violence.
 22    IR:              Fin'lly Mister Ambassador as you know
```

```
23        →     thuh critics say that thuh purpose of thuh
24              state of emergency thuh real purpose of thuh
25              state of 'merjuh- uh state of emergency is to
26              supress political dissent. those who are
27              opposed to the apartheid goverment of South
28              Africa. Is that so
29              (.)
30   HB:        I would haff to: uh- take issue with that
31              premise. because...
```

By counterbalancing IEs' opinions with divergent and contrasting points of view, IRs give voice to "the other side" of controversial issues. This practice is consistent with traditional standards of fairness in broadcast journalism (Epstein 1973: 59–77; Gans 1979). The footing shift enables IRs to perform this task without jeopardizing their neutralism.

3 *Generating disagreement between interviewees.* IRs also animate opinion statements to generate disagreement between IEs. Hence, after one IE has finished speaking, IR may formulate the gist of that response (or some aspects of it) and address it to a co-IE to solicit a contrasting response. These actions occur within an $IE_1/IR/IE_2$ turn sequence. In the following, after NM (a Black leader in South Africa) explains recent violent resistance to apartheid, IR encapsulates the gist of his account to solicit a disagreement from HB (a representative of the South African government) (arrowed).

```
(13) [MacNeil/Lehrer 7/22/85a: 13-14] (Simplified)
 1   NM:        Tch ˙hhhh WE have ha::d (0.6) many many year:s
 2              (0.8) of peace in South Africa. (1.1) Thuh
 3              present unrest (.) is of recent origin. (1.2)
 4              Since nineteen twelve (1.3) at thuh time of
 5              union: (.) when (0.3) thuh white minority.
 6              (0.3) took power (0.8) to thuh total exclusion
 7              of (0.4) people who're not white (0.9) thuh
 8              African National Congress (.) has petitioned
 9              (0.7) has campaigned peacefully (1.0) for MOre
10              than forty years now. (0.5) in an attempt
11              (0.3) to ame:nd thuh constitution. (1.3) in
12              an attem' to get (.) POwer sharing for thuh
13              black majority. (0.6) they have been totally
14              unsuccessful. (0.4) An' one hass to take this
15              into acCO:unt. (0.4) when on:e (0.2) speaks
16              abou:t (0.2) thuh present spate of violence
17              in South Africa.
```

```
18                  (0.4)
19    IR:    →       Peace has not worked he says Mister
20                   Ambassador,
21    HB:            ˙hhhh Well he's referring to: uh=ay- (0.2) ay
22                   duh (.) period of time in: (.) uh f:ar distant
23                   h past. ˙hh What I'm concerned about and what
24                   we should be concerned about Doctor Motlana
25                   and uh (0.2) myself is here and now....
```

Such practices are common in "debate interviews," where IEs are present to represent contrasting points of view (Clayman 1987: 150–200; Greatbatch, this volume). In this context the footing shift enables the IR to generate an informal debate between IEs without collaborating with either side (see Maynard 1986). Moreover, by mediating the debate through such animated assertions, IRs can also exercise a degree of control over their topical development. Unlike simple response invitations (e.g. *How do you respond to that?*), animated statements or "formulations" (Heritage and Watson 1980; Heritage 1985) can be used selectively to target specific aspects of the previous answer for subsequent discussion, while focusing those aspects into a single dramatic point (Heritage 1985: 102–3). Hence, by manipulating footing, IRs can actively shape the course of the debate without entering it as a participant.

Thus far, virtually all of the examples have contained overt attributions placed prior to the animated item (e.g. *X says* + assertion). Yet in this particular context attributions are a little more flexible; as the previous example illustrates, they may follow the focal item. Overt attributions may even be omitted altogether when soliciting disagreement. Consider the following, where the IR animates aspects of DM's answer to invite a disagreement from LH (arrowed).

```
(14) [MacNeil/Lehrer 6/11/85a:7]
 1    DM:            ... In the pa:st I don't believe the
 2                   administration's clearly indicated what their
 3                   policy is. ˙hh Now:- I believe they're
 4                   making concessions. uh they gave ih- gave in
 5                   on Salt Two:, they're givin' in on the MX,
 6                   ˙hh an I think ther givin' in on: uh:: thuh-
 7                   thuh contras....
 8    IR:            You don't believe, Congressman Hamilton, that
 9           →       thee administration is making concessions or
10           →       has clarified its aims
11    LH:            hhem Well let me:: (.) point ou:t that uh:
```

| 12 | the administration's objectives (0.3) have |
| 13 | never been crystal clear... |

What appears to be at work here is the transparent visibility of a
footing shift when the original version is proximately available.
Given that the IR is making a point that has just been expressed in
the immediately preceding turn, his remarks are self-evidently ana-
lyzable from the outset as "belonging to" the preceding speaker.
Moreover, IR takes steps to secure this analysis by preserving some
of DM's original words ("making concessions," a formulation
which DM used in line 4). Notice that this differs from the previous
example – extract (13) above – which does not preserve any of the
IE's original words, but which contains an overt attribution. The
local availability of the original version, together with the preservation of its specific words, are resources that enable speakers
accountably to report another's views without explicitly naming the
responsible party (see Sacks 1966; Goffman 1981: 150).

4 *Defending against criticism.* Finally, IRs shift footings in hostile
environments in order to defend themselves against critical attacks.
In the following, this strategy is used to respond to an accusation
that IR has "demeaned" the president. The IE making the accusation is Pat Buchanan, who was recently appointed White House
Director of Communications for Ronald Reagan. Buchanan's accusation is occasioned by IR's initial question (lines 6–10) concerning
a much-quoted line from a Reagan speech that morally equated the
Nicaraguan Contras with the founding fathers of the United States.
IR asks PB if he wrote that line for Reagan. Before asking the
question, however, he indicates in a preliminary statement (lines 1–
6) that he is interested in whether or not Buchanan's own ideology is
influencing the tone of White House rhetoric. This occasions the
following exchange.

(15) [Nightline 6/3/85: 5-6]

1	IR:	Arrigh. ˙hhh let's- let's talk a little bit
2		about uh:: about Pat Buchanan's ideology and
3		how that is reflecting itself now::, in:: what
4		wur seeing coming outta thuh White House,
5		˙hhhh or to what degree you're simply a
6		reflection o'thuh President. ˙hhh that li:ne
7		about the: uh thuh moral equivalent of our

```
 8                  founding fathers you're talking about the-
 9                  (er-) thuh President was talking about thuh
10                  contras there was that your line?
11      PB:         ˙hhhh No:, that was uh Pres'dent's own lin:e.
12                  Ted, I didn't put it into his spee:ch....
13                  ((18 lines omitted))
14                  ...nobody puts wor::ds intuh thuh mouth of
15                  Ronald Reagan he goes over every single speech
16                  he delivers. ˙hhh An' when 'e delivers it ˙hh
17                  those words are what he belie::ves. ˙hh And
18                  I think it is rilly uh- ˙hh it demea:ns thuh
19                  President tuh suggest thet someone say Pat
20                  Buchanan or anyone el:se ˙hh is running down
21                  there at night sneaking phrases or (lines)
22                  ˙hhh intuh speeches and thuh President
23                  doesn't know what he's sayi⌐ng. ˙hhh ⌐
24      IR:                                     ⌊No Pat ⌋ I don't
25      →           think anyone's sug ⌐gest ⌐ing that, I think=
26      PB:                           ⌊(sure)⌋
27      IR:   →     =what people are suggesting is thet thuh
28                  President of thuh United States perhaps more
29                  than any other man or woman in thuh country
30                  is terribly terribly busy cannot possibly
31                  write every speech of 'is own, ˙hh or for that
32                  matter go over every speech line by line as
33                  you suggest. ⌐˙hhh ⌐Uh- an when that happens,=
34      PB:                     ⌊Mhm ⌋
35      IR:         =then people in positions such as your own,
36                  ˙hh can sometimes get some of their own
37                  ideas across.
```

PB denies authorship of the "founding fathers" line, attributing it to
Reagan instead (lines 11–12). He then accuses IR of "demeaning"
the president (lines 18–23) by suggesting that "someone say Pat
Buchanan or anyone el:se ·hh is running down there at night sneak-
ing phrases or (lines) ·hhh into speeches and thuh President doesn't
know what he's saying." In response, IR denies the accusation by
first negating it (lines 24–5) and then recharacterizing his prior
action (lines 27–37) so as to mitigate its "demeaning" character; in
the process, he places it on a different footing. Thus, he presents
himself as merely the animator of his previous words, which he now
attributes to people in general; the IR says that he does not think
that "anyone's suggesting that" (lines 24–5) and that "what people
are suggesting ..." (line 27). Through these words he invokes the

professional journalistic identity of one who speaks on behalf of the citizenry when interacting with government officials. Hence, insofar as his prior question could be heard to express a point of view, the footing shift deflects ownership of this viewpoint away from the IR personally and onto people in general. Furthermore, insofar as the expressed view could be heard to "demean" the president, responsibility for that action is similarly deflected.

It would appear, then, that the footing shift can serve a crucial defensive function precisely because of the manner in which it shields IRs from having to accept responsibility for their words. This defensive function may be observed "in action" when IRs invoke the footing shift to respond to informal criticisms and complaints from IEs. But even when no criticisms are actually voiced within the encounter, the footing shift may be regarded as defensive in a more general sense, since its use presumably furnished IRs with plausible grounds to deflect criticisms that may arise at a later time.[3]

4 The interviewee's response

It was argued at the beginning of this chapter that footing is properly understood as an interactionally achieved phenomenon. While a speaker may advance a particular footing within a given turn, its subsequent fate is contingent on other parties to the encounter and how they choose to respond. In light of this observation, we turn now to consider how IEs deal with footing shifts in their responses.

Given that IRs regularly animate contentious and challenging assertions, it is not surprising that IEs typically seek to counter or refute them. But what is less obvious is that while doing so they ordinarily refrain from treating the focal assertion as expressing the IR's personal opinion. The standard response, then, is to preserve the IR's neutralistic posture. To this end, three alternative courses of action are employed with roughly the same frequency. These practices range in character from those that officially validate and advance the IR's proposedly neutralistic stance, to those that merely avoid undermining that footing.

4.1 Attributing the antecedent assertion to the same third party

In the most validating type of response, the IE duplicates the attributional pattern that the IR had initiated; that is, by overtly ascribing

the focal assertion to the same third party. IEs commonly do this
when referring to the previously animated assertion just prior to
refuting it, as in the following.

(16) [Nightline 7/22/85: 17-18]

```
 1    IR:           Reverend Boesak lemme a- pick up a point uh
 2                  the Ambassador made.
 3                  What- what assurances can you give u:s ˙hh
 4                  that (.) talks between moderates in that
 5                  country will take pla:ce when it see:ms thet
 6                  any black leader who is willing duh talk to
 7                  thuh government is branded
 8                  as the Ambassador said a collaborator
 9                  and is then punished.=
10    AB:    →      =Eh theh- thuh- thuh Ambassador has it wrong.
11                  It's not thuh people who want to talk with
12                  thuh government that are branded collaborators
13                  it is: those people ˙hh who are given powers
14                  by thuh goverment that they use in an
15                  oppressive fashion ˙hh within thuh township
16                  that are branded collaborators....
```

In this case the IE's initial response is to negate the antecedent
assertion, first by declaring it to be "wrong" (line 10), and then by
reformulating it in negative form ("It's not thuh people ...") (lines
11–12). Only then does he proceed to produce a contrasting version
of his own (lines 13–16). But in the process of negating the previously animated assertion, he himself animates it and attributes it to
the same person ("the Ambassador") that the IR initially cited
(compare lines 1–2, 8).

A similar outcome is achieved in the following example, although
in this case the IE does not negate the antecedent assertion. He
merely reformulates it as a way of highlighting which specific points
will be rebutted (lines 9–12), and to express token agreement with
some aspects of the viewpoint (lines 13–16), before countering it
with an alternative (lines 17–20).

(17) [Nightline 6/6/85: 19-20) (Discussing efforts to dispose of nuclear waste)

```
 1    IR:           You heard what Doctor Yalow said earlier in
 2                  this broadcast she'll have an opportunity to
 3                  express her own opinions again but she seems
 4                  to feel thet it is an EMinently soluble
 5                  problem, and that ultimately that radioactive
 6                  material cun be reduced, to manageable
```

```
7                    quantities, 'n put in thuh bottom of a
8                    salt mine
9      JS:    →      Thuh p- thuh point that she was making earlier
10                   about (.) reprocessing of: thuh fuel rods goes
11                   right to thuh heart (.) of thuh way a lotta
12                   people look at this particular issue. 'hh If
13            →      ya look at reprocessing thuh points she made
14                   earlier were I think very good in terms of
15                   'hh thuh problems we had with reprocessing in
16                   this country. 'h being the economic factors...
17                   What (.) was also true in thuh reprocessing
18                   venture we had in west valley 'hh is thuh
19                   fact that reprocessing was a technological
20                   failure....
```

But once again, in the course of referring to the IR's animated
assessment, the IE ends up attributing it to the same person
(arrowed) that the IR had originally cited (cf. lines 1–3). This type
of response maximally ratifies and advances the IR's proposedly
neutralistic footing.

The previous extract has an additional feature relevant to the
preservation of footing. The IE's reformulated version of the focal
assessment preserves little of IR's animated version (which makes
the general claim that radio-active material can be reduced), returning instead to the original version to resurrect specific points that IR
had merely adumbrated (that waste reduction, as the original
speaker characterized it, involves reprocessing fuel rods). This is in
direct contrast to what occurred in extract (16), where the IE's
reformulated version preserves the same points as the IR's version,
and even repeats many of his specific words. Returning to the above
example, when the IE modifies the wording and focus of the assertion in this way, he provides further evidence that what is being
addressed in the rebuttal is not the IR's viewpoint, but rather a
viewpoint that was originally advanced at an earlier time.

4.2 Referencing the antecedent assertion without attributing it to anyone

IEs can preserve the IR's neutralistic stance without going so far as
to ascribe the focal assertion to a third party. A similar outcome may
be achieved by referring to the assertion without attributing it to
anyone in particular (arrowed in the following extracts).

(18) [MacNeil/Lehrer 7/22/85a: 5]
```
 1    IR:              Finally Mister Ambassador as you know thuh
 2                     critics say that thuh purpose of thuh state
 3                     of emergency thuh real purpose of thuh state
 4                     of 'merjuh- uh state of emergency is to
 5                     supress political dissent. those who are
 6                     opposed to the apartheid goverment of South
 7                     Africa.  Is that so
 8                     (.)
 9    HB:              I would haff to: uh- take issue with
10          →          that premise. because…
```

(19) [MacNeil/Lehrer 7/22/85a: 21-22]
```
 1    IR:              But all thuh people around the world, the
 2                     Common Market foreign ministers today:, thuh
 3                     Secretary: uh General: of thuh forty seven
 4                     member: uh British Commonweal:th, uh members
 5                     of thuh af- banned African National Congress,
 6                     'hhhh our guest Doctor Motlana, all say that-
 7                     an' the American statement we've just heard,
 8                     'hhh that thuh reason for thuh violence that
 9                     thuh state of emergency: is designed to sto:p,
10                     thuh reason for that violence, is thuh policy
11                     of apartheid.
12    HB:    →         'hhhh Now if: that is being said 'n for the
13                     argument it's being accepted, 'hh then:…
```

When the IE in extract (18) negates the antecedent assertion, he
refers to it as "that premise." Noticeably absent here is a possessive
pronoun that would attach it to the IR or to anyone in particular.
Extract (19) has an added feature: an attributive verb is formulated
in the passive voice ("Now if: that is being said"), thereby leaving its
agent unspecified.

This kind of anonymous treatment might initially appear to be a
simple reflection of the form of the original attribution. In both of
the above extracts the IR cited a collectivity rather than a specific
individual ("thuh critics" in extract (18), lines 1–2, and "all thuh
people around thuh world . . ." in extract (19), line 1) (see Halkowski 1986), making an anonymous treatment by IE particularly
appropriate. However, the IE may deal with the assertion anonymously even when a specific individual was previously cited, as in
the following (arrowed).

(20) [MacNeil/Lehrer 7/22/85a:9-10]
```
 1   IR:            'hhhh Mister Ambassador?  How d'you respond
 2                  to thuh- to Mister Motlana's last point, thet
 3                  thuh real issue: is: (0.3) political power
 4                  for thuh blacks an' until thuh goverment
 5                  gives it to 'em there's gonna be violence.
 6                  (0.3)
 7   HB:     →      tch It is 'n: issue, (0.3) it is a valid one,
 8                  (0.2) is very legitimate. (0.2) thuh question
 9                  of uh (.) participation in thuh political
10                  process of thuh country, by: blacks. 'hhh But
11                  th:is is not at issue (.) at duh mo:ment....
```

Accordingly, the use of an anonymous response form is not limited to occasions when IRs use an anonymous attribution. Rather, it constitutes a generic means of doing strictly "impersonal" disagreement; that is, designing a disagreeing turn so that it is countering an anonymous point of view, a perspective in general, rather than one that belongs to any particular person. In the present context this implicitly ratifies the IR's animator stance, for the target assertion is not attached to the IR or to anyone in particular.

4.3 Withholding any reference to the antecedent assertion

Finally, IEs may simply produce a contrasting assertion without referencing the prior assertion in any way. In this way, they refrain from exhibiting any official orientation to whose position is being countered.

(21) [MacNeil/Lehrer 7/22/85a:4]
```
 1   IR:            What d'you say to Bishop Tutu and others who
 2                  have said since the state of emergency was
 3                  declared that this will cause even more
 4                  violence rather than t'stop thuh violence
 5                  that's in effect
 6                  (0.4)
 7   HB:            Well- (0.2) it is pretty clear that something
 8                  hass to be do:ne. h'hh in order to stop thuh
 9                  violence. 'hh Now thuh state of emergency: uh
10                  is inTENded 'hh to clamp down on that
11                  violence. h'hh Uh to stop it somehow to (0.3)
12                  p- uh protect hh innocent people's lives. 'hh
13                  To protect dem: as being thuh victims: of uh-
14                  uh radicals who (.) do not see any 'hh reason
```

```
15                    for participating in a process 'hh that can
16                    hopefully lead h'h to a solution of thuh
17                    country's (.) political problems.
```

Unlike the response forms examined previously, this one cannot properly be characterized as validating, explicitly or implicitly, the IR's proposedly neutralistic stance. But it does not undermine that stance either, and this it shares with the other response forms. In each case IEs refrain from taking actions that would imply that the prior assertion is an expression of the IR's own point of view.

The only exceptions to this pattern occur when the IR did *not* shift footings, or when the IR's footing might be construed as ambiguous. An example of the former is contained in extract (22) below, in which the IR follows an interrogative preface (lines 1–2) with a direct assertion (lines 3–6), which the IE in turn treats as expressing the IR's own views (line 7): "I do not agree with you . . ."

(22) [MacNeil/Lehrer 7/22/85a:19] (FW is Deputy Assistant Secretary of State for African Affairs in the Reagan administration.)
```
1    IR:    But isn't this (.) d  declaration of thuh
2           state of emergency:: (0.3) an admission that
3           the eh South African government's policies
4           have not worked, an' in fact that the um-
5           United States (0.4) administration's policy of
6           constructive engagement (0.2) has not worked.
7    FW:    I do not agree with you 'hhh that the approach
8           we have taken (.) toward South Africa is- ay-
9           is an incorrect approach. 'hhhhh We want.
10          (0.8) tuh see that s- system change....
```

And in the following extended turn the IR's footing seems somewhat equivocal, and the IE chooses to ascribe the assessment to him personally. The IE here is the South African ambassador to the United States, and just prior to this exchange he had justified his government's imposition of a state of emergency by arguing that it was intended to stop violence of Blacks against Blacks.

(23) [Nightline 7/22/85:3-4]
```
1    IR:    Arright lemme talk about this question then
2           fer a moment of violence (.) of blacks against
3           blacks. 'hh We live here in thuh United States
4           in a country that was 'hhh eh founded on a
5           revolution 'hh and I suppose looking- ehh at
6           that revolution that occurred in- in- in our
```

```
7              country an back at th- in the eighteenth
8              century 'hhh I suppo:se thuh British could've
9              said there was violence occurring at that time
10             an they could've dismissed it as saying this
11             is violence of Americans against Americans.
12             'hhh But thuh point was there was violence at
13             that time 'hh uh between: what we now call
14             Patriots 'hh an people in this country who
15             were considered to be allied with thuh
16             British. 'hhh And so when there is violence
17             of blacks against blacks ih- it may be
18             occCURring that way but nobody questions what's
19             causing it. 'hhh What is causing the anger an
20             thuh violence in South Africa is apartheid.
21             An that is something 'hh over which your
22             goverment obviously ha:s (0.2) control.
23      HB:    'hhhh Uhm (0.4) uh Charlie I will not quarrel
24             with you: that an important uh hh aspect here
25             an important issue 'hh 's thuh question of
26             dealing with thuh political situation....
```

The IR here is drawing an analogy between Black violence in South
Africa and political violence in revolutionary America. In detailing
the American case (lines 3–16), he produces several relatively non-
controversial or "factual" statements (that the United States was
founded on revolution [lines 3–5], and that there was violence then
between patriots and those allied with Britain [lines 12–16]) in an
unmitigated fashion, while he attributes a more evaluative assessment (that US violence amounted to violence of Americans against
Americans [lines 8–11]) to "thuh British." When he arrives at the
extended upshot of the analogy (lines 16–22), his footing is equivocal. He first notes that "nobody questions what's causing" the
present violence (lines 18–19), setting up a kind of puzzle that
works to slightly distance himself from the subsequent assessment
("What is causing the anger an thuh violence in South Africa is
apartheid") (lines 19–30) by implying that it is believed by "everyone" (the contrast category for "nobody"). However, the final
statement (lines 21–2) is asserted directly, without attribution. In
response to this equivocal footing, HB produces a "personal" form
of rebuttal ("Charlie I will not quarrel with you: ..."), thereby
selecting out one possible interpretation of the IR's assessment (as
representing the IR's own views) and incorporating that interpretation into his own turn.

As contrasting cases, these two examples further demonstrate that IEs, by commenting implicitly on the footing of the previous turn, contribute to its developing sense as "neutral" or otherwise. This is one implication of the standard response types examined in this section: they help to constitute and sustain retrospectively the footing of the antecedent turn by declining to treat it as expressing the IR's personal beliefs. Indeed, the first two response forms examined above actively deal with the prior assessment either as belonging to a third party or as belonging to no one in particular. As a result, the visibility of the footing shift, and the neutralism it proposes, is extended across the interaction by incorporating it presumptively into subsequent turns. It might be said that IEs actively collaborate to preserve the IR's neutralistic posture.

5 Constituting credibility

Although IRs ordinarily refrain from affiliating with their more opinionated statements, this does not mean that they produce such statements with equal weight. They can influence the truth value or epistemic weight of what they report by the terms used to characterize the responsible party.[4] Since there are a large variety of ways that any individual or collectivity may be formulated (see Sacks 1972a), IRs can select those formulations that either enhance or detract from the source's credibility. Note that this does not necessarily entail a departure from neutralism; IRs can comment on the party advocating a position without personally aligning with or against the position itself. But it does mean that positions may be endowed with varying degrees of credibility as they are animated. As we shall see, it is more common for IRs to enhance (rather than detract from) credibility in this manner, thereby placing IEs in the position of having to respond to compelling alternative points of view. Moreover, this proposed credibility often becomes an issue for IEs, who frequently attempt to undermine it in the course of responding.

5.1 Commenting on the source's authoritativeness

IRs may weight the credibility of a position by commenting on the authority of its source. Generally speaking, cited third parties in news interviews tend to be government officials, certified experts, or other authoritative spokespersons, and they are usually referenced

by their official titles (e.g. *Senator X, Doctor Y*). Other spokespersons tend to be referenced as *Mr./Ms.* where their authoritative
status has already been established. However, the IR may go to
extra lengths to comment on the authoritativeness of the source.

In the following, a critical assessment of the US government's
failure to join the Soviet Union's moratorium on nuclear-weapons
testing (lines 13–14) is endowed with credibility in this way (lines
8–12).

```
(24) [Nightline 10/6/86: CT5]
 1    FG:      ...We don't like hh (.) uh (.) having::
 2             arguments made which we feel are ˙hh uh (.)
 3             not only not (0.9) contributing to:: (0.3)
 4             positive and effective arms control, ˙hhh
 5             uh but we of course don't like having people
 6             (0.3) e- misrepresenting: our view of what
 7             would constitute (.) effective arms control.
 8    IR:      We:ll now when a former President of the
 9             United Sta:tes, and a man who knows a little
10             something about nuclear weapons, having
11             ser:ved on a nuclear submari:ne and was
12             himself an engineer, when Jimmy Carter calls
13             it an embarrassment. ˙hhh tuh have thee
14             United States not (.) match the ba:n, uh:
15             not exactly a lightweight.
16    FG:      ˙hhh Thuh President of the United States
17             today:, is Ronald Reagan. and the President
18             (0.3) has seen our problem very clearly, ˙hh
19             as one of ensuring:, (0.4) as long as we have
20             to rely upon nuclear weapons for deterrence,
21             ˙hh that we: (.) can do so with confidence.
22             and that requires testing them
```

Here an overt reference to the source's status as a former president
(lines 8–9), a formulation of his knowledge of the issue (lines 9–10),
and an enumeration of the experiential bases of that knowledge
(lines 11–12) each precede the reported assessment (lines 13–14).
Further, the assessment is followed by a statement (line 15) summarizing the cumulative upshot of these character descriptions: "not
exactly a lightweight." The negative characterization is the "least"
that can be said, given the prior descriptions, and thus stands as an
accountably understated assessment of competence, which the IR
has shown to be substantial.

This displayed credibility is not without its interactional consequences. As the IE constructs his rebuttal, he attends to the authority proposed through this device and attempts to outdo it by
ascribing his own counterassessment to the current president (lines
16–17). One president's views are thus invoked to counter another.
Indeed, the IE engages in a bit of one-upmanship here by noting,
prior to the counterassessment, that his presidential source is *presently* in office (note the stressed temporal formulation "today" in
line 17), thus implying that the counterassessment to follow is
perhaps a little more authoritative. In addition, when the IE actually
begins to deliver the counterassessment ("and the President has seen
our problem very clearly . . ."), he formulates its author as "the
President", thus choosing the full categorical reference form which
maximally accentuates the person's official status (cf. "President
Reagan," "he," etc.).

Now it could be argued that this move is not necessarily tied to
the credibility issue, since the IE is a defense department official and
is being interviewed as an administration spokesperson. But this
interactional identity does not require that IE's statements be attributed specifically to the president. It is perfectly possible for him to
speak on behalf of the administration by using the pro-term "we,"
which he employs in his previous turn (lines 1–2, 5–6). Hence,
reference to the president here appears to be responsive to the IR's
prior attribution, and the credibility exhibited through it, by proposing that the counterassessment is endorsed by someone who is at
least as authoritative, if not more so.

5.2 Commenting on the range of persons endorsing a position

Overt competence displays like the above are rare, and it is more
common for IRs to influence the credibility of what they report by
commenting on the range of persons who believe it. This procedure
plays on the common-sense dichotomy between the subjective and
variable nature of "mere impressions" versus the objective reality of
"hard facts." Given such a dichotomy, the number of persons
aligned with a given statement can be seen as an index of its facticity.
Thus, a widely endorsed viewpoint is not easily dismissed as the
idiosyncratic artefact of a particular person's understanding, for

such support endows it with a certain intersubjective validation (see
Pomerantz 1986).

In practice, animated assessments are often attributed to a single
individual, where the range of persons who might agree is left
unstated. However, assessments are sometimes ascribed to a collectivity, the nature of which can be indicative of the position's popu-
larity and, consequently, its facticity. For example, assessments may
be downgraded by indicating that they are not widely held (arrowed
in the following extract).

```
(25) [Nightline 6/5/85: 3]
 1    WA:           ...Business Week uh just about a week aGO:.
 2                  ˙h uh had a front (.) page story entitled ˙hh
 3                  do m:ergers really work ˙h An' the answer was
 4                  ˙h n:ot very oft┌en.            ┐
 5    IR:                           └Ya-┘ they- they clearly don't
 6                  believe it does, but Mister Forbes let me turn
 7                  to you because I must tell you in- in uh:
 8                  doing our research today we found very other
 9        →         (.) I=mean very few other people, ˙hh uh- who
10                  believe thet it is in any way BA:d.
11                  Now do you believe thet it- I me- uh- let's
12                  forget about bad for a moment=d'you believe
13                  its GOO:d. (0.4) Does it do anyone any good.
14                  (0.3) Does it do thuh public any good. Does
15                  it do thuh consumer any good.
16                  (0.7)
17    MF:           Sure it uh:- ub- ˙hh eh:: thuh PA:ST eh-
18                  you can learn from it....
```

In this example WA has been building the argument that corporate
mergers tend to be unproductive; he concludes by citing as evidence
a *Business Week* article making just this point (lines 1–4). The IR
solicits a response to this position from MF (lines 11–15), but he
first comments on the unpopularity of WA's position (lines 5–10).
His initial statement ("they- they clearly don't believe it does")
emphasizes the word "they," thus implying that others would probably disagree. He then says as much explicitly (lines 8–10) before
asking MF to respond.

In advocacy interviews, it is exceedingly uncommon for IRs to
downgrade the credibility of an expressed position in this manner.
More commonly, IRs enhance what they are saying by indicating
that the position has more general support. In the following an

assessment that South Africa is on the brink of violent disorder or
revolution (lines 7–9) is attributed to a collectivity of recent program guests (lines 5–6, arrowed).

(26) [MacNeil/Lehrer 7/25/85a: 6] (SD is advocating economic sanctions
against South Africa.)

```
 1   SD:          ...and we've got to try: thuh remaining
 2                steps that are open.
 3                (0.2)
 4   IR:          ˙hhhh Mister Chettle what d'you say duh those
 5        →       who: people who've said this on our program
 6        →       several times now:: uh in thuh last uh few
 7                weeks, that ˙hh TIMe is running out in South
 8                Africa. >that something must b- must be done:
 9                (.) or thuh whole thing is gonna go up
10   JC:          Well- eh that's been said fuh thuh last
11                twenty five years:. and I've heard it pretty
12                continuously ever since then:. uh: I don't
13                (.) uh think thet that's true....
14                ((9 lines omitted))
15                ...Freedom House issued (.) a statement uh::
16                the annual (.) survey of freedom around thuh
17                worl:d ˙h which showed that South Africa ˙h
18                >had only got< on:e country in thuh whole of
19                Africa that=had more freedom in it....
```

The generality of this view is subtly highlighted by several devices.
The I R appends a numerical formulation (the phrase "several times
now::" [line 6]) to characterize the "people who've said this on our
program", and this phrase is stressed intonationally. Moreover, it is
followed by a temporal formulation ("in thuh last uh few weeks"
[lines 6–7]) indicating that these convergent assessments have
emerged recently. Considered as a whole, the resulting attribution
proposes that the animated viewpoint is becoming increasingly
popular, and may represent an emerging consensus.

In rebutting this viewpoint, J C first orients to the credibility
proposed through the "emerging consensus" attribution and
attempts to undermine it (lines 10–13). He does not actually deny
that there is something of a consensus on the imminence of revolution, but he casts doubt on its credibility by noting that people have
been saying that South Africa is on the verge of violent disorder or
revolution "for thuh last twenty five years:." The upshot, which
remains implicit, is that since revolution has plainly not occurred
during this time, such predictions have regularly been misguided,

and the more recent predictions that the IR is referring to are apt to
be misguided as well. Note that this way of casting doubt is designed
specifically to show that the sheer number of persons endorsing a
position is no guarantee of its facticity. It is only after JC has
undercut the credibility of the "consensus" view in this manner that
he proceeds to counter it substantively (lines 15–19).

Finally, notice that in spite of the fact that the IR has upgraded
the credibility of the initial assertion, he has not personally affiliated
with it; and JC treats it "anonymously" (lines 10–13), that is, as an
anonymous point of view and not one that is held specifically by the
IR.

In a more extreme upgrading, the IR may straightforwardly
claim that a viewpoint is universally held. This occurs in the following (see especially line 7), when the IR animates a viewpoint to
dispute the explanation for the state of emergency in South Africa
offered by the South African ambassador to the United States (HB).

(27) [MacNeil/Lehrer 7/22/85a: 22]
```
 1    HB:          ... And that is thuh issue of (0.2) violence.
 2                 ˙hh An' if we can get out of that cycle
 3                 exactly to break hh that cycle. ˙hh I think
 4                 it'll be:- uh in the interest of everybody ˙h
 5                 to get then to thuh point (0.3) of dealing
 6                 with peaceful reforms.=
 7    IR:          =But all thuh people around thuh world
 8                 the Common Market foreign ministers today:
 9                 thuh Secretary: uh General: of thuh forty
10                 seven member: uh British Commonweal:th uh
11                 members of the af- banned African National
12                 Congress, ˙hhhh our- our guest Doctor Motlana
13                 all say that- an' the American statement we've
14                 just heard ˙hhh that thuh reason for thuh
15                 violence that thuh state of emergency: is
16                 designed to sto:p, thuh reason for that
17                 violence, is thuh policy of apartheid.
18    HB:          ˙hhhh Now if: that is being said 'n for the
19                 argument it's being accepted. ˙hh then: (0.3)
20                 uh- to do so: an to deal with it in ay
21                 peaceful manner. (0.4) you haff to get away
22                 from thuh point of violence. (0.2) As long as
23                 thuh violence 'uh cycle violence continues
24                 (0.2) there is no hope (0.3) to deal with
25                 it in any rational way.
```

After asserting the upcoming viewpoint is believed by "all thuh people around thuh world," the IR goes on to enumerate a list of five parties (lines 8–14) who "all say that-" apartheid is at the root of the current violence. Note that after the fourth party the IR begins to launch into the assessment component (line 13) but cuts off to add a fifth before proceeding. In one sense this list works to support the initial assertion that the viewpoint is universally endorsed by providing concrete instances of its adherants. But the listing format also seems to be a particularly strong way of doing this, in part because it plays off the rhetorical force associated with listlike constructions (Atkinson 1984; Heritage and Greatbatch 1986); the collection reads like a litany and is significantly longer than the three-part structure that lists ordinarily have (Jefferson 1990). Furthermore, by listing, the IR is also able to display each party's official status. But what is particularly interesting is that the resulting credibility is apparently consequential for HB's response. Notice that HB does not attempt to dispute the assessment directly; he "grudgingly" allows it (lines 18–19) and then resists its larger implications (that the state of emergency would not be necessary if apartheid were dismantled).

And like the previous examples, even though the IR has enhanced the credibility of this viewpoint quite dramatically, he has still not gone on record with a personal endorsement. Correspondingly, HB treats the assertion anonymously ("if: that is being said ...") (line 18), thus sustaining the IR's proposedly neutralistic footing.

6 Discussion

This analysis has implications for the nature and practice of journalistic neutrality within the framework of a news interview. More generally, there are ramifications for our understanding of the relationship between footing as a generic speaking practice and as a resource that can be adapted to, and is constitutive of, the work of professional journalism. I shall address these issues in turn.

6.1 Formal neutrality within the news interview

This has been a study of one method by which a neutralistic posture is produced and sustained in news interviewing. In pursuit of this stance, interviewers can shift footings when producing evaluative or controversial assertions. But this generates what is best understood as a provisional posture whose fate is contingent on how the interviewee subsequently deals with it. On occasion, an interviewee may treat the antecedent assertion as a reflection of the interviewer's own opinions; in the present data, this only happens when the interviewer does not shift footings, or when the interviewer's footing is recognizably ambiguous. Ordinarily, in the course of responding, interviewees decline to treat the antecedent assertion in this manner, thereby implicitly preserving the interviewer's neutralistic footing and extending its visibility across the interaction. This means that neutralism, insofar as it becomes a sustained feature of the encounter, requires the cooperation of the interviewee. Correspondingly, the footing through which it is achieved is also a collaborative production.

This analysis runs contrary to common-sense notions of neutrality as a trait inhering in interviewers as individuals, or an attribute of their conduct in specific situations. From an analytic perspective, the visibility of this journalistic "trait" is a joint achievement of interactants acting in concert to preserve a professional posture for interviewers. In other words, neutrality is a socially organized, or more specifically an interactionally organized phenomenon, something that parties to an interview "do together."

It is possible to conceive of the footing shift as a strategy that permits interviewers to smuggle their own beliefs into the discussion while claiming that they belong to someone else. Plainly, the footing shift *can* be used strategically in this sense; but it cannot be used with impunity, precisely because of the genuine resources that interviewees have to shape the interaction as it develops. Put simply, interviewers cannot say just *anything* and get away with it, for they are necessarily constrained by the interviewees and how they choose to respond. This should provide a corrective to the viewpoint that news interviewers are inherently powerful and able to dominate their guests at will (e.g. Owsley and Scotton 1984). Such work ignores the concrete opportunities that interviewees have to participate in the interaction and fashion whatever course it eventually takes.

It would be equally misleading to hold that interviewers are subservient to public figures, either those present as interviewees or those whose accounts are regularly imported into the encounter. It is sometimes argued that since professional standards of objectivity require that journalists ground all contentious assertions in the statements of institutional news sources, news inevitably comes to reflect official interpretations of events. While this does indeed capture an important and pervasive fact of journalistic life, it tends to overlook some important subtleties inherent in the news-production process. Although journalists are largely dependent upon source accounts, they determine precisely how those accounts will enter into the final news product, including the credibility with which they are endowed. Thus, in news interviews, the accounts of copresent interviewees are frequently subjected to challenge, while third-party accounts are frequently "weighted" as more or less credible. Hence news interviewers are dependent on the accounts of authoritative public figures, but they are not wholly subservient to them (see also Tuchman 1972; Fishman, 1980: 109–33). A comprehensive analysis of the news-production process must take into account not only the structural constraints that journalists confront, but also their enabling strategies and resources for achieving a measure of working autonomy.

6.2 Footing as interactional practice and journalistic skill

The footing shift is by no means restricted to the domain of journalistic practice. Across a variety of settings, interactants have the option of speaking on their own behalf, or on behalf of another or a collection of others, or on behalf of themselves and others jointly; and there are more or less standard ways of indicating which of these is being done. But the formal properties of this practice, and the fact that it is not setting-specific, should not blind the analyst to the diversity of specific tasks that may be pursued in and through it. For example, it is precisely because interactants are able to report the words and views of others that they can tell stories involving others as speakers; they can as a consequence recount a conversation, pass gossip, and so on. They may also act as the official or unofficial agent of a third party by representing that party in an ongoing negotiation; as a consequence, one member of a family can express the dining preferences of a nonpresent member, a lawyer can plea bargain on a client's behalf (Maynard 1984: 55–76), and so on. Finally, in the context of interpersonally "delicate" actions like disagreements,

criticisms, and accusations, interactants can be cautious or circumspect by attributing such actions to others (Pomerantz 1984b). What
specific activity is involved in any instance is discoverable by examining the detailed manner in which the footing shift is deployed in
its local context. The challenge for the analyst of news interviewing
(or any other institutional form of talk involving the footing shift) is
to determine its particular function for the practitioner, and what, if
anything, is "institutional" – or in this case "journalistic" – about it.

Even within a setting like the news interview, a variety of stable
and recurrent activities may be distinguished. Interviewers commonly shift footings to display provocative viewpoints for subsequent topical development, to counter an interviewee and thus
give voice to "the other side" of an issue, and to generate disagreement between interviewees. Such distinctions notwithstanding,
these are all standard interviewing tasks, and they share one feature
in common. Without the footing shift, they would each show the
interviewer to be taking a position on a controversial public issue;
with it the interviewer remains personally disengaged from the
substance of what he or she is saying. By virtue of these practices,
interviewers are able to give voice to controversial points of view
without going on record as endorsing such views. They can introduce opinions to challenge an interviewee, but not as a matter of
personal expression. Accordingly, they can fulfil the complex
journalistic requirement, put forth in the standard interviewing
textbooks (e.g. Lewis 1984: 117–28), of being interactionally
"adversarial" while remaining officially "neutral."

Further evidence that neutralism is specifically at issue can be
gleaned by reconsidering the precise manner in which such shifts are
actualized. When they are restricted to controversial opinion statements, when they are reiterated during specific evaluative words,
when interviewers self-repair to shift footings, and when they
decline to align themselves with or against the reported statements,
they methodically exhibit a concern to avoid the overt expression of
opinion. Correspondingly, interviewees appear to operate under the
auspices of a default assumption that interviewers' own opinions are
not at issue; hence, they regularly decline to implicate interviewers
or hold them responsible for what was said, thereby validating the
"journalistic" character of what is taking place. While recipient
responses to footing shifts have not yet been examined systemati-

cally in mundane conversation, it seems unlikely that such a default assumption of neutrality would be operative.[5]

So it is not the case that a generic practice like the footing shift can be straightforwardly imported into an institutional setting like the news interview and be expected to do that institution's distinctive work. If that were possible, then talking would be akin to laying bricks, and institutional talk would be a mere aggregate of immutable speaking practices. Such practices must be adapted and specialized in subtle ways, used in concert with other relevant practices, and thus tailored to the particular tasks at hand. Accordingly, it is through the context-sensitive deployment of formal interactional practices that a sequence of talk betrays its "institutional" character. And it is precisely through such specialized sequences of talk that social institutions are incrementally constituted.

Notes

1. By characterizing this as a *formally neutral* or *neutralistic* posture, I am following a usage initiated by Heritage and Greatbatch (1991) to distinguish descriptive analyses (like this one) from efforts to pass judgment on interviewers' neutrality in a *substantive* sense. Interviewers use certain formal speaking practices to avoid overtly expressing an opinion, and thus propose that they are being neutral, but whether this would hold up "in court" in light of all other aspects of program content is a matter that I do not claim to be addressing. It can be argued that "bias" enters in through a whole range of other channels: though the selection of topical agendas and interviewees, through differential treatment given to various categories of interviewees, through facial expressions and tone of voice, and so on. Nevertheless, it is possible to examine specific speaking practices that interviewers routinely employ to construct at least an appearance of neutrality as they interact with their guests, while making no ontological claims about whether such practices can be equated with neutrality in an absolute or ideal sense. Studies by Heritage (1985), Clayman (1988), Greatbatch (1988), and Heritage and Greatbatch (1991) approach the news interview from a similar analytic perspective. For complementary analyses of "objectivistic" practices in other arenas of journalistic work, see Tuchman (1972), Fishman (1980: ch. 5), and Robinson and Sheehan (1983).
2. The data were gathered from a variety of US network television news-interview programs in 1985. The primary corpus consists of ten full interviews taken from five different programs, for a total of approximately three hours of interviewing time. These interviews were transcribed in accordance with a system devised by Gail Jefferson. This

primary corpus was itself drawn nonsystematically from a much larger set of recordings amounting to thirty-three full programs. While only the three-hour subset was selected for detailed transcription and analysis, less detailed commercially prepared transcripts were obtained for the balance of the collection, and these were consulted on an *ad hoc* basis for exploratory purposes, and to verify the generality of particular phenomena.

3. For example, this practice might also be useful to address formal attacks that can be mounted after the occasion of the interview, such as legal charges of libel. On this point, see Tuchman (1972).

4. In a complementary analysis, Sacks (1992 [4 March 1971]) observes that when speakers are engaged in quoting others verbally, they can imply their own alignment towards what they are saying through the tone of voice they choose to adopt. In such cases, the speaker's views are conveyed without being stated explicitly.

5. Research on preference organization generally supports the idea that neutrality is not the operative assumption in ordinary conversation. Minimal and equivocal responses to invitations, offers, requests, and proposals are often *not* taken to be evidence of recipient's neutrality; such responses are instead hearable as constituting actual or potential rejection (Davidson 1984). Similarly, equivocal responses to assessments are treated as disagreement implicative (Pomerantz 1984a). As Paul Drew and John Heritage suggested to me in a personal communication, conversationalists seem to operate around a polarity of affiliation/disaffiliation, such that each acts under the assumption that the other is either "with me or against me."

6

Displaying neutrality: formal aspects of informal court proceedings

J. MAXWELL ATKINSON

1 Introduction: formality, informality, and conversation analysis

Debates about the relative merits of different types of court procedure are regularly based on assessments of the degree of "formality" involved at different points in the processing of cases. Such discussions are predominantly evaluative in character, and recent years have seen a number of moves, such as the introduction of various kinds of arbitration and conciliation procedures, which reflect a fairly widespread view that it is desirable to establish less formal methods for settling disputes.

Whether their interest in the relationship between formality and informality is evaluative or analytic, there are at least three important issues which are often ignored or taken for granted: the first is the question of just what it is about certain actions, events, and arrangements that gives rise to their being designated as "formal" rather than "informal"; the second has to do with why it is that participants sometimes produce actions which are instantly recognizable to others as "formal"; and the third is the question of what relevance, if any, such ways of behaving have for the just and efficient conduct of cases.

These questions have been central to the development of a program of empirical research into courtroom language and interaction at the Oxford Centre for Socio-Legal Studies. As has been discussed in more detail elsewhere (Atkinson and Drew 1979; Atkinson 1981, 1982; Pomerantz and Atkinson 1984), this work has depended heavily on a model for the analysis of "formal" interaction which derives from the discussion by Sacks, Schegloff, and Jefferson (1974: 729) about the potential for using the approach and findings of conversation analysis to develop a "comparative analysis of speech exchange systems."

The aim of the present chapter, however, is not to rehearse the theoretical and methodological case for working within such a framework. Rather, it is to present a brief report on one particular study, together with some fleeting reflections on the broader implications it might have for our understanding of the relationship between different ways of talking and the practical accomplishment of legal objectives.

2 Preliminary observations

The main data for this study are audio-tape recordings of hearings which took place in the London Small Claims Court before its closure through lack of financial support in 1981. It was one of several independent courts established throughout the United Kingdom and operated under the terms of legislation on arbitration procedures. In this particular court, both parties were required to agree beforehand to be bound by the decision of the arbitrator, and neither party was permitted to employ legal counsel to present a case. The hearings were usually conducted around a table in an office at the Polytechnic of Central London, with the parties to the dispute, the arbitrator, and the clerk of the court being the only persons present. On occasions, such as when the plaintiff was elderly or disabled, hearings would be held in people's own homes.

In the absence of legal counsel, parties were expected to present their own cases. In practice, however, evidence was usually elicited in the form of answers to questions from the arbitrator, and a typical sequence is reproduced below as fragment (1):

(1) London Small Claims Court: BS (Simplified Transcript)

Arbitrator:	So (0.2) you explained the design (0.3) that you wanted?
Plaintiff:	In very general terms, I said I had this kind of thing in mind and what did he think of it, and so on and so on – he drew the thing and said "Well that's OK. I can put that together for you" kind of thing. (0.3)
Arbitrator:	Certainly (0.3) And (.) did you specify any (0.4) particular material for the (1.0) sh– uh sandals? (.)
Plaintiff:	No I didn't. (1.4)

Arbitrator:	You left that up to his judgement?
	(.)
Plaintiff:	Yes (0.2) He showed me some of the materials he had in the shop, but actually I had no view about the materials used – I merely wanted a pair of wearable sandals.
	(0.7)
Arbitrator:	Certainly (1.2) And when you talk about a 'bespoke sandal' (0.2) this is one made (0.3) to your (0.3) order.
	(0.5)
Plaintiff:	Uh (0.4) when you say to my order, ehm I would expect to get a wearable pair of sandals out of it – ehm ah – it was done in discussion with Mr (NAME) he and I talked about it uhh (1.8) I think yes it's fair to say that he said that the sandals would be (0.3) acceptable.
Arbitrator:	Certainly (0.6) eh– can we now (0.3) look at the (0.2) uh (0.7) dispute between the two of you about fittings (1.0) You say that there was only one.

Although this may initially seem to bear a superficial resemblance to an examination sequence from any other type of court, there are several details which mark it out as being very different. One is that the arbitrator regularly starts his utterances by saying "Certainly," thereby acknowledging receipt of what the plaintiff has just said. By contrast, the use of such receipt markers is very rare in other types of examination sequences, where counsel more usually respond to a witness's answer by going straight ahead and asking an unprefaced next question, as in example (2):

(2) US Criminal Court (Simplified Transcript)

Counsel:	Did you ever receive any telephone calls from him?
Witness:	No.
Counsel:	Did the defendant ever request a date with you?
Witness:	No.
Counsel:	On February 14th, 1975, you were what, eighteen years old at that time?
Witness:	Yes.

Here, the only acknowlegments of the witness's answers are counsel's next questions, which are all she has to go on when it comes to analyzing his response. Under such circumstances, it is presumably difficult for a witness to come to any conclusions about what counsel made of a just-completed utterance until the next question has been asked. And this problem of trying to work out, solely on the basis of each next question, how counsel is responding to the answers is almost certainly one of the factors which give rise to the feelings of nervousness, bewilderment, and intimidation that are so often reported by people who have been subjected to court-room examination or cross-examination.

By contrast, the arbitrator's practice of acknowledging receipt before going on to the next question may be one way of helping to reduce or mitigate the kind of uncertainty that is involved in situations where the only acknowledgment an answer receives is an unprefaced next question. Unlike the situation where a witness has to wait to see what the next question consists of, starting a turn by marking receipt of what went before gives the other party at least some indication that the just-completed utterance was received and understood. If this is a technique which works to reduce some of the tensions normally associated with appearing in court, then two questions are worthy of further consideration: the first is that of whether it is something which Small Claims Court arbitrators do recurrently, or whether fragment (1) is merely an isolated instance; and the second is that of how this method of responding to witnesses compares with the methods used in other contexts. A search through the Small Claims Court tapes shows that cases where arbitrators mark receipt of a prior utterance as a preface to asking a next question are fairly common. And, as is evident from fragments (1) and (3)–(5), such sequences also recurrently exhibit various other common properties.

One is that they invariably occur after a plaintiff or defendant has elaborated his answer considerably beyond what had been projected by the question. The commonest form of this is where the question projects an answer of *yes* or *no*, but where the speaker in fact responds by doing something which is either different from, or additional to, the projected minimal response. For example, at one point in fragment (1) the plaintiff refrains altogether from producing a *yes* or *no*:

(1) (Excerpt)

Arbitrator:	So (0.2) you explained the design (0.3) that you wanted.
Plaintiff:	In very general terms. I said I had this kind of thing in mind and what did he think of it, and so on and so on – he drew the thing and said "Well that's OK. I can put that together for you" kind of thing. (0.3)
Arbitrator:	Certainly (0.3) And (.) did you specify any (0.4) particular material for the (1.0) sh– uh sandals?

Elsewhere, he carries on considerably beyond an initial "Yes":

(1) (Excerpt)
    Arbitrator: You left that up to his judgement?
              (.)
    Plaintiff: Yes (0.2) He showed me some of the materials he had in the shop, but actually I had no view about the materials used – I merely wanted a pair of wearable sandals.
              (0.7)
    Arbitrator: Certainly (1.2) And when you talk about a 'bespoke sandal (0.2) this is one made (0.3) to your (0.3) order.

From these examples, it can be seen that the arbitrator does not just mark receipt as soon as the prior speaker has finished, but delays slightly before doing so. He then pauses again before going on to ask the next question. As will be seen from the following, these details recur in different Small Claims Court hearings, and therefore emerge as constituting not just a particular type of turn, but a particular type of recurring *sequence* with six distinct stages:

1 *Arbitrator*: [PROJECTION OF MINIMAL RESPONSE]

2 *Litigant*:   [NON-MINIMAL RESPONSE]

3   [PAUSE]

4 *Arbitrator*: [RECEIPT]

5   [PAUSE]

6   [QUESTION]

Another example of such a sequence from the same hearing as fragment (1) occurs when the arbitrator is questioning the cobbler who made the allegedly faulty sandals:

(3) London Small Claims Court: BS (Simplified Transcript)
1.   Arbitrator: They'd be black leather with a cross front?
2.   Defendant: Yes, cross front (1.0) of soft leather as Mister (NAME) asked me to.
3.   (1.2)
4.   Arbitrator: Yes.
5.   (0.4)
6.   and the heel (0.8) is as for an ordinary shoe?

The following are some examples of the same sequence from other hearings presided over by different arbitrators:

(4) London Small Claims Court: DDC (Simplified Transcript)
1.   Arbitrator: The question is where on the belt is ⌈the damage?
2.   Plaintiff: ⌊Somewhere on the
                   belt. Somewhere on the back of this collar. I mean I don't
                   walk round like that all day long you know.
3.   (1.0)
4.   Arbitrator: Okay
5.   (.)
6.   And now if I can just briefly state what the law is on the
                   point …

(5) London Small Claims Court: RBA (Simplified Transcript)
1.   Arbitrator: I take it that the sign writing is done at the factory
                   premises.
2.   Defendant: Signwriting is done at the factory premises, the cover is
                   manufactured (0.5) it is then sign written by the sign
                   writer and then it's mounted on the frame that we
                   collected from (   ) Jewels.
3.   (1.5)
4.   Arbitrator: Yes.
5.   (.)
6.   Now are there any other points that you would like to
                   bring out, questions you want asked …

   The identification of a recurring sequence type raises a number of intriguing questions about its interactional implications, how it works, and whether or not it has any bearing on the practical accomplishment of any of the Small Claims Court's legal objectives. One way of beginning to shed some light on such issues is to compare what happens at this particular sequential position in a Small Claims Court with what happens at similar points in other contexts.

3 Avoiding disaffiliation

When confronted with a recurrent utterance or sequence type, it is sometimes analytically useful to consider what other things a speaker might have done at that particular point in the interaction. To this end, it is preferable, wherever possible, to look at examples of different options actually being implemented, rather than to rely on intuitive reflections about theoretical possibilities. This means, of course, that it is necessary to find comparable instances where speakers are producing and responding to similar actions in similar sequential positions. In the present context, therefore, an obvious first place to look is examination and cross-examination sequences from other types of court hearing. And a first question to ask is what happens when, as in the Small Claims Court examples seen above, speakers say something more than, or different from, what was projected by the prior question. What happens, in other words, when plaintiffs, defendants, and witnesses try to take the initiative by talking about matters which had not been projected as relevant by a prior question?

The short answer is that the production of such nonminimal or elaborative responses is one of the surest ways in which speakers in court can get themselves into trouble. This can come from different quarters, and may take different forms. In fragment (6), for example, saying something other than the projected *yes* or *no* gets a police witness at a Tribunal of Inquiry into immediate trouble with his interrogator − who discounts what he said and goes in pursuit of a minimal response:

(6) Scarman Tribunal (Official Transcript)

Counsel:	Did you make any attempt to persuade the Catholic crowd to go back before you baton-charged them?
Witness:	I do not see how you could persuade them to go back.
Counsel:	Never mind that, just answer the question first and then give your reason. Did you make any effort to persuade the Catholic crowd to go back before you baton-charged them?
Witness:	No.
Counsel:	Why not?
Witness:	I doubt if they could even hear me.

In some cases, the elaborative components of a witness's answer may prompt counsel to appeal to the judge to have them stricken from the record, as happens in the following excerpt from an American Criminal Court:

(7) US Criminal Court (Simplified Transcript)

Counsel:	. . didn't you tell the police that the defendant had been drinking?
	(0.2)

Witness: No, I told them there was a cooler in the car
                and I never opened it.
                (.)
Counsel: The answer uh (.) may the balance be stricken your
                honour and the answer is no?
Judge: The answer is 'No'.

In the following excerpt from a civil hearing in an English
County Court, the judge makes two attempts to get a minimal
response from a plaintiff. Then, when the plaintiff starts to elaborate beyond the "Yes," he is cut short by a judge who sounds
impatient to move on to the next question:

(8) English County Court: CvN (Simplified Transcript)
Judge: Have you seen him since he came back from Germany once
                or more than once?
                (1.0)
Plaintiff: Uhmm (.) I've only spoken with him once on this matter.
                (0.4)
Judge: Since you came back from Germany?
Plaintiff: Yes because I felt ┌that
Judge: └All right, all right, all right, very well
                (.) uh have you received ...

In these first three examples, saying more than was projected by
the question attracted a hostile or impatient response from the
person who asked the question. However, trouble can also come
from third parties, and nonminimal responses regularly prompt
objections from opposing counsel, as in the following example
from an American Criminal Court:

(9) US Criminal Court (Simplified Transcript)
Counsel A: Where did you first see Elaine?
Witness: When she first came back – she just came in and she was
                crying and was all ┌upset
Counsel B: └Well I object your Honour.
                (3.0)
Judge: Yes, it's not responsive to the question – where she first
                saw Elaine – she said she saw her come in and that may
                stand.

These examples of sequences where speakers in three different
types of court attempt to initiate talk beyond what was projected by
the prior question differ markedly from the earlier examples from
Small Claims Court hearings – in that the nonminimal responses

are all responded to with more or less explicit displays of hostility. By contrast, whatever else may be said about the Small Claims Court arbitrators' practice of receipting nonminimal responses, such acknowledgments can hardly be said to be overtly hostile, impatient, or disaffiliative. By marking receipt, rather than implementing one of the various other options seen above, arbitrators are therefore able to avoid displaying hostility when a prior speaker produces a nonminimal response.

It is also the case that, compared with what happens in other types of court, the response by Small Claims Court arbitrators is far more "permissive" when it comes to allowing speakers to initiate talk. They rarely attempt to interrupt or otherwise prevent speakers from elaborating beyond what had been projected as relevant by the previous question. And the fact that arbitrators routinely leave a gap before receipting the previous utterance suggests that their "permissiveness" extends to the point of not starting to speak until plaintiffs and defendants have had, as it were, one last chance to continue further with what they had been saying.

These observations about the way arbitrators refrain from interrupting when speakers introduce material other than what had been projected as relevant by the prior question are consistent with reports by people to the effect that they had felt they had been able to say what they had wanted to say at hearings of the Small Claims Court.

4 Avoiding affiliation

If the Small Claims Court arbitrator's practice of acknowledging receipt is a way of avoiding a range of alternative and more disaffiliative responses, it also has the effect of avoiding various more affiliative options of the kind that might be found at similar sequential positions in a conversation.

In pursuing this line of comparison, however, one of the problems is that extended question–answer sequences are fairly rare in conversation. Indeed, when they do occur, those finding themselves on the receiving end of a series of more than a few questions are likely to respond by asking why they are being "interrogated" or "cross-examined."

In other words, extended question–answer sequences are so

strongly associated with legal contexts that these latter may be invoked to describe and complain about such sequences when they occur in everyday conversational settings. And the fact that they are likely to be treated as grounds for complaint underlines the extent to which there is a widely entrenched view of interrogation and cross-examination as forms of talk which most people would prefer to avoid whenever possible.

To circumvent the problem of finding exactly comparable sequences from conversation which can be inspected with reference to the sequences where arbitrators' produce delayed receipts, it is possible to focus on the kinds of actions being produced by speakers at such points in the proceedings. When this is done, they can be seen to be engaged in one or more of at least three kinds of activity on which research findings from conversation analysis are available for comparative purposes: delivering news, making an assessment, and telling a story (or parts of a story) about some events in the world. Not all of these are always involved in every such turn, though elements of each are apparent in one of the plaintiff's utterances in fragment (1):

(1) (Excerpt)
  Plaintiff: . . when you say to my order, ehm I would expect to get
                  a wearable pair of sandals out of it – ehm ah – it was done
                  in discussion with Mr (NAME) he and I talked about it uhh
                  (1.8) I think yes it's fair to say that he said that the
                  sandals would be (0.3) acceptable.

Research in conversation analysis has shown that there are particular types of response which recurrently follow each of these activities – delivering news, making assessments, and telling stories – when they occur in conversation. For example, studies of news-delivery sequences (e.g. Heritage 1984b) show that recipients of a piece of news not only mark its receipt as news for them, but do so early (i.e. either in overlap with the news-delivery turn, or with no gap after its completion). In English, the most regularly used news-receipt token is almost certainly the particle *oh*:

(10) Conversation (Simplified Transcript)
  Hilda: . . she's got the application forms.
  Mary: Oh – so when's the interview, did she say?
  Hilda: She didn't uh– well uh– she's got to send the form
             back. Sh ⌈e doesn't know when ⌈the interview is yet.
  Mary: ⌊ Oh   ⌊Oh, it's just the form.

Ubiquitous though the use of *oh* may be for marking the receipt of news in conversational interaction, not a single instance of its being used by an arbitrator has been found in a corpus of twelve complete hearings, notwithstanding the fact that many utterances by the disputing parties plainly involve the presentation of news.

A similarly recurrent phenomenon has been described for assessment sequences by Pomerantz (1975, 1984a), who has shown that a first assessment by one speaker is regularly followed by a second assessment by another in the next turn. A major class of these involves not merely a display of agreement with the first assessment, but also an upgrade of it, as in fragments (11) and (12):

(11) Conversation (Simplified Transcript)
        Don: . . so it's a pretty good set up you know.
        Ken: Well my God it sounds marvellous, Don.

(12) Conversation (Simplified Transcript)
        Mike: . . it was fun the night we we ⌜nt down
        John: ⌞It was great fun ...

Again, even though utterances by plaintiffs and defendants frequently include assessments, the production of second assessments is something which the Small Claims Court arbitrators systematically refrain from doing.

Assessments are not the only type of conversational activity regularly followed by similar action by another party. As Sacks reported in his studies of story telling in conversation, a first story often prompts a second story in which a speaker displays his understanding and appreciation of the first by selecting a hearably relevant one with which to follow it. However, although plaintiffs and defendants in the Small Claims Court spend a good deal of their time telling stories, arbitrators never respond by telling a second story.

When the Small Claims Court arbitrators' practice of acknowledging receipt is compared with what happens at similar points in conversational sequences, it emerges that they systematically avoid a range of responses which are not just commonplace in conversation, but which also have generally *affiliative* implications.

Taken together with the earlier observations about their withholding the kinds of disaffiliative response that are found in various other courts, marking receipt therefore appears to be a highly effective way of avoiding displays both of affiliation and disaffiliation with the prior speaker. In other words, it would appear to work as a technique for displaying neutrality in the face of potentially controversial material.

5 Displaying neutrality and the role of arbitrator

Although the way Small Claims Court arbitrators display neutrality may make for a much less intimidating atmosphere than in other types of court, where overt displays of hostility are commonplace, it is doubtful whether the use of the technique described in this chapter is solely, primarily, or directly motivated by a concern with enhancing the "interactional comfort" of the participants. For it also provides a workable solution to a particular problem which arbitrators face by virtue of the specifically legal work for which they are responsible.

In many other types of court operating within the Anglo-American adversarial tradition, there is a clear division of labor between the tasks of examination and judging. Under this system, counsel are specifically detailed to take sides, and it is therefore hardly surprising to find them displaying affiliation and disaffiliation in response to what different witnesses say. By contrast, the arbitrator faces the problem of how to reconcile two potentially conflicting roles: he has to question both parties to the dispute and then, at the end of the hearing, he has to pass judgment. If he is to be seen as acting fairly in this latter capacity, it is therefore essential that he should not be seen to be taking sides while questioning either plaintiff or defendant. Otherwise, one or other of them would have grounds for complaining to the effect that the arbitrator was biased, and that justice had not been properly done.

Viewed in these terms, then, the practice described in this chapter appears to be one way in which arbitrators can effectively insulate themselves from any such accusations – and thereby contribute towards achieving the legal objective of ensuring that both parties to the dispute receive a fair hearing.

Insofar as the observations reported here show something of the detailed way in which the work of arbitration is carried out, they may also have broader practical and analytic implications. With regard to the former, they suggest that findings from this kind of study may be relevant both for policy debates about the relative merits of different types of court and for training programs in arbitration techniques.

As far as further research is concerned, the observations suggest that a potentially fruitful focus for future comparative research will be on sequences where participants are seeking to initiate, control, or otherwise direct what gets talked about. Roughly speaking, it appears that the more that people are permitted to say what they want to say, the less formal (and less intimidating) will the procedures be deemed to be, and vice versa.

However, as is evident from the range of examples included above, there is considerable detailed variation in the way lawyers respond to attempts by witnesses to develop their talk in directions not projected by the previous question. Particular practices may be found to cluster in one type of court rather than another, and to play a key part in its operation. Research aimed at identifying and describing such techniques may therefore help to improve our understanding both of how different court procedures actually work, and of their differential impact on those caught up in the legal process.

7

Answers as interactional products: two sequential practices used in job interviews

GRAHAM BUTTON

1 Introduction

This chapter addresses materials that are taken from the interview of a serving head of department in a comprehensive school in the southwest of England for the possible senior position of head of the arts faculty. In addition to the candidate, Mr. Carpenter (C), the other participants are the chairperson (who is a school governor) (CH); another school governor (D); the headmaster (HM); the deputy headmaster (DHM); and a subject adviser who is representing the local education authority. For non-UK readers it may be ethnographically relevant to know that the interview was more or less standard for British teacher interviews, with one candidate interviewed at a time by a panel consisting of the above categories of persons. The school governors who are on the interview panel are lay members of the public who, at the time this interview was conducted, were appointed by the local education authority (LEA). A subject adviser is a person appointed by the LEA as a specialist in a particular subject to advise all the schools in the county covered by the LEA on pedagogic matters relating to their subject.

The candidate's performance was discussed immediately after the interview and he was subsequently informed that he was not considered suitable for the position. His performance was discussed

This is a modified version of a paper originally published in a special issue of *Social Pscyhology Quarterly* on *Language and Social Interaction*, edited by Douglas W, Maynard, vol. 50, no. 2 (1987). I am indebted to John McNorton for the discussions we have had and for providing access to the interview that figures in this investigation. I am also indebted to the participants and all those who were involved at the school. Douglas Maynard and Emanuel A. Schegloff made detailed comments on previous drafts which were important for subsequent revisions. Some early thoughts on the issues introduced were first presented at the Institute for Ethnomethodology and Conversation Analysis, Boston University, August 1983.

with him in order to give him pointers for improving his "interview techniques." The whole of the interview was video-taped, but the interview panel would not allow any of the subsequent discussion to be recorded. Hence, the characterization of the candidate's answer that "it does not answer the question" was captured in note form. The major thrust of the criticism implied in this characterization – which will be examined in the analysis to follow – was that the candidate could not even understand what was being asked; the indictment became that he could not understand a simple question.

This chapter will, in part, address the grounds through which this characterization could be intelligibly made. Two issues that have been developed in two of the preceding chapters will overhang this consideration. The first concerns *relevance*: the relevance of a "special" categorization of persons – such as "interviewer" and "candidate" and the relevance of a "special" categorization of context, such as the "job interview" – for the description of participants' actions. Schegloff (this volume) discusses the way in which these issues can be confronted. He suggests that the relevance of such social structural features for the description of human action resides in the "procedural relevance" of ascribable categories and contexts for the construction of activities. That is, in order seriously to address questions abut the relevance of context and identity for the description of activity, it would be necessary to show how participants build into their actions and activities a sense of context and identity as relevant in and for their accomplishment. It is intended to show here that certain sequential structures are used which are designed to allow the interviewers to orient to a candidate's answers as "the candidate's answers," and thereby allow them to be used as a resource through which interviewers may objectively orient to the answers given. It is in their organization that participants may display an orientation to the "interview" as consistently relevant for, and built into, the construction of their actions. Further, it is through these displays that it becomes possible to ground the context of an interview as procedurally relevant for participants, and to provide a warrant for invoking the context of an interview in any case.

The second issue concerns "activity types" as described by Levinson (this volume). In his discussion, Levinson stresses the interrelationship between "social episodes" and language usage;

for example, the interrelationship between interviews, and the use of questions and answers. One of the features that Levinson underscores is the interactional character of questions which resides in the fact that they provide for answers. In this examination I want to extend his understanding of "interactional" and to suggest that to appreciate fully the interactional dimension of the interview, serious attention needs to be given to the fact that the interview is a form of speech exchange, the methodicity and orderliness of which imparts a methodicity and orderliness to the social setting as well as the activities and interactions which occur. As Levinson suggests, the interview is composed of sequences of talk, and, it can be added, it is only when their organization is examined that the social setting and social-setting activities and interactions can be rigorously grasped as analytic objects.

This chapter, then, is intended to make two particular points: (a) to provide for actions in the interview, such as answers to questions, to be understood as interactionally constructed in details of the contingent organization of a speech-exchange system;[1] and (b) to reveal an "interview orthodoxy" which is constituted in the organization of sequential structures. In the course of so doing, two further concerns will emerge as issues that require further attention: (a) that in the details of the organization of the speech-exchange system, there may reside a warrant for characterizing social settings, and that consequently there is a seriousness in systematically investigating a speech exchange system in itself as a method of addressing social structure; and (b) that it is necessary to display what it would take to invoke a social context or setting such as an interview as relevant for participants' actions, by investigating those activities for the ways in which they build in an orientation to the setting as systematically relevant for conduct.

2 Questions and answers

The interview overwhelmingly consists of talk that is organized into a series of questions and answers. Sacks (1992 [1972]) and Schegloff and Sacks (1973) show that some sequences of talk in ordinary conversation (such as questions and answers) form an interconnected pair of utterances that display particular characteristics which are not necessarily shared by any two adjacent utterances. One of these characteristics is that answers are sequential objects that have been occasioned by a prior activity – asking a question – and that their intelligibility as answers is dependent upon their position following a question. Consequently, persons do not systematically and regularly produce intelligible answers without questions having preceded them, whereas other classes of utterances, such as invitations, introductions, or even questions themselves, are not always preceded by one particular occasioning activity.

This means, furthermore, than an answer displays an understanding of the prior utterance in a way that is not necessarily claimed by an invitation, an introduction, or a question. In other words, answers are a resource whereby hearers can monitor a speaker's apparent understanding of the question. Hearers, therefore, have systematic grounds for finding that someone, though indeed talking after a question, has not "answered" it; for example, in terms of the questioner's or other hearers' understanding of the question, speakers may exhibit a "misunderstanding" of the question.

In this respect, we turn to the question and answer to be examined. Taking the question:

(1) [RMI 0077]
    P: … thank you Madam Chairman (.) Huhrm (.) What sort of sty::le do you see (.) yourself as– as a le::ader of– of (.) a– a team of teachers.

It is available for any hearer (or reader) to understand that this question is oriented to a person-management issue. The resources for arriving at this understanding all reside in features of the question. The interviewer invokes the perspective role of the candidate ("le::ader") in relationship to the group of people he would lead ("a- a team of teachers."), and directs the candidate to answering a question that pertains to how he would operate in this role ("What sort of sty::le do you see (.) yourself").

However, the beginning of the candidate's answer diverges from this.

(2) [RMI 0078]
    P: … a– ateam of teachers.
        (0.5)

```
C:              D'you mean how w'd I get other people to do it.
                (1.5)
C:              Well er:: (0.5) .mpt I think there are two ways of
                approaching tea::m teaching (0.5) ·hh it can either
                be a school based philosophy ...
```

Following the initiation of a repair (Schegloff, Jefferson, and Sacks 1977; Schegloff 1979b) of understanding ("D'you mean how w'd I get other people to do it") the answer shows that the candidate has understood the question to be one that is about a teaching style: "team teaching."

Like the first understanding, this understanding can also be located in the question. The interviewer refers to the personnel that the candidate would lead as a "team," a term that has technical referents in teaching vocabulary. Furthermore, the interviewer also uses the term "sty::le" when asking about how the candidate would perform his managerial role as a leader, and this is a term that can also be used to describe a particular form of teaching. So although the interviewer does not, in so many words, ask a question about "team teaching," it can be appreciated how the candidate might have taken it as such. Through the preservation of "team" the candidate displays that a resource for his answer was the question, and in answering as he does he claims an understanding of what this question possibly means for him. For hearers of his answer, however, it may display a misunderstanding of the question or at least a problem in understanding the question. Hearers who understand the question as one of person management may compare the candidate's answer, and the understanding of the question it displays, with this understanding and find that the candidate, although answering, is not answering the question that was asked. Methodic grounds thereby exist though which hearers of the candidate's answer could characterize it as one that "does not answer the question."

It can be observed, however, that the interviewers orient to the organization of the interview as a turn-taking system in the face of the above contingency. To appreciate fully how this is done, reference can be made to how problems of understanding may be oriented to in ordinary conversation.[2] In conversation, the questioner can monitor the recipients understanding of the question as the answer unfolds, and should there be a problem the questioner can initiate a repair of understanding. This may be done at the first turn-transition relevance place; the first place in an answer's utterance where a next speaker can legitimately start to talk (Sacks, Schegloff, and Jefferson 1974). For example, in excerpt (3) below, Tina displays that Mandy has misunderstood to whom the question refers, and does so at the first place where Mandy's utterance may be possibly complete. Mandy can then continue, and answer the question appropriately.

(3) [OEI]

Mandy:	There should be 'bout twuny or so people.	
Tina:	I hope– will Chris be coming?	
Mandy:	If she can:⌈: get	
Tina:	⌊No you ninny Christopher.	
	(.)	
Tina:	The insomniacs ultimate so ⌈lution.	
Mandy::	⌊Gawd I hope not.	

In the interview, the interviewers never undertook this sort of correction on occasions where understanding problems may have been possibly relevant. Interviewers not only did not start to speak at first possible places where a transfer of speakership could be coordinated, they neither, without a request from the candidate, intervened in the course of an answer. Once the candidate started to answer, the interviewers did not start to speak unless specifically requested to do so by the candidate. Yet, early in the candidate's answer, there is a place where the interviewer could have systematically and appropriately intervened. This is following "tea::m teaching."

(2) [RMI 0078]

> C: Well er:: (0.5) .mpt I think there are two ways of approaching tea::m teaching (0.5) ˙hh it can either be a school based philosophy ...

Although the talk to that place projects that there is more talk to come, and although, should an understanding problem be relevant, the continuation may undercut that relevance, nevertheless the relevance of an understanding problem may be displayed at that place. This was done in the previous excerpt of conversation, extract (3).

This is also a place that immediately follows the candidate's displayed understanding of the question, and is consequently a place that immediately follows a possible misunderstanding of the question. Further, the candidate leaves a space at this place where the interviewer could start to talk. Thus, following "teaching" is a space that could be systematically used to correct the candidate's understanding.

Consequently, although it may be heard that the candidate may have misunderstood the question, his understanding is, nevertheless, allowed to stand, and the possible lack of fit with the question is allowed to be a feature of the candidate's answer. Since the answer is open to assessment by the interviewers, whatever else might be assessed, it is open to assessment with respect to the competence of the candidate to understand what was being asked. The interviewers thereby constitute a resource for themselves which they can use to make attributions of personal deficiencies, that is, that the candidate "ducked the question."

However, it can be suggested that the understanding which the candidate arrives at, and which is oriented to by the interviewers as a resource with which to assess his competence to answer a question, is *interactionally constituted*, and derives from the interaction and not just from some supposed personal states such as "inner qualities" or "personal attributes." In ordinary conversation, displays of understanding are always open to correction should a co-participant display that there is a problem of understanding. Consequently, should no repair be initiated on their displayed understanding, understanding is not an issue. In ordinary conversation, then, understanding may not be an issue until it is made one, and speakers seemingly proceed on the basis that their displayed understanding is an appropriate one.

In the interview, the interviewer *let pass* the possible opportunity to correct the candidate's understanding of the question at a place where he might have displayed that there was a problem of understanding in the candidate's answer. Subsequently, the candidate may appropriately proceed on the basis of his displayed understanding. But, importantly, that understanding is *now* one that has been constituted through the interaction between the interviewer and the candidate, the interviewer letting pass the possible opportunity to correct a possible misunderstanding, and thus preserving as possibly appropriate the candidate's displayed understanding.

It can be suggested that the competence of the candidate to fit the

answer to the question is not something that can be fully appreciated outside of this interactional context. The eventual charge
that the candidate "does not answer the question" because of some
personal qualities derives from the decontextualization of the
candidate's answer from the interactional context in which it was
produced. The candidate's answer is being assessed outside of the
interactional particulars that occasioned and constituted part of its
course. It may well be appropriate to characterize the answer as one
that does not answer the question because, indeed, it does not fit the
question as asked. But that it may not do so is the *methodic* result
of the way that the participants have *organized their speech
exchange*, not just some idiosyncrasy on the part of the candidate.

3 Responses to answers

While in conversation an answerer's turn is monitorable as to how
a person understood the prior turn, so too may a recipient of the
answer have their response monitored for their understanding of
the answer. The reason for this again resides in conversational
organization. The shape or the design of a current turn at talk may
be organized with respect to the immediately prior turn and the
immediately next turn, and may not, unless specifically done and
marked, be organized with respect to other turns at talk (Sacks,
Schegloff, and Jefferson 1974).

Thus, questioners do not know what shape their answer-sub-
sequent turn will take, since this is dependent upon the intervening
answer. In the following fragment (4), for instance, it is not until
Alan produces a particular answer to Bill's initial query that Bill can
go on to deliver the invitation in that particular way. Had Alan not
answered in the way he did, Bill might not have been in a position
to deliver the invitation, or may have delivered it differently.[3]

(4) [OE II]

Bill:	Are you and Evelyn gonna be here for New Year?
Alan:	We don't know yet, if we stay for Christmas, no, if we go away for Christmas, yes.
Bill:	Well, if you are here we always 'ave a do (.) 'bout thirty people and you'd be welcome.

It is because of this organizational relationship that exists between adjacent turns that a current turn can display how the prior

turn was used as a resource in its production, and concomitantly how a speaker has understood the prior turn. Thus, although Bill, when taking his first turn in the example above might orient to his next turn as one in which he could go on and deliver an invitation (see Sacks 1992 [1966, 1967]), the form of the delivery displays that he has used the prior turn to structure that delivery – "Well, if you are here" – something he could not have projected from his first turn to speak. And this displays an understanding of Alan's answer as one that allows him to deliver an invitation.

Just as hearers inspect the answer to a question, recipients also monitor the response to an answer. This possibility furnishes the sequential opportunity for the *answerer to return to the answer* they had previously delivered. Should the response to an answer display some problem in co-participant's understanding, the original answerer can initiate some form of a repair. This can be accomplished by elaborating upon, or extending, or in some other way returning to the answer. Thus, answers may have the sequential opportunity to return to the answer, and consequently an answer's completion may be achieved over a course of a number of turns. An answer's actual completeness may, then, be an interactionally achieved matter.

In the example of Bill's invitation in extract (4), above, Alan clarifies the answer he gave following Bill's possible invitation. That is, Alan displays that Bill's invitation may pose some problem of acceptance, and uses Bill's response to the answer as grounds for returning to and attempting to clarify the issue.

```
(4a) [OE II]
        Bill:          Well, if you are here we always 'ave a do (.) 'bout
                       thirty people and you'd be welcome.
                       (0.5)
        Alan:          Oh:: well thanks it– Evelyn might work– I– what I
                       mean is that if she doesn't have to work Christmas
                       we'll go away but then she'll be working New Year's
                       Eve, and (0.5) if she has to work Christmas we'll (.)
                       be (.) away for New Year. (0.5) Is that right. Yeah.
        Bill:          Oh:::
        Alan:          But I'll co(h)me if she's working heh ⌐ heh.
        Bill:                                                 ⌊Oh::
```

Thus a response to an answer may indicate to an answerer some problem of understanding what the answer was getting at, in which case the answerer may return to the answer in an attempt at clarification.[4]

This opportunity to return to the answer is also afforded by another feature of the turn-by-turn organization of conversation, which is, since a current turn may use a prior turn as one of its resources for its production, aspects of the prior turn may be preserved in a current turn. Thus a response to an answer may preserve aspects of the answer; but, as talk unfolds, the current turn becomes a prior turn for the following or next turn. This following turn becomes a current turn and it may use its prior turn as a resource for its production. In doing so it may use parts of the immediately prior turn that were preserved from the turn before that. Thus a current turn may be marked as addressing, not just the turn before, but the turn before that. So, an answerer may be afforded the opportunity of returning to the original answer should aspects of that answer be preserved in the intervening turn, even where there is no understanding problem.

This can be seen in extract (5), which follows. Vera (line 5) uses Jenny's previous answer (line 3) in her response by challenging Jenny's answer that she "didn't go anywheh." Thus, rather than moving away from the prior turn, Vera preserves in her challenge aspects of that turn. This provides the sequential opportunity for Jenny (line 7) to return to the answer (now preserved in what is a prior turn in her next current turn) in the light of Vera's challenging response. She does this with an attempt to elicit information which she could use to modify her answer.

```
(5) [Rahman: I]
1.      Vera:       Whah didje get lahs ni:ght?
2.                  (1.0)
3.      Jenny:      Hahst– I dit (0.2) I didn't go anywheh.
4.                  (0.4)
5.      Vera:       W'l Mathew rrang t'see if you were here.
6.                  (0.7)
7.      Jenny:      ˙hh ˙Ohh:::. ˙hh well I wz in l'ahs' night.
```

Again, the organization of conversation at a turn-by-turn level means that an answerer may legitimately return to the answer. Thus the actual completeness of an answer is an interactional matter that may be determined over the course of turns at talk.

Returning to the interview from which the answer under consideration was taken, it can be found that the turns which follow the candidate's answers are used in one of three ways, all of which *preclude* the candidate from returning to the answer he had given in the manner that may occur in natural conversation. First, the current interviewer may signal that the questioning is at an end, by turning over speakership to the chairperson. This can be seen in the following two examples.

(6) [RMI 0105]
```
     C:         ... this week I have read s'm Balzac and I've read
                some Belrac poetry.
     P:         Thank you very much Madam Chairman. If– if you're
                appointed I– I hope you (.) won't (.) wish to take French on as
                part of the facul ⌜ty
     Ch:                           ⌞hhh heh ⌜heh
     HM:                                      ⌜H ⌜eh
     DHM:                                        ⌜Heh he
     C:                                         ⌞Heh
     P:         Thank you Madam Chairman
     Ch:        ˙hher(h)=Tha(h)nk you. Headmaster.
```

(7) [RMI 0225]
```
     C:         ... if I look around the schools that I've known in Waterford
                and so I am not aware::: ˙hhh that (.) they've stopped music
                or that they've stopped art or (.) whatever ⌜els e.
     HM:                                                     ⌞hrm
                (0.5)
     HM:        I– I– I will finish there but I think you'll find s'm dropped
                music ˙hh Madam Chairman thank you very much.
```

When the interviewers use their turns in this way, the candidate is offered only a limited resource for monitoring their understandings of his answers. Clearly, he knows that the interviewers understand, or propose, his answers to be finished. Also it allows him in some way to find how his answer has been taken; from extract (6) for instance: "If- if you're appointed I- I hope you (.) won't (.) wish to take French on as part of the faculty", and from extract (7) "but I think you'll find s'm dropped music." However, because the interviewers relinquish speakership to the chairperson, who is then the appropriate person to start to speak, the candidate is denied an opportunity to correct any problem that might exist. Consequently, the possibility that the candidate might return to his answer is systematically excluded. The candidate-complete answer is thus transformed into actual completeness.

Second, interviewers may ask a further question, but one which is "topically" disjunctive from both the prior question and the candidate's answer, as in the next two instances.

(8) [RMI 0311] Answering a question on discipline asked by DHM
C: ... ultimately (0.5) I would support teachers against pupils
                   otherwise yer whole (.) ethos of the– (wove) to the
                   discipline of school suffers.
                   (2.5)
DHM: Thank you Mister Carpenter ˙hhh Erm my next question is er
                   that er in your (0.5) experience is from your application
                   form that you have (.) (acted) as a form teacher and its's
                   possible that our– our facu::lty heads will not have to (.)
                   function in this way (0.5) but in the even::t of (.) your
                   having to:: fill the bre:ach as it were how might you spend on the
                   first twent-five minutes of the day: ˙hh hum if you had to fill in for
                   some one in a form teacher capacity.

(9) [RMI 0341] (Answering a question on time-tabling asked by DHM.)
C: ... block time tabling for– within the faculty (1.5) E' hI– I
                   think I could co::pe with that problem.
DHM: Thank you::u. hhh to what extent would you be (.) or– or
                   might you expect to control the expenditure on capitation due to the
                   five subjects within (.) yo:u:r faculty.

This type of response does not provide the candidate with a resource to monitor how he has been understood, and again, he cannot legitimately return to his answer. The interviewer asks a further question that uses neither a prior question nor the candidate's previous answer as a resource for its production, and thus directs the candidate away from what was previously said. This second use of turns following a candidate's answer also transforms a candidate-complete answer into actual completeness.[5]

A third way the turn position following a candidate's answer is used involves the current interviewer providing an assessment of the answer. This contrasts with the other two ways in as much as the interviewer preserves the "topicality" of the candidate's answer, and provides a resource that can be monitored for the interviewer's understanding of the answer.

(10) [RMI 0226]
           C: ... and dance drama is drama and you– I mean (.) what's
                              in a name (.) herhm.

HM: Uhm (0.5) Good. I'm pleased you mention dan<u>ce</u> becuz
I'm (.) <u>keen</u> that we should include that in our ˙hhh physical
education program and as you say it ˙hhh cl–>sly allied ˙hhh
WOULD you like to see <– (.) er– perhaps other subjects
br<u>ought</u> in::: to this area I– I know you have a p'ticular
interest in French but perhaps neglecti<u>ng</u> that I wonder if
you r'd other areas of the curriculum (.) br::<u>ought</u> into
this faculty if you had a <u>free</u> choice.

(11) [RMI 0212]

C: ... how do <u>I</u> get on with people I have worked with that's
what its about that's what– that's what <u>every</u> job is about
(.) it's not about structures.
(1.0)

HM: I would agree with you that schools are about <u>people</u> and
that is the (0.5) raw material (0.5) all the way through
Mister Carpenter. ˙hhh <u>Right</u> huhrm Well you <u>see</u> that for
histori<u>cal</u> rea:::so<u>ns</u> and reasons of philosophy we put
p'ticular group of sub<u>jects</u> together, English, Drama, Music,
Art and P.E. now hh I know that you have a particular
qualification is sever<u>al</u> of those areas and that must have
attracted you to this ˙hhh do you think that's rea::sonably
coherent bu<u>nch</u> of subjects to put together.

The assessment of an answer may afford the answerer the sequential opportunity to return to the answer. The assessment may be monitored for its degree of fit with the answer, and should this be found to be lacking, the answerer may confirm, or reaffirm, or elaborate upon, or extend, or modify the answer in light of the assessment. Further, in as much as the assessments in the above examples aim themselves at only part of the candidate's answer, the candidate might be able to underscore a point he finds the interviewer is keen on, or upgrade and elaborate other points which he might see as being possibly overlooked.

However, while it may appear that an assessment could afford these types of sequential opportunities, the ways in which the two examples are constructed are such that the candidate is *not* provided the sequential opportunity to return to his answer. That is, other features of the turn override the sequential implications that the assessments might otherwise have.

In extract (10) the interviewer increases the pace of his talk[6] as he approaches the end of his assessment: "Good. I'm pleased you mention dan<u>ce</u> becuz I'm (.) <u>keen</u> that we should include that in our

·hhh physical education program and as you say it ·hhh cl→sly allied." The increased pace can signal that he is continuing past the assessment. He then takes an inbreath – "·hhh" – which is also a way of holding a turn, and then at increased pace and loud volume – "WOULD" – a move is made into the beginning of the next question. It is only when he is well into the next question that the pace of his talk drops to what it has been throughout his previous talk: "WOULD you like to see ← (.)er."[7] All this has an interactional consequence because it is following the assessment that a possible turn-transition relevance place exists – or would, if this were ordinary conversation – where the transfer of speakership may be relevant, and where the candidate might start to speak to the assessment. Thus the interviewer moves across a possible turn-transition relevance place by speeding up his talk as it approaches, holds the turn, and continues, with the sequential result that the candidate is kept from legitimately speaking in the light of the interviewer's displayed understanding of the answer, and is directed to answering a new question.[8]

In the second instance, following the assessment part of the turn, a transition relevance place may be upcoming after "Mister Carpenter." Although there is a pause after "raw material," it is projectable that there is more to come, and indeed, Mr. Carpenter so orients in his own silence. However, after "Mister Carpenter," and after the assessment part of the turn, Mr. Carpenter might have possibly intervened. This possibility is attended to in the continued organization of the turn. The interviewer signals that the turn is being held with an inbreath, which can form a resource for finding continuation. The "Right" displays that the assessment activity is complete, and also pivots into a disjunctive matter which eventually emerges as the new question. The possibility of continuing is preserved by the throat clearing, which also holds the turn. Once more the turn is organized in such a way that the candidate may not appropriately speak in light of the understanding of the prior answer that the assessment may display.

The three ways in which turns following an answer are used in the interview have a sequential consequence for the candidate's answer. They determine that the answer he has given stands as complete. They do not afford the candidate an opportunity to elaborate upon his answer, to extend it, to modify it or in other ways return to the answer he had previously given in light of the interviewer's displayed understanding of his answer.

These uses of the turn position following the candidate's answer also have consequences for the issue that an answer may not answer the question. First the candidate is not afforded a resource through which he can determine how his answers are being understood. Thus, interviewers do not display in their subsequent activities that the answer does not fit the question, and is being heard as not answering the question. Second, because the turns that follow his answers provide for someone other than the candidate to be the next speaker, the candidate does not have the sequential opportunity to attend to any problem of a lack of fit between an answer and the question. Should he be able to return to an answer at a place where a possible problem with his answer may be displayed, he may then be able to correct, or in some ways remedy a displayed problem.

To return to the focal question–answer sequence introduced earlier, it was suggested that the candidate produced an answer that may not have correctly answered the question, in that it may not have properly fitted the question. Following the answer was one of the interviewers' sequential provisions described above. The interviewer employed the first sequential practice identified. He marks the receipt of the answer and moves into a further question, one which is disjunctive from both the answer and the prior question. The candidate is thereby deprived of a further resource with which he could deal with the possible problem his answer is later characterized as comprising.

(12) [RMI 0092]
      C: … and we have if you like a general discussion (.) ˙hh I
                  would try't instigate that (.) if:: we weren't blocked
                  time tabled for it.
      P: Mrm (0.5) mpt Thank you Mister Carpenter (2.5) what
                  herm (.) w'd– do you see the role of a head of department
                  or head of facu::lty in introducing:: a probationer (.) teacher
                  into the profession …

4 An orientation displayed by interviewers

The previous two sections have described two sequential practices used by the interviewers during the interview: first, the possibility of correcting a problematic understanding of the answer is passed over; and second, the response following the candidate's answer organized the talk in such a way as to prevent the candidate from returning to the answer.

These sequential practices both display the same orientation to the candidate's answers: the interviewers orient to *the candidate's answers as his answers*. Each practice is designed to constitute and preserve what the candidate says as what he had to say, and all that the candidate had to say, rather than what he was led to say, cajoled to say, prompted to say, and in other ways directed to say. In this manner, interviewers may achieve the objectivity of their position. These practices "distance" interviewers from the received answers. This can be briefly elaborated on for both practices.

The first sequential practice of letting pass the opportunity to correct a possible problem of understanding preserves the candidate's understanding, and, thus, the candidate's answers may be oriented to as a display of his *own* understanding and not one that observably has been a product of interviewers' direction. Any subsequent assessment of his answer can then be oriented to as assessing the *candidate*'s performance.

The second sequential practice, which prevents the candidate from returning to his answers and elaborating upon or extending them in the light of an interviewer's displayed understanding also preserves the candidate's answers as his answers. The answer the candidate gives is organizationally constituted as everything he had to say on the matter. He is not encouraged to say more, as he might be should interviewers, for example, assess his answer in such a way that he would be given the sequential opportunity to return to his answer following the assessment. Consequently, his answer can be objectively assessed as the one *he* gave.

In general, both practices sustain an interview orthodoxy: that the questions in the interview can reveal the personal characteristics, qualities, and deficiencies of a candidate. It may appear that all the candidate has as resources to answer the questions are the questions themselves, and his own "wit." If so, then an answer, since it is open to assessment, provides the interviewer with a resource to gain access to that "wit." So, as now a purely objective matter, the interviewers construct a setting where a characterization of the candidate as not answering the question is, legitimately, also a characterization of the candidate's deficiencies.

But, the sequential practices that the interviewers engage in are, in part, constitutive features of the social setting as an interview. These practices furnish part of the context within which the candidate's answers occur. A consequence of this for an activity such as "answering" is that the form of answering builds into it as relevant for its construction an orientation to the *context of the interview*, and that context thus elaborates upon that activity. Consequently, the sequential practices that the interviewers may orient to as objectively placing them outside of the candidate's answers may, actually, be constitutive features of the answers.

We have been experiencing this turn-around in the previous sections. So, letting pass the opportunity to correct a possible problematic understanding is an active constitutive feature of the candidate's understanding; it preserves a possible misunderstanding as part of the candidate's answer. To appreciate the candidate's understanding of the question it has to be examined in the interactional context within which it is embedded. Also, when the interviewers provide responses following answers that prevent a return to the answer, they are constituting the answer as complete. Although it may appear that their activities are oriented to preserving the candidate's answers as his answers, they are indeed interactionally part of the constitution of his answer as complete.

Thus, although the two practices that have been described may display an orientation to the candidate's answers as his answer, they are actually constitutive features of what an answer turns out to be. The charges that the candidate "does not answer the question" derive from the interactional particulars that occasioned and constituted it. The characterization, though, is of answers that are thoroughly grounded in the way in which the interview as a social occasion is organized, and in the way in which an orientation to the interview as a form of speech exchange is built into activities as relevant for their organization.

Notice, then, that what has been described in a description of the practices are orientations by participants to a turn-taking system for interviews. Thus, the first practice involves the "right" of a candidate to have multi-unit turns at talk as opposed to a single unit of talk, as in conversation. The second practice, in its first instantiation, organizes speaker selection through a specified person – Madam Chairman. In its second form it organizes speaker selection by providing for the candidate to speak next via a chain of questions and answers, as in its third form. Thus participants are organizing the interview as a social occasion by their contingent production of a turn-taking system for the interview. This has analytic ramifications for some of the issues in the introduction and which have overshadowed part of the above analysis: the warrantability of the relevance of a context such as interviews for the description of human conduct, and for the warrantable analytic use of categorizations such as "interviewer" and "candidate" in the first place. These concerns are returned to in the following discussion.

5 Discussion

By taking just one answer in an interview and attempting to ground a characterization of it in the situated, locally organized practices of participants, this chapter has attempted to show: (a) how activities accomplished in an interview are interactionally constructed in some of the situated details of the organization of speech exchange; and (b) that an interview orthodoxy is constituted in the organization of sequential structures. Rather than simply emphasizing this in a conclusion, two further issues which have been alluded to and which have become a prompt for further interest may be drawn out briefly in a discussion.

The first issue concerns the very characterizability of social-structural settings such as "an interview." What makes an interview recognizable? It is not the sign on the door, nor just the gathering together of certain people. It is, rather, what those people do, and how they structure and organize their interactions with one another, that achieves for some social settings its characterizability as an interview. This integrally involves the way in which the participants organize their speech exchange with one another. The practices that have been described here are used by the participants to organize and structure some part of their speech exchange and, consequently, become procedures through which the social setting of the interview is in part constituted. The practices have all involved activity on the part of interviewers, activity that is oriented to placing the interviewers outside of the candidate's answer so that it may be objectively examined. It might be suggested that this is a "job" of interviewers. These procedures may, then, be ones that are usable by interviewers to do their work, through which they achieve their status as interviewers, and through which they can be seen to be engaged in the business of interviewing. Thus, the warrantable use of categories such as "interviewer" and "candidate" – in the face of a multiple categorization possibilities for any person (an interviewer may be a father as well, for instance) – may reside in participants' orientation to and constitution of them as relevant categories in and for the construction of their activities. Although it remains to be seen what further orientations may be displayed, it is possible to suggest now that if the above has any credence then it is by revealing aspects of the methodic organization of relevant status as a situated categorization procedure done in actual talk that dimensions of social structure may be accordingly addressed.

This leads into a second issue, which is the relevance of invoking social-structural concerns as relevant for the organization of participants' action. The concern is that the activities are assumed to be the product of the context, since they take place in an invoked context such as an interview. Thus we would have the phenomenon of "interview talk." A problem is that just because the talk might be subsumed under the auspices of an interview does not mean that it is the product of that context. Rather, it becomes necessary to show that the context was procedurally relevant for the construction of participants' activities.[9] One way in which it has been seen here that participants display an orientation to the setting, indeed build into their activities a situated specification of the setting, is in the details of the organization of their talk. Thus, the two practices examined have been relevant to a *turn-taking* procedure. To reveal the practices it has been necessary to draw comparisons with ordinary conversation. It is in these comparisons that it might become possible to see participants' orientations to the context as relevant for their activities as described, and unless that can be shown, specification of a context as structuring human conduct is problematic. It is to that warranted specification that interest might turn.

Notes

1. See Atkinson, Cuff, and Lee (1978), Cuff and Sharrock (1986), Clayman (1988), Greatbatch (1988), and Heritage (1985) for considerations of other forms of interviews and meetings that are also concerned with the organization of speech exchange.

2. See Sacks, Schegloff, and Jefferson (1974), for a relevant description of the turn-taking system for conversation.

3. This section involves a presequence initiated in the first line, which can be used to get to a subsequent invitation sequence, see Sacks (1992 [1966, 1967]) and Terasaki (1976).

4. Alan's response to Bill's invitation appears to constitute rejection through the "speaker's reporting" practices described by Drew (1984).

5. Notice that in the extracts illustrating the two kinds of next activities, the interviewers include the component "thank you." In the first two extracts they are directed to the chairperson and are part of the display that the interviewer has concluded his questioning. In the second two extracts, they are aimed at the candidate and are a part of signaling a disjuncture with what is upcoming. The use of these "appreciations" in this way may build into participants' activities an orientation to the interview as a distinctive speech-exchange system, something which is alluded to later as a matter for further elaboration.

6. Marked by → in "cl→sly."

7. The end of the increased pace is marked with "←."

8. See Schegloff (1980) for a similar activity, which he describes as a "rush through."

9. See Schegloff (this volume) for an elaboration upon these matters.

PART 3

The activities of answerers

8

The delivery and reception of diagnosis in the general-practice consultation

CHRISTIAN HEATH

By the same institutional definition the sick person is not, of course, competent to help himself, or what he can do is, except for trivial illness, not adequate. But in our culture there is a special definition of the kind of help he needs, namely, professional, technically competent help. The nature of this help imposes a further disability or handicap upon him. He is not only generally not in a position to do what needs to be done, but does not "know" what needs to be done or how to do it. It is not merely that he, being bedridden, cannot go down to the drug store to get what is needed, but that he would, even if well, not be qualified to do what is needed and to judge what needs to be done. There is, that is to say, a "communication gap." (Parsons 1951: 441)

I should now like to suggest that social organisation of health care, overwhelmingly in modern societies, but particularly in North America, has come to be organised in terms of an asymmetrical hierarchy with respect to the functions of this particular system, of which the two polar aspects are the role of physician as the highest grade of publicly certified expert in health care and the role of sick person independent of the latter's status in other respects.   (Parsons 1975: 266)

1 Introduction

Parsons (1951, 1975) suggests that contemporary medical practice rests on an asymmetrical relationship between patient and doctor. Drawing from a specialized body of knowledge and technical skills,

I should like to thank Nigel Fielding, Paul Drew, John Heritage, and Douglas Maynard for their detailed comments on an earlier draft, Charles and Marjorie Goodwin for observations on some of the fragments discussed herein, and Agnes McGill and her careful editorial work. Different versions of this chapter have been presented at the following conferences: "When Patients and Doctors Meet," Cambridge, 1988; "Gemeiner Kongress Deutsche–Österreiche–Schweizerische Gesellschaft fur Soziologie," Zurich, 1988, and "Colloque Interdisciplinaire: Travail et Practiques Langagières," Paris, 1989. Audience comments on the data and the analysis were extremely helpful and, I am afraid, have been liberally integrated into various parts of the chapter. The chapter was prepared whilst the author was an doctors exercise expertise in determining the nature of a patient's condition and its appropriate management, and legitimize or preclude an individual's access to the "sick role." The relationship between the participants entails a "communication" or competence gap, in which the patient is unable to help himself and is ignorant of both the nature and the treatment of the disease. However, as Bloor and Horobin (1975) suggest, medical practice inevitably relies upon the "expertise" of the sick person (or their guardian) to decide when they should seek professional medical help, and provide relevant information to the doctor for the diagnosis and management of the condition.[1] The ways in which patient and doctor manage these potentially contradictory demands within the framework of diagnosis in the consultation forms the focus of this essay.

The asymmetrical relationship between patient and doctor, the tension between the lay person and professional expertise and the significance of medical authority to contemporary practice have infused studies concerned with the communication of diagnostic information by doctors to patients in the consultation. Research both in the United States and in Great Britain (e.g. Waitzkin and Stoeckle 1976 and Tuckett *et al.* 1985) has argued forcefully that the relative absence of diagnostic information provided by doctors in various types of medical interaction derives from the maintenance of authority and control by the practitioner or the profession over the patient and the consultation. It is, however, increasingly recognized by the profession itself that the relative absence of diagnostic and other forms of information provided by doctors to patients is consequential for compliance with treatment programs and undermines the possibility of encouraging prevention in medicine.

Byrne and Long's (1976) pioneering study of verbal behaviors of

Alexander von Humboldt Fellow at the University of Constance. I am very grateful to Thomas Luckmann for his generous support of, and comments on, the research discussed here.

The initial research upon which the chapter is based was undertaken as part of ESRC (HR/5148 and HR/8143) supported projects concerned with professional–client communication in primary health care, in particular general-practice consultations. The research was initially undertaken in collaboration with the late P.S. Byrne at the University of Manchester. Details concerning the projects, the methodological background and some analyses can be found in Heath (1986). I should like to thank Marshall Marinka and the MSD Foundation for assistance with data provision, and all those who kindly provided access to their consultations.

doctors in more than 2,000 general-practice consultations forms the basis of our current understanding of the presentation of diagnostic information to patients by doctors. They divide the consultation into six distinct phases: I, relating to the patient; II, discovering the reason for attendance; III, conducting a verbal or physical examination or both; IV, consideration of the patient's condition; V, detailing treatment or further investigation; and VI, terminating. The authors find that the phase of the consultation in which doctors present diagnostic information, consideration of the patient's condition, is relatively limited; indeed, in some cases it does not exist at all:

> What is curious is that when one talks to doctors about this behaviour [giving information or opinion], most claim that they use it frequently. Yet on tape one finds that the majority switch quickly from Phase III to V with hardly a word to the patient en route. They only give the information as a prelude to termination in explanation of the nature of the prescription they are about to hand over.
>
>   (Byrne and Long 1976: 50–1)

The authors describe the verbal behaviors used by medical practitioners during phase IV of the consultation and relate these utterance types to distinct communicative styles adopted by doctors. With their emphasis on patient- and doctor- "centered" knowledge and skills, Byrne and Long argue that the limited provision of diagnostic information in the consultation is intimately related to the asymmetries of the relationship and the maintenance of medical authority.

Drawing from Byrne and Long's important contribution, this chapter examines the delivery of diagnostic information in the general-practice consultation and the ways in which it is received by patients. The analysis explores how asymmetry between patient and practitioner is interactionally preserved and considers why relatively little diagnostic information is presented or discussed in the consultation. The data addressed in the chapter is drawn from a substantial collection of video recordings of general-practice consultants gathered in various settings throughout the British Isles.

It is through the diagnosis or medical assessment that doctors provide patients with information concerning the nature of the illness or disease. In the general-practice consultation, the doctor recurrently presents the diagnosis or medical assessment immedi-

ately following the physical examination. These summaries of the
patient's illness or state of health provide the basis to the management of the complaint and vary from a single word or phrase such
as "Bronchitis," "That's alright actually," through to a detailed
description and explanation of a particular condition. They include
"medical" assessments of the state of a condition, "He's not bad
you know," and specific diagnoses, "That's shingles," or "I'm
afraid she has tonsilitis again." These diagnoses and medical assessments occur both in "new appointments" and in circumstances in
which the patient returns to see the doctor with a particular condition.[2] As Byrne and Long (1976) find, some form of medical
assessment of the patient's condition is presented by the doctor in
the majority of consultations in our data corpus.[3] Indeed, if they
are not forthcoming immediately following the examination they
may be elicited by the patient.[4]

The diagnosis or assessment of the patient's condition forms a
pivotal position within the general-practice consultation. It marks
the completion of the practitioner's practical inquiries into the
patient's complaint and forms the foundation to management of
the difficulties. It stands as the "reason" for the consultation and is
routinely documented in the medical-record cards.[5] The status of
the diagnosis derives not just from the license and mandate ascribed
to the practitioner but from its sequential location, juxtaposed with
verbal and physical investigation into the nature of the condition.[6]
In cases where patients proffer candidate diagnoses of their complaint prior to the completion of the examination or interview,
practitioners routinely decline or delay consideration of their proposals.[7] The warrantable and objective character of the diagnosis
or medical assessment is accomplished in and through the investigation of the complaint and the location and design of the summary
of the condition. In interaction with the patient, the doctor systematically accomplishes the factual status of his professional opinion;
an objectivity which is rarely challenged.

2 Withholding reply to the diagnosis or medical assessment

As Byrne and Long suggest, the diagnosis or medical assessment
may be combined with an utterance in which the doctor addresses
the management of the condition. More usually, however, the

doctor's opinion of the patient's condition is presented in a distinct utterance or turn at talk which is solely concerned with the delivery of diagnostic information. Fragment (1) is drawn from a consultation in which the patient is suffering severe earache. We join the action as the physical examination draws to completion.

```
(1) (Ear examination)
    1    Dr:    →    er::::::::: Yeas:: (0.3) this one's: blocked
    2                (.) the other one's not.
    3           →    (1.2)
    4    Dr:         Well when would you like to have them done
    5                (.) next week some time:?
    6    P:          Yers: (.) yes please.
    7                (1.2)
    8    Dr    →     If you'd like, to:: (.) call at um::: (0.5)
    9                reception: (0.5) the girls (0.2) >on your way
   10                out (.) the girls will (0.7) sort out the
   11                appointment for you.
```

As the doctor steps away from the patient, having inspected both ears, he produces an assessment of the patient's condition "Yeas·· (0.3) this one's: blocked (.) the other one's not." The patient produces no response and after a 1.2 second silence, the doctor continues with a proposal concerning the treatment of the condition.

Fragment (2) is drawn from a consultation in which the patient has returned to the doctor for the assessment and treatment of a particular condition; fragment (3) from a consultation in which the patient presents a problem for the first time.

```
(2) (Chest examination)
    1    Dr    →    He's not bad you know
    2               (4.5)
    3    Dr:        What I would suggest we should do::: (.6) is
    4               simply continue with the:: (.5) Ventillin:
    5               (.2) at night.
```

```
(3) (Examination followed by questions)
    1    Dr:    →    ·hhh You know (0.2) I'm wondering if you've got
    2                a small:: ulcer:.
    3                (0.8)
    4    Dr:         And I'm wonderin if we ought to just have this
    5                looked into an:::,
```

```
6                    (0.2)
7    Dr:             (thoroughly) examined an::↑ (.) if this
8                    confirmed give you some special tablets that
9                    will help:.
```

In both cases the doctor presents a medical assessment or diagnosis of the patient's condition. In fragment (2), neither the child,
whose asthma has been examined, nor his father choose to respond
to the assessment, and after a 4.5. second silence, the doctor continues with a recommendation for treatment of the condition. In (3)
the doctor presents a candidate diagnosis to which the patient
produces no response. After a brief silence the practitioner continues by suggesting how the complaint might be managed.

In each instance the doctor presents the patient with information
concerning the nature or state of the condition. These "informings"
include descriptions of the condition, evaluations, and actual nam-
ings of the disease; they consist of actual diagnoses or medical
assessments of the complaint. In each case the doctor provides an
opportunity for the patient to respond to the informing by not only
delivering the diagnostic information within a distinct utterance or
turn at talk, but also by leaving a gap following the medical assessment in which the patient has an extended possibility to reply. The
patient withholds immediate response to the informing and remains
silent throughout the ensuing gap. In consequence, the practitioner
is able to move directly from the diagnosis of the condition to its
management.

Patients do not always remain silent following the delivery of the
diagnosis or medical assessment. An alternative way in which
patients deal with the presentation of diagnostic information by the
doctor is the production of a downward-intoned, often muffled, *er*
or *yeh*:

```
(4) (Chest examination)
1    Dr:      →    ˙hhhh You've got erm: (0.8) bronchitis::.
2    P:              °er:.
3                    (4.5) ((Dr begins to write prescription))
4    Dr:             ˙hhh (0.3) I'll give you antibiotics: to take
5                    for a week. hhh
6                    (.8)
7    Dr:             How long are you here for?
8    P:              We go back on Satur°day::
```

Both the downward-intoned *er* or *yeh* are "backward looking".
They operate retroactively, acknowledging the diagnosis or medical
assessment, passing the floor back "with dispatch," and providing
an undifferentiated opportunity to the doctor to develop the interaction in the way he might choose. In many cases, but by no means
all, withholding response, or producing a downward-intoned *er* or
yeh, to the presentation of information, leads to the doctor moving
directly from the diagnosis of the condition to its management.

The absence of patient participation in response to the delivery
of diagnosis or medical assessment severely curtails "phase IV" of
the consultation and contributes to the relative lack of diagnostic
information received by patients. Even in cases where doctors
provide extensive diagnostic information over successive utterances
we find patients withholding response to the informing and revealing remarkable passivity; consider, for example, fragment (6) presented at the end of this section.

Fragments (1)–(4) reveal one pattern of action which occurs in
phase IV of the general practice consultations within our data
corpus.[8]

    (Physical examination)
    Dr.   Diagnosis or medical assessment;
    P   No response, or downward-intoned *er* or *yeh*;
    Dr.   Recommended management, treatment, arrangements,
         and the like.

Thus, despite receiving the opportunity to respond to the diagnosis
or medical assessment, patients either withhold response altogether
or produce only the most minimal acknowledgment of the diagnostic information. Responses to informings which arise in conversational interaction appear to be used relatively rarely in reply to a
diagnosis or medical assessment in the consultation: for example, in
conversation, "informings" may be greeted with a response which
displays newsworthiness of the information and the "change in the
state" undergone by the recipient. Yet "newsreceipts," such as free-
standing *Oh*s, or more likely *Oh* in conjunction with additional
turn components (such as assessments), and "newsmarks" such as
Really or *Is it* (see Jefferson 1981a, 1981b; Heritage 1984b), do not
regularly greet diagnoses or medical assessments. It is also unusual
to find patients exploiting their opportunity to speak following a

diagnosis or medical assessment with an inquiry concerning the
nature of the illness, its relative seriousness or the course it is likely
to follow. Moreover, agreements, articulated through an explicit
yes or a second assessment, do not frequent replies to the diagnosis
or assessment.

Even in cases where the diagnosis of the patient's complaint is
relatively serious or problematic, patients remain reluctant to respond to the information presented by the doctor and apparently
unwilling to elicit further details. Consider the following instance
and note how the practitioner has to reconfirm the diagnosis before
a response is forthcoming from the patient. The patient initially
replies by simply recycling the diagnosis and only after the reconfirmation by the doctor does she begin to discuss the diagnosis.

```
(5) (Physical examination)
 1   Dr:            Yeah
 2                  (.3)
 3   Dr:      →     That's shingles.
 4                  (1.2)
 5   Dr:      →     <that's what it is:
 6                  (.2)
 7   P:             Shingles.
 8   Dr:            Ye⌈s
 9   P:             ⌊Oh: I (.) I did won: (.) be⌈cause the fact that it
10   Dr:                                        ⌊°no:
11                  that it(.) it's not itched↑ a lot
12   Dr:            No:::
13   P:             But: and I couldn't stand to touch it.
```

The relative absence of patient participation in phase IV of the
consultation is not solely explained by the behavior of the general
practitioner; indeed, the data suggest that doctors recurrently
provide an opportunity for patients (or guardians) to reply to the
diagnosis or medical assessment. However, it should be mentioned
that there are occasions when practitioners undermine the patient's
opportunity to respond to the diagnostic information. For instance,
as Byrne and Long (1976) suggest, the presentation of the diagnosis
may be designed to project further talk, not infrequently concerned
with the management of the case, and thereby to discourage the
patient's response. Moreover, doctors may combine the diagnosis
with the recommended treatment of the condition, excluding the
characteristic silence, and display both through the intonation and

pace that the utterance is incomplete. If the patient replies to the informing and recommendation, it is routinely the second item in the turn, the management of the case, which is addressed by the patient.

The patient's participation following the delivery of the diagnosis or medical assessment may be undermined by the nonverbal behavior of the general practitioner. Elsewhere (Heath 1986), I have documented the ways in which the bodily comportment of the doctor, through gaze and postural orientation, is consequential for the ways patients describe their problem and the information they provide. Parallel considerations apply to phase IV of the consultation: for instance, in presenting a diagnosis, a practitioner may undertake related activities such as writing a prescription or sick note and thereby discourage the patient from exploiting the opportunity to respond to the informing. Yet, in the cases discussed above and during the vast bulk of diagnostic informings, the practitioner is visually and interactionally available for patient contribution; indeed, the presentation of the diagnosis or medical assessment is not uncommonly accompanied by a shift of gaze towards the patients, an action which itself can serve to elicit talk from a co-participant (Heath 1986: ch. 2).

This relative absence of patients' participation can also be found in the management phase (phase V) of the general-practice consultation; the absence of response to each turn providing the doctor with an undifferentiated opportunity to draw the consultation from diagnosis, to management, and finally to closure. Consider the following fragment, in which the doctor provides the patient with a relatively extensive description of the state of his condition and its appropriate treatment.

```
(6) (P. blows into spirometer)
 1   Dr:        ˙hhh (0.2) erm:: (1.2) tth <You ought to be up
 2              the:re:::↑
 3              (1.0)
 4   Dr:        You are down: (0.2) there <which is not too
 5              ba:d.
 6              (0.6)
 7   Dr:        ˙thhh (0.5) er: (0.3) Still (.) <I'm a lot older
 8              an:: (al) a lot shorter than hhyouhh (.) ˙hhh and
 9              I'm (no) there::. (0.5) The difference between
10              us is partly yer. you got an attack of bronchitis
```

```
11                 which (0.3) drops it down::. (0.8) about that much:,
12                 (.) 'thhh (.) but er the rest is (even) these five
13                 cigarettes a day.'thhh (0.7) 'tt It would be a good
14                 idea:: (1.2) to take the opportun:(tu)ity just not
15                 to star:t again if you can:::,
16   P:            °mm mm::
17   Dr:           because it (0.3) 'hhh five fags a day is just enough
18                 to keep your toe in the door so that (1.2) later on
19                 when you can afford it you smoke more and more. (0.3)
20                 and er::: (0.3) it's easy to stop (your age).
21                 (0.5)
22   P:            °er::.
23   Dr:           So it's not a bad idea to have a go (.) 'thhh erm:::
24                 (1.5)
25   Dr:           thhhh
26                 (3.2)
27   Dr:           erm:::
28   P:            (26.3)
29   Dr:           I want you to take one of these tablets four times a
30                 day for the nex:t five days:: and lots of hot
31                 drinks to, (1.6) loosen the phlegm :. (0.7) 'thhh
32                 (4.2)
33   Dr:           and:: er: (1.2) I'll make this out to: resume: next
34                 Monday <I should think that you probably be
35                 alright by then bu⌐t I think you should be
36   P:                          ⌊mm
37   Dr:           off till then.
38                 (0.8)
39   Dr:           If you not alright then: come back an see me again
40                 then.
41   P:            (O::kay)
42                 (16.00)
43   Dr:           O:.kay:
44   P:            O.kay
45                 (0.3)
46   Dr:           Terra::
47   P:            Thanks.
```

The consultation progresses from the presentation of diagnostic information, to management and then to closure, with very little participation by the patient, despite a delivery of diagnostic information by the doctor which maximizes the opportunities for "recipient"-initiated intervention.

The relative passivity of patients in phase IV of the consultation does not seem to be directly related to the substance of the diagnos-

tic information, its relative seriousness or peculiarity, nor the length
of the utterance(s) through which it is provided. As the data reveal,
the informing may involve a description of the condition, an evaluation, a naming of the complaint, and various other objects; it may
consist of a single word or sentence, or a series of utterances which
describe and explain the illness. Yet patients may persist in withholding replies, sometimes over a very detailed summary of the
condition interdispersed with specific opportunities to respond.

This relative absence of recipient participation with informings
is also found in other interaction environments in which an expert
provides an opinion or assessment on matters of which the other
person is ignorant. Consider the following brief examples drawn
from a popular British television program, in which an expert
assesses the antiques and *objets d'art* brought along by members of
the *Roadshow* audience. The client begins by presenting his
personal knowledge of the article whilst it is subject to careful
inspection by the expert, who then delivers his expert opinion of the
object and discusses its provenance and such like.

(7) (Inspecting a grandfather clock)
1   E: →   It's <u>cert</u>ainly a Mediterranean scene there:
2   (1.2)
3   E: an:d: (1.2) you're absolutely right (0.2) it is
4   Maltese.
5   (1.7)
6   E: We talk basically about the history of the clock...

(8) (Inspecting silver candlesticks)
1   E: →   What you've got here is the most ma<u>r:vellous</u>
2   (0.7) pair (0.5) of mid nineteenth century
3   Russian candlesticks.
4   (0.7)
5   E: The m<u>arks</u> which (0.7) can you see that?
6   C: Yes:
7   (.)
8   E: They tuck them very neatly............

In both instances, the expert delivers his assessment of the object
and provides the client with the opportunity to respond. The client
provides no reply and the expert then continues. Note that in these
instances, the expert continues by elaborating specific details of the
object, rather than moving directly on to an action more akin to the

management phase of the "interview." The valuation, the hiatus of
each event, follows a detailed description during which clients systematically withhold response unless specifically encouraged to by
the co-participant.

Thus the pattern found in phase IV of the consultation may be
closely related to the asymmetrical relationship between patient
and doctor and in particular the relative distribution of expertise
between the participants; asymmetries which may be relevant to
and preserved in other types of interactional environment.

3 The design of a diagnosis or medical assessment

In the instances discussed so far, even fragment (6), where the
doctor specifically encourages the patient to respond, it can be
observed that the diagnosis or medical assessment is presented as a
factual, monolithic assertion concerning the state of health or illness of the other. The delivery of expert information by the doctor
can, however, be designed in such a way as to overcome the
patient's apparent reluctance to reply.

One such design is to pose the diagnosis or medical assessment
as a question, thereby inviting the patient to reply to the doctor's
professional assessment of the complaint.

```
(9)
 1    Dr:    →    If I was te say to you, (.) er I think that your
 2                getting:: (0.2) very re:al physical symptoms:,
 3                but (0.2) they're not symptoms of disease: (.)
 4                ˙hhh. th ey're symptoms of your
 5    P:                  mm
 6    Dr:        body (0.3) over reacting because of an:xiety:,
 7    P:         mmh
 8    Dr:        how would you feel about tha:t.
 9    P:         Yeah (0.2) I would say it:.
10               (1.0)
11    P:         I would say that (1.2) most could be it (1.2)
12               because.......
```

The informing suggests that the condition may be caused by
"anxiety" rather than disease, and invites the patient to respond to
the idea. The suggestion is accepted by the patient, who is encouraged to explain why he might be suffering from this type of condition. The more detailed response to the proposed diagnosis arises
in the light of the practitioner withholding further talk after the

initial response. In the next fragment, the medical assessment "Smoking:?" simultaneously proposes an underlying cause for the symptoms (breathlessness and coughing) and invites the patient to reply.

```
(10) (Physical examination)
 1    Dr:      →    Smoking:?
 2                  (1.2)
 3    Dr:           Ho ⌐w many?
 4    P:              └(Oh:) yes but I have (.) cut dow:n a lot.
 5                  (1.8)
 6    Dr:           To:?
 7                  (0.6)
 8    Dr:           From? (0.2) To:?
 9    P:            We ⌐ll I use to smoke about twenty a day but⌐I have
10    Dr:             └hhh                                     └erm
11    P:            cut °them dow:n:.
```

In both fragments (9) and (10), the medical assessment proposed by the doctor does not correspond to patients' version of the complaint. The assessments suggest that the symptoms are related to a different cause or condition than believed by the patient. As a way of attempting to secure the patient's acceptance of the diagnostic assessment, the practitioner delivers or implies a tentative summary of the condition and invites the patient to reply. The proposed assessment of the condition meets with more immediate success in fragment (9) than in (10). But in both cases, through the way in which the informing is designed, the doctor is able to encourage the patient to reply and address the proffered summary of the condition. The medical assessments generate further discussion of the complaint and an expansion of the phase of the consultation in which the "doctor considers the patient's condition."

Unlike instances discussed earlier, where the diagnosis or medical assessment is presented as a factual statement or report of the patient's state of health, in (9) and (10) the doctor displays, through his invitation, a certain tentativeness in the summary of the cause of the condition. Displaying uncertainty or tentativeness concerning the diagnosis or medical assessment can itself serve to encourage the patient to respond:

```
(11) (Physical examination)
 1    Dr:      →    ˙hhh It's not a totally typical story of a
 2                  wear and tear arthritis, but I think that's:
```

```
 3                    what it's going to turn ou⌐t to be::::.
 4    P:      →                                 └ (Well that (.) but
 5                    that en right wouldn') wife and nurse says hhh⌐h
 6    Dr:                                                           └oh
 7                    wel l⌐I think we ought to get an X. Ray as a
 8    P:                  └˙hh heh
 9    Dr:     check.
10    P:      Yers
11    Dr:     ˙hh You've not had this done on that ankle before?
12    P:      No:.
```

(12) (Physical examination)
```
 1    Dr:             °mm Fine
 2                    (0.7)
 3    Dr:     →       ˙hhhh Well there's a marked er:: (.)
 4                    conjunctivitis on both si:des there Mister
 5                    Banks, erm:
 6    P:              °er
 7                    (0.2)
 8    Dr:     →       ˙thhhh What set it off I wouldn't know:
 9    P:      →       I ⌐wouldn't either I thought what was it hay:
10    Dr:             └(he heh)
11    P:              fever or somit like this: (° __ __ mm) wi⌐th this
12    Dr:                                                      └You're
13                    not normally a hay fever suf⌐ferer are you?
14    P:                                          └No no ....
```

In (11) the doctor presents a qualified diagnosis of the condition;
it is marked with "I think" and a statement concerning the untypi-
cal nature of the condition's history. The patient does not directly
agree with the proposed diagnosis, but rather supports the doctor's
opinion by citing other sources. His wife and a second expert (a
nurse) had also thought it might be a "wear and tear arthritis." The
doctor does not respond to the patient's reply, but rather moves
directly to consider the management of the condition. In (12) the
doctor presents a diagnosis to which he receives a downward-
intoned "er." Rather than turning to the management of the condition, the doctor declares he does not know what caused the
condition. The patient treats the utterance as an invitation to
deliver his own thoughts on the matter, initially revealing his own
ignorance and then mentioning a possible cause. The reply serves to
generate further inquiries.

    In both these instances the way in which the diagnosis is presented encourages the patient to respond. The doctor displays his lack of certainty or relative ignorance and the patient offers support to the professional assessment of the condition. Despite the tentative nature of the diagnosis or medical assessment, patients do not allow their replies to compete with or challenge the medical assessment of their complaint. They do not agree explicitly with the doctor's opinion but rather, the patients preserve the differential status between their own version and the understanding of the expert, designing their contribution so that it supports the doctor's proposal but does not imply that their own assessment or knowledge of the condition is equivalent to the opinion of the expert.

There are significant differences between the ways in which the doctors present diagnosis in the two instances, the extent to which they encourage patients' participation, and the sequential trajectories which emerge from the medical assessments. Indeed, in (12) the postdiagnosis declaration of ignorance is specifically designed to elicit the patient's ideas, and the doctor uses the response to generate further discussion concerning the cause of the condition, whereas in (11) the doctor forestalls further consideration in this consultation of the "candidate" medical assessment (the patient is referred for further diagnostic tests).

By no means all the occasions in which patients reply to the diagnosis arise in circumstances where the doctor displays the uncertainty or tentative nature of the medical assessment. Various devices which generate patients' participation in this phase of the consultation underscore the factual basis of the summary of the condition: for instance, diagnoses or medical assessments prefaced by *In fact* or *Actually* or, as in the following instance, both, receive a response which displays that the doctor's opinion is news for the recipient. These "newsmarks" invite the doctor to reconfirm the medical assessment and lead to the informing being advanced in some way.[9]

(13) (Physical Examination)

```
1   Dr:    →    In fa:ct actu:ally (.) her tonsils an that
2                look (0.5) much more shrun:ken.
3                (0.4)
4   M:          Do they?=
5   Dr:         =Yeah: (.) they look quite (.) >have you? (0.6)
6                looked recently (.) ˙hhh⌈hhh They heh so (.) ˙hh
7   M:                               ⌊No
```

```
8     Dr:          want to show your mum:?
9                  (1.2)
10    M:           Le⌈ss than they usually are::? you mean::.=
11    Dr:            ⌊Show her
12    Dr:          =Oh yers:: (0.2) actually (.) ˙hhh open wi:::de
13                 (0.6)
14    Dr:          Can you see:: erm:: ⌈the bit down the mid⌈dle::
18    M:                               ⌊oh:::: yers::        ⌊yes::
19    Dr:          is⌈what we ca::ll: the: the uvula:::: >that's just
20      ⌊Yes
21    Dr:          the fancy name but either si:de…
```

Diagnoses or medical assessments in which the doctor contrasts
his findings with the patient's version of the complaint also receive
a display of the newsworthiness of the informing and are followed
by reconfirmation (and development) of the original assessment
from the doctor. In the next instance, the contrast "It's not ..., it's
a ..." draws the newsmark "Is it?" and reconfirmation of the
medical assessment by the doctor.

(14) (Physical examination)
```
1    Dr:    →     It's not a vein: (.) it's a muscle in spas:⌈m.
2    P:     →                                               ⌊Is it?
3    Dr:          Yeah
4    P:           Oh:
5    Dr:          and I think what's cau⌈sing it to be in spasm
6    P:                                 ⌊I've had it for about
7                 three or fou⌈r weeks, and n⌈ow (or something like
8    Dr:                      ⌊Yeah          ⌊Yeah
9    P:            that.)
10   Dr:          You've got a low grade inflammation of the eye::::
11                (0.3) the front of the eye and this is probaly
12                making the spasm co⌈me.
13   P:                              ⌊(°Right)
14   Dr:          ˙hh that's a nuisan⌈ce not anything serious,
15                                   ⌊°mm
16   Dr:          and I think w⌈e can settle it with some (__ __)
17   P:                        ⌊No (that's right he heh heh °not)
18                serious
```

The reconfirmation receives the freestanding "Oh:" and the doctor
responds with further details of the nature of the condition suffered
by the patient. It is worth noting that, in overlap with the elaboration of the medical assessment, the patient underscores his
grounds for seeking professional help by mentioning how long he
has suffered the complaint before turning to the doctor.

Prefacing the diagnosis or medical assessment with *In fact* and/ or *Actually*, or presenting a contrast, both serve to show that the doctor's summary of the condition differs from, or contrasts with, the anticipated version of the complaint. The display of newsworthiness to the informing by the patient may be less concerned with eliciting confirmation than with displaying to the doctor that the diagnostic assessment is unexpected and in particular contrasts with the patient's (or guardian's) understanding of the complaint. Prefaces to the diagnosis such as *In fact* and *Actually* are employed in circumstances in which the doctor fails to find evidence of the difficulties presented by the patient (or guardian), and contrasts, in cases where the diagnosis of the condition is other than suggested by the patient (or guardian). In and through the way he designs the diagnosis or medical assessment, the doctor displays his sensitivity to the incongruence between his qualified understanding of the condition and the version presented by the patient.

Other turn designs in the delivery of a diagnosis or medical assessment which serve to encourage or elicit a response also arise in circumstances where there is incongruence between the patient's and the practitioner's assessment of the condition: for example, it was noted earlier how the doctor in fragment (9) encourages the patient to accept an alternative conception of his symptoms by inviting him to consider a proposed diagnosis, and in fragment (10), how the doctor, through the assessment "Smoking:?," attempts to encourage the patient to reinterpret and reattribute her symptoms. In and through these and other devices (there is not the space to document them here) the doctor encourages the patient to respond to the diagnosis or medical assessment, and in various ways secures the patient's cooperation with, or commitment to, the professional understanding of their condition or state of health, in contrast to the lay standpoint of the patient (or guardian).

It is perhaps worth adding that the various turn designs found in these materials also serve to encourage particular forms of client co-participation in other environments in which experts provide an informed opinion concerning matters unknown to the other. Returning to the *Antiques Roadshow*, consider the following instance in which the expert prefaces his opinion with "in fa:ct," which marks the contrast between the professional assessment of the vase and the client's belief that it was North American.

(15) (Inspecting a grandfather clock)
```
 1   E:    →   `hhh Well in fa:ct it's Japanese:.
 2            (0.5)
 3   C:       Oh is it::?
 4   E:       Yes:: he's Japanese (.) `hh erm (0.3) there's
 5            a lot of characteristics about him which would
 6            would indicate that.> I think probaly the best
 7            piece (0.8) to indicate it is.......
```

4 Incongruency and accounts of illness

The medical consultation is, characteristically, organized in two
distinct sections; the interview or information-gathering phase,
followed by the diagnosis and management of the condition. This
organization is found within both new and return appointments,
and is reflected in the schematic description of the diagnostic phase
of the consultation provided earlier. Withholding response to or
acknowledging a diagnosis with the downward-intoned *er* or *yeh*,
contributes to this overall organization, providing the practitioner
with the opportunity to progress directly from the diagnosis to the
management of the condition and the termination of the consultation. Alternatively, a reply to the diagnosis may not simply stall
the progression of the consultation but reintroduce matters which
are more conventionally dealt with during the interview phase.

(16)
```
 1   Dr:   →   `hhh It's the sa:me as you've had all:: along
 2            rea::lly isn't it ⌐°with this:
 3   P:            ⌊Yes       ⌊ Yes it ishh
 4   Dr:      Yea h
 5            (.)
 6   P:       On:ly: if this: la:s:::ss:::t (0.2) (tch) (0.5)
 7            couple of month it's: been:: (.) `hhhhhh a(h)
 8            bihht (.) whether it be du⌐e to col:d weather:
 9   Dr:                   ⌊Yeah
10   P:       (.) I don't know whether that's anything to
11            do: with it.
12   Dr:      `hhhh Can I just listen in around your heart
14            and things right? (.) Just relax there if you
15            will.
16            ((Listens to chest))
```

The medical assessment treats the current symptoms as evidence of
an underlying, long-term illness (angina) and invites the patient to

respond. Prior to the actual completion of the medical assessment, the patient produces "Yes" in overlap with "rea::lly," and reiterates his agreement following the medical assessment with "Yes it is." Subsequently the patient produces an account in which he stresses how the symptoms have changed over the past few months and suggests that the complaint is sensitive to cold weather. As he delivers the account, the patient, through the ways he articulates the utterance and behaves visually, expresses his symptoms and especially the pain associated with the complaint.[10] Despite, therefore, the patient's apparent agreement with the diagnostic assessment, he delivers a description of his symptoms which suggest that the difficulties are not the "same as he has had all along"; his suffering is significantly worse and corresponds to certain climatic changes. The patient's account of his illness provides the possibility that the diagnosis and/or the management of the condition might be misconceived.

The patient's account proves relatively successful. In response, the practitioner temporarily abandons the management of the condition and returns to examine the patient. Following further inquiries, the doctor refers the patient for diagnostic tests in order to review the current medical assessment. Accounts in and through which patients attempt to counter (aspects of) the diagnosis or medical assessment do not always lead the doctor to reconsider his question.

(17) (Physical examination)
```
 1  Dr:          Slip (.) slip your things: on now::.
 2               (0.5)
 3  Dr:     →    ˙hhhh I'm sure: Doctor: Mckay's: right (.) I'm
 4               sure that these headaches:: yer gettin are::er
 5               associated with a bit of arthritis::, (0.5) in
 6               yerer:: (0.7) in yer neck (.) really:h (.) more
 7               than your (.) spine::. (.) er:m:. ˙thh I mean
 8               more than your lower spine it's the in your
 9               neck th⌐at's causin the::
10  P:            ⌊(°It is)
11  P:           It ⌐seems to be he:re:: anywa⌐y:.
12  Dr:            ⌊ the problem.        ⌊That's correct
13               (0.2)
14  Dr:          Yes mhhh
15               (3.2)
16  P:           That I could understood (.) because it (.)
```

```
17                 it's the headaches: was the thing that's:
18                 got me, (0.4) (More (....) than anything else)
19                 (1.2) >°More than the devil in hell< because
20                 they were gettin more or (.) less (.)
21                 permanent yer know:: (1.2) They were coming
22                 even when I was never pain in the back of me
23                 neck.
24                 (28.00)
25    Dr:          ˙hhhhhhh Right well I'll tell what we'll do
26                 Mister Tarrett (.) I'll give you......
```

The patient produces a possible agreement "(°It is)" with the medical assessment and follows the practitioner's explanation of the symptoms with an assessment "It seems to be he:re:: anyway:." The assessment provides a qualified agreement with the practitioner's opinion and, as the practitioner turns to write the prescription, the patient produces an account which stresses the increasing severity of the difficulties and underscores how the nature of the condition has been transformed since it was previously presented to a medical practitioner. The account fails to persuade the doctor to reconsider his assessment or treatment of the condition and the patient leaves the surgery with the prescription which was being prepared as he attempted to counter the practitioner's opinion of the condition.

Unlike the instances discussed earlier in this chapter, in both fragments (16) and (17), the patients initially respond to the diagnosis or medical assessment with an agreement. The agreements, however, foreshadow accounts in and through which the patient attempts to counter aspects of the professional opinion of the condition. The initial agreements and the accounts they foreshadow arise in response to medical assessments which suggest that the current symptoms and diagnosis (and, by implication, the management of the condition) are familiar to the patient; the presenting problem is "simply" evidence of a condition which the patient has suffered before and received medical advice and treatment for. In different ways the accounts stress the recent and increasing severity of the symptoms, and in particular reveal or emphasize the recent personal suffering experienced by the patient. Indeed, through their accounts and the subjective revelation of the symptoms, the patients attempt to suggest, even show, that their recent difficulties are not only more severe but different from hitherto. In (re)presenting and attempting to display the seriousness of their symptoms, patients not only encourage the doctor to reconsider his opinion of the condition and its management, but also bolster their grounds for seeking professional help in the face of a diagnosis which implies that their difficulties are familiar and relatively unproblematic.

Patients may not only be faced with a diagnosis which appears to question the severity of their symptoms and suffering, but a medical assessment which undermines the very existence of the condition for which they have sought the help of the doctor.

```
(18) (Physical examination)
   1   Dr:    →    Well yer ches:t is:: (.) absolutely cle:ar:
   2                today::,
   3                (1.0)
   4   Dr:          which is helpful:↑ (0.4) and your pulse is:
   5                (0.7) only eighty ˙thhh (.) which is er:::
   6                (1.2) not so bad.
   7                (1.2)
   8   P:     →    (Right it's::) there:: night time (uh) (.)
   9                it's:::ts not clear there, I've got er:::
  10                (            ) (1.4) (            )
  11                (0.3) I've more or less gone to bed when it
  12                starts:  on us:?
  13                (2.5)
  14   P:           I wake all the way through the night without
  15                getting any sleep (un open.)
  16                (0.5)
  17   Dr:          mm
  18   P:           (I don't know what's fetchin it up) during the
  19                nights (.) but it comes in at the nights.
  20                (0.5)
  21   Dr:          ˙thhhh You've not had any history of:er::: (.)
  22                allergy of asthma:: or: er::: (0.3) ˙hh hay
  23                fever °or anything like that?
```

Following a thorough physical examination, the practitioner declares that "today" the patient's chest is clear and his pulse rate reasonable. The medical assessment implies that there is little evidence for the presenting symptoms of the patient – breathlessness, a persistent cough, and a racing heart – but perhaps leaves the possibility open that the patient might indeed have been ill at some other time. In reply, the patient produces an account of his condition, describing when the symptoms arise and underscoring the severity of the difficulties and the discomfort they cause. The account details the patient's subjective experience of the illness and provides an explanation for the relative absence of symptoms during the consultation, namely that the difficulties are particularly severe at night when they are unavailable for examination by the doctor. By reasserting his symptoms and suffering and accounting for the absence of physical evidence, the patient encourages the doctor to undertake further inquiries into the difficulty, identify the nature of "the condition," and provide some form of treatment for the complaint. The account underscores the patient's grounds for seeking the doctor's help in the face of a medical assessment that threatens the legitimacy of the patient's claims to being sick and his grounds for seeking professional help and precludes his access to treatment and the sick role.

An alternative course of action undertaken by patients when faced with a medical assessment which fails to provide evidence of their difficulties is to accept that the condition does not exist and attempt to justify their decision to seek medical help. It will be recalled that in the following fragment the medical assessment prefaced by "In fa:ct actu:ally" receives "Do they?," which in turn elicits reconfirmation.

(13) (Physical Examination)
```
 1  Dr:      In fa:ct actu:ally (.) her tonsils an that
 2           look (0.5) much more shrun:ken.
 3           (0.4)
 4  M:       Do they?=
 5  Dr:      =Yeah: (.) they look quite (.) >have you? (0.6)
 6           looked recently: (.) ˙hhh ⌜hhh They heh so (.) ˙hh
 7                                     ⌊ No
 8  Dr:      >want to show your mum:?
 9           (1.2)
10  M:       Le⌜ss than they usually are::? you mean::.=
11  Dr:        ⌊Show her
12  Dr:      =Oh yers:: (0.2) actually (.) ˙hhh open wi:::de
13           (0.6)
14  Dr:      Can you see:: erm:: ⌜the bit down the mid ⌜dle::
18  M:                          ⌊oh:::: yers::          ⌊yes::
19  Dr:      is ⌜what we ca::ll: the: the uvula::: <that's
20  M:         ⌊Yes
21  Dr:      just the fancy name, (.) but either si:de,
```

```
22                  (0.9)
23     M:           Ye⌈ah
24     Dr:            ⌊it's quite shrunken down actually.
25     M:           Yes
26     Dr:          Good
27     Dr:          ((Examines patient's glands))
28                  (1.2)
29     Dr:          Good (0.2) an she hasn't any glands:: there
30                  (0.5)
31     M      →     Well there has been mum⌈ps at school:
32     Dr:                                  ⌊·thh
33     M:           you⌈see (an I) thought she was coming down
34     Dr:             ⌊Yeah
35     M:           with: (1.0) the mumps last week⌈an that.
36     Dr:                                          ⌊er yeh ·hhh
37     Dr:          I think she's ha::d (1.2) you know a throat
38                  infec⌈tion.
39     M:                ⌊Throat infection.
40     Dr:          ·hhh It's always (0.7) I find it difficult........
```

Following the reconfirmation of the medical assessment and its receipt, the doctor inspects the child's glands and declares there is no evidence of disease. In response to the medical assessments which fail to provide evidence of the symptoms suffered by the child, the mother produces an account. In the account she does not attempt to preserve the symptoms and (re)present the child's suffering, but accepts the findings of the physical examination and provides grounds for her decision to bring the child to the doctor: there are "mumps at school" and she was concerned that her daughter might have caught the disease. The doctor is sensitive to the mother's account, not only confirming that there might have been a "throat infection" (repeated by the mother), but later declaring she was wise to bring the child along in such circumstances.

In each instance, the patient produces an account in and through which he or she attempts to underscore the severity of the condition or explicitly justify the decision to seek professional medical help. The accounts reveal ways in which the patient (or guardian) is sensitive to the diagnosis or medical assessment, and in particular the import of the practitioner's findings for the patient's understanding of the complaint. The accounts arise in circumstances where the diagnosis or medical assessment fails to confirm the patient's (or guardian's) version of the difficulty and thereby jeopardizes the reasons for which they have sought professional help. By providing hitherto unmentioned details, asserting the severity of their symptoms and/or their reasons for concern, patients attend to and account for the incongruence between their own conception of the condition and the doctors' professional, medical assessment. Whether they attempt to stress the seriousness of the complaint, explain the absence of symptoms or justify their concerns, in each case the account attempts to (re)assert, either implicitly or explicitly, the patient's (or guardian's) reasons for seeking professional help. As a New Zealand general practitioner mentioned to Byrne and Long: "In order to have the privilege of talking to your doctor, you need to fulfil the essential precondition of being sick. Then you may go to him and ask him if he will perform his professional services upon you" (1976: 20).

Despite the "potential" conflict which underlies the delivery of postdiagnostic accounts by patients, actual disagreement with the doctor or altercation between the participants is extremely rare. In attempting to encourage the doctor to reconsider the assessment of the complaint, patients, through the ways in which they design their accounts, systematically preserve the differential between their own understanding of the complaint and the scientific or objective opinion of the general practitioner. In particular, by reinvoking, even expressing, their subjective experience of the symptoms and suffering incurred with the complaint, patients maintain a sharp distinction between their lay conception and individual knowledge of the illness and the technical competence and expertise of the doctor. The ways in which patients' accounts are designed to avoid explicit disagreement in the consultation are highly parallel to the ways in which discrepant claims are managed within other environments, such as the traffic courts studied by Pollner (1979). In the case at hand we can see how postdiagnostic accounts weave a delicate path through the tapestry of obligation and responsibility which underlies the delivery of medical help, preserving the asymmetries in the relationship between patient and doctor while on occasions encouraging (rather than demanding) reconsideration of the diagnosis or medical assessment of the condition.

Practitioners are also sensitive to the incongruence between their diagnosis or medical assessment of the complaint and the presenting problem of the patient. Indeed, in certain cases they elicit explanations from patients concerning their (misconceived) reasons for concern.[11] Moreover, in a number of the instances addressed here, it can be observed how the turn design of the diagnosis or medical assessment occasions patients' participation and encourages the presentation of an account. Both the diagnoses in (16) and in (17) are sensitive to the possibility of differing conceptions of the condition; and in (13), by specifically marking the factual basis of the medical assessment, the doctor displays his sensitivity to the potential conflict between the findings of the physical examination and the mother's version of the child's state of health. Indeed, even in (18) the delivery may be designed to encourage a response from the patient in which he accounts for the apparent incongruence between his presenting symptoms and the medical assessment. Similarly in the previous section, it can be seen that turn designs which systematically encourage patient response to the diagnosis or medical assessment may be employed in circumstances in which there is incongruence between the patient's version of the complaint (presented during the interview phase of the consultation) and the findings of the verbal and physical examination. The actual shape of the diagnosis or medical assessment is deeply consequential to the form of participation by the patient and the type of account which is presented.

One final point: through the ways in which the interview or physical examination are conducted, patients may be sensitive to the possibility that the diagnosis or medical assessment will fail to confirm their version of the condition prior to its actual delivery. Before the practitioner presents his opinion, the patient may attempt to explain the absence of physical signs and/or underscore their reasons for seeking professional help. Consider the following fragment. As the practitioner begins to deliver the diagnosis. "Yeah that's er::: (.) 'hhh" the patient enters in overlap, stressing that he has tried every solution before seeking help from the doctor.

```
(19)
1    P:          It's now going across my shoulders an:: (.)
2                it (it)(.) <I never worried about it until
3                somebody said ugh::::::::::: what's all
4                that over yo┌ur back?
5    Dr:                     └Yeh.
6    Dr:         Nyer it's nice (.) friends are good
```

```
 7              like th at (—) you know ugh :::::
                       ⌐
 8   P:               ⌊Yeh
 9   Dr:        ughh::::ee ⌐urgh they go.
10   P:                    ⌊Yeah
11             (0.7)
12   Dr:  →    Yeah that's er::: (.) ˙hh⌐h(———)
13   P:   →                          ⌊I've tried every
14             cream an if:: (.) I can't get rid of it.
15   Dr:       (Right)
16             (0.7)
17   Dr:       I'll give you some crea:m: ˙hh that ˙hh erm:::
18             (2.2)
19   Dr:       er: >You>you know th. that's (.) like er:::
20             (.) like an athletes: foot.
21             (0.5)
22   P:        Oh real⌐ly::?
23   Dr:             ⌊Ar:: (.) It's a f:::fungus: infection
```

5 Discussion: preserving asymmetries between patient and doctor

Diagnosis and assessment form the foundation to the general-practice consultation. The interview and the practitioner's examination of the patient are undertaken in order to produce a professionally warranted version of the condition or the state of health of the patient, and it is the diagnosis or medical assessment which determines the treatment of the difficulties. The diagnosis and medical assessment not only provide the basis to the management of the complaint, but also legitimize the patient's claims to being ill and, if necessary, access to the sick role and its incumbent rights and responsibilities. In this way the medical consultation and in particular the interaction between patient and practitioner provide an institutionalized basis to the management of illness within society.

Despite the significance of diagnosis and medical assessment, the phase in which the doctor "considers the patient's condition" constitutes a relatively brief phase within the medical consultation, often no more than a single utterance delivered by the practitioner. Both doctors and patients contribute to its brevity. The authoritative, monolithic assertions which present an expert opinion of the condition do not particularly encourage the patient to respond, despite the opportunity they provide immediately following their completion. For their own part, patients reveal an extraordinary "passivity" in receiving news or information concerning their illness. Withholding response, or producing a downward-intoned grunt or *yeh*, provides the doctor with the opportunity of progressing directly from diagnosis to management of the condition. Alternative forms of diagnosis or medical assessment do serve to encourage patients' participation and almost any response, other than the characteristic acknowledgment, foreshadows further contribution from the patient, and serves in various ways (and through different sequential trajectories) to generate further talk concerning the diagnosis or medical assessment.

Responses to the diagnosis or medical assessment other than the characteristic downward-intoned *er* or *yeh*, whether encouraged by the doctor or volunteered by the patient, appear to emerge on occasions in which there is incongruencey between the professional opinion and the lay understanding of the condition. Inviting the patient to respond to a tentative diagnosis, the use of contrasts and prefacing assessment with fact markers, and the delivery of accounts in which suffering is reasserted or reasons for contact explicated, are all in their different ways systematic attempts to manage incongruency between the patient's and the practitioner's assessment of the complaint. Replies to and discussion of the diagnosis of medical assessment tend to arise in circumstances in which the participants are attempting to reveal, reconcile, and manage incongruent versions of the illness or disease. Incongruency generates movement away from the simplest pattern and leads to an expansion of phase IV of the consultation in which "the doctor considers the patient's condition." Ironically, therefore, greater discussion concerning the diagnosis or medical assessment may occur and more "information is exchanged" in circumstances in which patient and doctor have differing and incongruent conceptions of the condition.

Patients' accounts of their illness or behavior, and in particular the different ways in which they attempt to justify having sought professional medical help, reveal a deep sensitivity to asymmetries in the relationship between patient and doctor. By describing and accentuating their subjective experience of the illness, qualifying their own version of the complaint or explaining why they were concerned, patients systematically preserve the differential status between their own understanding of the complaint and its professional assessment – between the expertise of the doctor and their own lay opinion. Indeed, even in cases where there is potential conflict between the different assessments of the condition, patients maintain the differential status of the participants' opinions whilst simultaneously introducing information which encourages the doctor to reconsider his opinion of the condition.

Incongruent versions of the illness, the designs of accounts, and the forms of response received by diagnoses and medical assessments in various ways embody the interactional asymmetry between patient and doctor in the medical consultation. Withholding reply to the diagnosis or medical assessment or producing a downward-intoned grunt or *yeh*, is one way in which patients display and accomplish their differential status with respect to the assessment and management of illness and the condition at hand. By withholding response, patients not only provide the doctor with the opportunity of developing the consultation as they so wish, but preserve the objective, scientific, and professional status of the diagnosis or medical assessment; the silence or acknowledgment operating retroactively to underscore the significance of the practitioner's "opinion" of the condition. The relative absence of a range of other objects which commonly greet informings, including news-receipts and newsmarks, inquiries, and certain forms of acknowledgment such as an explicit *Yes*, may not only reveal the patient's orientation to medical authority and "affective neutrality," but also a central concern to avoid any response which could serve to imply that the participants' versions and assessment of the condition had an equivalent status. Even in cases where the doctor displays uncertainty in diagnosis, and thereby encourages discussion of the medical assessment of the condition, it may be observed how the patient's contribution preserves the contrasting status of the two versions of the illness and in particular embodies the subjective and lay standpoint of their own opinion.

It is hardly surprising that patients, in receiving diagnosis or medical assessment, preserve the distinction between the technical expertise and skills of the practitioner and their own lay knowledge and experience of illness and medicine. Any response to the diagnosis or medical assessment which challenges the asymmetry between the participants' understanding of the condition inevitably undermines the patient's grounds for seeking professional medical help. If the lay assessment of the illness or disease is equivalent to the practitioner's, then a fundamental part of the reason for turning to the doctor and receiving technical expertise is removed. Even in cases of long-term chronic illness, involving repeated consultations concerning a particular illness (consider fragments [2], [17], and [18]) and the potential accumulation of lay knowledge and experience concerning the disease, patients continue to preserve the differential status between their own opinion and the diagnosis or medical assessment of the doctor.

As the burgeoning body of empirical studies concerned with "illness behavior" would suggest, there is not necessarily a correspondence between the patients' evaluation of their illness and reasons for seeking medical help, and the diagnosis or medical assessment of the practitioner. Indeed, given the increasingly specialized nature of medical expertise and practice, and its localization within a particular profession, it might be expected that incongruent assessments of symptoms and illness between patient and doctor recur within the consultation. In general practice this does not seem to be the case. Both doctors and patients are sensitive to potential incongruence in the assessment of a condition in the consultation and through the design of the diagnosis or medical assessment – the production of accounts of the illness and the like – attempt to accomplish a (presupposed) shared (not equal) orientation towards the difficulties as a basis for their management. For the patient, incongruent versions of the illness may well threaten their legitimacy to be sick (and undertake the various responsibilities and obligations it entails) and undermine their reasons for seeking professional medical help. Thus, in this situation of "labeling" *par excellence*, the contrast between the subjective orientation of the patient and the objective opinion of the doctor, the congruence of versions and the asymmetrical distribution of knowledge and technical competence, infuses the accomplishment of diagnosis, its presentation, and its receipt.

It was suggested earlier that the "mutually dependent and interrelated" roles of doctor and sick person place the patient under contradictory and potentially conflicting responsibilities and obligations. On the one hand, the patient is unqualified to diagnose or treat his condition and must place himself in the hands of technically competent help; on the other, contemporary medical practice relies upon the individual's ability and expertise to recognize illness, decide when it is appropriate to seek professional help, and describe competently their symptoms and suffering. In the ways in which patients respond to the diagnosis and medical assessment, they systematically manage these "competing" demands. By withholding response to the medical assessment of the condition, or tailoring accounts to embody their subjective orientation to the illness, patients relinquish or subordinate their knowledge and opinion concerning the illness (found within the interview phase of the consultation), and render the co-participant's version as the objective, scientific, and factual assessment of the condition. The asymmetrical relationship between the participants and the differential status of their opinions concerning illness, are accomplished in and through the interaction between patient and doctor in the consultation itself.

6 Postscript

In recent years there has been a growing interest in interpersonal communication in the consultation and a commitment to training general practitioners in behavioral skills. Studies by Byrne and Long (1976), Tuckett et al. (1985) and others have provided a rich body of procedures for monitoring and improving the individual practitioner's communication skills. It is, however, important that any initiative to transform behavioral features of the consultation is sensitive to the interactional organizations in and through which the diagnosis of disease and its management are accomplished. A brief glance at the phase in which general practitioners consider the patient's condition reveals that the relative absence of diagnostic information presented to the patient in the consultation is not solely a consequence of doctors' practice "only [to] give the information as a prelude to termination in explanation of the nature of the prescription they are about to hand over" (Byrne and Long 1976: 50–1). Indeed, despite receiving an opportunity to elicit additional diagnostic information, patients systematically undermine their chance to gain further details concerning the nature of their condition. It is critical that our practical recommendations to "modify" the behavior of medical practitioners, whether in the delivery of diagnostic information or the multitude of other activities which occur in the consultation, is thoroughly embedded in a detailed understanding of the local interactional organization and the various rights and responsibilities therein.

Notes

1. For the purposes of this chapter I have taken the liberty of slightly corrupting the very powerful argument of Bloor and Horobin. The authors suggest that in and through negotiation between patient and doctor during the consultation, these contradictions are managed. In one sense, the aim of this chapter is to explicate that negotiation within one phase of the interaction between patient and doctor.
2. A diagnosis does not necessarily occur in the first of a series of consultations, nor are medical assessments particularly found in subsequent consultations. Moreover, unlike many phenomena which occur in the interaction between patient and doctor, the position of these objects is insensitive to whether the consultation is "new" or a "return."
3. Byrne and Long (1976) find that in 30 percent of consultations, phase IV, "consideration of patient condition." does not occur and in 48 percent it occupies less than one-tenth of the time of the whole consultation. In our own data corpus, a diagnosis or medical assessment occurs in more than 80 percent of consultations; the only recurrent absences are those dealing with "psychosocial" problems. The difference in the observations might be explained by access to recordings of the physical examination in our recent data (the domain in which diagnosis and medical assessment is often presented) and the consideration within this research of single words or sentences uttered by the doctor prior to recommending management of the complaint. More importantly, however, it is interesting to note how our observations dovetail with Byrne and Long's discussion of the relative brevity of phase IV.
4. Utterances through which patients attempt to elicit a diagnosis or medical assessment from the doctor reveal various characteristics which display the speakers' reluctance, difficulty, embarrassment, etc. in delivering the request. Consider the following instance:

(Chest Examination)

```
1   P:    →    What is it doctor if yer (don't) think that's
2              a rude question, is it?
3   Dr:        Wehhhllh huh I don't think it's a ru:de
4              question I mean I think it's jus:t (.) you
5              know (.) (t) I think it is:: probably pai:n
6              from you hear::t.
```

5. See Heath (1982) for a detailed discussion concerning the documentation procedures used for the medical-record cards in general practice.

6. In the following instance which is taken from extract (10) above, the single word "Smoking:?" achieves its status as a candidate diagnosis of the cause of the patient's difficulties solely by virtue of its position in immediate juxtaposition to the completion of the physical examination and the doctor's inquiries. *Mutatis mutandi*, the object itself marks the shift in the business at hand.

(Physical examination)
```
1   Dr:    →    Smoking:?
2              (1.2)
3   Dr:         Ho w many?
4   P:            (Oh:) yes but I have(.) cut dow:n a lot.
```

7. In the following instance, as the doctor is about to manipulate the patient's foot, the patient proffers a candidate diagnosis of his complaint "touched off" by the question concerning his age. Note how the proffered diagnosis is declined at least until the completion of the examination, whereupon it turns out to be correct; see fragment (11).

```
1   Dr:         How old are you now?
2   P:    →     Forty nine just coming up to forty nine.
3              (0.5)
4   P:    →     (Your right) it could be
5              arthritis: (.) ˙hh (.) hhhhhhheh
6   Dr:         We : ll ::
7   P:          ˙hhoop There <er.er. I can just feel it there
8   Dr:             lets have a look first
```

8. It should be noted that there is an important bias in the analysis discussed here towards postexamination diagnosis and assessment and there are reasons to believe that diagnostic informings within this position are particularly prone to no response, given the patient's limited technical and sometimes visual access to the physical examination.

9. For a detailed discussion of "newsmarks" and "newreceipts," their interactional coordination, and the trajectories which emerge following their production, see Jefferson (1981a) and Heritage (1984b: with special reference to note 13, 339–44). Different forms of newsmark or newsreceipt following the diagnosis or medical assessment project different sequential trajectories, and involve varying opportunities for patient or practitioner to initiate further discussion of the matters at hand. Research is currently directed to locating these various trajectories, and it is planned that they will be dealt with in a future paper.

10. See Heath (1989) for an analysis of the ways in which the expression of pain can be embodied in talk and how doctors manage these revelations within the framework of diagnostic activity.

11. The doctor does this in the following excerpt from extract (19):

```
19   Dr:              er: >You>you know th. that's (.) like er:::
20                    (.) like an atheletes: foot.
21                    (0.5)
22   P:               Oh real ┌ly::?
23   Dr:                     └Ar:: (.) It's a f:::fungus: infection
24   Dr:              ˙hhhhhh
25   P:               Or ┌hhh
26   Dr:                 └(    )
27                    (0.6)
28   Dr:              which is
29   P:               °Good Lord.
30                    (.)
31   Dr      →        Yeh(.)˙hhh he wha.wha.wha.wha.what did you
32                    feel it was:: °yer know=
33   P:               =˙hhh I don't know (.2) because of the·
34                    crea:ms: I've ha:d on::: I was gettin
35                    worrie:d: I didn't know what it was:
36   Dr:              Yes(.) what sort of creams: have you had?
```

9

On the management of disagreement between news interviewees

DAVID GREATBATCH

1 Introduction

A number of studies have dealt with institutional settings in which the participants use a turn-taking system that restricts the incumbents of particular social roles to either asking or responding to questions. Courtroom examination (Atkinson and Drew 1979), formal classroom lessons (McHoul 1978; Mehan 1979, 1985), and news interviews (Greatbatch 1985, 1988; Clayman 1986, 1987; Heritage and Greatbatch 1991), for example, have all been shown to involve variations of this form of turn-type preallocation. In each of these settings there are constraints on the production of types of turns. Counsel, teachers, and news interviewers properly ask questions; whereas witnesses, pupils, and interviewees properly restrict themselves to responding to them.

Several of these studies have focused on the effect of various forms of turn-type preallocation on the design and management of the interactional activities they constrain. In particular, research has concentrated on the ways in which turn-type preallocation can result in modifications of the ordinary conversational ways of accomplishing particular activities. It has shown, for example, how this method of turn taking can result in interaction in institutional settings departing sharply from ordinary conversation in terms of the manner in which it is opened and closed (Atkinson and Drew 1979; Clayman 1989, 1991) and the methods that are employed to manage topic maintenance and shift (Greatbatch 1986a).

I am indebted to John Heritage and Paul Drew for their detailed comments on earlier drafts of this chapter.

In this chapter, I explore the relationship between the turn-taking provisions of the news interview and the management of disagreement between interviewees. This form of disagreement is central to many of the interviews conducted on British television and radio because of the widespread use of panel interviews, in which the advocates of opposed positions are invited to debate their differences.

2 Turn taking in news interviews

As noted, the turn-taking system used in news interviews differs from the one employed in mundane conversation in that it places constraints on the production of types of turns. These constraints function with respect to the institutional identities interviewer (IR) and interviewee (IE). They specify that incumbents of these roles should respectively confine themselves to asking and responding to questions (Greatbatch 1985, 1988; Clayman 1988).

These turn-taking procedures are associated with the management of a number of the basic tasks and constraints that are central to the practice of news interviewing. Most obviously, they preestablish the local roles of broadcast journalists as report elicitors and their guests as report producers. In doing this, they provide for the accomplishment of the central purpose of the news interview, that of providing a context in which broadcast journalists can elicit information or opinion from newsmakers, experts or other persons (Heritage 1985; Clayman 1987; Greatbatch 1988; Heritage and Greatbatch 1981).

The news-interview turn-taking system also provides for the maintenance of a convention concerning the status of the broadcast audience. Rather than attempting to create the impression that the audience are eavesdroppers on a supposedly private interchange (as is sometimes done in other types of broadcast interviews and discussion programs), news IRs sustain them as the primary addressees of the IEs' statements. They do so by avoiding actions which are characteristic of private conversation. Specifically, by respecting the constraint that they should confine themselves to asking questions, IRs withhold a range of responsive activities which are characteristically produced by speakers during and/or following responses to their questions in conversational contexts. These include acknowledgment tokens (*mm hm, uh huh, yes*, etc.) (Schegloff 1982; Jefferson 1984b) and news-receipt objects (*oh, really, did you*, etc.) (Jefferson 1981a, 1984b; Heritage 1984b). Given that by producing such objects speakers identify themselves as the primary addressees of the prior talk, their withholding by IRs operates to formulate IEs' statements as being expressly produced for the benefit of the overhearing audience (Heritage 1985; Greatbatch 1988; Heritage and Greatbatch 1991; Greatbatch and Heritage forthcoming).

In acting in accordance with the news interview turn-taking provisions, then, IRs maintain the role of report elicitor (by asking questions), but decline the role of report recipient (by withholding acknowledgment tokens and news receipts). They thereby sustain an interactional 'footing' (Goffman 1981c) which casts the audience in the role of primary addressees as opposed to eavesdroppers on a putatively private interchange.

Another task which the news interview turn-taking system is geared to handle is the legal requirement that broadcast journalists should maintain impartiality in their coverage of news and current affairs. This requirement is laid down in the charters, licenses and broadcasting act which set out the terms of reference for the television and radio organizations. In the context of news interviewing, it means that IRs should refrain from expressing their own opinions and should not overtly affiliate with or disaffiliate from those expressed by IEs.

The provisions of the news interview turn-taking system are geared to the management of this constraint in that, in so far as IRs and IEs act in accordance with them, IRs will automatically maintain a formally neutral or neutralistic stance (Heritage 1985; Greatbatch 1988; Heritage and Greatbatch 1991). On the one hand, by limiting themselves to asking questions, IRs avoid the overt expression of opinion and thereby occupy the neutralistic stance of one who merely solicits information and opinions. On the other, in confining themselves to furnishing the information and opinions solicited by IRs, IEs avoid challenging or commenting on the presuppositions or character of their questions and, in so doing, collaborate in preserving the IRs' neutralistic stance. That is to say, IEs treat the IR's questions as designed to solicit *their* opinions, rather than to express those of the IRs themselves (Heritage 1985; Clayman 1988, this volume; Greatbatch 1988; Heritage and Greatbatch 1981).[1]

In sum, the turn-taking system used in news interviews prespecifies that interaction in these settings should properly be conducted within a framework of IR questions and IE responses to those questions. These turn-taking procedures operate to manage a number of the key tasks and constraints associated with the news interview. They provide, in particular, for the maintenance of the discourse identities IR and IE, for the maintenance of the audience as the primary recipients of the talk, and for the maintenance of a neutralistic stance by IRs.[2]

3 The use of panel interviewing to display disagreement between interviewees

While the news-interview turn-taking system functions to provide for the maintenance of a formally neutral posture by IRs, it does not, of course, guarantee that an IR's conduct will be viewed as *substantively* neutral. IRs may obviously be accused of substantive bias even though they have avoided overt expressions of opinion. Such judgments can turn, for instance, on the use of aggressive and hostile lines of questioning, which may be taken as reflecting either a personal or, less commonly, an institutional hostility to the positions being espoused by their subject(s) (Clayman and Whalen 1988/9). Or relatedly, they may be based on apparent discrepancies between the manner in which different categories of IE are interviewed (Hall 1973; Schlesinger, Murdock, and Elliot 1983; Jucker 1986). These considerations concerning IR neutrality are of relevance to the present chapter in that they are implicated in a problem for which the use of panel interviews to display disagreement between IEs can be seen to offer a principled solution.

In Britain the occupational culture of broadcast journalists is one which stresses the values of immediacy, controversy, liveliness, and entertainment. In the context of news interviewing, one of the ways in which these objectives can be pursued is through the use of one-to-one interviews in which interviewees are subjected to investigative cross-questioning. A problem with the use of combative one-to-one questioning, however, is its inherent vulnerability to charges of bias. While IRs seek to sustain a neutralistic stance by operating within the provisions of the news-interview turn-taking system, their use of hostile questioning can be used as a basis for inferences of bias at a substantive level.

The use of "panel" interviews involving (two or more) IEs occupying different standpoints offers a way of reconciling these competing pressures. As a means of provoking debate between IEs, the panel interview can be a source of lively and combative interaction without the need for aggressive cross-questioning. By concerning themselves primarily with the task of getting the IEs to display and debate their differences, IRs can thus, on the one hand, generate vigorous interaction while, on the other, guarding against accusations of bias.

These properties of the panel interview may be one reason for the greater use of this format in the United Kingdom in recent years. During the 1960s broadcast journalists operated in a sociopolitical climate which provided them with increasing freedom. At the beginning of the next decade, however, political pressure led to their adopting a more circumspect approach (Tracey 1977; Cockerell 1988). And it has been noticeable that since this time there has been a steady retreat from the use of combative cross-questioning, with its vulnerability to charges of bias, and a growth in the use of panel formats which allow IRs to facilitate combative interaction through the airing of disagreements between the IEs themselves (Heritage 1985).

4 The objectives of this chapter

The aim of the present chapter is to identify and account for some of the characteristic features of the turn and sequence structures through which disagreements between news IEs are managed. The chapter (a) shows that their organization differs markedly from that of disagreements between speakers in conversation, and (b) proposes that this is largely due to considerations associated with the turn-taking practices used in news-interview settings.

In demonstrating that the manner in which IEs display and debate their differences in panel interviews is heavily structured by the news-interview turn-taking system and its attendant interactional footings, the chapter has two broad objectives: the first is to shed further light on the detailed management of the news interview *per se* and the way in which its constraints shape and influence the generation of news and opinion within it; the second is to provide a demonstration of the way in which essentially simple modifications of the conversational turn-taking system can have radical implications for the management of other interactional activities. So, although it is concerned with a particular institution-alized form of talk and the speaking practices that are constitutive of it, the chapter addresses an issue that is relevant in other types of institutional interaction in which specialized turn-taking pro-cedures are employed.

5 The organization of disagreement in mundane conversation

Disagreements between news I Es differ from those between speakers in conversation primarily in terms of (a) their positioning and design and (b) the way in which the sequences that embody them are exited. Before proceeding to the analysis, therefore, a brief summary of research on these aspects of the patterning of disagree-ments in ordinary conversation is necessary.

5.1 Positioning and design

In mundane conversation, the "alternative" actions of agreeing and disagreeing are routinely accomplished in distinctive ways. Whereas agreements are normally performed directly and with a minimum of delay, disagreements are commonly accomplished in mitigated forms and delayed from early positioning within turns and/or sequences. Within conversation analysis, these differences between the structural features of the turns and sequences in which agreements and disagreements are customarily packaged are de-scribed in terms of a preference organization, in which disagree-ments constitute the dispreferred actions (Pomerantz 1975, 1984a).[3]

In her research into disagreements, Pomerantz has identified a number of the procedures through which their production is sys-tematically delayed and mitigated in conversational interaction. One of these is delayed turn initiation (Pomerantz 1984a: 70), an example of which is located in (1). Thus, in this extract, B delays the production of a disagreement turn by pausing before beginning to speak.

(1) [NB:IV:11.-1]
    A: God izn' it <u>dreary</u>.
         →   (0.6)
    A: ⌜Y'know I don't think-
    B: ⌞·hh- It's <u>warm</u> though.

Disagreements are also regularly delayed in conversation through the production of utterances, such as requests for clarification and questioning repeats, which are designed to initiate repairs on proposed problems in hearing and/or understanding prior talk (ibid.: 71). For example, due to the production of a request for clarification, the disagreement in (2) is produced not in the turn adjacent to the one which established the relevance of agreement/disagreement, but rather in a later turn.[4]

(2) [TG:1]
  1   B: Why <u>wh</u>at'sa mattuh with y-Yih
  2   sou⌜nd <u>HA</u>:PPY, hh
  3   A: ⌞Nothing.
  4   A: →   I sound ha:p⌜py?
  5   B: ⌞<u>Ye</u>:uh
  6   (0.3)
  7   A: No:,

In addition to being delayed sequentially by the occurrence of preturn initiation gaps and/or the production of predisagreement turns, disagreements in conversation are also frequently delayed within the turns in which they occur (ibid.: 72). So, for example, disagreement components are often delayed and mitigated by the production of agreement prefaces, as in (3).

(3) [MC:1:.13]
    L: I know but I, I- I still say that the sewing
                  machine's quicker.
    W: →   Oh it c'n be quicker but it doesn't do the
                  jo:b,

As Pomerantz has shown, the fact that the production of disagreements is systematically delayed in conversation minimizes the likelihood of their occurrence (ibid.). This is because, as is illustrated in (4), in environments in which agreement/disagreement is relevant (and in which disagreement is dispreferred), a speaker may (a) analyze the occurrence of one or more of the devices associated with the delaying of disagreements (arrow 1) as implicating an unstated or as-yet-unstated disagreement and (b), having done so, attempt to forestall its anticipated production by backing away from a prior assertion (arrow 2).

(4) [SBL:3.1.-8]
```
      B:            . . . an' that's not an awful lotta fruitcake.
           1 →      (1.0)
      B:   2 →      Course it is. A little piece goes a long way.
      A:            Well that's right.
```

It only remains to be added to this brief consideration of the positioning and design of disagreements in conversation, that the preference features associated with their production provide a framework in terms of which disagreements can be upgraded. Since the features provide resources for the avoidance and mitigation of overt conflict, speakers can strengthen their disagreements by declining to use them (see, e.g., line 3 of [5] below).

5.2 Exits

Speakers in conversation frequently negotiate exits from their disputes through a process which involves them moderating their prior assertions (Pomerantz 1975). A sequence which serves to illustrate this is observable in (5) in which D is attempting to persuade C to abandon a plan to emigrate to Switzerland.

(5) [G:II:2:33] (C has informed D that one of the reasons for her wanting to emigrate to Switzerland is the high level of taxation in the USA)
```
1    D:      If y'go tuh Switzerland yer payin about
2            fifty per cent a' yer money in ta:xes.
3    C:      Not in Swi:tzerl'nd.
4    D:      (No) I think it i:s.
5    C:      ˙hhhh No:::,
6            (0.7)
7    D:      Well you pay awful high ta(h)xes over there,
8            (0.2)
9    C:      Wa:l, (.) There's ul awful lota'v other
10           benefits. t- t- to ⌜r:eap from it ⌝=
11   D:                        ⌊That might be.⌋
12   C:      =too ⌜:.
13   D:           ⌊That might be:.
```

```
14                (.)
15   D:           Connie I can' argue that c'z I've never been
                  there.
17                (1.0)
18   D:           Bu::t anyway::
19   C:           'h 'hhhhhh B't anyway: gimme a jingle Dee:,
20                but give me: please do try en give me a few
21                day's notice.
```

The extract opens with C furnishing an unqualified disagreement
with D's assertion that the level of taxation in Switzerland is "about
fifty per cent" (line 2). Following this disagreement, D immediately
backs away slightly from his initial position by incorporating a
qualifier ("I think") into his reassertion and thus accepting that
there may be some doubt about his estimate of the rate of tax (line
4). C, however, does not respond so as to progress this movement
towards a reduction of the discrepancy between their positions.
Instead, she produces an unmodified reassertion of her position
(line 5).

In the face of C's unyielding response, D again opts to take a
more conciliatory line by electing to produce a modified version of
his disputed assertion (line 7). In so doing, he further moderates his
initial position by producing an assessment which admits the possibility that Swiss taxes (while high) may not be as high as he previously estimated. In the next turn, C, in asserting the existence of
"other benefits," permits this moderated assertion to stand as
stated and initiates a movement away from the issue in dispute
(lines 9–10 and 12). As such, she now progresses the movement
away from disagreement by declining to dispute D's moderated
reassertion.

Subsequently, D initiates a further deescalation of the disagreement by acknowledging that there may, as she proposed, be other
benefits to be gained from living in Switzerland (lines 11 and 13).
He then proceeds to initiate an exit from the present disagreement
sequence by, first, overtly declining to pursue the dispute further on
the basis of his proposed limited knowledge (lines 15–16); and,
second, producing a "passing turn," that is a turn without topical
content, which provides for either the introduction of new topical
materials by C or a movement into a closing of the interaction (line
18) (Schegloff and Sacks 1973). C then collaborates in terminating
the disagreement sequence by moving to a consideration of future
arrangements.

In this sequence, then, the parties begin in outright disagreement. Across the sequence, however, they modify their stances so as to move closer together and, in so doing, they collaborate in exiting the dispute.

In sum, in mundane conversation disagreements are normally either forestalled or mitigated through the use of preference features. Moreover, sequences which embody disagreements are routinely exited through a process in which the speakers deescalate their disputes by moderating their positions. Correspondingly, disagreements are normally managed in ways that in the first instance function to minimize the likelihood of overt conflict and which, upon its actualization, operate to temper it in the interests of its subsequent resolution.

6 The organization of disagreements between news interviewees

The organization of disagreements between news IEs differs markedly from that of disagreements between speakers in ordinary conversation in a number of important respects. In the remainder of this chapter, I shall identify some of these differences and explicate their relationship to the turn-taking practices used in news interviews. In so doing, I begin by focusing on the positioning and design of disagreements between IEs, considering first those that are produced in accordance with the provisions of the news-interview turn-taking system.[5]

6.1 Disagreements produced in accordance with the news-interview turn-taking provisions

As noted above, the news-interview turn-taking system specifies that IEs should properly limit themselves to responses to IR questions. Disagreements with co-IEs are not exempt from this constraint. Thus, in contrast with disagreements in conversation, disagreements between IEs are not normally produced in adjacent turns at talk. Rather, they are ordinarily and properly elicited by and addressed to a third party, the IR.

Examples of IE–IE disagreements being performed as answers (or as parts of answers) to an IR's question are observable in (6), (7), and (8). In each case, an IR asks a question which provides for the relevance of an IE producing a statement which agrees or disagrees with one previously made by a co-IE (arrow 1). In each case, the recipient of the question subsequently elects to disagree with the other IE in the course of furnishing an answer (arrow 2).

```
(6) [WAO:17.1.80]
  1   IR:              But how does the government (.) curb
  2                    inflation which was a central ˙hhhh (.)
  3                    plank in its election policy:.=
  4   PH:              =It certainly wa:s and it will be:: a:nd
  5                    what is more the government is determined to
  6                    keep down the increase in the supply of
  7                    money which is the: ma:in determining factor
  8                    which er- concerns prices,
  9                       ⌈ that's wha-            ⌉
 10   IR:      1→        ⌊ Mister Radi⌋ce what's your answer to
 11                    that.
 12   GR:      2→      Well of course I don't agree with that,=bu-
 13                    er- as the: the: the: inflation rate has
 14                    increased by seven per cent since the
 15                    general election,=and ˙hh much of this in
 16                    fact about five per cent of this is
 17                    directly, hh attributable to what the
 18                    government has done. =The fact that they
 19                    increased . .
```

(7) [WW:6.6.79] (This is an extract from an interview conducted following the election of a Conservative government in 1979. The previous Labour administration had given substantial financial support to the publicly owned motor company, British Leyland. Such subsidies would apparently be precluded by the incoming administration's monetarist policies. Prior to the interview, however, a scenario has been shown suggesting that a situation might arise in which British Leyland would be unable to continue trading without further state support. The question is whether Prime Minister Thatcher would bail the company out. "Mister Edwards" is chairman of the company.)

```
  1   IR:              ˙hhh Supposing ou::r (.) scenario about
  2                    British Leyland (.) actually came about.
  3                    What do you think she would do: in the
  4                    circumstances of Mister Edwards coming along
  5                    and asking for further state dole.
  6   PC:              I don't think Mister Edwards would get
  7                    another state dole.
  8   IR:      1→      What d'you think Perg.
  9   PW:      2→      I think that in the circumstances that
 10                    you've described she would e : r give
 11                    way . . . (continues)
```

(8) [WAO:12.4.79]
```
 1   IR:              John Mackintosh an Autumn election?=or a
 2                    Spring election next year
 3   JM:              Oh I think an Autumn election,=but for quite
 4                    different reason.=I think the budget ˙hh⁻
 5                    does not- ˙hhh it's not an electioneering
 6                    budget.=It's a steady sensible budget. ˙hhh
 7                    and the case for an Autumn election is the:
 8                    ˙hh difficult position of the government in
 9                    Parliament. ˙hhh and I would have thought
10                    that the government would want to go for a
11                    proper majority in October.
12   IR:    1→        Teddy Taylor do you see an Autumn election.
13   TT:    2→        Actually I don't see an Autumn
14                    election.=Because I think we're going to have
15                    a lot of trouble by the Autumn. I think the
16                    government will stagger on until the last
17                    possible time:.
```

Disagreements produced in accordance with the provisions of the news-interview turn-taking system also differ from disagreements in conversation in that they are not systematically delayed and mitigated by the occurrence of the preference features that are associated with the latter. Thus they are rarely qualified and are not normally prefaced by agreement components or delayed sequentially by, for example, the use of preturn initiation gaps or repair initiators. Instead, as is illustrated in (6), (7), and (8) above, they are characteristically produced promptly and in a straightforward and unvarnished fashion.

As to why the features associated with dispreferred actions in conversation are rarely used, it may be suggested that their roles in the mitigation and forestalling of disagreement are largely bypassed here. Thus, by virtue of being addressed to a third party, disagreements which are produced as answers to an IR's questions are *automatically* mitigated, in that mediated disagreements are intrinsically weaker than unmediated ones. Moreover, because the news-interview turn-taking provisions make no allowance for the disagreeing parties, the IEs, directly addressing or responding to one another, the preference features cannot properly be produced or treated as "forestalling" devices.

The structure of turn taking in news interviews, then, means that disagreements between IEs are ordinarily elicited by and addressed to a third party, the IR, with whom neither party disagrees. Disagreements which are produced in this manner are not systematically mitigated or forestalled by the use of the preference features that are associated with disagreement in conversation. Such features are largely rendered redundant in these contexts due to the turn-type preallocated character of the turn-taking system and its attendant interactional footings. This system provides for the overt production of disagreements between IEs, but in a mediated and therefore mitigated form.

6.2 Disagreements produced via departures from the news interview turn-taking provisions

6.2.1 Sequential positioning

On occasion IE's opt to depart from the standard question–response structure of the news interview in order to disagree with their co-IEs. The structure of turn taking in news interviews means that there are four main positions in which they may do this. These are as follows.

(a) Following his/her response to an IR's question
If a question does not invite an IE to disagree with a co-IE, the IE may first respond to the question and then proceed to disagree with the co-IE's previous position. An IE does this, for example, in the following extract.

(9) [WAO:24.1.81] (Simplified) (In this case, a journalist referred to as Peter in the data, and a former defence minister (LC), are being interviewed about the implications of the Soviet Union's invasion of Afghanistan. 'Peter' has previously asserted (data not shown) that, since Afghanistan has been "for a long while within the Soviet sphere of influence", the invasion has not significantly altered the balance of power in the Middle East.)

```
1    IR:      Would you want Lord Chalfont would you like
2             to see ˙hhh bases built up to to to defend
3             from the arc of the crisis as it were.=
4    LC:      =Not formal bases in the old sense of Aden
5             or Singapore: in in the days of the British
6             presence east of Suez, what I would like to
7             see: is a strong military and naval maritime
8             presence by the West in that arc,
```

```
 9                 ⌈˙hhhh   e:r   in-    in-    in-    co-⌉
10    IR:          ⌊Which would involve bases wouldn't it ⌋
11    LC:          Well it wouldn't necessarily require
12                 ⌈a- a (      ) (      ) or⌉Persian kind of=
13    IR:          ⌊In (      ) or Persia⌋
14    LC:          =base. But it requires arrangements with
15                 (      ) perhaps in (      ) .hhh with the:
16                 Kenyans in Mombassa, perhaps with the
17        →        Somalies, ˙hhh but I want to make a point
18                 about what Peter said. ˙hhh a- And that is
19                 that surely the the invasion of (.)
20                 Afghanistan has made the whole difference=It
21                 is true as he says that since nineteen
22                 seventy-eight . . . (continues)
```

Having answered the second of the IR's questions concerning the
desirability of military bases being built (lines 11–12 and 14–17)
LC goes on to depart from the question–response format of the
news interview in order to disagree with PJ's earlier assertion that
the invasion of Afghanistan by the former Soviet Union has not
significantly altered the balance of power in the Middle East. That
is, he produces a disagreement with his co-IE by means of a post-
answer topical shift which he initiates at lines 17–18 ("but I want
to make a point about what Peter said").

(b) Prior to his/her response to an IR's question
IEs may produce a disagreement prior to, rather than after, a response to an IR's question which does not provide for the relevance
of its occurrence. For example:

(10) [AP:22.1.80] (Simplified)
(In this extract, two MPs are making the cases for (JK) and against (OM) a
proposed amendment to the 1967 Abortion Act. JK has asserted (data not
shown) that the present Act virtually allows abortion on request (pointing to
findings of a government select committee in support), and that as such it needs
to be tightened up by the addition of a clause which specifies that a woman
must have a 'serious' reason for wanting an abortion)

```
1    IR:        So in fact the clause has now got
2               ⌈two wo:rds ⌉
3    JK:        ⌊Now says seri⌋ous. Y⌈es. ⌉
4    IR                              ⌊s e ⌋rious and
5               substant⌈ial. ⌉
6    JK                 ⌊Yes.⌋That's right.
7    IR:        Oonagh what implications from your point of
```

```
8                    view=
9    OM:             =mhm=
10   IR:             =does that make,
11   OM:      →      I'd like to make my own position clear first
12                   of all. I support the sixty-seven Act. 'hhhh
13                   And abortion to be allowed on those
14                   particular grounds.    'h I don't believe that
15                   we have abortion on request,=still less do
16                   we have abortion on demand. 'hhh The
17                   implications of the words serious and
18                   substantially 'hhh are very grave indeed
```

In this extract, the IR directs a question to OM (lines 7–8 and 10)
which does not provide for the relevance of her agreeing/disagree-
ing with JK's earlier assertion (data not shown) that "we were-
have virtually got (.) abortion on request." Subsequently, however,
OM opts to temporarily suspend her response to the question (lines
11–12) in order to disagree with this assertion (lines 12–16). Having produced the disagreement, she then proceeds to address the
IR's question, overtly indicating that she is doing so by repeating
the IR's use of "implications" (lines 16ff.). Here, then, an IE disagrees with a fellow IE by means of a preresponse topical shift.

(c) Following a co-interviewee's turn
Rather than withholding a disagreement with a co-IE until an IR
has addressed a question to them, IEs may initiate it at a possible
completion of the co-IE's turn, as in (11).

```
(11) [WAO:15.2.79]
1    SB:             . . . and far less on incomes policy 'hh then
2                    he claims to be:.=
3    IR:             Do you think the implications of this
4                    document are a (.) tough budget.
5    SB:             'hhh We:ll 'hh again it is important how
6                    it's presented. I disagree with the idea
7                    'hhhh that you have to punish workers for
8                    wage claims.
                     .
                     .
                     .      ((13 lines of answer omitted))
                     .
                     .
22                   The most important thing 'hhh is that Mister
23                   Healey 'h  should stick to his gu:ns.=
```

```
24   PJ:    →      ⌈You   s ⌉ ee
25   IR:        =⌊Well  I-⌋
26                 (.)
27   PJ:    →      I disagree with- with Sam Brittan on a- in a
28                 most (.) fundamental way about this, (.)
29                 because (0.2) it may well be so.=I mean he
30                 would arg- Sam Brittan would argue from a
31                 monetarist point of vie:w.=But what Mister
32                 Healey does about the money supply over the
33                 next few months ˙hhh will... (continues)
```

Here an IE (PJ) self-selects at a possible completion of a question–
answer sequence in order to disagree with a point of view expressed
in his co-IE's prior answer (lines 24 and 27). He thereby subverts
both the standard turn type and the turn-order format of the news
interview. Not only does he depart from the role of responding to
IR questions, he does so in a context in which the news-interview
turn-taking system effectively restricts the right to speak to IRs:
that is, following the completion of question–response sequences
(Greatbatch 1988).

(d) Mid a co-IE's turn
IEs may initiate a disagreement interruptively, as an on-the-spot
response to statements in a yet-to-be-completed co-IE's turn. In this
context, then, an IE–IE disagreement is produced during the
course of a disagreed-with IE's turn, as in (12).

```
(12) [LRC:20.10.80] (Simplified)
     DW:           ...the government advertising campaign is ˙h
                   highly irresponsible. ˙h It's being given
                          ⌈u n d e r  hug ⌉e ... (continues)
     TD:    →      ⌊Utter rubbish⌋
```

In sum, IEs can depart from the standard structure of the news
interview in order to disagree with their co-IEs in four main positions: (a) following their responses to IRs' questions; (b) prior to
their responses to IRs' questions; (3) at the possible completions of
co-IE turns; and (4) in the midst of co-IE turns.

6.2.2 The production of mediated disagreements

Although disagreements produced in these four positions are not
solicited by IRs, they are nonetheless regularly mediated through

them. Insofar as they are produced in conjunction with their author's response to an IR's question, the IR will, of course, be the "default" addressee. However, IEs recurrently continue to direct their talk to IRs even when producing disagreements as direct responses to co-IE assertions. This is illustrated in (11) above, for example, in which the IE sustains the IR as the primary *in situ* recipient of his talk, most notably by referring to the IE with whom he is disagreeing in the third person (at lines 27 and 30).

When IEs depart from the provisions of the news-interview turn-taking system in order to disagree with a co-IE, then they routinely continue to conform with one of the central expectations established by and embodied within it – that an IE's talk will be addressed to an IR. Correspondingly, while they deviate from their role as "answerers," they nonetheless sustain a core aspect of their institutionalized footing. And, in so doing, they limit the extent to which their actions undermine both the status of the interaction as a news interview and the role of the IR within it.[6]

6.2.3. The redundancy of the preference features

The role of the preference features in the mitigation and forestalling of conflict is largely bypassed in the context of "violatively" produced disagreements, just as it is in the case of those produced as responses to IR questions. Insofar as IEs opt to sustain a core aspect of their institutional footing by continuing to direct their disagreements through an IR, the latter will be automatically mitigated. Moreover, by maintaining IRs as addressees, IEs neither project nor make relevant a response from the co-IE with whom they are in disagreement. This means that the features are effectively rendered redundant as forestalling devices.

The redundancy of the preference features also extends to unmediated disagreements. Unmediated disagreements require IEs to abandon their institutional footing. Since, as we shall show, this is strongly connected with the escalation of conflict, the preference features, which are associated with the mitigation of conflict in ordinary conversation, are largely redundant in the context of unmediated disagreements.

In sum, IEs sometimes depart from the provisions of news-interview turn taking in order to disagree with a co-IE. In so doing, however, they regularly mediate their disagreements through a third party, the IR, with whom neither disagrees. In doing so, even though they depart from the news-interview turn-taking system, they maintain the footing of an IE which the turn-taking system normally sustains. Irrespective of whether "violatively" produced disagreements between IEs are mediated or unmediated, the preference features associated with disagreement in ordinary conversation are not observed.

6.3 The upgrading of disagreements

In conversation speakers can strengthen or upgrade their disagreements by declining to use some or all of the preference features that are routinely used to mitigate and forestall their production. The redundancy of the preference features in the context of disagreements between IEs means that this resource is not available to news IEs. However, the turn-taking procedures for news interviews supply IEs with two alternative sets of resources for upgrading their disagreements: one concerns sequential positioning; the other, turn design.

6.3.1. Sequential positioning and the strength of disagreements

Upon hearing a co-IE statement with which they wish to disagree IEs have two basic options: (a) they can wait until an IR addresses a question to them and then produce the disagreement either in their response to the question or, if this is not provided for, before or after their response; (b) alternatively, they can elect not to wait for an IR to put a question to them, and produce the disagreement either interruptively or at a possible completion of the co-IE's turn.

These options , and the courses of action they embody, serve as a metric by which the IEs can mark the urgency and strength of their disagreements with co-IE positions. Thus, in the first place, IEs can upgrade the strength of their disagreements by producing them as direct comments on the remarks of their co-IEs. Such disagreements are hearably stronger than those that are withheld until a question has been asked in the following respects: (a) they are produced earlier; (b) unlike disagreements that are produced as answers to IR's questions, they represent departures from the news interview's normative question–response format; and (c) unlike those disagreements that are produced either before or after their authors' response to IRs' questions, they subvert the standard turn order as well as the standard turn-type format of the news interview.

If IEs elect to display the urgency of their disagreements by producing them as direct comments on co-IE statements, a supplementary means of intensifying them in terms of positioning is available to them. Thus IEs can further underline their disagreements by initiating them in the midst, rather than at the possible completion of the co-IE's turn. This positioning endows disagreements with greater strength in that it involves the motivated interruption of a turn in progress.

Turning to disagreements which are withheld until a question has been asked, the possibility of an IE varying their strength by way of their positioning can also arise here. If IEs withhold a disagreement until an IR has addressed a question to them, but find that the question does not provide for the relevance of its production, they have the option of strengthening it by producing it before responding to the question rather than after such a response. Pre-response disagreements are stronger because they (a) occur earlier and (b), in contrast to the latter, are given priority over, and thus displace, a normatively expectable response to the IR's question.

In this section, we have seen how the sequence of positions in which IEs can disagree with one another serves as a metric by which they can vary the intensity of their disagreements. We now turn to consider a second resource on which they can draw to emphasize their differences.

6.3.2. Turn design and the strength of disagreements

We have seen that when they depart from the provisions of the news-interview turn-taking system to disagree, IEs recurrently limit the extent to which they can be heard to shift away from their institutionalized footing by directing their talk not to the disagreed-with co-IE, but rather to the IR. In light of this, it can be seen that, apart from being able to upgrade disagreements in terms of the positions in which they are initiated, IEs also have the option of upgrading them by breaking with this convention and producing them in unmediated forms. That is, they can escalate or maximize them by opting to enter into direct, unmediated disagreement with a fellow IE, as in (13) and (14).

(13) [LRC:20.10.80]
    GM: . . . <u>that</u> <u>bud</u>get will inevitably gro:w, .h at
                    the ex<u>pen</u>se (0.2) of the West Midlands
                    region.
    JT: →   <u>N</u>o that isn'⌈t true.⌉
    GM: ⌊I beli ⌋eve . . . (continues)

(14) [LRC:20.10.80]
    DW: . . . . that's fa:r more important <u>and</u> (.) a
                    just way of going about matters, ˙hh than
                    selling off the best type of
                    Coun⌈cil   house.⌉
    TD: →   ⌊No rubbish,⌋ they're not <u>a</u>lways the
                    best.

This upgrading has two aspects: first, as noted earlier, because it is addressed directly to the party whose statements are being disputed rather than to a third party, an unmediated disagreement is intrinsically stronger than a mediated one; second, within the news interview, the production of such a disagreement involves IEs in a very real sense in abandoning their institutionalized footings. Not only do they depart from their role as "answerers," but they also cease to maintain the IR as the *in situ* addressee of their talk.

The strength of IE–IE disagreements, then, does not turn on the absence or otherwise of the preference features as it does in conversation; rather, it turns on their positioning in relation to the standard and expectable question–response format and in terms of the identity of the addressee. In other words, the strength of disagreements is determined in large part by the extent to which speakers opt to maintain or step out of their institutionalized footing in producing them.

6.4 Exits

As we have seen, exits from disagreement sequences in dyadic and multiparty conversation are normally initiated and accomplished by the disagreeing parties themselves. However, exits from disagreements between news IEs are usually either initiated or unilaterally accomplished by a third party: in the vast majority of cases disagreements are resolved not by the disagreeing parties themselves, but rather by an IR.

6.4.1 The initiation of exits

Cases in which IRs initiate, rather than unilaterally accomplish, such exits routinely involve IRs exercising their institutionalized right as questioners to direct the topical focus of the IEs' talk (Greatbatch 1986a). An example is located in (15), in which two political commentators are being interviewed a few days after the election of a Conservative government in 1979. The extract begins with the IR asking PC whether he believes the prime minister would be willing to contribute further government money to the publicly owned (and at that time ailing) British Leyland motor company in the event of its managing director ("Mister Edwards") requesting additional financial assistance.

```
(15) [WW:6.6.79] (Simplified)
 1   IR:      ˙hhh Supposing ou::r (.) scenario about
 2            British Leyland  actually came about. What
 3            do you think she would do: in the
 4            circumstances of Mister Edwards coming along
 5            and asking for further state dole.
 6   PC:      I don't think Mister Edwards would get
 7            another state dole.
 8   IR:      What d'you think Perg.
 9   PW:      I think that in the circumstances that
10            you've described she would e : r give
11            way. = Rather along the: the: the: the: the
12            Heath line. = So I think that the possibility
13            of ˙hhh having thousands of people laid off
14            in the Midlands which is a very ˙hh volatile
15            area I think. = (An) area where disagreeable
16            things can easily happen. = Birmingham. = Think
17            of that (.) awful place. ˙hhhh e::r The
18            thought of all those British Leyland workers
19            running rampage. = I think that she would
20            probably give way like Heath did.
21   IR:      I shall restrain myself er from
22            saying anything about your view of
23            Birmingham. ˙hhhh All right (.) we've got a
24            straight    disagreement between you on the
```

25		industrial thing. ˙h Let me bring something
26		else up. (.) For <u>both</u> of you. ˙hhhh What
27		about the civil service? ˙hhh All these
28		permanent secretaries, = you know they're not
29		great believers in radical changes and sharp
30		de<u>par</u>tures. And they <u>do</u> seem to have a great
31		impact on ministers = As Willie Armstrong
32		said. ˙hhh Doesn't that worry you Mister
33		Cosgrave?
34	PC:	I thi:nk ˙hhh that is an area which in many
35		respects is <u>far</u> more important than any
36		opposition she may meet from the trade
37		unions. ˙hhhh If Mrs Thatcher does not <u>break</u>
38		the civil service (.) she will not succeed.=
39	IR:	=How d'you mean break the civil service.

PC answers the IR's initial question by expressing the opinion that the prime minister would rebut an approach for additional money (lines 6–7). The IR then asks PW for his view (line 8) and, in answering, PW disagrees with his co-IE by suggesting that the prime minister would in fact be obliged to accede (lines 9–20). Having explicitly attended to the fact that there is a "<u>straight</u> disagreement" between the two IEs "on the industrial thing" (lines 23–5), the IR proceeds immediately to initiate an exit from the disagreement. He does this by (a) shifting topic to the issue of the civil service (lines 25–32), and then (b) producing a next question on that topic (lines 32–33). In the next turn, PC confines himself to responding to this question (lines 35–9). By declining to pursue the prior disagreement (e.g. by reasserting his disagreed-with position via a pre- or postresponse topical shift) he thus collaborates with the IR in the accomplishment of an exit from it.

Cases in which IRs' unilaterally accomplish exits from IE–IE disagreements normally involve them enacting their institutionalized right as broadcast journalists/questioners to close a news interview down when its allotted time expires (Greatbatch 1988; Clayman 1989). A case in point is located in (16), where a Labour MP (RH) and a trade-union leader (AS) are discussing Denis Healey's narrow victory over Tony Benn in the Labour Party's 1981 deputy-leadership election. In the run up to this election RH supported Healey, while AS backed Benn.

The extract opens with the IR asking RH if he believes in the voting system that was used (lines 1 and 3–4). This question is asked against the background of disagreement within the Labour Party over the election procedures and the practices adopted by some of those casting votes. The system was an electoral college in which the Labour members of parliament, trade unions, and ordinary constituency party members each had one-third of the votes. Supporters of Healey have argued that his victory would have been larger had certain trade-union delegations either consulted their members or followed the wishes of their members as expressed in such consultations. Supporters of Benn, by contrast, have insisted that the voting system should have given greater weight to the views of the party's ordinary constituency members and that, had it done so, Benn would have been elected.

(16) [P:28.9.81]

```
1    IR:        Mister Hatter┌sley do you believe in the=
2    RH:                     └hhh
3    IR:        =system that pro_du_ced (0.5) De_nis Healey by
4               nought ┌point  eight per cent,
5    RH:               └˙hhhh hhhh
6    RH:        Well very clea_rly if we have to trawl over
7               the vo_te.˙hhh I don't believe in the system
8               in which over a mi_llion members of the
9               Tra_nsport and General Workers U_nion ˙hhh
10              suggested by their consulta_tion that they
11              wanted Denis Healey: ˙hhh and then the
12              exe_cutive and the delegation didn't even
13              vote for him as their second choice. Ho_wever
14              I accept the point you made to Mister
15              Ki_nnock ˙hh that er:m (0.2) (though) some
16              unions vo_ted fo:r Denis Healey who didn't
17              consult their members at all:, ˙hh what I
18              wa_nt to see: ˙hh if we're going on with the
19              electoral co_llege .hhh is the ob_ligation on
20              every union (.) to consult its members and
21              then to respon:d to the wishes of their
22              members after they've been consulted.
23   AS:        Don't you think the most important thing is
24              to re_cognise that the Par:ty it_self ˙hhh had
25              a consultation process and ei_ghty two per
26              cent ˙hhh of ordinary Labour Party branches
27              voted in support of (.) Tony Benn. ˙hh And
28              se_condly don't- and secondly don't you think
29              ˙hh that the trade union movement it_self as
```

```
30                    Neil Kinnock says 'hh has got it's own
31                    constitution 'h which has been properly 'h
32                    derived over many years.=There's no problem
33                    with our constitution 'hh we can arrive at
34                    our decisions and those decisions we shall
35                    transl⌐ate on=
36   IR:                   └( )
37   AS:    =th⌐eir (         )⌐
38   IR:        └On that- on th┘at (.) rhetorical
39                    question which I'm afraid you can't answer
40                    'cause we've come to the end of our time
41                    thank you gentlemen very much indeed.
```

In responding to the IR's question, RH criticizes the conduct of some union leaders on the grounds that they cast their vote in line with their own, rather than their members', preferences – suggesting that Healey's victory would have been larger but for this (lines (6–22). Subsequently, AS subverts the normative question–response format of the news interview by initiating a turn in which he first asserts the importance of the preference of the party's ordinary constituency party members for Benn (lines 23–7) and then counters RH's criticisms of the conduct of the trade unions (lines 27–35). This disagreement, however, is not pursued, as the IR subsequently closes the interview down and, in so doing, unilaterally terminates it (lines 38–41).

In each of the above cases exits from sequences embodying disagreements between IEs occur following a first disagreement. It is by no means unusual, however, to find IRs initiating or accomplishing such exits following an *n*th disagreement. Accordingly, disagreements between IEs often extend over a series of turns.

6.4.2 Extended disagreement sequences

IE–IE disagreement sequences which extend over a series of turns stand in contrast to extended disagreement sequences in conversation in that they rarely involve the disputants moderating or, more generally, moving away from their disagreements. Indeed, IEs commonly *escalate* their disputes by (a) moving out of (and often quickly abandoning) their institutionalized footings, and by (b) producing their talk interruptively. This can be illustrated by reference to two examples drawn from an interview in which a Tory member of parliament (TD) and a Labour member (DW) are, respectively, arguing for and against the Conservative government's policy of giving local council tenants the right to purchase their accommodation.

Earlier in the interview, DW has argued that this policy is socially divisive. It will result in a serious reduction in the stock of dwellings available to house people who have little or no option but to look to the council to supply them with a home. Moreover, because it is primarily the tenants in better-quality properties who are opting to buy, the stock that remains will consist largely of low-grade properties, in particular flats in high-rise blocks. In his view, people living in council-owned properties who wish to own their own home should be encouraged and, where necessary, assisted to purchase properties in the private sector, so as to retain the existing stock of council-owned dwellings to accommodate people who are not in a position to buy a home.

The first of the examples begins with the IR asking TD a question which focuses on the possibility that the policy of selling council houses may, as DW has proposed, be a socially divisive measure.

```
(17) [LRC:20.10.80] (Simplified)
 1   TD:        ...You won't have a mixed
 2              soc┌i : e t y (          )┐
 3   IR:           └Aren't you creating ┘two nations though
 4              Tony Beau┌mont-Dark.┐
 5   TD:                 └  N   o  ┘on the contrary we're
 6              creating one nation, = we're giving people the
 7              right to stay tenants if they wish to do so.
 8              ·hhh That's creating one nation. ·hhh What
 9              creates two nations is saying that ·hh a
10              council tenant in some way or othe:r ·hh is
11              somewhat inferior to anybody else.=
12   DW:        =B┌ut-┐
13   TD:          └But┘this proves it is no:t.=
14   DW:        =Yes but what about those council tenants
15              that Tony must take into consideration ·h
16              who live in flats,=and very very few flats
17              are being sold off, ·h in Birmingham for
18              example the number of flats sold ·hh could
19              be counted on one of both hands. ·hh It's
20              the better type of home- accomodation. And
21              if there's a right (.) er as Tony has been
```

```
22                    telling us 'hh er er a fundamental right
23                    apparently for tenants to buy 'h why not for
24                    private tenants. 'hh When the matter was
25                    raised in the House of Commons 'hh when we
26                    asked the Tory ministers 'h why not give p-
27                    (.) private tenants the right to bu:y 'h
28                    then of course we were told it's out of the
29                    question. Why not give (.) council=
30     TD:            =We ⌜ll look-⌝
31     DW:               ⌞p r i ⌟vate ⌜tenants    as    well.
32     TD:                              ⌞Well no:w may I say
                      this (    ) to the:: to- to this subject,=i-
34                    it's a very interesting point because all
35                    can't do it 'hhh David says none should do
36                    it. 'hhh erm If I may ask- if you work on
37                    that basis you're alwa:ys going to have a
38                    a- a- a- a very divisive society,=what we're
39                    trying to do 'hhh is to give people the
40                    right to live their li:ves, 'hhh not the
41                    councils dictating whether the doo:rs 'hh
42                    all the doors are white, =or all the doors
43                    are blue, 'hh 'hh and it's not just the best
44                    (.) houses,=when 'hh I was chairman of
45                    housing here in nineteen seventy-eight in
46                    Birmingham 'hhh and (.) there were many
47                    hou:ses er in the nineteen twenties and
48                    early thirties that (are being) sold. 'hh
49                    They're not just the modern one ⌜s.
50     DW:                                            ⌞But how
51                    many fl ⌜ats have been sold off.
52     TD:                    ⌞And- may I say you can si- 'hh
53                    woul ⌜d- (  )-⌝
54     DW                    ⌞ H o w⌟many flats ha ⌜ve been sold=
55     TD                                          ⌞Well
56     DW:            =off and es ⌜pecially those flats in multi-=
57     TD:                        ⌞So because (         )-
58     DW:            =sto ⌜rey blocks.
59     TD:                ⌞So   b e c ause flats are=
60     ( ):            =mhm=
61     TD:            =aren't selling well it means that people
62                    who live in council houses shouldn't have
63                    the right to bu ⌜y them. I don't see the=
64     DW:                            ⌞N o :
65     TD:            =logic of th ⌜a t.
66     IR:                         ⌞L e-⌟let's talk about the right
67                    to buy in terms of money thou:gh, er some
```

68   tenants not a great deal but some have
69   found that the: ˙hhh offers of _discounts
70   are very attractive but when they get into
71   the owning market as they do (.) they find
72   that repairs are not discounted and that
73   they're something they really can't handle.
74   This is a growing problem isn't it.

In this case the disagreement extends over a series of turns, all of which involve the IEs departing from their role as answerers. The disagreement is initiated by DW. Selecting himself to speak after TD's response to the IR's question, he takes issue with TD's assertion that the policy of permitting council tenants to purchase their accommodation is not socially divisive (line 14). He begins by reasserting his position concerning the type of properties that are being sold, here formulating it so as to address TD's assertion that the policy is designed to give people the right to decide for themselves whether they wish to remain tenants (lines 14–20). Underpinning this point is a further aspect of the proposed social divisiveness of the policy. This is that the "right to buy" strongly favors tenants living in the better-quality properties. For these tenants, it is argued, the purchasing of their home is a good investment, whereas for others, living in poorer-quality dwellings, it is not. Following this, DW then goes on to introduce what he sees as a further dimension of the social divisiveness of the policy. This is the fact that private tenants do not have a similar right to buy their properties from their private landlords (lines 21–9 and 31). While this disagreement is produced "out of turn," DW nonetheless maintains, in large measure, the footing of an IE by continuing to mediate his talk through the IR. This is accomplished in part by the use of third-person reference (see lines 15 and 21).

In responding, TD does not modify his position with a view to minimizing or reducing the disagreement; rather, he pursues and maintains his initial position. Like DW, however, he continues to display an orientation to the footing of an IE. Thus he begins his utterance with a "token" request to speak (Greatbatch 1985, 1988), thereby acknowledging that he is speaking out of turn (lines 32–3). Moreover, he goes on to direct his disagreement through the IR, thereby displaying an orientation to the IR's status as the primary *in situ* recipient of IE talk (notice again the use of a third-person pronoun to refer to the co-IE with whom he is disagreeing [line 35]).

Having addressed DW's point about private tenants (lines 34–43), TD goes on to assert that, contrary to what DW has claimed, it is not just the better homes that are being sold (lines 43–9). He does not, however, refer here to the issue of the flats which was the focus of DW's criticism; rather, he confines his remarks to the sale of houses.

DW subsequently attends to this, directing a question to TD which treats TD's turn as having evaded the central thrust of his criticism and seeks to get DW to address this (lines 50–1). By asking a question, he initiates a wholesale departure from the normative format of the news interview, and, in so doing, hearably escalates the dispute by entering into direct, unmediated disagreement with his co-IE.

DW's question is partially overlapped by TD's continuation of his prior utterance (lines 52–3). DW, however, furnishes an elaborated reformulation of his question (lines 54, 56, and 58). and TD abandons his attempts at continuation in order to respond to the question (lines 55, 57, 59 and 61ff.). In so doing, he too vacates the institutionalized footing of a news IE, occupying instead the stance of one who is in direct, unmediated disagreement with his co-IE. However, following TD's response, the IR intervenes and, in reestablishing his institutionalized stance *vis-à-vis* the IEs, initiates an exit from the disagreement by producing a question which involves a topical shift (line 66ff.).

In this case, then, neither of the disagreeing IEs opts to moderate their position, or otherwise move away from or out of disagreement; rather, they pursue and escalate their dispute until the IR steps in to restore the standard question–response format.

Our second example follows on directly from the first.

(18) [LRC:20.10.80]

```
1    TD:        to bu ⌈y them. I don't see the logic=
2    DW:              ⌊N o :
3    TD:        =of th ⌈at.
4    IR              ⌊L e-⌋ let's talk about the right to
5               buy in terms of money thou:gh, er some
6               tenants not a great deal but some have
7               found that the: ˙hhh offers of _dis_counts
8               are very attractive but when they get into
```

```
 9                the owning market as they do (.) they find
10                that repairs are not discounted and that
11                they're something they really can't handle.
12                This is a growing prob⌈lem  ⌉ isn't it.
13    DW:                                ⌊mhm⌋
14    TD:         ˙hhh Well it u- it- it- I mean you talk
15                about this as a growing problem I think it's
16                something like ˙hhh you know between fi:ve
17                and ten a week er- e:r are being aske:d to:
18                ˙hh for the councils to buy their houses
19                back. ˙hh I don't think that matters,
20                (.)
21    IR:         Ye⌈s but- but-⌉
22    TD:           ⌊ s o m e ⌋ times people⌈s positions=
23    IR                                    ⌊mhm
24    TD:         =cha:nge either way: ˙hhh=
25    IR:         =(Bu⌈t)(    ) ⌉
26    TD              ⌊But  th⌋en
27                yo⌈u    have   the    flexibili:ty
28    DW:           ⌊But- but-but does the government
29                advertising campaign is ˙h highly
30                irresponsible. ˙h It's being given
31                ⌈u n d e r   huge
32    TD:         ⌊Utter rubbish.
33                (.)
34    DW:         Yes,
35                (.)
36    DW:         not at al⌈l,
37    TD                   ⌊Utter rubbis⌈h.
38    DW:                               ⌊It's not rubbish at
39                all,=the view is being given it's so easy so
40                simple ˙hh but as as⌈is pointed out i⌈n =
41    TD                              ⌊It i:s simple.  ⌋
42    DW:         the film ˙h many many people ˙h have had
43                difficulties with- they've bought a house
44                not knowing the responsibilities of er- er-
45                er- er
46    TD:         I⌈don't think  people arc  as idiots⌉
47    DW:          ⌊payments   and   the   rest. And⌋
48    TD:         ⌈as you seem to think they are:⌉
49    DW:         ⌊it's   very   important   to t⌋he present
50                economic climate ˙hh the redundancies and
51                the closures being brought on by the Tory
52                government ⌈˙h that people sh⌈ould think=
53    TD:                    ⌊huh   huh   ha ⌋
54    DW:         =very seriously ponder very seriously ˙h
```

```
55              before they decide to buy.
56   IR:        Gentlemen thank you both.  (.) ((Turns to
57              address the camera)) u- So much for the
58              moment at least for those getting a fair
59              deal from council housing... ((continues))
```

The extract begins with the IR initiating an exit from the preceding
disagreement. This involves him asking TD a question which
focuses on another putative problem with the government's policy.
This is that, having been tempted by the offers of discounts to buy
their homes, some erstwhile council tenants find that they cannot
afford to maintain their homes since the repairs, the cost of which
were previously covered by their rent, are much more than they had
anticipated (lines 4–12). This issue has been raised by opponents of
the policy, who have argued that the government, in pursuing an
ideological preference for home ownership, has failed to make clear
to council tenants the financial implications of their having to pay
for repairs to their properties once they have purchased them.

In responding to the IR's question, TD rejects his suggestion
that this is a growing problem, proposing that the numbers
involved are small and that, correspondingly, it does not undermine
the credibility of the policy (lines 14–19, 22, 24, and 26–7). DW
subsequently subverts the normative news-interview format to dispute TD's answer (lines 24 and 31ff.). In so doing, he begins by
asserting that the "government advertising campaign is ·h highly
irresponsible," thereby explicitly formulating the criticism mentioned above (lines 28–30). As he proceeds to provide the grounds
for this assertion (lines 30–1), TD interruptively rejects it (line 32).
While DW's turn was ambiguous as to whether it was directed to
the IE or IR, TD's counterassertion is clearly directly addressed to
his co-IE. And subsequently, with DW abandoning his projected
turn to address the disagreement (lines 34 and 36), the two IEs
continue in outright, unmediated disagreement[7] until the IR, in
intervening to shut the interview down, unilaterally terminates their
dispute (lines 56–59).

In sum, IEs rarely, if ever, deescalate their disagreements.
Instead, they pursue and frequently intensify their disputes by moving out of their institutionalized footings and entering into direct,
unmediated disagreement. Sequences embodying extended disagreements between IEs thus display trajectories that stand in

marked contrast to those recurrently following disagreement sequences in ordinary conversation. Specifically, they are characterized by the continuation and escalation of conflict rather than by its minimization and deescalation.

The absence of deescalation is underpinned, in part at least, by the fact that IEs do not have to contend with a key problem which arises in other interactional contexts, most notably conversation, when participants enter into disputes. This is the problem of negotiating an exit from them. Thus the deescalation of disagreements which frequently occurs in ordinary conversation can, amongst other things, be seen to be implicated in the handling of this matter. By moving to attenuate their disagreements, speakers can negotiate their way towards and collaboratively achieve an exit from their disputes.

In news interviews, however, IEs do not normally have to consider how they are going to exit their disputes. They are effectively released from this responsibility by an expectation deriving from the structure and constraints associated with these settings. This is that a third party, an IR, will not only maintain a neutralistic stance and thus refrain from entering into disagreements between IEs, but will also either initiate or unilaterally accomplish an exit from them. Unlike speakers in both dyadic and multiparty conversation, then, where no similar expectation exists, news IEs can pursue and escalate their disagreements secure in the knowledge that they will not have to negotiate their own way out of them. They can, in other words, maximize their disagreements because they know that sooner or later a nondisagreed-with, and formally impartial, third party will intervene and get them off the hook – since to do otherwise would involve that party failing to enact their institutional role.

7 Conclusion

In the context of panel interviews the IEs are normally there to debate and argue for their conflicting positions. The way in which IEs do this, however, is strongly constrained by the turn-taking practices used in news interviews, their underlying footings, and the expectances that they establish. This is most obviously the case when IEs furnish their disagreements in accordance with the provisions of the news-interview turn-taking system. As we have seen, however, even those disagreements that are not produced in this way are shaped by considerations and expectations deriving from and embodied within this system's structure. The news-interview turn-taking system has a pervasive influence over the management of disagreements between I Es, irrespective of whether they involve departures from the strict question–response format it operates to establish.

Of the various implications of turn taking for the management of disagreements between news I Es, two warrant particular emphasis. First, as noted, the news interview turn-taking system and its attendant footings supersede the preference features used in ordinary conversation. As such, an organization which operates to minimize the occurrence of overt disagreement in the latter is rendered redundant in news-interview settings.

But while the news-interview turn-taking system, through its displacement of this organization, provides for the production of overt disagreements between I Es, it also operates to attentuate them by requiring they be mediated through a third party, the I R. In other words, it provides for the production of overt disagreements, but in a mediated and therefore mitigated form. And, as we have seen, it is only through the total abandonment of its provisions *and* their underlying footings that I Es can furnish disagreements that are both overt *and* unmitigated.

Secondly, in the event of I Es entering into direct, unmediated and therefore unmitigated disagreements, the system establishes an expectation that I Rs will intervene to manage an exit from them, since to do otherwise would require that they abandon their institutional role. This means that I Es can escalate their disagreements without regard to a difficulty with which they would otherwise be presented: that of subsequently negotiating an exit from them. At the same time, however, the fact that I Rs normally initiate or unilaterally accomplish exits also operates to limit the extent to which the I Es' disagreements are intensified. Unmitigated disagreements are thus normally of limited duration with I Rs rarely allowing them to escalate "out of control." As such, the structure of turn taking and its associated expectances provide simultaneously for the escalation and limitation of overt disagreement.

The news-interview turn-taking system, then, results in a

patterning of disagreements between IEs which differs markedly from that of disagreements in ordinary conversation. It provides for the overt production of disagreements and supplies a context in which these can be readily upgraded and escalated. The framework it establishes for their management, however, is one which provides for, in the first instance, mitigation and, in the second instance, limitation of the disputes which occur within it.

These considerations may shed further light on the prevalence of panel interviews and their efficacy as a means of generating lively and combative broadcasting. From the broadcasters' perspective such interviews offer a framework which not only has a built-in potential for disagreement between IEs, but which also facilitates its overt production, pursuit, and escalation, while simultaneously enabling IRs to exercise a large measure of control over its focus and duration. From the IEs' perspective, these interviews permit them to display openly their disagreements and to do so without responsibility for negotiating their way out of them. Moreover, if their disputes break out of the confines of the normative interview format, IEs know that IRs will normally step in before they escalate to an extent that might seriously damage their public reputations.

Notes

1. It should be underlined that the terms "formally neutral" and "neutralistic" are used here to refer to patterns of conduct through which a party, in this case an IR, can avoid being seen overtly to express opinions. As should become clear presently, it is not being suggested that such patterns of conduct guarantee an IR's "neutrality" in a substantive sense. A range of the procedures implicated in the maintenance of formal neutrality by news IRs are well discussed by Clayman (1988, this volume).
2. For more detailed discussions of turn taking in news interviews in Britain, see Greatbatch (1988), Greatbatch and Heritage (forthcoming) and Heritage and Greatbatch (1991). For a discussion of turn taking in American news interviews, see Clayman (1987).
3. Although disagreement is dispreferred in the vast majority of contexts, there are a number of environments in which it is the preferred action. For example, as Pomerantz (1975, 1978) has shown, disagreement rather than agreement is the preferred activity in environments in which it constitutes an affiliative as opposed to a disaffiliative action – for example, following the production of self-deprecations.
4. Note, moreover, that, having been thus displaced over a number of

turns, the disagreement is further delayed by the occurrence of a preturn initiation gap following B's response to the request for clarification.

5. The data extracts employed in this study are drawn from a corpus of recordings of television and radio interviews which were broadcast on British news and current-affairs programs between 1978 and 1985.

6. For further discussion of this and other procedures which I Es use to limit the extent to which they shift away from their institutionalized footing when departing from the strict provisions of the news-interview turn-taking system, see Greatbatch (1988) and Heritage and Greatbatch (1991).

7. Notice that this is reflected in T D's use of first-person reference at line 46.

10

Interviewing in intercultural situations

JOHN J. GUMPERZ

This chapter reports on a comparative study of two job-training program interviews selected from a set of seven recorded in the early 1980s in the British Midlands. The proceedings were recorded by the interviewers who, along with three of the applicants, are native English speakers from the immediately surrounding region. The remaining four applicants are native speakers of various North Indian languages, who came to Britain some ten to fifteen years prior to the time the recordings were made, and have acquired an instrumentally adequate control of English. A principal concern in the analysis is with the subtle and often unnoticed ways in which linguistic and sociocultural knowledge interact in verbal encounters to bring about communicative outcomes characteristic of what Bernard Py (in Py and Jeanneret 1989) has called "minorization," the context-bound, interactive processes through which certain individuals are stereotyped as members of stigmatized minorities. The notion of minorization is particularly applicable to situations where one participant is bilingual or bidialectal and his/her talk is interpreted in terms of the other participant's culturally specific inferential practices, and where the differences in interpretive criteria has a perjorative effect on the outcome of the interaction.

In contrast to informal conversations and casual talk, selection interviews are goal-oriented instrumental encounters, where interviewers evaluate what is said in order to select candidates who have

I am grateful to Norine Berenz for her assistance at every stage of the transcription and analysis of the data, and also to John Heritage and Paul Drew for their encouragement and many helpful comments. This chapter is an extensively rewritten and expanded version of an earlier draft which appeared in *Minorisation linguistique et interaction* (Py and Jeanneret 1989).

the background and the ability to complete the course and find suitable employment, while interviewees seek to gain access to programs that provide training in marketable job skills as well as financial support during the training period. My basic assumption, one that is shared by most discourse and conversation analysts, is that interpretation of what a speaker intends to convey at any one point rests on socially constructed knowledge of what the encounter is about and what is to be achieved (Goffman 1974, 1981a; Heritage 1984b). But it can be shown that this knowledge goes beyond mere decontextualized description of what usually happens in similar encounters. Apart from general information of the kind given above, there are additional, taken-for-granted evaluative and interpretive criteria which only emerge in the course of an interaction as part of the ongoing conversational exchange and which play a key role in the interpretive process.

It is these tacitly applied and, by and large, unnoticed assessment processes that are, as I hope to show, of particular importance for the study of minorization processes. Since they are applied automatically without conscious reflection, they are difficult to describe in the abstract and can only be discovered indirectly through comparative analysis. What I intend to do in this chapter is to illustrate empirical methods for analyzing conversational exchanges, methods that enable us to demonstrate how minorization works or, more specifically, how and under what conditions culture-bound interpretive practices characteristic of minorization situations can affect individuals' lives.

The non-native English-speaking participants have a good, functional command of English, and they encounter few, if any, comprehension problems at the level of reference or propositional content. Interpretive difficulties, for the most part, arise at the level of illocutionary force, where a speaker's communicative intent is assessed. The reason for this is that situations like those analyzed here involve communicative complexities and make cognitive, interactive, and rhetorical demands on participants that are quite atypical when compared with what the South Asians are used to in their ordinary contacts with native speakers. I will argue that when bilinguals must face such unaccustomed communicative complexities, they tend to fall back on rhetorical strategies acquired in their own native-language environment, mapping these onto their

English speech in dealing with what, for them, are novel circumstances. Native English-speaking participants in turn, who find their communicative expectations violated and have difficulty in following the non-native speaker's arguments, react with interpretations characteristic of minorization situations. As a result, the bilinguals' chances of achieving their communicative ends are likely to be jeopardized.

Before going on to the actual examples, let me briefly give some details about the theoretical premises on which the analysis is based. Much of the basic research in the study of everyday conversational exchanges has been and continues to be done by sociologists interested in everyday communicative practices. Methods of transcription have been proposed which identify key features of language usage relevant to turn taking; procedures for in-depth investigation capable of revealing some of the features of language use that govern the conduct of conversation have been worked out. Results published so far provide convincing evidence to show that the conduct of verbal exchanges everywhere and in any language community is governed by regularities or, as I prefer to call them, principles of conversing which go beyond those investigated in established traditions of grammatical or discourse analysis. Since the conversation analysts' interactive perspective is basic to the approach I want to develop here, let me briefly summarize its import in terms of three notions: turn-taking organization, sequential organization, and conversational negotiation (Atkinson and Heritage 1984).

By *turn-taking organization*, I refer to the fact that all interaction requires speaker change. Allocation of turns at speaking is not automatically achieved but is always actively managed through talk. It follows that what speakers say at any one time cannot solely be studied in terms of an utterance's propositional content or even in terms of its illocutionary force. The positioning of an utterance and its timing in relation to preceding and following speaking turns as well as its role in accomplishing such conventional tasks as enlisting the other's attention, creating the interactive space to develop an argument, opening or closing conversations, or managing topic change are important to its interpretation.

The second notion, *sequential organization*, refers to that property of interaction by virtue of which what is said at any one time sets up expectations about what is to follow either immediately afterwards or later on in the interaction. This is perhaps best illustrated by what are commonly known as *adjacency pairs*, such as questions and answers, offers and acceptances or refusals, greetings and acknowledgments, and the like. In all such cases, once an initial member of a pair has been produced, other speakers are constrained to respond to or at least acknowledge expectations raised in the preceding speaker's talk. Adjacency pairs are merely special cases illustrating what is perhaps a much more general constraint on verbal interaction. If conversational involvement is to be maintained and the encounter is to be brought to a satisfactory conclusion, participants' contributions cannot be treated as semantically independent of each other and interpreted in isolation. Interaction is only possible by virtue of the fact that speakers conform to certain general principles of semantic or thematic coherence. So that coherence, like turn allocation, must be actively managed by means of discourse strategies.

The third term, *conversational negotiation*, refers to the processes or procedures by which shared understandings are arrived at and conversational-management tasks like those involved in sequential and preference organization are accomplished. It has been shown that the regularities of ordering that conversation analysts have discovered are produced without conscious effort on the part of speakers. Conversational principles, moreover, do not function like "all-or-none" grammatical rules. Nor is the negotiation process overtly marked by grammatical or lexical means. Negotiation is achieved indirectly and cooperatively through different speakers' moves and countermoves as a byproduct, so to speak, of the task of conveying content. Conversing, therefore, cannot simply be seen as a problem of putting information into words or, for that matter, of using the right grammar or choosing appropriate expressions. It is a collaborative enterprise involving the coordinated efforts of several speakers and listeners in the production of interactional outcomes (Goodwin 1991). I want to argue that it is this issue of eliciting and achieving conversational cooperation, as well as developing the shared understandings on which argumentation must rest, that is most centrally affected by the taken-for-granted cultural assumptions that underlie interpretation.

To see why this is the case, we need to adopt an analytical approach which differs in several respects from that of those analysts who in the past have been primarily concerned with general principles of conversational ordering. That is, we must turn to a speaker-oriented perspective and ask what it is speakers and listeners must know or do in order to be able to take part in a conversation or to create and sustain conversational involvement. By formulating the basic issues in this way, the focus shifts from the analysis of conversational forms or sequential patterns as such to the necessarily goal-oriented interpretive processes that underlie their production, processes that have some similarity to those discussed in earlier work by Garfinkel (1967) and Cicourel (1974), among others.

The following example from Drew's analysis of cross-examination testimony in a rape case (this volume) illustrates this point. When the victim, taking the witness stand, is asked by the defense counsel whether she had a "fairly lengthy conversation with the defendant," she replies, "We were all talking." The counsel then continues with, "You knew at the time that the defendant was interested in you," and she replies, "He asked me how I'd been." To the next question, "You went to a bar?" she replies, "It's a club." When he goes on, "It's where girls and fellas meet," she answers, "People go there." In interpreting what is conveyed at any one point in this encounter, participants as well as analysts draw upon indirect inferences based on understandings of what cross-examinations are about and on what they have learned through past experience about typical American defense attorney's strategies in rape cases. The very fact that an exchange is categorized as a "cross-examination" serves to retrieve historically and culturally based knowledge that can be brought to bear on the interpretation of constituent messages. We assume that the witness knows that the opposing attorney in a cross-examination seeks to challenge her testimony by bringing out inconsistencies and suggesting alternative interpretations. Presumably, therefore, she is aware that to give *yes* or *no* answers to the above questions, would be tantamount to agreeing to the specific envisionment of the activity that the attorney's expressions suggest. In substituting her own wording for the attorney's, she manages to change this envisionment to one which more closely reflects her version of the facts.

I use the term *conversational inference* to refer to the situated or context-bound process of interpretation by which participants in an exchange retrieve relevant background knowledge and assess others' communicative intentions or, to use a more familiar term, the illocutionary force of what is conveyed (Gumperz 1982). As the above example suggests, background knowledge acquired through past experience or communication with others includes both commonly known information about the encounter type as well as information about strategies that participants are most likely to employ. But the example also shows that retrieval is not just a function of the referential meaning of participants' messages. By substituting her own expressions for the attorney's expressions, the witness leaves their propositional content relatively unchanged. The shift in envisionment rests largely on the contrast between the idiomatic values of hers and her opponent's expressions. Thus, a third type of knowledge that enters into conversational inference is participants' command over the linguistic resources or contextualization cues by which to achieve such effects.

By *contextualization cues* I refer to those verbal signs that are indexically associated with specific classes of communicative activity types and thus signal the frame of context for the interpretation of constituent messages (Gumperz 1982, 1992). In the rape case, for instance, lexical choice as well as stress placement serve as contextualization cues.

Contextualization enters into conversing in two ways. At one level of generality, it affects the way we categorize the activities we enact and the interactive etiquette we employ. This is not just a matter of labeling what goes on as, for example, a discussion, committee meeting, classroom session, interview, and the like. It also serves to frame the interaction in such a way as to convey information on what is likely to transpire, what role relations and attitudes are involved, what verbal strategies are expected, and what the potential outcomes are. So that, by agreeing that an interaction constitutes an enactment of a particular set of activities, sociocultural information which has been acquired through previous communicative experience becomes available for use in a particular situated interpretive process. As Erving Goffman has argued, the set of assumptions associated with particular events or situations acts as a filter or lens by means of which we sift our general stock of knowledge in order to retrieve what we need to know for the purposes of the encounter at hand. At a second level of generality, categorization affects the interpretation of the utterance level signaling cues by which we identify the illocutionary force of a stretch of talk – as, for example, a question, request,

reply, interruption, etc. – so as to contextualize the sequential relationships among utterances or speaking turns.

Let me now turn to the data to illustrate this. The interviews
took place in a skills center, a publicly funded adult-education
institution that offers training in skills that are in short supply.
Courses may last anywhere from a few weeks to several months.
Applicants fill out forms in which they answer questions about their
background, their general state of health, and previous work experience. A certain proportion of the candidates are selected for an
interview which ultimately determines admission to the course.

In the interview, the candidate faces a panel of two or more staff
members and responds to queries dealing with matters that overlap
in part with material covered in the written application. It is frequently the case that relatively little new factual information is
transmitted. There is, furthermore, no opportunity for direct assessment of the applicants' technical skills. Whatever is learnt in the
interview is learnt through talk. Candidates, in other words, are
judged largely on the basis of how they present themselves through
verbal interaction, how they react to the interviewers' queries, and
how they describe what they can do. The analysis of the inferential
process by which participants judge each other's arguments is thus
clearly relevant both in determining how assessments are made and
in investigating why certain outcomes arise.

Example 1: the bricklayer

(1)
1	R:	come in. <2> hello mr T.
2	T:	==hello.
3	R:	==take a seat. [sigh] <1> and I'll introduce mr C,
		an instructor at the skills center,
4.	T:	==mhm.
5	H:	==how do you do.
6	R:	==at Akrington, I'm R D from the training services.
		and you understand that,
		.. the panel you're here, .. ehm, *at today,
		the purpose of it is to confirm,
		.. *finally that eh, you've chosen the right, *course.
7	T:	=={[lo] yeah.}
8	R:	==and to give you the opportunity,
		to ask any questions that you want to ask.

can I just check with you a few of the details?
are you still living eh .. in (xxxx)?

9 T: yeah, in (xxxx) .. {[hi] Bristol, Bar Mill.}
10 R: Bar Mill. Br– Brookside is it?
11 T: {[lo] Br– Brookside, yes.}
12 R: right.
13 T: mhm.

The greetings and introductions in the first few exchanges are marked by fast tempo, frequent latching of speaking turns, and relatively colloquial style, all of which convey an air of informality. In turn 6, when R begins to explain the purpose of the interview, her tempo slows, and her message is delivered in short phrases, some separated by pauses. She seems to be trying to make sure that the applicant understands the main points of her explanation and is informed of his rights. The applicant, who in turn 2 has responded to the casualness of the initial greeting with a similar loud, cheerful "hello," now shifts to a low pitched "yeah" by way of confirmation. The next part of the interview touches on potentially damaging information.

(2)
1 R: and can I {[ac] just,
       .. try} and follow one or two things on the form} {[lo] [dc] you completed?}
       ahm, .. you haven't served an apprenticeship?
2 T: {[lo] *no. .. no. no.}
3 R: {[lo] no. I think you just crossed the wrong ones there.}
       just ah, .. =(xxx)=
4 T: ={[lo] right,}=
5 R: == {[lo] one out.}
6 T: =={[lo] yeah.}
7 R: ... {[lo] and you haven't got any of these– .. illnesses, .. skin diseases.}
8 T: {[hi] *no, no illnesses.} ... {[lo] [ac] that sort of thing is alright.}

R's question "you haven't served an apprenticeship?" alludes to the possibility that T may have unintentionally given the wrong answer on his questionnaire. He responds with a low pitched and strongly accented "no," briefly pauses, and, when there is no reply, reinforces his denial with two more low pitches *nos*, whereupon R, using similar low pitch, goes on to supply a reasonable explanation for his apparent mistake. The fragment concludes with an exchange

of confirmations, indicating that both participants agree. Note the
applicant's speech here. In the previous fragment, which dealt with
largely uncontroversial, biographical facts, his responses alternately
employ low-pitch register for confirmation and high-pitch register
for new information. In the present fragment, he employs a similarly low-pitched response to deal with the apprenticeship question.
In this way, by the way he contextualizes his talk, he manages to
routinize the exchange and deflect attention from the potentially
damaging nature of the topic. The interview then continues in the
same relaxed tone in which it began. In the following set of
exchanges, R seeks to find out if the candidate has familiarized
himself with the training program.

(3)
```
1   R:   {[hi] have you visited the skills center?}
2   T:   {[hi] yep,} .. {[lo] I've been there. {[p] yeah.}}
3   R:   {[ac] so you've *had a chance to look around.}
         =={[lo] and did you look in at the, .. *bricks shop?}
4   T:   {[hi] *ah yeah.} well we had a look around the bricks shop,
         and um, .. ah it looks– it looks ok. … I mean it's–
5   R:   ==alr=ight.=
6   T:          =pretty=good. yeah.
7   R:   {[ac] are you quite happy about} the, um .. conditions at the center?
         ==you understand them, .. {[lo] I mean?}
8   T:   {[hi] oh yeah. I under=*stand them.}=
9   R:                      ={[lo] the require=ments of the =course,=
10  T:                                        =yeah.=
11  R:   =={[lo] and that the first three weeks are assessment weeks?}
12  T:   {[lo] yeah.}
```

R's initial turn is marked by high-pitch register and rapid tempo,
which T then matches. Although his answer in turn 2 is quite
general, R's response implies that she has decided that he has basically done what he needs to do. When T hesitates, as if searching
for words, R's latched "alright" supplies him with an appropriate
answer. He quickly follows up with a partially overlapping "pretty
good, yeah," giving the impression that that is the reply he would
have made anyhow. The frequent overlap, latching, and rapid
tempo suggest that both parties are collaborating in treating the
interaction as a routine, almost ritualized, exchange (Auer 1990).
In the next fragment C, the second interviewer, takes over with
more detailed questions about previous work experience.

(4)

 1 R: {[hi] ok}, [out-breath] eh .. {[lo] you can have a .. chat with mr C now.}
 2 T: hmm.
 3 C: alright. I see from the information that I've got (xxx)
        you, is that you spent eh, ... twelve months,
        working for a builder, {[hi] in the south of france?}
 4 T: {[f] [hi] uhm well yeah.} {[ac] I *did actually,}
        ==I s:– I spent .. two *years over there.
        {[lo] I worked in a boatyard for some time,}
        and [clears throat] I worked for a builder as well.
        and, you know, I did some brick laying, .. *over there.
        .. [in-breath] {[ac] I suppose that's what got me interested, you know.}
 5 C: yeah. ahm, alright, you did some bricklaying over there,
        ==what sort of things were you *doing.
 6 T: well, {[hi] all sorts of things} {[ac] we would do,} putting flats up you
        know.
        and ah, .. oh just laying bricks– n:– {[lo] and that sort of thing,
        you know.}
        {[hi] general building} really, {[ac] drain work, and that sort of thing.}
 7 C: {[lo] flagging, that type of thing.}
 8 T: {[lo] yeah, flagging.}
 9 C: and then, .. twelve months you spent with .. *Seville isn't it?
10 T: {[hi] Seville Construction,} yeah. {[lo] they're a building company
        as well.}
12 C: ==yeah,
13 T: ==mm. I *did some brick laying, .. eh {[lo] with them *too.}
        .. and, .. that was for about ah, .. {[lo] [ac] twelve months, I think.}
        ... but uh– {[hi] the *reason} {[lo] I– I wanted to *do bricklaying}
        was because uh, {[ac] I've always been interested in it. you know.}
14 C: {[lo] yeah, yeah. fine.} [clears throat]
        eh, .. the reason for coming into training as a *bricklayer?
        eh– {[lo] although you've only spent uh,}
        ... two years in total =(full time),=
15 T: =yeah,=
16 C: yeah, ahm– you don't feel yourself,
        or in yourself, competent enough to– to take a job *as a bricklayer,
        as things stand, at the *moment.
17 T: ==*no, not really.
        ==well, [clears throat] I could do with ah,
        .. {[ac] practicing the bottoms and that sort of thing,}
        ==you know. ... {[ac] in bricklaying itself.}
        that's– that's the reason I– I want to take the course. you know.

In replying to C's questions, T in 4 and 13 volunteers the information that he has already worked professionally as a bricklayer. He seems to understand that his answers here could be important for the success of his application. By choosing to introduce the topic himself, he gains the opportunity to design his presentation in such a way as to show himself in the best possible light. Note how he does it. His narrative account first brings up his work in a boatyard. He then clears his throat, as if trying to recall what else he had done, and goes on with "I worked for a builder as well." Finally, almost as an afterthought, he concludes: "and, you know, I did some brick laying, . . *over there, . . [in-breath], . . I suppose that's what got me interested, you know." The positioning of this item and his style of delivery indirectly convey the impression that brick-laying is something he did along with many other things, and that he has only now decided to specialize in it. Later on, in 13, after C's mention of the firm name "Seville," T again volunteers, copying the intonation pattern of the previous phrase about bricklaying: "I *did some brick laying . . eh with them *too" – that is, presumably not too much – and then, as if to confirm the impression that he had done only enough to make him want to learn more, he continues: "but the *reason I wanted to *do bricklaying was because I have always been interested in it. You know." By skillful use of idiomatic expressions and by the way he times and locates what he has to say within the ongoing interaction, T has indirectly managed to convey much of the message which C then, on his own initiative, proceeds to put into words for him in turns 14 and 16. Evidently, both interviewers have decided that T would make a good candidate and are cooperating with him in creating an interview record that will justify their decision.

Example 2: the electrician

The second applicant receives quite different treatment. A native speaker of Urdu born in Pakistan, he is applying for training as an electrician. As in example 1, the extract from the interview we are analyzing falls into four subsections: introductions, checking on questionnaire responses, determining familiarity with the training program, and checking on previous work background, although here topics 2 and 3 are brought up in reverse order.

(5)

| 1 | R: | hello =mr A.= |
| 2 | A: | =good=morning to =you.= |

3   R: =do–= .. do take a seat.
                     .. this is mr. C, an instructor at the skills center, and
4   C: ==hello mr =A.=
5   A: =(xxxx)=
6   R: =I'm R M,= from the training services.
7   A: yes.
8   R: and, .. {[hi] [dc] we're *here to*day:,}
           so that we can *confirm, that you *have chosen, the *right course.
9   A: yes.
10   R: =={[lo] before we can go any further.}
           ==and .. if there are an– any questions *you want to ask, {[dc]
           please *do so.}
11   A: .. yeah.

The interviewer opens with an informal "hello.". But when A
responds with a partially overlapping and, from a native English
speaker's perspective, somewhat unusual "Good morning to you,"
R pauses and adopts a stiffer mode of delivery. Then again in turn 7
following R's introduction of herself, A's "yes," which from a
native English speaker's perspective seems like an unusual response
to an introduction, evokes another pause on R's part. She slows
down perceptibly and then turns to a highly accented style of the
kind typically used with listeners who do not understand English
very well. It appears that the interviewee's responses have significantly affected the quality of the interaction, so that the initial
informality has by now been replaced by an air of tenseness, which
increases as the interaction goes on. In the next passage, A is asked
to report about his visit to the skills center.

(6)
 1 R: ok? {[hi] have you *visited the skills center?}
 2 A: yes, I did.
 3 R: so you've *had a look at the *workshops?
 4 A: yes.
 5 R: ==yeah. .. {[hi] you know what the .. training allowance is?} ... do you?
        ==you know how much you've got to live on, for the period of time?
 6 A: yeah.
 7 R: and ... [clears throat] {[hi] was it explained to you} *at the skills center,
        that the first three weeks are assessment weeks?
 8 A: yes.
 9 R: {[lo] and what *that entails.}
10 A: yeah.

In contrast to the bricklayer, who does not just answer questions
but also takes advantage of unfilled pauses and interviewers' hints

to make additional, elaborative comments that serve to put him in a
more favorable light, the electrician provides only minimal replies
and does not volunteer any new information. Even direct follow-up
probes like R's "so you've *had a look at the *workshops" in turn
3 produce only brief acknowledgments. The interviewer is com-
pelled to formulate ever more specific questions to draw out the
information she needs. This pattern continues in the next section.

(7)
1	R:	o.k. {[hi] can} we just *clarify, … one or two points, that .. you have here on your application form?
2	A:	yes.
3	R:	you did a capstan setting *operating course.
4	A:	yes.
5	R:	was that a skills center course?
6	A:	{[hi] yes.}
7	R:	{[ac] a six month one.}
8	A:	ah yes. ah {[lo] [dc] I, .. completed} only for ten weeks.
9	R:	{[lo] I: see.}
10	A:	{[lo] for operating.}

When asked about the course he had mentioned in his written
questionnaire responses, A provides no qualifying statement on his
own. The next question yields only a brief "yes," as does the
follow-up question. Finally, in response to R's second probe, "a six
month one." A comes up with a cryptic "I completed only for ten
weeks," leaving it up to the interviewer to draw her own inferences.
When R responds with "I see," A provides a similarly enigmatic
elaboration: "for operating." An analyst who has the time to check
out possible interpretations might guess that the applicant intends
to convey that the course had two parts, an initial ten weeks for
operating and a second part for setting, and that he left the course
after completing the first part, presumably to take a job. But interviewers, who must keep up with the ongoing exchange and have
little time to reflect on what they are hearing, will most probably be
confused by the way A contextualizes his reply. They are likely to
infer that the applicant is equivocating and perhaps trying to cover
up a failure on his own part. Since the interview has fallen into a
strict question–answer mode, the applicant has only limited opportunities to influence interpretation so that the information that
emerges is shaped by the interviewer's talk, with results that are far

from favorable to his case. In the next fragment, the interview turns
to some additional background questioning.

(8)
1	C:	… and that– … was that at B?
2	A:	B. yes. =skills center.=
3	C:	=who was your= instructor? ==mr S?
4	A:	um:: {[lo] mr F.}
5	C:	mister?
6	A:	F.
7	C:	… mr {[hi] ‾F::?}
8	A:	yeah. I think he was … {[hi] from P.} .. {[lo] the instructor.}
9	C:	… hm.

In turn 1 C, the second interviewer, breaks in with a question
and once more the exchange goes wrong. When asked, "Who was
your instructor?," A gives a name without further comment. C,
who does not recognize the name, asks for clarification, but A
provides no additional information, simply repeating the name in
the same tone of voice. When C asks again, this time with strong
accent and high-pitch register indicating that he is getting annoyed,
A seems to become confused. His pausing in turn 8 of fragment 7
already suggests that he realizes that something is wanted but is not
sure what that may be. Turn 8 in fragment 8 is interrupted by two
long pauses. A is doing his best to come up with a response that
meets with the interviewers' approval, but without success. Both
sides now seem frustrated and the interviewers give up. Whatever A
says from now on is likely to be challenged.

(9)
1	R:	and you *say here,
		that you want to ap*ply for the electrical installation course.
2	A:	yes.
3	R:	{[lo] right.} you do understand that that's a block *entry course?
		==which means that, .. the course *starts at a particular time every
		year, and it runs for, thirty-nine weeks.
4	A:	yeah.
5	R:	yeah.
		——four turns omitted ——
6	R:	… and you've put here, that you want to apply for that course,
		because there are more jobs in, … {[dc] the trade.}
7	A:	{[lo] yeah.}
8	R:	so perhaps you could explain to mr C,
		ahm … a*part– from *that rea:son,
		*why else you want to, .. apply for e*lectrical work.

9	A:	I think I like .. {[hi] this job .. in my–} .. as a {[hi] pro*fession.}
10	C:	.. {[lo] and *why do you think you'll *like it.}
11	A:	... why?
13	C:	could you explain to me *why?
13	A:	<1> why do I like it? well, I think is .. ah more job {[hi] prospect.}

R's comments in turns 1–5 highlight the problems that A will encounter should he be accepted. She most probably does not see him as a successful candidate and is trying to prepare him for failure. Her next question is one that in one form or other is used in many job interviews to determine what the applicant knows about his chosen profession. When her initial move once more evokes only a minimal acknowledgment, she tries to be more explicit: "a*part from that rea:son, 'why else (do) you want to apply for e*lectrical work." But again A merely paraphrases his own earlier words. At this point C takes over the questioning and, sounding clearly annoyed, twice asks A to explain his answer. Yet A, who again has not understood what is wanted, simply reiterates what he has just said. Abandoning this line of inquiry, C now turns to the topic of A's previous experience.

(10)

1	C:	... what sorts of work have you done be*fore, .. in this particular *field.
2	A:	.. what do you mean? please?
3	C:	well, ... electrical installation and maintenance, eh some of it in*vo:lves, ... ehm jobs done in your home, in your own *home. have you {[hi]*done} jobs {[lo] in your own home.}
4	A:	{[hi] yes sir.}
5	C:	yeah, and what sort of jobs have you *done.
6	A:	well I– ... I wired up my own {[hi] *house.}
7	C:	you've wired your own *house.
8	A:	yeah.
9	C:	yeah?
10	A:	it is passed, ... by the .. authority {[hi] electricity board.}
11	C:	yeah?
12	A:	first {[hi] time.}
13	C:	.. {[dc] so having wired your own *house, could you tell me what the con*sumer box is?}
14	A:	yeah. where ... the fuses is.
15	C:	{[ac] where the fuses are.} {[lo] alright. fine} ... have you done anything *other than .. wire your own house?

In response to A's request for clarification in 2, C emphasizes jobs done in the home and ends with a direct question: "Have you *done jobs in your home?" Once more A's "yes" responds only to the surface form of the question. He clearly does not understand what is intended. When C then follows with yet another, more specific query, he finally receives a minimally substantive answer: "I wired up my own house." But in view of what has just been said, this merely constitutes a claim without any supporting evidence. There follows another probe for more detail: "You've wired your own *house", to which A simply answers "Yeah." C's following "Yeah" has a strong rising intonation. He is obviously not convinced. In his response, A pauses twice. He is again searching for an appropriate answer. When C remains unconvinced, A tries another elaboration. Then a final question from C: "So having wired your own *house, can you tell me what the con*sumer box is?" In view of what has been said in turns 3 and 5, it is clear that what is wanted is an answer which refers to the operations involved in electrical installation. This sort of question is frequently asked as a request for corroboration of applicants' claims about work experience. Yet A's answer, instead of describing how fuse boxes enter into "wiring one's home," simply provides a gloss for the term "consumer box." In other words, he has given a layman's reply and not the sort of answer that the interviewer would have expected from someone who has the technical expertise to do the job the applicant claims to have done. Clearly not satisfied, the interviewer changes topic. But, by now, the candidate has little chance of repairing the damage, and, in their tape-recorded post-interview discussion, the two interviewers agree that A would not make a suitable candidate for the course.

Considering what we have learned about the applicants' backgrounds, we see no obvious reason why one was accepted for a course and the other one rejected. Although both have some previous relevant experience, the first candidate has already worked as a bricklayer in two firms and could presumably get another job in the trade based on this experience. The second candidate, on the other hand, has only done some electrical work in his home and would not qualify for an electrician's job without formal training. It is evident, therefore, that the interviews' outcomes are directly attributable to the talk. The two applicants' responses are quite differently received. The bricklayer, who comes across as responsive, interested in the program, and relatively capable and enterprising, is consistently given the benefit of the doubt. Although many of his answers are lacking in detail, interviewers frequently supply him with the words he needs and in other ways assist him in making his case. The electrician, by contrast, is seen as relatively passive, unnecessarily stiff, unresponsive to interviewers' overtures, and frequently not knowing what he is talking about. His answers are challenged at every turn and there are clear indications that much of what he says is just not believed.

Are the differences between the applicants matters of individual personality or individual style, or do they reflect culturally patterned distinctions? The following fragments, similar to (5) above but taken from other interviews in the data set, suggest that the latter is the case and tnat the interviewers' assessments are based in large part on systematic differences in contextualization strategies.

(5a)

1	T:	come in. [pause while M enters] hello M.
2	M:	hello.
3	T:	grab a seat. … now I .. first of all, this is H C, an instructor
4	H:	==hello M.
5	M:	==hi,
6	T:	==at skills center. .. and you know who I am, T C,
7	M:	==yep.

(5b)

1	H:	come in, G. [G enters] won't you take a seat, will you?
2	R:	hello G.
3	G:	hello.
4	R:	.. let me introduce to you mr H, an instructor at the skills center.
5	H:	==morning G.
6	G:	==morning.
7	R:	==and ah .. mr C, you may have met him,
8	G:	==morning.
9	C:	==morning G.

The native English speakers in the above fragments respond to the interviewers' informal style much as the bricklayer does, returning informality with informality, so that the exchanges are likewise fast-paced and routinized. The South Asian applicants in the following three fragments, however, respond quite differently.

(5c)
1 H: (take a seat.)
2 R: hello mr A.
3 A: =={[lo] [p] hello.}
4 H: ==(   )
5 R: ==take a seat.
6 A: good morning.
7 R: ... let me introduce to you mr H, an instructor at the skills center.

(5d)
1 T: come in.
2   ... [knock again]
3 M: oh:. .. good afternoon.
4 T: afternoon. .. take a seat. ... right.
5   well, first of all, let me introduce .. H C.
6 M: .. [mumbled response]
7 T: ==one of the .. instructors from the skills center,
8 M: right.

(5e)
1 H: come in K. [K enters] just take a seat, will you please?
2 R: hello K.
3 K: {[lo] hello.}
4 R: let me introduce you to mr H, an instructor at the skills center,
5   and ehm .. mr C, who.. works at the training services, in (   )
6 C: ==morning K.
7 R: I also .. work at the retraining services. and my name is R M.

In fragment (5c) turn 3, A's low and soft "hello" contrasts with the native applicants' higher pitched and more cheerful sounding delivery. When A counters R's "take a seat" with a formal "good morning," the latter reacts by pausing before going on with the introductions. In fragment (5d), M enters the room with an embarassed sounding "oh" and then, after an unfilled pause, offers a formal "good afternoon," to which T responds with a less formal "afternoon." But, in spite of the fact that T pauses twice, presumably expecting a response, M gives none. In turn 8 then, M replies with "right" to T's introduction of the second interviewer, just as the electrician does in fragment (5). K's "hello" in fragment (5e) is similar in tone to A's greeting in fragment (5c). Like the other South Asians, K barely responds to the interviewers' attempts to set a more informal tone. It seems evident that the South Asians' responses are patterned and that we are faced with culturally based differences in communicative style, differences which significantly affect the quality of the interaction.

(6a)

1	T:	alright, and you're unemployed.
2		... you visited the skills center, haven't you?
3	M:	==yeah, .. visited, yeah, I've been round.
4	T:	a:nd you've done the– .. the master paperwork?
5	M:	yeah.
6	T:	you had a good look *on the class?
7	M:	yeah,
8	T:	a:nd .. were you quite happy with what you saw there?
9	M:	yeah, I were quite happy, yeah.

(6b)

1	R:	you have visited the center, I believe, the skills center?
2	G:	yeah.
3	R:	yes.
4	G:	I've had =a=
5	R:	=so=
6	G:	look around.
7	R:	==you've had a look around. you had a–
8	G:	==yes.

During this phase of the interview (cf. [6] above) the native English speakers here use strategies like those in the bricklayer interview. The interviewers' words are frequently repeated or paraphrased by way of confirming what has been said. Also, seemingly formulaic phrases such as "look around" are strategically deployed again and again: by the interviewer then the applicant in fragment (3), by the applicant in (6a); and by the applicant then the interviewer in (6b). In this way, applicants present themselves as being sufficiently enterprising to have familiarized themselves with the training program in advance of the interview. Non-native speakers' strategies in the following fragments, by contrast, are quite different.

(6c)

1	T:	well, first of all, have you been to the .. skills center at A yet?
2	M:	yeah. I– I've been once.
3	T:	you've been once.
4	M:	yeah.
5	T:	and how long were you there?
6	M:	.. well, ... there?
7	T:	mhm.

8	M:	just a .. few hour.
9	T:	just for the visit?
10	M:	yeah. just for a visit.
11	T:	yeah? .. ehm: did you have a good look round the center?
12		or did you just go into one section (xxxx)?
13	M:	no I .. been there, around all– .. all center.
14	T:	yeah.
15	M:	[unintelligible response]
16	T:	so you saw *all the classes there?
17	M:	… well I came from college, .. just to .. {[hi] visit,}
18		.. m:: and ah I was in other course, .. that time.
19		in vocational preparation course.
20	T:	mhm.
21	M:	mr .. W was our teacher, and he sent us there.
22	T:	mhm.
23	M:	a::nd we came there, with course.
24	T:	yeah.
25	M:	yeah.
26	T:	alright.

(6d)

1	R:	have you visited the skills center?
1	A:	yeah, once,
1	R:	==you have?
1	A:	==before this, yeah.
1	R:	was that on a tuesday?
1	A:	yeah,
1	R:	==and you–
1	A:	==tuesday.
1	R:	… you looked around, did you have a look at the workshop, did you?
10	A:	[unintelligible response]
11	R:	yeah. you had a chance to: talk to the instructor?
12	A:	yeah.

When asked if he has been to the skills center, the applicant in (6c) answers, "I've been once." The interviewer, who seems somewhat skeptical, then seeks to elicit more information with the follow-up question: "how long were you there?," whereupon the applicant first hesitates before saying, "Just a few hour." When he is then asked, "Just for the visit," he replies, "Yeah. Just for the visit." The exchange goes on for several more turns with the interviewer asking more and more specific questions yet receiving only minimal or seemingly irrelevant answers. In fragment (6d), the question about visiting the skills center again elicits a minimizing response: "Yeah, once." And the follow-up queries elicit only a minimal "Yeah."

Whereas the native speakers are seen as showing initiative and willingness to cooperate, the non-native speakers appear to be inordinately reticent and seeking to downgrade or minimize what they have done, when judged by our English conventions. Note, for example, that M, in fragment (6c), when asked to elaborate on what he did on his visit to the center, says, "W was our teacher," and then goes on, "We came there, with course," as if he were trying to show that he was one of a group who were merely following the authorities' orders.

What are the contextualization processes or signaling mechanisms by which the above assessments are produced and what is their basis in speakers' linguistic and cultural background? I have already referred to native English speakers' use of pitch register, that is, the raising or lowering of pitch level in relationship to preceding talk. The interviewers and the bricklayer consistently use high pitch to indicate new information and, by inference in certain contexts, willingness to respond. They use low pitch to refer to known information or, by inference, to confirm what has been said. Furthermore, interviewers and interviewee readily respond to each other's pitch level and match changes in level to signal agreement. The electrician's practices differ significantly from this. In fragment (7) line 6, he responds to the question, "Was that a skills center course?" with a high-pitched "yes," and, below that in line 10, he uses low pitch to convey the new information that he completed only the operating portion of the course. Note also his use of pitch register in response to the emphatic question, "Mr. {[hi]⁻F::?}," in the segment from fragment (8): "Yeah, I think he was ... {[hi] from P.} . . }[lo] the instructor.}" Considering the fact that he is being asked to explain who Mr. F was, his use of pitch register here must seem odd indeed to anyone relying on native English expectations to process his talk.

Another important set of contextualization cues is found at the level of prosody both in the phrase-internal placement of accent or stress and in final pitch contour. Native English speakers rely on syllable stress (marked in the transcript by "*") to call attention to a particular item of information and, by inference, to suggest that the questioner would particularly like an answer to that aspect of the message. To put it in conversation-analytic terms, by virtue of the principle of preference organization, stressing sets up the expectation that the stressed items are in some way to be responded to. Consider R's question in fragment (3) of example 1: "so you've *had a chance to look around. And did you look in at the, . . *bricks shop?" "Had" here is stressed to suggest the speaker's assumption that the trip has already been made, so that the entire first part of the question becomes a preliminary to the second part, where "bricks shop" is highlighted as the item about which more information is wanted. As was pointed out above in describing how the candidate searched for words in his answers and how the interviewer responded, the candidate makes the expected inference and manages the interaction in such a way that the information emerges. Now consider the following from fragment (4). When the interviewer C asks, "I see from the information that I've got . . that you spent twelve months working for a builder in the south of France?," the candidate replies, "Well, yeah. I *did actually. I spent two *years over there." His stress on "did" suggests coreference with "spent" and the stress on "years" sets up a contrast with the interviewer's "months." Then a few turns later the interviewer asks, "Alright, you did some bricklaying over there, what sort of things were you *doing?," using stress to indicate that what is wanted is information about the operations the candidate performed. The candidate appropriately answers with a list of suitable operations. And so successful is his strategy that he manages to engage the interviewer in extending the list. In other words, here and elsewhere throughout these materials, stress placement is crucial in signalling coreference and alerting interlocutors to what is expected by way of an answer.

I have already cited several instances where non-native applicants failed to respond to the interviewers' use of stress as a cue. Recall R's use of contrastive stress in fragment (9): "A*part from *that reason, *why else do you want to apply for e*lectrical work?"; and A's reply, "I think I like . . job in my- . . as a profession," where A is clearly aware that there is something about his previous answers that the interviewer finds unsatisfactory, but seems unable to process the interviewer's use of stress as a guide to indicate what type of an answer is wanted. Other analyses of South Asian English discourse show that what we are dealing with here are far-reaching differences in ways of signaling emphasis and discourse level coreferentiality (Gumperz 1989).

There are other matters of pausing, pacing, and intonation that also contribute to the inferential process. Listening to the overall stream of talk of the native English speakers, we gain the impression of a smooth synchronized exchange where turn allocation is readily managed. Pausing or shifts in rhythm and tempo do not seem to interfere with the flow of the interaction. Yet pauses (marked in the transcript by two or three dots or, for timed pauses, a number in angle brackets) are quite frequent. R's introduction in fragment (1) turn 6, for example, contains three pauses: "I'm R D from the training services. And you understand that, . . the panel you're here . . ehm, *at today, the purpose of it is to confirm, . . *finally that eh, you've chosen the right, *course." Since pauses are possible turn-transition points which others may treat as opportunities to take the floor, how does the speaker manage to keep from being interrupted? The explanation lies in the way she contextualizes her pauses by syntactic positioning and intonation. Note that all three pauses are marked by slight rises in final intonational contour, which in English usually indicates that more is to come. The first and second clause, moreover, are syntactically incomplete and, in clause 2, "ehm" is used as a floor-holding device. We assume that listeners who perceive these signals infer that pausing serves as a strategy to gain time to find appropriate words or otherwise plan what is to be said next. This explanation also holds for C in fragment (4) turn 3, "you spent eh, . . twelve months, working for a builder"; and in turn 9, "and then, . . twelve months you spent with . . *Seville isn't it?," pausing here is used to gain time to check factual information.

T also employs similar time-gaining strategies, but there is an additional aspect of his use of pausing that is of particular importance for the way he manages the interaction. Consider the two exchanges from fragment (2) repeated below:

```
1   R:  .. you haven't served an apprenticeship?
2   T:  {[lo] *no. .. no. no.}

7   R:  ... {[lo] and you haven't got any of these– .. illnesses, .. skin diseases.}
8   T:  {[hi] *no, no illnesses.} ... {[lo] [ac] that sort of thing is alright.}
```

In each of these cases, pauses follow utterance-final falling-intonation contours and thus mark possible turn-transition points. But when interviewers fail to take their turn, the candidate, as was pointed out in the preceding discussion, takes advantage of the opportunity to take the floor once more and add further information to bolster his argument.

Sequential placement is also important in the case of conversation overlaps (here marked by "="). There are quite a number of these in the exchange, but they are concentrated in certain locations. In the introductory section of fragment (1) turns 1–7, all speakers' contributions overlap the previous speaker's turn. What is exchanged here are formulaic phrases providing little new information. There is evidence from other similar interviews that overlaps are frequent in such situations, and that in fact they have the effect of marking the sequence in question as a routine matter. Now note the use of overlap in fragment (2) turns 3–8. Here, information of importance for the candidate's evaluation is being conveyed. Yet, if overlap indicates a routine interaction, the fact that both speakers use it here suggests that they agree in treating the candidate's answer to the written question as a routine error, as if it were the sort of thing that could happen to anyone. The candidate's use of overlap thus becomes a strategy to forestall questioning that might lead to pejorative interpretation. In other words, interviewers and candidates rely on shared interpretations of intonational and other contextualization cues for purposes of conversational management.

In example 2, equivalent signaling mechanisms or contextualization cues are employed quite differently. From the very beginning of the interaction, the sequencing also differs. In fragment (5) turn 1, the electrician, like the bricklayer before him, is greeted with a "hello" as he comes in. But, whereas the bricklayer had returned the greeting, copying the interviewer's prosodic contour, the electrician replies in a slow tempo with the more formal-sounding and thus rather discrepant "good morning to you." When C next greets him with "hello," the candidate's voice is so low that the reply is inaudible.

Later, however, in turns 6–9, when R first identifies herself and then describes the purpose of the interview, A replies three times with a loud and relatively high "yes," using a prosodic contour that in England connotes information that the listener already knows. Note that the interviewer's talk overlaps the first two of A's replies. Apparently, she did not expect a reply at this point. In the next exchange, R's question, "If there are any questions *you want to ask, please *do so," is answered with some delay by a simple "yeah," which, given the context, also seems odd. Experience with similar Asian–English/English–English interview situations suggests that A may be using "yes" as a backchannel signal, equivalent to T's "hmm." But the interviewers clearly do not understand. (For more detailed discussions of contextualization processes and their cultural specificity, see Gumperz 1982a, 1982b, 1992.)

It seems evident, then, that the interviewers' reactions are in large part explained by inferences based on their own culture-bound interpretations of contextualization cues. There is, of course, always the possibility that the interviewers already have preexisting stereotypes and are prejudiced against Asians. This may or may not be the case. Yet, stereotypes are either confirmed or changed in the course of an interaction. In the cases I have examined, the interaction generally starts on quite a friendly note, but the atmosphere deteriorates noticeably as the interaction progresses. This suggests that whatever happens in the interaction itself materially affects its outcome. And it is in this sense that interpretive and conversational processes are important.

My argument, then, is that the problem lies in the failure of conversational negotiation processes such as the ones I have discussed. So that, in this and in many similar cases, we are not simply dealing with lack of linguistic knowledge or prejudice on the part of one or another of the participants. Both candidates and interviewers rely on different, taken-for-granted rhetorical strategies and as a result seem unable to negotiate shared understandings about matters that are crucial to the interview's success. As I have shown, the ability to negotiate shared understandings presupposes a shared system of cues or *contextualization conventions*. It is this difference in contextualization strategies which plays a major part in determining the different outcomes of the interviews. In situations of differential power and interethnic stigmatization, problems that in other cases might pass as simple instances of lack of shared linguistic knowledge come to be seen as reflecting the speaker's ability, truthfulness, or trustworthiness. The result is that speakers whose communicative practices are stigmatized tend to encounter much more difficulty in their institutional contacts with majority speakers. Such conditions if they persist over time, will, in all probability, have a significant effect on minority individuals' success in the society at large.

Appendix: transcription system

Symbol	Significance
.	Final fall
?	Final rise
,	Slight rise
-	Truncation (e.g. what ti- what time is it/)

. .	Pauses of less than 0.5 second
. . .	Pauses greater than 0.5 second (unless precisely timed)
<2>	Precise units of time (= 2 second pause)
=	To indicate overlap and latching of speakers' utterances; e.g.

<blockquote>
R: so you understand =the requirements=
B: = yeah, i under=stand them/
</blockquote>

<blockquote>
R: so you understand the requirements?
B: = = yeah, I understand them/
R: = = and the schedule?
B: yeah/
</blockquote>

with spacing and single "=" before and after the appropriate portions of the text indicating overlap and turn-initial double "=" indicating latching of the utterance to the preceding one.

::	Lengthened segments (e.g. wha::t)
~	Fluctuating intonation over one word
*	Extra prominence
{[ ]}	Nonlexical phenomena, both vocal and nonvocal, which overlay the lexical stretch; e.g. {[lo] text //}
[ ]	Nonlexical phenomena, both vocal and nonvocal, which interrupt the lexical stretch; e.g. text [laugh] text//

( )	Unintelligible speech
di(d)	A good guess at an unclear segment
(did)	A good guess at an unclear word
(xxx)	Unclear word for which a good guess can be made as to how many syllables were uttered with "x" = one syllable

PART 4

The interplay between questioning and answering

11

On clinicians co-implicating recipients' perspective in the delivery of diagnostic news

DOUGLAS W. MAYNARD

1 Introduction

In ordinary conversation, when there is bad news to tell, it can be organized so that the recipient rather than the bearer of the news ends up pronouncing it (Schegloff 1988a).[1] By prefacing the bad news, by giving pieces of information from which inferences can be made, and so on, the bearer alludes to the tidings, and thereby induces the recipient to guess at what they are. Schegloff (1988a) provides the following telephone-call examples. In the first, Belle conveys news to Fanny about a mutual friend by announcing "something terrible":

```
(1) [DA:2:10]
  1   B:         ...I, I-I had something (.) terrible t'tell
  2              you. So⌈u h :⌉
  3   F:             ⌊How t⌋errible⌈is it
  4   B:                       ⌊˙hhhhh
  5              (.)
  6   B:         Uh: ez worse it could be:.
  7              (0.7)
  8   F:         W'y'mean Eva?
  9              (.)
 10   B:         Uh uh˙hh=
 11   F:         =Wud she do die:?=
```

My thanks to Steve Clayman, and especially Paul Drew and John Heritage for extremely detailed and helpful comments on an earlier version.

    Data were collected under Grant No. HD01799 from the National Institute of Health, Stephan A. Richardson, principal investigator, and Grant No HD 17803–02, Douglas W. Maynard, principal investigator. Bonnie Svarstad, who worked on the former grant with Helen Levens Lipton, with permission generously made the Richardson data available to the present author.

331

```
12   B:        =Mmhm,
13             (.)
14   F:        When did she die,
```

The announcement and subsequent formulation that the news is "ez worse it could be" (line 6) are ways of clueing Fanny, who guesses at the news (lines 8, 11). Then Belle confirms these guesses (lines 10, 12). In the second example, Charlie informs Ilene, who wanted a ride, that a planned trip to Syracuse has been canceled. Referring to a third party, he starts the news delivery by citing a reason for the cancellation (lines 1, 5, 7):

```
(2) [Trip to Syracuse, 1-2]
 1   C:        She decidih tih go away this weekend.
 2   I:        Yeah:,
 3   C:        hhhh-
 4   I:        =kh⌈h
 5   C:            ⌊So that:⌈t
 6   I:                    ⌊k-khhh
 7   C:        Yihknow I really don't have a place tuh sta:y.
 8   I:        ˙hh Oh::::: ˙hh
 9             (0.2)
10   I:        hhh So yih not g'nna go up this weeken'?
11             (0.2)
12   C:        Nuh:: I don't think so.
```

This leads Ilene herself first to indicate a realization (line 8; see Heritage 1984b) and then to venture the bad news (line 10). Rather than announcing the trip's cancellation, Charlie now merely has to confirm Ilene's inference (line 12).

A deliverer's clues or preindications, as Schegloff (1988a: 444) points out, engage a recipient's common-sense knowledge of the world, the participants' "recipient-designed" mutual knowledge, and "their orientation to the occasion of the conversation." The practices of clueing, guessing, and confirming are also displayed in institutional settings – particularly medical ones – where professionals must convey bad news (Glaser and Strauss 1965; Sudnow 1967; McLenahan and Lofland 1976: 257). Thus, a mother recalls her experience of finding out that she has given birth to a Down's Syndrome child:

And you know he [the father] was just acting so strangely and by then you get all these apprehensive feelings which I had during the pregnancy anyhow. And then the doctor came in and he drew the curtains around my cubicle and I thought, oh no, you know. And he told me the baby was born completely healthy, but he's not completely normal. And I looked at him and I said, he's mongoloid. And I've never seen a mongoloid baby before in my life, but all of a sudden the flat features, the thrusting of the tongue, you know, just kind of hit me in the face. And that poor doctor couldn't bring himself to say the word. He said, it shouldn't have happened to you, not to your age bracket.

(Jacobs 1969: 5)

The doctor's clues here include drawing the curtains[2] and then alluding to abnormality. Based on her "feelings" and prior, unthematized noticings, the mother guesses that the baby is "mongoloid," a matter that the doctor, by reciting how unlikely the event was, confirms in an indirect way.

These excerpts demonstrate that a bringer of bad news may have difficulty stating the news outright. By avoiding the pronouncement and simply confirming a recipient's inference, a teller can manage the conveyance as a joint activity. The bearer does not claim completely independent knowledge, and instead elicits a display of what the recipients, through their own knowledge or beliefs, can infer. In medical settings where clinicians must routinely deliver bad diagnostic news, it appears that this pattern of confirming can be actualized more explicitly than by mere reliance on clues and guesses. Clinicians can use a "perspective–display series," a device that operates in an interactionally organized manner to *co implicate* the recipient's perspective in the presentation of diagnoses. Schematically, the series consists of three turns:

1 clinician's opinion–query, or perspective–display invitation;
2 recipient's reply or assessment;
3 clinician's report and assessment.

Because the clinician, in a manner analogous to the clueing and guessing activity described above, sets up a diagnostic telling to confirm the recipient's own perspective, a consequence of employing this series is to embed that perspective as a constituent feature of the telling.

2 The perspective–display series

The data for this chapter derive from "informing interviews" recorded in two clinics for developmental disabilities (mental retardation, autism, language and learning disabilities, etc.). At such clinics, children go through an extensive evaluation process, which may include speech, psychological, psychiatric, pediatric, educational, and other kinds of examinations. When these tests are completed, clinicians meet with parents to tell them about the clinic's findings and diagnoses, and to make recommendations as to how to handle identified problems. This meeting or informing interview may last from 20 minutes to 2 hours as participants discuss a wide variety of concerns. In delivering diagnoses, clinicians may do so either immediately and *straightforwardly* (see Maynard 1989b); or they may do so *circuitously*, through the perspective–display series (Maynard 1991a). Use of this series may relate to a generic conversational strategy for giving one's own report of assessment in a cautious manner by initially soliciting another party's opinion (Maynard 1989a, 1991b).

While this chapter is mostly about turns (2) and (3) in the perspective–display series, some preliminary comments about turns (1) and (2) will be helpful in our later analyses. First, these two turns are similar to what Sacks (1992 [1966]) has called a pre-sequence. Pre-sequences include the summons–answer type, by which participants provide for coordinated entry into conversation (Schegloff 1968); pre-invitations (*Are you busy Friday night?*), by which a speaker can determine whether to solicit someone's co-participation in a social activity (Sacks 1992 [1966]), and pre-announcements (*Have you heard?*) through which a speaker can discover whether some news-to-be-told is already known by a recipient (Terasaki 1976). Depending on what a speaker finds out by initiating a pre-sequence, the conversation, invitation, or announcement may or may not ensue. Thus, in ordinary conversation, the perspective–display invitation and its reply operate like a pre-sequence and seem to have alternative trajectories. Sometimes, the asker follows a reply with his own report, or with further questions and then with his report. In this case, the third-turn report is akin to a "news announcement" (Button and Casey 1985), providing for at least some "receipt" of the report or possibly a "topicalizer" in the next turn; this topicalizer then occasions elaboration of the topic by the one who initiated the series. At other times, the reply to a perspective–display invitation will be followed by further questions or other topicalizers that permit the recipient to talk at length on some topic. The questioner, never announcing any independent information or perspective, appears to "interview" a recipient and provide for that person to do extended topical talk. However, in the clinical environment, the relationship between the first two turns and the third-turn report in the perspective–display series appears more fixed or *rigid* than in conversation; only one of the alternative trajectories occurs. After asking parents for their view, clinicians unfailingly provide their assessment of the child (for discussion, see Maynard 1991a).

A second matter concerning turns one and two in this series: it is here that clinicians and parents may collaboratively establish an alignment regarding two matters on which the delivery of diagnostic news depends: the existence of a child's problem and the expertise of the clinic for dealing with it. Turn 1, the perspective–display invitation, elicits the parents' view of their child, and does so through a variety of forms. A major distinction is between those queries that are *unmarked* and those that are *marked*, depending on whether they initiate reference to a problem as a possession of the queried-about child. When an invitation itself proposes a problem or difficulty, it is marked:

(3) [8.013]
    Dr: What do you see? as- as his difficulty.
                        (1.2)
    Mo: Mainly his uhm: (1.2) the fact that he doesn't
                        understand everything (0.6) and also the
                        fact that his speech. (0.7) is very hard to
                        understand what he's saying.

When an invitation does not propose a problem in this way, it is unmarked:

(4) [9.001]
    Dr: Now that you've- we've been through all this I
                        just wanted to know from you:::. (0.4) ·hh how
                        you see Judy at this time
                        (2.2)
    Mo: The same.
                        (0.7)
    Dr: Which is?
                      (0.5)
    Mo: Uhm she can't talk . . .

Marked queries presumptively ask parents for their view and occasion, from the parents, an immediate account of the child's difficulty. Unmarked queries are less presumptive but nonetheless also
seek an eventual formulation of a child's problem. Once clinicians
and parents exhibit accord on the existence of a problem, this also
implies an alignment as lay and professional participants with
regard to expertise for understanding the problem's exact nature.
The very proposing of a "problem," that is, reflexively suggests a
course of action in which parents, in one way or another, have
sought out the clinic for its specialized knowledge. Establishing
these matters sets up a hospitable environment that allows clinicians to present the diagnosis relatively smoothly. Nevertheless, in
reply to a perspective–display invitation, a parent may resist a
problem formulation. This, as we shall see, necessitates a specific
kind of interactive work before the clinician can deliver the diagnostic news.

   After parents display their views, then, clinicians regularly
deliver diagnostic news as a *confirmation* of what has been said.
Depending upon the relation of the elicited perspective to the clinical position, such confirmation can be relatively simple or more
complex. If the parents formulate some problematic condition that
is perceivedly close to the clinical position, then the confirmation
will be accompanied only by a reformulation and technical elaboration of the parent's version. When the clinical diagnosis departs
significantly from that version, a diagnostic presentation will be
accompanied by work that, while still confirming and reformulating what parents have said, also "upgrades" the severity of a child's
condition. Overall, it is the possibility of confirming the parent's
view that seems central to the diagnostic news delivery done
through a perspective–display series. Furthermore, this confirmation is an *achieved* phenomenon. When parents go along with,
or themselves produce, problem proposals, the nature of this
achievement is somewhat hidden. But when parents are resistant
to problem proposals, we can clearly see that the alignment between clinician and parent is a matter of delicate interactional
management.

   To demonstrate these matters, I will begin by showing how
"simple" confirmations work, and how they are achieved features
of using a perspective–display series. Then I will take up progress-

ively more "complex" deliveries that involve "upgrading" the nature of a condition to which parents have alluded. With more complex diagnostic news deliveries, every step in the process of leading towards a diagnosis can involve or invoke the parent's view, such that when some ultimate diagnostic term is produced, it appears as something on which clinician and parent, in a variety of ways, converge. This convergence may include, in addition to their displayed, mutually reinforcing *views*, demonstrations of the parties' shared *reactions* to the condition. In the end, however, convergence and mutuality come to be based on the clinical position, not the parents' version or one that is in between. While clinicians may demonstrate agreement with, and/or understanding of the parents' perspective, a claim is mounted that the parents' view affirms the very diagnosis of which they are now being informed.

3 Diagnostic news as confirmation

Simple confirmations occur when a clinician displays agreement and offers to reformulate and elaborate the parent's displayed view along more technical lines:

$$\text{delivery of diagnosis} = \text{confirmation} + \text{reformulation} + \text{elaboration}$$

The next excerpt shows the pattern; it begins with a perspective–display invitation (line 1) and a reply (lines 3–7):

```
(5) [8.013]
 1    Dr:        What do you see? as- as his (0.5) difficulty.
 2               (1.2)
 3    Mo:        Mainly his uhm: (1.2) the fact that he
 4               doesn't understand everything. (0.6) and
 5               also the fact that his speech (0.7) is very
 6               hard to understand what he's saying (0.3)
 7               lot ⌈s of ti ⌉me
 8    Dr:           ⌊ right ⌋
 9               (0.2)
10    Dr:        Do you have any ideas wh:y it is? are you:
11               d⌈o yo⌉u? h
12    Mo:         ⌊No ⌋
13               (2.1)
```

```
14    Dr:        'h okay I (0.2) you know I think we basically
15               (.) in some ways agree with you: (0.6) 'hh
16               insofar as we think that (0.3) Dan's main
17               problem (0.4) 'h you know does: involve you
18               know language.
19               (0.4)
20    Mo:        Mm hmm
21               (0.3)
22    Dr:        you know both (0.2) you know his- (0.4) being
23               able to understand you know what is said to
24               him (0.4) 'h and also certainly also to be
25               able to express:: (1.3) you know his uh his
26               thoughts
27               (1.1)
28    Dr:.       'hh uh:m (0.6) 'hhh in general his
29               development . . .
```

In her reply, the mother (Mrs. C) formulates her son's problem, after which the clinician (Dr. E) produces an agreement token (line 8). This token may encourage continuation on the part of Mrs. C, which does not occur (silence at line 9). Next, Dr. E initiates a question–answer sequence concerning "why" there is a problem (lines 10–11), which is unsuccessful in eliciting further material from his recipient. Then, although qualifying himself, Dr. E more fully expresses agreement with Mrs. C's perspective (lines 14–15), and reformulates the parent's complaint about Dan's understanding and speech as involving a "main problem" the child has with "language" (lines 16–18). Dr. E also precedes the reformulation with emphasis on the verb "does," which is a way of tying to the parent's prior assessment and further marking agreement with it.[3] Following Mrs. C's continuer (line 20), Dr. E elaborates on the diagnosis (lines 22–6), incorporating one term ("understand") that repeats what Mrs. C has said (line 4) and also using another ("express his thoughts") that is hearably a close version of Mrs. C's reference to "speech" (lines 5–7). In this series, the clinician's activities of confirmation, reformulation, and elaboration are all present and they severally work to co-implicate the parent's perspective in the diagnostic news.

Not any or all parental replies to a perspective–display invitation will offer an auspicious context for a confirming diagnostic news delivery. For instance, in replying to a perspective–display invitation, parents may take a position that there is no problem.

Clinicians with "bad" diagnostic news to deliver are not, then, in a position of being able to confirm. Instead, they may have to work to *achieve* just that conversational environment which is ripe for a confirmatory delivery. Clinicians have a variety of devices for handling the "no problem" reply from parents, such as listening for or encouraging talk in which some diagnosable condition or difficulty is eventually broached (Maynard 1991a).

(6) [47.001] (Simplified)

```
 1   Dr:        How's Bobby doing.
 2   Mo:        Well he's doing uh pretty good you know
 3              especially in the school. I explained the
 4              teacher what you told me that he might be
 5              sent into a special class maybe, that I was
 6              not sure. And he says you know I asks his
 7              opinion, an' he says that he was doing
 8              pretty good in the school, that he was
 9              responding you know in uhm everything that
10              he tells them. Now he thinks that he's not
11              gonna need to be sent to another school.
12   Dr:        He doesn't think that he's gonna need to be
13              sent
14   Mo:        Yeah that he was catching on a little bit uh
15              more you know like I said I- I- I know that
16              he needs a- you know I was 'splaining to her
17              that I'm you know that I know for sure that
18              he needs some special class or something.
19   Dr:        Wu' whatta you think his problem is.
20   Mo:        Speech.
21   Dr:        Yeah. yeah his main problem is a- you know a
22              language problem.
23   Mo:        Yeah language.
```

This excerpt starts with an unmarked invitation, which initially obtains a positive assessment from the mother, Mrs. M (lines 2–3). However, in the course of reporting a conversation with her son's teacher (lines 3–11, 14–18), Mrs M exhibits a position implying that she sees Bobby as having a problem ("I know for sure that he needs some special class or something," lines 17–18). Dr. E immediately follows this with a marked invitation (line 19) or one that contains a problem proposal. With this, he takes up what Mrs. M had implied and asks her for an explicit problem formulation, which she provides at line 20.[4] Then Dr. E uses two "yeah" tokens to confirm her perspective, and yet reformulates what she has said by suggesting that the "main problem is ... a <u>language</u> problem" (lines 21–2).

Also note how the parent receives the diagnosis by changing her terminology to match the clinician's (line 23).[5] Subsequently (in talk not reproduced here), Dr. E elaborates the diagnosis using words that further incorporate Mrs. M's displayed perspective. Overall, then, the way in which the parent's perspective is co-implicated in the delivery of diagnostic news here is similar to the previous example, with the exception that the clinician must strategically deal with an initial positive assessment on the part of recipient. Thus, the confirmation type of delivery is an achievement in that it depends on parents presenting not just anything in reply to a perspective–display invitation, but just that material which allows agreement and confirmation to be done. When that material is not initially produced, clinicians will seek it out, which suggests that their use of the perspective–display series is oriented to developing a hospitable environment for delivering a diagnosis.

4 Upgrading a condition

Even when a clinical diagnosis departs significantly from a recipient's position, the delivery still can involve a confirmation. Once that confirmation is performed, clinicians may reformulate and then add the upgraded diagnosis onto what has already been said. It seems, then, that "complex" deliveries have a progressivity to them that is set off by confirming the parents' view:

delivery of diagnosis = confirmation + reformulation + upgraded diagnosis + elaboration

What distinguishes the upgraded diagnosis from reformulations or elaborations is evidence internal to the talk between clinician and parent showing that both may be oriented not just to a difference in vocabulary but to a difference in level of seriousness. That is, the distinction between lay and professional terminology in earlier examples appeared to be a technical one. However, in contrast to lay terminology, professional nomenclature can imply a more critical and potentially stigmatizing condition for a child. In this situation, parents may subtly resist a proffered diagnosis, and clinicians will show a sensitivity to this resistance.

For instance, in one interview, a clinician asked a mother how she felt about her daughter's "functioning in the school." The mother replied that the girl was "not right on her level that she should be," that the teachers "don't think she's on her level," and that "she is kinda slow":

```
(7) [3.047]
 1   Mo:    . . . and I have seen no progress, from
 2           September to June. For her learning
 3           ability, she is slow.
 4           (0.6)
 5   Dr:    That's what we uh:: also found on- on
 6           psychological testing. ˙hhhh That she was
 7           per- not performing like a normal (0.2) uh:::
 8           six and a half year old uh (0.4) should.
 9   Mo:    mm hmm
10   Dr:    And that she was performing more uh (0.3)
11          ˙hhhh what we call as a borderline (0.4)
12          rate of retardation ˙hhh uh:::˙m
13          (2.2)
14   Dr:    For a normal (0.4) kind of might use a
15          number ˙hhhh it's usually about hundred
16          (0.2) or more. (0.6) and anywhere between
17          uh:: (0.3) eighty two and (1.2) uh:::: (0.4)
18          ninety is kind of uh:: (0.4) borderline
19          (0.6) kind of uh:: (0.2) ˙hhh functioning.
```

Here, the clinician, Dr. H, employs another device for confirming the parent's perspective, suggesting (line 5) that the clinic has "also found" what the mother has just said about the child being slow. Then, the clinician proposes to reformulate this as "not performing like a normal ... six and a half year old" (lines 7 and 8). This reformulation is met with a continuer at line 9, following which, Dr. H, by way of the "and" (line 10) adds a clinical term, "borderline rate of retardation" (lines 11–12). Note, then, that reformulations may foreshadow the upgraded diagnoses they precede. After this, at line 13, there is a large silence. In systematic fashion (see Pomerantz 1984a; Sacks 1987), this at least shows, on the part of the parent, an unwillingness to endorse the clinic's terminology and can indicate a withheld disagreement (Maynard 1989b). Subsequently, while Dr. H appears to explain the diagnosis (lines 14–18), in returning to the diagnostic category, he no longer refers to "retardation," and instead pairs "borderline" with "kind of functioning" (lines 18–19). Thus, Dr. H *retreats* from using a term that was added on to a confirmation and reformulation of the parents' version, which indicates the clinician's understanding that it may not have been as acceptable as the previous reformulation. Indeed, just after line 19 above (in talk not reproduced here), Mrs. B says, "Well I think she will progress later," and suggests that the child will do better in second grade. Then, Dr. H shows a further orientation to the difference in positions, stating, "One of the reasons why we are having this conference is also to make you aware of her limitations, and not to agree with you in everything that you say, saying that she is going to catch up, and she is going to do well in second grade or third grade and such things like that."[6]

Another interview illustrates this same feature of a clinician retreating from the presentation of an upgraded diagnosis when the parents, Mr. and Mrs. H, show a lack of receptivity. In lines 1–5 below, the father is replying to a perspective–display invitation (see Maynard 1989b for a fuller account). Following this reply, the clinician, Dr. R, delivers a confirmatory report (lines 7–10). While Dr. R here reformulates "maturing" (line 4) as "development," he reproduces the father's term "stopped" and marks agreement with this term by stressing the word "has."

```
(8) [17.050]
 1   Fa:      You know I think basically the problem is as
 2            I also said to Ellen that uh when you reach
 3            the age of about four or four and a half
 4            (0.9) you more or less stop maturing right
 5            there.
 6            (0.4)
 7   Dr:      Yeah (1.6) Well that kind 'of leads into what
 8            we found uh (0.2) ˙hh essentially what we
 9            have found in Robert is that (0.4) at (0.4)
10            a certain point his development has stopped.
11            (0.2)
12   Fa:      Right
13            (0.2)
14   Dr:      A::nd uh::: (0.2) when tested (0.4) he then
15            tends to look to us: like a kid with
16            retarded development.
```

```
17   Mo:        Mm h┌mm ┐
18   Fa:             └ Mm ┘::=
19   Dr:        =This is a kid who's reached a certain point
20              and then he stopped.
21   Fa:        Right.
```

Following this confirmatory report, Mr. H produces an agreeing continuer (line 12), which, in turn, sets the stage for an additional, upgraded diagnosis (lines 14–16). But after the official term, "retarded development," is presented, the parents both produce neutral continuers (lines 17–18). Then, Dr. R retreats to the prior terminology of the child's development as "stopped" (lines 19–20). This utterance is followed by another agreement token (line 21) from Mr. H. In part, it is the contrast between agreement tokens in the environment of terms such as "stopped development" and neutral continuers in the context of "retarded development" that indicates a resistance to which the clinician seems responsive. And, as in the interview from which excerpt (8) is taken, there is later evidence in this interview that the parents disagree with the "retarded" term. At one point, after the parents had been extolling Robert's skills at school, a social worker who was present in the interview asked the parents, "So you don't think he's retarded?" Mrs. H replied, "No," and Mr. H answered, "No I wouldn't say he's retarded at all." It therefore seems clear that the neutral continuers in excerpt (8) are withholding a display of such disagreement in this particular environment of diagnostic news delivery. While at this point the clinician presumably does not fully know of the parents' opposition to the term "retarded," he nevertheless demonstrably orients to the "minimalness" of their responses. (See the discussion in Maynard 1989b.)

Examples (7) and (8) show how asking the parents for their view may obtain a problem formulation that indicates a relatively hospitable environment for a confirming type of diagnostic news delivery. However, while being able to confirm and reformulate a parent's view may go smoothly, adding an upgraded diagnosis may not result in felicitous treatment by parents. Anticipating this, clinicians may employ other devices that help prepare the way for an upgraded diagnosis. The result can be long and complex deliveries of diagnostic news. I will examine a complex delivery, which shows that, through the perspective–display series and related devices, it is possible to reduce very stark disparities between parental and clinical perspectives regarding the condition of a child.

5 Reducing disparity

If we were to categorize or code the parental and clinical perspectives in the interview from which the next excerpts (9a–f) derive,[7] these perspectives would appear far apart, if not contradictory. Objectively, in fact, the situation would seem to present a high probability of argument and conflict:

Summary codification – Example 9

Parent's perspective	*Clinician's perspective*
the basic condition is hyperactivity	hyperactivity is one condition among several
the problem is temporary	the problems are not temporary
there is no brain damage	there is brain damage, which is the basic condition

We might predict that clinician and parent would dispute the child's symptoms, the duration of his condition, and what the basic condition is. Instead, as the interview proceeds, the distance between the participants narrows and the clinician's informing occurs harmoniously and affirmatively rather than argumentatively or conflictually. In part, this may be because, after confirming and reformulating the parent's perspective, but before moving to present an upgraded diagnosis, the clinician engages in *converting* and *identifying*, which are two other forms of co-implicating the parent's perspective. These forms, along with the perspective–display series and its progressive manner of presenting diagnostic news, help reduce the disparity between parties' perspectives. However, they do not imply compromise between the parties, nor do they involve negotiation over the existence, nature, and duration of problems. By proposing to bring a recipient's perspective in line with the clinical position, these forms are persuasive devices.

The first excerpt from this interview starts with the parent, Mrs. L, attributing to the clinician a particular statement regarding the potential of her son (lines 1–3 below). When, at line 4, Dr. C seems

to disaffiliate from this attribution, Mrs. L backs down (line 5).
And after Dr. C completes her utterance at line 6, the parent acknowledges Dr. C's position (line 7). Then, the clinician probes
(lines 8–9) Mrs. L for her own view on the matter of her son's
potential, which she gives in lines 10–11:

(9a) [30.001] (simplified) (The mother, Mo, is referred to in
the text as "Mrs L")

```
 1   Mo:           ... from what I was told in the beginning
 2                 and you told me too, he will outgrow this as
 3                 he goes along.
 4   Dr:           Well. Yeah. It's not exactly-
 5   Mo:           more or les⌜s  h : : : : ˙hhhh ⌝
 6   Dr:               ⌞important what I⌟said.
 7   Mo:           Yea⌜:h      ⌝
 8   Dr:              ⌞Wh⌟at- what do you think, I mean do you
 9                 think Barry will outgrow his problems?
10   Mo:           Well! I think so, in way- I hope so! in
11                 ways. Because you know...
```

In a qualified way, then, Mrs. L indicates a belief that her son will
outgrow his problems (lines 1–3, 5, 10–11), and goes on (in talk
not reproduced here) to list several reasons why: he will get proper
preschooling, eventually go into a regular school, take medication,
and she had been told that his problems were childhood ones that
would only last until puberty.

After this, the clinician introduces a typical perspective–display
invitation:

(9b) [30.016]

```
     Dr:           What do you think is wrong with him.
                   (0.3)
     Mo:           Well:, he's hyperactive child.
     Dr:           Mm ⌜hmm  ⌝
     Mo:              ⌞˙hhhh⌟ so:::, the definition they said
                   when a baby's born the brain is developed,
                   to that certain point. ˙hhhhhh now with
                   hyperactive child, that brai- the brain
                   hasn't developed, to that certain point...
```

From here, Mrs. L goes on to explain her concept of hyperactivity,
and in reply to a question from the clinician, indicates hearing the
explanation and diagnosis from a cousin who had seen a pediatric
neurologist and psychiatrist because her child seemingly had similar

problems. Mrs. L's alluding to this seems to warrant an inference from Dr. C, which, however, is disconfirmed:

(9c) [30.070]

Dr:	So . . . you suspect there's something wrong with Barry's brain then?
Mo:	We:ll::, um (.) uh::::m, not really, I would say (.) learn::ing (.) difficulties. You know, like uh he wasn't grasping.

Mrs. L next describes when problematic behavior first started (at age two) and how she became more suspicious that something was wrong when B was age three because he still was not "talking right" and was resistant to toilet training.

Then, through various displays of agreement, Dr. C confirms Mrs. L's views. Below, at line 5, the clinician uses a formulaic expression ("we agree with you"), although she also qualifies it (lines 6–7). In addition, at line 9, redoing an utterance that was overlapped by Mrs. L's line 8 query, Dr. C emphasizes or accents the verb "is" before repeating the very term ("hyperactive") that Mrs. L has used. At line 11, the clinician also stresses the verb ("has") which prefaces a gloss ("trouble") of what the parent discussed earlier. As mentioned, such emphasis is a way of both tying to the prior talk and marking agreement with it.

(9d) [30.119]

```
 1   Mo:        ┌(So that's) how I th┐ought something was
 2   Dr:        └So that's why we-  ┘
 3   Mo:        wro┌ng th┐ere.
 4   Dr:           └right┘
 5   Dr:        And (0.3) you know, we (.) we agree with
 6              you, you know, we- ih- cer- to the certain
 7              degree. ┌W e  f e e l  t h a t┐
 8   Mo:                └Is he gonna be all   ┘ right. heh huh
 9   Dr:        We- we feel that (0.3) Billy is: hyperactive.
10   Mo:        Yeah.=
11   Dr:        =y'know:, and he has had trouble, (.) for a
12              long ti:me. ┌hhhh ┐
13   Mo:                    └Yeah.┘
14   Dr:        But we don't see this as something that's
15              just gonna pass:
16   Mo:        Y┌eah, well I know that,┐
17   Dr:         └ and an- go  away.    ┘
18   Mo:        Right.
```

Subsequently, at lines 14–15, Dr. C, using a contrast marker ("but") and contrast stress on the verb "don't" (see note 3), takes up a position that contradicts what the parent has said regarding the child outgrowing his problems, and thus reformulates Mrs. L's version of the problem. Technically, while this is a *disagreement* (Pomerantz 1984a; Sacks 1987), it follows the preference form in which it is packaged as *agreement*. That is, the disagreement is postpositioned within the turn it occupies by the occurrence of preceding agreements and the contrast marker.

In a sense, the confirmation and reformulation succeed here. That is, after Dr. C produces various terms and characterizations, Mrs. L gives indications of assent (lines 10, 13, 16) and seemingly aligns (at line 18) with the proposed reformulation (lines 14–15, 17) thereby apparently relinquishing her earlier-stated view regarding the temporariness of the problem (see example [9a] above), and also possibly defusing a potential argument.[8] So far, this excerpt is similar to examples (5) and (6) above, wherein the clinician confirms and then suggests a reformulation of what a parent has said. And here, as in (6), the parent clearly accepts the suggestion.

In this instance, however, the confirmation-reformulation is not the end of the line or the immediate prelude to an elaboration; it precedes a move to present more serious diagnostic terminology. Moreover, in contrast to examples (7) and (8), this move involves other work on the part of the clinician, who proposes *converting* the parent's formulation of the problem to being among items on a list of things. Below (lines 4–5), Dr. C suggests that hyperactivity is "one of the problems" that B has, and then proffers "another" difficulty of the child and details its characteristics (lines 7–8, 10–11, and 13–14).

(9e) [30.134]

```
 1   Dr:      He ha:s serious problems.
 2   Mo:      Hm::
 3   Dr:      A:nd, you know, we don't know:: what kind of
 4            term to apply ta these problems. One of the
 5            problems is that he is hyperactive. h⌈'h h h h ⌉
 6   Mo:                                          ⌊Mm hmm⌋
 7   Dr:      another is that he's just sort of
 8            disorganized, in the way he⌈takes ⌉in the
 9   Mo:                                 ⌊(Mya)⌋
10   Dr:      world, he doesn't take it in the way 'hh
```

```
11              other children,
12   Mo:        Y┌eah.┐
13   Dr:         └his-┘his age. ˙hhh He can't put things
14              together in his mi::nd the wa┌y othe┐r
15   Mo:                                     └Ye::ah┘
16   Dr:        children would.
```

Mrs. L, in providing continuers (lines 6, 9, 12, 15) that allow the production of these detailings, at least "goes along with" Dr. C's descriptions and, insofar as "yeah" (lines 12, 15) is stronger than "mm hmm" in this regard, may even agree with them.

The activity of converting, in short, involves the parent assenting to the assemblage of a list that incorporates her version of the basic problem as apparently equivalent to other members of that list. It is no longer that hyperactivity is the son's basic problem, as was the parent's initial perspective. Now, that is one item in an inventory, which also includes being "disorganized" in taking in the world, and having difficulty putting "things together in his mind." Such conversion figures in the Dr. C's delivery of the core diagnosis, which comes after the two participants go on to discuss how Billy is doing in the "readiness program" at school. Dr. C, upon stating that Billy will "progress and learn, but he will always have a definite problem," reintroduces the issue of something being "wrong with the brain" (lines 1–4 below; cf. [9c] above):

```
(9f) 30.186
 1   Dr:        Now when you say: uh you know, the ter:m
 2              something wrong with the brain, is very
 3              vague, we don't like it (.) you
 4              don┌'t like it.┐
 5   Mo:           └Yeah right.┘
 6   Dr:        But ˙hhhhh when we have to descri:be Barry's
 7              problems, we would have to say that there is
 8              something, that┌is not┐working right
 9   Mo:                        └Yeah ┘
10   Dr:        in the brain
11   Mo:        Mm
12   Dr:        that's causing these things. It's causing
13              the hyperactivity, ˙hhhh┌it's:┐causing him
14   Mo:                                 └Yeah┘
15   Dr:        ta see the wor::ld, in a different way, from
16              other children,
17   Mo:        Mm yeah
18   Dr:        It's causing him to be:- his (.) thoughts to
```

```
19                  be maybe a little disorganized, when he
20                  tries ta order the world,
21      Mo:         Mm::
22      Dr:         in his mind. And ˙hhhh if you know, we had
23                  ta say, uh if we had ta give a diagnosis
24                  (0.2) ˙hh you know when you write away to
25                  schools:: or ta other doctors, you have to
26                  write something down as a diagnosis. I feel
27                  that hyperactivity, just alone, wouldn't be
28                  enough.
29                  (0.2)
30      Mo:         Mm ⌐hmm⌐
31      Dr:            ⌊˙hhh⌋and that we would have ta say
32                  something like brain damage.
33      Mo:         Mm hmm
34      Dr:         in terms of (0.2) of Barry's problems
35      Mo:         Mmm.
36      Dr:         Because it's a kind of thing that's- it's
37                  not jus:t hyperactivity that's gonna be
38                  helped with a little medicine. ˙hhhh He- he
39                  is going to nee:d, (0.5) a s- special
40                  education: (.) all the way through.
41      Mo:         Uh ha.
42      Dr:         We feel.
43      Mo:         Yeah.
```

The beginning of this excerpt shows the phenomenon of *identifying*. As evident in numerous interviews, this involves procedures whereby a clinician construes the parents' feelings in regard to hearing projected diagnostic terminology. Here, there are two aspects to the proposed identifying. Firstly, at lines 2–4, Dr. C acknowledges that her own reference to "something wrong with the brain" is "very vague," claims not liking the phrase, and suggests that this attitude is shared by her recipient, who agrees (line 5). Thus, if it is agreed that "we" and "you" do not like something, it exhibits a mutuality in one attitudinal area for the otherwise-partitioned sets of people who are so categorized.

Secondly, in moving to the diagnostic presentation, Dr. C portrays herself as forced to do so. She invokes the phrase "have to" in reference to (a) describing "B's problems" (line 6) and (b) saying the brain is not "working right" (lines 8, 10). Recall that Mrs. L has already shown resistance to characterizations of the severity and nature of the child's problem (she thought the problem would eventually go away, and that it was not brain damage). Being forced to describe problems and to say the brain is not working right, while not disavowing such matters, at least mildly mimics Mrs. L's resistance to these characterizations. In summary, identifying with a recipient in these ways takes her perspective into account by intimating that the clinician can understand what it is like to confront the bad news that must be delivered. This is a slightly different way of co-implicating the parents' perspective than we have seen so far, for it means that the clinician has incorporated already-displayed and yet anticipated reactions to the diagnosis.

The co-implicating of a parent's perspective is also accomplished here in the more usual sense, when Dr. C reinvokes the converting and detailing from excerpt (9e), which include Mrs. L's view regarding the nature of the problem. At lines 8, 10, and 12, that is, Dr. C suggests that the brain problem may be "causing these things" (line 12), a phrase that ties to the previously named symptoms (hyperactivity, seeing the world in a different way, having disorganized thoughts) that are reassembled within a three-part list (lines 12–13, 15–16, and 18–20), a rhetorical device that implies a sense of coherence, completeness, and unity (Atkinson 1984:57; cf. Jefferson 1990) to the package of symptoms. Beyond the sheer content of the list, Dr. C thereby appeals for some other condition to be "causing" them. And each part of the list meets with continuers, including two agreement tokens (lines 14 and 17) that permit Dr. C to progress to delivery of the official diagnosis. Thus, as opposed to being some unilateral declaration of Dr. C, the listing is collaboratively produced. Accordingly, to the extent that this listing serves as a warrant for the upcoming diagnosis, the basis for the warrant is in the parent's as well as the clinic's perspective.

Finally, in arriving at the actual term, Dr. C again portrays herself as forced to give it (lines 22–6), and invokes the institutional context – having to "write away" to schools and doctors – as an explanation for such force. The theme of partial resistance is thereby once more salient, and serves as a prelude to Dr. C discounting the parent's term, "hyperactivity" (lines 26–8), before going on to pronounce the diagnosis of brain damage (lines 31–2). This diagnosis, in a variety of ways, is an "upshot" (Heritage and Watson 1979) of what has gone before, and, as Dr. C elaborates (lines 36–40), also projects a specific, recommended treatment (special education as opposed to medication). The proposal for treatment here illustrates how closely therapies are linked to diagnostic terms and may be driving their use. That is, the very careful movement away from the parents' perspective and towards the clinic's position reflects not just an abstract concern with correct terminology, but with concrete remedies for the problems (Teas 1989).[9]

In review, this informing interview begins with a query and a perspective–display invitation that succeed in eliciting the parent's view of her child's condition as being temporary and basically involving hyperactivity. The third part of the perspective–display series follows a format in which the clinician confirms, reformulates, and then upgrades the conditions that the parent has named. The confirmation entails the clinician agreeing with the parent's proposal of hyperactivity, while the reformulation contradicts what the parent has said regarding the temporariness of the problem. After the parent gives signs of changing her perspective on this issue, the clinician proposes additional problems to the hyperactivity, *converting* the latter to one among several symptoms. The parent also goes along with these proposals, and then the clinician delivers a term that is "upgraded" with respect to another aspect of the parent's perspective. Whereas Mrs. L had resisted the suggestion that something was "wrong with B's brain" (example 9c above), the clinician subsequently (9f) presents "brain damage" as the basic diagnosis. Dr. C prefaces this delivery by *identifying* with the parent and by invoking the agreed-upon symptomology.[10] Although the interview would objectively exhibit disparities between parent and clinician, the perspective–display series and related strategies of co-implicating parental perspectives in the delivery of diagnostic news permit positional differences between the deliverer and recipient to be publicly overcome.[11] The movement that overcomes such differences is in the direction of the clinical position, and thus the series may be a persuasive way that clinicians ratify and confirm a parent's own perspective even while suggesting, indeed using that perspective to affirm, the alternative.[12]

6 Conclusion

The perspective–display series is a means by which participants to a clinical informing engage a circuit of talk that displays recipient's view as a prelude to the delivery of diagnostic news. By way of this series, clinicians can deliver, as a product of talk and interaction, a diagnosis that confirms and co-implicates recipient's perspective. In initiating the series, a perspective–display invitation seeks material from parents with which agreement can be formulated, to thereby begin, with a confirmation of what the parents had to say, a progressive delivery of diagnostic news. Upon this confirmation, clinicians can build reformulations, upgraded diagnoses, and technical elaborations. As compared with the clueing, guessing, and confirming strategy identified at the outset of this chapter, the perspective–display series more explicitly engages the recipient's perspective for a bad news delivery, yet still has this confirmatory aspect as a central feature.

Devices such as identifying with the recipient and converting the recipient's formulation of the problem to a symptom of something more basic may be employed in service of a progressive news delivery. In all, these mechanisms allow for diagnostic presentations that contain a parent's perspective as an embedded feature, and may thus persuade a parent to align with the clinical position. A further effect of using the perspective–display series is to portray the clinician not as one whose assessment is an independent discovery, nor the parent as one who must be moved from a state of ignorance to knowledge. Rather, the parent is one who partially knows the truth and the clinician is one who, in modifying or adding to what a parent already knows or believes, proposes to ratify the displayed perspective.

We can highlight these matters by comparing this sequence and circuitous news deliveries to those that are more direct or straightforward (e.g. Heath this volume; Maynard 1989b). First, straightforward deliveries may be preceded by other devices that propose to co-implicate the parents' perspective. For example, in one instance, a clinician led up to a relatively blunt delivery of a mental-retardation diagnosis by congratulating the parents on the "extraordinary job" they had done with their son. As herself the mother of a physically disabled child, the clinician also engaged in identifying, remarking "You know Mrs. R [the mother] and I can talk as parents as well as my being a professional."[13] However, while such prefacing mechanisms may show the clinician's appreciation of the parents' situation, they do not draw out the parents' beliefs or knowledge in the way that the perspective–display series does.

Second, when a clinician presents a diagnosis directly and detects resistance from the parents, it is possible to handle the difficulty through a retrospective elicitation of their perspective (Teas 1989).[14] In the next excerpt, Dr. V's mention of "going through all this" (lines 1–2) refers to the findings from separate diagnostic examinations that other clinicians in the room have reported.

```
(10) (I:39:17)
 1    Dr:        'hh you know again 'hh a::hm (.) the reason
 2               for going through all this ah- obviously
 3               when you have a kid who's way behind you
 4               worry about mental retardation.
 5               (0.4)
 6    Dr:        That's what we're y'know (.) discussing that
 7               issue. 'hh A:hm 'h
 8               (2.0)
 9    Dr:        you do:n't- and when y'talk about me:ntal
10               retardation what (.) we usually mean is
11               something y'know y- what parents are always
12               saying y'know ih- is the permanence of this.
13               Okay I know he's behind. 'hh Fact you've
14               done a better job (1.0) 'hhh we didn't even
15               need to do our testing. ah Lyn reminded me
16               ah (.) that (.) horrendous form that you filled
17               out. (0.6) You kno(h)w that- whatever it was
18               two three hundred item ah- can he do this
19               can 'e do this can 'e do that, you're 'hhhh
20               getting the same numbers as we are.
21               (1.5)
22    Dr:        A:h when you score the stuff that you guys
23                          ⌈d i d  ⌉
24    Mo:        ⌊Right⌋I was wonderin bout that.=
25    Lyn:       =Yeah there was an iden ⌈tical   profile
26    Mo:                                 ⌊You know that⌋three
27               hundred twenty question,   ⌈I did
28    ( ):                                   ⌊((laughter))
29    Do:        And so- yeah. And when you score all that
30               ahm (.) y' yer yer what chu in effect said
31               was that in most areas of development (.)
32               he's looking like ah somewhere between two
33               ta three years. (0.5) In skills. (0.4) More
34               like what you've said that you feel yer
35               (1.5) yer three year old is (1.0) y'know
36               doing bout the same. . . . So wha chu've
37               generally done the first thing is that uh-
38               this evaluation has been a ti:me consuming
```

```
39              an an expensive confirmation (1.5) of what
40              you've been seeing, that he's functioning
41              between a two and three year level on most
42              things. That's what you've been hearing=
43    Mo:       Mm hmm
```

At line 3, when Dr. V broaches the diagnosis, mental retardation it is as a possible upshot of the reported findings. Both parents are present at this interview, and their postures are rigid, their faces impassive, as the term is mentioned. Then, at two points of transition relevance (lines 5 and 8), neither one elects to talk.[15] Following this, Dr. V begins to elaborate the term (lines 9–13), and quotes the parents as acknowledging that their child is "behind," which seems to "touch off" a series of utterances in which he compliments the parents (lines 13–17) for filling out a long form that he then suggests shows them getting the "same numbers" (lines 19–20) as the clinicians. Lyn, a special-education consultant on the case, agrees and further proposes that the parents' assessment is "an identical profile" (line 25). After reciting some specifics of the assessment, Dr. V characterizes "this evaluation" – the clinic's – as "an expensive confirmation of what you've been seeing" (line 39–40).

Thus, it is possible for a clinician to adduce a recipient's perspective in other ways than through asking for it, after the delivery rather than before it, and as a means of handling or repairing interactional difficulties, such as the impassiveness and silences of the parents in (10), which emerge at the point of this delivery. Then, "confirmation" occurs under the auspices of recovering from a diagnostic presentation rather than under those of anticipating it. As an overall matter, therefore, the delivery of diagnostic news, like the bearing of bad news generally, may be organized in a variety of ways to embed recipient's perspective as a constituent feature of the presentation. By comparison with other means of delivery, however, use of the perspective–display series accomplishes the co-implication of recipient's perspective in a strong fashion. Rather than contingently responding to emergent displays of resistance or emotion, and rather than simply appreciating the difficult situation of recipients, clinicians can preliminarily elicit their *view* of the situation. And no matter what the disparity between recipient and clinical perspectives, or how serious the condition, clinicians can work through the series in a way that proposes to confirm what recipients already know and believe, even while using the latter to affirm the diagnostic presentation itself.

The perspective–display series is not characteristic of clinical talk alone. Just as the clueing–guessing–confirming mechanism for telling bad news occurs in ordinary conversation and in clinical environments, so too does the perspective–display series appear in both contexts. In conversation, initiating the series is an inherently cautious maneuver that contrasts with the outright offering of a report or assessment (Maynard 1989a). For example, by way of this series, unacquainted parties who do not have prior knowledge of each other's attitudes can see whether and how one's report or assessment can fit with the other's views of some social object. Similarly, well-acquainted parties can employ the series when their circumstances warrant caution. That is, where persons have a previously unarticulated concern or opinion to express, and are not sure how well a friend or relative will understand or receive it, they can first "test the waters" for the degree of hospitality which the expression might meet. If the circumstances allow, then persons can deliver their report, assessment, or opinion in a confirmatory way. Among both unacquainted and acquainted parties, producing potentially controversial displays of perspective in this way shows the interactants' orientation to a kind of social solidarity in their relationships. It seems, then, that the perspective–display series is a conversational mechanism that is *adapted* to a clinical environment where professionals must inform parents or patients of highly charged diagnoses (Maynard 1991b). By co-implicating their recipients' knowledge or beliefs (and anticipated reactions) in the news they have to deliver, clinicians present assessments in a publicly affirmative and nonconflicting manner. In short, the series represents a solution to interactive problems that transcend the clinician–parent or doctor–patient relationship. At least in some ways, rather than being a unique species of interaction, talk in institutional settings is continuous with that in ordinary life.

Notes

1. This is a paraphrase of Schegloff (1988a: 443), who states: "Conveying information to another and telling that person something may be

quite different matters. It was my colleague Harvey Sacks I think who first pointed out that when it comes to bad news, the talk can be organized in such a manner that the recipient of the news can turn out to be the one who actually says it." See also Terasaki (1976: 28–9) and Drew (1984: 133–6).

2. Privatizing the encounter between physician and patient can, of course, mean many things, but in a context of ambiguity surrounding major events such as birth, accident, illness, and death, it seems particularly indicative that some bad news is to come. See, for example, Sudnow (1967: 126, 129).

3. Sacks (1992 [1967]: 12) discusses the use of accent or emphasis with respect to possessive pronouns such as "my," "mine," "our," "ours," etc. If any given utterance contains such accent, "that is a pretty sufficient signal that the utterance is tied, and tied via a contrast of that possessive pronoun (or the speaker of it) and some other: 'Let's take my car.' 'No, let's take MY car.' " With verbs, the pattern seems to be that emphasis on a "same" verb as prior marks agreement, while emphasis on the contrast verb indicates disagreement. See Sacks (1992 [1972], lecture 4:6, 10–11).

4. When the strategy of listening for talk in which the parents would allude to the existence of a difficulty is not successful, a regular practice is for the clinician to seek agreement on recipients' reason for visiting the clinic, which implicates "resistive" parents in producing or assenting to some particular complaint about their child because it is that which brought them to the clinic in the first place (Maynard 1991a). In other words, if parents think there is "no problem," and clinicians do think there is, the latter proceed to remind the parents of why they came to the clinic. In circumstances that mirror this, where doctors find "no problem" and patients believe there is, Heath (this volume: 256–7) shows that patients then offer to explain why they came to the clinic.

5. Thus, the series of turns may share the character of an "embedded" correction sequence (Jefferson 1987: 88):
   1   A speaker produces some object (X).
   2   A subsequent speaker produces an alternative (Y).
   3   Prior speaker produces the alternative (Y).

And therefore, it seems that a part of the clinician's job is to correct lay perspectives. However, the interjection of agreement tokens before the alternative term in example (3), rather than rejecting an initial formulation as in a correction sequence, initially accepts and thus confirms that formulation.

6 Dr. H nevertheless went on to praise the mother for "feeling that way" because it showed a "positive attitude," and neither party returned to a discussion of the retardation term. Further discussion centered on the girl's need for affection, praise, and other forms of reinforcement. However, when the clinicians later recommended taking the child out

of parochial school so that she could attend a special class in the public schools, the mother would not go along with this recommendation.

7 Analyzing this interview requires glossing some details and segments that would take excessive space. My goal is to be responsible to these details and what goes in those segments, so as not to distort excerpts that are abstracted herein, and yet to concentrate on these excerpts as showing patterns that are invariant across at least the present corpus of data.

8 See the discussions in M. H. Goodwin (1983: 665) and Maynard (1985: 5–7) regarding how oppositional utterances can be handled in ways that accomplish repair or correction rather than in ways that implicate dispute.

9 The clinical position with regard to diagnosis, therefore, may be relatively rigid due to the intractability of institutional remedies (Mehan 1991). Nevertheless, while such institutional intractability may partially explain the origins and rigidity of the clinic's position, it does not account for the manner in which it is presented to the parents. The perspective–display series and its related mechanisms are persuasive devices, that is, but of a particular type. As clinicians work to co-implicate recipients' view in the delivery of diagnostic news, it displays a mutuality of perspective that gives at least the appearance of social solidarity rather than institutional imposition. See Maynard (1991b) and the conclusion of this chapter.

10. In general, "identifying" and similar devices for co-implicating a parent's perspective do not occupy distinct positions in a diagnostic news delivery series, but rather are relatively "free-floating" resources that can be introduced in a contingent manner at relevant interactional junctures on behalf of confirming, reformulating, upgrading, or elaborating a recipient's perspective. Thus, in one interview (no. 52), a clinician, Dr. V, apparently noticed some emoting on the part of her recipient, and broke off from confirming a mother's view that her child had a language difficulty to acknowledge how "scary" it was to come to the clinic. Dr. V went on to say, "Now I am a parent, ... and when I come in the first you know moment in the day I'm very struck by the building and the sign on the door [which refers to mental retardation] and it turns me off too and it's a very nervous feeling." Mrs. S, the mother, replied, "I agree with you." Thus, Dr. V proposed to identify with Mrs. S through categorizing herself as a parent, and proffering feeling-state descriptors with which Mrs. S could expectedly affiliate. The agreement from Mrs. S would suggest that the proposed identification was successful. After this, Dr. V returned to confirming the parent's view of there being a language problem, and reformulated the condition as a "trouble in verbalizing, in speaking." She later upgraded the diagnosis to "learning disability." Thus, identifying is not just a preparatory or anticipatory technique to be employed in immediate conjunction with presenting an upgraded diagnosis, but can

be utilized at any point in the delivery sequence (here, before a confirmation) where a recipient's emotional state "leaks through." In the
conclusion of this chapter, see also the discussion of "identifying" as it
occurs in the context of a straightforward diagnostic news delivery.
And for a roughly similar organizational phenomenon, see Jefferson's
(1988: 427–8) discussion of how "big packages" in conversation
(such as troubles tellings) may not themselves have a strict ordering of
constituent parts, but consist of smaller sequences that are only "loosely linked," and sometimes "interchangeably positioned."

11. Of course, delivering the diagnosis of brain damage transpires at some
distance from the recipient's invited and initially displayed perspective.
The significance of this lies in the temporality that thereby becomes an
ineluctable aspect of the news-delivery process. Sequential distance
between recipient's perspective–display and clinician's delivery of an
official opinion translates not only into an increase in clock time
according to the number of devices employed to co-implicate recipient's perspective, but may then permit an "inner time" (see Garfinkel
1967: 166) of anticipation and expectancy to develop as the participants move towards the interview's culmination.

12. In a pediatric cardiology clinic, Silverman (1981) has identified a persuasive use of perspective–display sequences as used to discuss Down's
Syndrome children. By employing what I call unmarked queries, clinicians focused away from the children's medical difficulties and on their
value as family members. This was to encourage parents to avoid
having surgery done on the child and to respect his or her "social
utility." With parents of other (non-Down's Syndrome) children, clinicians more often used closed perspective–display invitations and
thereby displayed a willingness to deal with medical and particularly
heart problems.

13. See the "Roberts" example and discussion of it in Maynard (1989b).

14. See also Heath's (this volume: 250–1) discussion of how doctors may
propose an assessment and invite the patient's confirmation. Also,
patients will sometimes offer their version of things after the clinician's
delivery. But they do so without challenging the physician's assessment
(Heath this volume: 257–9).

15. In regular medical consultations, Heath (this volume: 240) demonstrates that patients often do not talk after practitioners provide an
assessment or diagnosis, "despite the practitioner specifically providing a position, immediately following its delivery, where the patient
might 'properly' speak."

12

Dilemmas of advice: aspects of the delivery and reception of advice in interactions between health visitors and first-time mothers

JOHN HERITAGE and SUE SEFI

1 Introduction

The British health-visitor service is the largest single element of the UK community-nursing program, comprising some 9,300 qualified nurses (Cumberlege Report 1986: 10).[1] The health visitor's role, as described by the Health Visitors' Association (1985), is to be "fully and completely involved in the giving of advice and support but only indirectly in the treatment of illness, environmental control and the provision of practical help." As this broadly worded description suggests, health visitors have very wide-ranging professional responsibilities comprising the following: the detection and prevention of ill-health in the community; the identification of health needs in the community; health teaching; and advice and guidance in cases of illness and in the care and management of children (Council for the Education and Training of Health Visitors 1977). These responsibilities – in which advice giving plays a primary role – are necessarily discharged through verbal interaction with members of the community.

In this chapter, we examine the management of advice giving in interactions between health visitors and first-time mothers (primiparae) during the course of visits to the mothers' homes. In particular, we will focus on the first of these visits, which normally takes place about ten days after the birth of the baby and which is widely believed to be particularly significant for the subsequent relationship between mother and health visitor. Our objective is to describe

We would like to thank Steve Clayman, Paul Drew, David Greatbatch, Berry Mayall, Manny Schegloff, and Candace West for valuable comments on an earlier draft of this chapter.

some basic aspects of the advice-giving sequences that occur in these first visits. Specifically, (a) we will sketch the main ways in which advice giving is initiated with a particular focus on how the parties arrive at the point where advice giving is begun. (b) We will discuss the main ways in which advice is received over its course, focusing on the ways in which the advice may be accepted or resisted.

We emphasize that this chapter offers a relatively gross overview of the basic features of these advice-giving sequences and does so with reference to a particular social context – first visits to the homes of first-time mothers. More detailed analyses of the design and trajectory of advice-giving sequences will be dealt with in subsequent studies as will comparisons of the initiation, design, trajectory, and reception of advice in these visits with those occurring in later visits to the same first-time mothers and in visits to mothers who have already had at least one child. Finally, while the health visitors exhibited significant individual differences in their approach to advice giving, individual comparisons are also beyond the scope of the present chapter. Below, after a description of our data base, we begin our discussion with a brief overview of the health-visiting service.

1.1 The data base

The data on which the present chapter is based are drawn from a substantial corpus of self-administered audio-tape recordings by health visitors in a large industrial city in central England.[2] The health visitors recorded their first six visits to a range of mothers evenly divided between first-time mothers and mothers who had previously had one or more children. In all some seventy-five visits were recorded. This chapter is based on data from eight initial or primary visits to first-time mothers conducted by five different health visitors and occupying a total of 4.5 hours.[3] These data contain some seventy instances of advice-giving sequences and, although any indications of a distributional kind should be treated with caution, we are confident that many of the main ways in which advice giving is managed in home visits are represented in the observations that follow.

1.2 The health visitor service: a brief overview

Health visitors, as Dingwall (1977: 21) has observed, "are a uniquely British contribution to the delivery of public health services." They are fully trained nurses who work in association with general practitioners and community health centers. However, unlike community nurses in other advanced countries, health visitors do not perform routine nursing tasks and concentrate instead on illness prevention, giving advice on health and social problems and case finding for other more specialized agencies (ibid.).[4] Although their range of responsibilities is, as noted above, exceptionally large, in practice they presently tend to concentrate their work in two main areas of need: families with children aged under five, who absorb about three-quarters of their time, and the elderly sick, who occupy another 10 percent. Their work is conducted through two major types of activities: (a) clinics focused on preventative aspects of health involving developmental assessments and immunization; and (b) visits to the homes of persons in some kind of need. As far as home visits are concerned, the largest proportion are made to mothers of new-born children, and it is these visits which are the subject of this chapter.

The British health-visiting service is distinctive in that, unlike other medical services in the United Kingdom and elsewhere, its provision is supply- rather than demand-driven.[5] This characteristic is particularly prominent in relation to the health visitor's work with children. Health visitors have a statutory obligation to perform routine visits to all mothers with children under five regardless of whether these visits are requested or not.[6] The supply-driven character of the service reflects the origins of the health-visiting service in the municipal sanitation movement of the nineteenth and early twentieth centuries. Strongly interventionist and directed towards working-class homes, this movement culminated in the development of a national sanitary inspectorate during the early decades of the twentieth century. The following quotation from the rule book of the Manchester and Salford Sanitary Association (c 1880) gives a flavor of the women inspectors' duties:

They must visit from house to house, irrespective of creed or circumstances, in such localities as their superintendents direct. They must carry with them the carbolic powder, explain its use and leave it where it is accepted; direct the attention of those they visit to the evils of bad smells, want of fresh air and impurities of all kinds; give hints to mothers on feeding and clothing their children; where they find sickness, assist in promoting the comfort of the invalid by personal help ... they must urge the importance of cleanliness, thrift and temperance on all possible occasions. They are desired to get as many as possible to join the mothers' meetings of their districts: to use all their influence to induce those they visit to attend regularly at their places of worship, and to send their children to school.

(Clark 1973: 11)

Today, long after her incorporation into the national health service and with a statutory obligation embracing the health needs of children of all social classes, the modern health visitor still carries at least a whiff of that interventionist carbolic into the houses of contemporary mothers and their babies. Although the health-visitor organizations downplay this aspect of their role, the health visitors' access to the homes of young children gives their visits an unavoidable dimension of surveillance and social control.

The general significance of this surveillance role, which is widely oriented to by mothers,[7] may be inferred from the fact that health visitors are the largest single source of information and referral in cases of child abuse and neglect in the United Kingdom (Dingwall, Eekelaar, and Murray 1983).

1.3 The home visit

Home visits occupy between a quarter and a third of health visitors' time (Clark 1981; Dunnell and Dobbs 1982). They begin when the new-born is about ten days old and the midwife has formally relinquished responsibility for the mother and baby. For the first month or so, and especially in the case of first-time mothers, they tend to occur on a weekly basis, subsequently diminishing in frequency in succeeding months.[8]

The home visit is an aspect of health-visitor (henceforth HV) practice that is largely hidden from public view. Its content and procedures have not been a focus of sustained social-scientific research in the past, nor have systematic principles of home-visiting practice been elaborated and taught as part of HV training programs. Insofar as specific interactional procedures for the conduct of visits are acquired in the course of initial training, they are largely learned tacitly through apprenticeship to more experienced practitioners (Dingwall 1977).

Robinson (1982) has proposed that the knowledge base on which HVs rely – incorporating clinical and nutritional principles, epidemiology, child development, and psychological and sociological views of the person and the family within social processes – could sustain two alternative models of HV practice:

The first model is founded on a clinical, problem oriented base. The health visitor engages in a search for health problems through an "identification, diagnosis and treatment" process. Students are taught that a good relationship with clients is essential in order to gain acceptance for their special expertise in preventive health care ... The second model is founded on a relationship centred base. The client is enabled to engage in the self-identification of factors operating against his health and well-being and is encouraged to join with the worker in a programme of help.

(Robinson 1982: 24)

To date, however, no empirical studies have been developed to assess the extent to which these models influence HV practice.

Notwithstanding its importance, there have been relatively few attempts to study the home visit in any detail. Previous studies of HVs' activities have largely been based on diary keeping and other self-reporting methodologies and have concentrated on how HVs allocated their time among their different responsibilities and on statistical analyses of the topics and activities of the home visit (see e.g. Clark 1973; Watson 1981; Dunnell and Dobbs 1982). These essentially cross-sectional studies give little access to the interactional processes of health visiting and there is almost no published information that deals in detail with the events of the home visit.[9]

Studies of client perspectives on health visiting have tended to be small scale and present results which are piecemeal and fragmentary. In general, however, they indicate that mothers tend to prefer home visiting rather than clinics as a site for interaction with their HVs (see Bax, Hart, and Jenkins 1980; Orr 1980; Foxman *et al.* 1982), but, predictably, dislike it when visits occur unannounced (Orr 1980; McIntosh 1986). At the same time however a substantial proportion of mothers, particularly in social classes IV and V, see the HV service largely in terms of social control and surveillance and attempt to minimize contact with its representatives (ibid.). Most surveys suggest declining levels of satisfaction with the

HV service over time (Graham and McKee 1979; Field *et al.* 1982; Moss, Bolland, and Foxman 1982; McIntosh 1986) and indicate that mothers tend to remain unclear about the role and value of HVs (Hunt 1972; Moss, Bolland, and Foxman 1973; Orr 1980; McIntosh 1986). A number of studies have found that mothers evaluate their HVs largely in terms of personality characteristics and interpersonal style. These studies also indicate that mothers have a strong preference for friendliness and informality in HV conduct and that HVs are quite commonly perceived as excessively authoritarian and didactic (Political and Economic Planning 1961; Wilson and Herbert 1978; Blaxter and Paterson 1982; Foxman *et al.* 1982; McIntosh 1986).

Although advice giving has been a central feature of health visiting throughout the existence of the service, there has been relatively little systematic study of its provision. A study by Davison (1956) argued that, in contrast with social-service case workers, HV advice "is offered by her, not requested by her clients," and this view has been somewhat reinforced by anecdotal evidence from clients. As one of the latter, in an article published in *World Medicine*, observed, "they never really listen to you. Oh they appear to listen – but inside they have already pigeon-holed you and are just waiting for a gap in the conversation in which to give the appropriate advice" (Clark 1973: 6). Clark's time study of HV activities (ibid.: 69–73) found that advice giving was more frequent and more assertive in relation to physical health-care topics and where the subject was a young child. Finally, two studies of working-class mothers have dealt with reactions to advice giving. The mothers in Orr's (1980) study saw advice as something that should be "done without pushing," and this view was strongly reinforced in McIntosh's (1986) study of first-time mothers in Scotland, in which unsolicited advice was viewed as patronizing and was associated with considerable hostility. The mothers reported that they simply ignored much of this advice, particularly if it was associated with conflict of any kind (McIntosh 1986: 25–8).

1.4 The general character of the first visits

Of the visits that make up our data base, most represented the first occasion on which the mother and HV had met one another and, although the mothers were expecting a visit from the HV at some time during the week of the first visit, all were unannounced.[10] In a number of cases, third parties – husbands, grandmothers, or female friends – were present during the course of part or all of the visit and in some of these they were significant participants. The visits varied in length from fifteen minutes to just under an hour.

Although the visits are quite diverse, their content contains a number of common features. A large majority of topics were initiated and terminated by the HV in a basically 'segmented' process of topical progression (Button and Casey 1984; Sefi 1988). In visits where no third parties were present, the HVs usually began with inquiries about the mothers' experience of the birth and its immediate aftermath. Where third parties were present, they began by admiring the baby and dealing with topics that could be an appropriate focus of third-party participation.

Substantial parts of these first visits were occupied with three bureaucratic tasks: (a) getting face-sheet data about the mother and baby for the records of the clinic to which mother and baby will be attached; (b) getting consent signatures for immunization injections for diphtheria, whooping cough, tetanus, polio, and measles; and (c) explaining clinic procedures and the various subsequent health checks that mothers and babies will go through in the ensuing months and years. In a number of cases, explicit form filling for the creation of bureaucratic records formed a "backbone" to the visit: it was initiated early and was intermittently departed from in a range of topical excursions and returned to as the topical content of these excursions was exhausted. In others, the face-sheet data gathering was confined to a specific segment of the visit. The visits were substantially diverse in terms of their overall trajectories, the type and ordering of the topics raised and in terms of the "tone" or "rapport" achieved between the parties.

1.5 Advice giving and the problem of competence

There is ample evidence, both from survey data and from the materials that form the basis of this study, that during these first visits mothers primarily orient to their HVs as "baby experts" – persons with particular expertise on the health and treatment of babies – rather than as "befrienders" with whom they can share problems or

troubles that are not directly connected with problems of baby
management. Moreover, HVs characteristically comport themselves as "baby experts" during these visits. Thus, insofar as the
initial visits can come to involve more than a simple initiation of
contact together with the collection of face-sheet data, both
mothers and HVs treat its possibilities primarily in terms of a
"service encounter" (Jefferson and Lee, this volume).

However, in these visits it is also clear that, to a greater or lesser
extent, the mothers saw their knowledge, competence, and vigi-
lance in baby care as an object of evaluation and, moreover, by a
person with officially accredited competences to judge their conduct. This orientation emerged in a wide range of contexts but is
transparently visible in the mothers' responses to comments in
which the HV raises something that is apparently untoward, as in
(1):[11]

```
(1) [5A1:2]
  1   HV:        ˙hh She likes it on her ba:ck does she.
  2   M:         I j'st put 'er on there while I was
  3              gettin' ┌ the  pram out.
  4   HV:              └( )
  5   HV:        Yeh. 'Cos sometimes they can uh
  6              (0.5)
  7   M:         choke. Ye ┌h.
  8   HV:                 └Yeh. When they're on their back ┌s.
  9   M:                                                  └Well
 10              she does like it on her ba:ck.
 11   HV:        Ye:s.  I think when it- when you- when you're
 12              lea:ving he:r
 13              (.)
 14   M:         Ye: ┌ah
 15   HV:           └You ought to put her on her tummy
 16              real ┌ly,
 17   M:            └Yea:h, oh yeah
```

At the beginning of this sequence, the HV comments on the baby's
posture using a question design (statement + tag question) that is
built towards the supposition that the baby generally prefers to lie
this way. Although the question does not overtly treat the baby's
posture as problematic, it is noticeable that the mother's initial
response (lines 2–3) downplays its significance. She depicts it as a
brief and incidental part of her own earlier course of action and, by

implication, not as evidence of the baby's general preference. She then exhibits an awareness of a potential danger associated with this posture through her collaborative completion (line 7) of the HV's next turn (line 5). Thus it is only *after* the mother has displayed an alertness to the dangers implicitly raised in the HV's initial question that she then produces a revised response to it (lines 9–10) that acknowledges that the baby does in fact prefer lying on her back. Here then, the mother defers dealing with the HV's question "at face value" in favor of an initial response that shows her awareness of the dangers implicitly raised by it.

A concern for the judgmental possibilities inherent in these first visits is still more vividly illustrated by (2) below. Here an apparently casual observation by the HV "He's enjoying that isn't he" (presumably referring to some sucking or "mouthing" behavior by the baby) elicits contrastive responses from the baby's father and mother. While the father takes the remark at face value and responds with an agreement, the mother's response is notably defensive:

```
(2) [4A1:1]
 1   HV:       He's enjoying that ⌈isn't he.
 2   F:                           ⌊°Yes he certainly is=°
 3   M:        =He's not hungry 'cuz (h)he's ju(h)st (h)had
 4             'iz bo:ttle ˙hhh
```

Here the mother's initial response treats the HV's observation as implying that the baby may be hungry and, by extension, as possibly implicative of some failure on her part. She denies that the baby is hungry and goes on to produce an account that justifies her claim. Her response is one that treats the HV as someone who, whatever other functions she may have, is evaluating her competence as a mother.

This orientation towards the HV as someone who may stand in judgment on the mother's competence in child care suggests, and our data confirm, that requesting and giving advice during these first visits can be highly problematic activities. Any request for advice constitutes an admission of uncertainty about an appropriate course of action. Such a request may, further, imply or display that its producer lacks knowledge or competence concerning the issue at hand or is unable to cope with a problem without external assistance. By the same token, it constitutes the recipient of the request as the knowledgeable, competent, and authoritative party in the exchange. Concerns with these issues of knowledgeability, and the "face" considerations they raise,[12] may be compounded when the requested advice concerns a baby for whom a mother has a direct responsibility to care in a knowledgeable and competent way and when the requestee may be viewed as someone who stands in judgment on her knowledge and competence in this matter.

Similar issues concerning the implications of advice giving for judgments of mothers' knowledgeability and competence in child care and related matters may also inhabit contexts where advice giving is volunteered or occurs unrequested. For the volunteering of advice may carry with it an assertion of the very same implications about the relative authority and competence of the advice giver and advice recipient that are acknowledged in contexts where the recipient requests advice. And such implications may be the more unwelcome because they are produced by persons whose claims – to knowledge and to rights to judge – may be effectively unchallengeable.

1.6 Advice giving during the first visit: preliminary observations

In examining patterns of advice giving during these visits we have focused on sequences in which the HV describes, recommends, or otherwise forwards a preferred course of future action. Our concern is with sequences in which the HVs were engaged in activities having an essentially normative dimension which, we propose, is central to advice giving as an activity.

In the majority of our advice sequences, advice was explicitly future oriented and was delivered in strongly prescriptive terms.[13] This prescriptiveness emerged in a number of ways:

First, it appears in the language of overt recommendation:
[3A1:15] "I would recommend giving her a ba:th every da:y"

[4B1:16] "The hospital recomme:nd that she shouldn't start solids until she's (.) four months."

[1C1:31] "Well my advice to you: is that ... you firmly put her do:wn"

Second: advice was often couched in the imperative mood:
[3A1:24] "No always be ve:ry very qui:et at ni:ght."

[1C1:13] (The reference is to an eye infection)
"If you think they're pussie then you must use boiled
wa:te:r"

Third: advice was often expressed using verbs of obligation:
[1C1:5] "And I think you should involve your husband as
much as possible no::w"

[5A1:2] "when you're lea:ving he:r you ought to put her on
her tummy really"

Less commonly, advice could be expressed as a "factual generalization," as in the following case, in which a mother's enthusiasm for
disposable nappies (or diapers) is met with a generalization about
the practice of other mothers, which amounts to a recommendation
of reusable ones:

(3) [1C1:6] (Readers should note that the term 'terries' refers to a reusable
cotton towelling nappy or diaper)
```
1    HV:          And uh disposable nappies are quite easy
2                 aren't they really no:w,=
3    M:           =They're a lot easier than the uhm (0.4)
4                 terries (          ) aren't they yeah.
5    HV:                     [Ye:s.
6    M:           They're easier to pu(t) on and quite simple=
7    HV:          =Mm
8    M:           You kno:w,
9                 (0.2)
10   HV:    →     Lots of mums do: progress to thuh (0.8)
11                terries when they're a bit older.
```

In general, though, the HVs delivered their advice explicitly, auth-
oritatively and in so decided a fashion as to project their relative
expertise on health and baby-management issues as beyond doubt.

In examining patterns of advice giving during the first visit, we
will first consider the main procedures by which advice giving is
initiated in these visits and subsequently turn to look at some
aspects of its reception.

2 The initiation of advice giving

In looking at initiations, it is useful to begin with advice which was
directly or indirectly requested by mothers.

2.1 Mother-initiated advice

2.1.1 Requests for advice

Mother-initiated requests for advice are, in principle, the most
straightforward in our data base. A request for advice establishes
the relevance of subsequent advice giving in three important
respects: first, it establishes the problem area for which advice is
requested; second, it establishes the requester's uncertainty about
some aspect of that problem area and her view of it as problematic;
third, a request establishes her alignment as a prospective advice
recipient and thereby legitimates the subsequent delivery of advice.

Mother-initiated requests for advice can take the form of simple
question–answer sequences. Thus in (4) below, the mother designs
her request for advice as a straightforward "open" question,
thereby acknowledging ignorance as to how to proceed:

(4) [5B1:21] (The inquiry concerns the management of breast feeding)
```
1   M:      →    How long should I leave him on the other
2                side (            )
3   HV:          Until he's finished.
4   M:           Guzzling awa:y.
5   HV:          Mm:. 'Till he's had that side really.
6   M:           mYea:h.
```

However, even in their direct requests for advice, mothers were
rarely prepared to acknowledge complete ignorance about an
appropriate course of action.

More commonly, they managed their requests so as to display a
measure of knowledge or competence in the management of their
activities and thus to circumscribe the scope of the advice
requested. One common procedure for achieving such displays
involves embedding a proposal about an appropriate course of
action within a question. This procedure was normally managed as
a "closed" (*yes/no*) question – a format that was generally used to
solicit support for the proposed course of action – as in (5) below:

(5) [1C1:29]
```
  1   M:          Shall I let her tell me when
  2                she's hung┌ry.
  3   HV:                     └Yes well that's sensible.
```

Here, rather than using a question format (e.g. "How often should I
feed her") that would overtly acknowledge a lack of knowledge
about how often to feed her baby, the mother's inquiry is one
through which she portrays herself as having independent knowledge or understanding of how to proceed. The issue is thus treated
as only residually problematic and the HV is merely invited to
confirm the viewpoint embedded in the mother's inquiry.[14] In this
case, the HV's advice is limited to a fleeting confirmation.

However, this course of action carries a significant risk that the
HV will reject the mother's viewpoint and thereby deny the competence and knowledge that is proposed with it. This risk is realized
in (6):

(6) [3A1:15]
```
  1   M:     →   I haven't ba::thed her yet. Is once a week
  2               enough.
  3              (0.7)
  4   HV:        We::ll (0.2) babies do: sweat a lo:t. (0.3) So
  5              (0.3)
  6   IIV:       So I would recommend giving her a ba:th
  7               every da:y
```

Here the mother's inquiry describes a past course of action and
proposes an appropriate interval for bathing her child. However,
the HV's response indicates not only that the mother's proposal
about how often a baby should be bathed is incorrect, but also that
she has already failed to bath her child with a frequency that the
HV judges to be appropriate. Notwithstanding these risks, however, most requests for advice were packaged as requests for confirmation of proposed courses of action.

In most cases, including the above, mother-initiated advice
sequences emerged within topical environments that had already
been established by HVs' questions. These contexts afforded a wide
range of opportunities for mothers to display their knowledge and
ability to cope with the problems for which they sought advice.
Thus in the following case, rather than asking for advice outright,
the mother details a problem connected with the taking of iron

tablets, expresses uncertainty about whether to continue with them, and offers a candidate solution to her problem.

(7) [5B1:14]
```
 1    HV:         Have you got some iron tablets l┌eft.
 2    M:                                          └˙hh We:ll yes
 3                I ha:ve (.) 'cos uh ˙hh uhm (0.5) I wasn't
 4                able to take them in pregnancy because they
 5                made me constipa:ted.
 6    HV:         Ye:s.=
 7    M:          =And I have had a fe:w over the last few days
 8                and it's happening agai:n.
 9    HV:         Is it.
10    M:     →    So I don't know whether to carry on or no:t.=
11           →    =Maybe have one every now and agai:n.
12    HV:         Ye:s. (.) I mea(n) i- you're ten point fou:r
13                which isn't too ba:d.
```

Similarly in the next case, after the HV has raised the topic of family planning and suggested various sources of help including herself, the mother indirectly requests some advice about when to restart the pill (arrow 2) but only after she has shown that she has independently dealt with the family-planning issue (arrow 1):

(8) [4B1:7]
```
 1    HV:         ˙hh And family planning you know you can get
 2                pregnant straight awa:y so if you wou:ld (.)
 3                like any: (.) help in that score you can
 4                always ask me: or see the G.P. or go to the
 5                family planning clinic.=
 6    M:     1→   =Well I- I've got some (0.4) things
 7                upstai:┌rs.
 8    HV:                └°Oh well done.°
 9    M:     2→   But (.) when I've got to take them I
10                do:n'know.
11    HV:         Well (.) uhm if you're not breast feeding
12                there's no reason why you shouldn't start them
13                when (.) she's fou:r weeks.
```

In sum, the significant feature of requests for advice is that they directly and overtly establish a context in which advice can be relevantly given and they do so *in advance* of its actual delivery. Through requests, mothers can display an orientation to a state of affairs as problematic, describe the state of affairs and establish themselves as requiring some advice or direction about the course of action they should take. However, this procedure, which involves an overt acknowledgment of some limitation in the mother's knowledge or competence as a carer, was not often adopted. Direct or indirect requests for advice amounted to no more than seven cases (approximately 10 percent of the total) in a set of interactions that, in total, occupied nearly 4.5 hours. Moreover, these requests were most commonly managed so as to preserve – as far as possible – the appearance of competence in baby management and related issues. Both the infrequency of these requests and their characteristic design suggest that mothers may be reluctant to request advice for fear that adverse judgments may be made about their knowledge or competence in baby management or mothering skills.

2.1.2 Soliciting advice by describing an "untoward" state of affairs

An alternative and more "cautious" procedure which mothers employed for soliciting advice was substantially more indirect. It consisted simply of detailing an untoward state of affairs which, without overtly requesting advice, they treated as potentially problematic.[15] The following case, in which a mother and grandmother depict a condition of the new baby is prototypical in this respect:

```
(9) [4B1:22]
 1    HV:          Bonnets are wo:rth ha⌐ving.
 2    G:                              ⌊·hhh Her hai::r it
 3                 seems a bit grea:s⌐y
 4    M:                           ⌊Yea:⌐:h.
 5    G:                                ⌊Every time we've
 6                 wa:shed it=
 7    M:          =Ye⌐a::h
 8    G:             ⌊when we give her a little ba::th it
 9                 looks lo:vely ·hhh=
10    M:          =b⌐y the end'v-
11    G:            ⌊and by the end of ⌐th'da:y
12    M:                               ⌊by-
13                 (.)
14    M:          by three o'clock in the afternoon it's all
15                 greasy on the to:p.=
16    HV:         =Is it?
17    M:          Yea::h she's a re:a⌐l swea(t)uh.
18    HV:    →                       ⌊D'ju think she's ho:t.
```

```
19   ?G:        She might be:.
20   M:         Wul we keep 'e ⌐r wrappin' round er
21   G:                        ⌊ We keep 'er in that li- uh
22              (0.5)
23   M:         and in this little nest ⌐here that she's go:t.
24   HV:                                ⌊Ri:ght.
25              (.)
26   HV:    →   Ri:ght. ˙hh (It) might be that she's too ho:t.
27              (1.2)
28   ( ):       (     )
29   HV:    →   Becuz this is certainly the- (.) the
30              temperature of the hospital isn't it.=
31   M:         =Yea:h.
32   HV:        And is it the sa:me throughout upstairs as
33              we:ll.
34              (0.2)
35   M:         We:ll I've got a little fi::re (.) ⌐upstairs
36   HV:    →                                     ⌊I would
37          →   slowly bring the temperature do:wn to sort of
38          →   no:rmal.
```

Here the mother and grandmother's collaboratively produced description of the baby's condition (lines 2–15) is apparently initially triggered (Jefferson 1978) by the conclusion of a previous advice-giving episode that culminates in the recommendation that "bonnets are worth having." The grandmother's initial comment about the baby's hair (lines 2–3) is collaboratively worked up into an extensive depiction of a sweating baby by line 18. However, while this description is developed as something noteworthy and possibly problematic, it is not associated with any overt request for advice. In this context, it is thus the HV who formulates a possible cause of the problem (at line 18) and, after a series of inquiries, proposes a remedy (lines 36–8).

In a range of other cases, too, the detailing of something untoward becomes an occasion for advice giving. The following sequence, which occurs just before (9) above, begins with the grandmother's "triggered" observation that the rain recurrently prevents her daughter from walking the new baby to the shops. While this state of affairs is reported as a "trouble," it is not depicted as a specific "problem" that requires advice. In particular, the grandmother offers no explanation of why the daughter has to return home when it rains. In this particular context, while there

may be a concern for the baby's welfare, there is also the possibility
that the daughter does not like walking in the rain, or that she is
anxious about her new baby carriage which, she has asserted a few
turns earlier (data not shown), "goes funny" in the rain.

```
(10) [4B1:22]
 1   G:           ˙hhh When she sta:rts off walking ou:(t) it
 2                always seems to r⌐ai::n.
 3   HV:   1→                     ⌊aO:::h.=
 4   M:           =Yea:h.
 5   G:           Ge⌐ts half wa:y and 'as to come ba:ck.
 6   M:             ⌊(        )
 7   HV:   2→    Oh what a pity.
 8   M:           Yea::h myea:h.
 9   HV:   3→    But if she's wrapped up well it won't do he:r
10                any ha⌐:rm
11   M:                 ⌊(harm)
12   G:           No:.
13   M:           No: that's what they (   ⌐    )
14   HV:   4→                             ⌊Babies loose a lot
15                of heh- heat through their hea:ds
                  ((continues with advice))
```

The HV's response to the grandmother's initial observations is one
of simple affiliation: a sympathetically intoned "Oh" (arrow 1) in
response to the grandmother's account of the rain and a subsequent
empathetic assessment (arrow 2) in response to her account of its
consequences. Subsequently, however, she shifts to a "baby relevant" treatment of the reported events (arrow 3) and continues by
describing the baby's head as a major source of heat loss, an observation which culminates in the advice that "bonnets are worth
having." Here, then, a general, and at best opaquely motivated,
description of the irritations of the British weather is responded to
in terms of its implications for the health of the baby and engenders
advice giving as its outcome.

And in the following sequence, a minimally problematic reference also attracts advice giving.

```
(11) [3A1:14]
 1   HV:          Listen to your 'iccups. Just listen to your
 2                'iccups.
 3   B:           ((hiccups))
 4   M:           I know what cures those.
```

```
5                    (.)
6    M:              More milk ┌o
7    HV:                       └More
8                    ┌mi:lk is-
9    M:              └heh heh heh heh
10   HV:             Huh
11                   (0.5)
12   HV:    →        Don't worry about hiccups. ((continues))
```

This fragment opens with the HV addressing a remark – in "baby-talk" register – to the baby. Whilst it is unclear whether this remark is intended as a means to draw the mother's attention to the baby's hiccups and thus to treat them as problematic, the mother nonetheless proceeds to describe what she proposes as a "cure" for the baby's condition. Although the term "cure" formulates the baby's condition as a "problem," her subsequent depiction of it – "More milko" – is offered lightly and she follows it with laughter to which the HV briefly affiliates. Here, while the mother portrays herself as able to manage this situation, her formulation of it as problematic appears sufficient to engender advice giving, which the HV begins after a short pause.

2.1.3 Summary

A number of basic points about mother-initiated advice sequences can now be made. First, requests for advice are relatively infrequent in our data base of first visits. Second, mothers commonly manage them so as to portray themselves, as far as possible, as competent and knowledgeable about the issues they raise. Third, mothers may solicit advice, as in (9), by reporting or describing untoward states of affairs and without overtly requesting it. However, in such cases, the matters that are made explicit in overt requests – that something is viewed as problematic, the nature of the problem, and the need for advice – are, to varying degrees, left implicit. It is thus left to the HV to determine whether the described state of affairs embodies a genuine problem that warrants advice and/or whether the description is offered as a means of soliciting advice. Describing an untoward state of affairs is, at best, an indirect means of soliciting advice and such descriptions may be variously motivated. Advice giving, which treats such a description as a means of deploying a "problem" in search of a "solution," is only one of a range of possible responses and may represent a course of action that is unlooked for or undesired (Jefferson and Lee, this volume).[16] In our data, the HVs tended to deal with such descriptions in terms of their relevance for health or baby-management issues and to respond with advice. Thus the report – or even mention (see (11) above) – of some problematic state of affairs may be sufficient to entrain the delivery of advice even in circumstances where it is unlikely that the report is being offered in search of advice. The readiness with which the HVs in our sample responded to such reports and mentions with advice indicates both their concern with any potential problem situation that may arise and their orientation to advice giving as a central task of these interactions.

2.2 Health-visitor-initiated advice

The vast majority of advice giving in our data base was initiated by HVs. Much of it arose from routine inquiries about baby- and health-related matters. In contrast to the mother-initiated advice sequences in which, by requesting advice, the mothers established both its relevance and its object, advice giving in the HV-initiated sequences often emerged prior to any clear indication that it was desired.

Below we show a range of the sequences through which the HVs initiated advice. These vary from relatively elaborate attempts to establish a "problem" – and thereby to construct a context in which advice could relevantly be offered – to cases in which no such attempt was made and advice was delivered to a completely unprepared recipient.

2.2.1 Stepwise entry in advice giving: developing a problem

We begin with cases in which a relatively complete series of steps in the construction of a "problem-requiring advice" are present. In (12) below, the mother's response to the HV's initial inquiry is indicative of a residual problem:

(12) [1A1:10-11]
```
1   HV:    1→   Is the co:rd ehm (1.0) dry now.
2   M:     2→   Ye:s it's- (.) it weeps a little bit.
3   HV:    3→   And what do you do⌈:.
4   M:                            ⌊(mYeah.)
```

```
 5   M:    4→   I've got some of those mediswab⌐s
 6   HV:                                    └Uh⌐huh
 7   M:    4→                                  └an' I use
 8         4→   it to clean it with and I put a bit of
 9         4→   talcum (powder on)
10   HV:   5→   Don't be frightened of uhr (.) the co:rd
11         5→   because it's uhm (1.5) it uh nothing awful
12   HV:   5→   will happen.
13   M:         Mm:.
14   HV:   5→   Uhm just make sure you clean right insi:⌐de
15   M:                                              └Yea:h
16   HV:   5→   with (.) with the mediswabs.=Pull- pull it
17         5→   apart with your fingers ˙hhh and give it a
18         5→   good (.) clea:n.
19              (.)
20   HV:   5→   And then put ye:r (.) sterile powder on.
21   M:         Ye⌐:h.
22   HV:           └'nd if you need any more we can give you
23              some more swabs,
24              (.)
25   M:         Ri::ght.
26   HV:        Uhm (0.3) and what about- her bottom's
27              alright?
```

The sequence is opened with the HV's inquiry "Is the co:rd ehm (1.0) dry now." The design of this inquiry – in particular, its explicit reference to the cord being "dry" – is managed so as to implicate an expectable or normal state of the cord, and thus gives the mother a standard against which to recognize anything that may be problematic in her own case. The mother initiates her response with a turn component ("Ye:s it's-") that is shaped to a trajectory that would assert that the cord is "fine" or "normal." However, she then revises this response so as to acknowledge that it is weeping "a little bit" (arrow 2) – a response that, in the context of the HV's inquiry, indicates an ongoing problem. The HV's second inquiry, "And what do you do:." (arrow 3), now accomplishes a range of tasks: first, it fixes the issue as problematic and requiring action; second, it moves the topical focus of the sequence from the problem to measures for its solution; third, it projects some detailing of her activities by the mother (arrow 4) to which the HV can relevantly fit appropriate advice on the course of action to be followed (arrow 5).

As noted above, this is a relatively extended "step-by-step" procedure which culminates in advice giving. The relevant steps may be summarized as follows:

Step 1: HV: initial inquiry.
Step 2: M: problem-indicative response.
Step 3: HV: focusing inquiry into the problem.
Step 4: M: responsive detailing.
Step 5: HV: advice giving.

This "step-by-step" approach to the initiation of advice giving is further illustrated in (13):

(13) [1C1:39]
```
 1   HV:   1→   And you feel- (0.3) you're alright ba:thing
 2              (.) her?
 3   M:    2→   I haven't bathed her ye:t.
 4   HV:         Haven't you real⌐ly.
 5   M:    2→                    ⌊No:. She had a bath when she
 6         2→   came home from hospital (0.2) but I top and
 7         2→   tail her.
 8   HV:         Ye:h=
 9   M:    2→   =but uhm: me mum's coming over tomorro:w (.)
10         2→   and I'm gonna ba:th her in front of me mum
11         2→   'cos I'm (still) a little bi:t (.) you
12         2→   kno:w⌐(    )
13   HV:   3→        ⌊Did they show you how to bath
14         3→   her ⌐°(when you were in)°
15   M:        ⌊They di::d but (0.9) I: (.) still
16         4→   wasn't- I said to me mum you know wuh- when
17         4→   you come over tomorrow would you sort'v give
18         4→   me a ha:nd you know if I nee:d it.
19              (.)
20   HV:   5→   The main thing is: that you have the things
21         5→   all together before you sta:rt.
              ((advice giving continues))
```

Here the HV's initial inquiry is built towards an affirmative, "no problem" response. However, the mother's reply indicates a potentially problematic state of affairs and the beginning of her – subsequently abandoned – account for not bathing her baby (lines 11–12) implies some uncertainty or lack of confidence about how to do it. The HV's focusing inquiry topicalizes this issue by asking whether the mother has been shown the procedure. It is noticeable that although the initial component of the mother's response

("They di::d but (0.9) I: (.) still wasn't-") is abandoned in favor of depicting her request to her mother (and through that depiction, an intimation of her needs), it is at least compatible with a continuing state of uncertainty about how to bath her baby. Subsequently, the HV begins to advise the mother how to go about the task.

Several significant features of this stepwise entry into advice giving may now be summarily noted. First, the relevance of advice giving is established in a successive process through which (a) a problem is unearthed and then (b) measures for its solution are topicalized through a focusing inquiry. By this means, the potential need for advice can emerge as the joint construction of the participants.

Second, the HV's focusing inquiry and the mother's response to it can enable the HV to develop her course of advice in a nonadversarial fashion and in a way that is fitted to the mother's account. For example, in (12), the mother's response to the HV's focusing inquiry enables the latter to build her advice so as to support and reinforce the mother's report of what she has been doing, rather than as a recommendation that would contrast with and implicate criticism of the mother's reported actions.[17]

However, third, the HV's inquiries are not managed in such a way as to determine clearly that the mother is ignorant or at fault. For example, in (12), although the HV's focusing inquiry and her subsequent advice imply that the mother may have failed to clean the cord in a satisfactory fashion, she does not attempt to establish this as a definite fact. Such an attempt would develop the interaction in an inquisitorial direction, while an overt finding that the mother's treatment of the cord had been at fault would be a problematic context within which to initiate a course of advice. Similarly, in (13), rather than attempting to have the mother overtly describe her anxieties or difficulties, the HV builds towards advice giving on the basis that the mother seems uncertain about bathing her baby. Thus, while advice giving may imply that the HV discerns a lack of knowledge or competence in the mother, the exact character of these deficiencies is left implicit.

2.2.2 Variations on the stepwise entry into advice giving

While (12) and (13) above represent a relatively extended step-by-step movement into advice giving, the sequence may be varied –

contracted or departed from – in a variety of ways. In what follows, we show an ordered series of such contractions and departures. Within this series, each contraction or departure involves a reduction in the amount of preparation for the consummatory advice-giving phase of the sequence and increases the risk that the advice, when it is finally delivered, may be redundant and/or undesired.

Variation 1
A minimal form of contraction in the sequence arises when a general inquiry gets a response from the mother that both indicates a problematic state of affairs (step 2) and volunteers some account of how she has dealt with it (step 4). In these sequences, the mothers' accounts of how they are dealing with the problem, while designed to display their competence and capacity to cope, nonetheless consolidate their view of the state of affairs they describe as a problem. Moreover, because they topicalize the matter of how to deal with the problem, these accounts establish interactional environments that are ripe for advice giving. The following instance is typical in this respect:

```
(14) [1C1:13]
 1   HV:    1→   Her eyes're oka:y.
 2                (0.7)
 3   M:     2→   They ge- th- they get a bit wee:py sometimes,
 4          4→   but that's normal isn't it.  And I swab th'm
 5          4→   with wool with cotton woo:l,
 6                (0.3)
 7   HV:    5→   Ye:s if they- if they: (0.2) if you think
 8          5→   they're pussie,
 9                (0.8)
10   M:           Yea:h.
11   HV:    5→    then you must use boiled wa:te:r
                  ((advice giving continues))
```

Here the HV's initial inquiry (arrow 1) gets a response that details a baby problem (arrow 2). Subsequently, the mother describes what she did to deal with the problem (arrow 4) and the HV initiates a course of advice in response to this account. In contrast to the "full" step-by-step sequence displayed in (12) and (13) above, the shortened sequence runs as follows:

Step 1: HV: initial inquiry.

Step 2: M: problem-indicative response.

      +

Step 4: M: additional detailing.
Step 5: HV: advice giving.

This sequence is also realized in (15) below:

(15) [1C1:19-20]
```
 1   HV:    1→   What are her motions li:ke.
 2                (0.6)
 3   M:     2→   Uh: uh:m they're softer no:w because she
 4          2→   was a l'ttle bit constipated (0.2) a few days
 5          2→   ago:,
 6   HV:          Mm hm,
 7   M:     4→   and the midwife advised me to put a teaspoon
 8          4→   of uhm
 9                (1.0)
10   HV:          brown ⌈sugar
11   M:     4→          ⌊brown sugar in alternate feeds
12   HV:          I s⌈ee.
13   M:     4→        ⌊and tha:t helped her an' they're a lot
14          4→   softer no:w,
15                (0.6)
16   HV:    5→   Oh I don't think you nee:d (1.2) you kno:w=
                 ((advice giving continues))
```

In these cases, then, the mothers' volunteering of how they dealt with the problem obviates the need for the HVs' focusing inquiries while nonetheless creating a topical environment in which advice giving may be initiated.

Variation 2

A further contraction of this sequence occurs when the HV's initial inquiry yields a problem and the HV proceeds to advice giving (step 5) without any focusing inquiry. In these cases the advice-initiation sequence runs:

Step 1: HV: initial inquiry.
Step 2: M: problem-indicative response.
Step 5: HV: advice giving.

as in (16):

(16) [1C1:30-31]
```
 1   HV:    1→   And you're able to put her down in between
```

```
 2                 1→   fee:ds are you:,
 3                      (1.0)
 4      M:         2→   No::. (0.4) She screams.
 5      HV:             uhhhh hah hah ⌈hah ˙uhhhhhhhhhh
 6      M:         2→                 ⌊if I put her in the:⌈re.
 7      Fr:                                               ⌊hhehhhh=
 8      HV:             =hah °hah°=
 9      Fr:             =eh hhnh
10                      (1.0)
11      M:             Ye:s.=
12      HV:        5→   =Well it is important you kno:w tuh: (0.2) get
13                 5→   it into a rou:ti:ne (0.2) otherwise she'll get
14                 5→   so used to sittin' on your lap she'll want to
15                 5→   do it all the ti:me.
                        ((advice giving continues))
```

In (16) the HV's initial inquiry again projects an affirmative "no
problem" response. After a substantial delay,[18] the mother briefly
responds by depicting a possibly problematic state of affairs which
is initially met with laughter from the HV. Subsequently, the HV
proceeds directly to the initiation of advice.

A similar pattern emerges in (17). Here an initial inquiry about
postnatal exercises is met with a response that indicates that while
the exercises have been begun, the mother did not start them until
relatively recently after her return home. The mother's subsequent
elaboration of this observation is intersected with the initiation of
advice giving.

```
(17) [1C1:33-34]
 1      HV:        1→   Are you doing your exercises.
 2      M:         2→   Yes I've started to do them (  ) no:w.
 3                 2→   =I didn't do them 'till I come ho:me
 4                      (.)
 5      M:         2→   °You kno:⌈w I uh°
 6      HV:        5→            ⌊I think it's quite important to uh
 7                 5→   particularly yer tail exercises which you can
 8                 5→   do: when yer just sitting do:wn
                        ((advice giving continues))
```

Here the mother's response apparently indicates insufficient
commitment to the postnatal exercises and creates sufficient doubt
for advice about the exercises to be initiated. The HV's advice is
designed to underscore their importance.

By contrast with the sequence types discussed previously, this contraction significantly reduces the chance that the relevance of advice giving can be appropriately established prior to its delivery. First, since no description of how she is dealing with "the problem" is volunteered by the mother or requested by the HV, it may not be clear from the mother's initial response that she regards the circumstances she describes as significantly problematic. For example, in (17) the mother may have described an approach to her exercises which is, from her point of view, perfectly adequate. Thus what is treated as a "problem in need of advice" by the HV, may not be regarded in the same way by the mother.[19]

Second, in the absence of a description of the mothers' responsive measures, the HV has no assurance that the advice she gives may not be already known, and indeed acted upon, by the mother and her advice stands a serious risk of appearing inappropriate or redundant.

The choice between moving to a step 5 advice giving or a step 3 focusing inquiry is nicely illustrated in (18) below. Here, the sequence opens with a problematic noticing by the HV of the baby's jaundice that is strongly confirmed by the mother. At line 9, the HV begins a turn with "Well I think eh-" and abandons this beginning in favor of a focusing inquiry about where the baby has been during the day.

```
(18) [3A2:1-2]
  1   HV:          We:ll I think her (.) jaundice has faded a
  2                little bit but it hasn't (.) h⌐asn't
  3   M:                                        ⌊Gone
  4   HV:          gone yet.=
  5   M:           =No:: her eye:s especially if you notice her
  6                eyes when she opens them.
  7   HV:          O:h.
  8   M:           You can tell.
  9   HV:    →     Well I think eh- Has she been outs- outdoors
 10                he- getting plenty of light.
 11                (0.3)
 12   M:           Well she's (.) been outdoors but I mean (0.5)
 13                I wrap her up so well and I always keep the
 14                hood up so that she doesn't get wi:nd (.)
 15   HV:          Y⌐es
 16   M:            ⌊on her.=So: (.) not rea:lly.
 17   HV:          I think you (know) (.) keep her near the
 18                window.=
```

```
19   M:          =Okay.=
20   HV:         =Keep her in light because um `hh I thought it
21               really would have gone this week.
```

A comparison of the beginning of line 9 with the HV's subsequent advice delivery (line 17) strongly suggests that the HV was beginning a step 5 advice giving which she then abandoned in favor of a step 3 focusing inquiry. Insofar as the HV intended to recommend what she subsequently inquired into (that the baby be placed outdoors), the inquiry enabled her to avoid proposing a course of action which, it turns out that the mother has been cautious about (see lines 12–16). She was thus able to design her final advice in a way that was fitted to the mother's account and the weather conditions that the account details. Here then it is likely that the HV's reversion to a focusing inquiry served to avert the proposal of a contestable or inappropriate course of action.

Notwithstanding the various contractions of steps 3 and 4 of the movement into advice giving, all the HV-initiated advice sequences examined thus far have been developed after at least a *possibly problem-indicative response* (step 2) to a HV inquiry. In these cases, an initial problem-indicative response has provided for the relevance of the subsequent move into advice giving.

Variation 3
In a variety of cases in our data base, however, advice giving was initiated in the absence of a problem-indicative "step 2" response. In a small subset of these cases the HV sustains a "problem orientation" as the basis for advice giving by herself, detailing a possible or potential problem and then going on to offer advice on how to deal with it. For example, in the following instance, the HV follows a "no problem" response to her initial inquiry by first describing a problem that "might" arise (lines 8–14) and then offering advice on it (lines 14–15).

```
(19) [4B1:3]
1    HV:    1→   `hh And has your discharge lessened.
2    M:     2→   Yeah.
3    HV:          Smashing. And it's sort of pinky brown.
4    M:     2→   Yeah there's hardly anything the:re
5                 no⌜w.
6    HV:         ⌊Lovely.=
```

```
7    M:              =S┌o
8    HV:    5→        └˙hh You might find if you start rushing
9           5→        around as you're feeling so fit and ˙hhh
10          5→        gallo- walking up to the sh- (.) up to the
11          5→        Cowley Centre and doing your shopping and
12          5→        carrying heavy ba- (.) bags back 'nd things
13          5→        you might fi::nd ˙hhh that it- it gets a
14          5→        little bit heavier in which case that's a
15          5→        goo:d si:gn tuh (.) slow down a bit.
```

The basic pattern in this sequence may be represented thus:

> Step 1: HV: initial inquiry.
> Step 2: M: "no problem" response.
> Step 5: HV: advice giving on "possible problem."

This pattern is also exhibited in (20) below:

```
(20) [1A1:11]
1    HV:    1→        Uh:m (.) anything that w's worrying you at
2                     a:ll.
3                     (1.5)
4    M:     2→        No: I don't think so?
5    HV:    5→        When you:'re breast feeding you're passing
6           5→        over some hormones to your baby.
7    M:               °Ye:h,°
8    HV:    5→        So some ba- so┌me little girl babies do
9    F:                             └((cough))
10   HV:    5→        have  ( . ) °some (blood)°
11                    (0.7)
12   M:               Oh:.
13   HV:    5→        In fact there are- occasionally you do get a
14          5→        little bit'v mi:lk out of their breasts.
15   M:               ˙hh Oh:. (˙hhh)
16   HV:    5→        So that's as well to know if you remember that
17          5→        in case ┌you do:n't 'n' you know it (.)
18   M:                       └Mm:
19   HV:    5→        ala:rms you,
```

In these cases, even though the mother's reply offers no overt warrant for advice giving – the (step 2) response is problem free – the HV provides such a warrant in association with the advice (step 5) by foreseeing a possible problem, one that "might" arise, or that happens to "some babies."[20]

Variation 4
In our final variation on the basic sequence, even the warrant for
advice giving found in (19) and (20) may be dispensed with. In the
following cases, neither the HV's initial inquiry nor the mother's
response to it is overtly problem oriented. The advice giving that
ensues is thus delivered to an unprepared recipient – as in (21)
below:

```
(21) [4B1:16]
  1   HV:   1→   ˙hh Now this (0.2) uh:m she started bottle
  2         1→   feeds from bi:rth.
  3   M:    2→   °Yeah.°
  4              (2.2)
  5   HV:   5→   The hospital recomme:nd that she shouldn't
  6         5→   start solids until she's (.) four months.
  7   M:         Four m┌onths.
  8   HV:   5→         └At lea:st.
  9              (.)
 10   HV:   5→   ˙hhh Some babies don't even need to start
 11         5→   before six months (0.2) ˙hh and really the
 12         5→   longer you can fob off solids the better for
 13         5→   he::r.
```

And in (22), a mother's "no problem" response to an inquiry about
her baby's sleeping is accompanied by an elaborate description of
her procedure for feeding the baby at night.

```
(22) [3A1:24]
  1   HV:   1→   We:ll whu- uhh what is she: uh like at ni:ght.
  2   M:    2→   Uh::m (0.4) she's alright she kno::ws the
  3         2→   difference between night and da:y (.) and I
  4         2→   don't tend to stimulate her at all in (.) at night
  5         2→   ti:me I jus┌t get straight into the little
  6   HV:              └°( )°
  7         2→   roo:m ┌in the bed the┌re and (.) put her in
  8   HV:          └Yes        └Mm
  9   M:    2→   with me: (0.2) and (.) she fee:ds and that's
 10         2→   it.=Not much (.) chatting or anything o┌r
 11   HV:                                        └No.
 12   HV:   5→   ˙hh No always be ve:ry very qui:et at
 13         5→   ni:gh┌t. ˙hh
 14   M:         └Mm
 15              (.)
 16   HV:   5→   Always uhm (0.4) on- have a dim li:ght,
```

```
17   M:            Yeh.
18   HV:    5→    And uhm (1.0) be ve:ry qui:et don't chat her
19          5→    up at a:ll ˙hh when you change her (.) change
20          5→    as quickly as possib⌐le, without any
21   M:                              ⌊Yeh
22                 (.)
23   M:            Yeh.
24   HV:    5→    palaver.
                   ((advice giving continues))
```

Here, notwithstanding the fact that the mother's account of her
night-feeding procedures is, as it turns out, substantially identical
with the HV's preferred procedure, the HV nonetheless elaborately
advises her about appropriate practice and in terms that are very
similar to those already used by the mother. In these last cases,
advice giving is initiated on a unilateral basis without any basis in
a previously depicted problem and, in (22) at least, it is clearly
redundant.

2.2.3 Summary

We have now seen a variety of ways in which advice giving may be
initiated in these first encounters between mothers and HVs. First,
and relatively infrequently, mothers may request advice, thereby
establishing the relevance of advice giving and their own prospective orientation as advice recipients. In overt requests for advice,
identification of a problem area, the character of the problem, and a
prospective alignment of the local roles of advice recipient and
advice giver are usually achieved in a straightforward and natural
way. As we have seen, the requests for advice that achieve these
objectives are most commonly shaped as requests for confirmation
of a proposed course of action. By this means, mothers display their
own putative competence and capacity to cope with the problem
for which they seek help and avoid the appearance of ignorance
or incompetence which might arise from a simple request for
information.

Second, the predominant form of advice initiation arises from
HVs. In HV-initiated advice giving, by contrast with mother-
initiated requests for advice, both the need for advice – and with it
the prospective alignment of the mother as advice recipient – and
the problem for which advice is sought are often less clearly estab-

lished. Most commonly, HVs initiate advice giving in the context of routine inquiries into a range of health and baby-management issues. These inquiry sequences may be arrayed on a continuum in terms of the degree to which a need for advice and its associated problem area are established prior to the initiation of advice giving. Within this continuum, the bulk of advice giving is initiated without an extended preparatory sequence. Indeed, the bulk of advice initiations falls close to the "unilateral" end of our continuum, in which the HV's initial question serves primarily to topicalize the issue for which advice is subsequently developed.

Across all these environments, the HV defines herself as a knowledgeable and authoritative "expert" *vis-à-vis* an advice recipient who is relatively ignorant or noncompetent. Although, as we have argued, HV-initiated advice sequences are almost always initiated without the mother's desire or need for advice having been definitively established, there is a wide range of variation in the degree to which advice giving is prepared for in advance of its actual delivery. However, a substantial majority of advice giving is initiated with only minimal preparation. The extent of this preparation, however, may strongly influence the subsequent reception of advice, to which we now turn.

3 The reception of advice

As we have already proposed, the initiation of advice giving carries problematic implications about the knowledge or competence of the intended recipient. A concern for these implications shapes both the design of requests for advice and mothers' conduct in sequences in which HVs move towards the initiation of advice. This concern is equally manifest in the reception of advice where, as we shall see, mothers tend to minimize the extent to which they acknowledge that advice has been "informative."

3.1 Receiving information

In ordinary conversation, the parties have a range of resources with which to receipt informing statements. Prominent among these are acknowledgment tokens (such as *mm hm*, *uh huh*, *yes*, etc.), which are normally used as "continuers" (Jefferson 1984b; Schegloff

1982); objects like *oh*, which treat the information as "news" for the recipient (Heritage 1984b); and "newsmarks" (Jefferson 1981a), which also treat prior talk as "news" and, to varying degrees, promote further informings. Some of the distinctiveness of these objects can be illustrated by reference to the following fragment, in which the component elements of an informing are receipted in a variety of ways:

```
(23) [Frankel:TC:I:1:2-3: simplified]
 1   S:           ='hhh  Uh:m::, .tch'hhhh Who w'you ta:lking
 2                to.
 3                . . .
 4                . . .
 5   G:           I: wasn't talking to a:nybody. Bo-oth Martin'n
 6                I slept until about noo:n,=
 7   S:      1→   =O h.
 8   G:              'hhhh An' when I woke up, I wanted to call
 9                my mother.
10   S:      2→   Mm hm
11   G:               'hhhh An' I picked up the pho:ne, a:n' I
12                couldn't dial out.'n  I thought our phone was
13   S:      3→                       Oh: (   ),
14   G:           out'v order.  'n I-
15   S:      4→               Yeh,
```

In this segment, S's inquiry follows her report of repeatedly trying to telephone G and getting a "busy signal."[21] However, her inquiry, which presupposes that G has been talking extendedly on the phone, yields the report that this was not the case. This is "oh" receipted as "news" for S (arrow 1). Subsequently, G initiates a narrative whose first component is receipted as a narrative background with the "passive" or "continuative" acknowledgment token "mm hm" (arrow 2). As the narrative develops, G reports her discovery that she "couldn't dial out" and this component is "discovery" receipted by S with "oh" (arrow 3). Subsequently, G then reports her "first" and projectably incorrect thought (Jefferson 1986b) that her phone was out of order and this is receipted with an agreement-implicative acknowledgment token "yeh" (arrow 4). In this short segment, the various receipt items accomplish a range of distinctive tasks across the telling in progress, and they are selected to be appropriately responsive to the specific story segments as they emerge.

While this kind of variegated, segment-by-segment receipt of an informing rarely occurs in HV–mother interactions, the acknowledgment tokens deployed in (23), together with others detailed below, play a predominant role in the receipt of advice, to which we now turn.

3.2 Receiving advice

We begin by noting three main ways in which advice may be received.

   1 *Marked acknowledgment*: Here mothers respond to advice in ways that acknowledge its character as advice and its informativeness for them. Marked acknowledgments normally convey acceptance of the advice offered.
   2 *Unmarked acknowledgment*: Here mothers respond to advice in ways that avoid acknowledging it as informative and that avoid overtly accepting it. Although they do not involve the overt rejection of advice, we shall argue that unmarked acknowledgments represent a response form that is resistant to advice giving and that may imply rejection of the advice that is given.
   3 *Assertions of knowledge or competence*: Here mothers respond to advice by asserting that they already know and/or are undertaking the advised course of action. While these assertions, like unmarked acknowledgments, do not reject the advice to which they respond, they are also resistant to its delivery and achieve this resistance by indicating that the advice is redundant.

Below, we consider each of these three main forms of advice reception in turn.

3.2.1 Marked acknowledgments

The pro forma "marked" advice receipt in our data base is *oh right* – the first *oh* component treating the prior advice as "news" for the advice recipient and adumbrating its acceptance (Heritage 1984b), the subsequent "right" component overtly marking its acceptance, as in (19):

(19 cont.) [4B1:3]

```
 1   HV:          Lovely. = ·hh And has your discharge lessened.
 2   M:           Yeah.
 3   HV:          Smashing. And it's sort of pinky brown.
 4   M:           Yeah there's hardly anything the:re
 5                no ⌈w.
 6   HV:             ⌊Lovely.=
 7   M:           =S⌈o
 8   HV:             ⌊·hh You might find if you start rushing
 9                around as you're feeling so fit and ·hhh
10                gallo- walking up to the sh- (.) up to the
11                Cowley Centre and doing your shopping and
12                carrying heavy ba- (.) bags back 'nd things
13                you might fi::nd ·hhh that it- it gets a
14                little bit heavier in which case that's a
15                goo:d si:gn tuh (.) slow down a bit.
16   M:    →      Oh right.
```

More elaborately, marked acknowledgments sometimes include
partial repeats of key components of the prior advice:

(8 cont.) [4B1:7]

```
 1   HV:          ·hh And family planning you know you can get
 2                pregnant straight awa:y so if you wo:uld (.)
 3                like any: (.) help in that score you always
 4                ask me: or see the G.P. or go to the family
 5                planning clinic.=
 6   M:           =Well I- I've got some (0.4) things
 7                upstai:⌈rs.
 8   HV:                  ⌊°Oh well done.°
 9   M:           But (.) when I've got to take them I
10                do:n'know.
11   HV:          Well (.) uhm if you're not breast feeding
12                there's no reason why you shouldn't start them
13                when (.) she's fou:r weeks.=On the da:y she's
14                four weeks you can ⌈start them straight away.
15   M:    1→                       ⌊Four weeks.
16   M:    2→     Ri:ght.=
17   HV:          =And then you'll be covered.
18   M:           Mm.
19   G:           ((cough))
20   HV:          Oka::y.=
21   M:           =Ri:ght.
```

In this sequence, the mother requests advice about when to restart
the pill. The HV's advice, "four weeks," is initially presented in a

negatively formulated turn component "Well (.) uhm if you're not breast feeding there's no reason why you shouldn't start them when (.) she's fou:r weeks." The same basic information is then immediately re-presented in an affirmatively packaged turn component as positive advice. In the course of this second turn component, the mother acknowledges the specific advice element that responds to her previous inquiry with an overlapped repetition of "four weeks" (arrow 1) and a subsequent accepting "Ri:ght" (arrow 2) at the completion of the H V's turn.[22]

A similar pattern of response also emerges in (6) below:

```
(6 cont.) [3A1:15]
 1    M:              I haven't ba::thed her yet. Is once a week
 2                    enough.
 3                    (0.7)
 4    HV:             We::ll (0.2) babies do: sweat a lo:t.
 5                    (0.3)
 6    HV:             So I would  recommend giving her a ba:th
 7                    every da:y.
 8    M:      1→      Every da::y,
 9    HV:             So that she gets used to it and sh- that's her
10                    little pl:aytime for he ⌐r.
11    M:      2→                             ⌊Oh ri::ght.
```

Here, the H V's contrastive recommendation of a bath "every day" is acknowledged by the mother with a repeat (arrow 1) and her elaborative continuation is receipted with a subsequent "Oh ri::ght" (arrow 2).

In only one case in our data base is "corrective" advice giving followed by an overt acknowledgment of error. This sequence is a continuation of (9) above and we pick it up at the point where the H V raises the question of whether a sweating baby may be too hot.

```
(9 cont.) [4B1:22]
 1    M:      Yea::h she's a re:a ⌐l swea(t)uh.
 2    HV:                         ⌊D'ju think she's ho:t.
 3    (G):    She might be:.
 4    M:      Wul we keep 'e ⌐r wrappin' round er
 5    G:                     ⌊We keep 'er in that li- uh
 6            (0.5)
 7    M:      and in this little nest ⌐here that she's go:t
 8    HV:                             ⌊Ri:ght.
 9            (.)
```

```
10   HV:        Ri:ght. ˙hh (It) might be that she's too ho:t.
11              (1.2)
12   ( ):       (        )
13   HV:        Becuz this is certainly the- (.) the
14              temperature of the hospital isn't it.=
15   M:         =Yea:h.
16   HV:        And is it the sa:me throughout upstairs as
17              we:ll.
18              (0.2)
19   M:         We:ll I've got a little fi::re (.) ⌈upstairs
20   HV:                                          ⌊I would
21              slowly bring the temperature do:wn to sort of
22              no:rmal.
23   (M):       Ye⌈ah.
24   (G):         ⌊Yeh
25   HV:        A::nd
26   (G):   1→  W' don't want her catching co:lds y' s⌈ee.
27   HV:                                              ⌊No:
28              that's right (.) that's ri:ght it's
29              so⌈ : difficult to deci:de
30   G:          ⌊(                    )
31   HV:        is⌈n't it.
32   M:           ⌊It could be.
33   HV:        ˙hh But- but I think it- it's as ba:d tuh have
34   HV:        i⌈t too: hot as it is to have it too co:ld.
35   G:     2→   ⌊(we probably (0.7) do over protect.)
36   M:         Yea:h.
```

Across the sequence of HV inquiries the mother and grandmother acknowledge the possibility that the baby may be too hot (lines 3–19). However, after the HV's recommendation that the house temperature be reduced and the mother's and grandmother's brief acknowledgment of the advice, the grandmother accounts for their actions in terms of the risk of the baby catching cold (arrow 1). It is only after the HV moves towards a further reassertion of her position that the grandmother interjectively acknowledges that they may have been in error (arrow 2).[23]

The significant feature of these marked acknowledgments of advice is that they overtly receipt the talk to which they respond *as advice*. In different ways, their component elements – *oh* receipts, repetitions of key advice elements in prior utterances, *right* acceptances, and acknowledgments of error – respond to prior informings as "news" for the recipient and as containing information which the recipient accepts and is prepared to act on. It is striking that these marked acknowledgments of advice are primarily found in environments in which the advice recipient has *already cast herself in the role of prospective advice recipient* by directly (e.g. [8] and (6) above) or indirectly (e.g. [9] above) requesting advice. In these cases, a request for advice – with its explicit or implicit acknowledgment of some deficiency in competence or knowledge – can permit marked acknowledgment and acceptance of the advice which follows without further loss of "face." Moreover, such marked acknowledgment may be required from a recipient who, having requested advice, has now had that request fulfilled.[24] Marked acknowledgments of advice, however, are comparatively rare in the environment of HV-initiated advice. In the latter, the predominant form of receipt is unmarked acknowledgment.

3.2.2 Unmarked acknowledgments

Unmarked acknowledgments of advice giving characteristically involve such receipt objects as *mm hm*, *yeh*, and *that's right*. These objects stand in contrast to marked acknowledgments (such as partial repeats, *oh*, etc.) in two main respects. (a) They do not acknowledge advice giving as "news" for the recipient – indeed, receipts like *that's right* specifically propose that the recipient was already aware of the information offered as "advice," while objects such as *mm hm* and *yeh* are, as already noted, primarily "continuative" in character (Jefferson 1984b; Schegloff 1982). (b) These objects do not constitute an undertaking to follow the advice offered. In short unmarked acknowledgments, while receipting the talk that constitutes an advice giving over its course, do not acknowledge or accept that talk *as advice*.

The use of this pattern of receipting was widespread in our data base. The following case shows the development of a sequence of advice giving from (22) above, in which the HV's advice largely repeated the mother's own account of her actions in feeding the baby at night.

(22 cont.) [3A1:24]
```
1   HV:            ˙hh No always be ve:ry very qui:et at
2                  ni:gh ┌ t. ˙hh
3   M:      →           └ Mm
```

```
 4                     (.)
 5    HV:              Always uhm (0.4) on- have a dim li:ght,
 6    M:        →      Yeh.
 7    HV:              And uhm (1.0) be ve:ry qui:et don't chat her
 8                     up at a:ll ˙hh when you change her (.) change
 9                     as quickly as possib┌le, without any
10    M:        →                          └Yeh
11                     (.)
12    M:        →      Yeh.
13    HV:              palaver.
14                     (0.2)
15    M:        →      That's ri:ght.
16    HV:              And (.) so she kno::ws that uh
17    M:        →      (Yeh)
18    HV:              people aren't keen on me: at this: uhm (0.2)
19                     hou:r ┌and uh once she gets that message it's
20    M:        →            └Yeh
21    HV:              a good thi:ng.
22                     (3.0)
23    M:               And she tends to settle do:wn straight awa:y
24                     at ni ┌:ght
25    HV:                    └Mm
26    M:               I mean (.) sometimes during the da:y she'll uh
27                     (0.2) she'll scream for five minutes and then
28                     she'll go °┌off.°
29    HV:                         └Mm
30                     (0.2)
31    M:               But uh
32                     (1.0)
33    HV:              °(Yes)°
34    M:               Y- you're alright really a:ren't you.
```

In this datum, the mother receipts recognizably redundant advice
with a series of unmarked acknowledgment tokens (arrowed). At
the completion of the HV's advice giving, however, the mother
permits a full three second pause to develop (line 22) without
verbally acknowledging its completion and then proceeds with
remarks (beginning at line 23) that indicate that the problem on
which the HV's advice has been focused (the baby's sleeping at
night) is not a significant one. In this case, then, unmarked acknowledgments over the course of an advice-giving sequence adumbrate
a form of "passive resistance" to the advice-giving episode that is
ultimately expressed as an implicit rejection of the relevance of the
advice that was given.

This association between unmarked acknowledgments of advice giving and subsequent resistance is not particular to this datum. In (24) below, an extended pattern of unmarked acknowledgment is followed by a turn (line 37) that implies that the advice being delivered is redundant. The mother's initial turn in this datum represents the renewal of an earlier telling about problems in getting her baby to sleep. After a minimal affiliation with the trouble (line 3) the HV inquires into how she handled the problem – an inquiry which is a standard precursor to advice (cf. (12) above).

```
(24) [1A1:7]
 1   M:          B't last night she j'st wouldn't go o:ff.=I
 2               think she'd about two hou:rs till six o'clock.
 3   HV:         O:h poor you.=So what did you do:.
 4                   . . .
 5               ((17 lines of data omitted in which Mother and
 6                 Father describe being up all night))
 7                   . . .
 8   HV:         I think there's a danger when you are breast
 9               feeding that (.) especially at night when
10               you're all sort of nice and cosy and wa:rm
11               ˙hhhh that you do: (0.4) uhm (0.8) you know
12               the baby feels so comf- comfortable and so
13               content,
14   M:          Mm:
15   HV:         Uhm being cuddled an' (0.6) and sucking at
16               your breast (0.4) that she falls asleep (.)
17               she forgets about feeding
18   M:          Mm ┌:::
19   HV:            └and falls to sleep without actually taking
20               he:r hhh┌h
21   F:                  └Mm.
22   HV:         uh required quantity,=
23   M:          =┌Ye::s.
24   HV:          └and therefore you've got to (0.5) do your
25               best to keep her awa┌ke when she's actually
26   M:      1→                      └Yea:h
27   HV:         feeding.
28               (.)
29   HV:         ˙hhhh Uhm (0.2) in hospital we encourage
30               babies khhhhh ˙hhh to keep awake by: sort of
31               tickling the ba┌ck of their neck or ˙hh
32   M:      2→                 └Mm::
33   HV:         tickling the soles of their feet,
```

```
34   M:    3→   Ye⌐:s.
35   HV:          Land not
36               (.)
37   M:    4→   They taught me (under the jaw) as well.=
38   HV:         =Yeh and not having them (.) mghm too wrapped
39               up.
40               (0.2)
41   M:          Mm:.
42               (1.0)
43   HV:         And uhm (.) I usetuh
44               (3.2)
45   HV:         You've got to get as much of a bosom in her
46               mouth ((continues))
```

In the advice delivery that follows (beginning at line 24), the mother responds with a series of unmarked acknowledgments (arrows 1–3) and then indicates (arrow 4) that she is already thoroughly aware of the advised procedure.[25] Subsequently, she retreats once more into (delayed) unmarked acknowledgment (line 41) as the HV continues. Shortly thereafter the HV shifts topic (lines 45–6). In this sequence, then, the mother's series of unmarked acknowledgments culminates in a response that, while confirming that she has heard and understood the substance of the HV's advice, specifically avoids treating it as "news" for her.

While we have so far proposed that unmarked acknowledgments are associated with subsequent resistance to advice, we may now note that they may be analytically treated as forms of resistance in themselves. Insofar as a would-be adviser shapes their talk as advice, then an appropriate form of receipt will involve the use of marked acknowledgments that treat the talk as advice. Unmarked acknowledgments, which do not involve such a treatment, are inherently resistant to the advice giving to which they respond regardless of what they adumbrate. This contrast between the two forms of acknowledgment is very apparent in the following sequence. The sequence opens with the HV's introductory remarks, which are hearably prefatory to the advice giving which follows. These remarks (lines 1–20) are appropriately "continuation" receipted (at lines 14, 18, and 20). Subsequently, however, a series of components of a lengthy advice sequence which generally favors immunization against whooping cough receive unmarked acknowledgments or no acknowledgments (arrowed 1), but the subsequent mention that the parents may defer making a decision about the

immunization receives marked acknowledgment (arrowed 2). The
HV's later remarks in support of vaccination yield a return to
unmarked acknowledgment (arrowed 3). Here the forms of acknowledgment are consistent with the tacit expression of the
parents' resistance to making a quick decision about their child's
vaccination. After this renewal of unmarked acknowledgment, the
HV shifts the topic (arrow 4).

```
(25) [4A1:14-15]
  1   HV:            Have you thought about the immunisations yet.
  2                  (0.5)
  3   F:             Not rea:lly 'ave we?
  4   M:             N┌o:.
  5   HV:             └The: ones on offer are diphtheria (.)
  6                  whooping cough (.) tetanus (.) polio and
  7                  measles.
  8                  (0.2)
  9                  'hh And the: (0.3) health authority
 10                  recommend (0.7) that unless there's a family
 11                  history on (0.4) the immediate side your
 12                  brothers and sisters or your brothers and
 13                  sisters 'hh with a history of epilepsy,
 14   F:             Mm:,
 15                  (0.2)
 16   HV:            Uh:m that's not febrile convulsions in babies
 17                  but- but
 18   F:             Mm.
 19   HV:            proper epilepsy,=
 20   F:             =Yes.
 21   HV:            'hhh Then there's no: reason fer: (.) a child
 22                  not to have whooping co┌ugh.
 23   F:       1→                           └Mm.
 24                  (.)
 25   HV:            'hh But if you deci:de (1.0) thatchu you don't
 26                  want him to have it (.) a little while ago
 27                  there was a sca:re then you- it's entirely up
 28                  to you nothing is compulsory,=
 29   M:       1→    =Mm hm,
 30   HV:            but it is recommended that if possible (0.2)
 31                  all of them are better than: (0.7) i- it's
 32                  better to have them all than (0.5) uhm:
 33                  (0.7) no:t,=
 34   F:             =(         )   ((to baby)
 35   HV:                      └whooping cough can be a killer in
 36                  the baby under one.
 37            1→    (1.0)
```

```
38   HV:          Uh:m (1.2) but it m- (0.2) maybe you'd like to
39                have a think about it and=
40   M:     1→    =Mm hm
41   HV:          uh:m talk it over with the doctor,
42          1→    (1.0)
43   HV:          when you see him at clinic.
44   M:     1→    Mm hm,
45                (0.6)
46   HV:          You don't need to make a decision really
47                before (0.2) ˙hh before he's (.) three months,
48   F:     2→    Thr ee months.
49   HV:             └which is when the first injections
50                sta: rts.
51   F:     2→         └Ri:ght.
52                (0.7)
53   HV:          And he might ask your families (0.7) whether
54                they know (0.2) of- of- of any reason and
55                indeed whether you yourselves had the whooping
56                cough vaccine as children.
57   F:           Mm.
58   HV:          Uhm (1.2) in my eleven years I've never seen a
59                reaction to it but people clearly have had
60                reactions,
61   F:     3→    Mm :
62   M      3→       └Yeah.
63                (0.2)
64   HV:    4→    Uhm (.) he's lovely isn't he?
```

If unmarked acknowledgments may be analytically considered as involving advice resistance, then we should expect to find cases in which HVs orient to them as such. Such evidence is present in (25) above, where, after a series of unmarked acknowledgments culminating in no acknowledgment (line 37) of a series of turns advocating whooping-cough vaccination, the HV revises her position (at line 38) by proposing that the parents talk to the doctor about the issue and introduces the possibility of their delaying their decision. It is noticeable here that the father's marked acknowledgments of the HV's revised position only begin after she has overtly stated (lines 46–8) that the parents do not need to make an immediate decision.

A similar process in which unmarked acknowledgments are treated as advice resistant is visible in (26) below. Here, after a sequence of unmarked acknowledgments (arrowed 1) to her

repeated advice about keeping the baby on milk for the first four
months, the HV shifts towards a position that suggests that the
parents may wish to start the baby on solids earlier than this
(arrowed 2). Unlike (25) above, however, this shift does not attract
any marked acknowledgment and the HV subsequently shifts topic
(arrowed 3). It may be noted that the sequence opens with a pre-
sequence about grandmothers that is later clumsily employed to
preemptively discount them as an alternative source of advice about
weaning babies.[26]

```
(26) [4A1:13-14]
 1   HV:            And did you breastfeed him at a:ll?
 2   M:             No:.=
 3   HV:            =No he went straight on to the bottle.
 4                  (5.2)
 5   HV:            At this stage I don't know whether you've got
 6                  grannies nearby,
 7                  (1.0)
 8   HV:            have you?
 9   M:             One yea:h.=
10   F:             =(One ⌜near Whitestone Close)
11   HV:                  ⌊Yes.
12   HV:            Uh:m (0.2) ˙hh The hospital at the moment
13                  recommend that you don't start solids (.)
14                  until (0.4) four months.
15                  (.)
16   HV:            ⌜and that's a long way off.
17   F:    1→       ⌊ Mm.
18   M:    1→       M⌜m hm,
19   HV:             ⌊ ˙hh But you might well- somebody might
20                  recommend that you do: (.) and indeed if he-
21                  if he (.) becomes a big baby you might well
22                  need to give him a little bit before (.)
23                  four months but ˙hh if it can be avoided=
24   F:    1→       =Mm.
25   HV:            milk is the only thing he needs really (0.2)
26                  or water between feeds.
27   M:    1→       Mm hm,
28   HV:            A:nd (1.0) he can have (0.7) uh juice
29   M:    1→       Mm hm,
30   HV:            about six weeks on.
31                  (0.7)
32   HV:            Uh:m (0.3) but I think just milk is all he
33                  needs really.
```

34	M:	1→	Mm hm,
35	HV:		Uh::m
36	F:		E's not a (water) baby are you?
37			(.)
38	HV:	2→	But if you <u>do</u> decide you want to start him on-
39		2→	on solids then that's- that's fi:<u>ne</u> (0.6) uhm
40		2→	and I'll (0.2) help you if I can.
41	M:		Mm hm,
42	HV	3→	Anything (.) you ought to know.
43			(1.0)
44	HV:		Uh:m
45			(4.0)
46	HV:	3→	And then at eight weeks (.) he has his first
47			developmental check

As already noted, unmarked acknowledgments, in the way that they avoid receipting advice as advice, constitute a form of resistance to its delivery. However, the resistance which they offer is essentially "passive." Unmarked acknowledgment does not involve the *rejection* of advice. Moreover, the fact that the advice is resisted is not stated outright, nor are the grounds on which it is resisted made overt. As we have seen, some, but not all, advice-giving sequences that involve unmarked acknowledgments culminate in some rather more overt expression of resistance at their conclusion. Unmarked acknowledgments are common in sequences in which advice has been initiated by the HV, and we suggest that they are well fitted to a social context such as these home visits, in which a mother may be able to do little or nothing to stem the flow of advice, where the HV is treated as having "rights" to advise on aspects of health and where the mother may not overtly reject the advice that is offered.

3.2.3 Assertions of knowledge and/or competence

Earlier in this chapter, we proposed that during these visits from the HV, mothers are concerned to display their knowledge, competence, and capacity to cope with matters concerning their babies' health. We proposed that this concern may underlie the relative infrequency of overt requests for advice during these first visits and that it informed the design of their requests for advice. We also suggested that similar issues may inhabit sequences in which advice is initiated by HVs. For the HV's initiation of advice may imply that the mother is ignorant or otherwise unable to cope with the matters raised in the delivery of advice. The mothers' preoccupation with these implications is vividly illustrated by a number of sequences in our data base in which the mothers respond to advice giving with some assertion of knowledge or competence.

A preliminary sense of this preoccupation may be developed from the following datum, which is a continuation of (14) above:

```
(14 cont.) [1C1:13]
 1   HV:           Her eyes're oka:y.
 2                 (0.7)
 3   M:            They ge- th- they get a bit wee:py sometimes,
 4                 but that's normal isn't it?  And I swab th'm
 5                 with wool with cotton woo:l,
 6                 (0.3)
 7   HV:    1→     Ye:s if they- if they: (0.2) if you think
 8          1→     they're pussie,
 9                 (0.8)
10   M:            Yea:h.
11   HV:    1→     then you must use boiled wa:te:r wi⌈th a
12   M:     2→                                       ⌊Yeah I
13          2→     kno:w
14   HV:    3→     little bit of salt i:n. (.) One teaspoonful of
15          3→     salt to a pint of boi:led wa:te:r (0.5) or
16          3→     half a teaspoon to half a pint. (.) Oka⌈:y?
17   M:     4→                                            ⌊(°Oh
18          4→     right I wi:ll do that (  ) . °)
19   ():           ˙hhh
20                 (0.3)
21   HV:    5→     And then you: (0.3) use clean cotton wool one
22          5→     swab for each ey:e.
23   M:            °Alri:ght.°
24                 (.)
25   M:     6→     Yeh I do that now. (0.2) I use a separate
26          6→     thi:ng (0.2) with a bit of wa:rm warm water.=
27   HV:           =Mm.
28   M:            The- Not so: much that I >y'know< to worry
29                 abou:t jist a little bit (in 'er ey⌈e) it's
30   HV:                                              ⌊Mm
31   M:            sticky: (0.4) ('er eye)
32                 (0.7)
33   HV:           Ye:s (.) we:ll (.) tha:t is pretty usual.
```

In this sequence, the HV details the procedure for treating mild eye infections. It is notable that each component of her advice is acknowledged by the mother in terms of whether or not she already knows what to do. Thus the first possible completion of the HV's advice – which ends at the recommendation "then you must use boiled wa:te:r" (arrow 1), is met by an assertion of knowledge (arrow 2). By contrast, the continuation of this advice that incorporates the reference to salt and an instruction as to quantity (arrow 3) is responded to with a marked acknowledgment and an undertaking to follow the advice (arrow 4). The final component of the HV's advice, which concerns using a separate swab for each eye (arrow 5), is initially met with an acquiescent "Alri:ght," which is then revised by the mother's subsequent assertion that this is what she does already (arrow 6). Across the segments of this advice giving, then, the mother deals with each segment in terms of an underlying concern to display her knowledgeability wherever possible.

A similar concern to display knowledgeability or competence emerges in the next several cases where, in each case, after an initiation of advice giving (arrow 1), the mother responds by indicating that she is already aware of and/or has already dealt with the matters that are in the course of being raised (arrow 2). In the first three of these cases in particular, it may be noted that the competence assertions occur very "early," that is, at or near the first point at which advice is recognizably being initiated.

```
(15 cont.) [1C1:19-20]
  1   HV:              What are her motions li:ke.
  2                    (0.6)
  3   M:               Uh: uh:m they're softer no:w because she
  4                    was a l'ttle bit constipated (0.2) a few days
  5                    ago:,
  6   HV:              Mm hm,
  7   M:               and the midwife advised me to put a teaspoon
  8                    of uhm
  9                    (1.0)
 10   HV:              brown ⌈sugar
 11   M:                      ⌊brown sugar in alternate feeds
 12   HV:              I s⌈ee.
 13   M:                  ⌊and tha:t helped her an' they're a lot
 14                    softer no:w,
 15                    (0.6)
 16   HV:    1→        Oh I don't think you nee:d (1.2) you kno:w=
 17   M     2→         =(I) stopped doing it no:w.=
```

(11 cont.) [3A1:14]
```
 1   HV:              Listen to your 'iccups. Just listen to your
 2                    'iccups.
 3   B:               ((hiccups))
 4   M:               I know what cures those. (.) More milk ┌o
 5   HV:                                                      └More
 6                    ┌mi:lk is-
 7   M:               └heh heh heh heh
 8   HV:              Huh
 9                    (0.5)
10   HV:     1→       Don't worry about (h)iccups.
11   M:      2→       Ye:ah ┌I kno:w (.) she ha┌s them nearly every,
12   HV:                    └( )              └( )
13   HV:              Does sh┌e.
14   M:      2→              └fee:d.
```

(10 cont.) [4B1:22]
```
 1   G:               ˙hhh When she sta:rts off walking ou:(t) it
 2                    always seems to r┌ai::n.
 3   HV:                               └aO:::h.=
 4   M:               =Yea:h.
 5   G;               Ge┌ts half wa:y and 'as to come ba:ck.
 6   M:                 └( )
 7   HV:              Oh what a pity.
 8   M:               Yea::h myea:h.
 9   HV:              But if she's wrapped up well it won't do he:r
10                    any ha┌:rm
11   M:                     └(harm)
12   G:               No:.
13   M:               No: that's what they (    ┌  )
14   HV:     1→                                 └Babies loose a lot
15           1→       of heh- heat through their hea:ds
16                    (0.3)
17   HV:     1→       ˙hh so:=
18   G:      2→       =Well she's alwa:ys got a hat on (    )
```

(16 cont.) [1C1:30-31]
```
 1   HV:              And you're able to put her down in between
 2                    fee:ds are you:,
 3                    (1.0)
 4   M:               No::. (0.4) She screams.
 5   HV:              uhhhh hah hah┌hah ˙uhhhhhhhhhh
 6   M:                           └if I put her in the:┌re.
 7   Fr:                                               └hhehhhh=
 8   HV:              =hah °hah°=
 9   F:               =eh hhnh
```

```
10                    (1.0)
11    M:              Ye:s.=
12    HV:    1→       =Well it is important you kno:w tuh: (0.2) get
13           1→       it into a rou:ti:ne (0.2) otherwise she'll get
14           1→       so used to sittin' on your lap she'll want to
15           1→       do it all the ti:me.
16    M:     2→       Well she di- that's what (.) I did in
17           2→       hospital: uh I realise (about) my mistake no:w
18           2→       but you (can't) keep them qui:et. I- (in fact)
19           2→       I don't like (    )=
20    HV:    1→       =Well my advice to you: is that when she's had
21           1→       a cuddle and you've changed her and you've fed
22           1→       her and she's brought her wind up (1.2) that
23           1→       you firmly put her do:wn,
24    M:     2→       I've sta:rted.
25    HV:             O⌜:n her ow:::n,
26    M:     2→        ⌊I did it this mo:rning.
```

And in the following case, an inquiry which raises a problem about cats (arrow 1) is preemptively dealt with at its first possible completion (arrow 2). The mother's subsequent recycle of her response (arrow 3) is met with advice (arrow 4) to which she, in turn, responds with a repetition of her previous response (arrow 5):

```
(27) [1C1:44]
 1    HV:              ˙hhh Two cats,
 2    M:               We've got three: actually.
 3    HV:              Oh goodness.
 4                     (1.0)
 5    HV:              ˙hhh What d'they think of the baby.
 6                     (1.0)
 7    M:               u- Uhr they j's have a little sniff and they
 8                     look at 'er when she cri:es but that's about
 9                     i:t.
10                     (0.2)
11    HV:    1→        You don't think they'll ever (.) jump up in
12           1→        the pra:m ⌜or anything (like that).
13    M:     2→                  ⌊I've got a cat-net.
14    HV:              ⌜(    )
15    M:     3→        ⌊Well: (0.4) I've got the cat-net and I'm you
16           3→        know I'm here all the ti:⌜me.
17    HV:    4→                                  ⌊˙hh I think if
18           4→        you've got three cats it might be a good idea
19           4→        to have a cat-net.
20    M:     5→        Yeh ⌜I've got one I've definitely got one
21    HV:              ⌊(Becau-)
```

```
22  M:    5→   anyw ┌a:y
23  HV:   6→         └Yes because uh (.) there's always the
24        6→   danger they might be attracted uh (.) ˙hh and
25        6→   sit on the (1.0) sit in there for warmth,
26  M:    7→   That's it when I go upstairs I put it on
27        7→   you know.=
28  HV:         =Mm,
29  M:    7→   But >I mean< I- when I'm in the kitchen I can
30        7→   sort'v see: you know.
31             (1.0)
32  HV:        What a lot of cats,=How did you get three cats
33             then.
```

Here, after the mother's third attempt to establish the fact that she has a cat-net (arrow 5), the HV develops her advice with an account of why cat-nets are necessary (arrow 6) and this is met by the mother with an elaboration of her earlier claim that she has the matter in hand (arrow 7). Subsequently, the HV initiates a shift of topical line.

In a number of these sequences, what starts as HV-initiated advice giving ends as a competence struggle. It is notable, in our data base at least, that once the HV has committed herself to a course of advice giving she may be reluctant to abandon it. In each of the following instances, which exhibit continuations of the data shown above, the HV persists in advice giving (arrow 3) in the face of competence claims (arrow 2) Thus in (15), the HV's continuation of advice giving (arrow 3) does not acknowledge the mother's assertion (arrow 2) that she has already stopped doing the advised-against procedure (putting brown sugar in the baby's feed to alleviate constipation).

(15 cont.) [1C1:19-20]
```
 1  HV:   1→   Oh I don't think you nee:d (1.2) you kno:w=
 2  M:    2→   =(I) stopped doing it no:w.=
 3  HV:   3→   =You shouldn't do it u:h (1.0) as a
 4        3→   regular thi ┌ng otherwise it would be
 5  M:               └Ooh no:.
 6  HV:   3→   ba:d for her tee:th.
 7  M:         It was jist a couple of da:ys and it
 8             helped (her).
 9             (1.5)    ((Tearing Paper))
10  HV:        Good.
```

Similarly, in (11), the HV persists in advising the mother, despite the latter's claim that she is not concerned about the baby's hiccups.

```
(11 cont.) [3A1:14]
  1   HV:    1→   Don't worry about (h)iccups.
  2   M:     2→   Ye:ah ⌈I kno:w (.) she ha⌈s them nearly every,
  3   HV:          ⌊(    )            ⌊(    )
  4   HV:          Does sh⌈e.
  5   M:     2→             ⌊fee:d.
  6   HV:    3→   Yes. Well you can always put them do:wn the-
  7          3→   you don't have to keep nu:rsing them for- ˙hh
```

In (10), the HV's advice-adumbrative observation that babies lose a lot of heat through their heads, culminates in the advice that "bonnets are worth having" despite the baby's grandmother's interjection that the baby always has a hat on.

```
(10 cont.) [4B1:22]
  1   M:            No: that's what they (    ⌈    )
  2   HV:    1→                            ⌊Babies loose a lot
  3          1→   of heh- heat through their hea:ds (0.3) ˙hh
  4          1→   so:=
  5   G:     2→   =Well she's ⌈alwa:ys got a hat ⌈on (    )
  6   HV:    3→              ⌊b-              ⌊Bonnets are
  7          3→   wo:rth having.
```

And in (16), the HV's advice that the mother "firmly put her do:wn" is augmented through three syntactically continuous accretions (lines 6, 8, and 10) despite the mother's interjected claims (lines 5 and 7) to be doing just that.

```
(16 cont.) [1C1:30-31]
  1   HV:    1→   =Well my advice to you: is that when she's had
  2          1→   a cuddle and you've changed her and you've fed
  3          1→   her and she's brought her wind up (1.2) that
  4          1→   you firmly put her do:wn,
  5   M:     2→   I've sta:rted.
  6   HV:    3→   O⌈:n her ow:::n,
  7   M:     2→     ⌊I did it this mo:rning.
  8   HV:    3→   preferably not right by you:
  9                (0.8)
 10   HV:    3→   and you can check her every (1.0) fifteen
                  minutes ((continues))
```

In the cases shown above, the HV's do not abandon advice giving in the face of the mothers' claims to knowledge or competence.

Moreover, in sustaining their advice giving, they sequentially delete the mothers' claims to competence. This conduct underscores other dimensions of the generally unilateral character of advice giving in these first visits and it suggests that, on occasion, the HVs may take little account of the mothers' claims to competence even when those claims are made clearly and assertively.

3.2.4 Summary

In this section, we have examined three major ways in which the reception of advice may be managed. While our data base contains only one instance in which advice is overtly rejected, only one class of receptions – marked acknowledgment – involves the full-fledged acceptance of advice *as advice*. The others – unmarked acknowledgment and competence assertions – in their different ways involve resistance to advice giving. Competence assertions resist advice through the claim that its content is already known and/or acted upon by the mother who, in this way, seeks to reject any implication of incompetence or lack of knowledge that may be carried by the initiation of advice. Unmarked acknowledgments, which receipt advisory talk but without acknowledging or accepting its character *as advice*, constitute a form of "passive resistance," whose motivation may remain opaque. In a substantial number of cases, unmarked acknowledgments were followed by more overt expressions of resistance to advice giving that challenged its relevance or informativeness to advisees.

4 Discussion

Taken as a whole, three facets of the advice-giving sequences in our data base of first visits are particularly striking. The first is the predominantly unilateral character of the ways in which the HVs both initiated and delivered advice. In the substantial majority of cases, the HVs began to deliver advice in the absence of any clear indication that it was wanted and, in a further substantial body of cases, in the absence of any clear indication of a "problem." In a large number of cases, little attempt seemed to be made to fit the advice giving to the particular interactional circumstances from which the advice emerged and, in many of them, it is difficult to resist the impression that the HVs would have initiated advice giving no matter how the mothers responded to their inquiries. Secondly, there was little effort to accommodate advice giving to the circumstances of individual mothers and, in particular, to acknowledge their competences and capacity for personal decision making. Indeed, in most of the cases in which the mothers asserted their knowledge of competence in some facet of health or baby management, their assertions received no acknowledgment or minimal acknowledgment and, in a number of cases, were positively resisted. Third, in this context it is significant that fully three-quarters of all the HV-initiated advice met with either passive or active resistance. While it is not possible to extrapolate from the mothers' conduct during the course of advice giving to their subsequent decisions about whether to follow the advice or not, their reception of it suggests that much of the advice may have been counterproductive.[27] The responses of the mothers in these sequences may perhaps be aptly summarized by the Scottish mothers in McIntosh's study, who observed:

I don't like the health visitors. I mean, it's no' like help or advice – they *tell* you. It wisnae, "Maybe you should do this," it was, "You *should* do this." Y'know, "You're doing it all wrong." That's how I never went to the clinic. I was sick o' bein' bossed about.

She keeps tellin' me, "Do this, do that." It makes ye feel like a moron, that yer no' capable o' lookin' after yer baby. It undermines yer confidence. Ah always feel guilty after she's been as if ah've been doin' everything wrong. It makes me mad. Ah don't say anything at the time, ah just mutter a few oaths when she's gone.

(McIntosh 1986: 26)

These mothers' accounts of the authority relations assumed in advice-giving sequences and the passive resistance with which this assumption is met ("Ah don't say anything at the time") appear to encapsulate the predominant pattern of advice giving and advice reception that emerges from our data.

In considering this pattern, we are left with the problem of explaining why it is that our HVs persisted in this – apparently unproductive – process of self-initiated advice giving. Although, in the present context, responses to this problem can only be speculative, a number of possibilities suggest themselves.

We begin, first, by recalling Robinson's (1982) contrast between a clinical problem-oriented approach to health visiting associated with a medical background and an approach based on the clients' identification of their own health needs, which might be favored by those whose training originates in social-work contexts (see Baldock and Prior 1981). HVs are, as previously noted, trained nurses – often with extensive clinical and hospital experience. This training and experience may incline them towards, in Robinson's (1982) terms, "an identification, diagnosis and treatment" approach to mothers rather than one in which mothers are encouraged to take the lead in defining their needs.

While this possibility is certainly attractive, it cannot by any means carry the whole burden of explanation. A preliminary analysis of interactions involving the same HVs with experienced mothers (with one or more previous children) suggests that, with these mothers, the HVs were less ready to initiate courses of advice unilaterally and more prepared to acknowledge the knowledge, experience, and competence of the mothers. This evidence, though yet to be fully developed, suggests that the "nursing background" of the HVs, while a possible factor in their orientations towards the first-time mothers, is by no means a factor that influences them to engage in unilateral advice giving regardless of who they are dealing with.

A second consideration arises out of the recognition that our findings are based on data involving interactions with first-time mothers who, in the nature of the case, are inexperienced in dealing with young babies. Much of our advice-giving data is consistent with the possibility that the HVs took up a "pessimistic" or "defensive" stance with respect to the knowledge and competence possessed by these mothers. This stance has a number of aspects.

First, with respect to issues which the mothers treated in some way as problematic, the readiness with which the HVs proceeded to advice giving suggests that they started from the "pessimistic" presumption that the mothers would, at best, have limited competence to deal with the problem. This presumption might also have "defensive" aspects insofar as the HVs are organizationally accountable for the health and welfare of both mother and baby and, in some subsequent context, may desire to assert the adequacy of their conduct with respect to some problem. Second, the HVs' readiness to engage in unilateral advice giving is also consistent with "pessimistic" presumptions about the knowledge of first-time mothers. Specifically, the HVs may believe that first-time mothers are unable either to recognize that they have a problem or, relatedly, to anticipate or imagine the range of problem contingencies to which they may become subject. And, to the extent that they take such a view, the relative lack of mother-initiated requests for advice – documented in this study – may confirm them in it. Such a perspective may encourage HVs to offer anticipatory or preemptive advice that addresses such contingencies before they are recognized or before they arise.

Third, the HVs' "pessimism" about the mothers' knowledge and competence may be matched by a correspondingly high valuation of their own expertise. Mayall and Foster (1989) have shown that HVs are confident in the superiority of their own knowledge base regardless of whether its origins were lay or professional in character. These survey-based findings are matched in our data where the HV's advice giving was marked by a significant tendency to assert their own authority and expertise over against the mother and other lay sources. This tendency is perhaps most particularly marked on the occasions in which they declined to acknowledge the independent knowledge and competence which the mothers attempted to display.

A final set of considerations arise from the broad and somewhat nebulous character of the HV role. It will be recalled that the HV role is centrally defined in terms of the provision of advice rather than in terms of direct practical nursing assistance and that the HV is nonetheless obliged to visit the homes of mothers with young children. Home visits conducted on this obligatory basis and in a context in which HVs have no practical nursing responsibilities must inevitably raise what might be termed the "ticket of entry" problem – the issue of what the recognizable purpose or point of home visits might actually be. This problem is one which may exercise both mother and HV alike and it may emerge with particular force on the occasion of first visits. As we have noted, a number of studies suggest that many mothers, rightly or wrongly, believe that home visits are conducted primarily for surveillance and social-control purposes. Regardless of the extent to which the HVs are aware of this belief or themselves recognize and accept this purpose, they are nonetheless confronted with the task of endowing their unsolicited visits with some basic (perhaps alternative) sense of purpose. The delivery of advice, to the extent that it sustains the parties' sense that the HV desires to be useful to the mother, may contribute to a resolution of this "ticket of entry" problem.

It is here, however, that the central dilemma of advice giving may reach its apotheosis. For advice giving must ordinarily constitute the advice recipient as being of at least doubtful knowledge or competence. As we have seen, rather than establishing that mothers definitely lack specific knowledge or competences in relation to health or baby-management issues, HVs tend to act on a presumption of systematic doubt about the mother's abilities. There are good interactional reasons for this. First, the inquiries that might be necessary to establish the mothers' knowledge or competences could readily undermine "rapport" between the parties and may focus attention on just the surveillance aspects of these visits that HVs may be most anxious to have disattended. Second, efforts at a clear determination that a mother is specifically ignorant or incompetent on some matter will, if successful, tend both to humiliate the mother and to sour the context in which the subsequent advice is delivered. Conversely, where the outcome of those inquiries is the finding that the mother is specifically knowledgeable and competent, the basis on which advice can appropriately be given will be undermined. In this case, the result of detailed inquiry would be the loss of the "ticket of entry" that advice giving represents.

Thus, insofar as HVs deploy advice giving as a central "ticket of entry" to mothers' homes, they may tend to initiate advice in contexts where the recipient's desire or need for advice is uncertain. Paradoxically, the HVs' need to make herself useful may result in the delivery of advice in interactional contexts where, at best, it is of indeterminate value to the recipient and, at worst, it is resented and resisted by her. The ultimate dilemma of advice giving as a ticket of entry may be that it can only be bought by spoiling the ball game.

Notes

1. These figures are presented in terms of "full-time equivalents" and thus the actual number of nurses working in the health-visitor service is rather larger than this figure.
2. Audio-recording was selected both because it was a straightforward technique for data collection to be used by the health visitors themselves and because video equipment and the additional persons who

would be required to operate it would have constituted an intrusive distraction in a delicate setting. The audio-record, however, has significant drawbacks. It is impossible to determine the spatial arrangement of the parties to the interaction and, on many occasions, the possibly important nonvocal activities of the parties. The significance of certain aspects of the audio-record is rendered equivocal by these lacunae. In developing our observations, we have avoided data manifesting these difficulties.

3. In the original data-collection process an attempt was made to restrict the social class of the mothers in the sample to IV and V. In the event, our sample is more broadly spread and incorporates persons with a wide range of occupations, including self-employed business persons, white-collar employees, skilled, semi-skilled, and unskilled manual workers, and persons who, at the time of the visits, were unemployed.

4. See Robinson (1982) for a summary account of the historical background to this unusual division of labor between health visitors and other community nurses, and Donzelot (1980) for an account of the ideological background of health visiting.

5. See, for example, Foster (1988) for a comparison of this feature of the British health visitor's role with her opposite number in France – the *puéricultrice.*

6. Although the health visitor has a statutory obligation to cater to the health needs of all children, she does not have a statutory right of entry into the parental home. In practice, however, the accountability of denying entry to the health visitor renders such a right unnecessary.

7. A range of studies from the 1960s onwards (e.g. Political and Economic Planning 1961; Cartwright 1979 cited in Robinson 1982; Graham 1979) have suggested that some mothers perceive health visitors in terms of a surveillance role. McIntosh's (1986) study of a working-class sample of mothers' attitudes to the health-visitor service showed that the majority of first-time mothers viewed the health visitors' role primarily in surveillance terms (McIntosh 1986: 15). Such outlooks occasionally emerged as a more-or-less overt feature of the interactions that form the data for this chapter.

8. For example, in our data base home visits were made on a weekly basis for the first month and subsequently on a monthly basis.

9. Indeed Dingwall (1977: 91) has observed that the complexity of the home visit vitiates the value of timing studies.

10. Although the HV service stresses the value of establishing contact with mothers before the birth of a baby and efforts are normally made to do so, only one HV in our sample (HV no. 5) had in fact made contact with her two first-time mothers prior to the first recorded visit.

11. The speakers in this and the data extracts that follow are labeled as follows: HV = health visitor; M = mother; F = father; G = grandmother; Fr = friend.

12. In Brown and Levinson's (1987) terms, advice giving threatens both

the positive face and negative face of the advice recipient. The recipient's positive face is threatened by the advice giver's implication that the recipient is not knowledgeable or competent concerning the matters that are advised upon. The recipient's negative face (desire to be unimpeded) is threatened by the obligation to follow the course of action recommended by the advice giver.

13. See Ervin Tripp (1976) and M. H. Goodwin (1991) for an analysis of directive forms. West (1990) describes similar features in the design of physicians' directives, though she also finds differences in their design that are strongly patterned by gender.

14. This procedure for requesting advice is not, of course, restricted to these materials. In the following datum, G has called E for a recipe for Tacos. Her initiation of the request is designed to show some knowledge of the relevant ingredients (arrowed):

```
[NB:IV:2:R]
    G:     →    ˙hhhhh So e- d'you nee:d you need uh
           →    hhamburger don't chu.
    E:          ˙hh Ye:u:us? e‑n y ‑uh need
    G:     →                  [E n]
    E:          ┌some: u ┐h :    ┐
    G:     →    └s-  ˙hh┘ sh:r┘edded lettuce?
    E.          Shredded lettuce en CHEE::SE?
```

15. See Drew (1984) for a discussion of other cases of reportings in which the relevance or implications of the reportings are left implicit. Drew notes that "the way in which an event is portrayed in a reporting establishes the relevance of a particular kind of involvement/co-participation by the recipient through some conventional tying between the kind of occasion/activity and a relevant action by the recipient" (1984: 149, n. 10).

16. As it turns out, in both (10) and (11) the offered advice is resisted, see pp. 404–5.

17. For a related discussion of a context in which a professional seeks to build an interactional environment in which the delivery of professionally expert information will not conflict with the lay perspective, see Maynard (this volume).

18. See Jefferson (1989) for an account of the distribution and "standard maximum" length of pauses in conversation.

19. We do not intend to imply in this paragraph that more complete stepwise approaches to advice giving always eventuate in appropriately designed giving. In (15), for example, while it is apparent that the mother presents the child's problem as past and presents her approach to it as the product of advice from another health professional, the HV nonetheless initiates advice giving.

20. In (20), the advice giving may be stimulated by intimations earlier in the visit that the mother is considering abandoning breast feeding.

21. See Pomerantz (1980) for a further discussion of this segment.
22. It may be noted that the mother's additional use of "right" at line 21 to acknowledge acceptance of the HV's advice after her acceptance has been resolicited (at line 20) is further evidence that "right" is a standard, but "minimal" form of marked acknowledgment for the acceptance of advice.
23. It is notable that this overt acknowledgment of past error is made by the grandmother rather than the mother. The grandmother does not have direct responsibility for the child's welfare and, moreover, is "experienced" and may have little to prove with respect to her competence in child-raising practices. Moreover, her account is couched in terms of conscientious, if misplaced, concern for the baby's welfare during a cold English winter.
24. For a parallel argument with respect to the receipt of answers to questions, see Heritage (1984b).
25. We particularly note here that the mother asserts that she was "taught" this procedure rather than, for example, "told about" it. The term "taught" here conveys not only that she was told about it, but that she learned the procedure or otherwise "took it on board."
26. This presequence illustrates a recurrent anxiety among the HVs in our data base about alternative sources of advice. In the following sequence, the HV receives no response (arrow 1) to a two-component advice delivery. Subsequently, she moves to undercut the baby-food packet as a source of advice about feeding (arrow 2).

```
[1C1:29-30]
     HV:              Don'(t)- (0.2) I think it- (.) it's sensible to
                      (1.0)
     HV:              you know tuh- (0.2) to use your common sense
                      and give 'er what what you think she nee:ds.
          1→         (0.3)
     HV:              ˙hh If she's (.) ˙hh happy: (.) she's not
                      being si:ck (0.6) she's not screaming the
                      place do:wn >you're doing the ri:ght thing.<
          1→         (0.5)
     HV:    2→       Don't take any notice of what it says on the
                      packet an' how many ounces (.) per how many
                      (.) weeks,
```

Here it is noticeable that the HV's elaboration of her first piece of advice is designed in terms of a three-part list format (Jefferson 1990) which is often used in talk designed to persuade (Atkinson 1984; Heritage and Greatbatch 1986). The failure of this advice component to get any response may be implicated in the HV's subsequent move to deny the value of the baby-food packet as a source of direction for the mother – a move that was possibly foreshadowed with her initial turn beginning *"Don*'t-" that was previously abandoned in favor of the subsequent, more constructive advice.

27. This is the clear conclusion of McIntosh's (1986) questionnaire-based study of first-time mothers' responses to their HVs. See McIntosh (1986: 60) and Carter *et al.* (1986) for a more general review.

13

The interactional organization of calls for emergency assistance

DON H. ZIMMERMAN

1 Introduction

Drawing on past work and research currently in progress (Sharrock and Turner 1978; Meehan 1983, 1989; Zimmerman 1984; M. Whalen and Zimmerman 1987; 1992: J. Whalen, Zimmerman, and Whalen 1988; M. Whalen 1990; J. Whalen 1990), this chapter examines the interactional organization of the talk that occurs in calls to 9–1–1 and other emergency telephone numbers operated by three emergency dispatch centers. Callers dialing emergency numbers ordinarily do so to get assistance for troubles they have witnessed or experienced, a project that is sometimes straightforward and sometimes not. And in turn, personnel answering such calls – called complaint takers or call takers – have a number of tasks to accomplish in order to determine in a timely manner what assistance (if any) is appropriate. It is important to note at the outset that calls are best

described as *ongoing and developing sequences of actions*, actions that systematically get formed up into "calls" ... [Calls] are observably oriented to by staff in innumerable ways to name, explain, describe, account for, and otherwise identify the events that make up their everyday work world. In this sense, "calls" appear as an essential feature of the sensibility of the work as an observable, orderly feature.

(J. Whalen, 1990: 6; emphasis in original)

Thus, the term "call" does not simply refer to instances of telephone contact, but to what is accomplished by parties to those

The author would like to express his deep appreciation for the comments and suggestions he has received from Paul Drew, Tim Halkowski, John Heritage, Robin Lloyd, Wayne Mellinger, Jack Whalen, Marilyn Whalen, and Thomas P. Wilson. They made the difference.

contacts as they interact in the pursuit of their respective concerns.[1] For staff, this involves managing the contingencies that attend the dispatch organization's attempt to conform its response to a wide range of reported troubles to its policies and protocols. The processing of a series of such calls constitutes the day's work for a call taker (see J. Whalen 1990). Drawing on data from three emergency dispatch centers, this chapter exhibits and analyzes such work.

In the case of calls collected from two of the centers that furnished the main data source for most of the earlier studies – Central County and in particular, Mid-City – the configuration of sequences organizing calls for help routinely, but by no means invariantly, assumed the shape shown in table 13.1 (Zimmerman 1984; Whalen and Zimmerman 1987). The circumstances of emergency calls vary within and across calls as well as between different dispatch organizations. With regard to the latter, for example, there may be policies which specifically shape call takers' (henceforth CTs[2]) answering turn. At the third organization, Lane County,[3] CTs ask callers (henceforth Cs) "What is your emergency?" immediately after categorically self-identifying in their first turn, thus initiating interrogation *prior* to a request for assistance by C.[4]

Table 13.1 *Configuration of sequences for managing calls for emergency services*

Pre-beginning
    Opening/identification/acknowledgment
        Request
             Interrogative series
        Response
    Closing

Across all three organizations, many callers remain anonymous, while some self-identify in their first turn prior to stating their problem or making their request. As will be evident below, self-identification plays a part in both constructing and extending Cs' opening turn, and in the case of *categorical* self-identification by a C, placing the call on a particular footing ("my organization to your organization"). CTs, for their part, sometimes say very little beyond issuing continuers, ask no questions, and allow Cs to provide information with minimum intervention. At other times they engage in extensive and lengthy interrogation.

A central task for this chapter, then, is to bring into focus the range of contingencies that Cs and CTs confront, and in showing how they manage these contingencies, provide a fuller sense of this genre of talk as a particular kind of *work*. For the work of the call consists of participants coping with (a) the call-processing requirements characterizing the particular dispatch organization and (b) the variable circumstances peculiar to each call. The general mechanisms of talk-in-interaction are the tools Cs and CTs employ to bring (a) and (b) into alignment on actual, particular, real-time occasions of telephone talk. It is important here to underscore the fact that aligning (a) and (b), that is, in managing the course of the interaction to get through the call (and perhaps achieve an accountably appropriate outcome), specifies the interactional task of both C and CT. This alignment or convergence is often routinely achieved. At other times, its accomplishment tests the patience and interactional skills of both parties. In either case, the alignment of (a) and (b) is the *work* that the talk performs in accomplishing the call for emergency services.[5]

The concern of this chapter, then, is to pursue a further examination of the organization of emergency calls, using preliminary data from another dispatching operation (Lane County) in addition to Mid-City and Central County. This will afford a closer examination of the interactional contingencies Cs and CTs produce and encounter in the course of a call and the machinery they deploy to manage them. Particular attention will be paid to the division of attention CTs must manage between monitoring Cs' talk and coding and passing on information pertinent to the assembly of the "dispatch package" (the codified information required to dispatch assistance). The design of Cs' first turn at talk will also receive more detailed attention, as will several newly encountered features of emergency dispatching at Lane County, including the already mentioned early initiation of interrogation. Before proceeding, a brief characterization of the three settings from which the data were obtained is in order.

2 Three dispatch centers

The corpus from which the data for this analysis is drawn consists primarily of telephone calls to an emergency number in the mid-western United States (Mid-City), supplemented by a further collection of calls[6] from (and observation in) "9–1–1" dispatch centers in two West Coast locations (Central County and, more recently, Lane County[7]). A less systematic collection of calls to other types of service organizations, public and private, also informs this analysis.

The Emergency Communications Center at Mid-City, like Lane County, employs a computer-assisted dispatch system (CAD). Both separate call taking from dispatch. Requests for police, fire, and medical assistance are taken by CTs who enter information received from Cs into a computer terminal for transmission to dispatchers (henceforth Ds) who further process the information and forward it to appropriate units in the field.[8] The Mid-City CAD provides CTs and Ds with valid intersections programmed into the computer. When, as often is the case in automobile accidents, location is reported in relation to an intersection, the computer will reject those it does not recognize. Accurate locational information is not only critical for the dispatch of assistance (see below) but also can be used to recognize multiple calls concerning a single event.

CTs at Central County, which did not have CAD, employed "incident cards" on which information was written. In addition, Central County combined the call-taking and dispatching functions. Depending on their work station, the call could be dispatched by the CT receiving the call or subsequently carried by hand to another CT staffing the appropriate station for dispatching fire, paramedic, or sheriff units.[9]

At Mid-City, if all CTs are busy and a call has been waiting for 5 seconds, a green light will go on; after 15 seconds, an orange light; and after 35 seconds a red light and a buzzer.[10] At Central and Lane Counties, CTs orient to the gongs or buzzers announcing incoming calls. When the volume of calls increases, Cs may be placed on hold if their problem is not urgent so that other incoming calls can be answered and similarly screened. Thus, the "state of the system" is available to CTs, with a high volume placing a premium on distinguishing between urgent and nonurgent calls.[11] As will be evident below, incoming calls, particularly those on 9–1–1 or other designated emergency numbers, are oriented to from the outset as virtual emergencies.

Whatever the technological and organizational differences between the three settings, the major task each addresses is functionally identical: to collect and codify the information necessary to dispatch police, fire, or paramedic units to the scene of a reported incident, and to do so accurately and quickly. This entails several related tasks, one of which is to ascertain the nature of the problem requiring emergency response, for example, a crime, a medical problem, or a fire. Further, in order to dispatch assistance, a location must be specified. This is ordinarily managed by eliciting an address or intersection (if C has not already volunteered this information). Information may also be elicited to assist responding units to locate quickly the scene of the incident, for example, whether the address is a house or an apartment building, etc.[12]

Beyond problem and location, there is often additional information to be elicited. In the case of criminal activity, for example, CTs have the responsibility to obtain and forward to responding officers descriptions of suspects, whether they are armed, whether they are still present at the scene or the direction and means of their flight, etc. Such information is sanctionably relevant to the production of good work; for instance, personnel in the field (whose safety is, or is perceived to be, contingent on adequate characterization of an emergency situation) will quickly make it known if the details provided in the dispatch prove incomplete or misleading.

The information collected by CTs provides the basis for the construction of what may be termed a "dispatch package" (cf. Meehan 1989 on "complaint packages"). As the assembly of the dispatch package is a major component of a CT's processing of a call, it will be examined in more detail in the following section prior to examining the management of specific classes of call contingencies.

3 The dispatch package

In answering a call the CT is involved in at least two parallel and interdependent lines of activity: (a) talking with and listening to the C; and (b), codifying and entering particular items of information (the nature of the problem, its location, etc.) that constitute the dispatch package into the computer (or writing it on an incident card) in preparation for its transmittal to a D. With regard to the latter task, CTs categorize Cs' descriptions of trouble by use of a coding system. Inspection of the problem codes available for the two-hour period from which the Mid-City calls were drawn reveals a total of forty-seven different codes, with almost half used more than once. There are undoubtedly more codes in use at Mid-City. At Lane County (which also employs CAD) there are 360 such codes which CTs must memorize and enter without error as the system will accept only the correct code or abbreviation (J. Whalen personal communication; see also J. Whalen 1990). Codes at Central County were drawn from the State Penal and Welfare codes.

The "dispatch package" at Mid-City took the following form:

(1)
23:03   2270 5 Av. N.
                         pergun p1
                         comp says people are shooting
                         guns at that address - no one shot
                         yet. Says they will shoot cops.
                         Then hung up.

The time of the dispatch is 23:03; the address is given, followed by the code for the type of problem, usually in the form of an abbreviation as, in this case, "pergun" – a person with a gun. The urgency of the call is indicated as "p1," or priority one, the highest of three levels. Priority codes associated with a particular type of problem are programmed into the computer and are assigned automatically. The assigned priority can be overridden by CTs if they believe a particular problem is more urgent than ordinary troubles of that type. Ds can override CTs' overrides as well as the preprogrammed priority code. (At Western and Central Counties CTs and Ds assign priorities.) Detail concerning the incident is then provided in the form of a brief narrative description.

3.1 Keyboard activity

The activity of entering information into the CAD is evident on the Mid-City tapes in the form of keyboard sounds. The occurrence of

these sounds at various points in the call can be related to the
requirements of the dispatch package. The following transcript
displays the keyboard sounds (marked as "kb" with a left bracket
"[" indicating onset and a right bracket "]" indicating termination)
directly below the relevant line of transcript. A series of dashes
marks the duration of the sounds.

```
(2) [MCE:21:1:1]
  1   CT:        Mid City=emergency:
  2              (.)
  3   C:         Yes.=I'd like tuh report ur
  4              disturbance, in an alleyway:, behind
  5              ar building?
  6   CT:        Okay, what's thee address there?
  7   C:         ˙hh Well- my building is twenty three oh one
  8              ˙hh Mills Way,
  9              [kb---------------
 10   CT:        Mnhm.
 11              --------
 12   C:         ˙hh an it- thuh building (.) right next to
 13              -----------------------------]
 14              ours (.) ah: (.) that would be (.) north of
 15                       [kb----]
 16              our building ˙hh so thuh building north of
 17                             [kb]
 18              our building ˙hhh an' the disturbance is- ah:
 19                                  [kb-------------------------
 20              (.) in thee- at thee carriage house
 21              -------------]
 22              area of that building (.) in thee (1.2)  at
 23                             [kb-------]
 24              thuh garage area (.9) carriage house=garage
 25              area ˙HH=
 26                [ k b - ]
 27   CT:        =umhm=
 28   C:         =What is- is- happening is that uh woman (.)
 29              has been screaming for thuh last twenty five:
 30              thirty minutes=gimme=my=money=gimme=my
 31                                         [k b ----------------
 32              =mon(h)ey ˙hh and uh: (.) just kept up too
 33              ----------------------------------- ]
 34              long and eh they're=they're assaulting each
 35              other physically and uh: I don't know what
 36              thee problem is (.) there,
 37                             [k b --]
```

38	CT:	Okay. We'll get somebody there=
39	C:	=>'kay thank you much=
40	CT:	=Umhm=bye

The keyboard sounds commence just after C utters "twenty three oh one" (lines 8–9) and continue until the brief pause after "building" (lines 12–13). Brief keyboard activity occurs in the vicinity of C's filled pause "ah:" (lines 14–15) and just after "our building" (lines 16–17). They resume as C begins to specify further the location of the disturbance "an' the disturbance is-" (lines 18–19) and stop after "in thee" (lines 20–1). Short spurts of sound occur in lines 22–3 and 25–6, with more extended activity beginning as C commences his account of what the woman has been screaming (lines 30–1). The last sounds begin and end before CT delivers her promise of assistance.

The dispatch package generated in interaction with this C looked like this:

(3)
11:04   2301 Mills Way S.
               unk trb p1
               behind building north of
               here...at carriage house...
               sounds of woman screaming

It seems reasonable to infer (allowing for some lag) that the initiation of keyboard activity in the immediate vicinity of address information, subsequent to further locational detail, and after descriptions of the trouble, is in response to these classes of information, and indeed, exhibits an orientation to them as elements of the dispatch package.

In the following call a similar alignment of keyboard activity and C's informings is apparent:

(4) [MCE:20:2:171]

1	CT:	Mid-City police and fire,
2		(.)
3	C:	Y̲hes I'd like to um: tst I'm at thirty one
4		seventeen uh tenth avenue sou:th?
5		[kb -----------
6	CT:	Mnhm

```
 7                     --------]
 8   C:              ˙hhh Uh there's uh (0.2) oh I think it's uh (.)
 9                    white jeep (.) ˙hh jeepster that pulled up here
10                                        [kb---------------
11                    uh in front.=An there's about (0.1) five Nihgro
12                    ----------------------------------------]
13                    guys tha' got out, I heard=um talkin about
14                                               [kb--------
15                    (0.1) ˙hh going (.) to thee next apartment
16                    -----------------------------------]
17                     building uh fur uh fight (0.2) ˙hh an I jus'
18                                       [kb----]
19                    am going down tuh check it out=I'm up
20                    here ˙hh (.) in my apartment, I thought I'd go
21                         [kb------------------]
22                    down an kinduh ˙hh look and see what was goin
23                                   [kb-----------------------------------
24                    on but uh ((clears throat)) you might bi-
25                    -----------]
26                    might not be tt anything but ih if it iz
27                    it's ˙hhh it sounded like they were angry an
28                         [kb--------------------------------------]
29                    ˙hh an  they talked about uh fight, there's an
30                    apartment building next to us=here.
31   CT:             Unhunh (.) is is yur uh (.) address=uh single
32                    family home there=
33   C:              =˙h Uh well it's uh: ˙hh cream colored mansion
34                                        [k b-------]
35                    I'm on twenty:: uh::: (.2) let's=see I'm on
36                         [kb--------------------]
37                    tenth avenue an' thirty second street
38                       [˙hh thirty one seventeen tenth avenue south=
39   CT:             [Umka-
40   CT:             =˚Okay do ya know thee uh address uv thee
41                    apartment building=
42   C:              =No: it's jus' right next door it's just one
43                    down it's probably be=um: (.2) thirty=one
44                    fifteen er ˙hh something like that
45   CT:             O:kay (.1) then kin I have your name please
46   C:              Uh Johnson
47                    (  0.5  )
48                    [k b-----]
49   CT:             An y'say they they did go inside already?
50   C:              Yeah
51   D:              ˚Oh shoot. Ahright we'll have um check it ⌐out
52   C:                                                      ⌊Fine
53                    thanks=
54   D:              =Mnhm
```

The dispatch package for this call assumed the following shape:

(5)
00:07   2117 2 Av S.
                         misc. p2
                         white jeep outfront
                         5 B/Ms got out
                         went into apt bldg next door
                         poss 2115s sounded angry
                         were talking about a fight

Notice that most of the information selected by CT (location, vehicle, description of involved parties, possibility of a fight) was provided by C by line 17 of the transcript. The balance of lines 17–31, where CT asks if his address is a single family house, is comprised of talk by C interspersed by keyboard activity by CT. C's utterances deal with his plan to go down from his apartment to see what is going on, coupled to the suggestion that the incident "might not be anything" (line 26). He goes on to review and elaborate the features of the original report: "it sounded like they were angry" (line 27) and "they talked about uh fight" (line 29).

Apart from her opening categorical identification and a single continuer (line 6), CT has focused her activity on keyboard entry of information. This activity is not continuous; for example, no keyboard sounds are evident from CT's continuer (line 7) following C's address (lines 3–4) to the mention of the "white jeep" (line 9). The point to be taken here is that C continues to develop his informing and CT monitors his talk, entering pertinent information as it is provided. At the possible conclusion of C's account of the trouble in line 17, CT says nothing while she continues her keyboard activity. After a pause of 0.2 second, C initiates his elaboration (lines 17–30), which, in the absence of a receipt or acknowledgment from CT, may be oriented to the possibility of some problem with his narrative. This is evident in his hedge in line 26 ("might not be anything") coupled to a review of the grounds for his original proposal that there was a possible policeable trouble in the making (lines 27–30). In so doing, C supplies one further piece of information in line 27 ("it sounded like they were angry") which was incorporated in the dispatch. After C's mention of the apartment building next to him on lines 29–30 (the site of the possible fight), CT initiates a locational query (lines 31–2).

With regard to the dual activities of interacting with C and

entering information into the computer, it is important to note that
CTs must orient not only to what Cs are saying, but what they may
be *about* to say, that is, whether Cs' current remarks are prefatory
to the delivery of pertinent information (e.g. on the occurrence of a
crime), in which case CTs may defer initiating inquiries.[13] CTs thus
attend to the development of Cs' remarks with an ear to satisfying
the requirements of the dispatch package.[14] What Cs' utterances
offer or project relative to such "satisfaction" furnish a critical
element in CTs' decision to initiate questioning or pass the opportunity to do so. How Cs shape their turns to project upcoming
informings is treated in more detail in section 6 of the chapter.

A directly relevant issue for CTs' construction of the dispatch
package is a given C's capacity or willingness to function as an
informant. When a C is hysterical, a CT must somehow realign that
C to the business at hand: providing information, or in the case of a
medical emergency, monitoring or rendering aid to the patient. This
may involve reassuring C ("help is on the way"), or asking that he
or she "calm down" or "stop shouting" or "answer questions." In
the following extracts, C calls to report that his wife has just shot
herself. C is shouting and is extremely upset.

```
(6)   [WC:EMS:1:JW]
 1    CT:      Nine one one what is yur emerg- ((cut off by
 2             transmit static))
 3             (.2)
 4    C:       GO::D MY WIFE JUST SHOT HERSELF (.3) TWENTY
 5             TWO SIXTY EIGHT (GRANT) AVENUE HURRY U:::::P
 6             (.2)
 7    CT:      What happened?
 8             (.2)
 9    C:       (AR:::)=SHE JUS SHOT HERSE::LF=
10    CT:      =SHE (SHEL   )?
11             (.2)
12    C:       SHE SHOT HER SELF WITH'A SHOTGUN
      .
      .        [[6 Turns Omitted]]
      .
13    CT:      We're notifying them
14             (.4)
15    C:       HURRY: U:::P
16             (.5)
17    CT2:     Tell'im to quit shouting.
```

```
18                      (.3)
19      CT:             Please stop shouting sir we're here ta-=
20      C:              =(WE:LL WHO'┌S BO:THERING, GO:D┌ain DA:MN
21      CT:                         └Sir             └Sir (.4) we're-
22      C:              FUCKIN'SH-=
23      CT:             =We're (   in') an ambulance there, where did
24                      she shoot herself
24                      (.4)
26      C:              SHE SHOT HERSELF IN=THE CHEST HURRY U::P
27                      (.4)
28      CT:             Okay we're (shotin') an ambulan┌ce there┐
29      CT2:                                           └I got it┘  i:n
30                      (.3)
31      C:              HURRY U:::P=
32      CT:             ='kay we have an ambulance on the way si:r
33                      (.3)
34      C:              MY WIFE'S DE:AD (SHE CAN'T     )
35                      (.2)
36      CT2:            Tell'er ta quit- tell'im to quit shouting.
37                      (.2)
        .
        .               [[19 Turns Deleted]]
        .

38      CT2:            Okay you're son and daughter are there, how old
39                      are they
40                      (.4)
41      C:              THEY'RE THREE AN' FOUR AN' NOW GOD DAMMIT
42                      (        ::N)=
43      CT2:            =Okay people are on the way right now sir don't
44                      shout I can't understand you when you shout
        .
        .               [[10 Turns Deleted]]
        .

45      CT2:            Okay quit (.3) don't shout, I can't understand
46                      you (   )
47      C:              WHAT=DO I DO::
```

As evident in the transcript, CT has difficulty understanding C,
which is attributed in line 44 to his shouting. (CT2 is CT's training
supervisor who is monitoring his management of the call). The
issue for CT is to secure C's cooperation in answering questions
and, in cases like the above, in attending to and following instructions for providing prearrival medical assistance.

In the call above, C is treated as "hysterical." When a C is
perceived as "uncooperative" (refusing to answer questions) CTs

may attempt realignment of C as interrogatee to their discourse role
as interrogator: (J. Whalen, Zimmerman, and Whalen 1988):

(7) [Dallas FD/B1]
```
1   N:           And whatis thuh problem there?
2   C:           I don't kno:w. if I knew I wouldn't
3                be needin'⸢y-
4   CT:                    ⌊Si:r: I- eh would you
5                answer my questions please? What iz
6                thuh problem?
```

CT's task is to secure the information necessary for determining if a
dispatch of some kind of assistance is warranted. Thus, a critical
contingency for those answering emergency phones is the demeanor
of the C: in those instances where C is not providing the needed
information, CT must find some means to align C as a resource for
acquiring the information. This may involve such things as directives ("stop shouting" or "answer my questions") or reassurances
("help is on the way"). Such turns by CT are locally occasioned and
constructed to address the interactional problem posed by "hysterical" pleading for immediate assistance or refusal to cooperate:
realigning the C for pursuit of an organizationally mandated, collaboratively accomplished activity (obtaining information and giving
instructions).

The work of aligning a distraught caller itself poses contingencies for the management of the call. Reassuring Cs that "help is on
the way"[15] (which ordinarily initiates closing[16]) could lead C to
hang up prematurely, the business of the call having been concluded as far as C is concerned. Several devices are used to deal with
this issue. Perhaps the most direct is to reassure the C and to
accompany this with instructions to stay on the line, or calm down
and talk to the CT as in the following:

(8) [Lane County]
```
1   CT:          We have units on the way, okay just stay on the
2                phone with me
3   C:           Okay
```

(9) [Central County 2:10:86]
```
1   CT:          Has .e got uh gun ma'am?
2   C:           YES HE DOES::
3                (1.5)
```

4	C:	ONE ONE FOUR LAKE VIEW HYPERION=SEND THUH
5		POLICE=<u>HURR</u>Y.
6	CT:	Ma'am they're <u>com</u>in=if you'll just quit
7		screaming an' take uh deep breath and talk tuh
8		me okay:?
9	C:	Okay ˙hh

In fragment (8) above, CT informs C in line 1 that units are on the way, and immediately tells C to stay on the line, a directive that C acknowledges. As the transcript notation in fragment (9) suggests, C is screaming. Moreover, she is repeating the address and her request for assistance (lines 4–5) punctuated by an urgency marker ("Hurry"); such repetitions appear to constitute *pleadings* (M. Whalen, 1990: 171–87, 290–4) which, insofar as they occupy turn space, displace informings which CTs seek, and thus must be dealt with. Note that CT asks C to acknowledge his directive in lines 7–8 ("take uh deep breath and talk tuh me okay:?"). It appears that directives and questions (including acknowledgment elicitors) which require a next-turn response move (or attempt to move) Cs beyond the closing implicative span of the reassurance and back into the sequence of informings or other actions (e.g. checking to see if the patient is breathing) that CTs orient to as the proper conduct of the call.[17]

In sum, the dispatch package consists of slots to fill with particular classes of information, and the activity of providing/eliciting the required items constitutes a potent contingency of the interaction. Moreover, acquiring, processing, and entering this information are largely parallel activities taking place over the actual course of the call. Thus, while the point may be obvious,[18] it is nevertheless important to exhibit the framework of nonvocal activities – listening for, coding, and entering information – within which CTs orient to what Cs say in the course of the call.

The dispatch package – the collated information necessary for dispatching assistance – is assembled over the course of handling the contingencies of a call. CTs' task of constructing this package begins when Cs initiate a call to an emergency number. The following section examines the organization of call openings and the contingencies that attend the beginnings of calls for emergency services.

4 Openings

4.1 Virtual emergencies: the pre-beginning

Like other telephone calls, the opening section of emergency calls provides participants with the interactional space to establish "the kind of call this is" (Schegloff 1979a). The organization of openings provides participants with a machinery for regulating access to, and shaping the trajectory of, conversational encounters of all sorts. In the calls of interest here, the process of projecting the character of the call is initiated through a "pre-beginning" constituted by a C's act of dialing an advertised emergency number.

The character of a call as a virtual emergency can be clearly seen in the case of "enhanced" 9–1–1 systems. Such a system was in place at Central County (but not at the other two dispatch operations). Enhanced 9–1–1 means that the telephone numbers, addresses, and other information (e.g. the various police and fire jurisdictions within which the telephone's location falls) are automatically displayed on a console in the dispatch center when the call is answered. This arrangement has obvious advantages in that, in the case of a broken connection, it allows CT to call back a C,[19] as in the following fragment reported in M. Whalen and Zimmerman (1987: 179):

```
(10) [Central County V5-B/017]
  1   CT:        County Emergency
  2              ((Caller hangs up))
  3              ((Phone being dialed and ringing))
  4   C:         Hello?
  5   CT:        Yes, this is nine one=one emergency calling
  6    .         back, do you have an emergency?
  7   C:         No we don't
```

Moreover, Cs may be somehow incapacitated or prevented from speaking, as suggested in fragment (11):

```
(11) [County Central field notes]
  1   CT:        Nine one emergency
  2              ((Loud voices in the background -- screaming
  3              and arguing))
  4              ((Click))
  5   CT:        Oo:::ps! Sounds like a domestic
```

```
6                  ((CT calls phone number from which call
7                  originated))
8     CT:          This is thuh Sheriff's Department. Is there
9                  a problem?
```

Call-backs thus exhibit CTs' orientation to the call as a virtual emergency even in the absence of an actual request for help. M. Whalen and Zimmerman (1987) suggest that the opening segment of emergency calls rests on a prior action presumed to have a particular relevancy: dialing an emergency number projects a need for help *prior* to the alignment ordinarily achieved by the identification/acknowledgment portion of opening sequence (see below). CTs answering a 9–1–1 call (or other emergency number) are primed to hear it as a request for help *before* the first word is spoken.

The pre-beginning thus establishes an alignment of identities which provides a particular footing for the call. This alignment is, of course, subject to change or modification in a call-back or in the subsequent course of an undisrupted call. In the following call, CT's attempt to sustain an organizationally appropriate alignment with C borders on the heroic:

(12) [MCE/20-10/196]
```
1     CT:          Mid-City police  an fire
2                  ((background noise and music on the line))
3     C:           (YA::H ) Thiz iz thuh (          ) ((voice
4                  is very slurred))
5                  (1.5) ((loud background noise))
6     CT:          Hello:?
7                  (0.4)
8     C:           YEA::H?
9     CT:          Wadidja want?
10                 (0.5)
11    C:           Yea::h we- we wan' forn'ca:y (h) heh
12                 (0.6) ((background voices, noise))
13    CT:          Bout wha::t?
14                 (5.3)
15                 ((noise, voice: "hey gimme dat..."))
16    C:           Hay=I've=uh ri:ddle for ya:
17                 (0.3)
18    CT:          HU:::H?
19    C:           I have uh ri:ddle for ya
20                 (0.3)
```

```
21   CT:        I don't have ti:me f'r riddles=do=ya wanna
22              squa:d'r no:t=
23   C:         =NO: jes' uh simple que::stion,
24              (0.4) ((loud music)) Wha' fucks an leaks
25              like uh ti:ger,
26              (0.2)
27   CT:        HU:H?
28   C:         What fucks an leaks like uh ti:ger,
29   CT:        Bye bye:
30   C:         Huh? ((background noise))
31   CT:        Good bye
32   C:         Why::?
33              ((disconnect))
```

As suggested earlier, an answerer responding to the telephone summons under the auspices of an official identity will attempt to deal with the call in official terms. The CT displays this orientation when, despite (or perhaps because of) the slurred quality of C's voice, she seeks to elicit grounds for dealing with the call with a request for service in line 9 ("Wadidja want?") and in line 13 ("Bout wha::t?"). When C then offers to tell her a riddle in line 16, CT informs him "I don't have ti:me f'r riddles" (line 21) but makes yet another attempt to orient C to official business with her "do=ya=wanna squa:d'r no:t?" (lines 21–2) query. When these attempts fail, CT terminates the call. (See Zimmerman 1990 for a more extensive analysis of this call.)

The point to be taken here is that the particular alignment of identities projected or achieved at a given point, such as the opening, establishes a footing for the call, the relevance of which continues in force until an alternative alignment is proposed through some action of the participants[20] (as with the initial alignment, realignment is an interactionally managed affair). In the call above, C's attempt to establish an alternative alignment is resisted, and as the proposed footing is incompatible with the official business of the line, CT's termination of the call is warranted.

4.2 Opening – identification – acknowledgment sequence

In calls that continue past the issuance of a summons signaled by the phone ringing in the dispatch center, the anonymous character of the interaction is then further constituted by the participants' systematic specification and reduction of the "core opening sequences" observed for mundane telephone calls (Schegloff 1986). The core sequences are comprised of a *summons/answer* sequence which provides for the initial availability of the parties to interaction; an· *identification/recognition* sequence that establishes and aligns the situated identities of the caller and answerer; a *greeting* sequence which establishes a mutually ratified state of talk; and a *howareyou* sequence which provides an opportunity to topicalize the current state of one or the other party. After the completion of these sequences there occurs a slot for the *reason for the call* ("first topic") in which the matter ostensibly motivating the call may be broached.

In ordinary telephone calls, one or the other ·speaker may preempt first topic, moving it forward and deleting one or more of the core opening sequences. In "institutional" calls such as those of concern to this chapter, the last two sequences are *routinely* absent (M. Whalen and Zimmerman 1987: 175–8; Heritage and Greatbatch 1991) for the reason that they are not relevant to essentially anonymous encounters.[21] Such calls routinely (and quickly) move from CT's opening categorical identification to C's acknowledgment and a following request for help or a report or description of a problem. This opening exhibits an oriented-to modification of the "core" opening sequences observed to occur in ordinary telephone calls, displaying participants' concern to get on with the "reason for the call," promoting this agenda to a very early point in the call's opening.

4.3 Reason for the call: requests, reports, descriptions

Following the acknowledgment of the CT's categorical opening (usually a *yes* or a *yeah*), Cs produce a second component which provides the reason for the call (alternatively, the "business at hand" – see Button and Casey 1988/9). The form of C's second component varies. It can be shaped as a report, description, or narrative account of some problematic event or activity, or a request for police, fire, or paramedic assistance.

Requests are routinely done in a format displaying C's need or desire for service or directly asking that such assistance be sent:

(13) [MCE:21:4a:4]
    C: I need the paramedics please?

(14) [MCE:21:21:28]
    C: (Say if you gotta) squad car could you send one
                         over to...

(15) [MCE:21:32:47]
    C: Would you send the police please to...

(16) [MCE:17:7:108]
    C: Could you have the police come out to...

(17) [MCE:21:24a:33]
    C: We'd like you to send an ambulance out,

(18) [MCE:20:7a:191]
    C: Can you get somebody over here right away.
                         We've got a gal that's just ready to pass out

The first five fragments (13–17) illustrate commonly occurring openings. Notice that these requests, while they intimate that some type of policeable trouble or medical emergency is involved, do not specify the exact nature of the problem.[22] Indeed, they project a particular response without providing for its warrant.[23] More than the mere statement of a desired response or need is required, however, as is illustrated in the following call from an Ambassador Hotel operator to the Los Angeles Police Department occasioned by the fatal wounding of Robert Kennedy in the hotel kitchen:

(19) [RFK]
```
 1   CT:     Police Department.
 2           ( )
 3   C:      Yes  This is the Ambassador Hotel Em-
 4           Ambassador Hotel?
 5           ((echo: Hotel))
 6   C:      Do you hear me?
 7           ( )
 8   CT:     Yeah ↑I hear you.
 9   C:      Uh they have an emergency=They want thuh
10           police to thuh kitchen right away.
11   CT:     What kind of an emergency?
12   C:      I don't know honey They hung up I don't know
13           ⌜what's happening
14   CT:     ⌞Well find out, (. ) We don't send out without=
```

15	C:	=I beg your pardon?
16		( )
17	CT:	We have to know what we're sending on,

While some embarrassment may have attended the subsequent public disclosure of delay in the dispatch of assistance to the scene, it is clear that the C, a hotel operator relaying information from the hotel's kitchen, is initially not in a position to provide the required information. The CT then presses her to obtain the information and explicitly formulates the overriding issue at this point: "We have to know what we're sending on." The mere characterization of an event as an emergency is, other things being equal, insufficient.[24]

Returning to fragment (18), the nature of the service requested is specified by a statement of the problem ("We've got a gal that's just ready to pass out"). As intimated in the discussion of the dispatch package, CTs monitor Cs' utterances for reports or descriptions of events that can be formulated as a medical emergency (e.g. *difficulty breathing, auto accident with injuries,* etc.), fire (e.g. *structure fire, grass fire,* etc.) or police business, (e.g. *burglary, domestic,* etc.). If such an event is not depicted, CTs will initiate interrogation in the next turn (*What's the problem?*). However, if an address is provided CTs may verify (or initiate repair, if required – see below) before proceeding to the problem query.

Reports ordinarily involve a report frame (*I'd like/want to report an X*):

(20) [MCE:21:16a:21]
       C: I want to report a real bad accident

(21) [MCE:21:22:29]
       C: I would like to report a break in

(22) [MCE:20:6:188]
       C: I want to report a three car accident at...

The report format appears to be routinely deployed as a framework for *naming* a trouble by use of a single category ("accident") or brief phrase ("break in"). Accidents,[25] for example, are frequently packaged as reports. Reports specify the nature of the problem directly and economically (but see below). In addition, by employing a report format, Cs explicitly orient to the character of the

activity at hand: relaying information on a trouble to a co-participant aligned as the proper recipient of such an informing. The
recipient-designed report format may thus be one way in which Cs
do "calling the police" (Schegloff 1991: 61). The activity of calling
the police is not, however, restricted to making reports, as informings delivered via other formats will also mobilize response. For
example, Cs may simply describe a trouble. *Descriptions* may take
the form of declarative sentences[26] which inform the dispatcher of
the existence of some problem along with at least some minimal
context:

(23) [MCE:21:9:12]
```
1   CT:        Mid-City Emergency:
2   C:         ˙hh Um: yeah (.) Somebody jus' vandalized
3              my=ca:r,
```

(24) [MCE:17:1:59]
```
1   CT:        Mid-City police and fi:re
2   C:         In thuh YWCA parking lot there uh bunchuh
3              teenagers right now vandalizing my ca:r,
```

C's description in (23), "Somebody jus' vandalized my=ca:r" specifies the criminal act, marks its recency, and establishes the relationship of the caller to the trouble ("my car"). Similarly, C in
(24) locates the trouble, provides a general (but serviceable)
description of the perpetrators ("teenagers"), indicates that the
event is in progress, and, finally, specifies the trouble.

Reports and descriptions appear to formulate troubles which C
can fairly succinctly characterize. *Narratives* are more extended,
chronologically organized descriptions or accounts leading up to a
characterization of a possible trouble:

(25) [MCE:20:15:207]
```
1   CT:        Mid City police an' fire
2   C:         Hi um (.) I'm uh (.) I work at thuh University
3              Hospital and I was riding my bike home
4              tanight from (.) work-
5   CT:        Mm
6   C:         bout (.) ten minutes ago, ˙hh as I was riding
7              past Mercy Hospital (.) which is uh few blocks
8              from there ˙hh ( ) um ( ) I think uh couple vans
9              full uh kids pulled up (.) an started um (.)
10             they went down thuh trail an(h)d are beating up
```

11   people down there I'm not sure (.) but it
12   sounded like (something) ˙hh

After his acknowledgment, C starts and aborts a component "I'm
uh" (possibly the beginning of a locational formulation, *I'm at* . . .
and initiates a narrative which furnishes an account of how he came
to observe a possible trouble. It appears that narratives are
employed when the event is impending or in someway ambiguous;
that is, it is something that has not yet transpired but may be about
to, or if it is in progress or has occurred, its features are such that C
cannot (or chooses not to) say, in so many words, just what has
happened or is about to happen. Notice that C's narrative in fragment (25) provides "in passing" for the mundane pathway that he
took to the encounter: he was on his way home from work (lines 2–
4) following (presumably) his usual route (lines 6–8) when he
observed/heard signs of a possible trouble (lines 10–11) which is
marked for uncertainty (lines 11–12) – "I'm *not sure* but it
sounded like (something) .hh" (Sacks 1984b; Jefferson 1986b). In
the course of providing this account he furnishes a context within
which both the features of the event and the grounds for claiming
knowledge of them (the practical epistemology of their discovery)
are provided (see M. Whalen and Zimmerman 1990).[27]

The narrative format appears to furnish Cs with the resources to
pursue the mobilization of response to a possibly ambiguous
problem, and to package their report in a way that exhibits their
status as ordinary, disinterested, reasonable witnesses (see Bergmann 1987). Cs' descriptions can thus not only involve succinct
reference to events ("vandalism") but more extended narrative
treatments which frame an event and its noticing so that the trouble
is seen to have imposed itself on someone otherwise minding their
own business.[28] Even the usually parsimonious report frame can be
used to introduce what turns out to be a more extended characterization of an ambiguous but potentially troublesome occurrence:

(26) [MCE:21:28:42]
1   C: I'd like tu:h report (.) something weird that
2   happened abou:t (.) uh five minutes ago? In
3   front of our apartment building?
4   CT: Yeah
5   C: On seven thirteen Tenth Avenue Southeast?
6   CT: [keyboard] Mnhm

```
7   C:        We were just um sittin' in thuh room an we
8             heard this clanking ya know like someone wuz
9             pullin' something behind their ca:r an we
10            looked out thuh window...
```

Thus, although a report frame is used, reference to the event in line 1 ("something weird") is preceded by a very brief pause, suggesting that some issue may attend the naming of the event. The characterization then selected ("something weird") assesses rather than names the problem, projecting a more extensive narrative treatment (see section 6 below) in which the problem is described rather than simply labeled. Notice here as well C's care to display the mundaneity of the circumstances under which the event became known: "We were just um sittin' in thuh room an we heard ..." (line 7).

As is evident from the above, narrative accounts of some course of action are also used to detail the sequence of activities leading up to the discovery or witnessing of some event. Narratives appear particularly useful for exhibiting that the possibly troublesome nature of some event or activity was encountered in the course of pursuing very routine, ordinary activities. In the following, C provides an exposition of how she came to discover her front door open, and how the open door came to be suspicious:

```
(27) [MCE:17-19:96]
1    C:       ˙hh Yeah hi, uh this is Mary Cooper
2             ˙hh um: my sister an I left our house earlier
3             tonight (.) tt and we were certain we locked
4             thuh doors and ˙hh when we came back
5             ˙hh oh: about uh half hour ago oh twenty
6             minutes=ago ˙hh we noticed thuh front door was
7             open hhh an so we jus didn' feel like uh
8             checkin' aroun: so I thought we'd call you=
9    CT:      =Okay give me yur address
```

The relevant sequence of actions here was leaving the house and locking the doors (lines 2–4) and returning after a period of time to find the door open (lines 4–7). Notice that C does not label the event as a burglary. Nor does CT intervene at the point where C's narrative arrives at the open door, which is followed by an exhalation that seems to signal completion.

Burglary is a crime that is most often discovered after the fact, as it is by design usually committed when the victim is not home. C's account nicely (if implicitly) depicts the circumstances of a "normal burglary" (see Sudnow 1965) but it could portray other scenarios as well, for example the door was not locked and blew open, etc. C's subsequently expressed reluctance to enter the house suggests her suspicion that burglary (or some other sinister act) accounts for the open door, and it is at that point CT acknowledges the account ("Okay") and inquires about the address.

Cs thus employ a range of first-turn[29] formats which CTs must manage; that is, decide whether to intervene ("What's the problem?"), to issue continuers and monitor Cs' developing turn for information relevant to the dispatch package. The design of CTs' opening turn at Mid-City and Central County provides Cs with the opportunity to produce first turns that may not directly state or report an "emergency"; for example requests, that, while proposing a need for assistance, may not specify the nature of the problem or its location. This notion is examined in the next section dealing with CTs' first turn at Lane County.

4.4 Moving the interrogative series forward

CTs at Lane County employ an opening turn format that is designed to determine the nature of the emergency as early as possible in the call:

(28) [LC:EMS:2]
```
1   CT:      Nine one one what is yur emergency?
2            (.3)
3   C:       It's my brother he had a bomb an' it blew up
4            in=h=hand=hh ˙hh h ⌈h
5   CT:                    Wh⌊at's⌋ the a:ddre:ss?=
6   C:       =Five two nine Cherokee
7            (.3)
8   CT:      Five. two. nine. Cher(odie)?=
9   C:       =Yeah=hhh=
```

(29) [LC:EMS:5]
```
1   CT:      Nine one one what is yur emer⌈gency?⌉
2   C:                                    ⌊.hhh ⌋ OH MY
3            GO:D I JUST GOT HOME AND MY WIFE SHOT
4            HERSELF ˙hhh (     ) NINE FORTY TWO EAST (GREEN)
5            RO:W
6            (.)
```

```
7    CT:        Ni:ne forty three (.) East Green?
8               (.)
9    C:         OH MY GOD YES
10              (.)
11   CT:        Okay is she conscious?=
12   C:         (UH) NO SHE'S DEAD I (  ) I JUS GOT HOME
13              PLEASE HURRY
14              (.)
15   CT:        ˙hh Okay we're gettin' help o:n the wa::y=
```

(30) [LC:EMS:6]
```
1    CT:        ┌Nine one one what is yur emergency=
2    ?:        └(            (.)     )=
3    C:         =Uh yeah we have a little boy who can't breathe
4               at sixty nine hundred Marvin Lane
5               (.2)
6    ?:         (Hold'em)
7               (.3)
8    CT:        Sixty nine hun: ┌dred Marvin Lane?┐ =
9    ?:                         └(      dammit)  ┘ =
10   C:         =Yes, Burleigh City
```

In Lane County, CTs' first turn contains two components: categorical identification (9–1–1) and the query *What is your emergency?* Such a question explicitly treats the placement of the call as a request for assistance (pre-beginning) and, by design, initiates the interrogative series *prior* to C's first opportunity to speak (but see below). Lane County's opening turn thus contrasts with Mid-City/ Central County by projecting a *specific* first action for C, namely, an answer, the content of which should be hearable as a report or description of some type of emergency. In addition, requesting an account of the C's "emergency" also explicitly frames the nature of the business appropriate to a call to 9–1–1 (which may allow early screening of nonemergency requests[30]).

In the Lane County calls reproduced above, Cs appear to relate their emergency quickly rather than, for example, using their opening turn to request a particular response, such as *Send the police* (but see below). Such "efficiency" in the opening of the call is undoubtedly one of the policy objectives behind the design of this opening. However, while Cs to Lane County do produce first turns that provide descriptions of their emergency, they do not always do so as the very first component of their turn:

(31) [LC:EMS:1]
```
 1   C:     GO::D                          [Exclamation]
 2          MY WIFE JUST SHOT HERSELF      [Description]
 3          (.3)
 4          TWENTY TWO SIXTY (GRANT)       [Address]
 5          AVENUE
 6          HURRY U:::::P                  [Urgency Marker]
 7   CT:    What happened?
```

(32) [LC:EMS:5]
```
 1   C:     hhh* OH MY GO:D                [Exclamation]
 2          I JUST GOT HOME                [Stance]
 3          AND MY WIFE SHOT
 4          HERSELF ˙hhh                   [Description]
 5          (      ) NINE FORTY THREE
 6          EAST (GREEN) RO:W              [Address]
```

(33) [LC:EMS:6]
```
 1   C:     =Uh yeah                       [Acknowledgement]
 2          we have a little boy           [On-Behalf-Of]
 3          who can't breathe              [Description]
 4          at sixty nine hundred
 5          Marvin Lane                    [Address]
```

(34) [LC:SSI:1]
```
 1   CT:    911 ⌐what's your
 2   C:         ⌊YES. I NEED�follow A         [Acknowledgement]
 3          AMBULANCE                      [Request]
 4   CT:    What is the problem ma'am      [Problem Query]
 5   C:     I DO:N'T KNOW::, MY SISTER:
 6          I DON'T KNOW WHAT'S WRONG WITH HER.
 7          ˙hh I'M AT THE HORSE SHOE INN hh ˙hh hh
 8          ˙hh I DON'T KNOW THE ADDRESS hh ˙hh OH: MY:
 9          GO::D hh ˙hh PLE::ASE HU:RRY
```

In fragment (31) C's turn contains a prefatory exclamation,[31] a description of the emergency, as well as an address and an urgency marker.[32] C in (32) also employs a prefatory exclamation, an account of his discovery of the problem (stance), the relational identity of the victim, and then a description of the event followed by an address. In (33), C employs an acknowledgment, a statement marking the call as "on behalf of" a third party, and then a statement of the problem followed by an address. And in (34) C begins her turn immediately after CT produces the identifying 9–1–1,

overlapping the beginning of the problem query with an acknowledgment and a request.

Although Lane County's opening is designed to move directly to
an account of the C's emergency, this outcome, however frequent,
is thus not assured. It is important to stress that the argument here
is not that Lane County's opening "fails" to achieve its purpose,
but rather (a) the opening design may be yet another contingency
for C and (b) C's treatment of the opening may be yet another
contingency for CT. For example, in fragment (34) C begins her
turn at virtually the earliest recognition point in the categorical self-
identification and requests an ambulance rather than stating the
problem. C's precisely placed initiation is merely one feature of a
call exhibiting other features of an urgent request for help.

In the following call C aborts her description of the problem in
favor of a request for help:

(35) [LC:EMS:3]
```
 1   CT:        Nine one one what is yur emergency?
 2              (.2)
 3   C:         (   cuz) my husband has ˙hh has p- has ha-˙hh
 4              hh ( ) I-I-I need some ˙hh hhh I need someone at
 5              fifteen twenty four Old Ranch Road ˙hh //(  )-
 6   CT:        What's the name of the road?
 7              (.2)
 8   C:         ˙hh I need someone at sixtee:n ˙hh thirty fou:r
 9              ˙hh Old Ranch Roa:d˙hh lot one three fi:ve,
10              it's in (Maple) wood townshipit's u:p from>up
11              from< Sargent ┌York's           ┐
12   CT:                      └What's t┘he problem there
13              (.1)
14   C:         ˙hh My husband has ˙hh consumed too much
15              alcohol
```

It is worth noting, first, that C produces an utterance (lines 3–4)
which appears to teeter on the verge of reporting that her husband
has passed out ("my husband has .hh has p- has ha- .hh hh"). This
formulation is aborted and a new utterance requesting help (and
providing an address) is produced (lines 4–5). C's statement of her
problem (eventually elicited by CT's second problem query) is
further deferred by CT's repair initiation (lines 6) which deals with
his problem in hearing a part of the address given by C (line 5).
Although speculative at this point, it appears that C's abandonment
of her initial formulation may be directly related to the problem

query in CT's first turn. The issue that query may have posed for C is: is passing out drunk an emergency?

Thus, asking a question, while it projects an answer as the next action, does not guarantee that the very next action will be an answer, there being procedures available to preface or otherwise prepare the ground for an eventual rather than immediate answer. And, as the preceding call suggests, requests for help can reemerge in a slot prepared for a statement of the problem for which help is sought. It appears to be the case, then, that whatever the intended constraints of a given call-taking format, Cs' manner of conveying information, marking urgency, and pressing their pleas for assistance may remain as contingencies to be managed on a turn-by-turn basis.

5 Repair and verification

CTs regularly engage in extensive interrogation and clarification through insertion and repair sequences. For example, in a call too lengthy (57 turns) to reproduce here, the CT's participation (apart from her opening identification, response, and closing) consists of ten questions eliciting information, seven other-repair initiations, and six verifications of C's responses (see below).[33] Such actions by CT occasion responses from C, while C may herself initiate repair requiring a response by CT.[34]

CTs are alert for what C *fails* to say (or fails to say clearly or completely). CTs' other-initiated repairs are directed to some trouble in the hearing or understanding of C's prior utterance, or to some defect in the utterance itself as in the following call, in which C leaves out a crucial element of the address:

```
(36) [MCE:21:17:23]
  1  CT:      Mid-City emergency
  2  C:       ·hh Yeah ·hh Unh wanna make uh call for uh
  3           hit='n=run?
  4  CT:      Where is it?
  5  C:       Forty thirty five College hh ·hh
  6  CT:      College what.
  7  C:       °North eas ·hh Northeast
```

Even when C may project an extended turn, for example by beginning with their address[35] (see below), the organization of repair prompts contiguous, that is next-turn, repair initiation:

(37) [MCE:17:9:111]

1	CT:	Mid-City police an FI:re
2	C:	Yes. Um: I'm um at fifty three seventy two
3		Marvin
4	CT:	Fifty three seventy two Marvin what

C's "informing" the CT of troubles and their location may occasion *verification* of this information (Mellinger and Zimmerman 1987).[36] Verification occurs in the same "repair initiation opportunity space" (Schegloff, Jefferson, and Sacks 1977) as other-initiated repair, that is in the next turn following some informing or other response by C.[37] Verification takes the form of a repetition of C's previous turn, or some portion of it, and thus displays the information that CT has received from C. Verification is often addressed to locational information:[38]

(38) [MCE:21:35:53]

1	C:	Okay (.) There seems tuh be some sortuv
2		argu:ment or potential fi:ght uh about tuh
3		happen in thee alley, ˙hh connecting Forty: ˙hh
4		Sixth and Forty Seventh Street between Tenth
5		and Eleventh Avenue South in Mid-City ˙hh
6	CT:	Okay that's between in thee alley between Forty
7		Sixth and Forty Seventh Street?
8	C:	Mnhm
9	CT:	Between Tenth and Eleventh Avenue=
10	C:	=Right

While verification and repair both occur in the same sequential position, verification differs from repair in that it is not offered as a candidate *correction* of C's prior turn or some element of it. Instead, it exhibits CT's *receipt* of C's informing which is displayed for inspection and possible correction. In alternative terms, verification involves producing a subsequent turn that repeats all or part of a prior turn so that the prior speaker (who possesses the requisite knowledge) is positioned to acknowledge (or repair) the verification in the third turn.

Another difference between verification and repair is that while repair is closely positioned relative to the trouble-source turn (Schegloff, Jefferson, and Sacks 1977), verification can occur (or reoccur) as a "closing issue," as in the following calls, in which CT's verification[39] is placed in virtually the last location in which it could occur (at the very last moment, so to speak):

(39) [MCE:21:7:8]
```
1   C:          This is thuh Kit Kat Club on eighty one
2               nineteen Pine?
3   CT:         Mmhm
4   C:          'hh and thuh laundrymat (.) Jim's laundrymat...
    .
    .           [13 turns omitted]
    .
5   CT:         'hh Okay you're eighty one nineteen Pine Avenue
6               North arn't=ch=
7   C:          =That's correct=
8   CT:         =O:kay we'll get somebody=there
9   C:          O:kay? Thank you=
10  CT:         =Mnhn bye.
```

(40) [MCE:21:15:20]
```
1   C:          Uh: yeah hi: This is uh: hh thuh City Pub
2   CT:         Mmhm
3   C:          an: 'hh I'm thuh manager here tanight
4   CT:         Mmhm
5   C:          an: 'hh there's not re:ally any trouble going
6               on...
    .
    .           [4 turns omitted]
    .
7   C:          ...I'm just afraid if they don't go I WILL have
8               trouble with them?=
9   CT:         =City Pub=
10  C:          =Right=
11  CT:         =O:kay ma'am=
12  C:          =Thankyou=
13  CT:         =Mnhm bye
```

The preceding calls permit the conjecture that verification (either initial or repeated) by CT at some turns distant from the first mention of an item of information by C has closing implications, that is, that it is prefatory to closing. This may arise from the fact that issues such as location and the nature of the problem tend to be dealt with as a package; that is, once initiated, they will be pursued until closure can be achieved. The parties to the call may orient to the resumption of a "topic" as something placed just prior to closing. Moreover, verification of locational information implicates a type of "arrangement", for the near future (in the present case, for contacting C or for dealing with a problem) which, even if made early in a telephone call, can recur as a feature of closings (see Schegloff and Sacks 1973; Button 1987a).

It is worth observing in this context that exact locational information is critical for emergency dispatching. "Small" errors in hearing or entering an address (e.g., transposing digits) or acting on an incorrect directional tag for an address could result in consequential increases in response time. Lane County, for example, covers an area with a large urban center and many small towns and rural districts. Consequently, the exact address or location has to be entered into the CAD to determine which local agency should respond. Verification of address or location is thus an important element of CT's task, perhaps more so than verification of the details of the problem, since with a correct address police or other emergency personnel can be dispatched to the scene to determine the exact nature of the emergency.[40]

CTs thus engage in repair and verification at those points where Cs' informings are in some way problematic or where CTs' receipt of them requires confirmation. Where informings are incomplete, CTs initiate questioning to elicit the required information (the interrogative series). And, as intimated earlier, for those calls in which Cs package the essential information in an extended opening turn which pose no problems of hearing or understanding, CTs may say little other than to provide continuers. C's "choice" of turn design as well as the talk *and* listening done by the CT is critical for information collection, processing, and data entry. Thus, the shape of particular calls emerges from the interactional deployment of different devices and strategies for packaging, eliciting, and processing information.

6 The design of extended tellings

While it may appear a simple matter for Cs to state a problem plainly, such a supposition assumes that it does not matter who is speaking to whom (categorically), nor how a particular event or situation is to be characterized such that it conveys C's understanding and assessment of the trouble in a way that CT can find it to be reasonable grounds for dispatching assistance.[41] Turn design for C is very much a matter of recipient design: how to package the trouble in a fashion that a particular sort of official recipient will understand and act on it (e.g. fragment [35], above). This section explores how the design of Cs' first turn intersects with CTs' concern to construct a dispatch package quickly.

Earlier, the rather minimal turn components deployed in C's first turn were reviewed: requests, reports, descriptions, and narratives which, with the exception of the last, may occasion CTs' intervention through initiation of the interrogative series directed to obtaining information on (or elaboration of) the problem or location. This section will also consider how C and CT cooperate to produce methodically an extended turn by C which provides most or all of the information CT needs to construct the dispatch package.

6.1 Caller self-identification

As suggested earlier, while many Cs remain anonymous, merely acknowledging the appropriateness of the identity alignment achieved in the call opening, some self-identify early in their first turn:

(41) [MCE:22:3a:136]
```
1   C:      Yes (.) This is Charlene Skolnick (.) I live at
2           eight four five one Xenon Avenue South 'hh I'm
3           sorry I'm uh little shaken, there's been an
4           accident (.) uh car is overturned across thuh
5           street.
```

(42) [MCE:17:12:118]
```
    C:      Yeah hh uh this is Beryl McKenna an' I'm at
            thuh Sherman Dell 'hh of uh highway eleven?
```

(43) [MCE:22:4:138]
```
    C:      Hello my name is Barbara Allen, I live at fifty
            sixth and an' Minerva South?
```

(44) [CDV3-B:9:20]
```
    C:      'hh Yes um:: (.) My name's Lavina Mello:n and
            um: hah- we're in Lake Minerva?
```

While names can be recognitionals (Sacks and Schegloff 1979), the offering of a name by Cs in fragments (41)–(44) is produced as an identification (C's name is not try-marked, for example). Self-identification may reflect the supposition of some Cs that it is necessary to identify oneself when speaking to the authorities. Caller self-identification may also be a cooperative gesture: the provision, up front, of an item of information that a C may believe CT to require. While it may turn out that the provision of a name has no relevance to further activities in connection with the call (e.g. C will not be contacted as a witness, or asked to sign a complaint,[42] etc.), the important point is that, as a feature of C's first turn, self-identification is hearable as a possibly prefatory element of the yet to be developed account of the call's business.

Note, however, that since C's name may at the outset not be relevant for the business at hand, its occurrence early in C's first turn may well be seen by CTs as a desultory utterance *delaying* arrival at pertinent matters rather than, strictly speaking, as prefatory to them (J. Whalen, personal communication). Yet there is little evidence to suggest that CTs are willing to intervene on the occurrence of early self-identification by C. Such early self-identification appears to achieve an extension of C's first turn even if participants entertain different relevances for that activity (see Jefferson and Lee [1981: 411–17] for a discussion of ambulance dispatching where divergence between caller and dispatcher relevances occasion certain difficulties in the call).[43]

Moreover, as is evident in these fragments, Cs also give their address or other locational information following the provision of their name.[44] Viewed together, the [name + address] format provides two possible items of information (even though, as noted above, there is a possible divergence between C and CT over the presumed relevance of name). By informing CT of who they are and where they are, Cs project further informings, allowing them to develop descriptions or narratives through which a problem is depicted. That is, self-identification followed by an address projects as a next item some statement of the problem occasioning the call. Such a statement itself may contain materials preliminary to specifying the problem as discussed earlier in connection with the narrative formatting of informings.

On occasion Cs open their turn with locational information. As indicated above, an address is one of the elements of the dispatch package; and when offered in C's first turn, it presents CT with information to enter or record, which is done while C continues her turn. That CTs closely attend to early offers of location even in the absence of information on the nature of the trouble is evident in the following call in which CT initiates repair of an incomplete address:

(45) [MCE:17:9:111]
```
1   CT:        Mid-City police and FI:re
2   C:         Yes. Um: I'm at fifty three twenty seven
3              Nelson
4   CT:        Fifty three twenty seven Nelson what
```

In addition to furnishing needed information for a response to the call, placement of an address as a lead or early element of C's first turn also appears to have a turn-design aspect, as is suggested in the following calls:

(46) [MCE:17:4:65]
```
1   C:         Yeah uh I live at thirty seven (.) fifty five
2              (.) Knollridge? South? and uh there's uh car
3              sittin' across thuh street from thuh house an
4              I can't tell from here fro'where I'm at ˙hh
5              kinduh hard- thuh see I don' know: it's kinduh
6              s:picious? Its sitting with its headlights on
7              an: everythin'...
```

(47) [MCE:17:9:111]
```
1   CT:        Mid-City police and FI:re
2   C:         Yes. Um: I'm at fifty three twenty seven
3              Nelson
4   CT:        Fifty three twenty seven Nelson what
5   C:         North
6   CT:        Yeah:
7   C:         An:d uh there's been uh ˙hh hh uh: uh young
8              fella,  he's been walking up an down thee alley
9              ˙hh (.) We had uh little trouble here
```

(48) [MCE:20:2:171]
```
1   C:         Yhes I'd like to um: I'm at twunty three
2              nineteen Eighth Avenue Nor:th
3   CT:        Hmhm
4   C:         Uh there's  uh (.) Oh I think it's
5              uh (.) white jeep ˙hh jeepster that pulled up
6              in front.  An there's about five Negro guys
7              that got out, I heard=um talking=about (.)
8              going (.) to thee next apartment uh fur uh
9              fight (.) an I jus am now going down tuh check
10             it out I'm up here (.) in my
11             apartment
```

Locational information appears to preface descriptions or narratives which depict events that are noticeable or troublesome in relation to C's location. The proximity of the event to C's residence is, of course, a basic warrant for calling in the incident. The locational terms of problem narratives, for example *across the street, walking up and down thee alley, pulled up in front, going to thee next apartment uh fur uh fight,* become anchored by specifying their coordinates via an address grid, landmark, or an intersection.

That Cs may be sensitive to the import of the placement of their address is suggested in the following fragment in which C self-interrupts what appears to be the beginning of a report format and replaces it with his address:

(49) [MCE:20:2:171]

1	C:	Yhes I'd like to um: I'm at twunty three
2		nineteen Eighth Avenue Nor:th
3	CT:	Hmhm
4	C:	Uh there's uh (.) Oh I think it's uh (.) <u>white</u>
5		<u>jeep</u> ·hh jeepster that pulled up in front.

Moreover, as will be evident in the following discussion of categorical self-identification, Cs are also attentive to the distinction between where they are and where the problem is, which is reflected in the placement of locational information in relation to other elements of their turn.

6.2 Categorical self-identification

Categorical self-identification (e.g. "This is the Kit Cat Club"; "This is the Riverdale Police") places the call on a particular footing ("my organization to your organization"), establishing a particular kind of warrant for Cs' knowledge of – and interest in – the trouble they report (M. Whalen and Zimmerman 1990). Like the use of personal names discussed above, when categorical self-identification occurs in C's first turn, it occurs either in turn-initial position, or as the second component following the acknowledgment token:

(50) [MCE:21:15:20]

1	C:	Uh: yeah hi: This is uh: hh thuh City Pub
2	CT:	Mmhm

```
3   C:          an: 'hh I'm thuh manager here tanight
4   CT:         Mmhm
5   C:          an: 'hh there's not re:ally any trouble going
6               on=except that I've asked=uh few people tuh
7               leave ( . )   They arn't ( . ) drunk they're just
8               belligerent
```

(51) [LC]
```
1   CT:         Nine one one what is your emergency?
2   C:          This is Merchant's Bank. We've had a customer
3               that was just knocked to the ground and robbed
4               outside of our facility.
```

(52) [LC]
```
1   CT:         Nine one one what is your emergency?
2   C:          Ah:: This is Trudy from Western States Bank (.)
3               We've just been robbed.
```

In fragment (50) C goes on to complain of belligerent customers whom she fears will make trouble for her. She has doubly identified herself, first by the [*This is* + name of organization] format (line 1) and second, by her position as "manager" (line 3). The former projects a report of some trouble within the precincts of the organization by someone speaking on behalf of that organization; the latter component specifically identifies C as one who is responsible for the orderly conduct of business in that establishment (and, not incidentally, one who is likely to have made such reports before). Thus, the categorical identification is prefatory to, and informative for, the nature of the reported trouble.

Fragments (51) and (52) reveal that categorical self-identification retains its early positioning in C's opening turn even when CT's first turn directly asks for the nature of the emergency. Moreover, if some other component is underway in C's opening turn, C will likely self-interrupt to produce the identification as an appropriately positioned prefatory move (line 1 in both [53] and [54]):

(53) [MCE:21:20:27]
```
    C:              'hh Hi we gotuh:  This is security at thuh
                    bus depot?=Greyhound bus depot?
```

(54) [MCE:17:1:98]
```
    C:              Yeah Thirty five six uh This is North Side.
                    Thirty five sixteen (.) Harvard 'hh There's
                    uh...
```

Thus, Cs exhibit an orientation to the early placement of self-identification in the turn by self-interrupting and reordering other components with respect to such identification. Such placement exhibits C's claim that the identity thus advanced is relevant to the subsequent course of the call.

When Cs categorically self-identify, CTs may say very little beyond issuing continuers, and allow the C to provide information with minimum intervention, as in the following call:

```
(55) [MCE 21:20:27]
  1   CT:        'hh Mid City emergency
  2   C:         'hh t Hi we gotuh: This is security at thuh
  3              bus depot?=Greyhound bus depot?=
  4   CT:        =Yes °Sir=
  5   C:         =An' we gotuh guy down here that's uh: (   )
  6              oh:ver intoxicated. 'hh He's jus he's passed
  7              out (.) and uh we'd tuh have 'im taken outuh
  8              here=
  9   CT:        =Okay=
 10   C:         =if we can.
 11   C:         hh Ahright we 'll see ya in a few minutes?=
 12   CT:        =O:kay
 13   C:         O:kay ⌈sounds good⌉Bye.
 14   CT:               ⌊Bye       ⌋
```

Note first that C begins the turn with the expression "We gotuh:" (line 2) which, for placement considerations mentioned just above, is aborted to produce a categorical self-identification "This is security at thuh bus depot" in lines 2–3. "We gotuh" is a form of the proprietary *We have* format which is routinely employed by Cs who speak in some special organizational capacity, for example as professionals, managers, public-safety personnel, etc. (Sacks 1992 [1967]). Note also that "at thuh bus depot" (lines 2–3) is also reformulated to the more specific, try-marked "Greyhound bus depot?" (line 3), which completes C's categorical self-identification. After acknowledgment from CT, C then reissues the *We have* format ("we gotuh" – line 5) which specifies the business at hand (a drunk) and proposes a course of action in lines 7–8 ("have 'im taken outuh here") to which CT assents in line 9. In line 11 C next proposes a prompt police response ("we'll see ya in a few minutes?") which also gains CT's assent (line 12). The call then rapidly closes. CT's very brief turns, apart from the opening identification, have consisted essentially in acknowledgments and assents to C's identification, description of trouble, and proposed solution. This clearly has markings of a very routine transaction between parties who, acting in mutually recognized capacities, have practiced ways of quickly disposing of familiar problems. In the following call from Mid-City General Hospital, C categorically self-identifies, describes the problem, and provides the address, which CT acknowledges as she begins to enter the information into the computer. CT's "thank you" following C's continuation of locational information is closing-implicative and the call is terminated at the end of the next turn.

```
(56) [MCE:21:14:19]
  1   CT:        Emergency
  2   C:         Hi ˙hh General, there's been an overdose. (.)
  3              Twenty three twenty three ˙hh
  4              I ⌈ daho: hh          ⌉upstairs apartment
  5   CT:          ⌊ (keyboard) O:kay ⌋
  6   C:         num:ber two:  .hh
  7   CT:        Thank you=
  8   C:         =Umhm bye
```

Such practiced – and laconic – dealings with routine events can also be seen in the following call between CT and an ambulance dispatcher over a direct line:

```
(57) [MCE:21:4b:5]
  1   A:         Amblunce
  2   CT:        ˙hh Yes sir. Inside the bookstore: on Boston
  3              and River=thuh adult bookstore? ˙hh We have an
  4              unconscious diabetic.
  5   A:         Unconscious disbetic inside thuh bookstore.
  6   CT:        Yes sir.
  7   A:         Alright.
  8   CT:        Thank you:
```

Direct lines connecting public-safety organizations, including other police jurisdictions and medical services such as private ambulance companies, are common in emergency dispatching operations. Use of the direct line in itself can be categorically identifying, allowing parties to the call to proceed directly to their business. The point to be emphasized here is that establishing a special capacity as entitled reporter and recipient, respectively, of particular types of information affords a basis for quickly accomplishing the transaction.

Like personal identification, categorical self-identification can also be followed by locational information:

(58) [MCE:21:7:8]
```
1   C:       ˙hh This is thuh Kit Kat Club on eighty one
2            nineteen Pine?
3   CT:      Mnhm
4   C:       ˙hh and thuh laundrymat (.) Jim's laundrymat?
5   CT:      Mnhm
6   C:       It's down thuh street here=a=bit...
```

(59) [MCE:17:14:87]
```
1   C:       Yes this is thee uh Quick Gas station on thirty
2            second and uh: Mason Avenue South?
3   CT:      Mnhm
4   C:       I gotuh woman here claiming that uh:...
```

(60) [MCE:21:6:7]
```
1   C:       Uh: this is uh: da g ˙h Knights of Columbus
2            Hall: at tuh nine twunty three west Haverford?
3            north=
4   CT:      =Umhm [keyboard]
5   C:       ˙hh Uh: we had some uh women's purses uh:
6            stolen?
```

(61) [MCE 21:20:27]
```
1   CT:      ˙hh Mid City emergency
2   C:       ˙hh t Hi we gotuh: This is security at thuh
3            bus depot?=Greyhound bus depot?=
4   CT:      =Yes °Sir=
5   C:       =An' we gotuh guy down here that's uh: (   )
6            oh:ver intoxicated. ˙hh He's jus he's passed
7            out
```

The format [self-identification + address + problem], like [name + address + problem], links C's location with the trouble about to be characterized, projecting that location or one defined in relation to it ("It's down the street here=a=bit ...") as the place to which assistance is to be sent. When the location of the problem is different from the one from which the call was placed, self-identification is separated from subsequent locational information by a statement of the problem, as in the following fragments:

(62) [MCE:22:5:139]
```
 1  C:          'hh Ye:s Tee Dee A calling 'hh hh I have uh
 2              silent alar:m (.) at three west River Street
 3  CT:         Mnhm
```

(63) [MCE:22:17:155]
```
 1  C:          Ye:s M T B calling?
 2  CT:         Umhm
 3  C:          Uh: are you aware of uh motorcycle accident on
 4              Summit Boulevard and Pier:ce Avenue? south
```

(64) [MCE:17:6a:106]
```
 1  C:          Fourth Precinct calling?
 2  CT:         Mnhm
 3  C:          We have un accident on uh Lighthouse an Central
 4              with injuries?
```

Thus, if an organization is calling to report the existence of a problem at a different location (as in TDA's report of a silent alarm), the components of the opening turn are ordered as [self-identification + problem + location].

The foregoing suggests that Cs' opening turn can exhibit an internal organization that permits CTs to monitor their development with respect to the provision of information relevant to assembling the dispatch package. Cs employing the report, description, or request format routinely occasion CTs' initiation of the interrogative series. However, the narrative format, particularly when C self-identifies and provides an address, signals that an organized informing is in process, one that CT can attend, glean (and enter) information, and, if needed, intervene to repair a problematic address or to initiate inquiry.

6.3 Divergent concerns: a postscript

The emphasis on the coordinated achievement of emergency calls should not be taken to suggest that the concerns (see Mandelbaum and Pomerantz 1991) of Cs and CTs are aligned at each point in the call. Earlier, this chapter examined calls in which Cs are so distraught that their pleas for immediate response to their problem interfere with CTs' attempt to assemble a dispatch package. J. Whalen, Zimmerman, and Whalen (1988) have observed that the deployment of the interrogative series involves a turn-positional (and real-time) delay in response to Cs' requests for help. The questions asked by CTs are intendedly relevant to mobilizing an appropriate response to the emergency, but may not be understood as such by anxious Cs. J. Whalen (1990: 9) points out that

For practitioners (call-takers and dispatchers), the intended effect of the standard ordering of work tasks (along with organizational procedures and policies ...) is to make the handling of calls as routine as possible, and in this way process "emergencies" as routine, expected, and even predictable events in practitioners' work lives. For nonpractitioners like citizen callers, however, "emergencies" are visibly experienced — that is to say, their "experiencing" of their circumstances is displayed in their talk — as anything but routine events. For them, it is overwhelmingly the case ... that the event is not expected, is hardly a "nothing special about it, just another one of those" occasions.

The task of practitioners like the CT is to transform what is from C's point of view (as exhibited in their speech and vocal quality) an urgent, threatening, deeply felt "right now, this moment, life-changing" event into a *routine* call, the features of which become standardized through the situated interactional process by which the organization puts in a day's work.

The divergence of concerns between Cs and CTs, is perhaps the master contingency for both parties, for this divergence poses potential obstacles to (for the parties) the timely and appropriate completion of the call: its accomplishment as an accountable sequence of actions making up both a unit of organizational activity and an efficacious act by an individual seeking help.

Not all divergencies portend difficulties in the interaction. It has already been observed that in the case of self-identification early in C's first turn, C and CT may have different orientations towards the relevance of identification, although in this instance there are no notable consequences other than the extension of C's turn (which extension serves as an opportunity for Cs to produce their troubles telling rather than to have it elicited piecemeal by CT's interrogation).

Divergent concerns can, however, be the source of marked difficulties in the course of a call. J. Whalen, Zimmerman, and Whalen (1988) describe a call in which the divergence between C and CT is of sufficient interactional seriousness that a dispute is touched off which leads to a serious delay in the dispatch of assistance. For the most part, however, it appears that a divergence of relevances between C and CT, while surfacing as issues in the course of a call, are amenable to practices which realign the participants so that the call can proceed, for example, by initiation of repair by C or CT and the issuance of directives by CT aimed at realigning C. Moreover, the interrogative series is to some extent a resource through which the requirements "driving" CTs' queries become visible to Cs; that is, the assembly of a call as a sequence of talk-in-interaction is, at least to some extent, a self-explicating enterprise (Pollner 1979; cf. J. Whalen, Zimmerman, and Whalen 1988; J. Whalen 1990).

7 Conclusion

A good deal of the work done on "institutional talk" has focused on modifications of the turn-taking system for ordinary conversation that organize talk *cum* action in classrooms, courtrooms, news interviews, employment interviews, clinical interrogations, mediation sessions, paramedic–base-station communications, business meetings, and congressional hearings (Atkinson and Drew 1979; Mehan 1979; Greatbatch 1985, 1986a, 1986b, 1988; Button 1987b; Clayman 1987, 1988, 1989, 1991; Garcia 1991; Halkowsky 1990; Lloyd 1990; Mellinger 1990; Heritage and Greatbatch 1991; Boden forthcoming). Orientation to, and achievement of, the variously constrained parameters of turn taking constitute different speech-exchange systems which provide procedures by which participants' can "do" distinctive types of talking together that activate and make observable settings of institutional activity (see Heritage and Greatbatch 1991). That maintenance of a particular configuration of turn taking is critical for producing recognizable activities such as news interviews is dramatically evident when such constraints are breached or abandoned, as in the notorious Bush–Rather interview (Clayman and J. Whalen 1988/9; Schegloff 1988/9).

The configuration of speech-exchange systems is not the only resource for producing "institutional" talk. Talk oriented to institutional settings usually involves repetitive occasions that, within a constrained range of variation, exhibit similar structures to those proposed here for emergency calls. There is a "density" or concentration of repeatedly deployed particular conversational machinery (e.g. interrogative-insertion sequences in emergency and other service calls). In addition, certain sequences may not occur (or be reduced or specialized in form) in the environments they ordinarily inhabit in everyday talk[45] (see Heritage 1984a: 238–40; M. Whalen and Zimmerman 1987: 175–8; Heritage and Greatbatch 1991).

A central assumption here is that organizational settings reflexively shape and are shaped by the deployment of general conversational mechanisms adapted to manage the interactional contingencies of locally executed task activities (Heritage, 1984a: 280–90; Zimmerman and Boden 1991). That is, the implementation of organizational policies and objectives are unavoidably undertaken in actual, situated encounters between participants using the machinery of conversational organization to do the interactional work that the organization's aims require. In this way the organization gets *done*, and the characteristic patterns of activity associated with the organization are produced.

It is important to note here that while specific tasks or projects may mobilize interactional mechanisms, it is those mechanisms which make the pursuit of such projects observable, actionable, and accountable in the first instance. Further, deployment of such sequential machinery carries with it its own constraints: whatever the agendas in question, they will have to be worked out, turn by turn, within the sequential context initiated by use of that machinery (see especially J. Whalen, Zimmerman and Whalen 1988; J. Whalen 1990). Moreover, participant concerns (see note 1), whatever their source, enter the situation as local "objects" produced by one party for recognition and response by another. As such, they become local matters to be managed by the participants, that is, interactional contingencies to be dealt with interactionally.

Three points need emphasis in the face of these and other variations. First, the accomplished shape of a given call is not a mechanical reproduction of some ideal–typical structure; nor is it a consequence of following (however imperfectly) a script or protocol. This is not to say that protocols play no part in the management of emergency calls. As has been noted, there are protocols for the provision of pre-arrival instructions for medical emergencies (e.g. how to perform CPR) employed in dispatch organizations like

Lane County. Nevertheless, the use of a protocol would itself be a contingency to be dealt with in the course of an actual call, for example gaining the attention of a distraught C, adapting the protocol to circumstances at the scene, and securing compliance with instructions.

It is pertinent in this context to recall Schegloff's remarks on the orderliness of singular instances:

in a great many respects, social action done through talk is organized and orderly not, or not only, as a matter of rule or as a statistical regularity, but on a case by case, action by action, basis. Particular complements of participants on singular occasions of interaction proceed in, to them, orderly ways; or failing this, have ways of coping with the apparent lack of order which operate on a single case basis. Both past analytic work and continuing ordinary experience testify to the relevance of the single occasion as the locus of order.

(1987b: 102)

Thus, in examining a range of contingencies across calls and across organizations, it is possible to obtain a glimpse of how an institutional context of activity is constituted in particular, locally managed, interactionally achieved occasions of telephone talk.

The second point ties directly to the first: both organizational policy and call-specific contingencies can pose particular issues to be resolved in a call. While sequences outlined in table 13.1 in the introduction to this chapter are responsive to common and recurrent contingencies of emergency calls (achieving identification, aligning identities, requesting assistance, eliciting information, promising help, and closing), they by no means address all of the circumstantial issues that Cs and CTs confront. Hence, with respect to any given call, the sequences displayed in table 13.1 do not function as a template but are rather resources that may be modified, augmented, used repetitively or not at all because the contingencies to which these components are responsive are altered, unusual, recurrent, or absent. As was seen earlier, Cs are sometimes "hysterical", and plead for immediate assistance. Distraught Cs are often difficult to understand, occasioning next-turn repair initiation. Moreover, CTs may repeatedly attempt to reassure Cs by telling them that help is on its way, an utterance that ordinarily functions as a closing implicative response, and poses a further contingency, keeping distressed Cs on the line, which requires additional work by CT.

Finally, the actual shape of a given call is produced by co-participants' selection, modification, and concentration of elements of the
"primordial" machinery of ordinary conversation to work through
the contingencies of particular encounters. Moreover, the provenance of these sequential components is interactional rather than
institutional. As a consequence, recurrent features of these calls can
be initially described without reference to so-called "larger" contexts. This permits the question of the relationship of the interactional organization of the call to its institutional setting and function
to be posed without confounding the one with the other.[46]

Notes

1. Mandelbaum and Pomerantz (1991) provide a set of conceptual distinctions that ground inferences about participants' "purposes" or
   "intentions" in the organizational detail of their actual interactions.
   Their scheme (which, for reasons of space, cannot be spelled out here)
   is not so much a classification of participants' concerns as a means to
   insist on a tight linkage between the notions of purpose, intention,
   goal, or agenda and the details of actual interaction. In alternative
   terms, if such motivational notions (whether individual or organizational) are to be invoked as an element of an analysis, they must be
   shown to be exhibited in the detailed organization of interaction.
2. At Mid-City, the civilian personnel who answer the emergency lines
   are called *complaint takers* (CTs) as distinguished from *dispatchers*
   (Ds), the police officers who actually dispatch police units. At Lane
   County, those answering the 9–1–1 and other telephone lines are also
   called CTs, with other civilian personnel doing the actual dispatching.
   At Central County, personnel answering the phone also dispatch, and
   are referred to as Ds. To avoid terminological confusion, personnel
   answering calls from the public in each of these settings will be referred
   to simply as CTs. It is by no means clear that Cs are aware of these
   occupational designations and the functional distinctions they mark,
   for example that a D may be initiating a response while the CT is still
   speaking with the C.
3. The dispatch organization at Lane County, Oregon is responsible for
   the city of Eugene and half of the county, serving a population of
   approximately 250,000. The dispatch operation itself is referred to as
   Central Lane, but as one of the other organizations is identified by the
   pseudonym "Central County," the Oregon operation will be referred
   to as Lane County. The author wishes to extend his thanks and appreciation to the administration and staff of the Eugene Department of
   Public Safety for making this data available. Particular thanks are due

to J. Whalen for allowing the author to benefit from his call-taking expertise.

4. Discussion based on the Lane County data must be treated as provisional, as the analysis of calls from this organization has just begun.

5. Both C and C T must cope with call-processing requirements, although from different perspectives. In so doing, C and C T reflexively modify the circumstances of the call (see Heritage 1984a: 106–110), for the nature of the coping C and C T engage in becomes another contingency of the call.

6. It should be noted here that the work of CTs and Ds is relatively well documented. All incoming calls are tape-recorded, as are all radio dispatches, with tapes being held for a month or more against the contingency that a particular call could be needed as evidence or be the subject of a citizen complaint. The records generated by the calls, for example the incident cards at Central County and the computer dispatch records generated at Mid-City and Lane County are similarly preserved. The call for emergency service, apart from its outcome (see J. Whalen, Zimmerman, and Whalen 1988), is thus accountable in detail over its course. This study and others like it are beholden to the existence of such tapes and records (see J. Whalen 1990).

7. In the case of Central County, the data derives from a year-long observational study (conducted with J. and M. Whalen) supplemented by tape recordings and transcripts of actual calls. Information on, and calls from, Lane County have been provided by J. and M. Whalen.

8. Police units ("squads") in Mid-City were equipped with computer consoles. Dispatch was thus fully computerized, although radio communication furnished a fall-back. Ambulances are dispatched by an ambulance D who is contacted by the C T by telephone. No fire calls were present in the Mid-City corpus, and no information is available concerning how fire equipment is dispatched. Ds at Central County and Lane County dispatch all three services by radio.

9. The Central County dispatch operation was organized into three stations: fire, medic, and sheriff dispatch. CTs dispatched by radio those calls appropriate to the station they staffed; other types of calls were hand-carried to a C T at the appropriate station. Central County has since begun conversion to a C A D system.

10. The author would like to acknowledge, and thank, Dr. Donileen Loseke, whose field notes form the basis of this discussion of Mid-City.

11. An orientation to the state of the system is exhibited in the treatment of the calls themselves, as in the following self-proclaimed "nonemergency" call that is put on hold at Mid-City:

[MCE 21:3a:3]
```
1   CT:      Mid-City emergency:
2   C:       Hi um I don' think this is really
3            emer gency
4   CT:           [Well then ] hold on please
```

Similarly, when a C asks to continue the call past the point at which it might routinely be transferred or otherwise disposed of, the CT may explicitly mark the time-limited character of the current interaction if the traffic in in-coming calls is heavy:

[MCE:22:16:153]

1	CT:	Emergency Center
2	C:	Oh. (.) Well this isn't really an emergency
3		there's jus' something I'd like tuh talk tuh ya
4		about
5	CT:	Do you need uh squad sent out?
6	C:	No: I guess not=
7	CT:	=Then you should call thee precinct in thee
8		area you live in.
9	C:	((background noise)) Wull cun I talk tuh you fur
10		uh second?
11	CT:	Very short one.

12. Obtaining locational information can sometimes pose a challenge. In one incident in the northeastern United States a man called on his car phone to report that he and his wife had suffered gunshot wounds. The man (who was gradually losing consciousness) was unable to specify the exact location of his car beyond the street name and area. Ds had police units in the area sound their sirens one by one until a siren could be heard over the car phone, thus permitting police to locate the victims.

13. CAD systems permit CTs to access a number of information sources, including data bases listing criminal histories and outstanding warrants or "wants" on individuals. At Lane County, CTs may review such information while dealing with Cs, or other CTs may listen in and initiate searches while the original CT interrogates the C. The interactional implications of this aspect of CTs' activities remain for further work to specify (J. Whalen, personal communication).

14. The actual dispatch of police, fire, or paramedic units may occur well prior to the termination of a call if the trouble is urgent, for example a life-threatening medical emergency or a crime in progress. Once the problem and location are known, a CT using a CAD system can electronically transmit the information to a D while gathering further information from the C. At Central County, other CTs would often listen in and dispatch the relevant units while the original CT dealt with the C.

15. CTs at Lane County are instructed to avoid telling Cs that help is on the way since this creates a "special relationship" under which Lane County would be liable should help be delayed or even not be dispatched as might be the case for apparently trivial or otherwise seemingly nonurgent calls. In practice, CTs at Lane County do inform Cs

(particularly if they are distraught) that help is on the way in calls which clearly command an urgent response, for example life-threatening medical emergencies, crimes in progress, etc. In other cases, Cs are told that CT will inform the dispatcher of the reported problem.

16. Calls for emergency assistance are focused on a single item of business: securing a response. When that business is concluded, and if no further information from or action (e.g. cardio-pulmonary resuscitation – CPR) by C is required, the call can, indeed should, be ended. CTs' promise of assistance, for example "We'll get somebody there," signals the accomplishment of that business, and thus initiates the closing. A brief exchange of *thank yous* and *byes* make up the terminal exchange in these calls. The main difference between closings in the police calls and in ordinary conversation is the compression of the closing section, which is possible because of the focused, "monotopical" character of the police call. These reduced closings are a good example of the adaptation of general organization of interaction to the exigencies of a particular class of encounters (see Clark and French 1981; Greatbatch 1988; Clayman 1989). Closings will receive only passing attention in this chapter.

17. The discussion of CTs' management of the closing implicative force of the reassurance is deeply indebted to an undergraduate research project conducted by K. C. Cooper.

18. That CTs enter information into a computer as they talk with Cs could be asserted without reference to any actual call; that is, it could be warranted by observation or through the use of informants' accounts. However, many of the pertinent features of the setting, including the operation of an aspect of CAD, are recoverable (at least in part) from the calls themselves. Indeed, were this not the case, it would be difficult to see how one could speak of an organization's influence on the conduct of those performing within its purview. That and how the organization's features (or some subset of features) are available *in* the calls *for* both *participants* and thereby, for *analysts* (Schegloff and Sacks 1973) specifies: (a) the *relevance* of the organization to the participants whose activities both animate and constitute that self-same organization; and (b) availability of that organization as an object of naturalistic inquiry.

19. There are alternative means by which a CT can reestablish contact with a C. At Lane County, calls to the 9–1–1 number are "seized" by the system until released which means that the line can be immediately rung back ("flashed") without knowing the phone number. Calls can also be traced if it is necessary – as it would be if a C was incapacitated and unable to answer – to determine the location of the phone from which the call was made. CTs at Lane County flash disrupted calls, indicating the same orientation to incoming calls as virtual emergencies.

20. The mechanism for sustaining an established footing is that described

by Heritage as an "architecture of intersubjectivity" (1984a: 254–60).
I am indebted to Thomas P. Wilson (1991) for this suggestion. See
Schegloff (1987a, 1991) for a discussion of participants' orientation to
their immediate, local circumstances and some of the issues that attend
the "range" of some initially achieved alignment.

21. When parties known to CT come on the line, the relevance of the
    otherwise reduced sequence is restored, and greeting/*howareyou*
    sequences reappear (Whalen and Zimmerman 1987: 176–7).

22. When Cs request that CTs *send* help, they routinely provide a destina-
    tion. When they simply request assistance, they routinely do not. In the
    former case, CTs intervene to inquire about the problem; in the latter
    case, the address.

23. This formulation derives from an observation by Gene Lerner.

24. The considerations that attend a decision to dispatch include organiza-
    tional policy determining under what conditions a dispatch may be
    made to an unknown trouble. Cs may be third parties asked to call for
    help but without the requisite knowledge, as in the case, initially, of
    the Ambassador Hotel Operator. Another factor is the CTs' assess-
    ment of Cs' credibility (see especially J. Whalen, Zimmerman, and
    Whalen 1988), or emotional state. Ambient noises such as screaming
    and cursing in the background, sounds of fighting, etc. may prompt a
    response even in the absence of a formulation of the trouble.

25. It is worth noting in passing that, in emergency calls (and probably in
    most other domains of discourse), the term "accident" is heard as
    "automobile accident" unless otherwise specified.

26. Consider, however, the following:

    [MCE:22:17:155]

1	CT:	Emergency center
2	C:	Ye:s uh MTB calling?
3	CT:	Umhm
4	C:	Uh: are you aware of uh motorcycle accident on
5		Summit Boulevard and Pier:ce Avenue? south
6	CT:	Summit Boulevard?

    In this call from a transit company, C shapes his informing as a
    question. Accidents and other highly observable events may draw
    multiple calls from the public. C's utterance orients to this possibility.
    Nevertheless, in posing the question, the trouble is described.

27. "Practical epistemology" involves how the person reporting or des-
    cribing the event came to know it; the adequacy of the description,
    given the features of the event to which the person has access; and the
    status of the person *vis-à-vis* the event, for example as witness, victim,
    or someone with a stake in framing the event as a policeable trouble
    (M. Whalen and Zimmerman 1990). See also note 28.

28. Sharrock and Turner (1978) note that police dispatchers are sensitive
    to the possibility that Cs may be motivated to settle scores with other
    individuals by getting them into trouble with the police.

29. Cs' actual first turn may be given over to work other than initiating the
    business of the call, for example dealing with ambiguities in CTs'
    categorical identification, as in the following:

[MCE: 21:25:35]
```
1   CT:        Mid-City emergency:
2   C:         Can I 've thuh police=please=
3   CT:        =This is police.
```

In the present context, first turn refers to Cs' first sequentially appropriate slot for introducing the reason for the call.
30. Suggested by J. Whalen (personal communication).
31. The positioning of exclamations (or "response cries" – see Goffman
    1981a: 78–122) like *God!* or *Oh God!* in the turn-initial position of
    Cs first turn appear to function as prefaces to the depiction of what is
    to C a distressing state of affairs. Notice that the opening turn at Lane
    County asks C to report directly the nature of the event that led to the
    call. Exclamations such as *Oh God!* may be occasioned precisely for
    the reason that C must now put in words and describe to another a
    terrible event, an event the implications of which may be just occurring
    (or reoccurring in vivid form) to them. The exclamation frames that
    report as one with momentous implications for the teller. In that
    respect, it would seem to affiliate with Heritage's (1984b) change-of-
    state token, although in this case it is the deliverer of "news" who
    employs the marker. Moreover, as exclamations like *God!* (and others
    such as *Shit!* or *Fuck!*) occur in other positions and in other sequential
    contexts, there is obviously much work to be done to understand the
    interactional placement and function of such devices. This is a task for
    another paper.
32. C is also screaming and CT has difficulty understanding what he has
    said.
33. The call in question is [MCE 17:9:74].
34. Cs may also initiate repair, often within the interrogative series as
    subinsertion sequences:

[MCE:21:33:49]
```
1   CT:    Mid-City emergency
2   C:     Uh yes I'd like tuh report a domestic argument
3          ˙hh on: thee fi:rst floor (.) of thuh house at
4          thuh corner of uh: let me see uh thurty second
5          avenue and twenty third stree:t (.) It's thee
6          Northeast wait uh second (.) Southeast corner
7          of thee intersection.
8   CT:    What color is it, do you know?
9   C:     What color is what?=
10  CT:    =Thuh house.
11  C:     Oh thuh house is yellow
```

35. Addresses in Mid-City carry a directional designation; if it is incorrect, response could be made to the "right" address in the wrong end of the city. A missing directional tag is a common trouble source in the Mid-City corpus.

36. "Verification" in this context is used in the sense that a recipient of information from a co-participant may verify or confirm that they have correctly "copied" that information. Addresses, for example, may be verified in that the address will in fact be copied (on an incident card, or into a CAD, for subsequent transmission by radio to responding units) and needs to be copied correctly. Verification is not limited to the issue of copying, but can extend to the issue of appropriate understanding, for example that a request for police to respond to a hotel is to be taken as a request for police to contact the desk clerk in the lobby of that hotel (Zimmerman forthcoming).

37. The discussion of verification has drawn upon work in progress in collaboration with M. Whalen. See also Mellinger (1990).

38. In the following call, the CT repeats one element of the previous turn and transforms another, displaying her understanding of the C's report of an accident with injuries:

[MCE:17:6a:106]
```
1   CT:        Mid-City police an fire
2   C:         Fourth precinct calling?
3   CT:        Mnhm
4   C:         We have un accident on uh Willow an
5              Cranmer with injuries?
6   CT:        Willow an Cranmer an its uh P. I. huh?=
7   C:         =Right
```

The object presented for confirmation thus involves two issues: the location and the nature of the problem (injury vs. noninjury accident).

39. Notice that in the call from the Kit Kat Club C gives the address of the club without the directional information while CT's verification includes that information. In the City Pub call, no address is given, and the verification turn consists in repetition of the club name. For bars, clubs, hotels, etc. the Mid-City computers apparently retrieve address information by name of establishment.

40. These considerations were provided by J. Whalen (personal communication).

41. For cases where this transfer of information was, for various reasons, problematic, see J. Whalen, Zimmerman, and Whalen (1988); M. Whalen (1990). The discussion above of a C's revision of a nearly uttered "passed out" to "consumed too much alcohol" also reflects some of the problematics of turn design in emergency calls. See Meehan (1989) for a discussion of recipient design in calls to the police.

42. Cs who report a loud party will often be asked for their name and

address, as in such cases, a signed complaint may be necessary to close the party down.

43. It may be that first turns, particularly the early components of first turns, may structurally provide a certain "grace space," if only for the fact that such early components frame or project the type of interaction proposedly upcoming. Such projections then furnish the occasion for co-interactant(s) to pass opportunities to speak (and thus participate in the extension of the ongoing turn), or to intervene at the earliest possible moment. Such a conjecture requires further investigation within the domain of mundane conversation as well as that of "institutional talk."

44. In some cases, Cs omit locational information, proceeding directly from their name to a narrative account of their trouble:

[MCE:17-19:96]
```
1    C:            ˙hh Yeah hi, uh this is Mary Cooper ˙hh um: my
2                  sister an I left our house earlier tonight...
```

45. Relative to the wide range of mundane conversations and the diversity of participants, occasions of "institutional talk" additionally involve, among other things, recurrent, specialized sets of situated identities (e.g. interviewer/interviewee; service seeker/provider) which in turn are founded in more basic discourse identities, for example questioner/ answerer, requestor/grantor, etc. (see Jefferson and Lee this volume; Zimmerman 1992).

46. The author is indebted to Thomas P. Wilson for this insight.

14

Contested evidence in courtroom cross-examination: the case of a trial for rape

PAUL DREW

1 Introduction

In the adversarial Anglo-American criminal-judicial system, cross-examination is essentially hostile. Attorneys test the veracity or credibility of the evidence being given by witnesses with questions which are designed to discredit the other side's version of events, and instead to support his or her own side's case. When being cross-examined, witnesses are, of course, conscious of this purposefulness behind the questions they are asked. They are alive to the possibility that a question or series of questions may be intended to expose errors or inconsistencies in their evidence, and hence to challenge and undermine it. This awareness on the part of witnesses is manifest in the guarded and defensive ways in which they answer certain questions. For instance, in this extract from a rape trial from which the data for this chapter are principally taken, the alleged rape victim gives an answer which is designed to manage what she perceives to be the damaging implications – for her version of

The analysis here is based in part on research I undertook whilst I was a visiting lecturer in Language and Institutions, Tilburg University, Netherlands, in the spring of 1983. I am most grateful to Tilburg University's Department of Language and Literature, and to Professor Konrad Ehlich, for giving me the opportunity to do this research. Versions of this chapter have been given at various places: I am grateful particularly to the EPOS group at UCLA for their comments and critical suggestions when I gave it there in 1987. I am grateful also to John Local and to John Heritage for their comments on an earlier draft.

I am much indebted to Brenda Danet, of the Hebrew University of Jerusalem, and to Mack O'Barr, of Duke University, North Carolina, for their generosity and colleagueship in making available to me data which they have so painstakingly collected. Most of the transcripts are my own, although in some cases they are based on those of Bob Dunstan.

470

events – of the defense attorney's questions. (In all the data extracts in this chapter, the attorney is designated as A, the witness as W, and the judge as J.)

(1) [Ou:45/3A:270]

```
1    A:         An du̲ring that enti̱:re: (0.3) e̲ve:ning. (0.8)
2               Miss ((name)), (0.5) its your testimo̲ny: (2.0)
3               that there was: (0.9) n̲o i̱ndication (.) as f̲ar
4               as you could te:ll, (0.3) that the defendant
5               had been drinking,
6               (0.2)
7    W:         N̲o:,
8               (2.2)
9    A:         Now: M̲iss: ((name)) (1.2) w̲hen you were
10              inte̱rviewed by (.) the poli̱:ce (.) some times
11              later (.) some time l̲ater that evening, (1.0)
12              didn̲'t you t̲ell the police (>) that the
13              defendant had been drinking?
14              (0.2)
15   W:         N̲o⌈::
16   A:             ⌊Didn' you tell 'em tha̱t=
17   W:         =I to̲ld them there was a c̲ooler in the ca̱:r
18              an I never o̲pened it.
19   A:         The a̲nswer: uh: (.) may the ba̲lance be: uh
20              stri̱cken y'r honour:, an the a̲nswer is n̲o:?
21   J:         The a̲nswer is n̲o:
```

The attorney's questions in this extract are plainly designed to imply an inconsistency in the witness's story – an inconsistency, that is, between her present testimony that the defendant had not been drinking, and what the attorney alleges she told the police shortly after the incident. The witness first denies that she told the police that the defendant had been drinking (line 15). However, she adds to that denial an explanation about what she actually told the police at the time (i.e. that there was a drinks cooler in the defendant's car; lines 17–18). In providing this supplementary explanation, which the attorney asks to be stricken from the record (lines 19–20), the witness constructs her answer in such a way that her versions then and now are consistent, whilst also implying an account for the attorney's "mistaken" interpretation of what she told the police, a matter which would not be resolved by her denial alone. Thus the defensiveness of the witness's answer orients to the potential inconsistency in her story which the questions are attempting to imply; it is designed also to rebut the damaging inferences which might otherwise be drawn about the apparent discrepancy between the attorney's version of what she told the police, and her own.

This chapter focuses on such disputes as these in cross-examination, when attorney and witness offer alternative and competing descriptions or versions of events. It will focus particularly on a device for producing inconsistency in, and damaging implications for, a witness's evidence. The device is therefore associated with an attorney's management of questioning to attempt to discredit a witness. A line of questioning[1] is designed in such a way that it ends by juxtaposing and contrasting items of discrepant information, as in extract (1), or information from which certain damaging inferences might be drawn about a witness's version of events. The systematic properties of this contrast device will be explicated.

Before beginning to analyze the data which are the focus of this chapter, it will be useful to review some general properties of verbal interaction in court settings.

2 Verbal interaction in courts and the "overhearing audience"

The conduct of criminal cases in the Anglo-American judicial system is conventionally depicted as "adversarial," involving a contest between two sides as to which can produce the more convincing story about whether and how some incident happened, and whether that incident was a violation of some law (i.e. of an interpretation of some law). The standard for deciding which side's story is the more convincing is, of course, the verdict of the jury. The crucial role in the adversarial system of testing one side's story against the other's, in some respects in contrast to many European "inquisitorial" legal systems, lies behind the condition that the only evidence that is admissable is that which can be orally attested in court. Except in special and infrequent circumstances,[2] a witness has to appear in court to testify verbally to anything which might count as evidence in a case, whatever observations, documents, signs, forensic traces, photographs, eye-witness accounts, findings, declarations, confessions, and the like which may be invoked on behalf of a side's case. For only when a witness can be called to testify about some piece of evidence can the opposing side have the opportunity to test the veracity, significance, relevance, and interpretation to be accorded that evidence. Thus there is a dual emphasis in an adversarial system upon evidence being produced verbally, and being given on behalf of and in the service of one of two competing sides, the prosecution or defense. Witnesses are regarded as being members of one or the other side's team: hence they are treated as giving evidence in support of their side's case, a view which is rather dramatically encapsulated in the legal rule that an attorney "may not impeach the credit of his own witness" (Cross and Wilkins 1980: 93–4).

This dual emphasis on the verbal character of evidence, given by witnesses called to attest on behalf of one of the competing sides, is nicely illustrated in the following extract from the direct examination (or examination-in-chief) of a police forensic scientist, called by the prosecution during a trial for an armed robbery in which a victim was shot.

(2) [O'B:St v Mason:1:22] (The non-examining attorney who interjects in line 13 is designated as DA, i.e. the defence attorney)

1	A:	Uh now, Sergeant ((name)), was the print put
2		on these before the shotgun shell was fired
3		or after?
4	W:	Before it
5	A:	Before?
6	W:	Yes sir
7	A:	Was it a revolver or a shotgun?
8	W:	Shotgun
9	A:	And you lifted it off of the brass casing?
10	W:	That is correct
11	A:	Well then why weren't there any prints on the
12		other shotgun shell-
13	DA:	If your honour please, he's uh harrassing
14		his own witness.
15	J:	Sustained.
16	A:	I'm trying to get to the truth.

Photographs have been produced in court both of the defendant's fingerprints and of the fired and unused shell casings from the gun alleged to have been used in the robbery. Such evidence is not allowed to "speak for itself"; what is to be made of those photographs, and what any comparison between them may amount to, has actually to be verbally attested by the scientist. The purpose of this direct examination is to elicit just those facts and interpretations about the photographs which the attorney expects will support the prosecution case. However, in this fragment the attorney appears to encounter a difficulty, which is to get from his witness an account for a discrepancy between finding finger prints on the unused but not on the fired shell casings. At just the point where the attorney's questions appear to be oppositional and almost to challenge his "own witness's" testimony, the opposing (defense) attorney objects that "he's uh harrassing his own witness," thereby invoking that sense of, and the evidentiary rule concerning, a witness belonging to a team.

It is a common complaint made by some legal practitioners and those (such as police officers and forensic scientists) who are regularly called as expert witnesses, as well as by legal reformers, that the store set in our adversarial system on the admissability of evidence only if it can be verbally represented in the service of one side's case can sometimes result in the derogation of the "truth" in a trial. (In this respect it might be noted that in [2], line 16, the examining attorney's explanation for his "testing" questioning of his own witness is that "I'm trying to get to the truth.") In this view the outcome of a case may depend rather less on "objective truth" than on the vagaries of courtroom examination – whether the right questions were asked, how they were asked, and how they were answered – and ultimately upon the ability of witnesses to tell credible "stories" in their testimony. It should be emphasized that in the analysis which follows the objective is not to decide or otherwise to assess the extent to which the "truth" satisfactorily emerges in courtroom (cross-)examination. The purpose of this discussion is only to review the principle in the adversarial system that evidence will be given orally, so that it may be tested and, if necessary, challenged by the other side in cross-examination. This is a backdrop to the expectation of witnesses that questions during cross-examination will be hostile, and may attempt to discredit their testimony. The aim of this analysis, in line with the ethnography of speaking, is to elucidate some of the technical, sequential, and pragmatic properties of participants' engagement in cross-examination.

The use of "participants" here needs to be qualified. Despite the presence in court of often quite large numbers of people, the number of those who (legitimately) participate by speaking is, of course, limited. During examination of a witness, for example, speakership is restricted to the examining attorney and the witness, though occasionally the nonexamining attorney and the judge may intervene, usually to make and to adjudicate an objection, as happens in (2). (The defense attorney's objection in [2] intervenes after a question has been asked and before it can be answered, and is thus interruptive. The format of such interventions/objections as interruptive is evidence for the *normative* character of the preallocated restriction of turns at talk to just the two parties in examination.)

However, the talk between attorney and witness in examination is, of course, designed to be heard, understood, and assessed by a group of nonspeaking overhearers, the jury. Whilst they do not ordinarily participate, at least verbally, in the interaction between attorney and witness,[3] they are required to make a decision on the basis of what they have heard during a trial. The structural feature that talk in (cross-)examination is designed for multiparty recipiency by nonspeaking overhearers can immediately be seen to have certain consequences for sequential patterns and activities in the talk. For instance, the major resource in conversation for displaying understanding, and for checking whether a recipient has properly understood, is what the recipient says/does in the next turn. A speaker may inspect a recipient's response in the next turn as a kind of proof procedure, to see whether that response displays a "correct" understanding of the speaker's prior turn:[4] and if it does not, the speaker can initiate repair in a third turn in a sequence, that is in his/her turn after recipient's response (see especially Schegloff 1992). But this resource is unavailable for checking the understandings of those nonspeaking overhearers whose decisions, based on what they hear and understand, play so crucial a role in court: for jury members do not produce "next turns" in which their understandings of what has been said may be exhibited and, if necessary, subsequently corrected.

This has a range of consequences for the management of the talk between attorney and witness: while space prevents detailed consideration of these consequences, a brief illustration may help to indicate how the talk's production for an overhearing audience can "shape" the management of sequences and the interactional work achieved in them. Since the overhearing audience are unable to exhibit (at least vocally) their understanding of an answer, an attorney may be unsure whether the jury have fully appreciated the force or significance of a witness's prior response. Hence in the "third turn" (i.e. the question after a question–answer sequence) is an opportunity to "emphasize" a point in the witness's answer by repeating all or part of that answer. The turn-taking constraints are such that such (partial) repeats are formed as questions which check or confirm the witness's response. In conversation partial repeats of what the prior speaker just said commonly indicate that the recipient has doubts about the correctness of what was said: they are used to initiate repair, to invite the speaker to "think again" and correct something in their prior utterance. But in examination, partial repeats are not generally associated with attorneys' doubt about prior answers, nor with witnesses' self-repair; instead they manage to have the witness affirm or repeat the point, simple repetition being a means of emphasizing a point for the benefit of the jury. An instance is to be found in (2):

```
(from 2)
1   A:        Uh now, Sergeant ((name)), was the print put
2             on these before the shotgun shell was fired
3             or after?
4   W:        Before it
5   A:        Before?
6   W:        Yes sir
```

So that partial repeats are recurrent both in direct and cross-examination: in each environment a (partial) repeat of an answer by the attorney provides an opportunity – indeed, the only opportunity before the closing speech[5] – to underscore or highlight a witness's prior answer. Zimmerman (this volume) notes that personnel taking calls for assistance from the emergency services may similarly repeat what the caller has just said (for instance, when the caller is giving an address): whilst such (partial) repeats are done in the space where in conversation repair may be initiated, Zimmerman shows that in emergency calls their purpose is confirming or verifying what the caller has just said. This is closely related to the work that partial repeats do in courtroom examination, though here verification is designed to ensure that it has been fully heard and appreciated by the nonspeaking overhearers.

Here, then, the production by attorneys of partial repeats, and the interactional work that is managed through such objects, are the result of participants' orientation to a structural feature of the talk in which they are engaged. That is, they are designed for the benefit of an overhearing audience, in circumstances where it is important that that audience take full cognizance of significant points in the questions and answers, but in which they are excluded from the turn-taking system in such a way that they are prevented from displaying their understanding. This briefly illustrates how the structural properties associated with turn taking in an "institutional context" may shape the interactional work which objects perform, and can shape also the sequential management of an activity.[6] Later in this chapter I will show that the production of contrasts, the purpose of which is to discredit aspects of the witness's testimony, is associated with a similar orientation to the overhearing audience.

As well as restricted rights as to who is permitted to speak in courtroom examination, there are constraints also on the type of speaking turn which each may produce, "question" and "answer" turns being allocated respectively to attorney and witness. The specialized speech-exchange system for courtroom examination has been described elsewhere (see Atkinson and Drew 1979: ch. 2; see also Greatbatch 1988 for a similar account of the preallocation system of question and answer turns in news interviews). Here it is only necessary to stress that although the types of turns are preallocated between the participants, the content – and particularly the activities – achieved in those turns are left to be interactionally managed by participants on a local turn-by-turn basis. That is to say, "questions" and "answers" are only minimal characterizations of the turns to which attorneys and witnesses are confined. Other activities may be done in the context of "questioning" and "answering," but those other activities are done through the format of questions and answers (Atkinson and Drew 1979: 68–76); so that the interactional work in which, as will become clear, attorneys and witnesses are engaged (accusing, discrediting, rebutting, defending, challenging, etc.) has to be fitted to the sequential environment which the specialized speech-exchange system allocates to each participant.

These properties of the specialized speech-exchange system in courtroom examination are relevant to the analysis which follows in the remainder of this chapter. The witness's attempts to deflect or challenge what are for her the damaging implications of the attorney's questions, and in turn the attorney's production of contrasts designed to discredit aspects of the witness's testimony, are all activities which are shaped by their structural environment. They are shaped, that is, by the constraints associated with the respective positions of the attorney and witness within the turn-taking system; and by their orientations to what is to be conveyed to the jury. The interaction between attorney and witness is influenced by the necessity of indicating points to the jury, but doing so in such a fashion as to avoid certain unwanted consequences for potential next questions or answers in the "current" interaction.

3 The data

The particular focus of the present analysis is an extract from a trial for rape, recorded in a municipal criminal court in a large city in the eastern United States. In this extract the alleged rape victim is being cross-examined by the defense attorney. Just before this the witness has agreed that she knew the defendant for "two or three years" before the alleged rape; and she has testified that he had been to her house before. The questions in this extract concern an occasion before the night of the alleged rape, when the witness met the defendant (not by arrangement) in a place which the attorney describes as a "bar" and the witness a "club" (about which more later).

(3) [Da:Ou:2:1]

```
 1   A:    An' at tha:t ti:me (0.3) he: asked ya to go
 2         ou:t with yu (0.4) isn't that c'rect
 3         (2.1)
 4   W:    Yea┌h
 5   A:       └With him. (.) izzn'at so?
 6         (2.6)
 7   W:    Ah don't remember
 8         (1.4)
 9   A:    W'l didn:'e: a:sk you if uh: (.) on that night
10         that uh::: (.) he wanted you to be his gi:rl
11         (0.5)
```

```
12   A:        Didn'e ask you that?
13             (2.5)
14   W:        I don't remember what he said to me that night.
15             (1.2)
16   A:        Well yuh had some uh (p) (.) uh fairly lengthy
17             conversations with thu defendant uh: did'n you?
18             (0.7)
19   A:        On that evening uv February fourteenth?
20             (1.0)
21   W:        We:ll we were all talkin.
22             (0.8)
23   A:        Well you kne:w. at that ti:me. that the
24             defendant was. in:terested (.) in you (.)
25             did'n you?
26             (1.3)
27   W:        He: asked me how I'(d) bin: en
28             (1.1)
29   W:        J- just stuff like that
30   A:        Just asked yuh how (0.5) yud bi:n (0.3) but
31             he kissed yuh goodnigh:t. (0.5) izzat righ:t.=
32   W:        =Yeah=he asked me if he could?
33             (1.4)
34   A:        He asked if he could?
35             (0.4)
36   W:        Uh hmm=
37   A:        =Kiss you goodnigh:t
38             (1.0)
39   A:        An you said: (.) oh kay (0.6) izzat right?
40   W:        Uh hmm
41             (2.0)
42   A:        An' is it your testimony he only kissed yuh
43             ('t) once?
44             (0.4)
45   W:        Uh hmm
46             (6.5)
47   A:        Now (.) subsequent to this...
```

What is plainly at issue in this extract, quite explicitly so in lines 23–4, is what the witness could or should have known about the defendant's "interest" in her. We do not need to be concerned here with the significance such knowledge might have for her subsequently agreeing, on the night of the alleged rape, to go for a drive with the defendant, in whatever circumstances "going for a drive" was proposed and accepted, with respect to her claim to have been raped, and the defendant's claim that she consented to intercourse.

It is not necessary here to become involved in a narrative reconstruction of how these issues raised during cross-examination, and more broadly during the trial, fit together, or what significance one issue has in relation to another. It is clear that what is being proposed in the attorney's questions in (3), and what the witness is contesting, is the matter of what she and the defendant "were to each other" prior to the incident in which it is alleged the witness was raped. What is therefore also being contested is whether as a result of what happened on this earlier occasion the witness had grounds for suspecting or anticipating that the defendant was (sexually) "interested" in her.[7]

In each of his questions in extract (3) the attorney attributes to the defendant behavior which might manifest sexual interest, namely asking her to go out, asking her to be his girl, having lengthy conversations together, that the evening they met was 14 February (i.e. Valentine's Day), being interested in her, and kissing her goodnight. It is also clear that in answer to these points the witness is being defensive, and is contesting whether from what happened on that occasion she would have been aware of the defendant's sexual interest in her. The analysis of these data will begin by considering the witness's defensiveness, before turning to focus on the point in lines 30–1 where the attorney employs the discrediting contrast device.

4 *I don't remember* as a way to avoid confirming

To begin with, we can notice something about the opening lines in this extract which make a considerable difference for what follows; in the sense that if the witness had stayed with what it looks as though her answer to the first question initially was (i.e. "Yeah," line 4), and not changed her answer to "Ah don't remember" (line 7), then it is conceivable that much of the subsequent questioning about what the defendant said to her might not have taken place.

(3) [Da:Ou:2:1]

```
1   A:        An' at tha:t ti:me (0.3) he: asked ya to go
2             ou:t with yu (0.4) isn't that c'rect
3             (2.1)
4   W:        Yea⌈h
5   A:           ⌊With him. (.) izzn'at so?
```

6   (2.6)
7   W: Ah don't remember

In line 4 the witness appears to confirm that the defendant did ask her to go out with him. However, the attorney just overlaps her answer/conformation with a postpositioned "prompting" (line 5), which might be responsive to her 2.1 second delay in answering, and in which he corrects an error in his initial question, substituting "With him" for the mistaken "with yu." Whereupon, in response to the attorney's prompting, the witness changes from confirming that he asked her out, to answering that she does not remember if he asked her out (line 7).

This is one of the several occasions during the cross-examination in which the witness answers that she "doesn't remember" or "doesn't know" something which the attorney proposes happened or was the case; she does so also in her next answer in line 14 of (3) when she answers that "I don't remember what he said to me that night." One sense of such answers is that the witness might be anticipating that what she is being asked to confirm will turn out to be prejudicial to her story and the prosecution's case. Though she may not be able to project precisely how some point is going to work against her story, her suspicion that it might do so may make her reluctant to agree to the point, and she attempts instead to prevent or obstruct that line of questioning. "Not knowing/remembering" can therefore be an object conveniently used to avoid confirming potentially damaging or discrediting information. And the apparent change from her initial answer in line 4 to her answer in line 7 can be grounds for considering that her claim not to remember is just such a "strategic" avoidance. Her self-repair might exhibit her recognition that the matter of whether the defendant asked her out is potentially troublesome for the version which seemingly she would prefer to convey of their having no special relationship.

As a sequential object *I don't remember* not only avoids confirming what is proposed in the question, but also avoids disconfirming it: that is, the witness thereby avoids directly challenging or disputing a version proposed by the attorney, but nevertheless neutralizes that version, at least for the present. The use of the object frustrates the attorney employing that version in a series of further questions, but without directly contesting what the attorney has asked. But as an object *I don't remember* has a particular content; it claims a particular cognitive state. Furthermore, it is noticeable that it is used by the witness with some frequency in response to questions about matters of "detail," for instance about the appearance of the defendant's car,

(4) [Da:Ou:5:1]

> A: <u>D</u>oes it have a <u>spoiler</u> on it,
>   (1.0)
> W: I don't remember.
>   (1.0)
> A: 'Scu<u>s</u>e me,=
> W: =I don't re<u>membe</u>r

about the temperature on the evening of the alleged rape,

(5) [Da:Ou:3:2]

> A: About <u>e</u>h:: (.) about how warm <u>wa</u>s it.
>   d'yu: (.) remember,
>   (0.3)
> W: <u>N</u>o=I don't.
>   (0.5)
> A: Seventies:? eighties:?
> W: I don't re<u>membe</u>r.

about the distance between her and the defendant when they talked,

(6) [Da:Ou:3:1]

> A: About <u>how far</u> awa:y was the defendant fro<u>m</u>
>   <u>y</u>ou when you <u>h</u>ad this <u>c</u>onver<u>sat</u>ion?
>   (0.5)
> A: In ⌈feet (.) if you can estimate it
> W: ⌊(I d-)
> W: I don't kno:w how many f<u>eet</u>

and about how many telephone calls she received from him between February and June.

(7) [Da:Ou:1:6]

> A: How many ph<u>o</u>ne <u>ca:</u>lls would you say that you
>   (.) had received from the defendant. betwee:n
>   (0.6) February and' June twenny ninth:,
>   (1.1)

W:	Ah don' know.
	(0.7)
W:	Ah didn't answer all of them.
	(0.8)
A:	'Scuse me?
W:	Ah <u>don't</u> re<u>mem</u>ber,=<u>I</u> didn't answer all of them.

Also, if *I don't remember* was to be analyzed only as a strategically deployed object to frustrate a line of questioning, that would not take into account its use by the witness in *direct* examination. Here, for example, she answers that she "doesn't remember" details about which she is asked by the prosecution attorney (i.e. her own side) in direct examination earlier in the trial.

(8) [Da:Ou:45/28:2]

A:	Uhm (.) did you (0.4) obs<u>erve</u> whether 'r not
	((City)) Tavern (0.9) (w-) was <u>open</u>.
	(0.4)
W:	Ah don't remember.
	(0.8)
A:	Did yuh observe any <u>car:s</u> parked there.
	(0.9)
W:	Ah don't remember.

A fuller analytic treatment of *I don't remember* has, then, to take account both of its cognitive claims, and its use in the environment of cooperative questioning as well as in hostile cross-examination. Considering the former, quite apart from what cognitively one can or cannot happen to recall, *stating* that one does not remember some detail can be a means of displaying the unimportance or lack of significance of that detail, and hence that it is the sort of thing one would not remember. By testifying that she is unable to recall them now, here in court, the witness is able to exhibit her having taken no account of such matters *at the time*. Such details are not recallable now because they were not things which she noticed then: which is to say that "not remembering" something attributes to it a kind of status, as unmemorable because it was unnoticed.

   A reason, perhaps the reason, for something to pass unnoticed is that it is unimportant, or seems to have no special significance. So that by claiming not to remember whether or not the tavern was open, whether there were any cars parked in the area, how many telephone calls the defendant made to her, how far he was across the street, whether his car had a spoiler, and so forth, the witness can display not only that she did not happen to notice these things, but that there was no reason for her to have noticed them. As one lives through an unfolding scene, there is a variety of things which, though potentially noticeable, go unnoticed. Some things only come to have a significance in retrospect, in the light of something which happened – some dramatic incident, for example – but which was unanticipated. It is only on looking back that the "true" significance of certain details can be discerned. At the time, as they occurred, and without knowing what was about to happen – a car crash, a murder in the street, or whatever – the details of a scene are just part of the unremarkable, unremarked, "seen but unnoticed" incidental details of daily life. For this reason those who are eye witnesses to unexpected dramas are often unsure about the details of what they saw. They give confused or inconsistent accounts of "what direction," "how far," "what speed," "how many," "what color," and so on, since those things only come to be important after they were experienced, by virtue of the subsequent dramatic occurrence. The taken-for-granted ordinariness of scenes,[8] up until a drama occurs, makes such details as may later be asked about unnoticeable, of no account, at the time: only subsequent inquiry into a drama constitutes those details as having been significant after all.

But crucial to this "seen but unnoticed" character of a scene's details is the standpoint of the observer. Such details may go unnoticed by people who have no reason to notice them, who have no suspicion of what is about to happen, and who therefore are *innocent* of the events they witness. It is this reflexive relationship between the unremarkable and unnoticeable character of a scene, and the perspective of the unsuspecting and innocent observer for whom they would be unnoticeable, which can provide for the witness's claims in (4)–(8) not to remember certain details as displays of innocence. To be unable to recall such details is to exhibit them as having been unnoticeable at the time *for the kind of observer she was*, that is someone who had no reason to suspect what in fact took place, the alleged rape. Questions about how far away the defendant was standing when he asked her to go for a drive, or whether there were other cars in the vicinity where they parked, constitute those details as retrospectively significant (e.g. for whether or not she could have smelled drink on the defendant's breath; or whether she might have been alarmed at his parking in an isolated spot). In contrast, in claiming not to remember such matters the witness treats them as having been of no account to her at the time, and in this way depicts herself as innocent, that is as not having suspected what his (sexual) intentions were.[9]

If the witness was to have confirmed that the defendant had asked her to go out with him (lines 1–2) or to be his girl (lines 9–10) on this earlier occasion, then she would be confirming grounds for suspecting, when he asked her to go for the drive during which the alleged rape took place, what his real intentions were. Alternatively, if she were to disconfirm that he had made such overtures she would directly contradict the version proposed in the question, thus setting up an opposition of her word against his. Answering that she "doesn't remember" avoids both these consequences in rather a neat way, because it relegates whatever the defendant did say to her then as unnoticeable, inconsequential. This displays herself, implicitly, as having had no reason to take any special notice of what the defendant asked her, and thereby as having had no special interest in him and having been innocent of his interest in her. But she simultaneously also manages to *imply* a disconfirmation of his having asked her out or to be his girl. Since being asked out might be regarded as the kind of matter one would not fail to notice or to remember, then "not remembering" amounts to suggesting that he probably did not ask her out. If her "not remembering" relegates what he said to the status of unnoticeable, and given that she might be expected to notice and remember being asked out, then her answers imply that it probably did not happen.

One further point about the implicitness with which the object *I don't remember* can work to convey her innocence of the defendant's intentions: in using this object, the witness manages to *exhibit* rather than to *claim* her lack of suspicion.[10] That is, she does not need to state in so many words that she was unaware of his intentions: her "not remembering" can provide recipients, especially the jury, with materials from which they can discover for themselves that she was unsuspecting. By having recipients do that work of discovering that conclusion for themselves, instead of stating or claiming it overtly, the witness manages to imply it *unofficially* through her answers. This preliminary consideration of the first few

lines of (3), in which she deflects the possibly damaging implications of agreeing that the defendant asked her out, begins to
reveal in the witness's answers a delicate management of withholding confirmation of, whilst not overtly contradicting or disagreeing
with, versions of events which the attorney proposes in his
questions. That is, she may design her answers so as to rebut the
attorney's versions of events, not by directly challenging his
versions, but by implying a different characterization of events.
This will become a main theme of the analysis which follows of the
unfolding interaction between attorney and witness in (3).

5 Alternative descriptions

After the witness's claims not to remember whether the defendant
asked her to go out with him, or asked her to be his girl, the
attorney pursues his line of questioning with two further formulations of the defendant's "interest" in her.

```
16    A:        Well yuh had some uh (p) (.) uh fairly lengthy
17              conversations with thu defendant uh: did'n you?
18              (0.7)
19    A:        On that evening uv February fourteenth?
20              (1.0)
21    W:        We:ll we were all talkin.
22              (0.8)
23    A:        Well you kne:w. at that ti:me. that the
24              defendant was. in:terested (.) in you (.)
25              did'n you?
26              (1.3)
27    W:        He: asked me how I'(d) bin: en
28              (1.1)
29    W:        J- just stuff like that
30    A:        Just asked yuh how (0.5) yud bi:n (0.3) but
31              he kissed yuh goodnigh:t. (0.5) izzat righ:t.=
```

When the attorney proposes that the witness had "fairly lengthy
conversations with thu defendant" (lines 16–19), she counters that
version with the answer that "we were all talkin" (line 21). And
again, her reply that "He: asked me how I'(d) bin: en j- just stuff
like that" in lines 27–9 appears to deny that she "knew that the
defendant was interested" in her (lines 23–5). That latter reply is
used by the attorney when he constructs the contrast in lines 30–1:

and that contrast will eventually be the focus of analysis in a later section.

But for now I shall focus on how the versions which the witness constructs in her replies work to dispute the versions which the attorney proposes in his prior questions. How, for instance, does her account that "<u>He:</u> asked me how I'(d) bin:. . ." manage to dispute the attorney's claim that she knew that the defendant was interested in her? Since this will involve a quite extended treatment of how her alternative descriptions are designed to compete with and rebut the attorney's versions, it may help if I summarize the stages in the analytic argument.

A first observation, discussed in the following subsection, is that although it is clear that the witness's versions are designed to rebut and replace those of the attorney, her answers in lines 21 and 27 above, as elsewhere, do not contain overt markers of rejection or correction. Thus the contrastive force of her versions derive almost entirely from properties of the descriptions which she constructs. That observation leads to a consideration of how a description of something that happened, for example her account in line 27–9 of the defendant's greeting, can be taken to represent or characterize the scene as a whole, or to stand as a gloss for the scene. But in order that her description/characterization be heard to differ from and rebut the attorney's versions, her description, again, for example, of the defendant's greeting to her, is required to be heard as representing "the most" that happened between them. This maximal property associated with the contrastive or disputatious force of her descriptions is discussed in the third subsection: after which the more general relevance, for conversation, of this maximal property of next and contrasting descriptions is considered in the final subsection.

5.1 The absence of overt correction markers

One option which the witness has as a way to dispute a version of events proposed in the attorney's question is explicitly to reject that version, with an overt negative marker (*No*) followed by a correction. ("Correction" should be understood as a candidate correction; that is, it is the version which that speaker, here the witness, believes to be or is offering as the correct version.) That option was

selected in extract (1), when the witness rejected the attorney's
version of what she had told the police regarding the defendant's
drinking, and then gave a correct version of what she told them.

```
 9   A:        Now: Miss: ((name)) (1.2) when you were
10             interviewed by (.) the poli:ce (.) some times
11             later (.) some time later that evening, (1.0)
12             didn't you tell the police (>) that the
13             defendant had been drinking?
14             (0.2)
15   W:        No ::
16   A:          [Didn' you tell 'em that=
17   W:        =I told them there was a cooler in the ca:r
18             an I never opened it.
```

This option of overtly rejecting and correcting the attorney's
version is likewise used in these fragments.

(9) [Da:Ou:6:2]

```
     A:        And it was at this point that you say that
               the defendant (2.0) started to kiss you
               is that right
     W:        No we started talkin'
```

(10) [Da:Ou:1:4]

```
     A:        He take you out to the ca:r?
               (1.3)
     W:        No he walked outsi:de with us.
```

An alternative option for disagreeing with a version proposed by
the attorney is, however, more indirect: the witness does not preface her version with a negative rejection marker, and the description she offers implies a different characterization of an event or
scene from that conveyed by the attorney's description. The witness
uses this option in (3), for instance, when she is asked about her
knowledge of the defendant's interest in her.

```
23   A:        Well you kne:w. at that ti:me. that the
24             defendant was. in:terested (.) in you (.)
25             did'n you?
26             (1.3)
27   W:        He: asked me how I'(d) bin: en
```

```
28              (1.1)
29    W:        J- just stuff like that
```

The witness is plainly disputing the attorney's contention that she knew that the defendant was interested in her: but she does so by producing an alternative description which implies that she did not know. Her alternative description competes with or challenges the attorney's account, but it does so by reporting something which implies a rather different relationship between her and the defendant than is proposed by the attorney's use of "interest" (line 24). Some other instances of this option of producing alternative competing descriptions without prefacing them with overt rejection markers occur elsewhere during this cross-examination.

(11) [Da:Ou:1:2]

```
      A:        An' you went to a: uh (0.9) ah you went to
                a ba:r? in ((city)) (0.6) is that correct?
                (1.0)
      W·        Its a clu:b.
```

(12) [Da:Ou:1:2]

```
      A:        Its where uh (.) uh gi:rls and fella:s
                meet isn't it?
                (0.9)
      W:        People go: there.
```

(13) [Da:Ou:1:3]

```
      A:        An' during that eve:ning: (0.6) uh: didn't
                Mistuh ((name)) come over tuh sit with you
                (0.8)
      W:        Sat at our table.
```

(14) [Da:Ou:6:1]

```
      A:        Some distance back into theuh (.) into the
                wood wasn't it
                (0.5)
      W:        It was up the path I don't know how far
```

In each of the extracts, as in lines 23–5 of (3), the question is designed to elicit an answer which is either *yes* or *no*; that is, which will either confirm or disconfirm the version proposed in the question. So the first thing to notice about her answers is that the witness is avoiding what the question asks, and declining either to confirm or disconfirm. Secondly, although her answers implicitly work to disconfirm the attorney's versions, her descriptions or versions are in some respects not intrinsically oppositional to his. In extracts (9) and (10), where the witness uses an overt disconfirmation marker, there was also a direct contrast between her versions and the attorney's, that is between "started talking" and "started to kiss you," and between "take you out" and "walked outside with us." However, in a case such as (13), not only is her version not prefaced as a disconfirmation, but the description she offers, "Sat at our table" does not intrinsically exclude the attorney's version, "sit with you." Whilst hers are qualified, guarded versions of what the attorney suggests, that they manage to be defensive as well as to rebut his versions is an almost entirely implicit property of the descriptions which she selects.

I have said "almost entirely" because there are elements of contrasting references in some of the witness's versions. For example, in lines 16–21 of (3) there are two such contrastive elements.

```
16   A:      Well yuh had some uh (p) (.) uh fairly lengthy
17           conversations with thu defendant uh: did'n you?
18           (0.7)
19   A:      On that evening uv February fourteenth?
20           (1.0)
21   W:      We:ll we were all talkin.
```

The first is the turn-initial component "We:ll", which marks a certain disjunction between the second speaker's opinion or position, and that expressed by the first speaker. That preface therefore projects that the witness's version will differ from and disagree with the attorney's position (Sacks 1987: 59; Pomerantz 1984a: 72 and n. 12). The second contrastive element is that the witness substitutes "we ... all" in place of "you . . . with the defendant"; whilst "we" in her answer would include her and the defendant, her adding "all" specifically includes others besides the two of them (i.e. the girlfriends she was with).

Despite the way in which her version of "we ... all" directly contradicts his version of "you two," such a straightforwardly exclusive contrast does not seem to capture how "all talkin" is designed to be heard as standing in place of "fairly lengthy conversations," and thereby as disputing the attorney's version. The terms "all talkin" and "fairly lengthy conversations" are not by themselves incompatible, and might easily be applied to the same activity or scene. It is possible to imagine one person having "lengthy conversations" with another in the course of a bunch of people "all talking." Clearly, one respect in which the witness's version is designed to challenge the attorney's version is the sheer matter of the sequential position in which it is produced. The witness produces her versions as next or second to the attorney's, by virtue of the sequential occurrence of answers; and insofar as she has declined to confirm the version in the question, and has instead produced in next position a different version of the "same" incident or circumstances, the descriptions which the witness reports can be heard as candidate replacements. They are not further specifications which add something to the attorney's versions, but are *alternative* versions designed to qualify and *replace* the versions initially produced by the attorney. Sequential position is, then, a primary interpretative resource in understanding that the witness's answers are designed to counter or to dispute his versions.[11]

5.2 Reporting a "detail" implies a characterization of the scene

Within that context of their sequential position, however, the witness's answers have other interpretative properties through which they are designed to dispute his versions. We can return to the observation that the alternative consecutive descriptions of the attorney and witness might appear not to be mutually exclusive. Even though the witness's answers contain alternative references, for example "people" in place of "girls and fellas" in (12), and "club" for "bar" in (11), nevertheless these alternative descriptions are not necessarily, inevitably, or invariably inconsistent or contrasting ways of describing the same thing. Just as on occasions two people having "fairly lengthy conversations" can go along with "we were all talking," so too "clubs" include "bars," albeit whose use is restricted in some ways associated with membership; and the term "people" certainly includes "girls and fellas." In (13) there is a mutual or necessary connection between "sitting with" someone and "sitting at" their table: and in (14) being "back into the wood" may also be "up the path." In each question–answer pair, therefore, the subsequent description by the witness does not exclude, in a directly contrastive sense, the prior description which she has been asked to confirm.

The witness's answers display a marked cautiousness insofar as she takes a stand, through her redescriptions or qualifications of the attorney's versions, on matters which might not otherwise, in other forms of discourse, seem to make much of a difference. For instance, in a conversational setting it may be doubted that in describing someone joining one at one's table for a drink, there is sufficient difference between that person "sitting with one" and "sitting at one's table" for it to be worth troubling to insist on the latter version. The two versions are not intrinsically mutually exclusive: "bars" may be located in "clubs," "sitting with" someone can involve "sitting at" that person's table, and in the circumstances where driving up a path leads into a wood, either may serve as a characterization of where one was.

These alternatives might, then, be used interchangeably as *equivalent*, as *partial* but equally adequate or correct descriptions of the same scene. However, in not allowing the attorney's versions to pass unamended, the witness orients to the differences between these versions for her story. Focusing on lines 16–29 of (3), her versions are designed not merely to add to or supplement those proposed by the attorney, but to replace his. In so doing, she is attempting to correct some impression or implication which might be conveyed by the attorney's portrayal of the facts. When in line 21 she answers "We:ll we were all talkin" and in line 27 that "He: asked me how I'(d) bin:," she is treating his prior versions not as having been partial and needing filling out, but as having been wrong. And a first requirement for treating her descriptions as combative, as correcting his, is that they are not just detailing more which could be said about a scene, but recharacterizing the scene as a whole.

The witness does not manage this recharacterization by disputing the attorney's version head on; by which I mean that she avoids some rather direct ways of challenging his version that she knew that "the defendant was interested in you." "Interested" here can be considered a *gloss* for some details of what was said between them that night, what the defendant did, the way he looked at her, how they acted towards one another, and so on – instances of which could be detailed as evidence in support of that gloss (Garfinkel and Sacks 1970). At least a couple of direct ways in which the witness might have challenged that gloss would have been simply to dispute it, along the lines of *No he didn't seem much interested in me*; or to have substituted her own contrasting gloss, for example *Well, he was interested in everyone that night; he was having fun.* Alternatively, she might have challenged the gloss "interested" in a more indirect fashion. Given that a gloss might be unpackaged into its constituent or component activities (Jefferson 1986a), the witness might have focused on one of those constituent activities or details as a means of challenging the gloss, for example by answering in lines 21 or 27 *Well he didn't talk to me any more than he talked to the others* (where comparative amounts of talk are routinely used as an index of the degree of interest conversationalists have in one another; as well as an index used by professional sociologists and social psychologists in sociometric studies of friendship).

In her answer in line 27 she does not use any of these methods of disputing the attorney's gloss "interested in you." Instead, she answers by reporting particulars of the occasion which stand as constituent or evidential details for a quite different gloss than that proposed by the attorney. In reporting "He: asked me how I'(d) bin:," the witness details a greeting which is conventionally one between people who know one another, but have not been in touch for some length of time (*How have you been?* indicates passage of time "since we last met"). It is a greeting which indicates acquaintance and familiarity but not close intimacy. Such a greeting would not be the kind of detail to be reported as evidence of the sexual interest of the one performing the greeting: so that the witness is detailing something about the scene – finding in the scene something to report – which would *not* be used as evidence to support the attorney's gloss or characterization of the scene. This has an important corollary which underlies the manner in which her version specifically but implicitly challenges the attorney's version: that is, selecting to report a detail which does not support his version implicitly asserts (provides the grounds for recognizing)

that there is nothing in what happened which *could* be reported in
its support.

A gloss with which a scene or someone's behavior is characterized (e.g. "interested in you") can be taken to stand for a collection
of particulars of that scene/behavior (for more on which see Garfinkel and Sacks 1970; Jefferson 1986a), particulars which, if necessary, can be cited as evidence in support of that gloss. Outside of
that collection are other details which may not "fit" the proposed
gloss, not in the sense that they necessarily contradict it (though
they may), but just because they are conventionally unconnected or
not associated with, or not constituent behaviors of, the gloss in
question. For example, the fact that the birds are singing might well
be reported as part of the evidence for the gloss that it is a "beautiful day"; but if the day being described as *beautiful* happened to be
a Tuesday, that fact would not ordinarily be included in a collection
of the particulars of a "beautiful day" (for related issues, again see
Sacks 1984b). Thus, if one speaker were to propose that *It's a
beautiful day* and the other replied *It's Tuesday*, the second speaker
would be heard to imply something like "What's beautiful about it,
it's Tuesday": where even if the first speaker did not know what it
was that the other had against Tuesdays, why for him it was a bad
day, the first speaker would at least be able to discern that it *was* a
bad day for the other, that the other was not assenting to it being a
"beautiful day," and might therefore perhaps ask in reply *Why,
what do you have on Tuesdays?*

Thus there is a reflexive property of reporting a detail outside of
the conventional collection of particulars for a proposed gloss;
which is that in so reporting an "unassociated" detail, that other
(second) speaker dissents by implying that an alternative gloss is the
correct version. So that the indirectness or delicacy of the witness's
method of disputing the attorney's characterization of the defendant as "interested" in her is that she does not dispute the characterization itself, nor even its supposed constituent particulars from
the collection of details reportable as evidence for that characterization. Instead, she reports a detail from *outside* that constituent
collection, thereby implying but not stating that nothing occurred
which could support the attorney's version. In coming to this
generic formulation of the methodical procedures which underlie
the manner in which the witness's answer disputes the version

proposed by the attorney, the aim is to free the methodical practices of reasoning from their local environment. In this way we can begin to discern the procedures for reasoning and for interpretation through which one version might be disputed by an alternative competing version, in an implicit fashion and without using explicit markers of rejection or correction.

5.3 The "maximal" property of descriptions

This brings us closer to an analytic account of how the witness's version in lines 27–9 is designed to dispute the attorney's prior version; but the account is not yet exhausted. Her report "He: asked me how I'(d) bin: en (1.1) j- just stuff like that" has a discernible property with respect to the attorney's prior version, which can best be approached by considering the attorney's subsequent question, and the contrast on which the analysis here is coming to focus.

```
23   A:        Well you kne·w at that ti:me. that the
24             defendant was. in:terested (.) in you (.)
25             did'n you?
26             (1.3)
27   W:        He: asked me how I'(d) bin: en
28             (1.1)
29   W:        J- just stuff like that
30   A:        Just asked yuh how (0.5) yud bi:n (0.3) but
31             he kissed yuh goodnigh:t. (0.5) izzat righ:t.=
```

The contrast in the attorney's question in lines 30–1 suggests an inconsistency between the version she offered in lines 27–9, that he just asked her how she had been, and another "detail" of the scene/ behavior to which she has previously attested, that the defendant kissed her goodnight. This inconsistency trades off an interpretation that when she claimed that the defendant asked her how she had been, she is reporting not just a detail of what happened, his greeting, but is suggesting that nothing more happened between them as regards intimacy, "interest," and so forth than might be depicted by that greeting. Whereas the attorney is proposing that something more intimate did occur, namely kissing. So that the contrast in the attorney's question displays his understanding that the witness is claiming that the defendant's behavior towards her was only as friendly (i.e. nonintimate) as his greeting indicates.

That is, of course, just what the witness's answer in lines 27–9 is designed to indicate. She reports this one detail, a friendly greeting, and then adds "just stuff like that." By completing her detailing with that generalized phrase, she makes explicit that whatever else occurred between them that evening was nothing more than is suggested in the lack of intimacy in the greeting. Jefferson's account of the work of such generalized completors in the context of three-part lists is relevant here also: "the [two item and generalized completor] lists may be 'relevantly incomplete'; i.e. not only do the named items not exhaust the possible array of nameables, but a third item would not do such work; i.e. there are 'many more' relevant nameables which will not, and need not, be specified" (Jefferson 1990: 68). Thus the generalized completor "just stuff like that" is informative about other unspecified details of the scene. It indicates that all the other reportable but unspecified details are commensurate with the nothing-more-than-friendly greeting (the "just" indicates "no more than," and "stuff like that" refers to the greeting).

The result of this is that the witness is indicating that everything that occurred between her and the defendant that evening is part of a collection which is adequately represented by the kind of greeting she reports. But we still need to account for the implication that the form of greeting she reports is as much by way of "interest" that the defendant showed towards her. This account rests on a further interpretative or pragmatic property of her description of his greeting, through which it can convey that "nothing more intimate happened" than that. This can be referred to as the "maximal" property of the description – "maximal" because the description "He: asked me how I'(d) bin:" depicts the most, in terms of intimate behavior, that happened between them.

I want to come at this "maximal" property from two rather different directions: the first involving another disputed version in cross-examination during a different trial; and the other in quite another context. First, the following is an extract from the cross-examination of a defendant charged with being an accessory to murder. She is accused of having aided her boyfriend to gain entry to the victim's apartment by persuading him to open the door to her: her defense is that she went ahead unnoticed by her boyfriend, with the intention of warning the victim that her boyfriend was coming with a gun and that he should get away.

(15) [Da:Ch:CE1]

A:	Remember some more after the second
	set of knocks,
	(5.0)
W:	I don't know I was just c:onstantly
	ba:ngin' an' ba:ngin'=
A:	=(Didj'yu) after the second set of knocks=
W:	=I didn't say that I said: (n)'in the
	beginning I kept bangin' I don't know how much

The exchanges in this fragment reveal an embedded dispute (Jefferson 1987) between the attorney and defendant about what to call the manner in which she struck the door of the victim's apartment; the attorney refers to it as "knocking," while the defendant refers to her "banging" on the door. The argument about this issue continues for some while: its obvious importance in the context of the accusation and her defense is that "banging" is commensurate with the urgency of her claimed intention to warn the victim of the danger, while "knocking" not only lacks that urgency, but would also be a way in which she might have disguised the danger by giving the appearance – to the victim inside – that nothing was amiss. So "knocking" and "banging" are not merely alternative descriptions; they each convey quite different versions of the activity in which the defendant was engaged, and hence of the scene (her intentions, whether or not there was an understanding between her and her boyfriend, etc.). For the defendant's version, "knocking" on the door is a bizarre description because it is not commensurate with how else she depicts her urgency and anxiety in trying to warn the victim.

Of course "banging" includes "knocking"; but from her perspective it is insufficient to describe adequately her urgency, because it implicitly proposes that she *did no more than* knock. Thus her disputing the term "knock" arises from her treating it as implying that all she did was to "knock": whilst "knocking" may theoretically be subsumed under "banging," the attorney's assertion that she "knocked" proposes that she *only* knocked. It is this property of the term "knocking," and how it obtains its contrastiveness with "banging" through conveying that the most that the defendant did was to "knock," that I am referring to as the description's maximal property. The description's adequacy relies not on how full or inclusive it is, but on its representing some essential character of the scene: from the defendant's perspective, her urgency in trying to warn the victim is not adequately represented in the term selected by the attorney.

The second direction to approach the maximal property of contrasting descriptions is to consider the making and understanding of invitations, to *Come over for dinner*, *Come over and have drinks this evening*, *You're invited for cocktails*, *Come and have coffee*, *Come and watch the game*, and the like.[12] An initial observation about any of these is that they are *partial* descriptions of, say, an evening. Drinking, dining, chatting, etc. are all activities used to formulate the invitations, although it is perfectly well understood that much else besides these may take place. In this respect it is not happenstance that the incident which resulted in the alleged rape which is the subject of the trial here began as an invitation to the witness/victim to "go and have a hamburger at MacDonald's": part of her account is that she was not initially alarmed when the defendant turned his car off the road before the shopping mall where the MacDonalds was located. So that, though sitting, wandering around the garden, listening to music, and many other activities besides are likely to take place and could therefore be other partial characterizations of an evening, they may not be used to formulate the invitation. The difference between *Come for dinner* and those other characterizations (i.e. listening to music etc.) is not that "dinner" is any less partial than those others: "dinner" is an equally partial account of an evening's activities.

The reason why "dinner," "cocktails," etc. are nevertheless not equivalent to such descriptions as "looking around the garden" is that "dinner" and "cocktails" are *informative* in ways to which both the givers and recipients of invitations mutually orient. For example, if one is invited for cocktails, or for coffee, one will not expect to be given a meal. Whatever else may take place, an invitation to "cocktails" informs recipients to make their own arrangements for eating.[13] The selection of "cocktails" to formulate the invitation is informative about other matters, such as whether the invitee should make arrangements to eat beforehand or afterwards.

Hence the selection of that characterization is treated as informative in that "if you select one, then it's not heard as just the one you're using, but as one selected in order to indicate something about other possible characterisations" (Sacks 1992 [1971]). Thus an invitation for "cocktails" or for "coffee" can be taken to mean "not dinner," although an invitation to dinner would not mean no cocktails or no coffee.

An illustration of this is provided in the following fragment: the "trouble" which arises about whether the invitation includes dinner nicely exposes the expectation that if the guests are going to be given dinner, then the invitation ought to say so, because otherwise they should not expect it.

```
(16)  [SF:2:5]
 1    Bob:      A:nd thee: U.S.C. U.C.L.A. football game's on
 2              Fridee night.
 3    (Mark):   .t'hhhh
 4    Mark:     It's o::n in the evening isn't it.
 5    Bob:      Yeah. Five uh'clo:ck. hh 'hhhh
 6              (.)
 7    Bob:      So::: we thought thet tihknow if you wanna come on
 8              on over early. c'mon over.
 9    Mark:     'hhhh- 'hhhh::::: Ah:::hhhh fer dinner yih mean?hh
10    Bob:      No not fer dinner'h=
11    Mark:     =Oh.
12              (0.3)
13    Mark:     Well five uh'⌐clock is dinner ti:me.
14    Bob:                   └W'l all have (munchies)er something,
15    Mark:     'hhhhh Might have wha:t?
16    Bob:      We might uh: go t'McDonalds er supm.
17              (.)
18    Mark:     ⌐Oh:.
19    Bob:      └Bt js c'm on over'n w'l si'dow:n'n watch th'ga:me
```

It looks as though Mark is being invited over just to watch the football game on television (lines 1–3): the invitation in lines 7–8 does not mention food, and Bob specifies "come on over early." And Bob's response, when Mark "pushes" the matter by asking whether he is being invited for dinner (line 9), makes it very clear that the invitation was indeed not meant to include dinner (line 10) – although it does include such "lesser" eats as are compatible with an invitation to come and watch the game on television (i.e. "munchies," line 14; later amended in line 16 to a similar kind of fast food). Here, then, "come over" and "dinner" stand in some sort of inclusionary/exclusionary relationship or hierarchy, in ways that other possible characterizations of an evening's projected activities do not. Although "come over" and "dinner" need not contrast with one another necessarily or in other circumstances, they count here as contrastive characterizations. Insofar as an invitation to come over to watch the game was designed to inform the recipient "not dinner," that has a maximal property, as standing for the most – in terms of food and drink – that will be provided. Of course "coming over (to watch the game)" may be accompanied by "munchies": but the recipient had better not depend on getting more to eat than the kind of food which may be associated with such an occasion. It is this property to which hosts and guests orient in making and understanding invitations: a host ought not to have to specify, explicitly, that dinner will not be provided, but instead should be able to rely on the maximal property of the terms of the invitation to do that work, to imply "not dinner" (and therein lies the sense of Mark attempting, through a show of uncertainty [line 9], to get himself invited for more than he was being asked for).

These examples in extracts (15) and (16) illustrate that when the relevance of paired alternative characterizations has been occasioned in the talk (or by the invitation), then when a speaker selects one characterization in preference to the other that can be informative about that speaker's position. The implication that the speaker is thereby rejecting the other prior characterization rests on attributing to the subsequently chosen description a maximal status in relation to the other. This maximal property has an exclusionary force: that is, the attorney's selection of "knock" in (15) is designed to exclude the witness's preferred version of "banging" by conveying that she did no more than (did only so much as) "knock." So also in (12)–(14) above; the witness's alternative versions contrast with those proposed by the attorney by conveying that "only so much as" this is the case. For example, when in (14) she answers that they were parked "up the <u>path</u> I don't know how far," her description implicitly dissents from the attorney's version that they were "Some distance back into theuh (.) into the wood" by indicating that as far as she was aware they were parked *only* "up the path." It will be recalled that in (13) the witness describes the defendant as having "Sat at our <u>table</u>," in place of the attorney's version that he "sat with" her. Again, she can be heard as indicating that nothing more, in terms of their relationship or intimacy, is to be associated with his sitting than that he joined her table/group.

In sum, the witness challenges the descriptive adequacy of the attorney's characterization by selecting an alternative candidate version which is informative about the "most that can be said" concerning some locally occasioned, contextually bound essential feature of the scene. The "maximal" property of a sequentially next description, produced in answer to the attorney's prior version, is then the interpretative device through which the witness's answers are designed to stand in place of, and hence to rebut, the attorney's versions. This is evident in two of the witness's answers in the target data.

```
16   A:        Well yuh had some uh (p) (.) uh fairly lengthy
17              conversations with thu defendant uh: did'n you?
18              (0.7)
19   A:        On that evening uv February fourteenth?
20              (1.0)
21   W:        We:ll we were all talkin.
22              (0.8)
23   A:        Well you kne:w. at that ti:me. that the
24              defendant was. in:terested (.) in you (.)
25              did'n you?
26              (1.3)
27   W:        He: asked me how I'(d) bin: en
28              (1.1)
29   W:        J- just stuff like that
```

Her answers in lines 21 and 27–9 are designed to specify details which, without directly negating or contradicting the attorney's prior versions, do not support his versions. Her subsequent characterizations are formulated to represent a scene in which there was no more intimate talk between her and the defendant than that they were "all talking," and no more interest shown in her by the defendant than is indicated by his friendly but not intimate greeting. Her alternative characterizations stand on behalf of a different gloss from that conveyed in the attorney's versions. Certainly, her characterizations do not assert that all that happened was that the defendant asked her how she had been, and that he did not speak to her after that greeting. Instead, they imply that whatever else did happen or was said, alluded to but not detailed in "just stuff like

that" in line 29, amounted to nothing more intimate than is indicated by that greeting. Just as an invitation to "come over to watch
the game" may not preclude "munchies," and perhaps beers, sitting, talking, and so on – but that nothing more in some essential
respect (i.e. dinner) will be provided – so too the witness's characterizations are partial in leaving unspecified whatever else happened, but assert that in some essential respect (i.e. intimacy)
nothing more than that happened.

It is precisely this maximal property of the witness's paired alternative characterizations, designed to dispute his versions, to which
the attorney orients in constructing the contrast "Just asked yuh
<u>how</u> (0.5) yud <u>bi:n</u> (0.3) but he kissed yuh good<u>nigh:t</u>" (lines 30–
1). But before considering further this contrast device and its interactional features, a note is in order about the generality of the
maximal property of a next, alternative description in disputing a
prior version.

5.4 Disputes and disagreement in conversation

Whilst these properties of the design of alternative and competing
versions have been explicated in the context of the witness's
answers during cross-examination, they have their origin and
natural site in ordinary conversation (for a more general consideration of the conversational origin of phenomena to be found in
institutional talk, see Schegloff 1987a). Research into disagreements (Pomerantz 1984a; Sacks 1987) has shown that their construction differs from that of agreements in a variety of ways associated with the dispreferred character of disagreement, and more
generally with the " 'bias' intrinsic to many aspects of the organisation of talk which is generally favourable to the maintenance of
bonds of solidarity between actors and which promotes the avoidance of conflict" (Heritage 1984a: 265). Very briefly, one important respect in which it has been shown that disagreements differ
from agreements is that disagreements, unlike agreements, are
generally delayed. Such delays may be sequential, as when a
speaker who disagrees with something their co-participant has just
said does not start speaking at the earliest opportunity after the
turn in which the disagreed-with assertion was made, resulting in
pausing before disagreeing (which the witness does in [3]; she

leaves pauses of 1 second or more before her disputatious replies in lines 14, 21, and 27–9). Furthermore, disagreements may also be delayed within the design of the turn in which they occur, by being preceded by such components as agreement prefaces, and by such brief components as *uh* and *well* (instances of the use of *well* are to be found in lines 9, 16, 21, and 23 of extract [3]).

The practice of delaying disagreements, both sequentially and in the construction of the turns in which they are done, is an important basis for characterizing disagreements as dispreferred responses. But additional features of their design are also responsible for regarding them as dispreferred; notably, disagreements may be expressed in mitigated or attenuated fashion, or in qualified or weak forms (Atkinson and Drew 1979: 57–60; Levinson 1983: 332–45; Heritage 1984: 265–9; Pomerantz 1984a: 74–5; Schegloff 1988). Pomerantz notes that one respect in which disagreement components are characteristically weak is that they are designed to avoid evaluations which are directly contrastive with the prior speakers' evaluations. We have seen that many of the witness's answers considered above similarly avoid directly contrastive or contradictory versions: for instance, it was noted that although in her answer in line 21 of (3) the witness did substitute the attorney's version of "you . . . and the defendant" with "we . . . all," her characterization of them as "talking" is a qualification and not a direct contradiction of their having had "fairly lengthy conversations."

One of the conversational extracts which Pomerantz cites (Pomerantz 1984a: 75) can be examined further in the light of the analysis above of the interpretative resources through which a subsequent version is produced to qualify, and hence reject, the prior version. In this extract from a telephone conversation, D is discussing with C, a female friend, the difficulties which have arisen in his marriage.

(17) [Goldberg:2:18]

1	C:	`hh D̲e̲finitely fo:r the: f̲i̲fteen years I:'ve
2		known you, (0.3) y̲i̲hknow you've r̲e̲ally bo:th
3		h̲o̲nestly gone yer own ways.
4		(0.8)
5	D:	Essentially:: ex̲c̲ept we've hadda good

```
 6                    relationship at home yihknow
 7    C:              Ye:s but I mean its a relationship whe:re
 8                    uh yihknow pa:ss the butter dear, hh
 9                    (0.5)
10    C:              Yihkno ⌜w make a piece (a) toa:st dear
11    D:                     ⌊N o not really
12    C:              this type'v thing.
13                    (.)
14    D:              We've actually hadda real health- I think
15                    we've hadda very healthy relationship y'know.=
16    C:              = ̇hhh Why: becuz you haven't knocked each
17                    other's tee:th ou:t?
18                    (0.7)
19    D:              Tha:t, a:nd we've::: hadda good communica:tion
20                    and uh: the whole- yihknow I think it's been
21                    healthy,
```

C quite evidently disagrees with D's evaluation that "we've hadda good relationship at home." Her response in lines 7–10 appears to dispute D's gloss of "good relationship"; but it does so by qualifying that description, through detailing some supposed breakfast-table talk between D and his wife. As we have seen for the way "he asked me how I'd been" disputes the attorney's claim that she knew that the defendant was "interested" in her, C counters D's claim that he and his wife had a "good relationship" by describing behavior which does not fit that gloss, which does not support the characterization "good relationship." The breakfast-time talk which C describes in lines 7–10, "pa:ss the butter dear, hh (0.5) yihknow make a piece (a) toa:st dear," implicitly suggests that this kind of banal, rather cold or formal talk (note the imperative forms, and a pretty cool, almost fusty, endearment term) is the most which passes between D and his wife, with respect to something like warmth or intimacy.

We saw that in (3) the witness reports only one thing that happened, the defendant's greeting "He: asked me how I'd bin:"; but she then adds a generalized completor, "just stuff like that," which indicates that everything else that occurred between them, whilst left unspecified, was commensurate with that greeting. Here too in (17) C adds a similar component, "this type'v thing." She does so after listing two supposed breakfast-time utterances, "pa:ss the butter" and "make a piece (a) toast," thereby producing a three-part list of the kind (two-item list plus generalized completor) analyzed by Jefferson (1990) (see the remarks above on the witness's use of "just stuff like that"). Through the generalized completor C implies – as the witness does in (3) – that *only* such talk as these polite, banal, or superficial utterances could be detailed in describing D's relationship with his wife. Thus C's detailing is designedly informative about their relationship in general, about everything else in D's and his wife's behavior towards one another but which does not need to be specified. And through the maximal property of her detailing, C implies that this is the most that can be said about their relationship: since this is less than a "good relationship," then it implies a qualified competing characterization to that offered by D.

This maximal device is evident also in C's response to D's subsequent defense. When he denies C's characterization of his relationship with his wife (line 11) and asserts instead that "I think we've hadda very healthy relationship" (lines 14–15), C challenges that by responding in lines 16–17 "Why: becuz you haven't knocked each other's tee:th ou:t?" This is perhaps a minimum condition for any marital relationship: so in detailing that, C manages to depict their relationship as only as good as the very least they could have for it still to count as a relationship at all (which is pretty much an exaggerated version of the procedure for "damning with faint praise").

The point of this brief excursion into disagreements in conversation is to suggest that this maximal property is a pragmatic property of alternative, "next" descriptions in talk-in-interaction generally, not limited to courtroom cross-examination. It is a conversational device whereby alternative characterizations can imply a contrast with and hence dispute a prior speaker's position/evaluation, whilst being designed in a mitigated or qualified fashion, and thereby avoiding contradicting the other speaker's position or evaluation head-on.

6 Contrast structures, and the "power of summary"

We can now turn to consider the attorney's question in lines 30–1 of (3), in which he appears to contest the witness's version that nothing more happened between her and the defendant that evening to suggest the defendant's "interest" in her than is indicated by his greeting.

```
27   W:          He: asked me how I'(d) bin: en
28               (1.1)
29   W:          J- just stuff like that
30   A:          Just asked yuh how (0.5) yud bi:n (0.3) but
31               he kissed yuh goodnigh:t. (0.5) izzat righ:t.=
32   W:          =Yeah=he asked me if he could?
33               (1.4)
34   A:          He asked if he could?
35               (0.4)
36   W:          Uh hmm=
37   A:          =Kiss you goodnigh:t
38               (1.0)
39   A:          An you said: (.) oh kay (0.6) izzat right?
40   W:          Uh hmm
41               (2.0)
42   A:          An' is it your testimony he only kissed yuh
43               ('t) once?
44               (0.4)
45   W:          Uh hmm
46               (6.5)
47   A:          Now (.) subsequent to this...
```

The contrast which the attorney proposes between "Just asked yuh how (0.5) yud bi:n" and the defendant having subsequently "kissed yuh goodnigh:t" is plainly designed to discredit the veracity of the witness's characterization of the defendant's lack of "interest" in her that evening. The attorney manages that contrast by bringing together two things to which the witness has already attested. Twelve lines before extract (3) the witness confirmed that the defendant kissed her goodnight:[14] and she has just in her prior answer (line 27) volunteered that version of the defendant's greeting.

Now the chance to "bring together" what has previously been said, pieces of prior evidence, and to juxtapose them to make a point, is available only to the questioner. Anyone in the position of answering is restricted to dealing with just what is asked in the prior question: though the question may be understood in the light of what has come before, and what is anticipated to be the line of questioning being developed, nevertheless it is the prior question which demands to be answered. And it will be recalled that this restriction is enforced in extract (1) when the witness, after disconfirming that she told the police that the defendant had been drinking, added to her answer an explanation of what she had told them:

the attorney's request to the judge that the "balance be here stricken" being a specialized instance of the familiar admonishment to witnesses to "Just answer the question, yes or no." As Sacks observed, the opportunity to bring together pieces of information to make a point gives to a questioner some sort of control.

> What we find ... is that the person who is asking the questions seems to have first rights to perform an operation on the set of answers. You can call it "draw a conclusion." Socrates used the phrase "add them up." It was very basic to his way of doing dialectic. He would go along and then say at some point, "Well, let's see where we are. Let's add up the answers and draw some conclusions." And it's that right that provides for a lot of what look like strugglings in some conversations, where the attempt to move into the position of questioner seems to be quite a thing that persons try to do ... As long as one is in the position of doing the questions, then in part one has control of the conversation.
>
> (Sacks 1992 [1964])

Bearing in mind what was said above about the preallocation of speaker turns in courtroom examination, the "strugglings" to which Sacks refers for the position of "doing the questions" in conversations do not occur. The specialized speech-exchange system allocates to the attorney and witness the fixed roles of questioner and answerer respectively: so that the element of control that Sacks describes, in which the questioner has "first rights" to pull together evidence and "draw conclusions," lies always with the attorney. The witness is left in the position of addressing and trying to deal with the attorney's selection of which items to pull together: she has no control over the connections which are made between pieces of information or testimony, nor over the inferences which may be drawn from such juxtapositioning – although she may attempt to rebut those inferences, as she does in extract (1), and in her answer to the attorney's contrast here (line 32, "Yeah=he asked me if he could?").

So out of the prior testimony the attorney selects two items to be pulled together, the descriptions of the greeting, "Just asked yuh how (0.5) yud bi:n," and of the farewell, "but he kissed yuh good-nigh:t." Greetings and farewells can, of course, have a special relevance for characterizing relationships, monitoring the current state of a relationship, and detecting changes in a relationship between the moments of arrival and departure. The wealth of sociological and anthropological studies of greetings has revealed much about their importance in displaying and negotiating relative status, regard, or intimacy (e.g. Goffman, 1971; Firth 1974; Irvine 1974; Kendon 1977; and Schegloff 1979, 1986). The significance for social organization of leave-taking has also received attention (e.g. Goffman 1963, 1971; Firth 1974). Goffman, especially, has shown that the form of greeting can betoken the kind of access which is being permitted, expected, or agreed upon: and he remarks that "taken together, greetings and farewells provide ritual brackets around a spate of joint activity – punctuation marks as it were – and ought therefore to be considered together" (Goffman 1971: 107). And in the contrast he constructs in his question in lines 30–1, the attorney does consider them together: as is so often the case, professional sociological concerns with greetings and farewells derive from and reflect ordinary speakers' practices for investigating and making sense of scenes.

In considering them together here, the attorney manages to juxtapose the claimed nonintimacy of the greeting with the acknowledged (or apparently acknowledged) intimacy of the farewell. The contrast achieved through this juxtaposition is a special kind of object, because it does not simply propose that if one is right (e.g. if the defendant did kiss her goodnight) then the other must be wrong (i.e. it must have been a warmer greeting than she is admitting). Whatever inconsistency is being implied in the contrast is not one which would be resolved by simply discounting one or other of the versions, of the greeting or farewell. Instead the difference between them in terms of intimacy/nonintimacy generates a puzzle about how it could have come about that the witness and defendant ended the evening on much warmer or closer terms than it is claimed they began it. Thus the manner of their farewell is represented in the contrast as *accountable*; not that it is being disputed, but insofar as it needs to be explained (for a more general consideration of which see Hart and Honoré 1959: ch. 2, especially p. 43). The puzzle which the contrast implicitly poses is, therefore, what happened between the greeting and the farewell which could account for the intimacy of the latter, when they had apparently begun on a nonintimate footing?

Whilst in other circumstances the change in intimacy between a greeting on arrival and a farewell on departure might be construed in a happier light, here that change is damaging for her having implicitly proposed – through the maximal property attributed to her detailing that "He: asked me how I'(d) bin:" – that everything else that happened between them that evening was "nothing more" intimate than is indicated by such a greeting. The damaging force of the puzzle which can be inferred from the contrast is that something else must have happened for them to have ended on such apparently intimate terms. The contrast works, then, to challenge not her characterization of the greeting itself, but the credibility of that as an adequate representation of everything else that happened, of all the scene's other essential particulars and how they are to be glossed.

This understanding of the implication conveyed in the contrast is displayed in the witness's reply in line 32, "Yeah=he asked me if he could?" She first confirms the descriptions out of which the contrast is built (she has, after all, already attested to these versions): but she then straightaway (note the latching of the second part of her reply to her confirmation) adds an explanation which attempts to account for the apparent and puzzling discrepancy. In that explanation she specifically details something else that happened, namely that the defendant asked to kiss her. She thereby constructs an account which attempts to "reconcile" the farewell, the kissing, with the greeting, just as in (1) she added an explanation which attempted to account for the apparent contradiction. She simultaneously holds on to her version that the greeting represents the "most" that happened between them; her characterization of how the defendant came to kiss her, that is after asking her permission, being rather too formal for intimacy, thus indicating that no special understanding had developed between them that evening such that he could have counted on kissing her (to ask permission for something is not to take it for granted).

So the attorney juxtaposes the witness's version of the greeting and what it "stands for" in terms of the defendant's interest in her, with the manner of their farewell. In this we can see that participants mutually orient to the properties underlying the disputatious work which the witness's detailing of the greeting is designed to accomplish. That is, the puzzle in his contrast trades off the understanding that her description of the greeting was designed to convey "all/the most that happened" between them. Hence the attorney's construction of the contrast builds on just those properties through which her detailing "He: asked me how I'(d) bin:" was deployed in challenging the attorney's alternative characterization. The same pragmatic resources which were available to the witness implicitly to rebut the attorney's version of the defendant's "interest" in her are equally available to the attorney in pulling together these two pieces of information and generating out of that a puzzle which is damaging to her version.

Although the attorney's construction of a contrast in lines 30–1 has been examined in some detail for this instance alone, such contrasts appear to be quite recurrent in cross-examination. The preallocation of speaker roles and turn types affords the attorney control over "putting facts together" from prior testimony. This is done in hostile cross-examination (i.e. apparently not, or not in this form, in direct examination) by juxtaposing "facts" in such a way as to achieve a contrast which has some damaging implication for the witness's testimony. The contrast in (3) is managed within a single speaking turn or single question: elsewhere during the same cross-examination similar contrasts are established in consecutive question–answer pairs, some instances of which are the following:

(18) [Da:Ou:45/2B:1]

A:	Now (.) subsequent to this: uh (0.6) uh you
	say you received uh (0.8) a number of
	phone ca:lls?
	(0.7)
W:	Yei:s
	(0.4)
A:	From the defendant?
	(1.2)
W:	Yeis
	(0.8)
A:	And isn't it a fa:ct (t)uh (.) Miss ((name))
	that you have an unlisted telephone number?
	(0.3)
W:	Yeis
	(1.2)
A:	An' you ga::ve the defendant your telephone
	number didn't you?
W:	No: I didn't
	(0.3)
A:	You didn't give it to ⌈ him
W:	⌊ No:.
	(10.2)
A:	Dur:ing the:se uh,...

(19) [Da:Ou:45/3A:7]

A:	And the defendant (.) took (.) the ca:r (1.0) an' backed it (1.0) into some trees did'n'e (0.5)
W:	Mm⌐hm
A:	⌊Underneath some trees
	(1.5)
A:	Now Miss ((name)) this time did you make any mention about turning around
W:	No
	(11.0)
A:	An' it was at this point that you say...

(20) [Da:Ou:3A:7]

A:	You dr<u>ove</u> (.) into the woods (1.0) with the defendant (1.1) did'n' say anything about MacDonald's (3.0) he started to kiss you (.) you did'n' kiss him back
W:	Right
	(3.9)
A:	And it was at <u>that</u> point that you (.) said you wanted to go home (0.4) is that right
	(1.2)
W:	Right
	(9.2)
A:	Now Miss ((name))

(21) [Da:Ou:45/3A:7]

A:	And isn't it a fact (1.0) Miss ((name)) (1.0) where you (1.1) went to (1.0) on this evening (1.9) was at least <u>a</u> quarter of a mile (0.5) from the main highway=
W:	=I don't know
	(2.5)
A:	Some distance back into the uh (.) into the wood wasn't it
	(0.5)
W:	It was up the <u>path</u> I don't know how far
	(4.0)
A:	And during this dri<u>:ve</u> up the pa:th (3.0) did <u>you</u> say anything to the defendant (1.0) about MacDonald's (0.5) where you were goin'=
W:	=No
	(10.6)
A:	And the defendant drove...

Each of the contrasts in extracts (13) and (18)–(21) differ with respect to their content, the pragmatic properties whereby one "fact" is being set against another, and the specific damaging implications which the contrast seeks to convey. Despite these differences in "local content," they have in common a number of organizational/structural and interactional features: for this reason they may be regarded as instances of a *contrast device* recurrently used in cross-examination (for an account of contrast structures used by political speech makers as applause-elicitation devices, see Atkinson 1984; there are close parallels between the interactional properties of contrasts in political speeches and in cross-examination). The features of this device's organization illustrated in the above cases are the following.

1 In consecutive questions the witness is asked to affirm or confirm a pair of "facts" or characterizations which are recognizably not discrete: taken together through their sequentially adjacent position, they are juxtaposed in such a way as to generate a puzzle. The puzzle arises from some "lack of fit" between one fact and the other, some discontinuity for which there should be, or needs to be, an explanation which is nevertheless not given. That is, the puzzle is created by implying that some discrepancy is accountable, without a possible account being provided. For instance, when in (18) the attorney establishes that the witness has an unlisted telephone number, what is made both puzzling and accountable by her answer to the next question is how did the defendant obtain her number if she did not give it to him? And in (19) the contrast between the defendant having parked somewhere other than the eating place to which she had agreed to drive with him, and her having made no "mention about turning around" implies the puzzle of why she did not say anything to him. The discontinuity or lack of fit achieved by putting together the two parts of the contrast is between her evidently ending up somewhere she did not think they were driving, and her not saying or asking anything about it.

2 In each instance the puzzle is left unresolved. Although the contrast has generated a puzzle which needs to be explained, the attorney does not subsequently ask what the explanation might be. Thus he breaks off that line of questioning at the point where an

explanation is relevant, but has not been given. By not asking the witness for her explanation, he withholds giving her the opportunity to provide an account which might satisfactorily resolve the puzzle. For example, in (18) the attorney finishes the line of questioning about the defendant telephoning her, at the point where the puzzle as to how the defendant obtained her unlisted number is left unresolved, unexplained.[15]

3 Whilst left unresolved at an official, explicit level, the puzzling discrepancy implies what might be termed an *unless* clause. For instance, in (18) the puzzle about how the defendant obtained her telephone number is only left unexplained unless the witness is dissembling in her answer that she did not give it to him: that way the puzzle is easily resolved – she gave it to him. And in (19) it is a puzzle that the witness made no mention of turning around when the defendant parked his car in some out-of-the-way spot, unless she perfectly well knew what he was intending when he parked the car there (similar accounts for her behavior are implicit in [20] and [21]). And the way this works for (3) has already been explicated· the defendant's kissing her goodnight is only puzzling unless something more happened between them in the course of the evening than the witness is admitting in her characterization of his not seeming to be particularly "interested" in her.

Nothing very technical is meant by the *unless* clause; it serves only to draw attention to the way in which the contrasts work to favor the implication of explanations which are prejudicial to the witness's accounts, or work to discredit aspects of her testimony. It might be that there are "innocent" explanations for what is inferable from the contrast, for example in (18) that one of her family or friends had given him the number, or that he had noticed it at her house.[16] The contrasts, however, are designed not to imply any such innocent circumstances or account. They are designed specifically and systematically to imply an *unless* clause which is damaging to the witness's testimony, by casting doubt upon her veracity, or upon the motives of her actions at the time.

4 However, these damaging inferences are only implied in the contrasts. They are not stated explicitly: it is left for hearers to recognize what the damaging implications are which arise from the con-

trast. The jury are thereby given the opportunity to draw their own conclusions and to find "for themselves" the discreditable implications of the contrast. By pulling together pieces of evidence in this way, the attorney manages not only to provide the jury with the materials with which to decide for themselves what conclusions to reach from the evidence in the contrast: he also avoids having to state explicitly what those conclusions (i.e. damaging implications) are. If he were to state them explicitly, given the turn-taking organization for (cross-)examination, he would have to formulate such conclusions/inferences in a question; which would then give the witness the opportunity to challenge or deny them.

Recalling the point made earlier in this chapter, that the talk between attorney and witness is designed to be understood by nonspeaking recipients, such contrasts are a means of conveying something to the jury over the head of the interaction with the witness. It is specifically in the contrasts where damaging conclusions from the evidence so far are implied: making out these implications is the work which nonspeaking recipients do.

5 Associated with the way in which contrasts are designed to enable the jury to draw their own conclusions from the testimony is that they are given time to do so. After the completion of each of the contrasts, the attorney then delays asking his next question for pauses of 6.5 seconds in line 46 of (3), and for 10.2, 11.0, 9.2, and 10.6 seconds in (18)–(21).[17] These are considerably longer pauses than are to be found elsewhere in cross-examination, the next longest pauses clustering around 3–4 seconds and occurring in quite different environments. This indicates a close connection between the clustering of pause lengths and the interactional work achieved in the prior question–answer pairs: the longer pauses of 6 seconds and more which occur in the environment of the production of a contrast appear to highlight the significance of the contrast, by giving the jury time to recognize and consider the damaging implications for the witness's testimony. Given the multiparty recipiency of the questions and answers, the pauses are designed to be slots for audience appreciation[18] of what they have just heard. As recipients, the jury do not display their understanding or appreciation verbally; therefore, in the absence of any means for the attorney to check the jury's comprehension, the pauses are extended to maxi-

mize the time in which they can assimilate the points implied in the contrasts.

6 Contrasts are summaries of sorts: they pull together some selected points from the prior testimony and complete that line of questioning. In each case, after the pause which follows the contrast the attorney moves on to question the witness about some other aspect of the case. The topic on which the attorney subsequently focuses may be related to the topic of the prior line of questioning, but it is nevertheless a distinct shift to a discernible next matter. For example, after the contrast in (3) which concludes his line of questioning about the defendant's "interest" in the witness on the evening they met in a club/bar, the attorney begins (line 47) to ask about the subsequent period between that meeting and the occasion of the alleged rape. Such shifts in the focus or topic of questioning after the contrast further deprive the witness of the opportunity to come back to the prejudicial point implied in the contrast. So to the earlier comment about the questioner exercising some control through having rights to summarize "where we are now," we can add that in cross-examination – unlike conversation – the attorney not only has first rights to perform that operation (see the above quotation from Sacks 1992 [1964]), but also has effectively the only right to do so. This is because he also has control over changing topic or topical shifts in questioning.

It is by virtue of these organized features of the production of contrasts that they can be considered to be devices, the use of which has a special and central role in the hostile, disputatious questioning of cross-examination. They are the means by which the attorney can selectively bring together points from the witness's testimony, and juxtapose them in such a way as to generate a puzzle, the implication of which is something discrediting about the veracity of the witness's evidence. The damaging inferences which may be drawn from the contrasts are not stated but left implicit. It is left to the jury to draw the conclusions which the contrasts are designed to convey. A contrast is a summary and completion of a line of questioning: hence the attorney manages to bring a line of questioning to a conclusion on what is, for the witness, a damaging point.

7 Conclusion

This chapter has focused on phenomena associated with "contrasting versions" produced by participants in courtroom cross-examination. The first sense of "contrasting versions" explored here
concerns the alternative and competing versions which the
attorney, and then the witness, produce to describe the "same"
action, event, or scene. A version is first proposed by the attorney in
a question: the witness, in her subsequent answer, produces an
alternative description, through which she is heard to dispute or
challenge the attorney's version. Without necessarily directly rejecting and contradicting the attorney's versions, the witness nevertheless disputes these by designing her descriptions in such a way that
they stand for a quite different characterization of a scene than that
proposed by the attorney. The witness's descriptions achieve their
(implicitly) disputatious force through a combination of their
sequential placement, as being done as "nexts" – and hence as
alternatives to – the attorney's; of their being qualified versions,
which do not endorse the attorney's prior versions; and of their
"maximal" property.

The second sense of "contrasting versions" explored here
concerns a device through which the attorney manages to convey to
the jury a contrast between the witness's account of what happened, and what is likely in fact to have happened. The attorney
designs a question, or a pair of adjacent questions, in such a way as
to juxtapose facts, the contrast between which implies a version
which is at odds with, and hence seeks to discredit, the witness's
versions of events. So in response to the witness's attempts to rebut
the attorney's versions, he produces contrasts which in turn are
designed to damage her rebuttals.

Both these kinds of contrasts are the products of the attempts by
each participant to challenge or discredit the other's version of
events. Their competing versions are implicated in, and portrayed
through, the descriptions of "facts" which each produces. In this
way "facts" are left to "speak for themselves"; or rather, their
production is designed to enable the jury to make the proper inferences from them. Descriptions are designed to provide the jury with
the materials from which they can discover for themselves what to
make of the facts. And both contrasts are associated with a measure

of control which each seeks to gain over what emerges from the cross-examination. Whilst this is perhaps more obviously the case for the contrasts which the attorney produces, as a procedure for summarizing by putting together facts in ways which are inconvenient or discrediting for the witness's position, the witness's attempts to counter the attorney's descriptive strategies, and hence herself control the information which is available to the jury, should not be overlooked. Her resistance to the attorney's versions is an attempt to deny him the materials with which he can develop a line of questioning towards some projected and, for her, awkward point: and therein lies the defensiveness of many of her answers.

Whilst the specialized speech-exchange system which is characteristic of cross-examination provides the necessary structural position and resource within which the attorney and witness respectively "fit" their turns, and hence their competing versions of events, this chapter has not focused on participants' management and implementation of the organization of turn taking for cross-examination. The focus has instead been the activities in which each is essentially engaged in cross-examination – those of substantiating and defending their respective versions of events, and disputing the other's versions. What has concerned me is not the management of turn taking itself, but the interactional management of activities in the turns which participants take.

Notes

1. For further discussion of how "lines of questioning" may be managed in cross-examination, and how witnesses attempt to counter perceived lines of questioning, see Atkinson and Drew (1979: esp. 173–81).
2. For the very few of which, under the English legal system, see Cross and Wilkins (1980).
3. Jury members have a legal right – of which they generally seem unaware, and which they almost never exercise – to ask questions during a witness's examination, for example to clarify a point.
4. This relies on an expectation that an utterance will attend to its adjacently prior turn, and hence that its production is based on an understanding of that prior turn. Hence "next position" is a basic structural position in talk-in-interaction. On how this operates, for participants primarily, but also for analysts, as a proof procedure, see Schegloff and Sacks (1973); Levinson (1983: 329–32); Heritage (1984a: ch. 8).
5. This is because there is a rule against repeating the same question: such

that attempts to do so may be disallowed on the grounds that "She's already given an answer to that question, and that answer will stand."

6. The questions asked by interviewers and answered by interviewees in news interviews are also, of course, produced for the benefit of non-speaking overhearers, the radio or television audience. Fuller consideration of these issues, and how this structural property shapes the details of such institutional talk, is to be found in Heritage (1985) and Heritage and Greatbatch (1991).

7. It is clear from the defense attorney's closing speech that this is the significance which he attaches to this line of questioning, and to aspects of the evidence about the defendant's claimed "interest" in the witness/alleged victim. Referring to this part of the testimony in his closing speech, he says: "Now it seems to me (a) situation that uhr: (0.5) that uhr, (0.7) uhr::, whe:re yuh have two (0.2) young people (0.6) who (0.6) appea:r, (0.4) from their testimony to be interested in each other ... he kissed her goodnight, (0.5) an' I reckon she wannah, (0.8) no question about that (0.3) a'right? here's two people who ar:e er interested in each other."

8. Sacks (1984b) explicates how the observability or perceived awareness of the "ordinariness" of scenes interlocks with, and is constituted through, the unnoticeability and unreportable character of many or most of the "infinite collection" of possible details that might be reported about a scene: "people, in reporting on some event, report what we might see to be, not what happened, but the ordinariness of what happened. The reports do not so much give attributes of the scene, activity, participants but announce the event's ordinariness, its usualness" (Sacks 1984b: 414).

   He goes on to suggest that there can be some considerable resistance to treating as "extraordinary" events which, even as they are happening, begin to appear to be "out of the ordinary." So it frequently happens that in reports of "really catastrophic events" such as hijackings, assassinations, and robberies, witnesses report that they initially believed that something else and much more ordinary was happening. "A classically dramatic instance is, almost universally, that the initial report of the assassination of President Kennedy was of having heard backfires" (Sacks 1984b: 419). Such "initial reports" commonly take the form *At first I thought* (mundane event), *and then I realized* (dramatic event). In one news story I have, someone who had been locked in the boot (trunk) of his car by people who had hijacked the car to use as a road block in a hold-up of a security van only realized after being in there for more than half an hour that it was not after all a gag for *Candid Camera*. And when the Oakland football stadium began shaking during the 1989 San Francisco earthquake, some of the football spectators at first attributed the shaking to the effects of a rock concert in a neighboring stadium. So there is a kind of preference to treat scenes which are obviously out of the ordinary as not as extraordinary as they may turn out to have been. For a development of these observations of Sacks, see Jefferson (1983): and on "at first I thought ..." in the context of accounts of paranormal experiences, see Wooffitt (1992).

9. For further consideration of the socially organized contexts of cognitive claims not to remember, and especially the social identity/category of speakers who report not remembering, see Bogen and Lynch (1989); Drew (1989); and with respect to displays of uncertainty/forgetfulness, Goodwin (1987).

10. On the differences between *claiming* and *exhibiting* understanding, see Sacks (1992) lectures of 2 October 1968; lecture 3, January 1969; 31 May 1971; and lecture 3, fall 1971.

11. This formulation makes reference both to a speaker's *production* of a turn/description, and to recipient's *interpretation* of that turn. There is an assumption here that there is a fundamental symmetry between production of conduct and its interpretation, because they are both "the accountable products of a common set of methods or procedures" (Heritage 1984a: 241), these common methods and procedures underlying the shared competence of participants, and thereby underlying "stable meanings." And it is clear in (3), though the data for extracts (11)–(14) are too extensive to be shown, that the attorney understands her answers to be disputing his versions. This is displayed in the manner in which he pursues an issue, by rephrasing the point of a question and asking it again.

12. Some of these issues associated with the design of invitations, with respect to their "informativeness," arise from Sacks's (1992) discussion in his lectures of 23 and 26 April 1971.

13. Sometimes invitations are rather unspecific about what will be provided in the way of food, or quite what kind of an occasion it is for. Often the main "clue" about what to expect is the time for which one is invited. So recipients may infer from the time at which they are invited whether or not they will be given a meal; and sometimes they can be mistaken, or be in doubt (see extract [16] below).

14. The attorney asked "Did'e kiss ya goodnight?," to which the witness replied "Yei:s."

15. The manner in which the contrast is constructed here puts the witness in a position somewhat akin to a "double bind." The witness's denial that she gave the defendant her telephone number is perhaps as damaging as an admission that she gave it to him would have been. Indeed her denial/disconformation was probably anticipated by the attorney, in a contrast through which a damaging point is won whichever way she answers the second question.

16. She has testified earlier that she and the defendant had known one another "since school," and that he had been to her house before.

17. In extracts (3) and (18) these long pauses do not immediately follow the second question–answer pair in the contrast. In (18) the attorney

repeats the witness's denial, thus helping to validate or emphasize it (see the earlier discussion of third-turn repeats in this context; and also note 15). In (3) the witness attempts to rebut the damaging implications of the contrast with an explanation, as discussed in the text. Once again, the attorney validates/emphasizes her answer, and that she agreed to kissing the defendant – points which arise directly out of her "additional" explanation in line 32 – before bringing that topic to a close with the 6.5 second pause.

18. A "slot for audience appreciation" identifies a structural position, after the production of a contrast, in which recipients perform some operation on what they have heard. The results of that operation may, in other contexts than this, be audible; for instance in political speeches this is a slot where the audience applaud (Atkinson 1984; Heritage and Greatbatch 1986; interestingly, the length of such applause is about the same as the pauses here in cross-examination, i.e. about 8–10 seconds). Of course, in cross-examination there is no verbal manifestation, no verbal equivalent of applause, of the audience's (jury's) appreciation of the point in that slot; video recordings of trials might, however, begin to identify some nonvocal manifestations of such appreciations.

The rejection of advice: managing the problematic convergence of a "troubles-telling" and a "service encounter"

GAIL JEFFERSON and JOHN R. E. LEE

1 Introduction

Over the past two years we have been engaged in a project funded by the British Social Sciences Research Council on the analysis of conversations in which "troubles" are expressed. Our data consists in transcriptions of tape-recorded conversations in "ordinary" settings, plus a small collection from "institutional" settings. Our basic concern is the ways in which "troubles" are talked about in the everyday world, in ordinary interaction.

The methodology we follow attempts to ground its analytical categories, its descriptions and formulations of procedure, upon the observable orientations of the co-participants themselves (see Sacks 1968: ch. 2). A constraint upon our research, then, is that our formulation of a phenomenon emerge from the data, rather than being imposed upon it as a preestablished theory or a preset operational definition. Indeed, it was only after months of consultations with the data that we felt secure in proposing that such a thing as "talk about a trouble" is a robust phenomenon, a specific organization of talk.

In the course of our first year's work, various aspects of talk about a trouble came to light in an unmotivated scan of the materials. We were not pursuing any particular aspect of troubles talk; rather, we made ourselves available to whatever might emerge as a possibly systematic feature. As we examined the range of conversations which constitute the current corpus, we began to get a sense that, although many of the conversations were long and multifaceted, they were not amorphous. There seemed to be a shape to them; a shape which recurred across the range of conversations; a shape which could be sensed to be rather well formed in some of the conversations and distorted or incomplete in others.

Furthermore, a series of utterance types were found again and again across the corpus, which seemed to "belong" in various positions within that, as yet dimly perceived, shape. And our work had already yielded a set of categories relevant to and generated in "troubles-talk" interaction; a set of categories to which co-participants could be seen to be orienting: a Troubles Teller and a "properly aligned" Troubles Recipient (see, e.g. Jefferson 1980a, 1984a). Thus, we had a strong, if vague, sense of troubles talk as a sequentially formed phenomenon, a seed collection of elements which might constitute the components out of which a troubles-telling "sequence" could be constructed, and a set of categories which might distribute the components across appropriate speakers. In short, we had the basis for a Troubles-Telling Sequence.

The prospect of gaining some analytic control over large chunks of conversation such as those we were confronted with was exciting, and we proceeded to direct our attention to an investigation of troubles talk as a coherent, sequentially organized unit. And indeed, a scan of the corpus yielded a series of recurrent, positioned elements which could be grouped into a rough segmental sort of order, on the basis of which we developed a candidate Troubles-Telling Sequence. However, a detailed examination of the materials did not yield a single instance of troubles talk in which the candidate sequence was present, element by element, or even segment by segment, in order. The actual instances of troubles talk comprised very messy versions of the candidate sequence (see Jefferson 1988).

Clearly, troubles talk did not occur as a consecutive sequence of ordered elements. On the other hand, the talk does tend to run off within a constrained set of elements; that is, the elements which were proposed to constitute the components of a Troubles-Telling sequence could be understood as recurrently present, but occurring in a "disordered" fashion. Secondly, although the elements might be "disordered," there is nevertheless a very gross sort of observable order; that is, the data tend to start off with elements which "belong" to early parts of the candidate sequence, and close with elements which "belong" to the latter parts of the candidate sequence. That is, our initial vague sense of a set of components occurring in order was not, as we supposed, vague because we had not yet carefully enough inspected the data; that is, the shape was not "dimly perceived," but, as it were, dimly manifested in the talk. Inasmuch as it is our aim to locate, describe, and then analyze objects which actually occur, our findings were problematic. A question was, is this vague shape a design feature of the "sequence," perhaps as a technique for managing the long stretches of talk it organizes, a flexibility which preserves coherence while absorbing a range of contingencies liable to develop over large chunks of conversation? Alternatively, is the design rather more strict, but on any given occasion of its use— as is so in occasional or frequent actual instances of the use of other strictly designed sequence types – is something happening in that interaction which is producing a "disruption" or "disordering" of a precisely ordered sequence?

Coming to terms with these possibilities required close analysis of talk about a trouble on a single instance by single instance basis. The results of those analyses suggest that in case after case a potentially strict sequence is encountering problems, and is thus becoming disordered. Further, it appears that the problems encountered by the sequence are not best characterized by reference to a particular interaction and its personnel and events, but by reference to general problem types which recur across the corpus of troubles talk.

At this point, then, we find ourselves provisionally treating the candidate Troubles-Telling Sequence as a "template" for the production of any given interaction in which "troubles" are talked about; a template which is massively subject to disordering or disruption as the result of specifiable and generalized problem types (for a fuller report, see Jefferson 1988).

This formulation is reminiscent of the methodological position Max Weber puts forth in his classic *The Methodology of the Social Sciences* (1949). While he was principally concerned with understanding large-scale sociohistorical movements rather than day-to-day social interaction in fine-grained detail, his epistemological arguments can equally well be posed for the latter.

In his program for the social sciences, Weber proposes that social organization should be studied via the construction of "ideal types" which, while not existing in the world, constitute a framework for the production of particular courses or sequences of action. And among his conditions for the construction of an "ideal type" were (a) that it be a logically possible course of action, which (b) adequately represents those actual instances indicated by it. Real-life "departures" from such a model do not necessarily disqualify the model, but may themselves be accounted for by an understanding of how the model has been departed from.

However, while akin to Weber's "ideal type," our "template" was not preformulated, but was grounded in and constructed from the data under inspection: in contrast to Weber's methodological program, we did not set out to find/construct a nonactual but representative model. Indeed, such a procedure is at variance with our own program which insists upon the description and analysis of actually occurring events in the very details of their occurrence. The notion of a "model" in this case is tentative and problematic; we are far more committed to its analytic sequelae.[1]

Our investigation of "disorderings" of, or "departures" from, the candidate Troubles-Telling Sequence yielded a range of phenomena which, singly or in combination, could be seen to be causing deep problems for the sequence. The various phenomena could be grouped into two major types: interactional "asynchrony," and activity "contamination."

Interactional "asynchrony" involves, roughly, that co-participants can be characterized as improperly aligned by reference to the categories provided for by, and crucial to, the orderly progression of the sequence. Following is a single, dramatic-to-the-point-of-pathological, instance.

(1) [JG:I:21:1–3] (F is caller, M is wife of intended call-recipient)
Marge: 'h We:ll uh may I: ha:ve about two minutes of your ti:me?
              (0.8)
Marge: I: would like to tell you that one of your: 'h uh brother
              er hu- you kno:w the Ma:sons down at your clu:b 'hhh
              uh::m::,h 'tlk 'hhh introduced my husband to a lady
              .
              .   (ca.20 lines omitted; straight monologue)
              .
Marge: 'hhhh An:d so when he went awa:y on Mother's da:y and 'hh
              he went away on Saturday evening of (0.3) Mother's Da:y
              'hh and he spent the night (.) with he:r and all: day
              Sunday and came home around about nine o'clock Sunday ni:ght
              'hhhh uh he didn:'t sa:y u-one word he just came in put his
              pajamas o:n 'hhh a:n:d uh sat on the couch for about five

```
                minutes and then he went in: to his bedroom and went to be:d.
                ˙hhhhh and:d uh u-so: uh then I,hh well you know I was
                questioning about what was go⌈i n g   o  :  n?⌉
Frank:   →                                    ⌊Well do you h⌋ appen to have
                his phone number?
                (0.2)
Marge:          ˙hhh u⌈No::? I do not have his ⌈phone>number<he: will-
Frank:                ⌊( )-                    ⌊Do you know where I might
                reach him?
```

We simply note, but do not explicate here, that a co-participant is observably not moving into alignment as a troubles recipient. Other materials collected as candidate instances of "troubles-talks" yielded far more delicate versions of interactional "asynchrony."

As to activity "contamination," we find that there are ranges of activities which converge with a troubles telling; activities which have rather different treatments of the event/situation which might constitute a "trouble," and rather different components and trajectories from those of a troubles telling *per se*. Among the range of "contaminants," we initially located three recurrent types: (a) building a case, in which the possible "trouble" constitutes a possible "misdeed" (or its consequence); (b) negotiating a plan, in which the possible "trouble" constitutes a possible "obstacle"; and (c) dispute, in which the possible "trouble" constitutes a "source of contention."

Simply enough, talk about a circumstance or event which might constitute a "trouble" and thus proceed in certain ways, that is as a troubles telling, may be very little, or not at all, a troubles telling, and very much or altogether the building of a case, the negotiating of a plan, or engagement in dispute. And it may, further, be ambiguous as to which is occurring.

Earlier we mentioned our concern as to whether or not "talk about a trouble" is a robust phenomenon. The alternative was that it is no more than a matter of "content," and otherwise no more than a "story," or a "topic," etc., like any other. The considerations of activity "contamination" were particularly informative on this issue. Specifically, a "content" which might be preclassified as "a trouble" occurs in talk which is not at all, or only partially, or ambiguously, a troubles telling, and in which, indeed, whether or not some event or circumstance *is* a "trouble," and whether or not the interaction *is* a troubles telling, is under negotiation. That is, it

is not the "content" *per se*, but the organization of the talk which
provides for a troubles telling; that same "content" may also be
talked of in ways which provide for other specifiable activities.

So, for example, in the following fragment, an instance of building a case with the possible "trouble" as a possible "misdeed,"
absence from work may be an index of a "trouble" or may constitute malingering. An announcement that "I got a real bad stomach
ache" occurs in the course of building a case for all good intentions
to go to work, and for the absence from work as warranted; that is,
an "excuse." On its occurrence, the event may be specifically
offered as a "trouble," but it is not received as such, and is reem-
bedded into the ongoing production of an "excuse," which, eventually, is received and accepted as such.

```
(2) [TCI(b):9:2]
  John:              I just called to make sure you were you know, (0.2) ˙hh I
                     didn't know whether you'd gone to work or what you kno ⌐w.
  Marcia:                                                                   ⌊I
                     was going to go: to wor:k,hh ˙hhhh I got a:fter you left
                     I thought well I'll eat some breakfast and then I will go:
                     to wor:k.hh
                     (0.3)
  Marcia:            ˙hhhhh A:nd so: I: a:te a muffin?hh ˙hhhh and chee:se,hh
                     (0.7) ˙hhhhh And then I went to the bathroo:m? (1.5) ˙t
                     ˙hhh There was,h (1.6) a::nd I had a spoonful of cereal,
  John:              Mm hm,
  Marcia:      →     ˙hhh And then I got a real bad stomach ache.
                     (1.7)
  Marcia:            Like (.) when: (.) someone tied a knot in my stomach.
                     (0.2)
  Marcia:            ˙hhh So I lay dow:n and the next thing I know it was
                     eleven o'clo:hh-hh
  John:              heh-heh-heh-heh-heh-hih-hih-heh=
  Marcia:            =So I didn't go:.
  John:              Ah,
                     (0.3)
  John:        →     No that's: okay,
                     (0.5)
  John:              Mh,
                     (1.2)
  John:              They can get along without you for a day or two,
```

In this case, the co-participant is perhaps a properly aligned
"excuse recipient," but not a "troubles recipient." And we note

that in subsequent talk he does some "interrogation," "You been laying down on the couch or in the bedroom," and still later, some "accusatory talk," "A̅re you gonna d̲o anything? or you just gonna: (2.3) lay arou̲:nd." The focus here is̲ not on the troublesomeness to the teller of a̅ circumstance or event, but on whether it constitutes an adequate excuse for absence from work, or a case of malingering (see also Jefferson 1986a).

And, for example, in the following fragment, an instance of negotiating a plan, with the possible "trouble" as a possible "obstacle," a recurrent midpoint element of the candidate Troubles-Telling Sequence, a heightened description of the "trouble," "O̅h:: my God I been ·hhh running the highest temperatures you ever sa̅:w," is followed by an offer to close the conversation altoge̅ther.

(3) [TCI(b):7:1—2] (Opening unrecorded; L is caller and is identifying herself to C, the call recipient)

```
Lily:              (I'm) Jo:dy's mothe̲:r?
                   (0.6)
Cora:              Oh ye┌h ((very hoarse, here and throughout the talk)
Lily:               ̅   └Jo:dy Lih-t̲empi,
Cora:              Oh:̲ yeh,
                   (0.2)⁻
Lily:              Are you si::ck,
Cora:        →     ·tc̅h u-Y̲eh I got the f̲lu.
Lily:              Ao̲h:::::.uh┌hnh┌hnh  ha┐ha-ha-ha ┐
                             └h-  └hhhhhh ┘hh-hh-hk┘
                   (.)
Cora:                         ┌·hh
Lily:        →     └Well that n̲i:ps it in the bu̲:d, ·hh I was gonna a̲sk you if
                   you could ke̲ep Jo:dy for a c̲(h)ouple hours but you can't
                   if you got the flu̲::.
Cora:              ·tch I wouldn't want him a̲round me ho:n, ·t┌·hhhhhh┐hh=
Lily:                                                         └nNo::::, ┘
Cora:              =c̲ause uh: I've r̲eally got it.
                   (.)
Lily:              y:Y̲o┌u sure-
Cora:                  └I-
                   (.)
Cora:              But I'd be glad to d̲o it if I wasn't sick.
Lily:              e-You s̲ure sound aw̲:ful.┌(        ho̲arse.)┐
Cora:        →                             └·t O̲h:: my G̲od┘I been ·hhh running
                   the highest temperatures you ever sa̲:w.
Lily:        →     O̲h my go̲:sh well let m̲e hang up and let you get back to bed=
```

Cora:	=eh <u>huh</u> ⌜uh uhh⌝h h h u- h h u-⌝=
Lily:	⌞<u>So</u>:rry ⌟I <u>d</u>isturbed you.⌟=
Cora:	=How <u>you d</u>oin hon=
Lily:	=Oh <u>j</u>ust <u>fi</u>:ne.

In this case, the co-participant may be properly aligned as the proposer of an inauspicious plan, and an intruder upon someone's "trouble," but certainly not as a "troubles recipient." As with the single dramatic instance of interactional "asynchrony," these single instances of two types of activity "contamination," building a case, and negotiating a plan respectively, are transparent for the problematic effect on a troubles telling. Again, other materials yielded far more delicate and ambiguous versions.

We come now to the third type of activity "contamination," that of dispute, in which the "trouble" becomes a source of contention. We had constructed an array of materials in which disputes, which were in various ways disruptive of what might otherwise constitute a troubles telling, occurred. The array was simply designed to point up the recurrent "dispute" outcome of the introduction of a possible "trouble." It was out of an inspection of the arrayed fragments that the issue with which we are concerned in this chapter emerged.

2 A precursor of dispute: the giving of advice

A recurrent feature of materials in which a possible troubles telling turned into a dispute was that there were greater or lesser degrees of "asynchrony" present; that is, recurrently a co-participant could be seen to be declining to align properly as a "troubles recipient" prior to the onset of dispute. And, recurrently, attendant to that "asynchrony" was the giving of advice. So, for example, in the following fragments, selected initially as simple instances of the onset of dispute in what might otherwise be a troubles telling, we see the combination of asynchrony, advice giving, and dispute. The arrows indicate advice or advice-relevant utterances, the asterisked arrows indicate the onset of dispute.

(4) [Frankel:US:1:57ff] (V is talking to someone other than J at the very start of this fragment)

Vic:	Cause that-that's (his policy).
James:	Hey <u>Vic</u>tor,
Vic:	So I (have to say)

James: The <u>n</u>ext time you see me I'm gonna be looking like <u>he</u>:ll
            you know why,
            (0.7)
James: Cause <u>e</u>:very damn one of these <u>t</u>eeth coming out.
( ):   (   ).=
James: =bottom and top.
            (0.7)
Vic: →   Doesn't matter you still be you <u>wo</u>:n't you James,
James: s-uh::::::, Yeh I guess so-<u>MA</u>YBE (   ) when <u>I</u> see that
            dentist (come at me) with that damn <u>n</u>eedle I'm ready to <u>r:run</u>
            like <u>he</u>:ll (.) <u>I</u> don't <u>mind</u> eh pulling them but he coming at
            <u>me</u> that <u>needle</u>'s what I can't stand.HAH ⌈HAH <u>HAH</u> HAH!⌉
Vic: →   ⌊(Use)- Tell him ⌋<u>gas.</u>
James: ˙hh Huh?
Vic: →   Tell him gas.
            (0.4)
James: Uh- No I don't (want no ga⌈s, no) I wi-I will take it.
Vic: →   ⌊Well let me ask you this question.
James: You know?
Vic: Let me ask ⌈you o n e ques⌈tion.
James: ⌊I'll take it.   ⌊Yeh righ⌈t
Vic: ⌊Let me ask you this
            question.
James: Yeh.
Vic: →   Are you getting toothaches?
            (0.4)
James: * → NO!
            (0.2)
Vic: →   ⌈(Then don't   )-
James: * → ⌊But I got cavities!

(5) [NB:I:6:13ff:r]

Lottie: <u>H</u>ow:'s your f<u>oo</u>:t.=
Emma: =˙t˙hh <u>O</u>h: it's <u>h</u>ealing <u>b</u>eautifully:.
Lottie: G<u>oo</u>: d.⌈
Emma: ⌊The <u>other</u> one may have to come o:ff on the <u>other</u> toe
            I've got it in <u>th</u>at but it's not in<u>f</u>ected.
            (0.8)
Lottie: →   Why don't you <u>use</u> some <u>stuff</u>⌈on it.
Emma: ⌊˙t <u>I've</u> got per<u>o</u>xide I put o:n
            it but uh ˙hhhh the <u>other</u> one is <u>h</u>ealing very w<u>e</u>:ll: I
            <u>l</u>ooked at it the other day I put a new t<u>a</u>:pe on it every
            d<u>a</u>:y so ˙hhhh⌈hhh
Lottie: →   ⌊Why don't you <u>g</u>et that <u>n</u>ay-u<u>h</u>::: Revlon
            nai⌈l:::
Emma: * →   ⌊˙hhh Well <u>th</u>at's not <u>t</u>herapeutic Lottie <u>r</u>eally it <u>s</u>ays

on the (0.4) thi:ng e-th-when you g-ah this pero:xide is:
uh: kind of uh,hh ˙hhh ⌈hh

Lottie: * →   ⌊What do you mean uh th-u do:ctors
use it,

(6) [SBL:2:1:8:2]

Faye: I was thinking this morning, I was having a little trouble
                     in the bathroom, and I thought oh, boy, I-n-I-uh uh this
                     business of getting up at six o'clock and being ready to eat,
                     is uh- is not for me, ⌈heh heh

Bea: →   ⌊Uh huh, Well, uh th-((clears throat))

Faye: Somehow you ⌈endure it.

Bea: →   ⌊There's an- there's an answer to that too.

                     (2.0)

Bea: hhhh A physical answer t(hh)o hhh

Faye: You mean taking laxative at night.

Bea: →   No, suppositories. ⌈That takes-

Faye: * →   ⌊Well, it doesn't always work for me Bea,

Bea: No?

Faye: It didn't work this morning.

(7) [TCI(b):9:1] (Opening unrecorded; J is caller)

John: (How are you) feeling now.

Marcia: Oh::? (.) pretty good I gue:ss, ⌈hh- hh⌉

John: ⌊Not so⌋hot?

                     (0.8)

Marcia: I'm just so:rt of: waking u:p,

                     (0.2)

John: Hm:m,

                     (3.6)

Marcia: Muh- ((hiccup)) (0.9) My: (   ),

John: Huh?

Marcia: My: (   ) doesn't hu:rt, (0.4) My head feels (.) better,

John: °Uh huh,°

                     (1.5)

Marcia: ukhhh ⌈uh ukhh

John: ⌊Well that's goo(h)d,

                     (1.4)

John: →   Take (.) you kno:w make sure you're taking (.) plenty of
                     vitamins and

                     (0.7)

Marcia: Ye:h?

John: →   you know drink plenty of wa:ter.

                     (1.0)

Marcia: * →   ˙t˙hhhh Can't drink water when you're slee:ping,

In the four above fragments, the giving of advice occurs very early in talk about a "trouble." And according to our candidate Troubles-Telling Sequence, the advice was specifically occurring "prematurely." That is, in our examination of the corpus we had found a recurrent later segment which we called the "work-up" component, in which a range of diagnostic, prognostic, etc., considerations of the "trouble" were produced, in which it seemed to us "advice" might properly be introduced. This segment not only occurs late in the sequence but is strongly close-implicative and is recurrently followed by closure of the troubles telling. Thus, it seemed to us that in the above fragments an element of a later and close-implicative segment is introduced before a troubles telling has really been started.

It seemed to us reasonable to wonder if the advice is being resisted as much for its prematurity and close-implicature as for, for example, the quality, applicability, etc., of the advice itself. We noted that various sorts of advice, suggestions, recommendations, of remedies, recipes, machinery, holiday venues, shortcuts, etc., may be accepted, the details copied down in great detail, although a recipient has no intention of using them. That is, acceptance or rejection may be in great part an interactional matter, produced by reference to the current talk, more or less independent of intention to use it, or actual subsequent use.

The four above fragments suggested that the presence of "asynchrony" and "sequential prematurity" at least in part might account for resistance to the advice, and was predictive of the emergence of dispute. And in the following fragment, we find advice being introduced in a way that exhibits an orientation to both those features; that is, a co-participant can be seen to be working to set up an interactional and sequential context which, according to our considerations, specifically would foster acceptance. Here we find advice being positioned in what would seem to be an appropriate Troubles-Telling Sequence segment; that is, in a work-up initiated by the troubles teller, and emerging as the logical outcome of a diagnosis offered by the troubles recipient and concurred in by the troubles teller; that is, the advice is sequentially appropriate and the talk is interactionally "synchronous." However, the advice, when it is delivered, is disputed.

532   Gail Jefferson and John R. E. Lee

(8) [Rahman:II:12—13]
```
Gwen:    You know he's a funny little in⌐secu:re  1⌐ittle boy:=
Myra:                                 ⌊ee Y e : h⌋
Gwen:    =isn⌐'t    he:.⌐
Myra:        ⌊Beh-uh b⌋ut the point is Gwennie don't forget no:w. ˙h
         (0.3)
Myra:    Eh:m (.) He was so: close to °Gordon° wa:sn't he.=
Myra:    =He wa⌐s v e r y : : .
Gwen:         ⌊°Well this is it⌋you see⌐::,°      ⌐Mm:,
Myra:                                ⌊And no⌊w he's  ↑go:ne. And
         he thinks ↑you're gonna go as well you s⌐ee:.
Gwen:                                            ⌊Well I think this
         is it⌐(but it- it's)
Myra: →      ⌊Well ih- S o :⌋=
Gwen:    =⌐ Oh ⌐::
Myra: → =⌊ ˙h ⌊be patient with him course we:: don't mi:nd,
Gwen: * →But it gets me down a bit you know⌐I: mean I ca:n't
Myra:                                       ⌊(Loo:k.)
Gwen:    I ca:n't mo:ve? you know he ⌐says where you goi:⌐n g,⌐
Myra:                                ⌊ (What)              ⌊Well⌋=
Gwen:    =⌐(          )
Myra: → =⌊I've t o : l d y⌋ou:.
         (.)
Gwen:    Mm⌐:?
Myra: →    ⌊Just send him round here for a⌐couple of: hou:⌐rs.
Gwen: * →                                 ⌊ehh! ˙hh      ⌊But then
         (tha-) But⌐you know ↑My:ra I⌐ never go anywhere⌐do I::.
Myra:              ⌊(          )⌋                        ⌊I:: ↓kn ow=
Myra:    =Ye:ah.
```

The disputed advice is abandoned, and reissued at a next appropriate place; namely, again after some diagnostic talk initiated by the troubles teller and participated in by the advice giver.

(8.a) [Rahman:II:13—14]
```
Gwen:    But he's alright if there's somebody else he::re,
         (.)
Myra:    °Ye⌐s y e s°        b e c a u s e⌐
Gwen:       ⌊Bit it's jus:t⌋u when he's on⌋his ow⌐n he d⌐oesn't like⌐
Myra:                                      ⌊he   ⌋ha:tes ⌋=
Gwen:    =⌐being on⌐his ow:n⌐
Myra:    =⌊t h a t ⌋house o⌋n his ow:⌐n.
Gwen:                                ⌊iYe::ah,
Myra:    He ha:tes it. ˙h⌐h
Gwen:                   ⌊I supp⌐o:se you know: i⌐t
Myra:                         ⌊Well        ⌊Yeh-
```

                        (.)
Myra: →   Ih-ih-it Let him cause I mean it's not all that long you
                        kn⌐ow   ⌐Jus:t
Gwen: * →   ⌊Yeh·h ⌊Well you see it's different for me:.<eh for (.)
                  the other boy:s be⌐cause they always had each othe:r.
Myra: ⌊Yeh
Myra: E:xactly.

On this round, the advice is utterly minimally acknowledged with
"Yeh" and the diagnostic talk returned to with "·h Well you see it's
different for me:.<eh for (.) the other boy:s because they always
had each othe:r." The advice-giver again participates in this next
round of diagnostic talk, and yet again offers the advice, which is,
again, disputed.

(8b) [Rahman:II:14—15]
    Gwen: be⌐cause they always had each othe:r.
    Myra: ⌊Yeh
    Myra: E:xactly. ⌐Where Tho⌐mas-⌉
    Gwen: ⌊(But) ⌊Ye:s,⌋
                (.)
    Myra: ⌐W e l l h e⌉
    Gwen: ⌊Well there's o⌋:nly Da:nny and they fight like the (devil)=
    Myra: =uWell thi⌐s is i:t.   ⌉E ⌐x ⌐a c ⌐tly, ya⌐s.
    Gwen: ⌊ehhhhh hh⌋ ⌊heh⌋heh⌋   ⌊·hhhh
    Gwen: An⌐d u h⌉
    Myra: →   ⌊So just⌋ (.) ulittle patience with him cause I: don't mind
                  you know that.
    Gwen: * → Yeh but ih-ih-⌐ it's ⌉
    Myra: ⌊Yas.⌋
    Gwen: *→ =You know it's I try: I try to be pa↑tient hh⌐a ha ha My⌐:ra⌉
    Myra: ⌊I kn::ow, ⌋and⌋=
    Gwen: ⌐eh!
    Myra: =⌊ it's easy for me to say th⌐is,
    Gwen: ⌊·hhhe:hhh Oh::⌐: dearie m⌐e:,
    Myra: ⌊ee: Y a h.⌋

In fragments (4)–(7) advice is proffered which has not been
conversation-locally processed to promote acceptance, and in those
fragments, the advice is rejected; but in fragment (8)–(8b) the
advice is, repeatedly, conversation-locally processed to promote
acceptance, and is, repeatedly, rejected. That is, whether or not the
advice is processed to promote acceptance, it gets rejected. And we
note again, current acceptance or rejection of advice can have little
to do with the quality, relevance, etc. of the advice itself, or with the

advice recipient's intentions to use it, and rejection is certainly not an automatic outcome of an advice giving.

We are, therefore, led to wonder if perhaps the problem lies in the particular environment into which the advice in these cases is being introduced; namely, that of a possible troubles telling.

In that regard we can notice that while the relevant local categories *troubles teller* and *troubles recipient* constitute a fitted pair, not only do the categories *troubles teller* and *advice giver* not constitute such a fitted pair, but in terms of the general conversational categories, speaker and recipient, both occupy the same category, that of speaker, with each speaker's co-participant as the intended recipient. Upon the proffering of advice by a prospective or to-this-point troubles recipient, a troubles teller is shifted into incumbency in the appropriate paired category *vis-à-vis* an advice giver, that of advice recipient, and in more general terms, is transformed from a speaker to a recipient in the current interchange.

Thus, the accepting of advice may bring with it removal from the category troubles teller and loss of whatever perquisites that troubles-relevant category and its attendant conversation-general category, speaker, may entail. Correlatively, the delivering of advice may bring with it removal from the category troubles recipient and acquittal from whatever obligations that troubles-relevant category and its attendant conversation-general category, recipient, may entail.

3 The convergence of a troubles telling and a service encounter

The proffering of advice in the course of a troubles telling, with its new, and reversed, set of categories and their attendant rights and obligations, may implicate an altogether different form of talk; that is, not a troubles telling, but that which various interaction analysts call the service encounter, in which the criterial categories are, say, service seeker and service supplier (the relevant subcategories in this case being advice seeker and advice giver).

In such an environment, someone with a "trouble" may conduct her- or himself as a recipient-elect until such time as the advice giver is prepared to deliver the sought-for advice, whereupon the advice seeker assumes full recipientship. In effect, the advice seeker delivers the particulars of his conditions only until he or she need no longer do so; only until the advice giver is prepared to start delivering advice.

And it may be that environment, and not the environment of a troubles telling, in which the emergence of advice as a logical outcome of description and diagnosis properly and harmoniously resides. Clearly, there is a strong convergence between a troubles-telling and the service encounter. But that convergence may be problematic in just the ways that the convergence of a troubles telling with building a case, and the convergence of a troubles telling with negotiating a plan are problematic; that is, it may provide for "contamination" of a troubles telling with components and procedures of the convergent business, and thus for disruption of a Troubles-Telling Sequence.

The recurrently found rejection of advice in talk about a trouble may, then, be accomplice to an attempt by a troubles teller to preserve the status of the talk *as* a troubles telling, with its particular structural and interactional properties, and to maintain incumbency in the category troubles teller, with its particular and general perquisites.

Similarly to building a case, in which the "trouble" alternates with "misdeed," and negotiating a plan, in which the "trouble" alternates with "obstacle," the service encounter's business may be characterized as solving a problem, in which, then, the "trouble" alternates with "problem." Attendant to this alternation, it might be seen that while in a troubles telling the focal object is the "teller and his experiences," in the service encounter the focal object is the "problem and its properties."

A glimpse of this distinction may be found in the following fragment. In this case, just after the announcement of a candidate "trouble," "My toenails are falling off," the prospective troubles recipient launches into a story of a third party's trouble which is relevant to, and exhibited as brought to mind by, the announcement. The outcome of the story is the recommendation of a remedy. In this case, perhaps in part because of its method of introduction, the recommendation is accepted. But it can be noticed that the advice recipient/intending troubles teller thereafter raises the issue of efficacy of the remedy for herself as compared to the third party (i.e., if not actually disputing the recommendation, at least providing for its status as rejectable), and uses that talk to reintroduce her

own circumstances, "Well, my toenails are getting bad Lottie."
This second attempt is countered by an utterly bland, continuing
attention to the remedy by the advice giver.

(9) [NB:IV:10:31—34]

Emma:		˙hhh Well honey I'm glad you had a guu- I thought about you and I m:<u>miss</u>ed you, but I been r- I've really had a <u>very</u> nice time. Sunday was kind of a long day, but uh, ˙hh ⌈hhh
Lottie:		⌊Yeah,
Emma:		<u>I'm</u> used to everything no:w, an::d,
		(0.6)
Lottie:		Yeah.
Emma:		I'm brea- hhh I- my toenails are falling off, I ⌈don't know,
Lottie:		⌊Oh::. <u>W</u>ait
		a minute. That's- I'm glad you mentioned that. You know Isabel had her <u>nail</u> taken off, like <u>you</u> had your <u>toe</u>nail=
Emma:		=⌈Yeah?
Lottie:		=⌊taken off? and it just about <u>kill</u>ed her you know,=
Emma:		=⌈Yeah,
Lottie:		=⌊ she nearly died a thousand times and I was telling her about you.
Emma:		<u>Yeah</u>,
Lottie:	→	˙hhhh So anyway, <u>she</u> got this, Vi:dafoam, and, I bought some down there and I put some on my nails last night and I put on some tonight, ˙hh And she said that was the only thing that <u>heal</u>ed them.
Emma:		<u>Vi</u>:dafoam.
Lottie:		Yeah. And I- I payed a dollar:: uh- eighty three for it but then it might be a little cheaper <u>here</u>. in some, drug ⌈store there.
Emma:		⌊˙hhhhh-
		(1.0)
Lottie:		⌈<u>V</u>idafoam.
Emma:	*→	⌊I- I w- I wanna ⌈get some.
		⌊Wuh- Wait a minute, let me, uh, let me- I got it right here, I know it's Vidafoam.
		(4.2)
Lottie:		Yea:h, (0.8) <u>Via</u>foam. It's V-i-o, f-o-r-m. Ointment.
		(0.9)
Emma:	*→	v:Viaform, Did <u>she</u> have the ba:d big thick thing like ⌈my toenail,
Lottie:		⌊ <u>Oh</u>:::::. <u>Go</u>:::d, <u>Ye</u>:::s. ⌈<u>And how</u>.
Emma:	*→	⌊˙hhhhhh But <u>she</u> didn't break out on her <u>body</u>,hh ˙hhh
Lottie:		No? but- course that's v- course she breaks out on her in her <u>ha:nds</u>. you know.

Emma:		She always <u>did</u> have those- `hhh No, but this goes with the toenail bit I think some of this- goes with the toenail-
	→	Well, my toenails are getting bad Lottie, those two big toenails, but ah- `hhh
Lottie:	→	It says, uh, soothing, antibi::: (0.8) oh something, and fungi, dayo preparation for the treatment of <u>inf</u>lamed condition of the skin such as eczema, `hhh athletics foot and other fungus, `hh infection. Your physician may, `hh prescribe Vidafoam for other conditions and other direction differing from those that appeared on this package. `hh Now this uh Doctor Allen gave this to <u>he:r</u>, `hh ⌈and uh, uh::,
Emma:		⌊Mm hm,
Lottie:		she uses it on her, uh <u>hands</u> too. you know,=
Emma:		⌈Yeah,
Lottie:		=⌊ like, uh yih-uh-yih- uh, well you have that and she said for you to use on the- on your uh psoriasis.

When, later in the conversation, the troubles teller produces a description of her circumstances, it is met again with an utterly bland attention to a "problem and its properties"; in this case, its distribution and possible causes. (And at this point we find the onset of dispute.)

(9.a) [NB:IV:10:48—49]

Emma:	→	Oh God it's <u>terrible</u> Lottie, my toenails- `hhh they just look so sick those big toenails it just makes me sick. You know, they're jus- dead. Everything's dead. I-I sat out today and I said my God am I just <u>dy</u>ing. It's- like I'm <u>os</u>sified.
Lottie:	→	No at- we were in some place, I don't know if it was Dane's or some place, (0.5) I guess it was Dane's. and, somebody was talking about it, and <u>I</u> bet there were `hhh ten people around there, and they all started to say well they had the same thing? And I know, like Doctor Compton says it's from the damp- detergent.
		(1.6)
Lottie:		It really is.
Emma:	*→	I, gotta believe it Lottie, but <u>how</u> would it be on your <u>toes</u> though ho:ney.

What emerges from such materials as fragments (4)–(9) may be characterized as the advice giver's "essential interest" in the problem and its properties, and "essential indifference" to the troubles teller and his or her experiences. To bring home this distinction, we turn to a phenomenon which made its appearance fifteen years ago and has been lying around in a notebook since.

The phenomenon was noticed in the course of transcribing tapes from an emergency ambulance service. Throughout these conversations there was a general sense of the "essential indifference" of the service agency to the troubled person, which became crystallized in an utterly recurrent sort of interchange between agency personnel and various parties phoning on behalf of a stricken person. The callers recurrently found themselves confronted with what we are calling the "cargo syndrome." Specifically, the agency wanted particular information about the caller and did not want that same information about the sick or injured person, who was simply the item being transferred.

The problematically distributed information was particularly "person indexical," someone's name. In terms of sheer efficiency, the agency might have benefitted by requesting the sufferer's name although they had no practical use for it, because callers on behalf of sufferers in various ways insisted upon the relevance of the sufferer's name. Following is an array of instances of the cargo syndrome.

In the first place, the relevance of sufferer's name generated inquiries on that issue after a series of form questions had been gone through and the agency had not solicited the sufferer's name.

(10) [FD:IV:57]

Desk:	May I have your name please,
Caller:	Missuz Bradley?
Desk:	First- name?
Caller:	Loretta?
Desk:	Oka:y?
	(pause)
Desk:	And the phone number you're calling from.
Caller:	Broadway seven, one six, three three.
Desk:	Okay,
Caller:	And this is for Doctor Edletack.
Desk:	Okay, this is to⌐uh-
Caller: →	└Do you need the patient's name,
Desk: →	Uh, no.

(11) [FD:I:87]

Desk:	He is landing at Orbison Field.
Caller:	Right.
Desk:	Okay,
Caller: →	A:nd uh do you need the patient's name.
Desk: →	No::, no it won't be necessary,

And recurrently, callers volunteered the name, thus disrupting the orderly progression of the form-relevant questioning (transparently so in fragments [13] and [14] below.)

(12) [FD:IV:35]
Desk: What's your name again please sir,
Caller: ⌊D. R. Banning. B-a-n-n-i-n-g,
Caller: →   And uh it's uh:: the man's name is Bob DeMott.

(13) [FD:IV:74]
Desk: May I have your name please,
Caller: →   Yes. This is uh Missiz Lowe. L-o-w-e? and the child's name
               is Bartholemew, fifteen months old.
                        (pause)
Desk: →   And now your first name.
Caller: Jeannette.

(14) [FD:I:20]
Desk: I'll have them out there approximately at six then,
Caller: O⌈kay.
Desk: ⌊·hhhh⌈and-
Caller: →   ⌊And the employee's name is Randall.
Desk: →   Uh no. May I have your name please.

    In the following fragment, caller volunteers the name, and sub-sequently produces a pre-completion uptake of the "thrust" of a question which has broken off ("What's the-"). The pre-completion uptake shows the question to have been heard as a request for the sufferer's name.

(15) [FD:I:35]
    Caller: →   I have a lady who came over from next door, Missiz Effie
                   Ellis, and her husband is on the jo:b. And I called a
                   doctor and he say to get her to the hospital right away.
                            ⌈So-
    Desk: ⌊What's the-
    Caller: →   Effie Ellis.

    Finally, in the following fragments, the relevance of the sick or injured party as a namable "person" is consequential for the hearing of the request for caller's name. Specifically, callers are not certain that it is their name which has been requested. In the first of these fragments we find a combination of indices of an orientation to the relevance of sufferer's name; first, a checkout as to which name was being requested, and subsequently a volunteering of the name as in the above fragments (12)–(15).

(16) [FD:I:14]

Desk:		May I have your name please,
Caller:	→	My na:me?
Desk:		Yes.
Caller:		This is Missuz McCoughlin.

.
.

Caller:		M-c-c-o-u-g-h-l-i-n.
Desk:		i-n. Okay.
Desk:		Your first ⌐name-
Caller:	→	⌊And the lady's name is Miss⌐uz-
Desk:	→	⌊Your first initial.
Caller:	→	My n- my name is uh Beth, B-e-t-h,

(17) [FD:IV:113]

Desk:		What is your name please,
Caller:	→	My name? (.) is Ginny Selmur.hh
Desk:		S-e-l, m-u-r,
Caller:		Yes sir.

(18) [FD:I:98]

Desk:		And uh, may I have your name please?
Caller:	→	Uh, my name's Rostermann.
Desk:		How you spell that,
Caller:		R-o-s. T-e-r. M-a, n-n.
Desk:		Okay, and uh, first name.
Caller:	→	Mine, Fred.hh

(19) [FD:IV:41]

Desk:		Could I have your name and phone number in case⌐I have to=
Caller:		⌊( )
Desk:		⌐call you back,
Caller:	→	=⌊My name?
		(pause)
Caller:	→	It's- I:: didn't hear you sir,
Desk:		Could I have your name and phone number in case I have to call you back,
Caller:	→	Oh yes. Uh::m, my name is Missiz Budd, B-u-d-d.

(20) [FD:IV:3]

Desk:		What was your first name please,
Caller:	$\rightarrow$	Mi:ne? Eleanor.
Desk:		Eleanor, Baxter.
		(pause)
Caller:	$\rightarrow$	<u>My</u> first name? (.) or <u>her</u> first ⌐name.
Desk:		⌊Yours.
Caller:		Ya::h, Eleanor, hhh
Desk:		O:ka:: ⌐y,
Caller:		⌊hehh

It appears that the "essential concern" of a service supplier is the dispatching of a task, and whatever activities, information, etc., are critical thereto. In the above fragments we see the agency confronted again and again with a "nonessential matter." We take it that the confrontation in these fragments is a fine-grained index of a crucial distinction between a troubles telling and the service encounter; that is, the distinction between a focus on the "troubled person" versus a focus on the "problem and its properties," respectively.

A similar sort of "confrontation" may be occurring in fragments (4)–(9). Upon the offering of advice, an incipient or ongoing troubles telling converges with a service encounter, with the concomitant shift of relevant categories and activities, and, as well, the concomitant shift of focus, away from the troubles teller and his or her experiences, to the trouble itself, as a "problem to be solved." Again, then, the rejection of advice may be accomplice to a rejection of those shifts; an attempt to preserve the interaction's status as a troubles telling with its particular categories and activities, and its focus upon a matter to which the service encounter is "essentially indifferent"; that is, that of the teller himself, in contrast to, say, the teller as a mere bearer of the object of "essential concern," the trouble itself.

While we take it that the alternation as between "troubled person" and "troubles bearer" matters, we are not suggesting that the service encounter become "essentially concerned" with the troubled person. Such a concern carries with it an "essential indifference" to the trouble, which generates a stringent requirement from which the service encounter may specifically offer relief. As is abundantly evidenced in the current corpus of talk about a trouble, a "person" is one among others, one who participates in the ongoing everyday activities of the community; one who goes to work, gets together with his or her friends, listens to their stories, rejoices in their good times, tells them of his or her own good times, etc. A merest glimpse of this feature is available in the materials assembled here. For example, in fragment (1), an abandoned wife is nevertheless held responsible for carrying out her routine telephone-call duties; in fragment (2) a husband presses his not-yet-recovered wife to rejoin the workforce; in fragment (3) a candidate baby-sitter in the throes of a severe flu attack inquires into her co-participant's circumstances, and that inquiry is taken up with perfect alacrity; and in fragment (9) someone suffering a variety of troubles nevertheless provides appropriate attention to her sister's comings and goings, and warrants a prior report of her sister's splendid vacation with a reciprocal "I've really had a very nice time."

Thus, the caveat to a focus on someone with a trouble as a "person" is that he or she remain one among others, answerable to the requirements of the community. If he declines to do so, he may cease to be a "person"; that is, he may find himself abandoned by his cohort of candidate troubles recipients. Which is to say that while the concerns of the service supplier might be simplistically characterized as "repair and maintenance," the concerns of the troubles recipient might be, equally simplistically, characterized as "continued function, regardless." Thus, while the service encounter may be deficient in "human" terms, its alternative may be "materially" pernicious.

Further, it appears that sufferers of a trouble do not welcome the "humanizing" of a service encounter. We have noted the misfittedness of the two categories, troubles teller and advice giver. And we have seen, in the instances initially collected as disputes, that various forms of resistance occur when a prospective or to-this-point troubles recipient offers advice, an activity which may specifically "belong" to the service encounter. Correlatively, it may be noted that the categories advice seeker and troubles recipient are misfitted. And, likewise, activities which may specifically "belong" to a troubles telling are resisted when they occur in the environment of a service encounter.

Again, a merest glimpse of this proper distribution of activities may be seen in a comparison of two fragments, one from a troubles telling and one from a service encounter. A recurrent and ordered series in the Troubles-Telling Sequence is an exposition of the trouble by the troubles teller (see fragment [21] below, arrow 1), followed by an affiliation by the troubles recipient (see arrow 2), followed by an affiliation response, in which the troubles teller is observably "letting go" (see arrow 3); that activity warranted and elicited by troubles recipient's prior affiliation (Jefferson 1988). As our single instance we have chosen an interchange between the participants of fragment (9). On this occasion, and in contrast to that from which fragment (9) was extracted, an optimum troubles telling is in progress.

(21) [NB:IV:14:2]
Emma:	1→	I have to take two tub baths with tar in it every hhhhhh da:y?
Lottie:		Yea:h?
Emma:	1→	˙hhhhh And I have to have ointment oy put on four times a da:y and I'm under:: violet ra:y for a few seconds, a:nd I got a shot in the butt of vitamin: (0.2) A::. ski:n
		(0.5)
Lottie:	2→	Jee:sus.
Emma:	3→	Lo:ttie, honest to Go:d you know, I just broke out terribly a:uh- hh when I le-eft ho:me. An:d, I just- just my le:gs were just covered.hh

Such emotional reciprocity may be unwelcome by an advice seeker *vis-à-vis* an advice giver. So, for example, in our small corpus of institutional talk about a trouble, we find one practitioner who, in a range of ways, strikes us as "soft." At one point in the course of an advice seeker's "exposition," he produces an utterance which is unique in our limited institutional corpus, a mild version of an "affiliation," "Oh my:," an object which stands in contrast to the ubiquitous, perhaps definitive "Uh huh" and "I see" of the service encounter.[2] At that point, we find the advice seeker declining to produce an "affiliation response," that is, declining to "let go," and instead, working to continue with interactionally independent expositional talk.

(22) [SPC;10:3:4]
Caller:	1→	And he has gotten to the point now where he: (.) is so confused and everything that he gets (.) the two: people mixed u:p and he thinks this daddy's the other one.
Desk:	2→	Oh my:.

Caller: 1→   Then he doesn't want him to get close to him and that's (.)
                     one reason why he wants ((sounds like she is fighting tears
                     from now on)) to: uh:: ˙hhh right at the ti:me when he's
                     having an- wuh- one of these (0.2) uh: I don't know whether
                     you'd call it spell or what (0.7) ˙t but when he feels like
                     this, (0.3) that's when he wants to kill himself.

By characterizing the advice seeker's subsequent talk as "working" to continue with interactionally independent expositional talk,
we are noticing that she may specifically be resisting the "letting
go" provided for by the prior "affiliation"; that is, it is possible that
the mild but perhaps in this environment powerful "Oh my:" has
brought her to the tears she is now fighting.

Fragment (22) may constitute a delicate instance of a service
supplier's attempt to "humanize" the service encounter. A rather
more elaborate attempt can be seen in the following misbegotten
hybrid which tries to combine a troubles telling's "affiliation" with
a service encounter's "advice." These materials are excerpted from
a BBC radio broadcast in which a panel of experts offers advice to
telephone callers. A woman is reporting difficulty in handling her
young children, exacerbated by a tendency to depression, for which
her doctor prescribes antidepressants, which she would prefer to
manage without. Two of the panel respond: the first prefaces advice
with a formal "sympathy" token and a report of common experience; the second formats the advice as an outcome of a common
experience.

(23) [JRE:A:1—4]
    Caller: ˙hhhh And I want to know if there's anything that you can
                       do:, or you can help me with uh:m (.) coping with a
                       situation like this withou-ah- (   ) resorting to pi:lls.
                       (0.3)
    Desk 1:   →   We:ll Harriet. May I say you know first of all: how (.)
                       sympathetic I am to your difficulties. Uh:: I understand
                 →   them very well in fact my children were born while I was
                       still a studen:t. and in many ways I: spent as much time
                       looking after the young children as m(h)y wi(h)fe did.
                       ˙hhhh A:nd uh: (.) you kno:w, the strength of (.) young
                       children's deman:ds. ever on one's ti::me they're never
                       satisfied with anything simple there's always some
                       difficulty and always some problem. ˙hhhh Now whilst we
                       hear a great deal of sympathy indeed as we did from an
                       earlier caller about men having stressful difficulties in

their lives I'm <u>sure</u> that women have just as much if not
<u>mo</u>:re. ˙hh Now <u>having said</u> tha:t (.) <u>let</u>'s jump a little
bit <u>fu</u>:rther and if I can ex<u>plain</u> to you a little <u>why</u>
people get de<u>press</u>ed.

.
.   (ca 34 lines omitted; elementary explanation of
.   depression and antidepressants)
.

Desk 1: → It's <u>rather</u> like a <u>bandage</u> round an ankle. The <u>bandage</u> is
            doing no good to the ankle at <u>all</u> if it's been <u>strained.</u>
            But it's <u>giving</u> it a bit of su<u>ppo</u>:r⌈t.
Caller: ⌊<u>Ye</u>:s: <u>well</u> (.) Well
            that's what I <u>fee</u>:l:. But I <u>feel</u> that (.) uh:m ˙hh I k<u>now</u>
   *→   they will <u>help</u> me. I'm a:- a <u>trained</u> nurse mys<u>e</u>:lf.=
Desk 1:   =<u>Y</u>⌈ah?
Caller: ⌊And I k<u>now</u> I've <u>seen</u> (   ) a lot of people but (.) I
            know perfectly <u>we</u>:ll. that if <u>I</u> take the tablets for a
            period of time (.) they <u>will</u> help me.
Desk 1:   Mm hm
Caller: But- uhm- they <u>won</u>'t be a definite <u>a</u>:nswer. to my <u>problem,</u>
            a:nd when I <u>stop</u> taking them I can't see any reason why: I
            shan't revert to feelin:g, exactly the same as I <u>have</u> been
            feeling.
Desk 2:   <u>No no</u>⌈ah- <u>I</u> g- <u>I</u> guess I can offer an <u>a</u>:nswer.=
Caller: ⌊(   )
Desk 2: → =<u>A</u> different answer cause <u>I</u> had (difficulty with) number
            three:.
            (.)
Caller: ⌈(   )
Desk 2:   ⌊ <u>A</u>::nd I since had a <u>fou</u>::rth. ˙hhhh And <u>while</u> I (.) that
         → <u>During</u> that ti:me my <u>weight</u> went up to twelve <u>stone</u>.=Now in
            fact I'm:: uh only five foo:t. ˙hh⌈h
Caller: *→   ⌊Well <u>I</u> don't ha⌈ve a <u>weight</u>
Desk 2:   ⌊<u>A</u> : n : d
Caller: ⌈problem
Desk 2:   =⌊<u>u</u> h : m,
            (.)
Desk 2: → ee- <u>Well</u> you <u>may</u> not have a <u>weight</u> problem but <u>that</u> was <u>my</u>
            form of stre:ss. I⌈mean you've got your dep<u>r</u>(h)ession.=
Caller: ⌊<u>Ye</u>:s.
Desk 2:   =˙hhh Uh:m:: and it- <u>it</u> (.) really <u>I</u> looked terrible I'm
            only five foot. Now my <u>weight</u> now is eight and a <u>ha</u>:lf. Now
            the ↑<u>way</u> we <u>did</u> it . . .

The various services being offered here are in no way designed
for this recipient, and are shown by the recipient to be ill-designed;

that is, the elementary explanation of antidepressants is followed by an announcement that the recipient is "a trained nurse myse:lf," and the introduction of overweight as an experience in common is argued to be irrelevant, "Well I don't have a weight problem."[3] Inasmuch as the advice turns out to be ill-designed and inappropriate for this recipient, the affiliation work is revealed as presumptuous. The attempt to undercut the anonymity of servicing with the intimacy of troubles recipiency results in an elephantine travesty which is effectively neither troubles telling nor service encounter but a worst possible version of each; namely, unwarranted affiliation compounded by inept servicing.

4 Conclusion

In short, it appears that it is from appropriate troubles recipients, in the environment of a troubles telling, that a troubles teller properly receives and accepts emotional reciprocity, and from appropriate advice givers, in the environment of a service encounter, that an advice seeker properly receives and accepts advice. Cross-environment profferings of reciprocity or advice turn out to be problematic.

Unless, as in the archetypal tribal situation, the advice giver one is consulting happens also to be a proper troubles recipient (e.g., a friend or relative), it appears that adequate management of a "trouble" must be achieved by a shunting between two distinctive but problematically convergent environments. And the occurrence of elements of one environment in talk appropriate to the other may constitute attempts to repair perceived inadequacies of each. Thus we find participants to a troubles telling attempting to rationalize their talk; to provide for it as more than a merely "phatic" exchange, with what turn out to be problematic attempts at problem solving. An alternative might be to recognize and enhance the deeply remedial potential of emotional reciprocity. Correlatively, we find participants to a service encounter attempting to humanize their talk; to provide for it as more than a merely "instrumental" exchange, with what turn out to be problematic attempts at reciprocity. An alternative might be to recognize and enhance the intensely relational potential of the instrumental colloquy.

Notes

1. The similarity, unsought and recognized after the fact, may not be altogether coincidental in that Harvey Sacks, who developed the methodology which we follow, was both a scholar, and critic, of Weberian methodology (see Sacks 1963). In effect, by enjoining us to avoid "ideal types," "models," etc., he made us familiar with them.

2. In the following fragment, a caller to a suicide-prevention agency is specifically seeking the affiliation she feels she will not get from her cohort of candidate troubles recipients; that is, she is soliciting and defining alignment by a service supplier as a troubles recipient. Not getting it, she focuses on and complains of the agency's definitive response type: "It sounds like a real professional uh huh uh huh uh huh."

[SPC:NYE:1964:1—2:Sacks Transcript]

Caller:	I can't call any of my friends or anybody cause they're just gonna say oh that's silly or that's stupid I guess
Desk:	Uh huh
Caller:	I guess what you really want is someone to say yes I really understand why you want to commit suicide I do believe you I would too
Desk:	Uh huh. Well tell me about it
Caller:	Bou I a funny thing I know it's emotionally immature except that doesn't help
Desk:	Uh huh
Caller:	I've got a date coming in a half hour and I ((sob))
Desk:	I see
Caller:	I can't go through with it I can't go through with the evening I can't ((sniffle))
Desk:	Uh huh
Caller:	You talk. I don't want to talk
Desk:	Uh huh
Caller:	((laugh sob)) It sounds like a real professional uh huh uh huh uh huh ((sniffle))
Desk:	Well perhaps you want to tell me uh why you feel like committing suicide

3. In response to this utterance, the service supplier *cum* troubles recipient produces a device which is indexical of problems in an interaction. Having brought an utterance to a completion point, she starts to talk again with a "continuation", "A:n:d uh:m." That object is introduced after a recognizable "disagreement initiation," "Well I don't ..." That is, seeing that a "disagreement" is under way, a prior speaker produces talk which utterly disattends that a response has been initiated at all. For a consideration of this phenomenon, see Jefferson (1981a). Having noticed the work of this object at this rather dramatic point in the

conversation, we can notice the only other occurrence, just after desk 1 has made a little joke, "I: spent as much time looking after the young children as m(h)y wi(h)fe did," which he follows by "·hhhh A:nd uh: (.) you kno:w." One thing which it is not followed by is the caller's laughter. Analysis has shown that the insertion of laugh particles in some ongoing talk can serve to "invite" a co-participant to join in a "laughing together," and thereupon, laughter by co-participant is relevant until/unless some work is done to revise the current relevancies (see Jefferson 1979: 82ff.). That article concentrates on some work a co-participant might do to revise the current relevancies. Here we see a device used by the one who had invited laughter and has received no uptake, to revise the current relevancies; that is, to provide that laughter by co-participant is not due and, in fact, the utterance was not designed to achieve a "laughing together," as it might have appeared upon its initial completion, but was simply a privately enjoyed parenthetical on the way to further, "serious" talk. Thus, the two occurrences of "A:nd uh:" in this segment are deployed to manage an advice seeker's rejection of affiliative work by advice givers.

References

Abell, P. and G. N. Gilbert, (eds.) 1983. *Accounts and Action*. Aldershot: Gower.

Adelsward, V., K. Aronsson, L. Jonsson, and P. Linell 1987. The unequal distribution of interactional space: dominance and control in courtroom interaction. *Text*, 7(4): 313–46.

Albert, E. 1964. "Rhetoric," "logic," and "poetics" in Burundi: culture patterning of speech behavior. *American Anthropologist*, 66, pt. 2(6): 35–54.

Argyle, Michael 1974. *The Social Psychology of Work*. Harmondsworth: Penguin.

Arvey, R. and J. Campion 1982. The employment interview: a summary and review of recent research. *Personnel Psychology*, 35: 281–322.

Atkinson, J. M. 1979. Sequencing and shared attentiveness to court proceedings. In G. Psathas (ed.) *Everyday Language: Studies in Ethnomethodology*. New York: Irvington, pp. 257–86.

　　1981. Ethnomethodological approaches to socio-legal studies. In A. Podgorecki and C. J. Whelan (eds.) *Sociological Approaches to Law*. London: Croom Helm, pp. 201–23.

　　1982. Understanding formality: notes on the categorisation and production of "formal" interaction. *British Journal of Sociology*, 33: 86–117.

　　1984a. *Our Masters' Voices: the Language and Body Language of Politics*. London: Methuen.

　　1984b. Public speaking and audience responses: some techniques for inviting applause. In J. M. Atkinson and J. Heritage (eds.) *Structures of Social Action: Studies in Conversation Analysis*. Cambridge: Cambridge University Press, pp. 370–409.

Atkinson, J. M. and P. Drew 1979. *Order in Court: the Organisation of Verbal Interaction in Judicial Settings*. London: Macmillan.

Atkinson, J. M. and J. C. Heritage (eds.) 1984. *Structures of Social Action: Studies in Conversation Analysis*. Cambridge: Cambridge University Press.

Atkinson, M., E. Cuff, and J. R. E. Lee 1978. Meeting talk. In J. Schenkien (ed.) *Studies in the Organization of Conversational Interaction*. New York: Academic Press, pp. 133–54.

549

Austin, J. L. 1962. *How to Do Things with Words*. Oxford: Clarendon Press.

Baldock, J. and D. Prior 1981. Social workers talking to clients: a study of verbal behaviour. *British Journal of Social Work*, 11: 19–38.

Bateson, G. 1972. *Steps to an Ecology of Mind*. New York: Ballantine.

Bauman, R. and J. Sherzer 1974. *Explorations in the Ethnography of Speaking*. Cambridge: Cambridge University Press.

Bax, M., H. Hart, and S. Jenkins 1980. The health needs of the pre-school child. London: Thomas Coram Research Unit.

Belnap, N. D. 1963. *An Analysis of Questions*. Systems Development Corporation TM–1287.000.00, Santa Monica, CA.

Bergmann, J. R. 1987. *Klatsch: Zur Sozialform der diskreten Indiskretion*. Berlin: de Gruyter.

Berlin, B. and P. Kay 1969. *Basic Color Terms*. Berkeley and Los Angeles: University of California Press.

Blau, P. M. 1977. *Inequality and Heterogeneity: a Primitive Theory of Social Structure*. New York: Free Press/Macmillan.

Blaxter, M. and E. Paterson 1982. *Mothers and Daughters: a Three Generational Study of Health Attitudes and Behaviour*. London: Heinemann.

Bloor, M. J. and G. W. Horobin 1975. Conflict and conflict resolution in doctor–patient interactions. In C. Cox and A. Mead (eds.) *A Sociology of Medical Practice*. London: Collier Macmillan, pp. 271–85.

Blount, B. and M. Sanches (eds.) 1975. *Sociocultural Dimensions of Language Use*. New York: Academic Press.

Boden, D. forthcoming. *The Business of Talk: Organizations in Action*. Cambridge: Polity Press.

Boden D. and D. H. Zimmerman (eds.) 1991. *Talk and Social Structure*. Cambridge: Polity Press.

Bogen, D. and M. Lynch 1989. Taking account of the hostile native: plausible deniability and the production of conventional history in the Iran–Contra hearings. *Social Problems*, 36: 197–224.

Brazil, D., M. Coulthard, and C. Johns 1980. *Discourse Intonation and Language Teaching*. London: Longman.

Brown, G. and G. Yule 1983. *Discourse Analysis*. Cambridge: Cambridge University Press.

Brown, P. and S. C. Levinson 1978. Universals in language usage: politeness phenomena. In E. Goody (ed.) *Questions and Politeness*. Cambridge: Cambridge University Press, pp. 56–310.

 1987. *Politeness: Some Universals in Language Usage*. Cambridge: Cambridge University Press.

Brun-Cottan, F. 1990. Coordinating cooperation. Paper presented at the 89th American Anthropological Association Annual Meeting, New Orleans, LA.

Button, G. 1987a. Moving out of closings. In G. Button and J. R. E. Lee (eds.) *Talk and Social Organisation*. Clevedon: Multilingual Matters, pp. 101–51.

1987b. Answers as interactional products: two sequential practices used in interviews. *Social Psychology Quarterly*, 50(2): 160–71. Reprinted in this volume.

1990. On members' time. In B. Conein, M. de Fornel, and L. Quere (eds.) *Les Formes de la conversation*, vol. I. Paris: CNET, pp. 161–82.

Button, G. and N. Casey 1984. Generating topic: the use of topic initial elicitors. In J. M. Atkinson and J. Heritage (eds.) *Structures of Social Action: Studies in Conversation Analysis*. Cambridge: Cambridge University Press, pp. 167–90.

1988/9. Topic initiation: business at hand. *Research on Language and Social Interaction*, 22: 61–92.

Button, G. and J. R. E. Lee (eds.) 1987. *Talk and Social Organisation*. Clevedon: Multilingual Matters.

Byrne, P. S. and B. E. L. Long 1976. *Doctors Talking to Patients: a Study of the Verbal Behaviours of Doctors in the Consultation*. London: HMSO.

Carter, W. B., L. R. Beach, T. S. Inui, J. P. Kirscht, and J. C. Prodzinsky 1986. Developing and testing a decision model for predicting influenza vaccination compliance. *Health Services Research*, 20: 897–932.

Cazden, C. 1970. The situation: a neglected source of social class differences in language use. *Journal of Social Issues*, 26: 35–60.

Charniak, E. 1972. *Towards a Model of Children's Story Comprehension*. Massachusetts Institute of Technology, Artificial Intelligence Laboratory A1 TR–266.

Cicourel, A. W. 1974. *Cognitive Sociology: Language and Meaning in Social Interaction*. New York: Free Press.

1983. Language and the structure of belief in medical communication. In S. Fisher and A. D. Todd (eds.) *The Social Organization of Doctor–Patient Communication*. Washington DC: Center for Applied Linguistics, pp. 221–40.

Clark, H. H. and J. W. French 1981. Telephone goodbyes. *Language in Society*, 10: 1–19.

Clark, J. 1973. *A Family Visitor: a Descriptive Analysis of Health Visiting in Berkshire*. London: Royal College of Nursing.

1981. *What Do Health Visitors Do? A Review of the Research 1960–80*. London: Royal College of Nursing.

Clayman, S. 1986. Making news through talk: the organisation of turn taking in televised news interviews. Paper presented at the Conference on Talk and Social Structure, Santa Barbara, CA.

1987. Generating news: the Interactional organisation of news interviews. Unpublished PhD dissertation, Department of Sociology, University of California, Santa Barbara.

1988. Displaying neutrality in television news interviews. *Social Problems*, 35(4): 474–92.

1989. The production of punctuality: social interaction, temporal organization and social structure. *American Journal of Sociology*, 95(3): 659–91.

1991. News interview openings: aspects of sequential organisation. In P. Scannell (ed.) *Broadcast Talk: a Reader*. Newbury Park: Sage, pp. 48–75.

Clayman, S. and J. Whalen 1988/9. When the medium becomes the message: the case of the Rather–Bush encounter. *Research on Language and Social Interaction*, 22: 241–72.

Cockerell, M. 1988. *Live from Number 10: the Inside Story of Prime Ministers and TV*. London: Faber and Faber.

Cole, P. and J. Morgan (eds.) 1975. *Syntax and Semantics*, vol. 3: *Speech Acts*. New York: Academic Press.

Conley, J. M. and W. M. O'Barr 1990. *Rules versus Relationships: the Ethnography of Legal Discourse*. Chicago: University of Chicago Press.

Coulthard, M. 1977. *An Introduction to Discourse Analysis*. London: Longman.

Coulthard, M. and M. Montgomery (eds.) 1981. *Studies in Discourse Analysis*. London: Routledge.

Council for the Education and Training of Health Visitors (CETHV) 1977. *An Investigation into the Principles of Health Visiting*. London: CETHV.

Cross, R. and N. Wilkins 1980. *An Outline of the Law of Evidence*, 5th edn. London: Butterworths.

Cuff, E. and W. W. Sharrock 1986. Meeting talk. In T. A. van Dijk (ed.) *A Handbook of Discourse Analysis*, vol. III: *Discourse and Dialogue*, New York and London: Academic Press, pp. 149–60.

Cumberlege Report 1986. *Neighbourhood Nursing: a Focus for Care*. London: HMSO.

Davidson, J. A. 1984. Subsequent versions of invitations, offers, requests and proposals dealing with potential or actual rejection. In J. M. Atkinson and J. Heritage (eds.) *Structures of Social Action: Studies in Conversation Analysis*. Cambridge: Cambridge University Press, pp. 102–28.

Davis, K. 1988. *Power under the Microscope*. Dordrecht: Foris.

Davison, E. H. 1956. Health visiting and case work. *Nursing Times*, 52: 1087–9.

Deutscher, I. 1973. *What We Say; What We Do; Sentiments and Acts*. Glenview IL: Scott Foresman.

van Dijk, T. (ed.) 1985. *Handbook of Discourse Analysis*, vol. III: Discourse and Dialogue. London: Academic Press.

Dingwall, R. 1977. *The Social Organisation of Health Visitor Training*. London: Croom Helm.

Dingwall, R., J. Eekelaar, and T. Murray 1983. *The Protection of Children: State Intervention and Family Life*. Oxford: Blackwell.

Donzelot, J. 1980. *The Policing of Families*. London: Hutchinson.

Drew, P. 1981. Adults' corrections of children's mistakes: a response to Wells and Montgomery. In P. French and M. MacLure (eds.) *Adult–Child Conversation: Studies in Structure and Process*. Croom Helm, pp. 244–67.

    1984. Speakers' reportings in invitation sequences. In J. M. Atkinson and J. Heritage (eds.) *Structures of Social Action: Studies in Conversation Analysis*. Cambridge: Cambridge University Press, pp. 129–51.

    1989. Recalling someone from the past. In D. Roger and P. Bull (eds.) *Conversation: an Interdisciplinary Approach*. Clevedon: Multilingual Matters, pp. 96–115.

    1991. Asymmetries of knowledge in conversational interactions. In I. Markova and K. Foppa (eds.) *Asymmetries in Dialogue*. Hemel Hempstead: Harvester Wheatsheaf, pp. 29–48.

Dunnell, K. and J. Dobbs 1982. *Nurses Working in the Community: a Survey Carried out on Behalf of DHSS in England and Wales in 1980*. London: HMSO.

Duranti, A. 1988. Ethnography of speaking: towards a linguistics of the praxis. In F. J. Newmeyer (ed.) *Language: the Sociocultural Context (Linguistics: The Cambridge Survey IV)*. Cambridge: Cambridge University Press, pp. 210–28.

Duranti, A. and C. Goodwin (eds.) 1992. *Rethinking Context: Language as an Interactive Phenomenon*. Cambridge: Cambridge University Press.

Emerson, R. 1969. *Judging Delinquents*. Chicago: Aldine.

    1981. On last resorts. *American Journal of Sociology*, 87: 1–22.

Epstein, E. J. 1973. *News from Nowhere*. New York: Random House.

Erickson, F. and J. Shultz 1982. *The Counselor as Gate Keeper*. New York: Academic Press.

Ervin-Tripp, S. 1969. Sociolinguistics. In L. Berkowitz (ed.) *Advances in Experimental Social Psychology*, vol. IV. New York: Academic Press, pp. 93–107.

    1976. "Is Sybil there?": the structure of some American English directives. *Language in Society*, 5: 25–67.

Ferguson, C. 1964. Diglossia. In D. Hymes (ed.) *Language in Culture and Society*. New York: Holt, Rinehart, and Winston.

Field, S., J. Draper, M. Kerr, and M. J. Hare 1982. A consumer view of the health visiting service. *Health Visitor*, 55: 299–301.

Fillmore, C. 1975. *Santa Cruz Lectures on Deixis*. Bloomington: Indiana University Linguistics Club.

Firth, R. 1974. Verbal and bodily rituals of greeting and parting. In J. S. La Fontaine (ed.) *The Interpretation of Ritual*. London: Tavistock, pp. 1–38.

Fisher, S. 1983. Doctor talk/patient talk: how treatment decisions are negotiated in doctor–patient communication. In S. Fisher and A. D. Todd (eds.) *The Social Organization of Doctor–Patient Communication*, Washington DC: Center for Applied Linguistics, pp. 135–57.

Fisher, S. and D. D. Todd (eds.) 1983. *The Social Organization of Doctor–Patient Communication*. Washington DC: Center for Applied Linguistics.

Fishman, M. 1980. *Manufacturing the News*. Austin: University of Texas Press.

Foster, M-C. 1988. The French puericultrice. Paper presented to a Conference on Health Visiting: Theory and Practice, Thomas Coram Research Unit, London.

Foxman, R., J. Draper, G. Boland, and C. Owen 1982. A consumer view of the health visiting service at six weeks postpartum. *Health Visitor*, 55: 302–8.

Frankel, R. 1989. "I wz wondering – uhm could *Raid* uhm effect the brain permanently d'y know?": some observations on the intersection of speaking and writing in calls to a poison control center. *Western Journal of Speech Communication*, 53: 195–226.

1990. Talking in interviews: a dispreference for patient-initiated questions in physician–patient encounters. In G. Psathas (ed.) *Interaction Competence*. Lanham MD: University Press of America, pp. 231–62.

Frazer, B. 1975. Hedged performatives. In P. Cole and J. Morgan (eds.) *Syntax and Semantics*, vol. III: *Speech Acts*. New York: Academic Press, pp. 187–210.

Gans, H. 1979. *Deciding What's News*. New York: Random House.

Garcia, A. 1991. Dispute resolution without disputing: how the interactional organization of mediation hearings minimizes argumentative talk. *American Sociological Review*, 56: 818–35.

Garfinkel, H. 1967. *Studies in Ethnomethodology*. Englewood Cliffs, NJ: Prentice Hall.

1988. Evidence for locally produced, naturally accountable phenomena of order, logic, reason, meaning method, etc. in and as of the essentially quiddity of immortal ordinary society (I of IV): an announcement of studies. *Sociological Theory*, 6: 103–9.

Garfinkel, H. and H. Sacks 1970. On formal structures of practical actions. In J. C. McKinney and E. A. Tiryakian (eds.) *Theoretical Sociology*. New York: Appleton Century Crofts, pp. 338–66.

Garfinkel, H., M. Lynch, and E. Livingston 1981. The work of a discovering science construed with materials from the optically discovered pulsar. *Philosophy of the Social Sciences*, 11: 131–58.

Gazdar, G. 1976. On performative sentences. *Semantikos*, 1(3): 37–62.

Gilbert, G. N. and M. Mulkay 1984. *Opening Pandora's Box: an Analysis of Scientists' Discourse*. Cambridge: Cambridge University Press.

Glaser, B. G. and A. L. Strauss 1965. *Awareness of Dying*. Chicago: Aldine.

Goffman, E. 1959. *Presentation of Self in Everyday Life*. New York: Doubleday.

1961a. Fun in games. In E. Goffman, *Encounters*. Indianapolis: Bobbs-Merrill, pp. 15–81.

1961b. *Encounters*. Indianapolis: Bobbs-Merrill.

1963. *Behavior in Public Places*. New York: Free Press.

1964. The neglected situation. *American Anthropologist*, 66: 133–6.

1971. *Relations in Public*. New York: Basic Books.

1974. *Frame Analysis*. New York: Harper and Row.

1981a. *Forms of Talk*. Oxford: Blackwell.

1981b. Replies and responses. In E. Goffman, *Forms of Talk*. Oxford: Blackwell, pp. 5–77.

1981c. Footing. In E. Goffman, *Forms of Talk*. Oxford: Blackwell, pp. 124–59.

1983. The interaction order. *American Sociological Review*, 48(1): 1–17.

Goodwin, C. 1984. Notes on story structure and the organisation of participation. In J. M. Atkinson and J. Heritage (eds.) *Structures of Social Action: Studies in Conversation Analysis*. Cambridge: Cambridge University Press, pp. 225–46.

1987. Forgetfulness as an interactive resource. *Social Psychology Quarterly*, 50(2): 115–30.

Goodwin, C. and A. Duranti 1992. Rethinking context: an introduction. In A. Duranti and C. Goodwin (eds.) *Rethinking Context: Language as an Interactive Phenomenon*. Cambridge: Cambridge University Press, pp. 1–42.

Goodwin, C. and M. H. Goodwin 1992. Context, activity and participation. In P. Auer and A. di Luzio (eds.) *The Contextualization of Language*. Amsterdam: John Benjamins.

Forthcoming. Formulating planes: seeing as a situated activity. In Y. Engestrom and D. Middleton (eds.) *Cognition and Communication at Work*. Newbury Park: Sage.

Goodwin, M. H. 1983. Aggravated correction and disagreement in children's conversations. *Journal of Pragmatics*, 7: 657–77.

1990. *He Said She Said: Talk as Social Organization among Black Children*. Bloomington IN: Indiana University Press.

1991. Announcements in their environment: back-to-back interaction in a multi-activity work setting. Unpublished mimeo: Xerox PARC, Palo Alto, CA.

Goody, E. 1972. "Greeting", "begging" and the presentation of respect. In J. S. La Fontaine (ed.) *The Interpretation of Ritual*. London: Tavistock, pp. 39–72.

1978. Towards a theory of questions. In E. Goody (ed.) *Questions and Politeness*. Cambridge: Cambridge University Press, pp. 17–43.

Gordon, D. and G. Lakoff 1975. Conversational postulates. In *Papers from the Seventh Regional Meeting of the Chicago Linguistic Society*, Chicago: University of Chicago Press, pp. 63–84.

Graham, H. 1979. Women's attitudes to the child health services. *Health Visitor*, 52: 175–8.

Graham, H. and L. McKee 1979. *The First Months of Motherhood*. London: Health Education Council.

Greatbatch, D. 1985. The social organisation of news interview interaction. Unpublished PhD dissertation, University of Warwick, England.

1986a. Aspects of topical organisation in news interviews: the use of agenda shifting procedures by interviewees. *Media, Culture and Society*, 8: 441–55.

1986b. Some standard uses of supplementary questions in news interviews. In J. Wilson and B. Crow (eds.) *Belfast Working Papers in Language and Linguistics*, vol. VIII. Jordanstown: University of Ulster, pp. 86–123.

1988. A turn-taking system for British news interviews. *Language in Society*, 17: 401–30.

Greatbatch, D. and J. Heritage forthcoming. *The News Interview: Studies in the History and Dynamics of a Social Form*, London: Sage.

Grice, H. P. 1975. Logic and conversation. In P. Cole and J. L. Morgan (eds.) *Syntax and Semantics*, vol. III: *Speech Acts*. New York: Academic Press, pp. 41–58.

Gumperz, J. 1972. Introduction. In J. Gumperz and D. Hymes (eds.) *Directions in Sociolinguistics*. New York: Holt, Rinehart, and Winston, pp. 1–31.

1978. The conversational analysis of inter-ethnic communication. In E. Lamar Ross (ed.) *Interethnic Communication*. Proceedings of the Southern Anthropological Society, Atlanta: University of Georgia Press.

1982a. *Discourse Strategies*, Cambridge: Cambridge University Press.

1982b. *Language and Social Identity*, Cambridge, Cambridge University Press.

1992. Contextualization and understanding. In A. Duranti and C. Goodwin (eds.) *Rethinking Context: Language as an Interactive Phenomenon*, Cambridge: Cambridge University Press, pp. 229–52.

Gumperz, J. and E. Herasimchuk 1975. The conversational analysis of social meaning: a study of classroom interaction. In B. Blount and M. Sanches, M. (eds.) *Sociocultural Dimensions of Language Use*. New York: Academic Press, pp. 81–115.

Gumperz, J. and D. Hymes (eds.) 1972. *Directions in Sociolinguistics*. New York: Holt, Rinehart, and Winston.

Gumperz, J. and D. Tannen 1979. Individual and social differences in language use. In C. Fillmore, D. Kempler, and W. Wang (eds.) *Individual Differences in Language Ability and Language Behavior*. New York: Academic Press, pp. 305–25.

Halkowski, T. R. 1986. Talk about the mentally ill: collectivity categorization and the interactional construction of "deviance." Unpublished Masters' thesis, University of Wisconsin, Milwaukee.

1990. Hearing talk: the social organization of a congressional hearing. Unpublished PhD dissertation, University of California, Santa Barbara.

Hall, S. 1973. A world at one with itself. In S. Cohen and J. Young (eds.) *The Manufacture of News*. London: Constable, pp. 85–94.

Hamblin, C. L. 1973. Questions in Montague English. *Foundations of Language*, 10: 41–53.

Hanks, W. F. 1990. *Referential Practice: Language and Lived Space Among the Maya*. Chicago: University of Chicago Press.

Harrah, D. 1961. A logic of questions and answers. *Philosophy of Science*, 28: 40–6.

Harris, S. 1986. Interviewers' questions in broadcast interviews. In J. Wilson and B. Crow (eds.) *Belfast Working Papers in Language and Linguistics*, vol. VIII. Jordanstown: University of Ulster, pp. 50–85.

Hart, H. L. A. and A. M. Honoré 1959. *Causation in the Law*. Oxford, Oxford University Press.

Health Visitors' Association (HVA) 1985. *Health Visiting and School Nursing: the Future*. London: HVA.

Heath, C. 1981. The opening sequence in doctor–patient interaction. In P. Atkinson and C. Heath (eds.) *Medical Work: Realities and Routines*. Aldershot: Gower, pp. 71–90.

1982. Preserving the consultation: medical record cards and professional conduct. *Sociology of Health and Illness*, 4: 56–74.

1986. *Body Movement and Speech in Medical Interaction*. Cambridge, Cambridge University Press.

1988. Embarrassment and interactional organization. In P. Drew and A. Wootton (eds.) *Erving Goffman: Exploring the Interaction Order*. Cambridge: Polity Press, pp. 136–50.

1989. Pain talk: the expression of suffering in the medical consultation. *Social Psychology Quarterly*, 52(2): 113–25.

Heringer, J. T. 1972. *Some Grammatical Correlates of Felicity Conditions*. Ohio State University Working Papers in Linguistics, II: 1–110.

Heritage, J. 1984a. *Garfinkel and Ethnomethodology*. Cambridge: Polity Press.

1984b. A change-of-state token and aspects of its sequential placement. In J. M. Atkinson and J. Heritage (eds.) *Structures of Social Action: Studies in Conversation Analysis*. Cambridge: Cambridge University Press, pp. 299–345.

1985. Analyzing news interviews: aspects of the production of talk for an "overhearing" audience. In T. van Dijk (ed.) *Handbook of Discourse Analysis*, vol. III: *Discourse and Dialogue*. London: Academic Press, pp. 95–119.

1987. Ethnomethodology. In A. Giddens and J. Turner (eds.) *Social Theory Today*. Cambridge: Polity Press, pp. 224–72.

Heritage, J. and D. Greatbatch 1986. Generating applause: a study of rhetoric and response at party political conferences. *American Journal of Sociology*, 92: 110–57.

1991. On the institutional character of institutional talk: the case of news interviews. In D. Boden and D. Zimmerman (eds.) *Talk and Social Structure*. Cambridge: Polity Press, pp. 93–137.

Heritage, J. and D. R. Watson 1979. Formulations as conversational objects. In G. Psathas (ed.) *Everyday Language: Studies in Ethnomethodology*. New York: Irvington, pp. 123–62.

1980. Aspects of the properties of formulations in natural conversation: some instances analyzed. *Semiotica*, 30: 245–62.

Hintikka, J. 1974. Questions about questions. In M. K. Munitz and P. K. Unger (eds.) *Semantics and Philosophy*. New York: New York University Press, pp. 103–58.

Holstein, J. 1988. Court ordered incompetence: conversational organization in involuntary commitment hearings. *Social Problems*, 35: 458–73.

Horn, L. 1972. On the semantic properties of logical operators in English. Unpublished PhD dissertation, University of California, Los Angeles.

Hudson, R. A. 1975. The meaning of questions. *Language*, 51(1): 1–31.

Hughes, D. 1982. Control in the consultation: organizing talk in a situation where co-participants have differential competence. *Sociology*, 16: 359–76.

Hull, R. D. 1975. A semantics for superficial and embedded questions in natural language. In E. L. Keenan (ed.) *Formal Semantics of Natural Language*. Cambridge: Cambridge University Press, pp. 35–45.

Hunt, M. 1972. The dilemma of identity in health visiting. *Nursing Times* (Occasional Papers), 68(5): 17–20, and (6): 23–3.

Hymes, D. 1962. The ethnography of speaking. In T. Gladwin and W. Sturtevant (eds.) *Anthropology and Human Behavior*. Washington DC: Anthropological Society of Washington, pp. 13–53.

1964. Introduction: towards ethnographies of communication. *American Anthropologist*, 66: 12–25.

1972a. Models of the interaction of language and social life. In J. Gumperz and D. Hymes (eds.) *Directions in Sociolinguistics: the Ethnography of Communication*. New York: Holt, Rinehart, and Winston, pp. 35–71.

1972b. On communicative competence. In J. B. Pride and J. Holmes (eds.) *Sociolinguistics*. Harmondsworth: Penguin, pp. 269–93.

1974. *Foundations in Sociolinguistics*. Philadelphia: University of Pennsylvania Press.

Irvine, J. 1974. Strategies of status manipulation in the Wolof greeting. In R. Bauman and J. Sherzer (eds.) *Explorations in the Ethnography of Speaking*. Cambridge: Cambridge University Press, pp. 167–91.

1978. Formality and informality in speech events. *Texas Working Papers in Sociolinguistics*, no. 52, Austin TX: Southwest Education Development Laboratory.

Jacobs, J. 1969. *The Search for Help: a Study of the Retarded Child in the Community.* Washington DC: University Press of America.

Jefferson, G. 1974. Error correction as an interactional resource. *Language in Society*, 2: 181–99.

1978. Sequential aspects of story telling in conversation. In J. N. Schenkein (ed.) *Studies in the Organization of Conversational Interaction.* New York: Academic Press, pp. 219–48.

1979. A technique for inviting laughter and its subsequent acceptance/ declination. In G. Psathas (ed.) *Everyday Language: Studies in Ethnomethodology.* New York: Erlbaum, pp. 79–96.

1980a. On "trouble-premonitory" response to inquiry. *Sociological Inquiry*, 50: 153–85.

1980b. The analysis of conversations in which "troubles" and "anxieties" are expressed. Final report to the (British) Social Science Research Council: Report nos. HR 4805/1–2.

1981a. The abominable "ne?": a working paper exploring the phenomenon of post-response pursuit of response. University of Manchester, Department of Sociology, Occasional Paper, no. 6. An abridged version appears in P. Schröder and H. Steger (eds.) *Dialogforschung. Jahrbuch 1980 des Instituts für deutsche Sprache*, Düsseldorf: Schwann, 1981: 53–88.

1981b. "Caveat speaker": a preliminary exploration of shift implicative recipiency in the articulation of topic. Final report to the (British) Social Science Research Council.

1984a. On the organisation of laughter in talk about troubles. In J. M. Atkinson and J. Heritage (eds.) *Structures of Social Action: Studies in Conversation Analysis.* Cambridge: Cambridge University Press, pp. 347–69.

1984b. Notes on a systematic deployment of the acknowledgement tokens "yeah" and "mm hm." *Papers in Linguistics*, 17: 197–206.

1986a. On the interactional unpackaging of a "gloss." *Language in Society*, 14: 435–66.

1986b. At first I thought. Unpublished mimeo, University of York.

1987. On exposed and embedded correction in conversation. In G. Button and J. R. E. Lee (eds.) *Talk and Social Organisation.* Clevedon: Multilingual Matters, pp. 86–100.

1988. On the sequential organisation of troubles talk in ordinary conversation. *Social Problems*, 35(4): 418–41.

1989. Notes on a possible metric which provides for a "standard maximum silence" of approximately one second in conversation. In D. Roger and P. Bull (eds.) *Conversation: an Interdisciplinary Perspective.* Clevedon: Multilingual Matters, pp. 166–96.

1990. List construction as a task and resource. In G. Psathas (ed.) *Interaction Competence.* Lanham MD: University Press of America, pp. 63–92.

Jefferson, G. and J. R. E. Lee 1981. The rejection of advice: managing the problematic convergence of a "troubles teller" and a "service encounter." *Journal of Pragmatics*, 5: 399–422.

Jessup, G. and H. Jessup 1975. *Selection and Assessment at Work*. London: Methuen.

Jordan, B. 1990. The organization of activities and the achievement of competent practice in a complex work setting. Paper presented at the 2nd International Congress for Research on Activity Theory, Lahti, Finland.

Jucker, A. 1986. *News Interviews: a Pragmalinguistic Analysis*. Philadelphia: John Benjamins.

Karttunen, L. 1977. Syntax and semantics of questions. *Linguistics and Philosophy*, 1: 3–44.

Kasanin, J. S. (ed.) 1944. *Language and Thought in Schizophrenia*. Berkeley: University of California Press.

Katz, J. 1977. *Propositional Structure and Illocutionary Force*. Sussex: Harvester Press.

Keenan, A. 1977. Some relationships between interviewers' personal feelings about candidates and their general evaluation of them. *Journal of Occupational Psychology*, 50: 275–83.

Keenan, E. O. 1977. Why look at unplanned and planned discourse? In E. O. Keenan and T. L. Bennett (eds.) *Discourse Across Time and Space* (Southern California Occasional Papers in Linguistics, no. 5). Department of Linguistics, University of Southern California, Los Angeles.

Keenan, E.O., B. Schieffelin, and M. Platt 1978. Questions of immediate concern. In E. N. Goody (ed.) *Questions and Politeness*. Cambridge: Cambridge University Press, pp. 44–55.

Kelly, J. and J. Local 1989. *Doing Phonology: Observing, Recording, Interpreting*. Manchester: Manchester University Press.

Kendon, A. 1977. *Studies in the Behavior of Social Interaction*. Bloomington IN: Indiana University Press.

1979. Some theoretical and methodological aspects of the use of film in the study of social interaction. In G. P. Ginsburg (ed.) *Emerging Strategies in Social Psychological Research*. New York: Wiley, pp. 67–91.

1982. The organization of behavior in face-to-face interaction: observations on the development of a methodology. In K. R. Scherer and P. Ekman (eds.) *Handbook of Methods in Nonverbal Behavior Research*. Cambridge: Cambridge University Press, pp. 440–505.

1990. *Conducting Interaction*. Cambridge: Cambridge University Press.

Kenny, A. 1973. *Wittgenstein*. Harmondsworth: Penguin.

Kollock, P., P. Blumstein, and P. Schwartz 1985. Sex and power in interaction: conversational privileges and duties. *American Sociological Review*, 50: 24–46.

Korsch, B. M. and V. F. Negrete 1972. Doctor–patient communication. *Scientific American*, 227: 66–74.

Labov, W. 1966. *The Social Stratification of English in New York*. Washington D C: Center for Applied Linguistics.

1972a. *Sociolinguistic Patterns*. Philadelphia: University of Pennsylvania Press.

1972b. Rules for ritual insults. In D. Sudnow (ed.) *Studies in Social Interaction*. New York: Free Press, pp. 120–69.

Labov, W. and D. Fanshel 1977. *Therapeutic Discourse: Psychotherapy as Conversation*. New York: Academic Press.

Lakoff, G. 1971. Presuppositions and relative well-formedness. In D. Steinberg and L. Jacobovits (eds.) *Semantics: an Interdisciplinary Reader in Philosophy, Linguistics and Psychology*. Cambridge: Cambridge University Press, pp. 329–40.

1975. Pragmatics in natural logic. In E. Keenan (ed.) *Formal Semantics of Natural Language*. Cambridge: Cambridge University Press.

Lerner, G. 1987. Collaborative turn sequences: sentence construction and social action. Unpublished PhD dissertation. University of California, Irvine.

Levelt, W. J. M. 1983. Monitoring and self-repair in speech. *Cognition*, 14: 41–104.

Levi, J. and A. G. Walker (eds.) 1990. *Language in the Judicial Process*. New York: Plenum.

Levinson, S. C. 1977. Social deixis in a Tamil village. Unpublished PhD dissertation, University of California, Berkeley.

1979. Activity types and language. *Linguistics* 17: 356–99. Reprinted in this volume.

1980. Speech act theory: the state of the art. *Language Teaching and Linguistics: Abstracts*, 13: 5–24.

1981a. Some pre-observations on the modelling of dialogue. *Discourse Processes*, 4: 93–110.

1981b. The essential inadequacies of speech act models of dialogue. In H. Parret, M. Sbisa, and J. Verschueren (eds.) *Possibilities and Limitations of Pragmatics*. Amsterdam: John Benjamins, pp. 473–92.

1983. *Pragmatics*. Cambridge: Cambridge University Press.

1988. Putting linguistics on a proper footing: explorations in Goffman's concepts of participation. In P. Drew and A. J. Wootton (eds.) *Erving Goffman: Exploring the Interaction Order*. Cambridge: Polity Press, pp. 161–227.

Lewis, C. D. 1984. *Reporting for Television*. New York: Columbia University Press.

Lewis, D. 1969. *Convention: a Philosophical Study*. Cambridge M A: Harvard University Press.

1972. General semantics. In G. Harman and D. Davidson (eds.) *Semantics for Natural Language*. Dordrecht: Reidel, pp. 169–218.

Linell, P. 1990. The power of dialogue dynamics. In I. Markova and K. Foppa (eds.) *The Dynamics of Dialogue*. Hemel Hempstead: Harvester Wheatsheaf, pp. 147–77.

Linell, P. and T. Luckmann 1991. Asymmetries in dialogue: some concep-
 tual preliminaries. In I. Markova and K. Foppa (eds.) *Asymmetries in
 Dialogue.* Hemel Hempstead: Harvester Wheatsheaf, pp. 1–20.
Linell, P., L. Gustavsson, and P. Juvonen 1988. Interactional dominance in
 dyadic communication: a presentation of initiative-response analy-
 sis. *Linguistics,* 26: 415–42.
Litman, R. E. 1972. Experiences in a suicide prevention center. In
 J. Waldenstrom, T. Larsson, and W. Ljungstedt (eds.) *Suicide and
 Attempted Suicide.* Skandia International Symposia, Stockholm:
 Nordiska Bokhandelns Forlag, pp. 217–29.
Lloyd, R. M. 1990. Yucky secrets: the social organization of adults interro-
 gating children. Unpublished PhD dissertation, University of Califor-
 nia, Santa Barbara.
Luce, R. D. and H. Raiffa 1957. *Games and Decisions: Introduction and
 Critical Survey.* New York: Wiley.
McHoul, A. 1978. The organisation of turns at formal talk in the class-
 room. *Language in Society,* 7: 183–213.
 1990. The organisation of repair in classroom talk. *Language in
 Society,* 19: 349–77.
McIntosh, J. 1986. *A Consumer Perspective on the Health Visiting Service.*
 University of Glasgow: Social Paediatric and Obstetric Research
 Unit.
McLenahan, L. and J. Lofland 1976. Bearing bad news: tactics of the
 deputy U.S. Marshal. *Sociology of Work and Occupations,* 3: 251–
 72.
Malinowski, B. 1923. The problem of meaning in primitive languages. In
 C. K. Ogden and I. A. Richards (eds.) *The Meaning of Meaning.*
 New York: Harcourt, Brace, and World, pp. 296–336.
 1966. *Coral Gardens and their Magic.* London: Allen and Unwin.
Mandelbaum, J. and A. Pomerantz 1991. What drives social action? In K.
 Tracy (ed.) *Understanding Face-to-face Interaction: Issues Linking
 Goals and Discourse.* Hillsdale NJ: Erlbaum, pp. 151–66.
Marlaire, C. and D. Maynard 1990. Standardized testing as an interac-
 tional phenomenon. *Sociology of Education,* 63: 83–101.
Mayall, B. and M.-C. Foster 1989. *Child Health Care.* London:
 Heinemann.
Maynard, D. 1984. *Inside Plea Bargaining: the Language of Negotiation.*
 New York: Plenum.
 1985. How children start arguments. *Language in Society,* 14: 1–30.
 1986. Offering and soliciting collaboration in multi-party disputes
 among children (and other humans). *Human Studies,* 9 (2/3): 261–
 85.
 1989a. Perspective–display sequences in conversation. *Western Journal
 of Speech Communication,* 53: 91–113.
 1989b. Notes on the delivery and reception of diagnostic news regarding mental disabilities. In D. T. Helm, W. T. Anderson, A. J. Meehan

and A. W. Rawls. (eds.) *The Interactional Order: New Directions in the Study of Social Order*. New York: Irvington, pp. 54–67.

1991a. Perspective–display sequences and the delivery and receipt of diagnostic news. In D. Boden and D. H. Zimmerman (eds.) *Talk and Social Structure*, Cambridge: Polity Press, pp. 164–92.

1991b. On the interactional and institutional bases of assymetry in clinical discourse. *American Journal of Sociology*, 92(2): 448–95.

Maynard, D. W. and D. Zimmerman 1984. Topical talk, ritual and the social organization of relationships, *Social Psychology Quarterly*, 47: 301–16.

Meehan, A. J. 1981. Some conversational features of the use of medical terms by doctors and patients. In P. Atkinson and C. Heath (eds.), *Medical Work: Realities and Routines*. Aldershot: Gower, pp. 107–27.

1983. For the record: organizational and interactional practices for producing police records on juveniles. Unpublished PhD dissertation, Boston University.

1989. Assessing the "police-worthiness" of citizen's complaints to the police: accountability and the negotiation of "facts." In D. T. Helm, W. T. Anderson, A. J. Meehan, and A. W. Rawls. (eds.) *The Interactional Order: New Directions in the Study of Social Order*. New York: Irvington, pp. 116–40.

Mehan, H. 1979. *Learning Lessons: Social Organization in the Classroom*. Cambridge MA: Harvard University Press.

1985. The structure of classroom discourse. In T. van Dijk (ed.) *Handbook of Discourse Analysis*, vol. III: *Discourse and Dialogue*. London: Academic Press, pp. 120–32.

1991. The school's work of sorting students. In D. Boden and D. Zimmerman (eds.) *Talk and Social Structure*. Cambridge: Polity Press, pp. 71–90.

Mehan, H., A. Hertweck, and J. L. Meihls 1986. *Handicapping the Handicapped: Decision Making in Students' Educational Careers*. Stanford: Stanford University Press.

Mellinger, W. M. 1990. Negotiated orders: the social organization of paramedic calls for emergency Field orders. Unpublished PhD dissertation, University of California, Santa Barbara.

Mellinger, W. M. and D. H. Zimmerman 1987. The production of organizational records: the case of the dispatch package. Paper presented at the American Sociological Association Annual Meetings, Chicago IL.

Merritt, M. 1976. On questions following questions (in service encounters). *Language in Society*, 5: 315–357.

Mishler, E. 1984. *The Discourse of Medicine: Dialectics of Medical Interviews*. Norwood NJ: Ablex.

Moerman, M. 1988. *Talking Culture: Ethnography and Conversation Analysis*. Philadelphia: University of Pennsylvania Press.

564 References

Moss, P., G. Bolland, and R. Foxman 1982. *Transition to Parenthood Project*. London: Thomas Coram Research Unit.

Munby, J. 1978. *Communicative Syllabus Design*. Cambridge: Cambridge University Press.

New York Times 1973. *The Watergate Hearings: Break-in and Cover-up*. Toronto: Bantam.

Ochs, E. 1988. *Culture and Language Development: Language Acquisition and Language Socialization in a Samoan Village*. Cambridge, Cambridge University Press.

Oevermann, U. 1983. Zur Sache. Die Bedeutung von Adornos methodologischem Selbstverständnis für die Begründung einer materialen soziologischen Strukturanalyse. In L. v. Friedeburg and J. Habermas (eds.) *Adorno-Konferenz 1983*, Frankfurt-on-Main: Suhrkamp, pp. 234–89.

Orr, J. 1980. *Health Visiting in Focus: a Consumer View of Health Visiting in Northern Ireland*. London: Royal College of Nursing.

Owsley, H. H. and C. M. Scotton 1984. The conversational expression of power by television news interviewers. *Journal of Social Psychology*, 123: 261–71.

Parsons, T. 1937. *The Structure of Social Action*. New York: McGraw-Hill.

1951. *The Social System*. New York: The Free Press.

1975. The sick role and the role of the physician reconsidered. *Milbank Memorial Fund Quarterly*, 53: 257–78.

Perakyla, A. 1991. Invoking a hostile world: patients' "future" in AIDS counselling. Paper presented at the International Conference on Current Research in Ethnomethodology and Conversation Analysis, Amsterdam, July 1991.

Perakyla, A. and D. Silverman 1991a. Reinterpreting speech exchange systems: communication formats in AIDS counselling. *Sociology*, 25(4): 627–51.

1991b. Owning experience: describing the experience of other persons. *Text*, 11(3): 441–30.

Perls, F. 1969. *Gestalt Therapy Verbatim*. Lafayette CA: Real People Press.

Political and Economic Planning (PEP) 1961. *Family Needs and Social Services*. London: PEP.

Pollner, M. 1974. Mundane reasoning. *Philosophy of the Social Sciences*, 4: 35–54.

1975. "The very coinage of your brain:" the anatomy of reality disjunctures. *Philosophy of the Social Sciences*, 5: 411–30.

1979. Explicative transactions: making and managing meaning in traffic court. In G. Psathas (ed.) *Everyday Language: Studies in Ethnomethodology*. New York: Erlbaum, pp. 227–53.

Pomerantz, A. M. 1975. Second assessments: a study of some features of agreements/disagreements. Unpublished PhD dissertation, University of California, Irvine.

1978. Compliment responses: notes on the co-operation of multiple constraints. In J. N. Schenkein (ed.) *Studies in the Organization of Conversational Interaction*. New York: Academic Press, pp. 79–112.

1980. Telling my side: "limited access" as a "fishing" device. *Sociological Inquiry*, 50: 186–98.

1984a. Agreeing and disagreeing with assessments: some features of preferred/dispreferred turn shapes. In J. M. Atkinson and J. Heritage (eds.) *Structures of Social Action: Studies in Conversation Analysis*. Cambridge: Cambridge University Press, pp. 57–101.

1984b. Giving a source or basis: the practice in conversation of telling "how I know." *Journal of Pragmatics*, 8: 607–25.

1986. Extreme case formulations: a way of legitimizing claims. *Human Studies*, 9: 219–30.

1988. Offering a candidate answer: an information seeking strategy. *Communication Monographs*, 55: 360–373.

1988/9. Constructing skepticism: four devices used to engender the audience's skepticism. *Research on Language and Social Interaction* 22: 293–313.

1990/1. Mental concepts in the analysis of social action. *Research on Language and Social Interaction*, 24: 299–310.

Pomerantz, A. M. and J. M. Atkinson 1984. Ethnomethodology, conversation analysis and the study of courtroom interaction. In D. J. Muller, D. E. Blackman, and A. J. Chapman (eds.) *Topics in Psychology and Law*. Chichester: Wiley, pp. 283–94.

Pope, E. 1975. Questions and answers in English. Indiana University Linguistics Club Mimeo.

Psathas, G. (ed.) 1979. *Everyday Language: Studies in Ethnomethodology*. New York: Erlbaum.

Py, B. and R. Jeanneret (eds.) 1989. *Minorisation linguistique et interaction*. Geneva: Droz.

Roberts, C. 1985. *The Interview Game and How It's Played*. London: British Broadcasting Corporation.

Robinson, J. 1982. *An Evaluation of Health Visiting*. London: Council for the Education and Training of Health Visitors.

Robinson, M. J. and M. Sheehan 1983. *Over the Wire and on TV: CBS and UPI in Campaign '80*. New York: Russell Sage.

Ross, J. 1970. On declarative sentences. In R. A. Jacobs and P. S. Rosenbaum (eds.) *Readings in English Transformational Grammar*. Waltham MA: Ginn, pp. 222–72.

Sacks, H. 1963. On sociological description. *Berkeley Journal of Sociology*, 8: 1–16.

1968. Aspects of the sequential organization of conversation. Unpublished MS.

1972a. An initial investigation of the usability of conversational data for doing sociology. In D. Sudnow (ed.) *Studies in Social Interaction*. New York: Free Press, pp. 31–74.

1972b. On the analyzability of stories by children. In J. Gumperz and D. Hymes (eds.) *Directions in Sociolinguistics*. New York: Holt, Rinehart, and Winston, pp. 325–45.

1975. Everyone has to lie. In M. Sanches and B. G. Blount (eds.) *Sociocultural Dimensions of Language Use*. New York: Academic Press, pp. 57–80.

1979. Hotrodder: a revolutionary category. In G. Psathas (ed.) *Everyday Language: Studies in Ethnomethodology*. New York: Erlbaum, pp. 7–14. (Edited by G. Jefferson from an unpublished lecture: Spring 1966, lecture 18.)

1984a. Notes on methodology. In J. M. Atkinson and J. Heritage (eds.) *Structures of Social Action: Studies in Conversation Analysis*. Cambridge: Cambridge University Press, pp. 21–7.

1984b. On doing "being ordinary." In J. M. Atkinson and J. Heritage (eds.) *Structures of Social Action: Studies in Conversation Analysis*. Cambridge: Cambridge University Press, pp. 413–29.

1987. On the preference for agreement and contiguity in sequences in conversation. In G. Button and J. R. E. Lee (eds.) *Talk and Social Organisation*. Clevedon: Multilingual Matters, pp. 54–69.

1989. Harvey Sacks – Lectures 1964–1965. Edited by Gail Jefferson. *Human Studies*, 12(3/4): 183–404.

1992 (1964–72). *Lectures on Conversation*, 2 vols., edited by G. Jefferson. Oxford: Blackwell.

Sacks, H. and E. A. Schegloff 1979. Two preferences in the organization of reference to persons in conversation and their interaction. In G. Psathas (ed.) *Everyday Language: Studies in Ethnomethodology*. New York: Erlbaum, pp. 15–21.

Sacks, H., E. A. Schegloff and G. Jefferson 1974. A simplest systematics for the organization of turn-taking for conversation. *Language* 50(4): 696–735.

Sadock, J. 1974. *Toward a Linguistic Theory of Speech Acts*. New York: Academic Press.

Schank, R. and B. L. Nash-Webber (eds.) 1975. *Theoretical Issues in Natural Language Processing*. Cambridge MA: duplicated conference proceedings.

Schegloff, E. A. 1972. Notes on a conversational practice: formulating place. In D. Sudnow (ed.) *Studies in Social Interaction*. New York: Free Press, pp. 75–119.

1979a. Identification and recognition in telephone openings. In G. Psathas (ed.) *Everyday Language: Studies in Ethnomethodology*. New York: Erlbaum, pp. 23–78.

1979b. The relevance of repair to syntax-for-conversation. In T. Givón (ed.) *Syntax and Semantics*, vol. XII: *Discourse and Syntax*. New York: Academic Press, pp. 261–88.

1980. Preliminaries to preliminaries: "Can I ask you a question?". *Sociological Inquiry*, 50(3/4): 104–52.

1982. Discourse as an interactional achievement: some uses of "uh huh" and other things that come between sentences. In D. Tannen (ed.) *Analyzing Discourse: Text and Talk.* Georgetown University Roundtable on Languages and Linguistics, Washington DC: Georgetown University Press, pp. 71–93.

1984. On some questions and ambiguities in conversation. In J. M. Atkinson and J. Heritage (eds.) *Structures of Social Action: Studies in Conversation Analysis.* Cambridge: Cambridge University Press, pp. 28–52.

1986. The routine as achievement, *Human Studies*, 9: 111–52.

1987a. Between macro and micro: contexts and other connections. In J. Alexander, B. Giesen, R. Munch, and N. Smelser (eds.) *The Micro–Macro Link.* Berkeley and Los Angeles: University of California Press, pp. 207–34.

1987b. Analyzing single episodes of interaction: an exercise in conversation analysis. *Social Psychology Quarterly*, 50(2): 101–14.

1987c. Some sources of misunderstanding in talk-in-interaction. *Linguistics*, 25: 201–18.

1988. On an actual virtual servo-mechanism for guessing bad news: a single case conjecture. *Social Problems*, 35(4): 442–57.

1988/9. From interview to confrontation: observations on the Bush/Rather encounter. *Research on Language and Social Interaction*, 22: 215–40.

1989. Harvey Sacks' lectures on conversation: an introduction/memoir. *Human Studies*, 12: 185–209.

1990. On the organization of sequences as a source of "coherence" in talk-in-interaction. In B. Dorval (ed.) *Conversational Organization and Its Development.* Norwood NJ: Ablex, pp. 51–77.

1991. Reflections on talk and social structure. In D. Boden and D. Zimmerman (eds.) *Talk and Social Structure.* Cambridge: Polity Press, pp. 44–70.

1992. Repair after next turn: the last structurally provided defence of intersubjectivity in conversation. *American Journal of Sociology*, 97: 1295–1345.

In press. Reflections on quantification in the study of conversation. *Research on Language and Social Interaction*, 1993.

Schegloff, E. A., G. Jefferson, and H. Sacks 1977. The preference for self-correction in the organization of repair for conversation. *Language*, 53: 361–82.

Schegloff, E. A. and H. Sacks 1973. Opening up closings. *Semiotica* 8(4): 289–327.

Schenkein, J. N. (ed.) 1978. *Studies in the Organization of Conversational Interaction.* New York: Academic Press.

Schiffrin, D. 1987. *Discourse Markers.* Cambridge: Cambridge University Press.

Schlesinger, P., G. Murdock and P. Elliot 1983. *Televising "Terrorism": Political Violence in Popular Culture.* London: Comedia.

Scollon, R. and S. Scollon 1983. Face in inter-ethnic communication. In

I. C. Richards and R. W. Schmidt (eds.) *Language and Communication*. London: Longman, pp. 156–88.

Searle, J. 1969. *Speech Acts*. Cambridge: Cambridge University Press.

   1975. Indirect speech acts. In P. Cole and J. L. Morgan (eds.) *Syntax and Semantics*, vol. III *Speech Acts*. New York: Academic Press, pp. 59–82.

   1976. The classification of illocutionary acts. *Language in Society*, 5(1): 1–24.

   1979. Literal meaning. In J. Searle, *Expression and Meaning: Studies in the Theory of Speech Acts*. Cambridge: Cambridge University Press, pp. 117–36.

Searle, J. et al. (eds.) 1991. *(On) Searle on Conversation*, compiled and introduced by Herman Parret and Jef Verschueren, Amsterdam/Philadelphia: John Benjamins.

Sefi, S. 1988. Health visitors talking to mothers. *Health Visitor*, 61: 7–10.

Sharrock, W. W. 1974. On owning knowledge. In R. Turner (ed.) *Ethnomethodology*. Harmondsworth: Penguin, pp. 45–53.

Sharrock, W. W. and R. Turner 1978. On a conversational environment for equivocality. In J. Schenkein (ed.) *Studies in the Organization of Conversational Interaction*. New York: Academic Press, pp. 173–98.

Shuy, R. 1983. Three types of interference in an effective exchange of information in the medical interview. In S. Fisher and A. D. Todd (eds.) *The Social Organization of Doctor–Patient Communication*. Washington DC: Center for Applied Linguistics, pp. 189–202.

Silverman, D. 1981.The child as a social object: Down's Syndrome children in a paediatric cardiology unit. *Sociology of Health and Illness*, 3: 254–74.

   1987. *Communication and Medical Practice*. London: Sage.

Simmel, G. 1908. Der Arme. In Simmel's *Soziologie: Untersuchungen über die Formen der Vergesellschaftung*. Berlin: Duncker and Humblot, pp. 345–74.

Sinclair, J. McH. and M. Coulthard 1975. *Towards An Analysis of Discourse: the English Used by Teachers and Pupils*. Oxford: Oxford University Press.

Sorjonen, M.-L. and J. Heritage 1991. And-prefacing as a feature of question design. In L. Laitinen, P. Nuolijarvi, and M. Saari (eds.) *Leikkauspiste*. Helsinki: Suomalaisen Kirjallisuuden Seura, pp. 59–74.

Stenius, E. 1967. Mood and language games. *Synthese*, XVII: 245–74.

Stimson, G. and B. Webb 1975. *Going to See the Doctor*. London: Routledge.

Strong, P. M. 1979. *The Ceremonial Order of the Clinic*. London: Routledge.

Stubbs, M. 1976. *Language, Schools and Classrooms*. London: Methuen.

   1983. *Discourse Analysis: the Sociolinguistic Analysis of Natural Language*. Oxford: Blackwell.

Suchman, L. forthcoming. Constituting shared workspaces. In Y. Enges-trom and D. Middleton (eds.) *Cognition and Communication at Work*. Newbury Park NJ: Sage.

Suchman, L. and B. Jordan 1990. Interactional troubles in face-to-face survey interviews. *Journal of the American Statistical Association*, 85: 232–41.

Sudnow, D. 1965. Normal crimes. *Social Problems*, 12: 251–76.

1967. *Passing On: the Social Organization of Dying*. Englewood Cliffs NJ: Prentice Hall.

Tannen, D. and C. Wallat 1987. Interactive frames and knowledge sche-mas in interaction: examples from a medical examination/interview. *Social Psychology Quarterly*, 50: 205–16.

Taylor, T. and D. Cameron 1987. *Analyzing Conversation: Rules and Units in the Structure of Talk*. Oxford: Pergamon Press.

Teas, V. 1989. Labeling and the delivery of diagnostic news. Unpublished Master's thesis, University of Wisconsin, Madison.

ten Have, P. 1991. Talk and institution: a reconsideration of the "as-symetry" of doctor–patient interaction. In D. Boden and D. Zim-merman (eds.) *Talk and Social Structure*. Cambridge: Polity Press, pp. 138–63.

Terasaki, A. K. 1976. Pre-announcement sequences in conversation (Social Science Working Paper, no. 99), School of Social Science, University of California, Irvine.

Tiffin, J. and E. McCormick 1975. *Industrial Psychology*. London: George Allen and Unwin.

Toner, B. 1977. *The Facts of Rape*. London: Arrow.

Tracey, M. 1977. *The Production of Political Television*. London: Rout-ledge.

Tuchman, G. 1972. Objectivity as strategic ritual. *American Journal of Sociology*, 77: 660–79.

Tuckett, D., M. Boulton, C. Olson and A. Williams 1985. *Meetings be-tween Experts: an Approach to Sharing Ideas in Medical Consul-tations*. London: Tavistock.

Turner, R. 1972. Some formal properties of therapy talk. In D. Sudnow (ed.) *Studies in Social Interaction*. New York: Free Press, pp. 367–96.

(ed.) 1974. *Ethnomethodology*. Harmondsworth: Penguin.

1976. Utterance positioning as an interactional resource. *Semiotica*, 17: 233–54.

Waitzkin, H. 1985. Information giving in medical care. *Journal of Health and Social Behavior*, 26: 81–101.

Waitzkin, H. and J. D. Stoeckle 1976. Information control and the micro-politics of health care. *Social Science and Medicine*, 10: 263–76.

Watson, D. R. 1990. Some features of the elicitation of confessions in murder interrogations. In G. Psathas (ed.) *Interaction Competence*. Lanham MD: University Press of America, pp. 263–95.

Watson, P. 1981. A time study of health visitors' work. Unpublished PhD dissertation, Aberdeen University.

Weber, M. 1949. *The Methodology of the Social Sciences*. New York: Free Press.

West, C. 1979. Against our will: male interruptions of females in cross-sex conversation. *Annals of the New York Academy of Science*, 327: 81–97.

 1984. *Routine Complications: Troubles in Talk Between Doctors and Patients*. Bloomington IN: Indiana University Press.

 1990. Not just "doctors' orders": directive–response sequences in patients' visits to women and men physicians. *Discourse and Society*, 1: 85–112.

West, C. and R. Frankel 1991. Miscommunication in medicine. In N. Coupland, H. Giles, and J. M. Wiemann (eds.) *Miscommunication and Problematic Talk*. Newbury Park: Sage, pp. 166–94.

West, C. and D. Zimmerman 1983. Small insults: a study of interruptions in cross-sex conversations with unacquainted persons. In B. Thorne, C. Kramarae, and N. Henley (eds.), *Language, Gender and Society*. Rowley MA: Newbury House, pp. 102–17.

Wieder, D.L. 1974. *Language and Social Reality*. The Hague: Mouton.

Whalen, J. 1990. Processing "emergencies" in 9–1–1 communications. Unpublished paper, Department of Sociology, University of Oregon.

 1991. Technology as a pre-eminent contingency in the co-ordination of human activity: computer-aided dispatch systems and the work of 9–1–1 call takers. Paper presented to the conference on Current Work in Ethnomethodology and Conversation Analysis, University of Amsterdam, July 1991.

Whalen, J. and D. H. Zimmerman 1990. Processing "emergencies" in 9–1–1 communications. Paper presented at the American Sociological Association Annual meetings, Washington DC.

Whalen, J., D. Zimmerman, and M. Whalen 1988. When words fail: a single case analysis. *Social Problems*, 35(4): 335–62.

Whalen, M. 1990. Ordinary talk in extraordinary situations: the social organization of interrogation in calls for help. Unpublished PhD dissertation, University of California, Santa Barbara.

Whalen, M. and D. H. Zimmerman 1987. Sequential and institutional contexts in calls for help. *Social Psychology Quarterly*, 50(2): 172–85.

 1990. Describing trouble: practical epistemology in citizen calls to the police. *Language in Society*, 19: 465–92.

 1992. Telling trouble: citizen calls to the police. In R. Frankel (ed.) *Language in Institutional Settings*. Norwood NJ: Ablex.

Wilson, H. and C. Herbert 1978. *Parents and Children in the Inner City*. London: Routledge.

Wilson, T. P. 1985. Social structure and social interaction. Unpublished paper, Department of Sociology, University of California, Santa Barbara.

 1991. Social structure and the sequential organization of interaction. In

D. Boden and D. H. Zimmerman (eds.) *Talk and Social Structure.* Cambridge: Polity Press, pp. 22–43.

Wilson, T. P. and D. H. Zimmerman 1980. Ethnomethodology, sociology, and theory. *Humboldt Journal of Social Relations*, 7: 52–88.

Wittgenstein, L. 1921. *Tractatus Logico-Philosophicus.* London: Routledge and Kegan Paul.

1958a. *Philosophical Investigations.* Oxford: Blackwell.

1958b. *The Brown Book.* In L. Wittgenstein, *The Blue and Brown Books.* Oxford: Blackwell, pp. 75–185.

Wooffitt, R. 1992. *Tales of the Unexpected: Accounts of Paranormal Experiences.* Hemel Hempstead: Harvester Wheatsheaf.

Wootton, A. 1977. Sharing: notes on the organization of talk in a therapeutic community. *Sociology*, 11: 333–50.

Zimmerman, D. 1969. Tasks and troubles: the practical bases of work activities in a public assistance agency. In D. H. Hansen (ed.) *Explorations in Sociology and Counseling.* Boston MA: Houghton Mifflin, pp. 237–66.

1984. Talk and its occasion: the case of calling the police. In D. Schiffrin (ed.) *Meaning, Form, and Use in Context: Linguistic Applications.* Georgetown University Roundtable on Language and Linguistics. Washington, DC: Georgetown University Press, pp. 210–28.

1988. On conversation: the conversation analytic perspective. In J. A. Anderson (ed.) *Communication Yearbook 11.* Newbury Park NJ: Sage, pp. 406–32.

1990. Prende position. In I. Joseph (ed.) *Le Parler frais d'Erving Goffman.* Paris: Les Editions de Minuit, pp. 218–30.

1992. Achieving context: openings in emergency calls. In G. Watson and R. Seiler (eds.) *Text in Context: Contributions in Ethnomethodology.* Newbury Park NJ: Sage.

Zimmerman, D. H. and D. Boden 1991. Structure-in-action: an introduction. In D. Boden and D. H. Zimmerman (eds.) *Talk and Social Structure*, Cambridge: Polity Press, pp. 3–21.

Zimmerman, D. H. and C. West 1975. Sex roles, interruptions and silences in conversation. In Barrie Thorne and Nancy Henley (eds.) *Language and Sex: Difference and Dominance.* Rowley MA: Newbury House, pp. 105–29.

Subject index

accounts and accountability 17
  in courtroom interaction 508
  of news interviewers 164, 195
  in patient receipt of medical
    diagnosis 252–60
action 7, 10, 11, 104
  and turn design 33–6
  and utterances as "context shaped"
    and "context renewing" 18
activity types 22, 54, 66–79, 213–14,
    231n.
  in cross-examination 82–6
  defined 69
  structures of 70–1
address terms 6, 69
adjacency pairs 305
advice, see news delivery
affiliation 352–4, 357n.
  see also "footing"; neutrality
agreement 273
  see also disagreement, preference
    organization
anthropology 101, 132n.
  see also ethnography of speaking
    tradition
assessments 208–9, 223–6
  see also doctor–patient interaction;
    news delivery
asymmetries, see interactional
    asymmetries
authority 145–6, 153, 188–9
  in doctor–patient interaction 236,
    260–2
  in emergency calls 449–50
  in health visits 410–12
  see also interactional asymmetries

bad news, see news delivery
bilingualism, see cross-cultural
    communication; "minorization"
Birmingham discourse-analysis group
    13–14, 19
bodily comportment 243

category terms 107, 357n.
  in courtrooms 113
  see also relevance
cautiousness, see professional
    cautiousness
classroom interaction 15
  initiation–response feedback in 13–
    15
  question–answer sequences in 40–1,
    86–92
closing
  of disagreement: in ordinary
    conversation 275–7; in news
    interviews 287–98
  in emergency calls 465n.
comparative perspective of CA 4, 38–
    9, 41, 53
context 9, 15, 16–17, 18–19, 21, 23,
    102, 110, 128, 132n.
  breakdowns in institutional 61n.,
    117–27, 133n.
  "bucket" theory of 19, 21
  in linguistics 6–7, 8
  see also procedural consequentiality;
    relevance
"contextualization cues" 8, 307, 326
  pitch level and prosody as 322
contrast structures, see courtroom
    interaction
conversation analysis (CA) 4, 16–53,
    101–6
  activity focus of 17
  methodology 20–1, 146–8
  and social structure 103–4
conversation maxims 76, 78–9
conversational organization 305, 308–
    12
cooperation
  and inference 76–9
  in job interviews 308–12
  securing, in emergency calls 428–31
courtroom interaction 55–6, 58, 112–
    13, 199–211, 470–520

Index of names